ECONOMIC FORECASTING

ECONOMIC FORECASTING

GRAHAM ELLIOTT AND
ALLAN TIMMERMANN

PRINCETON UNIVERSITY PRESS
PRINCETON AND OXFORD

Copyright © 2016 by Princeton University Press
Published by Princeton University Press, 41 William Street,
Princeton, New Jersey 08540
In the United Kingdom: Princeton University Press, 6 Oxford Street,
Woodstock, Oxfordshire OX20 1TW

press.princeton.edu

All Rights Reserved
ISBN: 978-0-691-14013-1
Library of Congress Control Number: 2015959185

British Library Cataloging-in-Publication Data is available

This book has been composed in Minion Pro and Helvetica Neue

Printed on acid-free paper. ∞

Typeset by S R Nova Pvt Ltd, Bangalore, India
Printed in the United States of America

1 2 3 4 5 6 7 8 9 10

FOR OUR FAMILIES
◇◇◇◇◇◇◇◇◇◇◇◇◇◇◇◇

Jason and Shirley
Henry, Rafaella
and Solange

Contents

Preface

We started working on this book more than 10 years ago after teaching courses on forecasting techniques at University of Aarhus, Denmark, and in Bertinoro, Italy, to groups of PhD students and assistant professors. Since then, we have developed the material through courses offered to participants at many institutions, including at CREATES (University of Aarhus), American University, Edhec, Bank of Italy, SoFiE (Oxford University), and Universidad del Rosario.

Our idea was to provide a unified perspective that takes both the economics and statistics of the forecasting problem seriously. The intention was to write a forecasting book that could be used by masters and Phd students as well as professionals in places such as central banks, financial institutions, and research institutes. The book can be used as a textbook. Indeed, the first section of the book provides a unified theoretical discussion of the basic approach to forecasting that is grounded in the standard statistical practice of minimizing the "risk" (expected loss) of any method. The remainder of the book can be used both as a text and as a reference to a wide range of forecasting methods. We have tried as much as possible to provide detailed descriptions of how to construct forecasts, how to evaluate such forecasts, and how to compare them across different methods. This allows the book to serve as a single source for many widely employed forecasting methods. Through empirical applications and reviews of the empirical literature, we also shed light on which methods work well in different circumstances. We use examples ranging from stock returns to macroeconomic variables and surveys of forecasters.

Nearly all researchers who are interested in developing new forecasting methods through theoretical analysis or improving their empirical performance through data analysis work within a decision-theoretic framework. For example, the provision of point forecasts is a special case of point estimation and the provision of distributional forecasts is a special case of density estimation. We use this connection as a foundation for understanding the statistical basis for forecasting analysis and gaining a better understanding of how to think about the many forecasting methods in practical use. Thus, the first premise of the book is that taking seriously the economics underlying the forecasting problem means that the forecaster's loss function should be the starting point of the analysis.

The second premise of the book is that the joint density of the random variables that generate the observed data used to build and evaluate a forecasting model is far more complicated than we understand theoretically or empirically. As a consequence, all forecasting models are misspecified in the sense that they are approximations to the best possible forecasting model. In practice, this means choosing forecasting methods based on their risk functions (the expected loss given the data), but acknowledging that these risk functions are themselves very complicated objects that depend on the underlying (unknown) data-generating process. It is exactly the difficulties in understanding the risk functions that allow so many different forecasting approaches to be used in empirical work.

In addition to the students in our forecasting courses who have provided valuable feedback, throughout the years we have also benefitted from discussions on forecasting with many individuals. Without implying that they necessarily agree with the points of view expressed in the book, we thank our colleagues at UCSD (past and present) including Brendan Beare, Robert Engle, Clive Granger, Jim Hamilton, Ivana Komunjer, Andres Santos, Yixiao Sun, Rossen Valkanov, and Hal White. More widely in the profession we thank Frank Diebold, Peter Hansen, Andrew Patton, Hashem Pesaran, Ulrich Müller, Jim Stock, Mark Watson, and Ken West for their insights and support. We thank all of them for the inspiration they have offered over the years. This book has also benefitted more directly from the input of many friends and colleagues. In particular, we thank Peter Hansen, Kirstin Hubrich, Simone Manganelli, Andrew Patton, Davide Pettenuzzo, Barbara Rossi, and four anonymous reviewers for comments on the book. A number of PhD students provided exceptionally capable research assistance with the empirical analysis, notably Leland E. Farmer, Antonio Gargano, Rafael Burjack, Hiroaki Kaido, and Christian Constandse. Thanks also goes to Naveen Basavanhally for help with formatting the manuscript, to Alison Durham for doing an excellent job at copyediting the manuscript, and to Ali Parrington and the team at Princeton University Press for ensuring a smooth production process.

For collaboration on forecasting papers over the years we also wish to thank several former PhD students and colleagues, including Marco Aiolfi, Ayelen Banegas, Gray Calhoun, Carlos Capistran, Luis Catao, Tolga Cenesizoglu, Leland Farmer, Antonio Gargano, Veronique Genre, Dahlia Ghanem, Ben Gillen, Clive Granger, Niels Groenborg, Massimo Guidolin, Peter Reinhard Hansen, Geoff Kenny, Ivana Komunjer, Robert Kosowski, Fabian Krueger, Robert Lieli, Asger Lunde, Aidan Meyler, Andrew Patton, Bradley Paye, Thomas Pedersen, Gabriel Perez-Quiros, Hashem Pesaran, Davide Pettenuzzo, Marius Rodrigues, Steve Satchell, Larry Schmidt, Ryan Sullivan, Russ Wermers, Hal White, and Yinchu Zhu.

Last, but not least, we wish to thank our families for their understanding and inspiration during the years it took to complete the book. The book would not have been possible without their unwavering support.

I
Foundations
◇◇◇◇◇◇◇◇◇◇◇◇◇◇◇◇◇

1

◇◇

Introduction

Our aim with this book is to present an overview of the theory and methods underlying forecasting as currently practiced in economics and finance, but more widely applicable to a great range of forecasting problems. We hope to provide an overview that is useful to practitioners in places such as central banks and financial institutions, academic researchers as well as graduate students seeking a point of entry into the field. The assumed econometric level of the reader is that of someone who has taken a graduate or advanced undergraduate course in econometrics.

Whenever a forecast is being constructed or evaluated, an overriding concern revolves around the practical problem that the best forecasting model is not only unknown but also unlikely to be known well enough to even correctly specify forecasting equations up to a set of unknown parameters. We view this as the only reasonable description of the forecaster's problem. Some methods do claim to find the correct model (oracle methods) as the sample gets very large. However, in any problem with a finite sample there is always a set of models—as opposed to a single model—that are consistent with the data. Moreover, in many situations the data-generating process changes over time, further emphasizing the difficulty in obtaining very large samples of observations on which to base a model. These foundations—using misspecified models to forecast outcomes generated by a process that may be evolving over time—generate many of the complications encountered in forecasting. If the true models were fully known apart from the values of the parameters, Bayesian methods could be used to construct density and point forecasts that, for a given loss function, would be difficult or impossible to beat in practice.

Without knowing the true data-generating process, the problem of constructing a good forecasting method becomes much more difficult. Oftentimes very simple (and clearly misspecified) methods provide forecasts that outperform more complicated methods that seek to exploit the data in ways we would expect to be important and advantageous. As a case in point, simple averages of forecasts from many models, even ones that on their own do not seem to be very good, are often found empirically to outperform carefully chosen model averages or the best individual models.

1.1 OUTLINE OF THE BOOK

The approach of this book is for the most part based on forecasting as a decision-theoretic problem. By this we mean that the forecaster has a specific objective in mind (i.e., wishes to make a decision) and wants to base this decision on some data. Setting up this approach comprises most of the first part of the book. This part details the basic elements of the decision problem, with chapters on the decision maker's loss function, forecasting as a decision-theoretic problem, and an overview of general approaches to forecasting employing either classical or Bayesian methods. This part of the book provides foundations for understanding how different methods fit together. We also provide details of methods that are subsequently applied to many of the issues examined in the next part of the book, e.g., model selection and forecast combination.

The second part of the book reviews various approaches to constructing forecasting models. Methods employed differ for many reasons: lack of relevant data or the existence of a great deal of potentially relevant data, as well as assumptions made on functional forms for the models. In these chapters we attempt, as far as possible, to present the methods in enough detail that they can be employed without reference to other sources.

The third part of the book examines the evaluation of forecasts, while the fourth part covers forecasting models that deal with special complications such as model instability (breaks) and highly persistent (trending) data. This part also discusses data structures of special interest to forecasters, including real-time data (revised data) and data collected at different frequencies.

Finally, the fourth part of the book presents various extensions and refinements to the forecasting methods covered in the earlier parts of the book, including forecasting under model instability, long-run forecasting, and forecasting with data that either take a non-standard form (count data and durations) or are measured at irregular intervals and are subject to revisions.

1.1.1 Part I

The first part of the book motivates that point forecasting should be thought of simply as an application of decision theory. Since much is known about decision theory, much is also known about forecasting. This perspective makes point forecasting a special case of estimation, a field where excellent texts already exist. What makes economic forecasting interesting as a separate topic is the particular details of how decision theory is applied to the problem at hand. To apply this approach, we require a clear statement about the costs of forecast errors $e = y - f$, where y is the outcome being predicted and f is the forecast. The trade-off between different forecasting mistakes is embodied in a loss function, $L(f, y)$ which is discussed in chapter 2, with additional material on the binary case available in chapter 12. We regard loss functions as realistic expositions of the forecaster's objectives, and consider the specification of the loss function as an integral part of the forecaster's decision problem.[1] Different forecasters approaching the same outcome may well have different loss functions which could result in different choices of forecasting models for the same outcome.

The specification of loss functions is often disregarded in economic forecasting, and instead "standard" loss functions such as mean squared error loss tend to

---

[1] An alternative literature considers features of loss functions and attempts to suggest a good loss function for all forecasting problems. We do not consider this approach and view loss functions as primitive to the forecaster's problem.

be employed. This can prove costly in real forecasting situations as it overlooks directions in which forecast errors are particularly costly. Nonetheless, much of the academic literature is based on these standard loss functions and so we focus much of our survey of methods throughout the second part of the book on these standard loss functions.

Chapter 3 provides a general description of the forecaster's problem as a decision problem. It may strike some readers, more used to the "art" of forecasting, as unusual to cast point forecasting as a decision-theoretic problem. However, even readers who do not explicitly follow this approach are indeed operating within the decision-theoretic framework. For example, most forecasting methods are motivated in one of two ways: either the methods are demonstrated to provide better performance given a loss function (or set of loss functions) through Monte Carlo simulations for reasonable data-generating processes, or alternatively, the forecasting methods are shown to work well for some loss function for a particular set of empirical data $z = (y, x)$, where x represents the set of predictor variables used to forecast the outcome y. Both ways of measuring performance place the forecasting problem within the decision-theoretic approach.

To illustrate this point, consider Monte Carlo simulations of a data-generating process (joint density for the data) regarded as a reasonable representation of some data of interest. The simulation method suggests constructing N independent pseudo samples from this density, constructing N forecasts and evaluating $N^{-1} \sum_{n=1}^{N} L(f^{(n)}, y^{(n)})$, where $y^{(n)}$ is the outcome we wish to forecast, $f^{(n)}$ is the forecast generated by a prediction model, and $L(f, y)$ is the loss function which measures the costs of forecast inaccuracies. Superscripts refer to the individual simulations, $n = 1, \ldots, N$. The simulated average loss is usually thought of as a measure of the performance of the forecasting method or model for this data-generating process. This is reasonable since as N gets large, the sample average is, by standard laws of large numbers, a consistent estimate of the risk at the point of the parameter space for the data-generating process chosen for the Monte Carlo, i.e., as long as $E[L(f, y)]$ exists,

$$N^{-1} \sum_{n=1}^{N} L(f^{(n)}, y^{(n)}) \to^{P} E[L(f, y)], \tag{1.1}$$

where the Monte Carlo estimates a point on the risk function and $\to^{P}$ means convergence in probability. Finding a forecast that minimizes the risk is precisely the setup of a decision-theoretic problem.

The third part of the book discusses methods for evaluation of sequential out-of-sample predictions. In each case, one obtains from the data set T observations of the "realized" loss from the data. One then evaluates the time-series average $T^{-1} \sum_{t=1}^{T} L(f_t, y_t)$, where the t subscript refers to time, as a measure of the expected loss. In this case the assumptions that underlie results such as (1.1) are much more stringent because the sequence of expected losses generated from data are not independently and identically distributed (i.i.d.) as in the Monte Carlo simulations. However, under suitable assumptions again this method estimates risk. When using real (as opposed to simulated) data, we do not know the true parameter values of the data-generating process. Analyzing a variety of economic variables, we get a sense of how well different forecasting methods work for different types of data.

The general setup in chapter 3 is common to forecasters basing their estimation strategies either on frequentist or on Bayesian approaches. Chapters 4 and 5 build on this setup separately for these two approaches. Chapter 4 examines the typical frequentist approaches, explaining general pitfalls that can occur as well as highlighting special cases arising later in the book. Chapter 5 does the same for the Bayesian approach.

Viewing forecasting as a decision-theoretic problem sometimes means that the best forecasting model, despite working well in practice, may actually be a model that is very difficult to interpret economically. This becomes a problem when the forecasting exercise is a step in a decision process, and the forecaster must "explain" the forecast to decision makers or forecast users. In these cases an inferior point forecast that tends to be further away from the outcome may be preferred because it is easier to explain and may be seen to be more credible. Of course in situations where we suspect a lot of overfitting or instability in the relationships between the variables, we might prefer forecasting models that conform to economic theory since they are expected to be more robust. Practically, economically motivated restrictions on forecasting models can just be seen as following the decision-theoretic approach for a restricted set of models.

The final chapter of the first part of the book, chapter 6, examines issues related to model selection. By now the econometrics literature has a very good understanding of the merits and limitations of model selection, which we discuss for general models. From the perspective of forecasting, however, we regard model selection as simply part of the model estimation process. Of interest to the forecaster is the risk of the final forecasting model computed in a way that accounts for the full estimation process. Given the complexity of the distributions of estimators obtained from models whose selection is driven by the data, this issue is difficult to address analytically although it is still of direct relevance to the forecaster.

1.1.2 Part II

Part II of the book provides an overview of the various approaches to forecasting that have become standard in many areas, including the economic and finance forecasting literature. Chapters are based around either the amount of information available—from only the past history of the predicted variable through very large panels of variables—or the general estimation approach, principally parametric or nonparametric methods. To the extent possible, we provide details of how to go about constructing forecasts from the various methods, or alternatively direct readers to explanations available in the literature. We also discuss the trade-offs between different methods. In this sense we endeavor to provide a "first stop" for practitioners wishing to apply the methods covered in this section.

An important insight that arises from the decision-theoretic approach is that there is no single best or dominant approach to constructing a forecast for all possible forecasting situations. We discuss the types of forecasting situations where each individual method is likely to be a reasonable approach and also highlight situations where other approaches should be considered.

Throughout the book, we use a variety of empirical applications to illustrate how different approaches work. In most applications we use so-called pseudo out-of-sample forecasts which simulate the forecast as it could have been generated using data only up to the date of the prediction. This method restricts both model selection and parameter estimation to rely on data available at the point of the forecast. As time progresses and more data become available, the forecasting method, including the parameter estimates, are updated recursively. Such methods are commonly used to evaluate the usefulness of forecasts; a critical discussion of such out-of-sample forecasting methods versus in-sample methods is provided in part three of the book.

When building a forecasting model for an economic variable, the simplest specification of the conditioning information set is the variable's own past history. This leads to univariate autoregressive moving average, or ARMA, models. Since Box and Jenkins (1970) these models have been extensively used and often provide benchmarks that are difficult to beat using more complicated forecasting methods. Linear ARMA models are also easy to estimate and a large literature has evolved on how best to cover issues in implementation such as lag length selection, generation of multiperiod forecasts, and parameter estimation. We discuss these issues in chapter 7. The chapter also covers exponential smoothing, unobserved components models, and other ways to account for trends when forecasting economic variables.

Chapter 8 continues under the assumption that the information set is limited to the predicted variable's own past, but focuses on nonlinear parametric models. Examples include threshold autoregressions, smooth threshold autoregressions, and Markov switching models. These models have been used to capture evidence of nonlinear dynamics in many macroeconomic and financial time series. Unlike nonparametric models they do not, however, have the ability to provide a global approximation to general data-generating processes of unknown form.

Chapter 9 expands the information set to include multivariate information by considering a natural extension to univariate autoregressive models, namely vector autoregressions, or VARs. VARs provide a framework for producing internally consistent multiperiod forecasts of all the included variables. As used in macroeconomic forecasting VARs typically include a relatively small set of variables, often less than 10, but they still require a large number of parameters to be estimated if the number of included lags is high. To deal with the resulting negative effects of estimation errors on forecasting performance, a large literature has developed Bayesian methods for estimating and forecasting with VARs. Both classical and Bayesian estimation of VARs is covered in the chapter which also deals with forecasting when the future paths of some variables are specified, a common practice in scenario analysis or contingent forecasting.

The emergence of very large data sets has given rise to a wealth of information becoming readily available to forecasters. This poses both a unique opportunity—the potential for identifying new informative predictor variables—but also some real challenges given the limitations to most economic data. Suppose that N potential predictor variables are available, and that N is a large number, i.e., in the hundreds or thousands. Including all variables in the forecasting model—the so-called kitchen sink approach—is generally not feasible or desirable even for linear models since parameter estimation error becomes too large, unless the length of the estimation sample, T, is very large relative to N. Standard forecasting methods that conduct comprehensive model selection searches are also not feasible in this situation. If the true model is sparse, i.e., includes only few variables, one possibility is to use algorithms such as the Lasso, covered in chapter 6, to identify a few key predictors. Another strategy is to develop a few key summary measures that aggregate information from a large cross section of variables. This is the approach used by common factor models. Chapter 10 describes how these methods can be used in forecasting, including in factor-augmented VAR models that include both univariate autoregressive terms along with information in the factors. Finally, we discuss the possibility of using methods from panel data estimation to generate forecasts.

While chapters 7–10 focus on parametric estimation methods and so assume that a certain amount of structure can be imposed on the forecasting model, chapter 11 considers nonparametric forecasting strategies. These include kernel regressions and sieve estimators such as polynomials and spline expansions, artificial neural networks, along with more recent techniques from the machine-learning literature such as boosted regression trees. Although these methods have powerful abilities to approximate many data-generating processes as the number of terms included by the approach gets large, in practice any given estimated nonparametric model is itself an approximation to this approximation. Notably, the number of terms that can be successfully included in empirical applications will often be severely restricted by the available data sample. These approximate models thus do not have the same approximation ability as the models and thus themselves are approximations. Once again, the algorithm used to fit these forecasting models—along with the loss function used to guide the estimation—become key to their forecasting performance and to avoiding issues related to overfitting.

Forecasts of binary variables, i.e., variables that are restricted to take only two possible values, play a special role in decisions such as households' choice on whether or not to buy a car, the decision on whether to pursue a particular education, or banks' decisions on whether to change interest rates for short-term deposits. Restricting the outcome to only two possible values has the advantage that it crystallizes the costs of making wrong forecasts, i.e., false positives or false negatives. Chapter 12 takes advantage of these simplifications to cover point and probability forecasts of binary outcomes and discusses both statistical and utility-based estimators for such data.

The decision-theoretic approach embodies a loss function that is appropriate for the decision to be made and not, as is so often the case, chosen for convenience. It results in a decision, i.e., a choice of an action to be made. This directs itself to basing estimation on an objective of providing the best decision. Alternatively, we might consider provision of a predictive distribution (density forecast) for an outcome as the objective of the forecasting problem. In chapter 13 we see that this perspective is useful for a wide range of decisions.[2] Distribution forecasts also serve the important role of quantifying the degree of uncertainty surrounding point forecasts.

Distributional forecasting fills an important place in any forecaster's toolbox but it does not replace point forecasting. First, although density forecasts can be used to construct point forecasts, typically it is the point forecast or decision that is required. Second, distributional forecasts rely on the distribution being estimated from data. This brings the loss function or scoring rule—the loss function used to estimate the

---

[2] Dawid (1984) introduced what he termed the "prequential" approach to statistics, where prequential is a fusing of the words "probability" and "sequential." This approach argued that rather than parameters being the object of statistical inference, the proper approach was to provide a sequence of probability forecasts for an outcome of interest. Hence, the provision of a density is important not just for forecasting, but for statistics in general.

density—back into the problem. Often ad hoc loss functions are employed to estimate the distributional forecast, leading to problems when the distributional forecast is subsequently used to construct the point forecast.

Given the plethora of different modeling approaches for construction of forecasts throughout chapters 7–13, it is not surprising that forecasters frequently have access to multiple predictions of the same outcome. Instead of aiming to identify a single best forecast, another strategy is to combine the information in the individual forecasts. This is the topic of forecast combinations covered in chapter 14. If the information used to generate the underlying forecasts is not available, forecast combination reduces to a simple estimation problem that basically treats the individual forecasts as predictors that could be part of a larger conditioning information set. Special restrictions on the forecast combination weights are sometimes imposed if it can be assumed that the individual forecasts are unbiased. If more information is available on the models underlying the individual forecasts, model combination methods can be used. These weight the individual forecasts based on their marginal likelihood or some such performance measure. Bayesian model averaging is a key example of such methods and is also covered in this chapter.

1.1.3 Part III

The third part of the book deals with forecast evaluation methods. Evaluation of forecast methods is central to the forecasting problem and the difficulties involved in this step explain both the plethora of methods suggested for forecasting any particular outcome and the need for careful evaluation of forecasting methods.

To see the central issue, consider the simple problem of forecasting the next outcome, y_{T+1}, in a sequence of independently and identically distributed data y_t, $t = 1, \ldots, T$ with mean μ, variance σ^2, and no explanatory variables. It is well known that under mean squared error (MSE) loss the best forecast is an estimate of the mean, μ, such as the sample mean $\bar{y}_T = T^{-1} \sum_{t=1}^{T} y_t$. Since the outcome y_{T+1} is a random variable whose distribution is centered on μ, the forecast is typically different from the outcome even if we had a perfect estimate of μ, i.e., if we knew μ, as long as $\sigma^2 > 0$. Observing a single outcome far away from the forecast is therefore not necessarily indicative of a poor forecast. More generally, methods for forecast evaluation have to deal with the fact that (in expectation) the average in-sample loss and the average out-of-sample loss differ. To see this, suppose we use the sample mean as our forecast. For any in-sample observation, $t = 1, \ldots, T$, the MSE of the forecast (or fitted value) is

$$E[y_t - \bar{y}_T]^2 = E\left[(y_t - \mu) - T^{-1} \sum_{t=1}^{T}(y_t - \mu)\right]^2$$
$$= \sigma^2 \left(1 + \frac{T}{T^2} - 2\frac{1}{T}\right)$$
$$= \sigma^2(1 - T^{-1}).$$

Here the third term in the second line comes from the cross product when we compute the squared terms in the first line.

In contrast, the MSE of out-of-sample forecasts of y_{T+1} is

$$E[y_{T+1} - \bar{y}_T]^2 = E\left[(y_{T+1} - \mu) - T^{-1}\sum_{t=1}^{T}(y_t - \mu)\right]^2$$

$$= \sigma^2\left(1 + \frac{T}{T^2}\right)$$

$$= \sigma^2(1 + T^{-1}).$$

Here there is no cross-product term. Comparing these two expressions, we see that estimation error reduces the in-sample MSE but increases the out-of-sample MSE. In both cases the terms are of order T^{-1} and so the difference disappears asymptotically. However, in many forecasting problems this smaller-order term is important both statistically and economically. When we consider many different models of the outcome, differences in the MSE across models are of the same order as the effects on estimation error. This makes it difficult to distinguish between models and is one reason why model selection is so difficult. The insight that the in-sample fit improves by using overparameterized models, whereas out-of-sample predictive accuracy can be reduced by using such models, strongly motivates the use of out-of-sample evaluation methods, although caveats apply as we discuss in part III of the book.

In the past 20 years many new forecast evaluation methods have been developed. Prior to this development, most academic work on evaluation and ranking of forecasting performance paid very little attention to the consideration that forecasts were obtained from recursively estimated models. Thus, often studies used the sample mean squared forecast error, computed for a particular empirical data set, to give an estimate of a model's performance without accompanying standard errors. An obvious limitation of this approach is that such averages often are averages over very complicated functions of the data. Through their dependence on estimated parameters these averages are also typically correlated across time in ways that give rise to quite complicated distributions for standard test statistics. For some of the simpler ways that forecasts could have been generated recursively, recent papers derive the resulting standard errors, although much more work remains to be done to extend results to many of the popular forecasting methods used in practice.

Chapter 15 first establishes the properties that a good forecast should have in the context of the underlying loss function and discusses how these properties can be tested in practice. The chapter goes from the case where very little structure can be imposed on the loss function to cases where the loss function is known up to a small set of parameters. In the latter case it can be tested that the derivative of the loss with respect to the forecast, the so-called generalized forecast error, is unpredictable given current information. The chapter also shows how assumptions about the loss function can be traded off against testable assumptions on the underlying data-generating process.

Chapter 16 gives an overview of basic issues in evaluating forecasts, along with a description of informal methods. This chapter examines the evaluation of a sequence of forecasts from a single model. Critical values for the tests of forecast efficiency depend on how the forecast was constructed, specifically whether a fixed, rolling, or expanding estimation window was used.

Chapter 17 extends the assessment of the predictive performance of a single model to the situation with more than one forecast to examine and so addresses the issue of which, if any, forecasting method is best. We review ways to compare the forecasting methods and strategies for testing hypotheses useful to identifying methods that work well in practice. Special attention is paid to the case with nested forecasting models, i.e., cases where one model includes all the terms of another benchmark model plus some additional information. We distinguish between tests of equal predictive accuracy and tests of forecast encompassing, the latter case referring to situations where one forecast dominates another. We also discuss how to test whether the best among many (possibly thousands) of forecasts is genuinely better than some benchmark.

Chapter 18 examines the evaluation of distributional forecasts. A complication that arises is that we never observe the density of the outcome; only a single draw from the distribution gets observed. Various approaches have been suggested to deal with this issue, including logarithmic scores and probability integral transforms. We discuss these as well as ways to evaluate whether the basic features of a density forecast match the data.

1.1.4 Part IV

The fourth part of the book covers a variety of topics that are specific to forecasting. Chapter 19 discusses predictions under model instability. This chapter builds on the earlier observation that all forecasting models are simplified representations of a much more complex and evolving data-generating process. A key source of model misspecification is the constant-parameter assumption made by many prediction models. Empirical evidence suggests that simple ARMA models are in fact misspecified for many macroeconomic variables. The chapter first discusses how model instability can be monitored before moving over to discuss prediction approaches that specifically incorporate time-varying parameters, including random walk or mean-reverting parameters and regime switching parameters.

The previous chapters deal with cases where the forecast horizon is relatively short. Chapter 20 directly attacks the case where the forecast horizon can be long. Oftentimes a policy maker or budget office is interested in 5 or 10-year forecasts of revenue or expenditures. Interest may also lie in forecasts of the average growth rate over some period. From an estimation perspective, whether the forecast horizon is short or long is measured relative to the length of the data sample. We discuss these issues in chapter 20.

Real-time forecasting methods emphasize the need to ensure that all information and all methods used to construct a forecast would have been available in real time. This consideration becomes particularly relevant in so-called pseudo out-of-sample forecasts that simulate a sequence of historical forecasts. Many macroeconomic time series are subject to revisions that become available only after the date of the forecast. Since the selection of a forecasting model and estimation of its parameters may depend on the conditioning information set, which vintage of data is used can sometimes make a material difference. Similar issues related to data availability are addressed by a relatively new field known as nowcasting which uses filtering and updating algorithms to account for the jagged-edge nature of data, i.e., the fact that data are released at different frequencies and on different dates. These issues are covered in chapter 21.

This chapter also covers models for predicting data that take the format of either counts, and so are restricted to being an integer number, or durations, i.e., the length of the time intervals between certain events. The nature of the dependent variable gives rise to specific forecasting models, such as Poisson models, that are different from the models covered in the previous chapters of the book. Count models have gained widespread popularity in the context of analysis of credit events such as bankruptcies or credit card default, while duration analysis is used to predict unemployment spells and times between trades in financial markets.

1.2 TECHNICAL NOTES

Throughout the book we follow standard statistical methods which view the data as realizations of underlying random variables. Objective functions and other functions of interest are then also functions of random variables. Further, we assume that all functions are measurable, including functions that arise from maximizations of functions over parameters. We are rarely explicit about these assumptions, though this is seldom an issue for the functions examined in the book.

The decision-theoretic approach relies on the existence of risk or expected loss. For loss functions that are bounded, this is usually not problematic, but many popular loss functions are not bounded. For example, mean squared error loss and mean absolute error loss are the most popular loss functions in practice, and neither is bounded. It is fairly standard in the forecasting literature to simply assume that the expected loss exists, and further assume that the asymptotic limit of expected loss is the expected value of the limiting random variable that measures the loss. Throughout the book we follow this practice without giving conditions. Forecasting practice in some instances does seem to enforce "boundedness" of a sort on forecast losses; for example, in evaluating nonlinear models with mean squared error loss, often extreme forecasts that could lead to very large losses are removed and so the loss is in effect bounded.

Throughout the book we tend not to present results as fully worked theorems but instead give the main conditions under which the results hold. Original papers with the full set of conditions are cited. The reasons for this approach are twofold. First, often there are many overlapping sets of conditions that would result in lengthy expositions on often very straightforward methods if we were to include all the details of a result. Second, many of the conditions are highly technical in nature and often difficult or impossible to verify.

2

Loss Functions

Short of the special and ultimately uninteresting case with perfect foresight, it is not possible to find a method that always sets the forecast equal to the outcome. A formal method for trading off potential forecast errors of different signs and magnitudes is therefore required. The loss function, $L(\cdot)$, describes in relative terms how costly it is to use an imperfect forecast, f, given the outcome, Y, and possibly other observed data, Z. This chapter examines the construction and properties of loss functions and introduces loss functions that are commonly used in forecasting.

A central point in the construction of loss functions is that the loss function should reflect the actual trade-offs between different forecast errors. In this sense the loss function is a primitive to the forecasting problem. From a decision-theoretic perspective the forecast is the action that must be constructed given the loss function and the predictive distribution, which we discuss in the next chapter. For example, the Congressional Budget Office must provide forecasts of future budget deficits. Their loss function in providing the forecasts should be based on the relative costs of over- and underpredicting public deficits. Weather forecasters face very different costs from underpredicting the strength of a storm compared to overpredicting it.

The choice of a loss function is important for every facet of the forecasting exercise. This choice affects which forecasting models are preferred as well as how their parameters are estimated and how the resulting forecasts are evaluated and compared against forecasts from competing models. Despite its pivotal role, it is common practice to simply choose off-the-shelf loss functions. In doing this it is important to choose a loss function that at least approximately reflects the types of trade-offs relevant for the forecast problem under study. For example, when forecasting hotel room bookings, it is hard to imagine that over- and underpredicting the number of hotel rooms booked on a particular day lead to identical losses because hotel rooms are a perishable good. Hence, using a symmetric loss function for this problem would make little sense. Asymmetric loss that reflects the larger loss from over- rather than underpredicting bookings would be more reasonable.

There are examples of carefully grounded loss functions in the economics literature. For example, sometimes a forecast can be viewed as a signal in a strategic game that is influenced by the forecast provider's incentives. Studies such as Ehrbeck and Waldmann (1996), Hong and Kubik (2003), Laster, Bennett, and Geoum (1999), Ottaviani and Sørensen (2006), Scharfstein and Stein (1990) and Trueman (1994) suggest loss functions grounded on game-theoretical models. Forecasters are assumed to differ in their ability to predict future outcomes. The chief objective of the forecasters is to influence forecast users' assessment of their ability. Such objectives are common for business analysts or analysts employed by financial services firms such as investment banks or brokerages whose fees are directly linked to clients' assessment of their forecasting ability.

The chapter proceeds as follows. Section 2.1 examines general issues that arise in construction of loss functions. We discuss the mathematical setup of a loss function before relating it to the forecaster's decisions and examining some general properties that loss functions have. Section 2.2 reviews specific loss functions commonly used in economic forecasting problems, assuming there is only a single outcome to predict, before extending the analysis in section 2.3 to cover cases with multiple outcome variables. Section 2.4 considers loss functions (scoring rules) for distributional forecasts, while section 2.5 provides some concrete examples of loss functions and economic decision problems from macroeconomic and financial analysis. Section 2.6 concludes the chapter.

2.1 CONSTRUCTION AND SPECIFICATION OF THE LOSS FUNCTION

Let Y denote the random variable describing the outcome of interest and let $\mathcal{Y}$ denote the set of all possible outcomes. For outcomes that are either continuous or can take on a very large number of possible values, typically $\mathcal{Y}$ is the real line, $\mathbb{R}$. In some forecasting problems the set of possible outcomes, $\mathcal{Y}$, can be much smaller, such as for a binary random variable where $\mathcal{Y} = \{0, 1\}$. For multivariate outcomes typically $\mathcal{Y} = \mathbb{R}^k$ for some integer k, where k is the number of forecasts to be evaluated.

Point forecasts are denoted by f and are defined on the set $\mathcal{F}$. Typically we assume $\mathcal{F} = \mathcal{Y}$ since in most cases it does not make sense to have forecasts that cannot take on the same values as Y or, conversely, have forecasts that can take on values that the outcome Y cannot. There are exceptions to this rule, however. For example, a forecast of the number of children per family could be a fraction such as 1.9, indicating close to 2 children, even though Y cannot take this value. We assume that the predictors Z (as well as the outcome Y and hence the forecast f) are real valued. Formally, the loss function, $L(f, Y, Z)$, is then defined as a mapping $L : \mathcal{Y} \times \mathcal{Y} \times \mathcal{Z} \mapsto \mathcal{L}$, where $\mathcal{L}$ is in $\mathbb{R}^1$, and $\mathcal{Z}$ contains the set of possible values the conditioning variables, z, can take. Often $\mathcal{L} = \mathbb{R}^1_+$, the set of nonnegative real numbers. Alternatively, we could constrain the forecasts to lie in the convex hull of the set of all possible outcomes, i.e., $\mathcal{F} = \text{conv}(\mathcal{Y})$. We discuss this further below.

A common assumption for loss functions is that loss is minimized when the forecast is equal to the outcome—$\min_f L(f, y, z) = L(y, y, z)$. The idea is that if we are to find a forecast that minimizes loss, then nothing dominates a perfect forecast. In cases where the loss function does not depend on Z, so $L(f, Y, Z) = L(f, Y)$, it is natural to normalize the loss function so that it takes a minimum value at 0. This can be done without loss of generality by subtracting the loss associated with the perfect forecast $f = y$, i.e., $L(f, Y) = \tilde{L}(f, Y) - \tilde{L}(Y, Y)$ for any loss function, $\tilde{L}$. For $f = y$ to be a unique minimum we must have $L(f, y) > 0$ for all $f \neq y$.[1] More generally, when the loss function $L(f, Y, Z)$ varies with Z, it may not be possible to

---

[1] In binary forecasting this condition is often not imposed. This usually does not affect the analysis but only the interpretation of the calculated loss figures.

rescale the loss function in this manner. For example, a policy maker's loss function over inflation forecasts might depend on the unemployment rate so that losses from incorrect inflation forecasts depend on whether the unemployment rate is high or low. For simplicity, in what follows we will mostly drop the explicit dependence of the loss function on Z and focus on the simpler loss functions $L(f, Y)$.

2.1.1 Constructing a Loss Function

Construction of loss functions, much like construction of prior distributions in Bayesian analysis, requires a careful study of the forecasting problem at hand and should reflect the actual trade-offs between forecast errors of different signs and magnitudes. Laying out the trade-off can be straightforward if the decision environment is fully specified and naturally results in a measurable outcome that depends on the forecast. For example, for a profit-maximizing investor with a specific trading strategy that requires forecasts of future asset prices, the natural choice of loss is the function relating payoffs to the forecast and realized returns. Other problems may not lead so easily to a specific loss function. For example, when the IMF forecasts individual countries' budget deficits, both short-term considerations related to debt financing costs and long-term reputational concerns could matter.[2] In such cases one can again follow a Bayesian prior selection strategy of defining a function that approximates a reasonable shape of losses associated with decisions based on incorrect forecasts.

Loss functions, as used by forecasters to evaluate their performance, and utility functions, as used by economists to assess the economic value of different outcomes, are naturally related. Both are grounded in the same decision-theoretic setup which regards the forecast as the decision and the outcome as the true state and maps pairs of outcomes (states) and forecasts (Y, f) to the real line. In both cases we are interested in minimizing the expected loss or disutility that arises from the decision.[3]

The relationship between utility and loss is examined in Granger and Machina (2006), who show that the loss function can be viewed as the negative of a utility function, although a more general relation of the following form holds:

$$U(f, Y) = k(Y) - L(f, Y), \tag{2.1}$$

where $k(Y)$ plays no role in the derivation of the optimal forecast.[4]

Example 2.1.1 (Squared loss and utility). *Granger and Machina (2006) show that a utility function $U(f, Y)$ generates squared error loss, $L(f, Y) = a(Y - f)^2$, for $a > 0$, if and only if it takes the form*

$$U(f, Y) = k(Y) - a(Y - f)^2. \tag{2.2}$$

It follows that utility functions associated with squared error loss are restricted to a very narrow set.

---

[2] Forecasts can even have feedback effects on outcomes as in the case of credit ratings companies whose credit scores can trigger debt payments for private companies that affect future ratings (Manso, 2013).

[3] The first section of chapter 3 examines this issue in more detail.

[4] Granger and Machina (2006) allow decisions to depend on forecasts without requiring that the two necessarily be identical. Instead they require that the function mapping forecasts to decisions is monotonic.

Academic studies often do not derive loss functions from first principles by referring to utility functions or fully specified decision-theoretic problems, though there are some exceptions. Loss functions that take the form of profit functions have been used to evaluate forecasts by Leitch and Tanner (1991) and Elliott and Ito (1999). West et al. (1993) compare utility-based and statistical measures of predictive accuracy for exchange rate models. Examples of loss functions derived from utility are provided in the final section of this chapter.

2.1.2 Common Properties of Loss Functions

Reasonable loss functions are grounded in economic decision problems. Under the utility-maximizing approach, loss functions inherit well-known properties from the utility function. Rather than deriving loss functions from first principles, however, it is common practice to instead use loss functions with a "reasonable shape." For the loss function to be "reasonable," a set of minimal properties should hold. Other properties such as symmetry or homogeneity may suggest broad families of loss functions with certain desirable characteristics. We cover both types of properties below.

Trade-offs between different forecast errors when $f \neq y$ are quantified by the loss function. To capture the notion that bigger errors imply bigger losses, often it is imposed that the loss is nondecreasing as the forecast moves further away from the outcome. Mathematically, this means that $L(f_2, y) \geq L(f_1, y)$ for either $f_2 > f_1 > y$ or $f_2 < f_1 < y$ for all real y. Nearly all loss functions used in practice have this feature.

For loss functions that depend only on the forecast error, $e = y - f$, and thus take the form $L(f, y) = L(e)$, Granger (1999) summarized these requirements:

$$L(0) = 0 \text{ (minimal loss of 0);} \tag{2.3a}$$

$$L(e) \geq 0 \text{ for all } e; \tag{2.3b}$$

$L(e)$ is nonincreasing in e for $e < 0$ and nondecreasing in e for $e > 0$:

$$L(e_1) \leq L(e_2) \text{ if } e_2 < e_1 < 0, \qquad L(e_1) \leq L(e_2) \text{ if } e_2 > e_1 > 0. \tag{2.3c}$$

As in the case with more general loss, $L(f, y)$, condition (2.3a) simply normalizes the loss associated with the perfect forecast ($y = f$) to be 0. The second condition states that imperfect forecasts ($y \neq f$) generate larger loss than perfect ones. Most common loss functions depend only on e; see section 2.2 for examples.

Other properties of loss functions such as homogeneity, symmetry, differentiability, and boundedness can be used to define broad classes of loss functions. We next review these.

Homogeneity can be used to define classes of loss functions that lead to the same decisions. Homogeneous loss functions factor in such a way that

$$L(af, ay) = h(a)L(f, y), \tag{2.4}$$

for some positive function $h(a)$, where the degree of homogeneity does not matter. For loss functions that depend only on the forecast error, homogeneity amounts to $L(ae) = h(a)L(e)$ for some positive function $h(a)$. Homogeneity is a useful property when solving for optimal forecasts since the optimal forecast will be invariant to different values of $h(a)$.

Symmetry of the loss function refers to symmetry of the forecast around y. It is the property that, for all f,

$$L(y - f, y) = L(y + f, y). \tag{2.5}$$

For loss functions that depend only on the forecast error, symmetry reduces to $L(-e) = L(e)$, so that over- and underpredictions of the same magnitude lead to identical loss.[5]

Most empirical work in economic forecasting assumes symmetric loss. This choice reflects the difficulties in putting numbers on the relative cost of over- and underpredictions. Construction of a loss function requires a deeper understanding of the forecaster's objectives and this may be difficult to accomplish. Still, the implicit choice of MSE loss by the majority of studies in the forecasting literature seems difficult to justify on economic grounds. As noted by Granger and Newbold (1986, page 125), "an assumption of symmetry about the conditional mean... is likely to be an easy one to accept... an assumption of symmetry for the cost function is much less acceptable."

Differentiability of the loss function with respect to the forecast is again a regularity condition that is useful and helps simplify numerically the search for optimal forecasts. However, this condition may not be desirable and is certainly not required for a loss function to be well defined. In general, a finite numbers of points where the loss function fails to be differentiable will not cause undue problems at the estimation stage. However, when the loss function is extremely irregular, different methods are required for understanding the statistical properties of the loss function (see the maximum utility estimator in chapter 12).

Finally, loss functions may be bounded or unbounded. As a practical matter, there is often no obvious reason to let the weight the loss function places on very large forecast errors increase without bound. For example, the squared error loss function examined below assigns very different losses to forecasts of, say, US inflation that result in errors of 100% versus 500% even though it is not obvious that the associated losses should really be very different since both forecasts would lead to very similar actions. Unbounded loss functions can create technical problems for the analysis of forecasts as the expected loss may not exist, so most results in decision theory are derived under the assumption of bounded loss. In practice, forecasts are usually bounded and extremely large forecasts typically get trimmed as they are deemed implausible.

2.1.3 Existence of Expected Loss

Restrictions must be imposed on the form of the loss function to make sense of the idea of minimizing the expected loss. Most basically, it is required that the expected loss exists. Suppose the forecast depends on data Z through a vector of parameters, β, which depends on the parameters of the data generating process, θ, so $f = f(z, \beta)$. From the definition of expected loss, we have

$$E_Y[L(f(z, \beta), Y)] = \int L(f(z, \beta), y) p_Y(y|z, \theta) dy, \tag{2.6}$$

---

[5] A related concept is the class of bowl-shaped loss functions. A loss function is bowl shaped if the level sets $\{e : L(e) \le c\}$ are convex and symmetric about the origin.

where $p_Y(y|z, \theta)$ is the predictive density of y given z, θ. When the space of outcomes $\mathcal{Y}$ is finite, this expression is guaranteed to be finite. However, for outcomes that are continuously distributed, restrictions must sometimes be imposed on the loss function to ensure finite expected loss. The existence of expected loss depends, both, on the loss function and on the distribution of the predicted variable, given the data, $p_Y(y|z, \theta)$, where θ denotes the parameters of this conditional distribution. Existence of expected loss thus hinges on how large losses can get in relation to the tail behavior of the predicted variable, as captured by $p_Y(y|z, \theta)$.

A direct way to ensure that the expected loss exists is to bound the loss function from above.[6] From a practical perspective this would seem to be a sensible practice in constructing loss functions. Even so, many of the most popular loss functions are not bounded from above. In part this practice stems from not considering the loss related to the forecasting problem at hand, but instead borrowing "off-the-shelf" loss functions from estimation methods that lead to simple closed-form expressions for the optimal forecast.

It is useful to demonstrate the conditions needed to ensure that the expected loss exists. Following Elliott and Timmermann (2004), suppose that L depends only on the forecast error, $e = y - f$, and lends itself to a Taylor-series expansion around the mean error, $\mu_e = E_Y[Y - f]$:

$$L(e) = L(\mu_e) + L'_{\mu_e}(e - \mu_e) + \frac{1}{2}L''_{\mu_e}(e - \mu_e)^2 + \sum_{k=3}^{\infty}\left(\frac{1}{k!}\right)L^k_{\mu_e}(e - \mu_e)^k, \quad (2.7)$$

where $L^k_{\mu_e}$ denotes the kth derivative of L evaluated at μ_e. Suppose there are only a finite number of points where L is not analytic and that these can be ignored because they occur with probability 0. Taking expectations in (2.7), we then get

$$E[L(e)] = L(\mu_e) + \frac{1}{2}L''_{\mu_e}E_Y[(e - \mu_e)^2] + \sum_{k=3}^{\infty}\left(\frac{1}{k!}\right)L^k_{\mu_e}E_Y[(e - \mu_e)^k]$$

$$= L(\mu_e) + \frac{1}{2}L''_{\mu_e}E_Y[(e - \mu_e)^2] + \sum_{k=3}^{\infty}\left(\frac{1}{k!}\right)L^k_{\mu_e}\sum_{i=0}^{k}\binom{k}{i}E_Y[e^{k-i}\mu_e^i]$$

$$= L(\mu_e) + \frac{1}{2}L''_{\mu_e}E_Y[(e - \mu_e)^2] + \sum_{k=3}^{\infty}L^k_{\mu_e}\sum_{i=0}^{k}\frac{1}{i!(k-i)!}E_Y[e^{k-i}\mu_e^i].$$

$$(2.8)$$

This expression is finite provided that all moments of the error distribution exist for which the corresponding derivative of the loss function with respect to the forecast error is nonzero. This is a strong requirement and rules out some interesting combinations of loss functions and forecast error distributions. For example, exponential loss (or the Linex loss function defined below) and a student-t distribution with a finite number of degrees of freedom would lead to infinite expected loss since all higher-order moments do not exist for this distribution. What is required to make

---

[6] This is sufficient since we have already bounded the loss function (typically at 0) from below.

the higher-order terms in (2.8) vanish is that the tail decay of the predicted variable is sufficiently fast relative to the weight on these terms implied by the loss function.

2.1.4 Loss Functions Not Based on Expected Loss

So far we have characterized the loss function $L(f, Y)$ for a univariate outcome, and defined its properties with reference to a "one-shot" problem. This makes sense when forecasting is placed in a decision-theoretic or utility-maximization context. This approach to forecasting is internally consistent, from initially setting up the problem to defining the expected loss and conducting model estimation and forecast evaluation.

Some loss functions that have been used in practice are based directly on sample statistics without relating the sample loss to a population loss function. In cases where such a population loss function exists and satisfies reasonable properties, this does not cause any problems. Basing the loss function directly on a sample of losses can, however, sometimes yield a loss function that does not make sense in population or for fully specified decision problems. Loss functions that do not map back to decision problems often have poor and unintended properties. We consider one such example below.

Example 2.1.2 (Kuipers score for binary outcome). *Let $f = \{1, -1\}$ be a forecast of the binary variable $y = \{1, -1\}$ and let $n_{j,k}$, $j, k \in \{-1, 1\}$ be the number of observations for which the forecast equals j and the outcome equals k. The Kuipers score is given by*

$$\frac{n_{1,1}}{n_{1,1} + n_{-1,1}} - \frac{n_{1,-1}}{n_{1,-1} + n_{-1,-1}}. \tag{2.9}$$

This is the positive hit rate, i.e., the proportion of times where $y = 1$ is correctly predicted less the "false positive rate," i.e., the proportion of times where $y = 1$ is wrongly predicted. This can equivalently be thought of as

$$\text{KuS} = \frac{n_{1,1}}{n_{1,1} + n_{-1,1}} + \frac{n_{-1,-1}}{n_{1,-1} + n_{-1,-1}} - 1, \tag{2.10}$$

which is the hit rate for $y = 1$ plus the hit rate for $y = -1$ minus a centering constant of 1. The Kuipers score is positive if the sum of the positive and negative hit rates exceeds 1. For a sample with a single observation, this definition makes no sense, as one of the denominators in (2.10) is 0: either $n_{1,1} + n_{-1,1} = 0$ or $n_{1,-1} + n_{-1,-1} = 0$.

For a single observation, this sample statistic does not follow from any obvious loss function. The first term in (2.10) is the sample analog of $P[f = 1|Y = 1]$ and the second is the sample analog of $P[f = -1|Y = -1]$. However, they do not combine to a loss function with this sample analog. This failure to embed the loss function into the expected loss framework results in odd properties for the objective. For example, the definition of KuS in (2.9) implies that the marginal value of an extra "hit," i.e., a correct call, depends on the sample proportion of hits. To see this, consider the improvement in KuS from adding a single successfully predicted observation $y = 1$, $f = 1$.

The resulting improvement in the hit rate is

$$\Delta \text{KuS} = \frac{n_{1,1} + 1}{n_{1,1} + 1 + n_{-1,1}} - \frac{n_{1,1}}{n_{1,1} + n_{-1,1}}$$

$$= \frac{n_{-1,1}}{(n_{1,1} + n_{-1,1})(n_{1,1} + 1 + n_{-1,1})}.$$

Thus the marginal value of a correct call depends on the total number of observations and the proportion of missed hits prior to the new observation. The Kuipers score's poor properties arise from the lack of justification of its setup for a population problem.

2.2 SPECIFIC LOSS FUNCTIONS

We next review various families of loss functions that have been suggested in the forecasting literature. The vast majority of empirical work on forecasting assumes that the loss function depends only on the forecast error, $e = Y - f$, i.e., the difference between the outcome and the forecast. In this case we can write $L(f, Y, Z) = L(e)$. In general, loss functions can be more complicated functions of the outcome and forecast and take the form $L(f, Y)$ or $L(f, Y, Z)$.

2.2.1 Loss That Depends Only on Forecast Errors

The most commonly used loss functions, including squared error loss and absolute error loss, depend only on the forecast error. For such loss functions, $L(f, Y, Z) = L(e)$, so the loss function takes a particularly simple form.

2.2.1.1 Squared Error Loss

By far the most popular loss function in empirical studies is squared error loss, also known as quadratic or mean squared error (MSE) loss:

$$L(e) = ae^2, \quad a > 0. \tag{2.11}$$

This loss function clearly satisfies the three Granger properties listed in (2.3). When viewed as a family of loss functions—corresponding to different values of the scalar a—squared error loss forms a homogeneous class.[7] It is symmetric, bowl shaped, and differentiable everywhere and penalizes large forecast errors at an increasing rate due to its convexity in $|e|$. The loss function is not bounded from above. Large forecast errors or "outliers" are thus very costly under this loss function.

2.2.1.2 Absolute Error Loss

Rather than using squared error loss, which results in increasingly large losses for large forecast errors, the absolute error is preferred in some cases. Under mean absolute error (MAE) loss,

$$L(e) = a|e|, \quad a > 0. \tag{2.12}$$

---

[7] While the scaling factor, a, does not matter to the properties of the optimal forecast, it is common to set $a = 0.5$, which removes the "2" that arises from taking first derivatives.

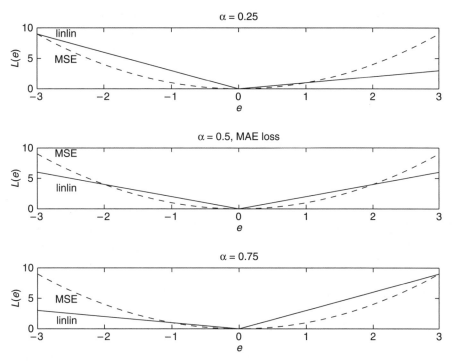

Figure 2.1: MSE loss versus lin-lin loss for different values of the lin-lin asymmetry parameter, α.

Like MSE loss, this loss function satisfies the three Granger properties listed in (2.3). The loss function is symmetric, bowl shaped, and differentiable everywhere except at 0. It is again unbounded. However, the penalty to large forecast errors increases linearly rather than quadratically as for MSE loss.

2.2.1.3 Piecewise Linear Loss

Piecewise linear, or so-called lin-lin loss, takes the form

$$L(e) = \begin{cases} -a(1-\alpha)e & \text{if } e \leq 0, \\ a\alpha e & \text{if } e > 0, \end{cases} \quad a > 0, \tag{2.13}$$

for $0 < \alpha < 1$. Positive forecast errors are assigned a (relative) weight of α, while negative errors get a weight of $1 - \alpha$. The greater is α, the bigger the loss from positive forecast errors, and the smaller the loss from negative errors. Again, this loss function forms a homogeneous class for all positive values of a. It is common to set $a = 1$, so that the weights are normalized to sum to 1.

Lin-lin loss clearly satisfies the three Granger properties. Moreover, it is differentiable everywhere, except at 0. Compared to MSE loss, this loss function does not penalize large errors as much. MAE loss arises as a special case of lin-lin loss if $\alpha = 0.5$, in which case (2.13) simplifies to (2.12).

Figure 2.1 plots lin-lin loss against squared error loss. The middle window shows the symmetric case with $\alpha = 0.5$, and so corresponds to MAE loss. Small forecast errors ($|e| < 1$) are costlier under MAE loss than under MSE loss, while conversely large errors are costlier under MSE loss. The top window assumes that $\alpha = 0.25$, so negative forecast errors are three times as costly as positive errors, reflected in the steeper slope of the loss curve for $e < 0$. In the bottom window, $\alpha = 0.75$ and so positive forecast errors are three times costlier than negative errors.

2.2.1.4 Linex Loss

Linear-exponential, or Linex, loss takes the form

$$L(e) = a_1(\exp(a_2e) - a_2e - 1), \quad a_2 \neq 0, a_1 > 0. \tag{2.14}$$

Linex loss is differentiable everywhere, but is not symmetric. Varian (1975) used this loss function to analyze real estate assessments, while Zellner (1986a) used it in the context of Bayesian prediction problems.

The parameter a_2 controls both the degree and direction of asymmetry. When $a_2 > 0$, Linex loss is approximately linear for negative forecast errors and approximately exponential for positive forecast errors. In this case, large underpredictions ($f < y$, so $e = y - f > 0$) are costlier than overpredictions of the same magnitude, with the relative cost increasing as the magnitude of the forecast error rises. Conversely, for $a_2 < 0$, large overpredictions are costlier than equally large underpredictions.

Although Linex loss is not defined for $a_1 = 0$, setting $a_1 = 2/a_2^2$ and taking the limit as $a_2 \to 0$, by L'Hôpital's rule the Linex loss function approaches squared error loss:

$$\lim_{a_2 \to 0} L(e) = \lim_{a_2 \to 0} \frac{\exp(a_2e) - e}{2a_2} = \lim_{a_2 \to 0} \frac{e^2 \exp(a_2e)}{2} = \frac{e^2}{2}.$$

Figure 2.2 plots MSE loss against Linex loss for $a_2 = 1$ (top) and $a_2 = -1$ (bottom). Measured relative to the benchmark MSE loss, large positive (top) or large negative (bottom) forecast errors are very costly in these respective cases. This loss function has been used in many empirical studies on variables such as budget forecasts (Artis and Marcellino, 2001) and survey forecasts of inflation (Capistrán and Timmermann, 2009). Christoffersen and Diebold (1997) examine this loss function in more detail.

2.2.1.5 Piecewise Asymmetric Loss

A general class of asymmetric loss functions can be constructed by letting the loss function shift at a discrete set of points, $\{\bar{e}_1, \ldots, \bar{e}_{n-1}\}$:

$$L(e) = \begin{cases} L_1(e) & \text{if } e \leq \bar{e}_1, \\ L_2(e) & \text{if } \bar{e}_1 < e \leq \bar{e}_2, \\ \vdots & \vdots \\ L_n(e) & \text{if } e > \bar{e}_{n-1}. \end{cases} \tag{2.15}$$

Here $\bar{e}_{i-1} < \bar{e}_i$ for $i = 2, \ldots, n - 1$. It is common to set $n = 2$, choose $\bar{e}_1 = 0$ and assume that both pieces of the loss function satisfy the usual loss properties so that the loss is piecewise asymmetric around 0 and continuous (but not necessarily

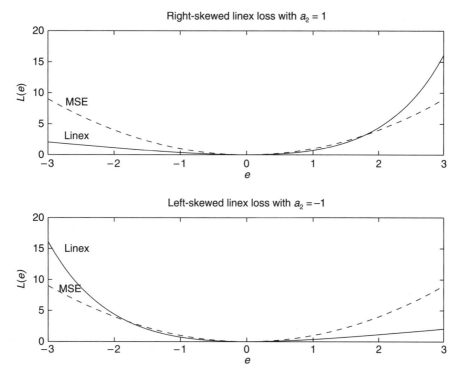

Figure 2.2: MSE loss versus Linex loss for different values of the Linex parameter, a_2.

differentiable) at 0. Lin-lin loss in (2.13) is a special case of (2.15) as is the asymmetric quadratic loss function

$$L(e) = \begin{cases} (1-\alpha)e^2 & \text{if } e \leq 0, \\ \alpha e^2 & \text{if } e > 0, \end{cases} \qquad (2.16)$$

considered by Artis and Marcellino (2001), Newey and Powell (1987) and Weiss (1996).

A flexible class of loss functions proposed by Elliott, Komunjer, and Timmermann (2005) sets $n = 2$ and $\bar{e}_1 = 0$ in (2.15), while $L_1(e) = (1-\alpha)|e|^p$ and $L_2(e) = \alpha|e|^p$, where p is a positive integer, and $\alpha \in (0, 1)$. This gives the EKT loss function,

$$L(e) \equiv [\alpha + (1-2\alpha)\mathbb{1}(e < 0)]|e|^p, \qquad (2.17)$$

where $\mathbb{1}(e < 0)$ is an indicator function that equals 1 if $e < 0$, otherwise equals 0. Letting α deviate from 0.5 produces asymmetric loss, with larger values of α indicating greater aversion to positive forecast errors. Imposing $p = 1$ and $\alpha = 0.5$, MAE loss is obtained. More generally, setting $p = 1$, (2.17) reduces to lin-lin loss since the loss is linear on both sides of 0, but with different slopes. Setting $p = 2$ and $\alpha = 0.5$ gives the MSE loss function which is therefore also nested as a special case, as is the asymmetric quadratic loss function (2.16) for $p = 2$, $\alpha \in (0, 1)$. Hence, the EKT family of loss functions nests the loss functions in (2.11), (2.12), (2.13), and (2.16) as special cases and generalizes many of the commonly employed loss functions.

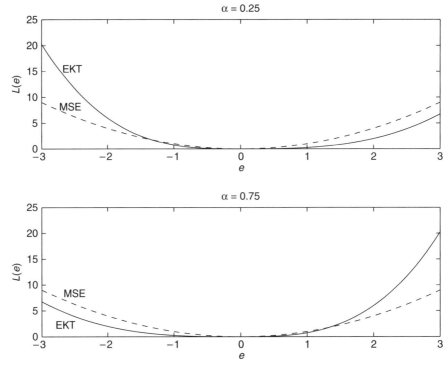

Figure 2.3: MSE loss versus EKT loss with p=3 for different values of the asymmetry parameter, α.

Figure 2.3 plots the EKT loss function for $p = 3$, $\alpha = 0.25$ (top) and $\alpha = 0.75$ (bottom). Compared with MSE loss, substantial asymmetries can be generated by this loss function.

Empirically, the EKT loss function has been used to analyze forecasts of government budget deficits produced by the IMF and OECD (Elliott, Komunjer, and Timmermann, 2005), the Federal Reserve Board's inflation forecasts (Capistrán, 2008), as well as output and inflation forecasts from the Survey of Professional Forecasters (Elliott, Komunjer, and Timmermann, 2008).

2.2.1.6 Binary Loss

When the space of outcomes $\mathcal{Y}$ is discrete, the forecast errors typically take on only a small number of possible values. Hence in constructing a loss function for such problems, all that is required is to evaluate each of a small number of possibilities. The simplest case arises when forecasting a binary outcome so that $\mathcal{Y} = \{-1, 1\}$ or $\mathcal{Y} = \{0, 1\}$. In this case there are only four possible pairings of the point forecast and outcome: two where the forecast gives the correct outcome and two errors. If we restrict the loss function to not depend on Z (this case is examined below) and also restrict the problem so that a correct forecast has the same value regardless of the value for Y, then the binary loss function can be written as[8]

$$L(f, y) = \begin{cases} 0 & \text{if } f = y = 0, \\ (1 - c) & \text{if } f = 0, y = 1, \\ c & \text{if } f = 1, y = 0, \\ 0 & \text{if } f = y = 1. \end{cases} \tag{2.18}$$

Here we have set the loss from a correct prediction to 0 and normalized the losses from an incorrect forecast to sum to 1 by dividing by their sum; see Schervish (1989), Boyes, Hoffman, and Low (1989), Granger and Pesaran (2000), and Elliott and Lieli (2013).

For (2.18) to be a valid loss function, we require that $0 < c < 1$. This ensures that the properties of the loss function listed in (2.3) hold. Notice that the binary loss function can be written as $L(e)$, since the loss is equal to

$$L(f, y) = c\mathbb{1}(e < 0) + (1 - c)\mathbb{1}(e > 0).$$

2.2.2 Level- and Forecast-Dependent Loss Functions

Economic loss is mostly assumed to depend on only the forecast error, $e = Y - f$. This is too restrictive an assumption for situations in which the forecaster's objective function depends on state variables such as the level of the outcome variable Y. More generally, we can consider loss functions of the form $L(f, y) \neq L(e)$. The most common level-dependent loss function is the mean absolute percentage error (MAPE), given by

$$L(e, y) = a \left| \frac{e}{y} \right|. \tag{2.19}$$

Since the forecast and forecast error have the same units as the outcome, the MAPE is a unitless loss function. This is considered to be an advantage when constructing the sample analog of this loss function and employing it to evaluate forecast methods across outcomes measured in different units. If the loss function is well grounded in terms of the actual costs arising from the forecasting problem, dependence on units does not seem to be an important issue—comparisons across different forecasts with different units should be related not through some arbitrary adjustment but instead in a way that trades off the costs associated with the forecast errors for each of the outcomes. This is achieved by the multivariate loss functions examined in the next section.

Scaling the forecast error by the outcome in (2.19) has the effect of weighting forecast errors more heavily when y is near 0 than when y is far from 0. This is difficult to justify in many applications. Moreover, if the predictive density for Y has nontrivial mass at 0, then the expected loss is unlikely to exist, hence invalidating many of the results from decision theory for this case. Nonetheless, MAPE loss remains popular in many practical forecast evaluation experiments.

More generally, level- and forecast-dependent loss functions can be written as $L(f, y)$ but do not reduce to $L(e)$ or $L(e, y)$. Although loss functions in this class

---

[8] See chapter 12 for a comprehensive treatment of forecast analysis under this loss function.

are not particularly common, there are examples of their use. For example, Bregman (1967) suggested loss functions of the form

$$L(f, y) = \phi(y) - \phi(f) - \phi'(f)(y - f),$$ (2.20)

where ϕ is a strictly convex function, so $\phi'' > 0$. Squared error loss is nested as a special case of 2.20.

Differentiating (2.20) with respect to the forecast, f, we get

$$\frac{\partial L(f, y)}{\partial f} = -\phi'(f) - \phi''(f)(y - f) + \phi'(f)$$
$$= -\phi''(f)(y - f),$$

which generally depends on both y and f. This, along with the assumption that $\phi'' > 0$, ensures that the conditional mean is the optimal forecast. Bregman loss is further discussed in Patton (2015).

In an empirical application of level-dependent loss, Patton and Timmermann (2007b) find that the Federal Reserve's forecasts of output growth fail to be optimal if their loss is restricted to depend only on the forecast error. Rationalizing the Federal Reserve's forecasts requires not only that overpredictions of output growth are costlier than underpredictions, but also that overpredictions of output are particularly costly during periods of low economic growth. This finding can be justified if the cost of an overly tight monetary policy is particularly high during periods with low economic growth when such a policy may cause or extend a recession.[9]

2.2.3 Loss Functions That Depend on Other State Variables

Under some simplifying assumptions we saw earlier that the binary loss function takes a particularly simple form. More generally, if the loss function depends on Z and the loss associated with a perfect forecast depends on the outcome Y, then the loss function for the binary problem becomes

$$L(f, y, z) = \begin{cases} -u_{1,1}(z) & \text{if } f = 1 \text{ and } y = 1, \\ -u_{1,0}(z) & \text{if } f = 1 \text{ and } y = 0, \\ -u_{0,1}(z) & \text{if } f = 0 \text{ and } y = 1, \\ -u_{0,0}(z) & \text{if } f = 0 \text{ and } y = 0, \end{cases}$$ (2.21)

where $u_{i,j}(z)$ are the utilities gained when $f = i$, $y = j$, and $Z = z$.

In this general form, the loss function cannot be simplified to depend only on the forecast error. Again restrictions need to be imposed on the losses in (2.21). First, we require that $u_{0,0}(z) > u_{1,0}(z)$ and $u_{1,1}(z) > u_{0,1}(z)$ so that losses associated with correct forecasts are not higher than those associated with incorrect forecasts. We might also impose that $\min\{u_{0,0}(z), u_{1,1}(z)\} > \max\{u_{1,0}(z), u_{1,0}(z)\}$ so that correct forecasts result in a lower loss (higher utility) than incorrect forecasts. Finally, it is

---

[9] Some central banks desire to keep inflation within a band of 0 to 2% per annum. Inflation within this band might be regarded as a successful outcome, whereas deflation or inflation above 2% is viewed as failure. Again this is indicative of a nonstandard loss function; see Kilian and Manganelli (2008).

quite reasonable to assume that correct forecasts are associated with different losses $u_{0,0}(z) \neq u_{1,1}(z)$, in which case normalizing the loss associated with a perfect forecast to 0 will not be possible for both outcomes. This is an example of level-dependent loss being built directly into the loss function.

2.2.4 Consistent Ranking of Forecasts with Measurement Errors in the Outcome

Hansen and Lunde (2006) and Patton (2011) consider the problem of comparing and consistently ranking volatility forecasts from different models when the observed outcome is measured with noise. This situation is common in volatility forecasting or in macro forecasting where the outcome may subsequently be revised. The volatility of asset returns is never actually observed although a proxy for it can be constructed. Volatility forecast comparisons typically use realized volatility, squared returns, or range-based proxies, $\hat{\sigma}^2$, in place of the true variance, σ^2.

Hansen and Lunde establish sufficient conditions under which noisy proxies can be used in the forecast evaluation without giving rise to rankings that are inconsistent with the (infeasible) ranking based on the true outcome.

Patton defines a loss function as being robust to measurement errors in the outcome if it gives the same expected-loss ranking of two forecasts whether based on the true (but unobserved) outcome or some unbiased proxy thereof. Specifically, a loss function is robust to such measurement errors if, for two forecasts f_1 and f_2, the ranking based on the true outcome, y,

$$E[L(f_1, y)] \gtreqqless E[L(f_2, y)]$$

is the same as the ranking based on the proxied outcome, $\hat{y}$:

$$E[L(f_1, \hat{y})] \gtreqqless E[L(f_2, \hat{y})],$$

for unbiased proxies $\hat{y}$ satisfying $E[\hat{y}|Z] = y$, where Z is again the information set used to generate the forecasts.

Patton (2011, Proposition 1) establishes conditions under which robust loss functions must belong to the following family:

$$L(f, \hat{y}) = \tilde{C}(f) + B(\hat{y}) + C(f)(\hat{y} - f), \tag{2.22}$$

where B and C are twice continuously differentiable functions, C is strictly decreasing, and $\tilde{C}$ is the antiderivative of C, i.e., $\tilde{C}' = C$.[10] In Patton's analysis f is a volatility forecast and $\hat{y}$ is a proxy for the realized volatility. Examples of loss functions in the family (2.22) include MSE and QLIKE loss:

$$\text{MSE} : L(f, \hat{y}) = (\hat{y} - f)^2,$$

$$\text{QLIKE} : L(f, \hat{y}) = \log(f) + \frac{\hat{y}}{f}.$$

---

[10] If $B = -\tilde{C}$, this family of loss functions yields the Bregman family in equation (2.20).

2.3 MULTIVARIATE LOSS FUNCTIONS

When a decision maker's objectives depend on multiple variables, the loss function needs to be extended from being defined over scalar outcomes to depend on a vector of outcomes. This situation arises, for example, for a central bank concerned with both inflation and employment prospects.

Conceptually it is easy to generalize univariate loss functions to the multivariate case, although difficulties may arise in determining how costly different combinations of forecast errors are. How individual forecast errors or their cross products are weighted becomes particularly important.

The most common multivariate loss function is multivariate quadratic error loss, also known as multivariate MSE loss; see Clements and Hendry (1993). This loss function maps a vector of forecast errors $e = (e_1, \dots, e_n)'$ to the real number line and so is simply a weighted average of the individual squared forecast errors and their cross products:[11]

$$\text{MSE}(A) = e'Ae. \tag{2.23}$$

Here the $(n \times n)$ matrix A is required to be nonnegative and positive definite. This is the matrix equivalent of the univariate assumption for MSE loss that $a > 0$ in (2.11).

As noted in the discussion of MAPE loss, the loss function in (2.23) may be difficult to interpret when the predicted variables are measured in different units. This concern is related to obtaining a reasonable specification of the loss function whose role it is to compare and trade off losses of different sizes across different variables. Hence this is not really a limitation of the loss function itself but of applications of the loss function.

The loss function in (2.23) is "bowl shaped" in the sense that the level sets are convex and symmetric around 0. It is easily verified that (2.23) satisfies the basic assumptions for a loss function in (2.3). If the entire vector of forecast errors is 0, then the loss is 0. A positive-definite and nonnegative weighting matrix A ensures that losses rise as forecast errors get larger, so assumption (2.3c) holds.[12]

A special case arises when $A = I_n$, the $(n \times n)$ identity matrix. In this case covariances can be ignored and the loss function simplifies to $\text{MSE}(I_n) = E[e'e] = \text{tr } E[(ee')]$, i.e., the sum of the individual mean squared errors. Thus, a loss function based on the trace of the covariance matrix of forecast errors is simply a special case of the general form in (2.23). In general, however, covariances between forecast errors come into play, reflecting the cross products corresponding to the off-diagonal terms in A.

As a second example of a multivariate loss function, Komunjer and Owyang (2012) provides an interesting generalization of the Elliott, Komunjer, and Timmermann (2005) loss function in (2.17) to the case where $e = (e_1, \dots, e_n)'$.

---

[11] While the vector of forecast errors could represent different variables, it could also comprise forecast errors for the same variable measured at different horizons, corresponding to short and long-horizon forecasts.

[12] Positive-definiteness alone is not sufficient to guarantee that the multivariate equivalent to (2.3) holds. Suppose $n = 2$ and let A be a symmetric matrix with 2 on the diagonals and -1 in the off-diagonal cells. A is positive definite but the marginal effect of making a bigger error on the second forecast is $4e_2 - 2e_1$, where $e = (e_1, e_2)'$. Hence if $e_2 < e_1/2$, increasing the error associated with the second forecast would reduce loss, thus violating (2.3).

Let $||e||_p = (|e_1|^p + \cdots + |e_n|^p)^{1/p}$ be the l_p norm of e and assume that the n-vector of asymmetry parameters, α, satisfies $||\alpha||_q < 1$. Further, let $1 \leq p \leq \infty$ and, for a given value of p, set q so that $1/p + 1/q = 1$. The multivariate loss function proposed by Komunjer and Owyang takes the form

$$L(e) = (||e||_p + \alpha' e)||e||_p^{p-1}. \tag{2.24}$$

As in the univariate case, the extent to which large forecast errors are penalized relative to small ones is determined by the exponent, p. However, now the full vector $\alpha = (\alpha_1, \ldots, \alpha_n)$ characterizes the asymmetry in the loss function, with $\alpha = 0$ representing the symmetric case. Since α is a vector, this loss function offers great flexibility in both the magnitude and direction of asymmetry for multivariate loss functions.

Other multivariate loss functions have been used empirically. Laurent, Rombouts, and Violante (2013) consider a multivariate version of the family of loss functions introduced by Patton (2011), and apply it to volatility forecasting.

2.4 SCORING RULES FOR DISTRIBUTION FORECASTS

So far we have focused our discussion on point forecasts, but forecasts of the full distribution of outcomes are increasingly reported. Just as point forecasting requires a loss-based measure of the distance between the forecast f and the outcome Y, distribution forecasts also require a loss function. These are known as scoring rules and reward forecasters for making more accurate predictions, i.e., predictions that are "closer" to the observed outcome get a higher score, where closeness depends on the shape of the scoring rule. Gneiting and Raftery (2007) provide a survey of scoring rules and discuss their properties.

Scoring rules, $S(p, y)$, are mappings of predictive probability distributions, p, and outcomes, y, to the real line. Suppose a forecaster uses the predictive probability distribution, p, while the probability distribution used to evaluate the "goodness of fit" of p is denoted p_0. Then the expected value of $S(p, y)$ under p_0 is denoted $S(p, p_0)$. A scoring rule is called strictly proper if the forecaster's best probability distribution is p_0, i.e., $S(p_0, p_0) \geq S(p, p_0)$ with equality holding only if $p = p_0$. In this situation there will be no incentive for the forecaster to use a probability distribution $p \neq p_0$ since this would reduce the score. The performance of a given candidate probability distribution, p, relative to the optimal rule, can be measured through the so-called divergence function

$$d(p, p_0) = S(p_0, p_0) - S(p, p_0). \tag{2.25}$$

Notice the similarity to the normalization in equation (2.3a) for loss functions based on point forecasts in (2.3): the divergence function obtains its minimum value of 0 only if $p = p_0$, and otherwise takes a positive value. The forecaster's objective of maximizing the scoring rule thus translates into minimizing the divergence function.

Several scoring rules have been used in the literature. Many of these have been considered for categorical data limited to discrete outcomes $y = (y_1, \ldots, y_m)$ with associated probabilities $\{p_1, \ldots, p_m\}$. Denote by p_i the predicted probability that corresponds to the range that includes y_i. The logarithmic score,

$$S(p, y_i) = \log(p_i), \tag{2.26}$$

gives rise to the well-known Kullback–Leibler divergence measure,

$$d(p, p_0) = \sum_{j=1}^{m} p_{0j} \log(p_{0j}/p_j). \tag{2.27}$$

Similarly, the quadratic or Brier score,

$$S(p, y_i) = 2p_i - \sum_{j=1}^{m} p_j^2 - 1, \tag{2.28}$$

generates the squared divergence

$$d(p, p_0) = \sum_{j=1}^{m} (p_j - p_{0j})^2. \tag{2.29}$$

For density forecasts defined over continuous outcomes the logarithmic and quadratic scores take the form

$$\log S(p, y) = \log p(y),$$

$$S(p, y) = 2p(y) - \left(\int p(y)^2 \mu(dy) \right)^{1/2},$$

where $\mu(\cdot)$ is the probability measure associated with the outcome, y. Both are proper scoring rules. By contrast, the linear score, $S(p, y) = p(y)$, can be shown not to be a proper scoring rule; see Gneiting and Raftery (2007).

Which scoring rule to use in a given situation depends, of course, on the underlying objectives for the problem at hand and the choice should most closely resemble the costs involved in the decision problem. To illustrate this point, we next provide an example from the semiconductor supply chain.

Example 2.4.1 (Loss function for semiconductors). *Cohen et al. (2003) construct an economically motivated loss or cost function for a semiconductor equipment supply chain. Supply firms are assumed to hold soft orders from clients which may either be canceled (with probability π) or get finalized (with probability $1 - \pi$) at some later date, y_N, when the final information arrives. Given such orders, firms attempt to optimally determine the timing of the production start, y_π, where $y_N > y_\pi$ due to a production lead-time delay. If an order is canceled, the supplier incurs a cancelation cost, c, per unit of time. Let y denote the final delivery date in excess of the production lead time. If this exceeds the production date, the supplier will incur holding (inventory) costs, h, per unit of time. Conversely, if the production start date, y_π, exceeds y, the company will not be able to meet the requested delivery date and so incurs a delay cost of g per unit of time. Cohen et al. (2003) assume that suppliers choose the production* *date, y_π, so as to minimize the expected total cost*

$$E[L(y_\pi, y, y_N)] = \pi \times c \int_{y_\pi}^{\infty} (y_N - y_\pi) d P_N(y_N)$$

$$+ (1 - \pi) \left[h \int_{y_\pi}^{\infty} (y - y_\pi) d P_y(y) + g \int_{-\infty}^{y_\pi} (y_\pi - y) d P_y(y) \right],$$

where $P_y(y)$ and $P_N(y_N)$ are the cumulative distribution functions of y and y_N, respectively. Provided that this expression is convex in y_π, the cost-minimizing production time, y_π^*, can be shown to solve the first-order condition

$$\pi \times c \times P_N(y_\pi^*) + (1 - \pi)(g + h) P_y(y_\pi^*) = \pi \times c + (1 - \pi)h, \tag{2.30}$$

and so implicitly depends on the cancelation probability, cancelation costs, inventory and delay costs, in addition to the predictive distributions for the finalization and final delivery dates. Cohen et al. (2003) use an exponential distribution to model the arrival time of the final order, P_N, and a Weibull distribution to model the distribution of the final delivery date, P_Y. To estimate the model parameters and predict the lead time, the authors use data on soft orders, final orders, and order lead time. Empirical estimates suggest that $\hat{g} = 1.0$, $\hat{h} = 3.0$, $\hat{c} = 2.1$, indicating that holding costs are three times greater than delay costs, while cancelation costs are twice as high as the delay costs. This in turn helps the manufacturer decide on the optimal start date for production, y_π^*.

2.5 EXAMPLES OF APPLICATIONS OF FORECASTS IN MACROECONOMICS AND FINANCE

Forecasts are of interest to economic agents only in so far as they can help improve their decisions, so it is useful to illustrate the importance of forecasts in the context of some simple economic decision problems. This section provides three such examples from economics and finance.

2.5.1 Central Bank's Decision Problem

Consider a central bank with an objective of targeting inflation by means of a single policy instrument, y_t, which could be an interest rate such as the repo rate, i.e., the rate charged on collateralized loans. Svensson (1997) sets out a simple model in which the central bank's loss function depends on the difference between the inflation rate (y_t) and a target inflation rate (y^*). Svensson shows that, conditional on having chosen a value for its instrument (the repo rate), the central bank's decision problem reduces to that of choosing a forecast that minimizes the deviation from the target. Although the forecast does not enter directly into the central bank's loss function, it does so indirectly because the actual rate of inflation (which is what the central bank really cares about) is affected by the bank's choice of interest rate which in turn reflects the inflation forecast.

Specifically, the central bank is assumed to choose a sequence of interest rates $\{i_\tau\}_{\tau=t}^\infty$ to minimize a weighted sum of expected future losses,

$$E_t \sum_{\tau=t}^\infty \lambda^{\tau-t} L(y_\tau - y^*), \qquad (2.31)$$

where $\lambda \in (0, 1)$ is a discount rate and $E_t[\ ]$ denotes the conditional expectation given information available at time t. Both current and future deviations from target inflation affect the central bank's loss.

Following Svensson's analysis, suppose the central bank has quadratic loss

$$L(y_\tau - y^*) = \tfrac{1}{2}(y_\tau - y^*)^2. \qquad (2.32)$$

Future inflation rates depend on the sequence of interest rates which are chosen to minimize expected future loss and hence satisfy the condition

$$\{i_\tau^*\}_t^\infty = \arg\min_{\{i_\tau\}_t^\infty} \sum_{\tau=t}^\infty \lambda^{\tau-t} E_t \left[(y_\tau - y^*)^2\right]. \qquad (2.33)$$

Complicating matters, inflation is not exogenous but is affected by the central bank's actions. Solving (2.33) is therefore quite difficult since current and future interest rates can be expected to affect future inflation rates. Because inflation forecasts matter only in so far as they affect the central bank's interest rate policy and hence future inflation, a model for the data-generating process for inflation is needed. Svensson proposes a tractable approach in which inflation and output are generated according to the equations[13]

$$y_{t+1} = y_t + \alpha_1 z_t + \epsilon_{t+1}, \qquad (2.34)$$

$$z_{t+1} = \beta_1 z_t - \beta_2(i_t - y_t) + \eta_{t+1}, \qquad (2.35)$$

where z_t is current output relative to its potential level, and all parameters are positive, i.e., $\alpha_1, \beta_1, \beta_2 > 0$. The quantities ϵ_{t+1} and η_{t+1} are unpredictable shocks to inflation and output, respectively. The first equation expresses the change in inflation as a function of the lagged output, while the second equation shows that the real interest rate $(i_t - y_t)$ impacts output with a lag and also allows for autoregressive dynamics assuming $\beta_1 < 1$. Using these equations to solve for inflation two periods ahead, we obtain the following equation:

$$y_{t+2} = (1 + \alpha_1\beta_2)y_t + \alpha_1(1 + \beta_1)z_t - \alpha_1\beta_2 i_t + \epsilon_{t+1} + \alpha_1\eta_{t+1} + \epsilon_{t+2}. \qquad (2.36)$$

Notice that the policy instrument (i) impacts the target variable (y) with a two-period delay. Moreover, each interest rate affects one future inflation rate and so a solution to the infinite sum in (2.33) reduces to choosing i_t to target y_{t+2}, choosing i_{t+1} to target y_{t+3}, etc. Hence, the central bank's objective in setting the current interest

---

[13] We have simplified Svensson's model by omitting an additional exogenous variable.

rate, i_t, simplifies to

$$\min_{i_t} E_t \left[\lambda^2 (y_{t+2} - y^*)^2 \right].$$

Using the quadratic loss function in (2.32), the first-order condition becomes

$$E_t \left[\frac{\partial L(y_{t+2} - y^*)}{\partial i_t} \right] = E_t \left[(y_{t+2} - y^*) \frac{\partial y_{t+2}}{\partial i_t} \right] = 0. \tag{2.37}$$

From (2.36) this means choosing i_t so that $E_t[y_{t+2}] = y^*$, which can be accomplished by setting

$$i_t^* = y_t + \frac{(y_t - y^*) + \alpha_1(1 + \beta_1)z_t}{\alpha_1 \beta_2}. \tag{2.38}$$

It follows that the optimal current interest rate, i_t^*, should be higher, the higher the current inflation rate as well as the higher the output relative to its potential, i.e., the lower the output gap.

Under this choice of interest rate level, the argument in the loss function reduces to

$$y_{t+2} - y^* = (\epsilon_{t+1} + \alpha_1 \eta_{t+1} + \epsilon_{t+2}).$$

This is just an example of certainty equivalence, which relies heavily on the chosen squared error loss function in (2.32). If the original loss function did not have a first-order condition (2.37) that is linear in inflation, then the solution would not be so simple and the expected loss would not be a straightforward function of the expected inflation rate.

2.5.2 Portfolio Choice under Mean–Variance Utility

As an illustration of the relationship between economic utility and predictability, consider the single-period portfolio choice problem for an investor who can either hold T-bills which, for simplicity we assume pay a zero risk-free rate, or stocks which pay an excess return over the T-bill rate of y_{t+1}. Assuming that the investor has initial wealth $W_t = 1$, and letting ω_t be the portion of the investor's portfolio held in stocks at time t, future wealth at time $t + 1$, W_{t+1}, is given by

$$W_{t+1} = \omega_t y_{t+1}. \tag{2.39}$$

The portion of wealth held in stocks, ω_t, is the investor's choice variable. To analyze this decision we need to specify the investor's utility as well as how accurately y_{t+1} can be predicted.

Suppose the investor has mean–variance utility over future wealth and maximizes expected utility:

$$E[U(W_{t+1})|Z_t] = E[W_{t+1}|Z_t] - \frac{a}{2} \text{Var}(W_{t+1}|Z_t), \tag{2.40}$$

where a captures the investor's risk aversion. The quantities $E[W_{t+1}|Z_t]$ and $\text{Var}(W_{t+1}|Z_t)$ are the conditional mean and variance of W_{t+1} given information at time t, $Z_t = \{z_1, \dots, z_t\}$. Under this utility function, the investor's expected utility increases in expected returns but decreases in the amount of risk, as measured by the conditional variance of wealth. We can think of expected loss as the negative of (2.40).

Following Campbell and Thompson (2008), consider the following data-generating process for excess returns on stocks:

$$y_{t+1} = \mu + z_t + \varepsilon_{t+1}, \tag{2.41}$$

where $z_t \sim (0, \sigma_z^2)$, $\varepsilon_{t+1} \sim (0, \sigma_\varepsilon^2)$ and $\text{Cov}(z_t, \varepsilon_{t+1}) = 0$. Here z_t represents a potentially predictable return component which may be known at time t, while ε_{t+1} is an unpredictable shock to returns. For an investor without information on z_t, the expected value of y_{t+1} is μ, while the variance of y_{t+1} is $(\sigma_z^2 + \sigma_\varepsilon^2)$, and so

$$\omega_t^* = \arg\max_{\omega_t} \left\{ \omega_t \mu - \frac{a}{2} \omega_t^2 (\sigma_z^2 + \sigma_\varepsilon^2) \right\},$$

which implies the following optimal holdings of stocks:

$$\omega_t^* = \frac{\mu}{a(\sigma_z^2 + \sigma_\varepsilon^2)}. \tag{2.42}$$

Given this weight on stocks, the average (unconditional expectation) of the excess return on the uninformed investor's stock holdings becomes

$$E[\omega_t^* y_{t+1}] = E\left[\frac{\mu(\mu + z_t + \varepsilon_{t+1})}{a(\sigma_z^2 + \sigma_\varepsilon^2)} \right] = \frac{\mu^2}{a(\sigma_z^2 + \sigma_\varepsilon^2)} = \frac{S^2}{a}, \tag{2.43}$$

where $S = \mu / \sqrt{\sigma_z^2 + \sigma_\varepsilon^2}$ is the unconditional Sharpe ratio, i.e., the expected excess return per unit of risk (volatility). Similarly, $\text{Var}[\omega_t^* y_{t+1}] = \mu^2 / [a^2(\sigma_z^2 + \sigma_\varepsilon^2)]$, and so the expected utility, evaluated at the optimal stock holdings, ω_t^*, is

$$E[U(W_{t+1}(f_t^*))] = \frac{\mu^2}{2a(\sigma_z^2 + \sigma_\varepsilon^2)} = \frac{S^2}{2a}. \tag{2.44}$$

Turning to the informed case where the investor exploits the predictable component in stock returns, z_t, the conditional expectation and variance of future wealth are $E[W_{t+1}|Z_t] = \omega_t(\mu + z_t)$ and $\text{Var}(W_{t+1}|Z_t) = \omega_t^2 \sigma_\varepsilon^2$, respectively, and so this investor's optimal stock holding is

$$\tilde{\omega}_t^*(z_t) = \frac{\mu + z_t}{a\sigma_\varepsilon^2}. \tag{2.45}$$

This investor's expected average excess return becomes

$$E\left[\frac{(\mu + z_t)(\mu + z_t + \varepsilon_{t+1})}{a\sigma_\varepsilon^2} \right] = \frac{\mu^2 + \sigma_z^2}{a\sigma_\varepsilon^2}. \tag{2.46}$$

Noting that the predictive R^2 in (2.41) is given by $R^2 = \sigma_z^2/(\sigma_z^2 + \sigma_\varepsilon^2)$, the informed investor's average (unconditionally expected) excess return in (2.46) can be written as

$$E[\tilde{\omega}_t^*(z_t)y_{t+1}] = \frac{S^2 + R^2}{a(1 - R^2)}. \tag{2.47}$$

Comparing expected returns under the unconditional forecast in (2.43) to the expected return under the conditional forecast in (2.47), the proportional increase in the investor's expected excess returns is

$$\frac{E[\tilde{\omega}_t^*(z_t)y_{t+1}]}{E[\omega_t^* y_{t+1}]} = \frac{1 + (R^2/S^2)}{1 - R^2}, \tag{2.48}$$

whereas the simple return difference (2.47)–(2.43) amounts to $R^2(1 + S^2)/(a(1 - R^2))$.

Empirical work indicates that predictive return regressions have an R^2 close to 0, so the ratio in (2.48) is close to $(1 + R^2/S^2)$, suggesting that the magnitude of the predictive R^2 should be evaluated relative to the squared Sharpe ratio. Campbell and Thompson (2008) use historical data to estimate a squared monthly Sharpe ratio of 0.012 or 1.2%. Hence, even a monthly R^2 of "only" 0.5% would increase the average portfolio excess return by a factor 0.5/1.2, i.e., by roughly 40%. Given their historical data, this corresponds to an increase in the expected portfolio return of approximately 1.7% per annum assuming a risk aversion coefficient of $a = 3$. Even small R^2-values can thus make a considerable difference to portfolio performance in this case. Moreover, the predictive R^2 can be used as a measure of the expected return gains arising from predictability. [14]

Mean–variance investors are concerned with expected utility rather than expected returns. For uninformed investors their expected utility is given by (2.44). For informed investors, using the optimal stock holdings in (2.45), we have

$$E[\tilde{\omega}_t^*(z_t)y_{t+1}|Z_t] = E\left[\left.\frac{(\mu + z_t)(\mu + z_t + \varepsilon_{t+1})}{a\sigma_\varepsilon^2}\right|Z_t\right] = \frac{(\mu + z_t)^2}{a\sigma_\varepsilon^2},$$

$$\text{Var}[\tilde{\omega}_t^*(z_t)y_{t+1}|Z_t] = \frac{(\mu + z_t)^2\sigma_\varepsilon^2}{a^2\sigma_\varepsilon^4} = \frac{(\mu + z_t)^2}{a^2\sigma_\varepsilon^2},$$

so that

$$E[U(W_{t+1}(\tilde{\omega}_t^*(z_t)))|Z_t] = \frac{(\mu + z_t)^2}{a\sigma_\varepsilon^2} - \frac{a}{2}\frac{(\mu + z_t)^2}{a^2\sigma_\varepsilon^2} = \frac{(\mu + z_t)^2}{2a\sigma_\varepsilon^2}.$$

The average (unconditional expectation) value of this expression is

$$E\left[E[U(W_{t+1}(\tilde{\omega}_t^*(z_t)))|Z_t]\right] = \frac{\mu^2 + \sigma_z^2}{2a\sigma_\varepsilon^2}. \tag{2.49}$$

---

[14] Of course, these calculations ignore transaction costs associated with portfolio turnover, as well as parameter estimation error which can be expected to be considerable.

Comparing (2.49) to (2.44), it is clear that the two are identical only when $\sigma_z^2 = 0$, otherwise (2.49)>(2.44), and the increase in expected utility due to using the predictor variable is given by

$$\text{CER} = \frac{\sigma_z^2}{2a\sigma_\varepsilon^2} = \frac{R^2}{2a(1 - R^2)}.$$

This is the certainty equivalent return (CER), i.e., the additional guaranteed return which, if paid to uninformed investors, would equate their expected utility with that of investors with access to the predictor variable. Using the earlier empirical numbers, for $R^2 = 0.005$ and $a = 3$, this amounts to an annualized certainty equivalent return of about 1%.

2.5.3 Directional Trading System

Forecasters' objectives reflect their utility and action rules. As a third example, consider the decisions of a risk-neutral market timer whose utility is linear in the payoff, $U(\delta(f_t), y_{t+1}) = \delta_t y_{t+1}$, where y_{t+1} is the return on the market portfolio in excess of a risk-free rate at time $t+1$ and δ_t is the investor's holding of the market portfolio which depends on his forecast of stock returns as of time t,

$$U(\delta(f_t), y_{t+1}) = \delta_t y_{t+1}. \tag{2.50}$$

Again, we can think of the market timer's loss as the negative of (2.50). Moreover, assume that the investor follows the decision rule, $\delta(f_t)$, of going "long" one unit in the risky asset if a positive return is predicted ($f_t > 0$), otherwise going short one unit. In this case the investor's decision, $\delta(f_t)$, depends only on the predicted sign of y_{t+1}:

$$\delta(f_t) = \begin{cases} 1 & \text{if } f_t \geq 0, \\ -1 & \text{if } f_t < 0. \end{cases} \tag{2.51}$$

Trading profits depend on the sign of y_{t+1} and f_t as well as on the magnitude of y_{t+1}. To see this, let $\mathbb{1}(f_t > 0)$ be an indicator function that equals 1 if $f_t > 0$ and otherwise equals 0. Then the return from the trading strategy in (2.51) becomes

$$U(\delta(f_t), y_{t+1}) = (2\mathbb{1}(f_t > 0) - 1)y_{t+1}. \tag{2.52}$$

As one would expect from (2.51), both the sign (in relation to that of the forecast, f_t) and magnitude of excess returns, y_{t+1}, matters to the trader's utility, while only the sign of the forecast enters into the utility function. Note that large forecast errors for forecasts with the correct sign lead to smaller loss than small forecast errors for forecasts with the wrong sign.[15] This example also raises the issue of which forecast approach would be best suited given the directional trading rule. Since the trader ignores information about the magnitude of the forecast, an approach that focuses on predicting only the sign of the excess return could make sense.

---

[15] In related work, Elliott and Lieli (2013) derive the loss function from first principles for binary decision and outcome variables. This setup does not admit commonly applied loss functions for any possible utility function.

How the forecaster maps predictions into actions may thus be helpful in explaining properties of the observed forecasts. Leitch and Tanner (1991) studied forecasts of Treasury bill futures contracts and found that professional forecasters reported predictions with higher MSE than those from simple time-series models. At first, this seems puzzling since the time-series models presumably incorporate far less information than the professional forecasts. When measured either by their ability to generate profits or to correctly forecast the direction of future interest rate movements the professional forecasters did better than the time-series models, however. A natural conclusion to draw from this is that the professional forecasters' objectives are poorly approximated by the MSE loss function and are closer to a directional or "sign" loss function. This would make sense if investors' decision rule is to go long if an asset's excess payoff is predicted to be positive, and otherwise go short, i.e., sell the asset.

2.6 CONCLUSION

In any nontrivial forecasting situation, any forecasting method is going to make errors as the forecast will not equal the outcome with probability 1. As a consequence, forecasters need to assess the impact these errors will have on decisions based on imperfect forecasts. The loss function quantifies how costly forecast errors are for the decision maker. Formally, loss functions map the space of outcomes and decisions (forecasts) to the real number line (which is typically normalized to the nonnegative part of the real number line, although this is just a convenience) and so allow us to directly measure the economic effects of forecast errors.

In many situations the step of formally constructing a loss function that is relevant to the particular forecasting problem is skipped, and instead an informal statistic—often an intuitive function of the outcomes and forecasts assessed over a number of forecast situations or time periods—is used to evaluate forecasting performance. We showed above (using the Kuiper's score as an example) that such approaches can be difficult to interpret and often the resulting measures of loss have poor properties. This approach is therefore to be avoided.

Instead, any approach to a real decision or forecasting problem should carefully consider the relevance of the loss function to the real costs of the errors that are sure to arise when the forecasting method is put into practice. In some cases this involves constructing a loss function that is specific to a particular problem. In situations with a financial outcome that can be directly measured, this can and should be employed as the loss function. In other situations care needs to be taken to ensure that the loss function employed approximates to a reasonable extent the actual costs associated with the forecast errors.

In the next few chapters, as well as later in the book when we examine forecast evaluation, we show that loss functions matter for every step of the classical forecasting process. This includes estimation of parameters, choice of models, and the eventual evaluation of the forecasting method. It follows that the best forecasting method plausibly will depend on the choice of the loss function and a forecasting model built for one loss function may be inferior when evaluated on a different loss function. This is highly suggestive of taking seriously the step of constructing the loss function when building a forecasting model.

There are situations where it might be relevant to simply choose an "off-the-shelf" method, many of which we discuss in this chapter. Often forecasts are "intermediate" inputs provided to higher-level decision makers (e.g., the Greenbook forecasts computed by the Federal Reserve) or to the public (e.g., public weather forecasts provided by the government). Sometimes the end use is either not known with sufficient precision or the end uses are diverse enough across different agents that it is simply not possible to construct the loss function of the end user. In these cases it is typical to use mean squared error or similarly simple loss functions. This is a useful approach, although (a) perhaps a density forecast in this situation makes more sense, and (b) there are costs from not matching the forecast with the loss function. Indeed, the density forecasting approach is becoming more prevalent in these situations as weather forecasts are given as probabilities and government agencies make increasing use of fan charts, etc.

3

The Parametric Forecasting Problem

The forecaster's objective is to use data—outcomes of the random variable Z—to predict the value of the random variable Y. Let T be the date when the forecast is computed and define $\mathcal{I}_T$ as the sigma algebra generated by $\{Z_t\}_{t=1}^T$, so $\mathcal{I}_T$ is a filtration ($\mathcal{I}_{T-1} \subset \mathcal{I}_T$). Following conventional terminology in the forecasting literature, we refer to $\mathcal{I}_T$ as the information set at time T. We define Z as $\{Z_t\}_{t=1}^T$ when the timing of the forecasting problem is clear and as Z_T when we need to be clearer about the time subscript, and write objects as conditional on Z or conditional on $\mathcal{I}_T$ as meaning the same thing. By $E[Y|z]$ we mean $E[Y|Z=z]$ or $E[Y|\mathcal{I}_T]$. The random variable Z typically includes past values of the predicted variable, as well as other possibly useful variables, X_t, so often $\{Z_t\}_{t=1}^T = \{Y_t, X_t\}_{t=1}^T$. In some cases (such as ARIMA and VAR forecasts, which we discuss in more detail in chapters 7 and 9), the information set might include only past values of the predicted variable(s). The outcome, Y, may be a vector or could be univariate.

We assume throughout the analysis that a joint distribution for $\{Y, Z\}$ exists, which can be written as $p_Y(y|z, \theta)p_Z(z, \theta)$, where the vector θ comprises all the parameters of the joint distribution. Through a small abuse of notation we refer to the true parameters as θ regardless of whether we are referring to the conditional distribution for Y given Z or to the joint distribution. We refer to this joint distribution as the data-generating process or true model.

This chapter focuses on the construction of optimal point forecasts, i.e., finding the best possible $f(Z)$ for a general forecasting problem. There are many reasons for considering the optimality of a forecast. First, clearly we want the best possible forecast. Second, questions related to forecast optimality can be complicated and there will not be a single best forecasting approach even in the simplest of problems. Selecting a good forecasting approach often requires deeper thinking about the problem than merely stating a loss function and it need not be straightforward to determine a reasonable set of models for a realistic forecast problem. This point motivates the wide range of approaches considered in the empirical forecasting literature (and in part II of this book), with different approaches being tailored to different data-generating processes and forecast objectives. Claims of forecast optimality are typically limited to restrictive classes of models and so can be very weak—optimality often does not extend too far in the sense that there may be better forecast models available, given the same data.

We use "risk" as our measure of the performance of a forecasting method, as well as the best measure for distinguishing between methods. Using jargon from the statistics literature, the risk of a forecasting method is simply the expected loss when integrating over both Y and Z. This focus on risk is unlikely to be controversial. Many forecasting papers motivate their methods through Monte Carlo experiments that examine risk at a few, carefully chosen points in the space of the parameters and data-generating processes. Such risk evaluation exercises require us to think carefully about the model spaces and to avoid assuming that methods that work for some Monte Carlo studies will necessarily work more generally, especially for quite different data-generating processes. It also highlights the role of the loss function; results favoring a particular forecasting model for one loss function need not generalize to other loss functions.

Examining in a single chapter the forecasting problem in the context of decision theory requires us to cut many corners. Hence, this chapter is really an overview of some key points from decision theory and estimation theory adapted to the forecasting problem and using language from forecasting. We demonstrate results not by proofs with technical conditions but through relevant examples.[1]

Forecast models may be parametric, semiparametric or nonparametric. Parametric models for the forecast are fully specified up to a finite-dimensional unknown vector, β. Nonparametric models typically have an infinite-dimensional set of unknown parameters. Semiparametric models fall in the middle. Throughout this chapter we assume that the true joint distribution of the data, or data-generating process, has a parametric representation with a joint density for the outcome variable and the conditioning information used by the forecaster. This is the setting that the title of the chapter refers to.

An alternative to examining point forecasts is to provide a predictive density. The construction of a predictive density arises naturally under the Bayesian approach. From the classical perspective, the estimation problem will be different from that of point forecasting. We will see below that point forecasts are features of the predictive distribution in the sense that knowing the predictive distribution allows the construction of the optimal point forecast. Hence, generating a predictive distribution is in a sense a harder problem since the estimation problem is to construct something more informative than the point estimate. For this reason it is often suggested that provision of a predictive distribution (known as density forecasting in the forecasting literature) is better than provision of a point forecast. However, when the predictive distribution must be estimated, additional concerns arise.

The chapter restricts our focus to forecasts with loss functions of the form $L(f, Y)$, i.e., we drop the dependence of L on Z, except through f. This reduces the notation and, as we saw in the previous chapter, most commonly used loss functions simplify in this manner.

The chapter proceeds as follows. Section 3.1 examines optimality of point forecasts under known model parameters. Section 3.2 considers classical (frequentist) approaches when parameters are estimated, again focusing on optimality issues. This is followed in section 3.3 by an examination of Bayesian methods for constructing point forecasts. Section 3.4 relates the two approaches and discusses density forecasts.

---

[1] Many books are useful for understanding the basics of decision theory; examples include Ferguson (1967) and Girshick and Blackwell (1954).

Section 3.5 compares the methods in the context of an empirical portfolio decision problem. Section 3.6 concludes.

3.1 OPTIMAL POINT FORECASTS

The forecaster's objective is to use data—outcomes of the random variable Z—to predict the value of the random variable Y. We next show how this can be formalized in the context of the forecaster's loss function.

3.1.1 Expected Loss

The forecaster's objective can be reduced to finding a decision rule $f(Z)$ that will be used to "choose" a value for the outcome of Y. The forecast is the decision rule. The notion of closeness of the forecast to the outcome is to make the loss small "on average," i.e., across different values of Y. For any decision rule we would like a forecast to minimize expected loss,

$$E_Y[L(f(Z), Y)|Z].\qquad(3.1)$$

Here the expectation E_Y is computed over the unobserved outcome, Y, holding Z constant. This expected loss is a function of the forecast rule, Z, and the parameters of the conditional distribution of Y given Z.[2] This explains why expected loss is a function of θ and the chosen forecasting rule, f. A sensible decision rule has low risk and hence minimizes expected loss.[3]

Using the conditional density for Y given Z, denoted $p_Y(y|z, \theta)$, the expected loss in (3.1) can be written as

$$\int_y L(f(z), y) p_Y(y|z, \theta) dy.\qquad(3.2)$$

This is the expected loss that we attempt to control and minimize.

When the expected loss exists, it follows from (3.2) that an optimal point forecast, $f^* \in \mathcal{F}$, satisfies[4]

$$f^*(z) = \arg\min_{f \in \mathcal{F}} \int_y L(f(z), y) p_Y(y|z, \theta) dy.\qquad(3.3)$$

Closed-form solutions to (3.3) can be established for many commonly used loss functions.

[2] We refer to these parameters generically as θ, although more generally we consider θ to be the parameters of the joint distribution of all the data, so expected loss is likely to depend only on a subset of θ since we condition on Z.

[3] This representation of the problem further limits choices of the loss function and requires assumptions on the underlying random variables to ensure that the risk exists.

[4] This minimizes risk since $f(z)$ varies for different values of z. Hence the minimization occurs inside the expectation over $p_z(z|\theta)$ in (3.2).

Example 3.1.1 (Optimal forecast under mean squared error (MSE) loss). *Under MSE loss, $L(f(z), y) = (y - f(z))^2$, and the risk in (3.2), reduces to*

$$\int_y (y - f(z))^2 p_Y(y|z, \theta) dy = \int_y (y - E(Y|z) + E(Y|z) - f(z))^2 p_Y(y|z, \theta) dy$$

$$= \int_y (y - E(Y|z))^2 p_Y(y|z, \theta) dy$$

$$+ \int_y (E(Y|z) - f(z))^2 p_Y(y|z, \theta) dy$$

$$= \text{Var}(Y|z) + (E(Y|z) - f(z))^2. \tag{3.4}$$

Since the first term in (3.4) does not involve the forecast $f(z)$ and the second term is nonnegative, the optimal forecast rule is to set

$$f^*(z) = E(Y|z), \tag{3.5}$$

which is thus the general form of an optimal forecast under MSE loss. The conditional mean will be a function of the underlying parameters, θ, and the data, z, or a subset thereof. Setting $f(z) = E(Y|z)$ does not guarantee that the outcome, y, will be close to the forecast, $f(z)$, since there is no guarantee that a particular outcome, y, is close to its conditional mean. However, on average y will be close to the conditional mean and hence the forecast in (3.5) makes sense.

Under MSE loss we can derive the optimal forecast without exploiting the differentiability of this loss function. More generally, provided we can pass differentiation through the integral (with respect to y), an optimal forecast must solve

$$\frac{d}{df(z)} \int_y L(f(z), y) p_Y(y|z, \theta) dy = \int_y \frac{d}{df(z)} L(f(z), y) p_Y(y|z, \theta) dy$$

$$= E[L'(f(z), Y)|Z = z]$$

$$= 0, \tag{3.6}$$

and so an optimal forecast, $f^*(z)$, solves

$$E[L'(f^*(z), Y)|Z = z] = 0.$$

This expression can be used to derive the optimal forecast rule. In some cases a closed-form solution will be available, although for complicated loss functions or densities we may not be so lucky.

Example 3.1.2 (Optimal forecast under MSE loss, continued). *Under MSE loss,* $L'(f(z), y) = 2(y - f(z))$, *so the first-order condition in (3.6) becomes*

$$\frac{1}{2} E[L'(f(z), y)|Z = z] = \int_y (y - f(z)) p_Y(y|z, \theta) dy$$

$$= \int_y y p_Y(y|z, \theta) dy - f(z) = 0.$$

Hence, $f^*(z) = \int_y y p_Y(y|z, \theta) dy = E[Y|Z = z, \theta]$, *and the optimal forecast is the conditional mean given the data, z, the forecasting model, and its parameters,* θ, *as in Example 3.1.1.*

While the conditional mean is the most frequently used prediction rule, it is typically not the optimal rule under asymmetric loss, as the next example shows.

Example 3.1.3 (Optimal forecast under lin-lin loss). *The expected loss under lin-lin loss* $L(e) = \alpha e \mathbb{1}(e > 0) - (1 - \alpha) e \mathbb{1}(e \leq 0)$, $0 < \alpha < 1$, *where* $\mathbb{1}(e > 0)$ *is an indicator function that equals 1 if* $e > 0$, *and otherwise equals 0, is given by*

$$\int_y L(f(z), y) p_Y(y|z, \theta) dy = \alpha \int_{f(z)}^{\infty} (Y - f) p_Y(y|z, \theta) dy$$

$$- (1 - \alpha) \int_{-\infty}^{f(z)} (Y - f) p_Y(y|z, \theta) dy. \quad (3.7)$$

Differentiating (3.7) with respect to $f(z)$ *yields the first-order condition for an optimal forecast,*

$$-\alpha \left(1 - P_{Y|Z}(f(z))\right) + (1 - \alpha) P_{Y|Z}(f(z)) = 0,$$

where $P_{Y|Z}(x) = \int_{-\infty}^{x} p_Y(y|z, \theta) dy$. *This simplifies to* $P_Y(f^*(z)) = \alpha$, *or*

$$f^*(z) = P_{Y|Z}^{-1}(\alpha), \quad (3.8)$$

and $P_{Y|Z}^{-1}(\alpha)$ *is the quantile function for Y given Z. If* $\alpha = 0.5$ *as with MAE loss, the optimal forecast is the median of the predictive distribution of Y. This makes intuitive sense since positive and negative forecast errors are assigned identical weights in the symmetric case. As* α *decreases towards 0, the optimal forecast moves further to the left of the tail of the predicted outcome distribution. This happens because negative forecast errors (overpredictions) are now penalized more heavily than positive errors, and so the optimal forecast gets shifted to the left to reduce the likelihood of overpredictions. For example, if* $\alpha = 0.25$, *the optimal forecast is no longer the median of Y but instead the first quartile of the distribution of Y.*

As an illustration, figure 3.1 plots the optimal forecast as a function of α *for a standard normal random variable, N(0, 1). Even though the predicted variable has a mean of 0, the optimal forecast is large and positive for large values of* α. *This corresponds to imposing strong penalties on positive forecast errors, so as to reduce the chances of observing such errors. Conversely, the optimal forecast is strongly negative for values of* α *close to 0.*

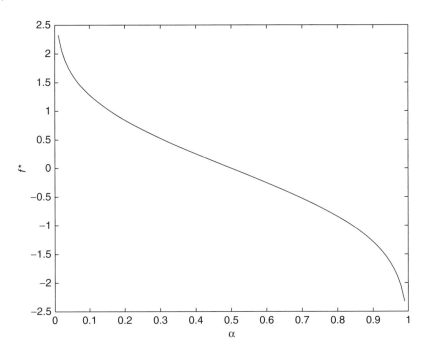

Figure 3.1: Optimal point forecast, f^*, of a standard normal random variable, N(0,1), under the lin-lin loss function for different values of α.

Linex loss is another case where we can hope to get a closed-form solution for the optimal forecast, particularly when combined with distributional assumptions such as (conditional) normality of the outcome.

Example 3.1.4 (Optimal forecast under Linex loss). *For the Linex loss function,*

$$L(f(z), y) = \exp(a(y - f(z))) - a(y - f(z)) - 1,$$

and so

$$\int_y L(f(z), y) p_y(y|z, \theta) dy = \exp(-af(z)) M_{Y|z}(a) - a(E(Y|z, \theta) - f(z)) - 1,$$

where $M_{Y|z}(t)$ is the moment generating function for Y conditional on Z which we assume exists and $a \neq 0$ is a parameter of the loss function. We want to minimize this, holding $Z = z$ constant. Differentiating with respect to $f(z)$ under the integral gives the first-order condition

$$0 = -a \exp(-af(z)) M_{Y|z}(a) + a$$
$$= -\exp(-af(z)) M_{Y|z}(a) + 1,$$

and so the closed-form solution for the optimal decision rule is

$$f^*(z) = a^{-1} \ln M_{Y|z}(a). \tag{3.9}$$

As we shall see in Example 3.2.1, this can be distinctly different from the conditional expectation of Y given z, $E[Y|z]$.

3.1.2 Interpretation of Forecast Optimality

The notion of an optimal forecast that minimizes the expected loss in (3.2) has several implications. First, taking expectations over Y in (3.2), it follows that optimal point forecasts aim to work well on average rather than for a particular value (single draw) of the outcome. In this sense the forecast attempts to estimate not the realization of the outcome, but rather a function of its predictive or conditional distribution. The optimal forecast itself is a function of z and can be considered a parameter of the conditional distribution, $p_Y(y|z)$. Under MSE loss the relevant function is the conditional mean; under MAE loss the relevant function is the conditional median; for Linex loss it is a feature of the moment generating function for the conditional random variable. The optimal forecast in this sense is unique. However, as we show below, when we move to estimating this function (or parameter), there will be no unique optimal forecast since there are many estimators for these features of the conditional distribution for Y, none of which are the single optimal estimator.

That the optimal forecast minimizes the average conditional loss also highlights the distinction between statistically bad forecasts and economically bad forecasts. A statistically bad forecast comes from constructing a poor model given the available data, while an economically bad forecast provides forecasts that are too imprecise for useful decision making. Forecasts are often viewed as "poor" if they are far from the observed realization of the outcome variable. However, in practice even good forecast models occasionally produce forecasts that are far from the outcome. For example, this will happen when we use an estimate of the conditional mean as our forecast but observe an outcome, y, drawn from the tails of its conditional distribution $p_Y(y|z, \theta)$. We do not necessarily view this as a bad forecast in the sense that such outcomes can occur even when the model is correctly specified.

Second, the optimal forecast in all these examples depends on the conditioning variables used to produce the forecast, Z. Conditioning on different predictor variables generally leads to different optimal forecasts given those predictor variables. This is true regardless of the forecasting problem. Any claims of optimality for a particular forecast model should be restricted to optimality for the given set of predictor variables used to construct the forecast.

Third, the optimization in (3.3) is with respect to a class of functions $\mathcal{F}$. The set of possible functions is often too wide to suggest the form of a reasonable forecast. Consider, for example, MSE loss for which we know that the optimal forecast takes the form of the conditional mean. However, the class of possible models for the conditional mean is immensely large, and hence does not actually define the form of the conditional expectation, (3.5), even up to a finite set of unknown parameters. Results can sometimes be established when the search over functions is restricted, but the notion of forecast optimality is clearly weaker.

Example 3.1.5 (MSE loss and linear projections). *Under MSE loss the optimal forecast takes the form $f^* = E[Y|z]$. Computing the conditional mean requires knowledge about the true relationship between y and z. Forecasts commonly use simple regression models based on linear projection of y on z: $f(z) = \beta'z$, where β are the parameters from the linear projection. Such projections are a subset of all possible prediction models so $\mathrm{MSE}(f(z)) \geq \mathrm{MSE}(E[Y|z])$ and linear projections are* *generally suboptimal in population. By construction, forecast errors and projections are orthogonal within the class of linear projections:*

$$E_Y[(Y - \beta'z)z'] = 0.$$

Within the class of linear models, linear projection is therefore optimal.

We might limit the set of forecast models $\mathcal{F}$ to specific parametric models rather than extending it to a wide class of functions. As in the previous example, this set may or may not include the optimal model when all possible functions are considered. When this restricted class can be written in parametric form as a function of the unknown parameters β and the data z, the optimal forecast in this restricted class is given by $f(z, \beta^*)$ where

$$\beta^* = \arg\min_{\beta \in \mathcal{B}} E_Y[L(f(Z, \beta), Y)]. \tag{3.10}$$

We refer to β^* as the pseudo-true value for β.[5] However, β^* need not be unique because the expected value of the loss function may obtain a minimum at a number of different values for β. Note that the value of the pseudo-true parameter, β^*, depends on θ, the parameters of the predictive distribution $p_Y(y|z, \theta)$, so the expected loss is still a function of θ rather than simply β.

While reduced-form expressions for the optimal forecast are often unavailable, some results can be shown for restricted classes of loss functions and conditional distributions for Y given $Z = z$. For error-based loss functions Granger (1969b) establishes that the conditional mean $E_Y[y|z]$ is the optimal forecast if the loss function is symmetric about 0 and the conditional distribution of the outcome is symmetric about $E_Y[y|z]$ so that $\bar{p}_Y(y) \equiv p_Y(y - E_Y[y|z])$ is symmetric about 0. This result also requires that either (i) the derivative of the loss function, L', is strictly monotonically increasing or (ii) the conditional density $p_Y(y|z)$ is continuous and unimodal. We show the result in the first case. The expected loss is given by

$$\int_{-\infty}^{\infty} L(y - f) p_Y(y|z) dy = \int_{-\infty}^{\infty} L(y - \alpha) \bar{p}_Y(y|z) dy, \tag{3.11}$$

where $f = E_Y[y|z] + \alpha$ and $\alpha = f - E_Y[y|z]$ is the forecast bias. Differentiating (3.11) with respect to α, we have

$$\int_{-\infty}^{\infty} L'(y - \alpha) \bar{p}_Y(y|z) dy = 0. \tag{3.12}$$

Using the assumed symmetry of $\bar{p}_Y(y)$ and the antisymmetry of $L'(y)$,[6] we have

$$\int_{-\infty}^{\infty} L'(y) \bar{p}_Y(y|z) dy = 0. \tag{3.13}$$

---

[5] Often the term "pseudo-true" is restricted to the maximum in quasi-maximum likelihood estimation. Here we are using a definition that is similar in spirit but broader given the wider set of criteria we consider.

[6] The antisymmetry of L' follows from the assumed symmetry of L around 0, i.e., $L(y) = L(-y)$.

This means that $\alpha = 0$ is a solution to (3.12). As pointed out by Granger, the solution to (3.12) is a unique minimum. To see this, suppose that there is another value of α that satisfies (3.13), i.e.,

$$\int_{-\infty}^{\infty} \left[L'(y - \alpha) - L'(y) \right] \bar{p}_Y(y|z) dy = 0. \tag{3.14}$$

Because L' is increasing, we have $L'(y - \alpha) - L'(y) > 0$ if $\alpha < 0$, while conversely $L'(y - \alpha) - L'(y) < 0$ if $\alpha > 0$. Because $\bar{p}_Y(y|z) \geq 0$ and integrates to 1, this means that (3.14) cannot hold unless $\alpha = 0$. The second-order condition for the optimum forecast guarantees that $f = E_Y[y|z]$ is a minimum.

3.1.3 Optimal Forecasts Conditional on Future Variables

Often we are interested in conditional forecasts, i.e., forecasts of Y conditional on a specific future path taken by another random variable, W. In the above analysis and in what follows, the results can be extended to this case by replacing $p_Y(y|z, \theta)$ and $p_Z(z|\theta)$ with the distributions conditional on setting the outcome of W to w, i.e., $p_Y(y|z, w, \theta)$ and $p_Z(z|w, \theta)$. For example, the Federal Reserve might want to forecast inflation conditional on a path of future Federal funds rates. While this extension may seem trivial conceptually, it can be difficult to implement in practice. The difficulty arises in constructing $p_Y(y|z, w, \theta)$. Typically a structural model of the data is required to understand the distribution of the outcome given future values of the variables we are conditioning on. In the case of inflation forecasting conditional on the Federal funds rate, we require a model for the structural relationship to understand how inflation reacts to the Federal funds rate without feedback effects from inflation.

3.2 CLASSICAL APPROACH

Applying any of the results of the previous section requires estimating the form of the model for the appropriate feature of the conditional distribution of Y given z along with the unknown parameters that arise in this estimation. Suppose we have a parametric model for the optimal forecast, $f(z, \beta)$, where β are parameters of the model, which in turn are a function of θ. Our (infeasible) optimal forecast model $f(z, \beta)$ must be estimated and now becomes $f(z, \hat{\beta})$, where $\hat{\beta}$ will be a function of z, the data available to construct estimates of the forecast model. Because the parameter estimates are a function of the available data, z, we can write $f(z, \hat{\beta}) = f(z)$. In the classical approach, a good estimator and hence a good forecasting model will be one that results in low average loss, where we average over Z as well as Y. This is an estimator (or forecast model) that has low risk, where risk is defined as

$$R(\theta, f) = E_{Y,Z} \left[L(f(Z), Y) \right]$$

$$= \int_z \int_y L(f(z), y) p_Y(y|z, \theta) p_Z(z|\theta) dy\, dz. \tag{3.15}$$

This is the risk that classical forecasting methods—methods for choosing $f(z)$—attempt to control and minimize.

3.2.1 Loss-Based versus Two-Step Approaches

The classical (or frequentist) approach to construction of forecasting models falls into two broad areas: either working directly with the sample analog of the loss function or using a two-step approach that first finds the form of the optimal forecast, then uses plug-in estimates for the unknown parameters. This section examines general issues that arise under these approaches. Much of the remainder of the book examines forecast construction in the context of more specific forecasting problems.

The sample analog approach requires finding the sample analog to (3.15) and constructing a forecast model $f(z, \beta)$, where β are unknown parameters with values that depend on θ, although as we discuss in chapters 6 and 11 the forecast model is typically also unknown. If $f(z, \beta)$ is identical to the optimal forecast (i.e., $f(z, \beta)$ equals the conditional mean of Y under MSE loss), then the forecast model is correctly specified. In practice, this should be considered an unlikely event. More likely, $f(z, \beta)$ is an approximation to the correct specification.

The two-step approach approximates the relevant feature of the conditional distribution of the predicted variable—e.g., under MSE loss this feature is the conditional mean of Y given $Z = z$—by a forecast model $f(z, \beta)$. Again, if this model is identical to the relevant feature of $p_Y(y|z)$, then the model is correctly specified, although more likely $f(z, \beta)$ is an approximation. In the second step, an estimate for β, denoted $\hat{\beta}$, is used to generate a forecast $f(z, \hat{\beta})$. The two-step approach therefore requires that the relevant feature of $p_Y(y|z)$ can be determined whereas the sample analog approach can always be used. Nevertheless, the two-step approach is more ubiquitous in practice. This is largely because the majority of forecasting studies is undertaken under MSE loss, reducing the forecast analysis to attempts at estimating the conditional mean of the outcome.

Example 3.2.1 (Linex loss, continued). *Let $Z_T = \{y_t\}_{t=1}^{T}$, so the data only comprise past values of the dependent variable. If we assume that $y_t \sim ind \; N(\mu, \sigma^2)$, then*

$$M_{y|Z} = \exp\left[a\mu + a^2\sigma^2/2\right], \tag{3.16}$$

and we have $f^\star(z) = a^{-1}\left[a\mu + a^2\sigma^2/2\right] = \mu + a\sigma^2/2$. A plug-in estimator might use the forecast

$$f_{T+1|T}^\star(Z_T) = \bar{y}_T + a\hat{\sigma}^2/2, \tag{3.17}$$

where $\bar{y}_T = T^{-1}\sum_{t=1}^{T} y_t$ and $\hat{\sigma}^2$ is some estimator of the variance, i.e., $(T-1)^{-1}\sum_{t=1}^{T}(y_t - \bar{y}_T)^2$.

Since we are estimating a feature of a conditional distribution such as its mean, it follows that point forecasting is really an estimation problem. Most of the results on risk and forecast optimality are analogous to those in parameter estimation theory. For the remainder of this section we go through some of these basic results, adapted to the forecasting problem.

First, consider the case where the forecast model is correctly specified, so $f(z, \beta)$ is equal to the correct feature of $p_Y(y|z)$. The analog procedure or the second step of the plug-in approach requires that β be estimated from data, so the actual forecast model is not $f(z, \beta)$ but $f(z, \hat{\beta})$. Calculation of the risk for a forecasting method involves taking the expectation over z and so gets affected by estimation of the unknown parameters. Because the additional randomness induced by parameter estimation increases the risk, the estimated forecast model will never obtain the optimality properties discussed in the previous section.

Example 3.2.2 (MSE loss given the observed history of the outcome). *Consider forecasting y_{T+1} under MSE loss using $Z_T = \{y_t\}_{t=1}^T$, where $y_t \sim \text{ind N}(\mu, \sigma^2)$ so that the data comprise past observations drawn independently from the same distribution. The population optimal forecast is μ. This produces a risk of $R(\theta, \mu) = E(y_{T+1} - \mu)^2 = \sigma^2$. When μ is unknown, we might instead use the sample mean $\bar{y}_T$ computed over T observations as our forecast, where $\bar{y}_T \sim (\mu, T^{-1}\sigma^2)$. The risk of this forecast is*

$$R(\theta, \bar{y}_T) = E_Y(y_{T+1} - \mu)^2 + E_Z(\bar{y}_T - \mu)^2$$
$$= \sigma^2(1 + T^{-1}).$$

This is strictly greater than the risk of the population forecast, σ^2.

The risk measure in (3.15) typically differs from the conditional expected loss measure in (3.2) since z_t varies with t. We illustrate this point in the next example.

Example 3.2.3 (MSE loss for linear forecasting model). *Consider a linear fore-casting model $y_{t+1} = \beta' x_t + \varepsilon_{t+1}$, where $\varepsilon_{t+1} \sim iid(0, \sigma^2)$ is independent of $Z_T = (x_0', \ldots, x_T')'$. Under squared error loss the expected loss is*

$$E[(\varepsilon_{T+1}^2 + (\hat{\beta}_T - \beta)' x_T x_T' (\hat{\beta}_T - \beta))].$$

Conditional on the data, Z_T, and a forecast $f_{T+1|T} = \hat{\beta}_T' x_T$, for the least squares estimator $\hat{\beta}_T = \left(T^{-1} \sum_{t=0}^{T-1} x_t x_t' \right)^{-1} \left(T^{-1} \sum_{t=0}^{T-1} x_t y_{t+1} \right)$ this becomes

$$E_Y[(y_{T+1} - \hat{\beta}_T' x_T)^2 | Z_T] \approx E[(\varepsilon_{T+1}^2 + (\hat{\beta}_T - \beta)' x_T x_T' (\hat{\beta}_T - \beta)) | Z_T]$$

$$= \sigma^2 \left(1 + T^{-1} x_T' \left(T^{-1} \sum_{t=0}^{T-1} x_t x_t' \right)^{-1} x_T \right), \quad (3.18)$$

which depends on all values of x up to time T. The unconditional expected loss, obtained by integrating over all z_T-values, becomes

$$R(\theta, \hat{\beta}_T' X_T) = E \left[\sigma^2 \left(1 + T^{-1} x_T' \left(T^{-1} \sum_{t=0}^{T-1} x_t x_t' \right)^{-1} x_T \right) \right]$$

$$\approx \sigma^2(1 + T^{-1}K), \quad (3.19)$$

where $K = \dim(x_t)$.

Risk functions that assume a correct specification, $f(z, \beta)$, and a known value of θ (and hence β) can be considered infeasible lower bounds on risk or "limiting" approximations to risk in large samples. At the same time when considering the optimality of a forecast procedure, parameter estimation error should be taken into account. A direct consequence of this is that even in the simplest forecast environments—and even with a correct model specification—there is no single optimal procedure that minimizes risk for all possible values of θ. Instead, the risk functions of different procedures will typically cross for different regions of θ. The next example illustrates this point.

Example 3.2.4 (MSE loss for shrinkage estimator). *Consider the forecasting problem in Example 3.2.2. Rather than use the sample mean estimator, $\bar{y}_T$ we could consider the shrinkage estimator $\gamma \bar{y}_T$ where $0 < \gamma < 1$. In this case the risk is*

$$R(\theta, \gamma \bar{y}_T) = E_{Z,Y}(y_{T+1} - \gamma \bar{y}_T)^2$$

$$= E_Y(y_{T+1} - \mu)^2 + \gamma^2 E_Z(\bar{y}_T - \mu)^2 + (1-\gamma)^2 \mu^2$$

$$= \sigma^2(1 + \gamma^2 T^{-1}) + (1-\gamma)^2 \mu^2. \tag{3.20}$$

For μ in the range $\pm\sqrt{T^{-1}\sigma^2(1+\gamma)/(1-\gamma)}$ the forecast $\gamma \bar{y}_T$ has lower risk than the sample mean $\bar{y}_T$; outside this range $\bar{y}_T$ has lower risk.

The results above were all predicated on the forecast model being correctly specified up to a set of unknown parameters, β. However, as discussed in the previous subsection, we may restrict our search to a subset of possible models that does not include the optimal model. For example, a forecaster with MSE loss might restrict models to linear projections even though the conditional mean is not linear in the conditioning variables. In this case, optimality is established with reference to this limited set of models.

Standard notions of risk for estimators extend to forecasts, including issues related to optimality of estimation methods. In parallel to estimation methods, a forecast method belongs to a family of optimal procedures if there exists some region of the parameter space, θ, for which no other forecast method has lower risk. It should be clear from the above examples that this concept of optimality generally defines a set of forecast methods as opposed to a single forecast method. Hence it is generally not possible to claim that there is a single optimal forecast method for any problem, unless θ is restricted to a point, in which case it must be known.

These considerations also raise the possibility that some forecast procedures are dominated by other forecasts for every value of θ and so are inferior and should never be used. This notion corresponds to the idea of inadmissible estimators.

Example 3.2.5 (MSE loss for shrinkage estimator, continued). *Allowing the shrinkage factor γ in Example 3.2.4 to take on any value in a set such as the real line, $\mathbb{R}$, generates a family of estimators which we denote $\{\gamma \bar{y}_T\}$. For $|\gamma| > 1$, it follows from (3.20) that there is no range of μ for which $\gamma \bar{y}_T$ dominates the sample mean $\bar{y}_T$, since the associated risk is strictly larger. Such estimators should thus never be employed. However, there is no such ranking when $0 < \gamma \leq 1$, in which case stronger shrinkage leads to lower risk for μ near 0.*

3.2.2 Risk and the Information Set

The way risk is defined in equation (3.15) means that its precise form depends on the specification of the information set. How the information set is specified is thus important for risk, just as it is in the evaluation and comparison of forecasts, as we shall see in the third part of the book.

The specification of the information set is particularly important to the notion of a trade-off between bias and variance that is key to understanding many forecasting problems. We next use the special case with a linear forecasting model and MSE loss to illustrate this point. We assume that not all possible predictor variables have been included in the model.

Suppose there are K potential predictor variables and let Z_T be the random variable that captures current and past values of all the K potential predictor variables, including past and present values of the outcome, y. Similarly, let Z_{kT} be the random variable generated by a subset of $k < K$ predictors. Finally, define Z_{-kT} as the random variable generated by the subset of omitted variables, so $Z_{-kT} \cup Z_{kT} = Z_T$. Note that different expressions are obtained in equation (3.15), depending on whether we integrate over all of Z_T or over only a subset of it.

Example 3.2.6 (Risk for subset regressions). *Consider the same problem as in Example 3.2.3. However, suppose that the forecasting model includes only $k < K$ regressors, including a constant unless all variables (including y) have mean 0.*

The least squares estimators for β can be written as $\hat{\beta}_{kT}$, where $\hat{\beta}_{kT}$ has the same dimension as β with 0s in place of estimates for the omitted variables and the least squares estimators from a regression of y_{t+1} on the included regressors in the remaining places partitioned according to x_t. Accounting for estimation, the forecast error is given by

$$y_{T+1} - \hat{\beta}'_k x_T = \varepsilon_{T+1} + (\beta - \hat{\beta}_k)' x_T$$
$$= \varepsilon_{T+1} + (\beta - E[\hat{\beta}_k | Z_{-kT}])' x_T + (E[\hat{\beta}_k | Z_{-kT}] - \hat{\beta}_k)' x_T,$$

where $E[\hat{\beta}_k | Z_{-kT}]$ is the expected value of $\hat{\beta}_k$ conditional on the omitted regressors. This is the standard omitted variable bias formula, where the mean of the ordinary least squares (OLS) estimates is a function of the omitted variables.

Integrating the squared forecast error only over (y_{T+1}, Z_{kT}) conditional on Z_{-kT} the expected loss becomes

$$E\left[\left(\varepsilon_{T+1} + (\beta - E(\hat{\beta}_k | Z_{-kT}))' x_T + (E(\hat{\beta}_k | Z_{-kT}) - \hat{\beta}_k)' x_T\right)^2 | Z_{-kT}\right]$$
$$= \sigma^2 + E\left[(\hat{\beta}_k - E(\hat{\beta}_k | Z_{-kT}))' x_T x'_T (\hat{\beta}_k - E(\hat{\beta}_k | Z_{-kT})) | Z_{-kT}\right]$$
$$+ \left[(\beta - E(\hat{\beta}_k | Z_{-kT}))' E[x_T x'_T | Z_{-kT}](\beta - E(\hat{\beta}_k | Z_{-kT}))\right]. \quad (3.21)$$

The second term is a variance term related to estimation error. Using the same math as in Example 3.2.3, this second term is approximately equal to $\sigma^2 k / T$. The third term is a bias term.

We refer to the second and third terms in (3.21) (the terms inside the large square brackets) collectively as the "estimation effect terms." Notice that nothing (apart from collecting more data and hence further enlarging Z_T) can be done to improve on the first term, although this avenue for improving forecasts should never be neglected.

This formulation of the problem results in the usual bias–variance trade-off that is common in calculations of the MSE. When forecasts are built from linear regressions and a constant is included, one can consider the notion of a biased forecast only when conditioning on potential omitted predictors. Nearly all of the choices that arise in the construction of forecasting models, regardless of the loss function, revolve around the cost and benefit from adding predictor variables. Under MSE loss we see that there is a trade-off between the variance (the second term in (3.21)) and the squared bias (the third term).

Adding variables increases the loss through the variance term, which increases by σ^2/T. However, the potential benefit is that the bias term $(\beta - E(\hat{\beta}_k|Z_{-kT}))$ could well be smaller as a result of the estimation of an extra parameter of $\hat{\beta}$.

The variance term disappears at rate T and so is of a smaller order (as a function of the sample size) than the first term in (3.21). For egregiously misspecified regressions, the bias term could be of the same order as the first term, and hence for large enough biases this term can dominate the variance term by an order of magnitude. Note, however, that sensibly applied statistical tests can usually be used to rule out such situations. Recall that under standard assumptions (and certainly for our i.i.d. examples) the power of hypothesis tests for the significance of the regression coefficients grows at rate $\sqrt{T}$. This means that statistical tests for model misspecification have good power in situations where the bias term is of a greater order than the variance term. When statistical tests find it difficult to distinguish between models, the bias–variance trade-off becomes more complicated.

Notice that the risk in (3.21) is a function of Z_{-kT}. Alternatively, we could have considered integrating over all of Z_T, to obtain a different expression for the risk, as we show in the next example.

Example 3.2.7 (Risk for subset regression, continued). *Consider the same problem as in Example 3.2.6. We can write the full regression as*

$$y_{t+1} = \beta'x_t + \varepsilon_{t+1}$$
$$= (\beta - \beta_k^* + \beta_k^*)'x_t + \varepsilon_{t+1}$$
$$= \beta_k^{*'}x_t + u_{t+1},$$

where $u_{t+1} = (\beta - \beta_k^*)'x_t + \varepsilon_{t+1}$ and β_k^* minimizes $E[(y_{t+1} - \beta_k'x_T)^2]$, where the expectation is computed over all random variables. The variance of u_{t+1} is $\sigma_u^2 = \sigma^2 + (\beta - \beta_k^*)'\Sigma_X(\beta - \beta_k^*) \geq \sigma^2$, where $\Sigma_X = E[x_t x_t']$. Now the regression to be run is seen to be a "short" regression with a larger variance. It follows directly from the result in Example 3.2.3 that the risk is

$$R(\theta, \hat{\beta}_k'x_T) = \left((\beta - \beta_k^*)'\Sigma_X(\beta - \beta_k^*)\right)(1 + k/T) \tag{3.22}$$

$$= \sigma_u^2(1 + k/T). \tag{3.23}$$

Hence the scaling variable σ_u^2 is larger than for the expression in Example 3.2.6.

The expression in (3.23) is the average of (3.21), averaged over the omitted variables, Z_{-kT}. In this version where we integrate out the omitted variables, the "estimation effect terms" are convoluted with the unpredictable component. The first approach is often more useful for comparing models. For methods where the variance term vanishes asymptotically as the sample size becomes large, often the result amounts to a comparison of σ^2 versus σ_u^2. This holds, for example, for many approaches to out-of-sample forecast evaluation, covered in the third part of the book.

3.2.3 Minimax and Average Risk

As with estimation, we might also consider minimax forecasting strategies. Rather than choosing the forecast to minimize the expected loss, an alternative is to choose the forecast with the smallest risk across all possible values of the unknown parameters, $\theta \in \Theta$. This is the minimax rule. Formally, one forecast, f_1, is preferred to another forecast, f_2, under the minimax notion of optimality if

$$\sup_{\theta \in \Theta} R(\theta, f_1) < \sup_{\theta \in \Theta} R(\theta, f_2).$$

More generally, f^m is the minimax decision rule if it minimizes $\sup_\theta R(\theta, f)$ among all decision rules: $\sup_{\theta \in \Theta} R(\theta, f^m) = \inf_{f \in \mathcal{F}} \left(\sup_{\theta \in \Theta} R(\theta, f) \right)$. Minimax rules are often difficult to identify outside very restricted sets of problems.

Example 3.2.8 (MSE loss given the observed history of the outcome, continued). *Consider the set of estimators* $\{\gamma \bar{y}_T\}$ *for* $0 < \gamma \leq 1$, *and notice from (3.20) that for all* $\gamma < 1$ *the risk is unbounded as* μ *becomes large. For* $\gamma = 1$, *the risk does not depend on* μ, *and hence the worst case scenario over* μ *for any* σ^2 *is infinite risk for* $\gamma < 1$ *or* $\sigma^2(1 + T^{-1})$ *for* $\gamma = 1$. *Hence choosing the forecasting method* $\bar{y}_T$ *is minimax over* μ *in this set.*

Minimax results extend beyond this example. For instance, OLS parameter estimates often yield minimax forecasts with bounded risk among linear predictors and predictive densities with finite second moments.[7]

Since there is typically no single optimal procedure that minimizes risk over all regions of θ, choosing between forecast methods comes down to a view as to which regions of θ are most likely. In the examples above where the choice is over $f_\gamma(z)$, we might use the sample mean if we think it likely that μ is large in absolute value. Conversely, if we think μ is unlikely to be large relative to the bounds derived in Example 3.2.4, then we might choose a shrinkage estimator. The optimal choice of the shrinkage parameter γ depends on how close we believe μ is to 0. More generally, the choice between forecasting approaches critically depends on the family of models thought to be possible for any forecasting problem. "Kitchen sink" regressions that include all available variables in the forecast model and use least squares estimation offer a robust strategy over a wide set of parameters, θ. In practice, however, this strategy tends to provide extremely poor forecasts with very high risk because much of the parameter space for which this approach would work well might reasonably be deemed irrelevant. All of the methods discussed in the second part of the book are directed at different forecast situations and can be thought of as providing models that work well for different regions of θ.

---

[7] Note that first performing a model search to decide which predictors to include and then using least squares yields a different estimator with a different risk function that is not flat in θ. See chapter 6 for details.

It is common to run Monte Carlo experiments to compute the average loss for different values of the parameters and compare competing estimation methods. One can then choose the "least bad" method or alternatively choose the method that seems to be doing best for the majority of cases. We can also consider a more formal approach to decide between methods. Denoting the weighting function by $\pi(\theta)$, one can choose the forecast method that minimizes $\int R(\theta, f)\pi(\theta)d\theta$, i.e., the risk averaged over all relevant parameters. The weighted average risk is a single number, enabling direct comparisons across different forecast methods.

3.3 BAYESIAN APPROACH

The Bayesian approach starts with the idea of averaging risk over all possible models, using a weighting function or prior, $\pi(\theta)$, for the parameters. This leads to Bayes risk which is defined by

$$r(\pi, f) = \int_{\theta} R(\theta, f)\pi(\theta)d\theta, \tag{3.24}$$

where $R(\theta, f)$ is given by (3.15). Any forecast, $f(z)$, that minimizes Bayes risk is a Bayes decision rule. Notice that this concept of risk is identical to the weighted average risk of the previous section.

To construct a Bayes decision rule (i.e., a forecast), we need a weighting scheme or prior, $\pi(\theta)$, over the parameters of the model. This prior tells us which parameter values are likely and which are not. As in the classical approach, a model for the outcome variable, $p_Y(y|z)$, is also required. Finally, we also need a model for the data used to construct the forecast $p_Z(z|\theta)$. Given the prior and the model for the data, we can calculate the posterior density for the parameters

$$\pi(\theta|z) = p_Z(z|\theta)\pi(\theta)/m(z), \tag{3.25}$$

where $m(z) = \int_{\theta} p_Z(z|\theta)\pi(\theta)d\theta$ is the marginal likelihood of the data, z. Using (3.15) and the posterior density in (3.25), Bayes risk can then be computed as

$$r(\pi, f) = \int_z \left(\int_{\theta} \left\{ \int_y L(f(z), y)p_Y(y|z, \theta)dy \right\} \pi(\theta|z)d\theta \right) m(z)dz. \tag{3.26}$$

Conditional on $Z = z$, we can choose the forecasting rule that, for each z, minimizes the conditional risk

$$\int_{\theta} \left\{ \int_y L(f(z), y)p_Y(y|z, \theta)dy \right\} \pi(\theta|z)d\theta.$$

To see why this delivers a forecast that minimizes Bayes risk, consider the expected loss conditional on $Z = z$. A Bayesian approach would be to choose $f(z)$ to minimize this for any $Z = z$. Since this rule minimizes the conditional expected loss, it also minimizes the unconditional expected loss, i.e., it minimizes Bayes risk and is hence a Bayes decision rule.

Example 3.3.1 (Bayes risk under MSE loss, continued). *From (3.4) we get the Bayes risk*

$$r(\pi, f) = \int_z \left(\int_\theta \text{Var}(Y|\theta, z)\pi(\theta|z)d\theta \right) m(z)dz$$

$$+ \int_z \left(\int_\theta [E(Y|\theta, z) - f(z)]^2 \pi(\theta|z)d\theta \right) m(z)dz.$$

The first term does not depend on the forecast. Minimizing the second term conditional on z, and so ignoring the outer integral, yields the first-order condition

$$\int_\theta E(Y|\theta, z)\pi(\theta|z)d\theta = f(z) \int_\theta \pi(\theta|z)d\theta$$

$$= f(z).$$

The optimal forecast is the conditional mean using the posterior, $\pi(\theta|z)$, as weights. When y_{t+1} given x_t is normal with unknown mean $\theta'x_T$ and known variance σ^2, and the posterior distribution for θ is $N(\tilde{\theta}, V)$, the optimal forecast reduces to $f(z) = \int \theta'x_T\pi(\theta|z)d\theta = \tilde{\theta}'x_T$, i.e., we replace the unknown parameters with their posterior mean.

Example 3.3.2 (Bayes risk under Linex loss). *Again assume that $z = \{y_t\}_{t=1}^T$ and $y_t \sim ind \, N(\mu, \sigma^2)$, with $\theta = [\mu, \sigma^2]$. For simplicity, also assume that σ^2 is known. Suppose the prior, $\pi(\mu)$, is such that $\mu \sim N(\mu_0, \tau^2)$ with τ^2 known. The posterior distribution is then*

$$\mu|z \sim N\left(\frac{T\tau^2}{T\tau^2 + \sigma^2}\bar{y}_T + \frac{\sigma^2}{T\tau^2 + \sigma^2}\mu_0, \frac{\tau^2\sigma^2}{T\tau^2 + \sigma^2} \right), \qquad (3.27)$$

where $\bar{y}_T = T^{-1}\sum_{t=1}^T y_t$. For notational convenience, write this posterior as $\mu|z \sim N(\tilde{\mu}, \tilde{\sigma}^2)$. To derive the optimal forecast we need to integrate out the unknown parameter, μ. Note that from (3.9) and (3.16),

$$f(z) = a^{-1} \ln \int_\theta M_Y(a)\pi(\theta|z)d\theta$$

$$= a^{-1} \ln \int_\mu \exp\left[a\mu + a^2\sigma^2/2 \right] \frac{1}{\sqrt{2\pi}\tilde{\sigma}} \exp\left[-\frac{1}{2\tilde{\sigma}^2}(\mu - \tilde{\mu})^2 \right] d\mu.$$

Combining the exponential components and completing the square yields the optimal rule

$$f(z) = a^{-1} \ln \left(\exp\left[\frac{1}{2}a^2(\sigma^2 + \tilde{\sigma}^2) + a\tilde{\mu} \right] \right)$$

$$= \tilde{\mu} + \frac{a}{2}(\sigma^2 + \tilde{\sigma}^2).$$

Plugging the results for $\tilde{\mu}$ and $\tilde{\sigma}^2$ into (3.27) yields the rule

$$f(z) = \frac{T\tau^2}{T\tau^2 + \sigma^2}\bar{z} + \frac{\sigma^2}{T\tau^2 + \sigma^2}\mu_0 + \frac{a\sigma^2}{2}\left(1 + \frac{\tau^2}{T\tau^2 + \sigma^2}\right). \qquad (3.28)$$

When $\tau^2 \to \infty$, we move towards a flat prior and

$$f(z) = \bar{z} + \frac{a\sigma^2}{2}\left(1 + \frac{1}{T}\right).$$

Notice the close relationship between the classical plug-in method that minimizes average risk over all relevant models and the more formal Bayesian approach which chooses the forecast rule to directly minimize the weighted average risk. In the example with MSE loss the forms of the models are the same, so differences arise only through the estimation of θ. In the Linex example there is also a difference in the coefficient multiplying the variance term.

3.4 RELATING THE BAYESIAN AND CLASSICAL METHODS

For any weighting scheme, $\pi(\theta)$, over the possible parameter values, the Bayesian approach finds the best average method. The classical approach, due to its typically ad hoc use of plug-in estimators, may or may not achieve the same weighted average risk. Even in settings with identical loss functions and predictive densities, one might therefore find a Bayesian method with equal or smaller risk than the classical procedure for all possible values of θ. Conversely, if the two methods are equivalent, then the classical approach cannot be beaten.

Example 3.4.1 (Comparing classical and Bayes risk under Linex loss with Gaussian data). *To compare the classical and Bayesian results, assume the variance is known. The classical plug-in estimator in (3.17) is*

$$\hat{f}(z) = \bar{y}_T + \frac{a\sigma^2}{2}.$$

For any normal prior this yields higher risk than the optimal rule. To see this, note that for the optimal rule in (3.28),

$$R(\theta, f) = \frac{a\sigma^2}{2}\left(1 + \frac{1}{T}\right) - 1,$$

while for the classical plug-in rule,

$$R(\theta, \hat{f}) = \exp\left[\frac{a^2\sigma^2}{2T}\right] + \frac{a\sigma^2}{2} - 1.$$

The difference between these two risk measures is

$$R(\theta, \hat{f}) - R(\theta, f) = \exp\left[\frac{a^2\sigma^2}{2T}\right] + \frac{a\sigma^2}{2} - \frac{a\sigma^2}{2}\left(1 + \frac{1}{T}\right)$$

$$= \exp\left[\frac{a^2\sigma^2}{2T}\right] - \frac{a^2\sigma^2}{2T} > 0.$$

This follows because the loss function is positive for arguments away from 0.

In the classical setting the plug-in method for constructing $f(z)$ through the estimate $\hat{\theta}(z)$ may be ad hoc rather than directed towards minimizing average loss. Often forecasters choose estimators that yield nice properties for the parameters themselves. For example, estimators that are individually consistent, asymptotically normal, and asymptotically efficient for θ are often employed. Such features of the estimators ignore potential trade-offs between parameters that could be used to generate forecasts with better risk properties. Plug-in methods may therefore not yield good forecasting rules for constructing the forecast, $f(z)$, even for reasonable weighting functions, $\pi(\theta)$. Ultimately, the goal of forecasting is not to estimate θ, but instead to minimize a function of these parameters.

In practice, differences between the risks of optimal and ad hoc methods need not be large. In the very simple example above, the difference is small for large values of the sample size, T. Even if a method is not strictly admissible, it might well be "close enough" that the classical method works reasonably well.

Admissibility—using the best forecast method given some weighted average over the parameters $\pi(\theta)$—is a less exciting property if the particular weights, $\pi(\theta)$, are not empirically plausible for the particular problem at hand.

Finally, all such comparisons of forecast methods require that the model $p_Y(y|z, \theta)$ be correctly specified up to the unknown parameters. This goes against both the spirit and practice of modern forecasting. Typically, the true model is unknown. Still, the Bayesian approach offers a method for forecast construction that is guaranteed to be admissible for the specified model, should it be true. Even if the true model is not necessarily the one used to construct the forecasts, provided that the forecasting model is close to the true model we are assured of using a method that works well for this particular model.

It follows from this discussion that it is difficult to find optimal solutions even for very simple forecasting problems. Hence for different combinations of distributions of the data and values of the model parameters, there is scope for alternative methods to dominate. This lack of a single dominant approach explains much of the burgeoning interest in empirical comparisons of different forecasting approaches.

3.4.1 Density Forecasts

The search for a solution to minimize $E_Y[L(f(z), Y)|Z]$ across different decision rules requires choosing a forecast, i.e., a function of the forecast density that minimizes the risk

$$f^*(z) = \arg\min_{f(z)} \int_y L(f(z), y) p_Y(y|z) dy. \tag{3.29}$$

This expression is suggestive of two ways in which density rather than point forecasts are useful. First, forecasters with different loss functions will generally construct different optimal forecasts even though the true density for the data is the same for all forecasters. Under some loss functions (e.g., piecewise linear loss), the optimal forecast will be a quantile of the outcome for which the quantile depends on the degree of loss asymmetry; see Example 3.1.3. Two forecasters with different loss functions in this family will want different quantiles of the predictive distribution, so an agency that merely reports a single number could never provide both with an optimal forecast.

Second, point forecasts are often criticized on the grounds that they fail to communicate the degree of uncertainty surrounding the forecast. For example, a point forecast of changes in future property prices might be positive although the forecast density could place significant weight on a price fall.

An alternative to providing point forecasts is thus to report an estimate of the predictive density $p_Y(y|z)$. When closed-form solutions are available, point forecasts can be directly computed from summary statistics of the provided distribution. More generally, numerical integration over the density forecast is required to find the optimal point forecast.

Density forecasts solve the first problem since two forecasters requiring different quantiles of the distribution would both be able to construct their optimal forecasts from the densities provided. Predictive densities also work for an MSE forecaster interested in the conditional mean. This forecaster can compute the conditional mean from the density forecast and examine how reasonable the mean is as a summary statistic for the center of the conditional distribution of Y given Z.

It would appear that it is sufficient to provide the entire predictive distribution (density forecast) for all possible outcomes. A number of caveats arise for this solution, however. While there seems to be a clear gain in generality from providing density forecasts rather than point forecasts, this is somewhat illusory since typically the predictive density depends on parameters, θ, that must be estimated. Hence an estimated predictive density will be provided, with different estimators of the density (e.g., different estimators of θ for parametric densities), resulting in different density estimates. Forecasters with different loss functions will generally prefer different estimators. The provision of the predictive density does not avoid the issue that the best estimator ultimately depends on the loss function. From the perspective of forecasters with piecewise linear (lin-lin) loss, a density estimator might well trade off accuracy near the median for accuracy at the tails (or vice versa). Hence a forecaster requiring a quantile near the mean will prefer a different estimate of the predictive density than a forecaster requiring a quantile in the tails.

The Bayesian equivalent to the predictive density is constructed via the posterior distribution for θ. The Bayesian approach chooses $f(z)$ to minimize

$$r(\pi, f) = \int_z \left(\int_\theta \left\{ \int_y L(f(z), y, z) p_Y(y|z, \theta) dy \right\} p_Z(z|\theta) \pi(\theta) d\theta \right) dz$$

$$= \int_z \left(\int_\theta \left\{ \int_y L(f(z), y, z) p_Y(y|z, \theta) dy \right\} \pi(\theta|z) d\theta \right) m(z) dz$$

$$= \int_z \left(\int_y \left\{ L(f(z), y, z) \int_\theta p_Y(y|z, \theta) \pi(\theta|z) d\theta \right\} dy \right) m(z) dz. \quad (3.30)$$

Here we allow the integral over θ to pass by the loss function since the loss function is not explicitly a function of the parameters, θ. Also, $\int_\theta p_Y(y|z, \theta)\pi(\theta|z)d\theta = p_Y^p(y|z)$ is the predictive density obtained by integrating over θ, using $\pi(\theta|z)$ as weights.

3.5 EMPIRICAL EXAMPLE: ASSET ALLOCATION WITH PARAMETER UNCERTAINTY

To illustrate and compare the use of classical and Bayesian prediction methods, consider the asset allocation problem of a buy-and-hold investor studied by Barberis (2000). There are two assets: T-bills and a stock market index. T-bills pay a constant, continuously compounded risk-free rate of r_f. Suppose the continuously compounded excess return on stocks, y_t, is independently and identically distributed:

$$y_t = \mu + \varepsilon_t, \quad \varepsilon_t \sim \text{ind } N(0, \sigma^2). \tag{3.31}$$

Consider a buy-and-hold investor's asset allocation decision at time T for an h-period investment horizon. Setting the investor's initial wealth to $W_T = 1$ and letting $\omega(z)$ be the allocation to the stock index, the investor's terminal wealth at time $T + h$ is given by

$$W_{T+h} = (1 - \omega(z)) \exp(r_f h) + \omega(z) \exp\left(r_f h + \sum_{\tau=1}^{h} y_{T+\tau}\right). \tag{3.32}$$

Suppose the investor has power utility over terminal wealth:

$$u(W_{T+h}) = \frac{W_{T+h}^{1-A}}{1 - A}, \tag{3.33}$$

where A is the coefficient of relative risk aversion. This utility function plays the role of the loss function with the difference that we seek to maximize expected utility rather than minimizing expected loss.

The investor chooses $\omega(z)$ as

$$\omega^*(z) = \arg\max_{\omega(z)\in[0,1)} E\left[\frac{W_{T+h}^{1-A}}{1 - A}\middle| Z_T\right], \tag{3.34}$$

where $E[.|Z_T]$ is the conditional expectation, given information at time T, $Z_T = \{y_1, \ldots, y_T\}$. To rule out bankruptcy and unbounded expected utility, the weight on stocks is restricted to lie in $[0, 1)$.

The classical and Bayesian methods differ in how they compute the expectation in (3.34). Under the classical plug-in approach, the investor conditions on the parameter estimates $\hat{\theta} = (\hat{\mu}, \hat{\sigma}^2)$ and solves

$$\max_{\omega(z)\in[0,1)} \int \cdots \int u(W_{T+h}(\omega(z))) p_Y\left(\sum_{\tau=1}^{h} y_{T+\tau}|Z_T, \hat{\theta}\right) dy_{T+1} \ldots dy_{T+h}. \tag{3.35}$$

It follows from (3.31) that $p_Y(\sum_{\tau=1}^{h} y_{T+\tau} | \hat\theta, z_T) = N(\hat\mu h, \hat\sigma^2 h)$.[8] This solution ignores that θ is not known but typically estimated with considerable error.

The Bayesian approach deals with parameter uncertainty by integrating over the posterior distribution $p_Y(\theta|z_T)$ which summarizes the uncertainty about the parameters given the observed data sample z_T. This leads to a predictive distribution which is conditioned only on the observed sample (and not on any estimate $\hat\theta$):

$$p_Y\left(\sum_{\tau=1}^{h} y_{T+\tau} | Z_T\right) = \int p_Y\left(\sum_{\tau=1}^{h} y_{T+\tau} | Z_T, \theta\right) p(\theta|Z_T)d\theta. \qquad (3.36)$$

The Bayesian investor therefore solves

$$\max_{\omega(z)\in[0,1)} \int \cdots \int u(W_{T+h}(\omega(z))) p_Y\left(\sum_{\tau=1}^{h} y_{T+\tau} | Z_T\right) dy_{T+1} \ldots dy_{T+h}$$

$$= \max_{\omega(z)\in[0,1)} \int \cdots \int u(W_{T+h}(\omega(z))) p_Y\left(\sum_{\tau=1}^{h} y_{T+\tau} | Z_T, \theta\right) p(\theta|Z)dy_{T+1} \ldots dy_{T+h}d\theta.$$

$$(3.37)$$

This can be evaluated by sampling from the posterior distribution for θ, and, conditional on this draw, sampling from $p_Y(\sum_{\tau=1}^{h} y_{T+\tau} | Z_T, \theta)$, and finally averaging $u(W_{T+h})$ across those draws.

Barberis (2000) assumes an uninformative prior, $p(\mu, \sigma^2) \propto \sigma^{-2}$, and utilizes a normal-inverse gamma (IG) posterior distribution (see, e.g., Zellner (1971)),

$$\sigma^2|Z_T \sim IG\left(\frac{T-1}{2}, \frac{1}{2}\sum_{t=1}^{T}(y_t - \bar{y}_T)^2\right), \qquad (3.38)$$

$$\mu|\sigma^2, Z_T \sim N\left(\bar{y}_T, \frac{\sigma^2}{T}\right), \qquad (3.39)$$

where $\bar{y}_T = (1/T)\sum_{t=1}^{T} y_t$ is the sample mean. To solve for the optimal $\omega(z)$, Barberis considers a grid of values $\omega = 0, 0.01, 0.02, \ldots, 0.99$ and computes the integrals in (3.35) and (3.37) by numerical simulation. The idea is to draw a large number of (cumulated) returns $\{y_{T+1:T+h}^i\}_{i=1}^{I}$ and then compute

$$\bar{U}(\omega(z)) = \frac{1}{I}\sum_{i=1}^{I} \frac{\left((1-\omega(z))\exp(r_f h) + \omega(z)\exp(r_f h + \sum_{\tau=1}^{h} y_{T+\tau}^i)\right)^{1-A}}{1-A}. \qquad (3.40)$$

This calculation is straightforward in the classical case, given the assumption of normally distributed data: simply draw I times from $N(\hat\mu h, \hat\sigma^2 h)$; for each draw compute $\sum_{\tau=1}^{h} y_{T+\tau}$, evaluate the utility function for a given value of $\omega(z)$ and

---

[8] Density forecasting methods are described in more detail in chapter 13.

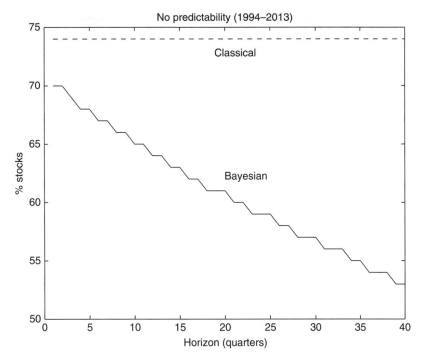

Figure 3.2: Optimal allocation to stocks under classical and Bayesian approaches.

average this across I. The value of $\omega(z)$ that yields the highest value of (3.40) is then the optimal allocation to stocks, $\omega^*(z)$.

To sample from the predictive distribution for long-horizon returns in the Bayesian case, $p_Y(\sum_{\tau=1}^{h} y_{T+\tau}|Z_T)$, first generate a sample (μ, σ^2) from the posterior distribution for the parameters $p(\mu, \sigma^2|Z_T)$. Then sample from the distribution of long-horizon returns conditional on past data and the parameters, $p_Y(\sum_{\tau=1}^{h} y_{T+\tau}|\mu, \sigma^2, Z_T)$. Finally, each of these draws is plugged into the utility function and averaged across the I draws to get an estimate of the average utility for a given value of $\omega(z)$.

Sampling from the posterior return distribution is very easy. First, we sample from the marginal distribution, $p(\sigma^2|Z_T)$, which by (3.38) is an inverse Gamma distribution. Given a value for σ^2, we next sample from the conditional distribution $p(\mu|\sigma^2, Z_T)$ which by (3.39) is a normal distribution. Finally, we sample from the distribution of returns conditional on the parameter values $p_Y(\sum_{\tau=1}^{h} y_{T+\tau}|\mu, \sigma^2, Z_T)$. From (3.31) it follows that conditional on (μ, σ^2) the cumulated return distribution is $N(\mu h, \sigma^2 h)$.

Comparing the solutions in (3.35) and (3.37) gives a measure of the importance of parameter uncertainty for the investor's optimal asset allocation. Figure 3.2 illustrates the difference in the percentage allocation to stocks (listed on the vertical axis) for the classical and Bayesian approaches for different investment horizons, h, measured in quarters and listed on the horizontal axis. The analysis uses quarterly returns data on a value-weighted portfolio of US stocks and a three-month T-bill rate over the 20-year period 1994Q1–2013Q4. The computations assume a coefficient of relative risk aversion of $A = 5$. The flat line shows the classical investor's allocation to stocks.

This line is constant and so under i.i.d. returns the classical investor's allocation to stocks is independent of the investment horizon. In contrast, the allocation to stocks under the Bayesian approach declines quite sharply from 70% at the 1-month horizon to around 55% at the 40-quarter (10-year) horizon.[9]

Such differences in asset allocations are a direct reflection of differences between how the classical and Bayesian approaches handle parameter uncertainty. Parameter uncertainty introduces another long-lasting source of risk; the true parameters could be worse than indicated by the sample, in which case long-run returns would be particularly adversely affected as the variance of the cumulative return distribution increases faster than linearly with the investment horizon, h. This leads risk-averse buy-and-hold investors to scale back their holdings of stocks and introduces horizon effects even under i.i.d. returns.

3.6 CONCLUSION

This chapter discusses how to find an optimal forecasting model by minimizing expected loss in situations with a known parametric forecasting model for the outcome given a set of predictor variables. In situations where the forecasting model is known except for a finite set of parameters, the expected loss can be computed by taking the expected value of the loss with respect to the conditional distribution for the outcome. Under MSE loss the optimal forecast is simply the conditional mean of the outcome.

When the model is unknown, past data must be employed to construct estimates of the model. Defining risk to be the expected loss integrated over both the outcome and the data employed to construct the forecast, the chapter discusses how classical forecasting approaches attempt to minimize this risk. Even in the simplest of forecasting situations, the presence of estimated parameters means that there is no unique forecasting model that minimizes risk over the entire parameter space. Different views on the relevant parameter space motivate different forecasting models. Although the Bayesian approach conditions on the data, different priors can be appropriate for different views on the parameter space, hence again leading to a range of possible forecasting models. Thus for both the classical and Bayesian approaches, there is not a single optimal approach to constructing a forecasting model.

The next two chapters elaborate on the classical and Bayesian approaches to constructing forecast models.

---

[9] The step features of the plot reflect the discrete grid used in our computations.

◇◇

Classical Estimation of Forecasting Models

It is rare for a forecaster to know the exact form of the best forecasting model or the values of its parameters. For example, under MSE loss we want to compute the conditional mean of Y, but typically do not know the true functional form of this. In practice, going from a forecasting model to an operational forecast—i.e., a single number or a density forecast—requires consulting with data that will help in both tasks. This chapter deals with general issues related to the classical approach to forecasting when parameters must be estimated while the next chapter discusses Bayesian estimation methods. We focus on the general approaches and how they relate to notions of forecast optimality as discussed in the previous chapter. Model selection is covered in chapter 6.

Using the setup from chapter 3 we are looking for a forecasting model, $f^*(z)$, that minimizes the expected loss

$$f^*(z) = \arg\min_{f \in \mathcal{F}} \int L(f(z), y) p_Y(y|z, \theta) dy. \tag{4.1}$$

Solving (4.1) involves a search over a space of functions, $\mathcal{F}$. Chapter 3 gave examples of how the optimal forecast can be constructed when the conditional density, $p_Y(y|z, \theta)$, and the parameters, θ, are known.

When the parameters of the forecasting model β must be estimated, the risk of the forecasting model will depend on the estimation procedure even if the model, $p_Y(y|z, \theta)$, is known. Even in the most trivial examples there will not be a uniquely optimal forecast procedure over all ranges of θ. Hence different approaches to constructing forecast methods coexist, even when the form of the joint density of Y and Z is known with only the parameters, θ, to be estimated.

More realistically, $p_Y(y|z, \theta)$ is not even known up to a set of parameters $\theta \in \Theta$, in which case the model itself is an approximation, thus further restricting notions of optimality. Often what is referred to as an "optimal" forecast in the forecasting literature is much weaker than the notion of forecast optimality given in (4.1) and instead refers to a set of possible forecasts that solve a much more restricted problem.

Classical estimation methods are the dominant approach in forecasting analysis. The simplest classical approach to constructing a forecast model is to use the sample analog of the forecast objective function, i.e., the loss function, and base the model on estimates that maximize this objective function. This makes estimation of forecast models a special case of M-estimation in statistics. An alternative and very popular approach, described in the previous chapter, is to first formulate the forecast model (which, from the previous chapter is a feature of the conditional distribution of the predicted variable) and then plug in estimates for the unknown parameters possibly obtained by minimizing some other objective function such as mean squared errors.

Sections 4.1 and 4.2 examine different estimation procedures when the forecasting model is approximated by the parametric specification $f(z_T, \beta)$ for some vector $\beta \in \mathcal{B}$. Many approaches have been considered, including M-estimation based on the loss function, maximum likelihood estimation, and various ad hoc methods. These methods compute an average of the loss function over all the observed data points, rather than the loss function at the time where the forecast is being generated, which is at the end of the sample, at time T. The chapter also examines popular estimation methods that have had some success in using penalized loss functions. Here the intent is not to interpret the limiting value of $\hat{\beta}$, but instead to reduce parameter estimation error and its effect on risk. Section 4.3 briefly examines issues that arise when the forecast model is not specified parametrically. This section serves primarily as a bridge to subsequent chapters that cover the material in greater detail. Finally, section 4.4 concludes.

4.1 LOSS-BASED ESTIMATORS

A straightforward approach to constructing a forecasting model[1] is to specify the model up to a set of unknown parameters, $\beta \in \mathcal{B}$, where $\mathcal{B}$ is the set of possible parameter values, and then estimate these parameters directly using the sample analog for the model's expected loss based on data $\{z_t, y_{t+1}\}_{t=0}^{T-1}$. This procedure, usually described as an M-estimator, yields[2]

$$\hat{\beta}_T = \arg \min_{\beta \in \mathcal{B}} T^{-1} \sum_{t=0}^{T-1} L(f(z_t, \beta), y_{t+1}). \tag{4.2}$$

The forecast of next period's outcome, y_{T+1}, denoted by $f(z_T, \hat{\beta}_T)$, is then constructed using the estimates, $\hat{\beta}_T$. Notice that there is no assumption (or expectation) that the forecast model $f(z_t, \beta)$ is correctly specified.

Under relatively general conditions it can be established that

$$T^{-1} \sum_{t=0}^{T-1} L(f(z_t, \beta^{**}), y_{t+1}) - T^{-1} \sum_{t=0}^{T-1} L(f(z_t, \hat{\beta}), y_{t+1}) = o_p(1), \tag{4.3}$$

---

[1] For simplicity we assume throughout this chapter that the forecast horizon is one period and so focus on one-step-ahead forecasts.

[2] Notice that we estimate the parameters of the forecasting model using the full sample; recursive, out-of-sample forecasting approaches are covered later in the book.

where

$$\beta^{**} = \arg\min_{\beta \in B} \lim_{T \to \infty} T^{-1} \sum_{t=0}^{T-1} E\ [L(f(z_t, \beta), y_{t+1})]. \tag{4.4}$$

Here we use the notation β^{**} to denote the average (over the sample) best choice for β, as opposed to β^{*} defined in the previous chapter as the best choice at time T. As discussed below, these may differ. Proofs of results such as (4.4) are typically broken into two steps: first show that the objective function converges uniformly in β, then show that $\hat{\beta}_T \to^P \beta^{**}$. A wide range of assumptions can be used to establish the result. Differences in the required assumptions reflect the form of stationarity of the data (strict, second order, or global) and type of time-series dependence assumed for the data (mixing conditions, near epoch dependence, summability assumptions, etc.), and the degree of smoothness of the objective function. Because of such differences, any attempt to write down assumptions and prove general results will be both lengthy and incomplete. For i.i.d. data, a summary of results is provided in Newey and McFadden (1994). For dependent data, Wooldridge (1994) is an excellent source for results.

Drawing on Wooldridge (1994, Theorems 4.2 and 4.3), we simply present a set of assumptions that both illustrate the character of the results and are general enough to cover many forecast situations. Assume the following.

1. $\beta \in \mathcal{B} \subset \mathbb{R}^k$, where $\mathcal{B}$ is compact.
2. $L(f(Z_t, \beta), Y_{t+1})$ and $f(Z_t, \beta)$ are measurable functions in β and continuous in $\{z_t, y_{t+1}\}$ on $\mathcal{B}$.
3. For each $\beta \in B$, $L(f(Z_t, \beta), Y_{t+1})$ satisfies a weak law of large numbers (LLN).
4. There exists a function $c_t(z_t, y_{t+1}) \geq 0$ such that

   (a) for all $\beta_1, \beta_2 \in \mathcal{B}$,

   $$|L(f(z_t, \beta_1), y_{t+1}) - L(f(z_t, \beta_2), y_{t+1})| \leq c_t(z_t, y_{t+1})||\beta_1 - \beta_2||.$$

   (b) $c_t(Z_t, Y_{t+1})$ satisfies a weak LLN.

Under these assumptions

$$\max_{\beta \in \mathcal{B}} \left| T^{-1} \sum_{t=0}^{T-1} L(f(z_t, \beta), y_{t+1}) - T^{-1} \sum_{t=0}^{T-1} E[\ L(f(z_t, \beta), Y_{t+1})] \right| \to^P 0. \tag{4.5}$$

This result gives a uniform weak LLN for the objective function over the possible parameters of the forecast model. The result is for a stronger case than that in Wooldridge (1994) because we assume that the loss function does not vary over time, which is a typical assumption for most forecast problems, although the results can be extended to allow the function itself to change.

Application of the result in (4.5) still requires proof of the two weak LLNs in the theorem, which in turn requires stationarity and dependence assumptions. Weak LLN results follow fairly directly from general assumptions, for example if (2) above holds, $[y_{t+1}, z_t]'$ is ϕ-mixing of size $-r/(2(r-1))$, $r \geq 1$ or $[y_{t+1}, z_t]'$ is α-mixing of size $-r/(r-1)$, where $r > 1$, and $E|L(f(z_t, \beta), y_{t+1})|^{r+\delta} < \Delta < \infty$ for some $\delta > 0$ and all t, then (3) above holds (see White, 2001, Corollary 3.48), where the addition of assumption (2) ensures that $L(f(z_t, \beta), y_{t+1})$ is mixing for any β. Given these assumptions and the assumption that there is a unique maximizer to $\lim_{T \to \infty} T^{-1} \sum_{t=0}^{T-1} E\left[L(f(Z_t, \beta), Y_{t+1})\right]$, it follows that $\hat{\beta}_T$ in (4.2) is consistent for β^{**} in (4.4). [3]

Results such as (4.5) suggest that—given enough data—the average loss from using $\hat{\beta}$ in the forecasting model is close to the smallest possible value of $\lim_{T \to \infty} T^{-1} \sum_{t=0}^{T-1} E\left[L(f(Z_t, \beta), Y_{t+1})\right]$, holding the forecast model $f(z_t, \beta)$ constant. What we really want is a forecast model $f(z_t, \hat{\beta})$ that comes close to obtaining the smallest possible conditional expected loss $E[L(f(Z, \hat{\beta}), Y)]$; in our notation this is $E[L(f(Z_T, \hat{\beta}_T), Y_{T+1})]$. An alternative way to make this point is to note that we want $\hat{\beta} \to^p \beta^*$, but (4.5) establishes convergence at β^{**} which need not be equal to β^*.

The objective we have minimized and the objective we would like to minimize are the same if the data are strictly stationary, i.e., under the assumption that the data are drawn from a strictly stationary process so $T^{-1} \sum_{t=0}^{T-1} E\left[L(f(Z_t, \beta), Y_{t+1})\right] = E\left[L(f(Z_T, \beta), Y_{T+1})\right]$. This is a very strong assumption, and unlikely to hold for most forecasting applications. For parameter estimators such as linear projections that depend only on the first two moments of $\{Y, Z\}$, the assumption of covariance stationarity suffices. More likely in any forecast situation, the data are heterogeneous in the sense that the data-generating process changes over time. Using past data to estimate the forecast model in such situations yields an estimator that works "on average," as opposed to being tailored towards the current forecasting problem. We illustrate this point in the following example.

Example 4.1.1 (Best average versus best current model under MSE loss). *Suppose that $Y_{t+1}|z_t \sim N(\beta_1 z_t + \beta_2 z_t^2, \sigma^2)$ and z_t is mean 0 with heterogeneous second and third moments denoted σ_{zt}^i, i=2, 3. Let the forecast model $f_t(z_t, \beta) = \beta z_t$. Then under MSE loss $E[L(f(Z_T, \hat{\beta}_T), Y_{T+1})] = E(Y_{T+1} - \beta Z_T)^2$ which is minimized at $\beta = \beta_1 + \beta_2 \sigma_{zT}^3 / \sigma_{zT}^2$. In this model $E[L(f(Z_t, \beta), Y_{t+1})] = C_t + (\beta_1 - \beta)^2 \sigma_{zt}^2 + 2(\beta_1 - \beta)\beta_2 \sigma_{zt}^3$, where C_t does not depend on β. Assuming that $\bar{\sigma}_z^i = \lim_{T \to \infty} T^{-1} \sum \sigma_{zt}^i$ is finite, $\beta^* = \beta_1 + \beta_2 \bar{\sigma}_z^3 / \bar{\sigma}_z^2 \neq \beta_1 + \beta_2 \sigma_{zT}^3 / \sigma_{zT}^2$ at T. As usual the OLS coefficient gives the best "average" fit and here this differs from the best current model.*

Note that (4.5) holds for a broad class of loss functions and forecast models, including loss functions that are not differentiable everywhere. This generality comes at a cost—some of the assumptions are stronger than we might prefer for some often-used loss functions. For example, under MSE loss where both the loss function is differentiable and a closed-form solution for $\hat{\beta}_T$ is available, we might not assume that the parameter space is compact. Indeed, for this simple problem, consistency results that do not require compactness are available for the least squares estimator.

For more complicated forecasting models (e.g., nonlinear models) the assumption of compactness fits well with the common forecasting approach of using an "insanity filter," which ignores the forecast if the forecast is deemed too far from the current outcome. Given the data, this could be considered a bound on the parameters that one is willing to entertain, which essentially amounts to a compactness assumption.

---

[3] This result follows from Wooldridge (1994, Theorem 4.3).

Some results have been established for particular combinations of loss functions and forecast models. The following example illustrates this.

Example 4.1.2 (*M*-estimator under lin-lin loss). *Consider the piecewise linear (lin-lin) loss function with $\alpha \in (0, 1)$ and a linear forecast model of the form $\beta' z_T$:*

$$L(f(z_T, \beta), y_{T+1}) = \alpha(y_{T+1} - \beta' z_T)\mathbb{1}(y_{T+1} > \beta' z_T)$$
$$- (1 - \alpha)(y_{T+1} - \beta' z_T)\mathbb{1}(y_{T+1} \le \beta' z_T).$$

Loss-based estimation of the forecasting model suggests using the analog

$$\hat{\beta} = \arg \min_{\beta} T^{-1} \sum_{t=0}^{T-1} \alpha(y_{t+1} - \beta' z_t)\mathbb{1}(y_{t+1} > \beta' z_t)$$
$$- (1 - \alpha)(y_{t+1} - \beta' z_t)\mathbb{1}(y_{t+1} \le \beta' z_t).$$

This is the M-estimator for the quantile α. Komunjer (2005) gives assumptions under which the M-estimator of $\hat{\beta}$ is consistent for β^{**}, including results for more general models.

When the loss function is twice differentiable everywhere, we can use expansions to establish the above results. A second-order mean value expansion yields

$$T^{-1} \sum_{t=0}^{T-1} L(f(z_t, \beta^{**}), y_{t+1})$$

$$= T^{-1} \sum_{t=0}^{T-1} L(f(z_t, \hat{\beta}), y_{t+1}) - \left[T^{-1} \sum_{t=0}^{T-1} \frac{\partial L(\cdot)}{\partial \beta} \bigg|_{\beta=\hat{\beta}} \right] (\hat{\beta} - \beta^{**})$$

$$+ \frac{1}{2}(\hat{\beta} - \beta^{**})' \left[T^{-1} \sum_{t=0}^{T-1} \frac{\partial^2 L(\cdot)}{\partial \beta \, \partial \beta'} \bigg|_{\beta=\bar{\beta}} \right] (\hat{\beta} - \beta^{**})$$

$$= T^{-1} \sum_{t=0}^{T-1} L(f(z_t, \hat{\beta}), y_{t+1}) + \frac{1}{2}(\hat{\beta} - \beta^{**})' \left[T^{-1} \sum_{t=0}^{T-1} \frac{\partial^2 L(\cdot)}{\partial \beta \, \partial \beta'} \bigg|_{\beta=\bar{\beta}} \right] (\hat{\beta} - \beta^{**}),$$

for some intermediate value, $\bar{\beta}$, between $\hat{\beta}$ and β^{**}. Here we used the first-order optimality condition, $E[\partial L(\cdot)/\partial \beta] = 0$, when evaluated at $\beta = \hat{\beta}$. Provided that $\hat{\beta}$ is consistent for β^{**} and $T^{-1} \sum_{t=0}^{T-1} (\partial^2 L(\cdot)/\partial \beta \, \partial \beta')\big|_{\beta^{**}}$ does not diverge, it follows that the average loss evaluated at the pseudo-true value and estimated value, $\hat{\beta}$, become similar.

The assumption of a unique maximizer may not hold in practice. For example, consider estimation of the parameters of an ARMA–GARCH model (discussed further in chapters 7 and 13) under MSE loss. Under this type of loss, the optimal forecast is simply the conditional mean and so the GARCH volatility parameters (other than the intercept) are unidentified. It may not be obvious that a lack of identification of the model is of practical concern for the forecaster since this simply means that two forecast models are equally good in terms of their expected (or average) loss. Using an unidentified model could, however, make it difficult to explain the forecast if two models yield the same expected outcome.

Finally, notice that a key assumption here is that we can formulate a parametric forecast model. We examine nonparametric methods in chapter 11.

4.2 PLUG-IN ESTIMATORS

The plug-in approach is commonly used in classical forecasting. Any estimator of θ or β requires the use of some form of objective function, which may or may not relate to the loss function for the forecasting problem. Here we break down plug-in estimators into three groups—those estimated using the correct loss function to construct parameter estimates; those that use a different loss function to estimate the parameters; and those that use the correct loss function but with restrictions imposed. First we present a simple application of a plug-in estimator.

4.2.1 Plug-In Estimators Based on the Forecaster's Loss Function

Given a loss function and an assumed joint density for the data, (Z, Y), we can sometimes construct a forecast model, $f(z, \beta)$, that captures the relevant feature of the predictive density. For example, a linear model might arise under MSE loss if the joint density of the data is normal. Typically, however, the joint density for the data is unknown and so both the form of the function, $f(z, \beta)$, and β are unknown. In practice, we must therefore use an approximation to the correct form of the forecast model $f(z, \beta)$ and choose some estimator for β.

In many situations where $f(z, \beta)$ takes the form of a parametric model, loss-based or plug-in methods will result in the same or very similar estimators. By this we mean that $|\hat{\beta}_{T,\text{PI}} - \hat{\beta}_T| \to^p 0$, where $\hat{\beta}_{T,\text{PI}}$ is the plug-in estimator. This would hold, for example, under MSE loss and a model for the conditional expectation with the plug-in estimator based on OLS. This follows directly as the OLS estimator minimizes the sum of squared residuals, $\sum_t (y_{t+1} - f(z_t, \beta))^2$, and so the objective functions are the same.

Aside from squared error loss, forecast models that use estimates from least squares problems may not have this property. The biggest concern with plug-in estimators is therefore that the loss function used to estimate the model parameters may not line up with the forecaster's loss function. We examine this issue in the next subsection.

A second concern is related to data heterogeneity which could mean that $\hat{\beta}_{T,\text{PI}} \to^p \beta^{**}$ rather than $\hat{\beta}_{T,\text{PI}} \to^p \beta^*$. In practice this means that the forecast model is good "on average" rather than being good at predicting next period's realization conditional on the current value of Z.

Example 4.2.1 (Mean-variance investor's use of plug-in estimators). *Consider the portfolio choice of an investor with initial wealth, $W_T = 1$. The investor chooses portfolio weights, $\omega_T = f(Z_T)$, which gives rise to future wealth, $W_{T+1} = \omega_T' y_{T+1}$, where y_{T+1} is a vector of gross returns on a set of risky assets. Given the investor's information at time T, Z_T, the distribution of future asset returns is $y_{T+1} \sim (\mu_T, \Sigma_T)$, so $E[W_{T+1}|Z_T] = \omega_T' \mu_T$, $\text{Var}(W_{T+1}|Z_T) = \omega_T' \Sigma_T \omega_T$. Suppose the investor has* *mean–variance preferences*

$$U(W_{T+1}) = E[W_{T+1}|Z_T] - \frac{a}{2} \operatorname{Var}(W_{T+1}|Z_T), \qquad (4.6)$$

where $a > 0$ captures the investor's risk aversion. Taking conditional expectations of (4.6), we have

$$E[U(W_{T+1})|Z_T] = \omega_T' \mu_T - \frac{a}{2} \omega_T' \Sigma_T \omega_T.$$

Maximizing expected utility subject to the constraint $\omega'(z_T)\iota = 1$, we get the optimal portfolio weights, (see Aït-Sahalia and Brandt (2001)),

$$\omega_T = \frac{\Sigma_T^{-1}\mu_T}{a} + \Sigma_T^{-1}\iota\left(\frac{a - \iota'\Sigma_T^{-1}\mu_T}{a\iota'\Sigma_T^{-1}\iota}\right). \qquad (4.7)$$

A two-step plug-in approach could be to first obtain estimates of μ_T and Σ_T, e.g., $\hat{\mu}_T = T^{-1}\sum_{t=1}^{T} y_t$, and $\hat{\Sigma}_T = (T-1)^{-1}\sum_{t=1}^{T}(y_t - \hat{\mu}_T)(y_t - \hat{\mu}_T)'$. In a second step, these estimates can be substituted into (4.7) to get the plug-in estimate of the portfolio weights:

$$\omega_T = \frac{\hat{\Sigma}_T^{-1}\hat{\mu}_T}{a} + \hat{\Sigma}_T^{-1}\iota\left(\frac{a - \iota'\hat{\Sigma}_T^{-1}\hat{\mu}_T'}{a\iota'\hat{\Sigma}_T^{-1}\iota}\right). \qquad (4.8)$$

Notice that ω_T is a highly nonlinear function of $\hat{\mu}_T$, $\hat{\Sigma}_T$ and so the sampling distribution of the estimated parameters may well lead to undesirable sampling properties of the associated expected utility function.

4.2.2 Estimation Based on Functions Other Than the Loss Function

An alternative to loss-based estimation is to use plug-in estimators derived from a variety of popular estimation methods. The leading case is perhaps to use maximum likelihood methods to estimate the model parameters and then plug these into the forecast model. Alternatively, often estimates obtained from least squares regression are used in forecast problems involving very different loss functions.

Maximum likelihood estimates for θ or β are commonly used in forecasting. Maximum likelihood methods typically require the construction of a likelihood for the data, although limited information maximum likelihood methods might be employed when models are complicated or it is thought that some of the predictor variables can be treated as exogenous. We can then construct forecasts from the model $f(z_T, \hat{\beta}_{\text{MLE}})$, using that $\hat{\beta}_{\text{MLE}}$ is typically easily derived from $\hat{\theta}_{\text{MLE}}$ and often is just a subset of the latter.

Example 4.2.2 (Forecast of a binary outcome variable). *Suppose Y is a binary variable that takes values of either 0 or 1 so the optimal forecast is a function of the "success" probability, $P[Y = 1|Z] = E[Y|Z]$. To generate a forecast of Y we might use a linear index model, $P(Y = 1|Z) = F(z'\beta)$ for some c.d.f., F. Popular choices are probit and logit models, the maximum likelihood estimates for which $\hat{\beta}_{\text{MLE}}$ can* be employed in a decision rule such as $\mathbb{1}(F(z'\hat{\beta}_{\text{MLE}}) > c)$, which forecasts $y = 1$ if the predicted probability falls above a certain threshold, c, and otherwise forecasts $y = 0$.

Using maximum likelihood estimates to construct a forecast model requires some knowledge of the form of $p_Y(y|z)$ and $p_z(z)$. When the likelihood is correctly specified so the entire joint density of Y and Z posited by the forecaster is the true data-generating process, under fairly general conditions the maximum likelihood estimators for the parameters $\hat{\theta}_{\text{MLE}}$ will be consistent for the true parameters of the data-generating process, θ. Assuming that the random variables from which the data are drawn have absolutely continuous distributions, and that the expected likelihood exists and is continuous in θ, the consistency result follows provided that (i) the model is identified (so the expected likelihood has a unique maximum at the true θ for the data-generating process) and (ii) the suitably scaled log-likelihood

$$\log \left\{ \prod_{t=0}^{T-1} p_Y(y_{t+1}|z_t, z_{t-1}, \ldots, \theta) p_Z(z_t|z_{t-1}, z_{t-2}, \ldots, \theta) \right\}$$

satisfies a uniform law of large numbers. This result follows from White (1996, Theorem 4.2).

In practice, the assumption that the likelihood is correctly specified is unlikely to hold and we can instead view the estimator as a quasi-maximum likelihood estimator (QMLE). QMLEs may still prove to have good properties, as discussed in White (1996), although their properties must be established in relation to the forecaster's loss function. When the kernel of the likelihood function agrees with the forecaster's loss function, the results from above apply.

Example 4.2.3 (Quasi-maximum likelihood estimation with a normal distribution). *The pseudo MLE from a model that assumes normality can be equivalent to a forecast that minimizes mean squared errors. To see this, let $\theta = (\beta, \sigma^2)$, so*

$$\hat{\theta}_{\text{MLE}} = \arg\max_{\theta \in \Theta} \left(\ln(\sigma^2)^{-T/2} \exp\left\{ -\frac{1}{2\sigma^2} \sum_{t=0}^{T-1}(y_{t+1} - f(z_t, \beta))^2 \right\} \right),$$

and

$$\hat{\beta} = \arg\min \sum_{t=0}^{T-1}(y_{t+1} - f(z_t, \beta))^2.$$

Here the estimates of the forecasting model $f(z_t, \hat{\beta}(\hat{\theta}_{\text{MLE}})) = f(z_t, \hat{\beta})$ and so forecasts based on the MLE values may be reasonable even when the density is misspecified.

Example 4.2.4 (QMLE for tick-exponential family). *Example 4.1.2 showed that the M-estimator for the relevant quantile provided an estimator for the forecast model under lin-lin loss. Komunjer (2005) examines QMLEs for the tick-exponential family whose pseudo densities take the form*

$$p_t^\alpha(y, \eta) = \exp\left[-(1-\alpha)(b(y) - a(\eta))\mathbb{1}(y \le \eta) + \alpha(b(y) - a(\eta))\mathbb{1}(y > \eta) \right],$$

where η is the model for the conditional quantile. When the tick-exponential is an asymmetric Laplace (double exponential) density, the tick-exponential QMLEs coincide with the conventional quantile regression estimator. Setting $b(y) = y$ and $a(\eta) = \eta = \beta'z$ yields a likelihood that is an order-preserving transform of the M-estimator based on the log function. It follows from Komunjer's results that the QMLE provides the best forecast among linear models.

Equivalence results such as those in the previous examples do not hold more generally. Rather, the forecasts based on MLEs will differ from those that minimize the loss function. Under reasonable conditions forecasts based on the correct loss function have the property that—at least in large enough samples—they yield losses that are approximately the smallest possible ones given the loss function and the forecasting model. In general we therefore expect forecasts based on the correct loss function to be superior to those based on MLEs. In small samples, efficiency may be more of an issue and it is possible that utility- or loss-based estimators are more sensitive to outliers than MLE-based estimators and so could lead to worse finite-sample performance. This issue has to be evaluated in each individual case.

Another case where the parameters are estimated under objective functions other than the forecaster's loss arises when standard econometric methods such as least squares estimation are used even though the forecaster has a different loss function such as mean absolute error loss or perhaps is interested in predicting turning points of the data. Indeed, the large literature on turning point prediction often examines forecasts in the context of logit or probit models; see, e.g., Chauvet and Potter (2005). It follows directly from the fact that β^* differs for different loss functions (see the examples in chapter 3) that this approach can easily lead to forecast models that do not achieve average losses that converge to the average expected loss given β^*. For further discussion and examples, see Weiss (1996).

Example 4.2.5 (Least squares estimates under absolute error loss). *Suppose least squares estimates are employed to generate forecasts under an absolute error loss function*

$$(T-1)^{-1} \sum_{t=1}^{T-1} \left| y_{t+1} - \hat{\beta}'_{\text{ols}} x_t \right| \to^P E\left[\left| Y - f(Z, \beta^*_{\text{ols}})\right|\right] \geq E\left[\left| Y - f(Z, \beta^*)\right|\right], \quad (4.9)$$

where $\beta^* = \arg\min_\beta E_Y[|Y - f(Z, \beta)|]$. Equality in (4.9) holds when the conditional mean and conditional median are equivalent, e.g., when the conditional distribution of Y given X is symmetric. Equality of the expected loss need not hold, however, for skewed or asymmetrical distributions.

4.2.3 Estimation Based on Penalized Loss Functions

The need to estimate the parameters of the forecasting model adds to the risk of the associated forecast. Under squared error loss, parameter estimation error usually adds a term of order T^{-1}. Although this term is asymptotically irrelevant, in practice it can still be a significant addition to risk. This is particularly true in practical forecast problems with monthly, quarterly, or even annual data where the sample size is not all that large and estimation errors can be important.

An alternative to choosing $\hat{\beta}$ to minimize the in-sample loss is to use a method that penalizes the in-sample average loss or constrains the dimension of the forecasting model. In this case we choose $\hat{\beta}$ as the minimizer of the Lagrangian

$$\hat{\beta} = \arg\min_{\beta} T^{-1} \sum_{t=0}^{T-1} L(f(z_t, \beta), y_{t+1}) + \lambda k(\beta), \qquad (4.10)$$

with $\lambda \geq 0$. We can view (4.10) as a penalized loss function with a penalty term $\lambda k(\beta)$. Applying this method to squared error loss and linear models, we have

$$\hat{\beta} = \arg\min_{\beta} T^{-1} \sum_{t=0}^{T-1} (y_{t+1} - \beta' z_t)^2 + \lambda k(\beta),$$

where variation in the choice of the function $k(\beta)$ results in different procedures. Ridge regression sets $k(\beta) = \sum_{i=1}^{k} \beta_i^2$, while the extended Ridge method uses $k(\beta) = \beta' A \beta$ for some matrix A. Ridge regression was originally introduced to deal with multicollinearity in linear regression. Even though multicollinearity is not a problem for forecasting, the Ridge estimator turns out to be a shrinkage estimator which can be useful in forecasting.

The Lasso (least absolute shrinkage and selection operator) method introduced by Tibshirani (1996) sets $k(\beta) = \sum_{i=1}^{k} |\beta_i|$ and also yields a shrinkage estimator. This method is often used for variable selection (see chapter 6) and so is useful in cases with large sets of possible predictors, few of which have sufficient predictive power to be included in the model. Bai and Ng (2008) consider Lasso methods to predict US inflation, while Elliott, Gargano, and Timmermann (2013) provide an application of both the Lasso and Ridge methods to predictability of US stock market returns.

Another, more recent, approach is the elastic net estimator proposed by Zou and Hastie (2005). This uses a penalty term $k(\beta) = \lambda_1 \sum_{i=1}^{k} |\beta_i| + \lambda_2 \sum_{i=1}^{k} \beta_i^2$, for $\lambda_1, \lambda_2 \geq 0$ which is a convex combination of the Lasso and Ridge penalty terms. By using such a combination of penalty terms, the hope is to avoid the tendency of Lasso to perform poorly when many predictors within a group have similar predictive power and Lasso tends to select an arbitrary predictor from the group. Bai and Ng (2008) use this approach to construct an inflation forecast from more than 100 variables.

A variation on these methods, due to Breiman (1995), is the Garrote, which chooses the parameters to solve

$$\hat{\beta} = \arg\min_{\beta} T^{-1} \sum_{t=0}^{T-1} \left(y_{t+1} - \sum_{i=1}^{k} w_i \hat{\beta}_i z_{it} \right)^2,$$

$$\text{subject to} \quad w_i > 0 \text{ for all } i, \quad \sum_{i=1}^{k} w_i < K,$$

where $\hat{\beta}_i$ are least squares estimates. This method has not, however, gained much use in the economic forecast literature.

Constrained optimization methods are examples of shrinkage estimators which shrink the coefficients of the unconstrained optimization methods to a particular point, usually 0. This can be seen in the following examples.

Example 4.2.6. *Let $y_t \sim iid(\mu, \sigma^2)$ and consider forecasting the mean of y_t. We can use the in-sample estimator with the lowest MSE subject to the constraint that $\mu^2 \leq K$ which prevents μ from becoming too large. This produces a penalized loss function of the form*

$$\min_{\mu} \left(T^{-1} \sum_{t=1}^{T} (y_t - \mu)^2 + \lambda \mu^2 \right), \tag{4.11}$$

where $\lambda \geq 0$. The solution to (4.11) yields the estimator

$$\hat{\mu} = \left(\frac{T}{T + \lambda} \right) \bar{y},$$

so the estimator shrinks the sample mean towards 0.

A second example is the generalized Ridge estimator.

Example 4.2.7. *Consider observations $\{Y, X\}$, where Y is $T \times 1$ and X is $T \times k$. Let $k(\beta) = \beta' A \beta$, where A is such that $A + X'X$ is positive definite. Then the solution to*

$$\hat{\beta} = \arg \min_{\beta} \left[(Y - X\beta)'(Y - X\beta) + \lambda \beta' A \beta \right]$$

is $\hat{\beta} = (X'X + \lambda A)^{-1} X'Y$ which is the generalized Ridge estimator; the simple Ridge estimator sets $A = I_k$.

4.3 PARAMETRIC VERSUS NONPARAMETRIC ESTIMATION APPROACHES

Restricting the set of forecast models $f(z)$ to a specific parametric form $f(z, \beta)$ results in a weaker notion of forecast optimality. This follows directly from the notion of maximization, since maximizing over a wider set of models cannot result in a worse choice in sample. In practice, forecasters often choose between alternate parametric models in some reduced set, $\mathcal{M}$. Limiting $\mathcal{M}$ to include only a finite number of models yields what is known as a model selection problem. When the set of models is infinite-dimensional, we refer to the model choice as a semi-nonparametric problem.

Chapter 6 examines the problem of model selection in far more detail, including discussions of properties of different methods and conditions under which these properties hold. Here we make only a few points that are pertinent to the current discussion. First, although there are often methods that can consistently select the correct model—assuming that it is included in the set under consideration—it does not follow that the risk function is the same as that obtained if the model were truly known. Notions of forecast optimality under model selection are therefore again much weaker, if they can even be established.

When the joint distributions of the outcome Y and predictors Z are unknown, it is popular to use sieve M-estimation to obtain a forecast model. Such methods generalize the estimation procedure in (4.2) by replacing a known or hypothesized forecast function, $f(z, \beta)$ with approximating functions that take the form $\tilde{\beta}_0' z_T + \sum_{j=1}^{J_T} \tilde{\beta}_j g(z_T, \gamma_j)$ so $\beta = (\tilde{\beta}_0', \tilde{\beta}_1, \ldots, \tilde{\beta}_{J_T}, \gamma_1, \ldots, \gamma_{J_T})'$, where the size of the parameter vector depends on the sample size, T, through the number of terms, J_T. Typically the functional form for g is chosen to have good approximating properties for a wide set of potential forecast functions. We examine these methods in more detail in chapter 11. Chen (2007, Theorem 3.1) gives results for consistent estimation of $\hat{\beta}$ for β^{**} under general conditions. The conditions are similar to those stated for M-estimation above— identification of the model at a single point β^{**}, continuity of the loss functions in the parameters, and uniform convergence— although since we now deal with sequences of models, results are somewhat more difficult to establish. In addition, there are restrictions on the parameters of the sieve models, i.e., the β's. While consistency of the model is of course useful to establish, the relationship between the forecast $f(z, \beta^{**})$ and $f(z, \beta_0)$ is not obvious in any practical forecast situation.

4.4 CONCLUSION

This chapter relates notions of forecast optimality under the classical approach, when the conditional distribution $p_Y(y|z, \theta)$, including the parameters θ, is known, to what we obtain in practice when the model and its parameters are unknown. Model and parameter uncertainty fundamentally affect our understanding of forecast optimality in several ways.

First, estimation methods that use objective functions different from the forecaster's loss function should generally be avoided since there is no obvious reason why the parameter estimates should be good at minimizing the forecaster's risk. This is the reason why Granger (1993) warns against basing estimation and evaluation on different criteria, a point that has been made a number of times in the forecasting literature (e.g., Weiss (1996).) The only exception to this arises when the forecast model is based on MLE estimates from a correctly specified model. However, we view correct specification of the joint density of the data to be highly unlikely for most forecasting problems.

Second, even when a model is correctly specified up to an unknown set of parameters and the parameters are estimated with the relevant loss function, at best only a family of minimum risk forecast methods, rather than a single optimal forecast method, can be established. This point was established in the previous chapter, and applies more generally to all of the results here.

Third, even when a forecast is constructed from a parametric model, the best-case scenario is that we obtain the optimal forecast from a restricted set of forecasting models even when we use the correct loss function.

Fourth, even when the forecast is based on the correct loss function, heterogeneity in the data means that it is likely that the estimator $\hat{\beta}$ for β^* (the best parameter for the current forecasting problem) actually converges to β^{**} (the average best parameter for the forecasting problem) with averages taken over the random variables that generated the data. In practice this difference could be small, but this is not necessarily the case. Of course if the data heterogeneity can be modeled, then improvements can be made in this direction. Chapter 19 examines examples of this nature.

Fifth, among forecast models estimated with the correct loss function, different estimators trade off risk across different regions of the parameter space in order to reduce the effect of parameter estimation error. This is the reason for considering restricted loss functions. Much of the effort in constructing good forecasts with limited data samples—such as the use of Bayesian vector autoregressions—comes from examining these second-order effects.

5

Bayesian Forecasting Methods

Bayesian forecasting methods typically involve calculating the predictive density for the outcome variable, Y, given both observables and assumptions on so-called unobservables. The observables are the data we condition on, i.e., z, which are outcomes of the random variables generating the data, Z. The unobservables are a given model, $M(\theta) \in \mathcal{M}$ and associated parameters θ, for the joint density of the data and outcome along with a prior distribution over the parameters of this joint density, $\pi(\theta)$. Using Bayes' rule, these can all be combined to construct the forecast distribution of Y given z and the choices on the unobservables, $P_Y(Y|Z, M)$.

The forecaster's loss function is generally not involved in the construction of the predictive density, although robustness to variations in either the proposed model or the prior can (and should) be viewed from the perspective of the loss function. Point forecasts can be formed by taking summary statistics of this predictive density with respect to the loss function in a manner analogous to the "known distribution" results presented in chapter 3. In practice, the known distribution is replaced with the predictive density and the point forecast is chosen to minimize the expected loss given the predictive density. In turn, predictive densities can themselves be used as density forecasts for the outcome of interest.

Several practical difficulties arise in implementing Bayesian forecasting methods. First on the list is how to specify the joint density of the data which is typically unknown. Properties of the forecast will depend on the choices made for this joint density. To address uncertainty about the form of the correct density, one possibility is to consider multiple models and use Bayesian model averaging—see chapter 14. In this chapter we assume that there is a single model, M, and although the results depend on the model choice, we suppress this dependence in the notation. Second, priors must be elicited for both the parameters and the unobservables. A third problem for forecasters is the construction of point forecasts, a process that involves summary statistics of the predictive density.

Section 5.1 introduces the basic theory behind Bayes risk as used in Bayesian forecasting analysis. Section 5.2 covers Ridge and shrinkage estimators while Section 5.3 provides a brief review of computational methods and discusses Bayesian modeling of predictive densities. Section 5.4 discusses economic applications of Bayesian forecasting methods and goes through an illustrative portfolio allocation example. Section 5.5 concludes.

5.1 BAYES RISK

Chapter 3 introduced Bayes risk as the weighted average of risk with weights chosen as the priors over the possible parameter values $\pi(\theta)$:

$$r(\pi, f) = \int_\theta R(\theta, f)\pi(\theta)d\theta. \tag{5.1}$$

Any forecast $f(z)$ that minimizes Bayes risk is a Bayes decision rule.

Using the notation for risk introduced in chapter 3, we have

$$R(\theta, f) = \int_z \int_y L(f(z), y)p_Y(y|z, \theta)p_Z(z|\theta)dy\,dz, \tag{5.2}$$

and so Bayes risk can be written as (see (3.26))

$$r(\pi, f) = \int_z \left(\int_\theta \left\{ \int_y L(f(z), y)p_Y(y|z, \theta)dy \right\} \pi(\theta|z)d\theta \right) m(z)dz. \tag{5.3}$$

Here we constructed the posterior for the parameters using Bayes' rule $\pi(\theta|z) = p_Z(z|\theta)\pi(\theta)/m(z)$, where $m(z) = \int p_Z(z|\theta)\pi(\theta)d\theta$ is the marginal likelihood. This can be viewed as a prior predictive distribution, i.e., a predictive distribution that does not depend on the observed data, z.

Minimizing (5.3) over forecast methods $f(z)$ conditional on $Z = z$ is the same as minimizing

$$\int_\theta \left\{ \int_y L(f(z), y)p_Y(y|z, \theta)dy \right\} \pi(\theta|z)d\theta$$

$$= \int_y L(f(z), y) \left(\int_\theta p_Y(y|z, \theta)\pi(\theta|z)d\theta \right) dy$$

$$= \int_y L(f(z), y)p_Y^p(y|z)dy,$$

where the minimization is over $f(z)$ and we used that the loss function does not depend on θ. Here $p_Y^p(y|z) = \int_\theta p_Y(y|z, \theta)\pi(\theta|z)d\theta$ is the (posterior) predictive density for Y. The optimal Bayesian point forecast is the forecast that minimizes expected loss with respect to this posterior predictive density.

Obtaining the posterior density of the parameters, $\pi(\theta|z)$, involves the usual Bayesian posterior density estimation problem for the model parameters. Hence, Bayesian forecasting can utilize a set of well-established methods. Many expositions cover this general problem and explain how to go about constructing the posterior density; see, e.g., Geweke (2005). The next example illustrates how the Bayesian predictive density can be derived in a simple case.

Example 5.1.1 (Computing the predictive density for an i.i.d. Gaussian series). Let $y_i \sim ind\ N(\mu, \sigma^2)$ with σ^2 known, and suppose the prior on μ is $N(\mu_0, \tau^2)$.

Using observations $z = (y_1, \ldots, y_T)$ to construct the forecast, the posterior density for μ is

$$\mu | (y_1, \ldots, y_T) \sim N \left(\frac{T\tau^2}{T\tau^2 + \sigma^2} \bar{y}_T + \frac{\sigma^2}{T\tau^2 + \sigma^2} \mu_0, \frac{\tau^2 \sigma^2}{T\tau^2 + \sigma^2} \right) \equiv N(\tilde{\mu}, \tilde{\sigma}^2),$$

where $\bar{y}_T = T^{-1} \sum_{t=1}^{T} y_t$ is the sample mean. The predictive density for y_{T+1} given z then follows from

$$p_{y_{T+1}}^p (y_{T+1} | z) = \int f(y_{T+1} | \mu, \sigma^2) \pi(\mu | z, \mu_0, \tau^2, \sigma^2) d\mu,$$

which results in

$$y_{T+1} | z \sim N(\tilde{\mu}, \sigma^2 + \tilde{\sigma}^2), \tag{5.4}$$

where the variance $\sigma^2 + \tilde{\sigma}^2 = \sigma^2 (1 + \tau^2/(T\tau^2 + \sigma^2))$. This distribution is the Bayesian density forecast $p_y^p(y|z)$.

Just as in the classical case, for some problems the predictive density may be considered a more useful summary of the forecast than a point forecast. In many practical forecast situations this is what most Bayesians would consider to be the objective of a forecasting problem because of the generality of the solution.

Once we have the predictive density, $p_Y(y|z, \beta)$, the best forecast can be constructed using the equivalent to the first step of the two-step classical approach, but with the predictive density in place of the unknown conditional density. For example, under MSE loss, the best estimator is the conditional mean of y given z. The Bayesian equivalent is the mean of the predictive density $p_Y^p(y|z)$. Similarly, for the lin-lin loss function we could report the relevant quantile of the predictive density.

Example 5.1.2 (Forecasting the mean of an i.i.d. Gaussian series under MSE loss). *Under MSE loss and using the setup in Example 5.1.1, the forecast becomes*

$$f(z) = E[y_{T+1} | z] = \tilde{\mu} = \frac{T\tau^2}{T\tau^2 + \sigma^2} \bar{y}_T + \frac{\sigma^2}{T\tau^2 + \sigma^2} \mu_0.$$

This is a shrinkage estimator that shrinks the sample mean, $\bar{y}_T$, towards the prior mean, μ_0, with weights that depend on the information in the prior (τ^2) and the sample (σ^2, T). In large samples the weight on the sample mean gets closer to 1. A similar result occurs for a more diffuse prior, i.e., a larger value of τ^2.

Example 5.1.3 (Forecasting the mean of an i.i.d. Gaussian series under Linex loss). *Under the Linex loss function, the optimal forecast given the conditional density is the mean plus $(a/2)$ times the variance. Using the predictive distribution in (5.4), this is*

$$f(z) = \tilde{\mu} + \frac{a}{2} \left(\sigma^2 + \tilde{\sigma}^2 \right),$$

which is the Bayesian point forecast.

Both Examples 5.1.2 and 5.1.3 use the same predictive density to construct point forecasts under different loss functions. Provision of the predictive density would therefore have been sufficient for forecasters in each of these cases.

Finally, when specifying the likelihood function used to construct the predictive density we required a model for both y and z, the choice of which will influence the results. This assumption of a known model is also implicit when we use the same θ for both the model and the true joint density of the data. Extension of Bayesian methods to allow for an unknown model often involves averaging over different models with weights reflecting the posterior likelihood that a particular model is "true." We examine such approaches in chapter 14.

In addition to providing the predictive density or Bayesian point forecasts, we can also examine the expected loss through the risk function. Expressions for these objects can be obtained by plugging the optimal forecast, $f(z)$, into either Bayes risk (equations (5.1) and (5.3)) or the risk function (5.2) which depends on θ. First, consider the risk function, $R(\theta, f(z))$. Denoting the optimal forecast by $f^*(z)$, the risk becomes

$$R^*(\theta, f) = \int_z \int_y L(f^*(z), y) p_Y(y|z, \theta) p_Z(z|\theta) dy \, dz. \tag{5.5}$$

Given the function $f^*(z)$, this reduces to a function of θ—just as in the classical case. For a given forecast, $f^*(z)$, the risk function can be examined for various values of θ to consider the associated risk.

Example 5.1.4 (Forecasting the mean of an i.i.d. Gaussian series under MSE loss, continued). *For this example, $f^*(z) = \tilde{\mu}$, so we need to evaluate*

$$R^*(\mu, f^*) = \int_z \int_y (y - \tilde{\mu})^2 p_Y(y|z, \theta) p_Z(z|\theta) dy \, dz.$$

We know that the conditional density is $y_{T+1}|z, \theta \sim N(\mu, \sigma^2)$. Integrating over this, we obtain $\int_y (y - \tilde{\mu})^2 p_Y(y|z, \theta) dy = \sigma^2 + (\mu - \tilde{\mu})^2$, i.e., the variance plus the squared bias. Here $\tilde{\mu}$ is a function of z since it depends on $\bar{y}_T$. Integrating over z, we have

$$R^*(\mu, f) = \int_z \left(\sigma^2 + (\mu - \tilde{\mu})^2 \right) p_Z(z|\theta) dz$$

$$= \sigma^2(1 + T^{-1}a^2) + (\mu - \mu_0)^2(1 - a)^2, \tag{5.6}$$

where $a = T\tau^2/(T\tau^2 + \sigma^2)$. This risk function shows the trade-off between using an informative prior versus using the sample mean. The sample mean is obtained from (5.6) by letting $\tau^2 \to \infty$, so $a \to 1$, corresponding to a flat prior. From (5.6), we have $R(\mu, \bar{y}_T) = \sigma^2(1 + T^{-1})$. Since $a < 1$, the prior reduces the variance component but adds a squared bias component $(\mu - \mu_0)^2(1 - a)^2$. When the prior mean, μ_0, is sufficiently close to the true value, μ, this will reduce risk. However, for more distant values the squared bias term can be greater than the estimation risk from using the least squares forecast.

For the simplest of forecast situations, this example again shows the lack of a single approach that is optimal across all models. Different choices of prior result in different estimators and different risk functions, but none is uniformly better than the others.

To reduce risk from a function of θ to a single number, and hence a measure that allows us to rank different methods, we need to weight all the possible values for θ. This requires a distribution over θ. Using the prior distribution, $\pi(\theta)$, we have

$$r^*(\pi, f^*) = \int_\theta R^*(\theta, f^*)\pi(\theta)d\theta.$$

Since $f^*(z)$ was chosen to minimize this weighted average risk, clearly the Bayes approach both minimizes the risk for this weighting and provides a constructive method for deriving the best forecasting rule. Indeed, under any weighting over the parameters, the Bayes' rule constructed for priors that are identical to that weighting provides an optimal forecast method. Classical methods can also be optimal if they are equivalent to some Bayes' rule.

Example 5.1.5 (Forecasting the mean of an i.i.d. Gaussian series under MSE loss, continued). *Using the prior density $\pi(\mu) \sim N(\mu_0, \tau^2)$, we have*

$$r^*(\pi, f^*) = \int_\mu \left(\sigma^2(1 + T^{-1}a^2) + (\mu - \mu_0)^2(1 - a)^2\right)\pi(\mu)d\mu$$

$$= \sigma^2(1 + T^{-1}a^2) + (1 - a)^2\tau^2.$$

For any choice of τ^2, $r^*(\pi, f^*) \leq r(\pi, \bar{y}) = \sigma^2(1 + T^{-1})$. Equality holds as $\tau^2 \to \infty$.

5.1.1 Empirical Bayes Methods

Forecasts or forecast distributions generally depend on so-called hyperparameters that must be chosen by the forecaster. This can readily be seen for the point forecasts in the above examples. For example, for the normal regression forecast in (5.10), we must choose the hyperparameters β_0 and Σ_0 to construct the forecast $\tilde{\beta}'x_T$. In empirical Bayes methods, the hyperparameters are estimated from the data in a model consistent way, rather than being imposed by the forecaster.

The typical empirical Bayes approach is to use the marginal density of the (observed) data that arises from integrating out the prior density, i.e., $m(z) = \int p_Z(z|\theta)\pi(\theta)d\theta$. Since this is a function of the hyperparameters in $\pi(\theta)$, this relates the distribution that generates the observed data, z_t, to the hyperparameters. For many problems the hyperparameters can therefore be estimated from the observed data in a simple and intuitive way.

Empirical applications in economics or finance that use so-called g-priors often involve estimating hyperparameters and priors based on the data and then determining the "strength" of the prior as some fraction of the information available in the data sample at hand. For a discussion of both parametric and nonparametric empirical Bayes methods in the context of forecast models with many predictors, see Stock and Watson (2006).

5.1.2 Bayesian Modeling of the Predictive Distribution

Construction of the predictive distribution, $p_Y(y_{T+1}|Z_T)$, i.e., the posterior distribution of the variable we wish to forecast conditional only on the current data, $Z_t = \{Y_t, X_t\}$, $t = 1, \ldots, T$, is the main object of interest in Bayesian forecasting. Having constructed a posterior density for θ, $\pi(\theta|Z_T)$, the predictive density is the average density for y after integrating out the unknown parameters. Formally, we have

$$p_y^p(y_{T+1}|Z_T) = \int p_y(y_{T+1}|\theta, Z_T)\pi(\theta|Z_T)d\theta. \tag{5.7}$$

An illustration of this point is the result in Example 5.1.1, where for the i.i.d. normal case the predictive density is a normal distribution with mean equal to the posterior mean and variance equal to the sum of the variance of y_t plus the variance from the posterior for the mean.

Just as in the classical case, uncertainty over the parameters of the model results in greater risk and less certainty over the location of the forecast. In the previous example this shows up in a strictly larger variance than if the mean were known.

How the forecast is constructed differs depending on the difficulties involved in the computation of the integral in (5.7) and also in the construction of the posterior which itself requires computing an integral. Closed-form solutions are rarely available in interesting forecasting problems and so instead the predictive distribution is computed using numerical methods that can be tailored to the specific problem at hand.

5.2 RIDGE AND SHRINKAGE ESTIMATORS

Under MSE loss, the Bayesian point forecast will be the average of the conditional mean given the parameters, weighted by the posterior distribution of the parameters. Letting $\mu(z, \theta)$ be the model for the conditional mean of y given z, the Bayesian point forecast under MSE loss is therefore

$$f(z) = \int_\theta \mu(z, \theta)\pi(\theta|z)d\theta, \tag{5.8}$$

where $\pi(\theta|z)$ is the posterior distribution of θ given z. To derive (5.8), start with

$$L(f(z), y) = (y - f(z))^2 = (y - \mu(z, \theta))^2 + (\mu(z, \theta) - f(z))^2$$
$$+ 2(y - \mu(z, \theta))(\mu(z, \theta) - f(z)).$$

The first term affects the risk regardless of our choice of forecast $f(z)$ and so we can ignore this term when choosing $f(z)$ to minimize risk. Given the definition of $\mu(z, \theta)$, the expected value of the third term equals 0. Bayes risk is then a constant plus the second term,

$$r(\pi, f) = \int_z \int_\theta \int_y (\mu(z, \theta) - f(z))^2 \, p_Y(y|z, \theta)p_Z(z|\theta)\pi(\theta)d\theta \, dy \, dz \tag{5.9}$$

$$= \int_z \int_\theta (\mu(z, \theta) - f(z))^2 \, p_Z(z|\theta)\pi(\theta)d\theta \, dz,$$

where we used that the squared loss term is independent of y. Assuming that the distributions allow us to differentiate under the integral, the first-order condition yields

$$2 \int_z \int_\theta (\mu(z, \theta) - f(z)) \, p_Z(z|\theta) \pi(\theta) d\theta \, dz = 0.$$

Rearranging, we have, conditional on z,

$$f(z) = \int_\theta \mu(z, \theta) \frac{p_Z(z|\theta)\pi(\theta)}{\int p_Z(z|\theta)\pi(\theta)d\theta} d\theta$$

$$= \int_\theta \mu(z, \theta)\pi(\theta|z)d\theta,$$

which is (5.8). Hence, under MSE loss we can combine the model for the conditional mean with the posterior to compute the Bayesian point forecast.

For the linear prediction model we have $\mu(z, \theta) = \beta' z$. Note that $\int_\beta (\beta' z)\pi(\beta|z)d\beta = \tilde{\beta}'z$, where $\tilde{\beta} = E_\pi[\beta|z]$, so $\tilde{\beta}$ is the mean of the posterior distribution for β. It follows that the Bayesian point forecast simply uses the posterior mean in place of the unknown β. The following example illustrates this result for a general regression with known variances and shrinkage.

Example 5.2.1 (Shrinkage estimator for multivariate regression model). *Let $y \sim$ N$(X\beta, V)$ and consider the conjugate normal prior, $\beta \sim$ N(β_0, Σ_0). Suppose that V is known and the marginal distribution for X does not involve β. Then the posterior distribution for β is $\beta|Y, X \sim$ N$(\tilde{\beta}, \Sigma)$, where $\Sigma = (X'V^{-1}X + \Sigma_0^{-1})$ and*

$$\tilde{\beta} = (X'V^{-1}X + \Sigma_0^{-1})^{-1}X'V^{-1}X\hat{\beta} + (X'V^{-1}X + \Sigma_0^{-1})^{-1}\Sigma_0^{-1}\beta_0. \tag{5.10}$$

The posterior mean is a general shrinkage estimator where the weights depend on the prior and the (generalized) least squares estimator, $\hat{\beta} = (X'V^{-1}X)^{-1}X'V^{-1}y$, is shrunk towards the mean of the prior, β_0.

Interesting special cases arise directly from this formulation. Setting $V = \sigma^2 I$ and $\Sigma_0 = \tau^2 I$ yields the posterior mean

$$\tilde{\beta}_{\text{Ridge}} = (X'X + \lambda I)^{-1}(X'X)\hat{\beta} + (X'X + \lambda I)^{-1}\lambda\beta_0, \tag{5.11}$$

where $\lambda = \sigma^2/\tau^2$. This is the standard Ridge estimator discussed in the previous chapter when, as is customary in Ridge regression, we set $\beta_0 = 0$. Less informative priors correspond to larger values for τ^2 and thus smaller λ which results in less shrinkage towards the prior. The generalized Ridge estimator of the previous chapter arises when we set $V = \sigma^2 I$ and use a prior $\tau^2\Sigma_0$ with $\beta_0 = 0$. This Bayesian motivation for the Ridge estimator can guide the choice of the shrinkage parameter λ in empirical applications.

Another popular special case is to use Zellner's g-prior. Under this approach consider setting the prior variance $\Sigma_0 = g\sigma^2(X'X)^{-1}$. When $V = \sigma^2 I$, using this prior in equation (5.10) yields

$$\tilde{\beta}_g = \frac{1}{1+g}\left(g\hat{\beta} + \beta_0\right). \tag{5.12}$$

For example, setting $g = 1$ gives an estimator that is an average of the least squares estimator and the prior mean. Rewriting (5.12) as $\hat{\beta}_g = \hat{\beta} + (1+g)^{-1}(\beta_0 - \hat{\beta})$, it readily follows that the larger the value of g, the more diffuse the prior is.

When both the mean and variance of the normal model, $\theta = (\beta, V)$, are unknown, it is common to write the prior as $\pi(\theta) = \pi(\beta|V)\pi(V)$, where $\pi(\beta|V)$ is the Gaussian distribution as in the above example and $\pi(V)$ is an inverse Wishart distribution; see Zellner (1971).

5.3 COMPUTATIONAL METHODS

Obtaining a Bayesian point forecast is straightforward in cases, such as those examined above, where we have both conjugate priors and point forecasts that depend on a known function of the parameter distribution. In such cases it is also simple to calculate predictive distributions or density forecasts. Such distributions can be useful in many ways—we can compute averages of posterior distributions of the model parameters, compute the average loss to understand the properties of the forecast, and construct density forecasts or make probability statements on how likely it is that the outcome falls in a specified range.

More generally, however, numerical methods are required to make these calculations. Numerical methods can be employed to obtain estimates of posterior distributions for the parameters $\pi(\theta|z)$, predictive densities $p^p(y|z)$, as well as summary statistics of these distributions. For example, the posterior density of the model parameters can be used to compute the mean outcome and construct one-step-ahead forecasts under MSE loss. Alternatively, $\pi(\theta|z)$ could be used to generate the predictive density, the mean of which can be used in multistep forecasting.

The standard problem in Bayesian estimation is to compute the posterior density of the parameters, $\pi(\theta|z)$. This is frequently very involved with different methods tailored to the particular model that needs to be evaluated. Since many texts are devoted to this subject, we give only a cursory overview of the methods to help the reader access the literature. Later chapters are clearer on the specific methods used for a range of forecasting problems.

The basic idea is to design a computational method for constructing draws from the posterior distribution $\pi(\theta|z)$ even though its exact density is unknown in cases where we are unable to describe it as a known distribution of the parameters of the prior and the data. Instead of directly working with the posterior, typically $p(z|\theta)\pi(\theta)$ is examined without normalizing by the marginal distribution of z. Normalization of this density is easily achieved using numerical approximation. In any particular application, $p(z|\theta)$ and $\pi(\theta)$ are both known since the forecaster must decide on a likelihood for the observed data z and a prior over the parameters, θ.

The next step is to sample from the distribution $p(z|\theta)\pi(\theta)$, given the data. This involves sampling from the prior multiplied by the likelihood, both of which are fully known as z is observed and θ is a draw from the prior. This can then be normalized using the draws. To enhance efficiency, often steps are taken to narrow down the support of the posterior so that sampling is undertaken in the correct range. Unfortunately, this approach is not very efficient or easy to use when θ is large-dimensional and contains more than a few parameters. For this common case, numerical methods that draw from a distribution that converges to the posterior are employed, rather than drawing θ directly from the posterior. Monte Carlo

Markov Chain (MCMC) methods typically involve refinements such as the Gibbs sampler or the Metropolis algorithm for drawing from the underlying distributions.

The Gibbs sampler is useful for situations where we cannot find a closed form for $\pi(\theta|z)$ but can split θ into subsets, say $\theta = (\theta_1, \theta_2)$ partitioned in such a way that there is a closed-form solution for $\pi(\theta_1|z, \theta_2)$ and $\pi(\theta_2|z, \theta_1)$. For a given starting value for θ_1, say θ_1^0, we can set up an iterative procedure that allows us to draw a value for θ_2 (denoted θ_2^1) given $\theta_1 = \theta_1^0$. We then obtain a draw of θ_1 (denoted θ_1^1) for the given $\theta_2 = \theta_2^1$. Proceeding iteratively, we obtain a sequence of numerical draws for $\theta = (\theta_1, \theta_2)$. After the effect of initial conditions wears off, in many situations it can be shown that these draws are draws from the desired joint density $\pi(\theta|z)$. Hence, after discarding a set of early draws, we can save the latter draws and use them to numerically characterize the posterior distribution for the parameters.

Example 5.3.1 (Least squares regression and the Gibbs sampler). *Suppose y_{t+1} is independently normally distributed conditional on x_t and θ with mean $\beta' x_t$ and variance $v^{-1} I_k$, where $k = \dim(x_t)$ and $\theta = (\beta, v)$, both of which are unknown. Suppose we set the prior for the conditional mean $\beta \sim N(\beta_0, \tau^2 I)$ independent of y_{t+1} and the prior for the inverse of the variance, so v is a χ^2_ω divided by a constant, s_0, and the mean of the prior for the variance becomes s_0/ω. The hyperparameters are then $\theta_0 = (\beta_0, \tau^2, \omega, s_0)$. For this problem there is no simple analytical or closed-form solution for $\pi(\theta|z)$, and numerical methods are required. It can be shown (Geweke, 2005, example 2.1.2) that*

$$\beta|z, v, \theta_0 \sim N(\tilde{\beta}(v), W(v)),$$

$$s^2(\beta)v \sim \chi^2_{\tilde{\omega}},$$

where $W(v) = \left(\tau^{-2} I_k + v \sum_{t=0}^{T-1} x_t x_t'\right)$, $\tilde{\beta}(v) = W^{-1}\left(\tau^{-2}\beta_0 + v \sum_{t=0}^{T-1} x_t y_{t+1}\right)$, $\tilde{\omega} = \omega + T$ and $s^2(\beta) = s_0^2 + \sum_{t=0}^{T-1}(y_{t+1} - \beta x_t)^2$. *Since it is straightforward to draw from the normal and χ^2 distributions, we can easily compute a sequence of values from these conditional distributions.*

Using draws of θ generated from $\pi(\theta|z)$, it is straightforward to either directly construct the forecast when this is a known function of $\pi(\theta|z)$, or alternatively construct draws of the forecast, $p^P(y|z, \theta)$. In the first case the forecast $f(z)$ is a known function of features of the distribution $p(y|z, \theta)$ and of the distribution for θ. For example, the linear regression case requires only the posterior means of θ given z which are easily computed. These can be used as the "coefficient estimates" in constructing the linear forecasting model.

The forecast density, $p_y^P(y|z)$, can be constructed from the draws of $\pi(\theta|z)$ and the known model, $p_y(y|z, \theta)$, drawing a value for the prediction for each of the draws of θ, while holding z constant. As noted in chapter 3, this approach can be used for any loss function, with different features of the estimated forecast distribution being relevant for different loss functions.

Suppose we are interested in the actual forecast rather than the predictive density, but there is no closed-form solution for the forecast as a function of this density. In this case we need to compute $f^*(z) = \arg\min r(\pi, f(z))$. Conditional on z, this requires finding the rule that minimizes $\int L(f(z), y) p_Y^P(y|z) dy$. Using the draws from $p_Y^P(y|z)$, for any forecast rule, $f(z)$, we can compute the average loss.

This follows because for any such forecast rule and any draw for y, we can compute a value for $L(f(z), y)$ with the average of these draws being the expected loss. Thus we can directly compute the expected loss associated with any forecasting rule. From among a set of such rules we can then choose the best rule as that with the lowest expected loss.

Zellner (1971) gives an early exposition of the Bayesian analysis of regression models including many of the models typically used in forecasting. More recent treatments and discussions of algorithms and numerical methods are provided in Koop (2003), Geweke (2005), and Karlsson (2013).

5.4 ECONOMIC APPLICATIONS OF BAYESIAN FORECASTING METHODS

There are too many examples of applications of Bayesian methods in the economic forecasting literature for a brief review to do any justice, so instead we comment on some of the main areas where such methods have proved particularly successful. Dating back to the work undertaken in the late 1970s as summarized by Litterman (1986), Bayesian methods have made up a large part of macroeconomic forecasting with multivariate models such as vector autoregressions which require the estimation of many unknown parameters. The main reason for the success of Bayesian methods in this area is that the loss associated with least squares estimation can be very large relative to the loss that arises when shrinkage or Bayesian methods are applied. Classical and Bayesian forecasters alike have found Bayesian methods to be a useful way to deal with parameter estimation error. Estimation of dynamic factor models is another area where Bayesian forecast methods have been extensively used; see, e.g., De Mol, Giannone, and Reichlin (2008). Finally, Bayesian methods are used extensively to estimate dynamic stochastic general equilibrium (DSGE) models and generate forecasts from such models. These topics are covered more extensively in chapter 9.

Forecast models with unobserved components are a second area where Bayesian models are now routinely used. Updating formulae used in Kalman filters follow from Bayes' rule under joint normality of the innovation terms and so are naturally given a Bayesian treatment; see Durbin and Koopman (2012) for an extensive treatment of such models. One such application is to specifications affected by discrete, unobserved breaks to the model parameters. Kim and Nelson (1999) cover Bayesian estimation of Markov switching models with recurring regimes, while Koop and Potter (2007) and Pesaran, Pettenuzzo, and Timmermann (2006) are examples of models where the breaks can be unique, with parameters drawn from some continuous meta distribution.

Return prediction and portfolio choice is a third area where Bayesian methods are commonly used. To form optimal portfolios, investors have to account for parameter uncertainty and the posterior predictive density provides a natural way to accomplish this. Compared with classical plug-in approaches which condition on a set of parameter estimates, the Bayesian solution that accounts for estimation error often leads to less extreme asset allocations, particularly for risk-averse investors. Examples of Bayesian applications to asset allocation include Kandel and Stambaugh (1996), Barberis (2000) and Pettenuzzo and Timmermann (2011).

Model combination is a fourth area of forecasting where Bayesian methods have been used extensively. Bayesian model averaging provides a way to handle model uncertainty and allows researchers to integrate out uncertainty about a particular dimension of the model choice. An early example is the study by Min and Zellner (1993) which considers forecasts of international growth rates. Bayesian model averaging is covered in chapter 14.

5.4.1 Bayesian Investor's Asset Allocation

To illustrate Bayesian decision making in the context of a simple prediction model, we use the example provided by Kandel and Stambaugh (1996) of a single-period investment decision. Consider an investor who, at time t, can allocate a fraction of his wealth, ω, to stocks which pay continuously compounded returns y_{t+1} or hold risk-free T-bills which for simplicity we assume pay zero returns. For simplicity assume that the investor's initial wealth at time t is $W_t = 1$. Then the future wealth at time $t + 1$, W_{t+1}, is given by

$$W_{t+1} = 1 + \omega \left[\exp(y_{t+1}) - 1\right].$$

The investor is assumed to have logarithmic utility over future wealth,

$$U(W_{t+1}) = \ln(W_{t+1}),$$

and maximizes expected utility conditional on current information, $Z_t = \{z_1, \ldots, z_t\}$:

$$\max_{0 < \omega < 1} \int U(W_{t+1}) p_Y(y_{t+1}|Z_t) dy_{t+1}.$$

To choose asset holdings, the investor therefore requires the conditional density of y_{t+1}, $p_Y(y_{t+1}|Z_t)$. This is assumed to be known up to a set of unknown parameters, θ.

The predictive density for y_{t+1} can be obtained by integrating the return distribution over the conditional density of θ, $p(\theta|Z_t)$:

$$p(y_{t+1}|Z_t) = \int_\theta p_Y(y_{t+1}|\theta, Z_t) p(\theta|Z_t) d\theta,$$

where, from Bayes' theorem, the posterior density of θ conditional on Z_t is $p(\theta|Z_t) \propto p(\theta) p(Z_t|\theta)$, $p(\theta)$ is the prior on θ, and $p(Z_t|\theta)$ is the p.d.f. for the data given the parameters.

As an illustration, consider the binary case where stock returns take two possible values: $y_{t+1} = +20\%$ or $y_{t+1} = -20\%$. Suppose the information consists of a sequence of i.i.d. binomial state variables, s_t, that take the value $s_t = 1$ (state 1) or $s_t = 2$ (state 2): $Z_t = \{s_t, \{s_{i-1}, r_i\}_{i=1}^t\}$. The model is parameterized through the probability that the high return state will occur next period given that state i is observed at time t, i.e., $\theta = \{\theta_1, \theta_2\}$, where $\theta_i = P(y_{t+1} = 20|s_t = i)$.

Following Kandel and Stambaugh (1996), assume that the investor's prior joint distribution is the product of two independent distributions for θ_1 and θ_2 each of which is given by

$$p(\theta_i) = \frac{[\theta_i(1 - \theta_i)]^{c-1}}{B(c, c)}, i = 1, 2, \tag{5.13}$$

where $c \geq 1$, and $B(\cdot)$ is the beta function. Hence, the prior depends on a single parameter, c.

Suppose the investor observes the following sample information presented in a (2×2) contingency table.

	State 1 $(t-1)$	State 2 $(t-1)$
$y_t = 20\%$	11	8
$y_t = -20\%$	5	8

If the economy has been in state i in T_i months during the observed sample, the probability that the high return state is realized in n_i of those months has a binomial likelihood function:

$$p(n_i | \theta_i, T_i) = \binom{T_i}{n_i} \theta_i^{n_i} (1 - \theta_i)^{T_i - n_i}, \, i = 1, 2. \qquad (5.14)$$

Combining the likelihood function in (5.14) with the prior in (5.13), the posterior for θ_i can be shown to follow a beta distribution:

$$
\begin{aligned}
p(\theta_i | Z_t) &= p(\theta_i | n_i, T_i) \\
&= \frac{\theta_i^{n_i + c - 1} (1 - \theta_i)^{T_i - n_i + c - 1}}{B((n_i + c), (T_i - n_i + c))}, \quad i = 1, 2.
\end{aligned}
$$

Letting $\hat{p}$ be the probability of observing the high return state conditional on Z_t, Kandel and Stambaugh (1996) show that, from properties of the beta distribution,

$$\hat{p} = \frac{n_j + c}{T_j + 2c}.$$

Moreover, the expected stock return can be calculated from

$$\hat{y}_{t+1} = E[y_{t+1} | Z_t] = 0.2\hat{p} - 0.2(1 - \hat{p}).$$

The investor's constrained optimization problem therefore becomes

$$\max_{0 < \omega < 1} (\hat{p} \ln(1 + 0.2\omega) + (1 - \hat{p}) \ln(1 - 0.2\omega)).$$

This has solution

$$
\omega^* = \begin{cases} 0 & \text{if } (2\hat{p} - 1) < 0, \\ (2\hat{p} - 1)/0.2 & \text{if } 0 < 2\hat{p} - 1 < 0.2, \\ 1 & \text{if } (2\hat{p} - 1) \geq 0.2. \end{cases}
$$

Suppose the signal $s_t = 2$ is observed at time T. Since $n_2 = 8$, $T_2 = 16$, then $\hat{p} = 0.5$ independent of which value c takes in the prior. In this case the conditional risk premium on stocks equals 0, and so risk-averse investors choose not to hold any stocks.

Next, suppose $s_t = 1$. Using that $n_1 = 11$, $T_1 = 16$, $\hat{p} = (11 + c)/(16 + 2c)$, we have the following.

c	$\hat{p}$	$\hat{y}_{t+1}$	ω^*
1	0.67	0.067	1.00
10	0.58	0.033	0.83
20	0.55	0.021	0.54

Even though it cannot be rejected from a statistical point of view that there is little information in receiving the signal $s_t = 1$ (under the null that $\theta_1 = 0.5$, the probability of drawing $n_1 \geq 11$ "up" states in $T_1 = 24$ draws exceeds 10%), Bayesian investors change their asset allocation decisions quite strongly based on the observed signal, with the allocation to stocks varying from 54 to 100% in the above example, depending on the strength of the investors' prior beliefs.

5.5 CONCLUSION

The Bayesian approach to forecasting is becoming increasingly popular in applied forecasting. Bayesian forecasting models build directly on standard Bayesian foundations for model construction. In particular, when the model is known up to a finite set of unknown parameters, the posterior distribution for the predicted outcome given the data is easily derived from the posterior distribution of the model parameters. As with the construction of posterior distributions for parameters, only the simplest situations lead to closed-form solutions for the posterior distribution of the outcome given the observed data. This means that numerical methods are at the forefront of most Bayesian applications to forecasting. Further details of these methods are provided in chapter 9.

6

Model Selection

Only a very optimistic forecaster trusts that his model is correctly specified and includes all variables that are relevant for forecasting. This underscores the idea that a set of models, rather than just a single model, might reasonably be considered in constructing a forecast of a particular outcome. Models could differ by their dynamic specification given a set of predictor variables, in which case model selection simplifies to lag length selection. Models could use different subsets from a long list of potential predictor variables, in which case model selection involves choosing which covariates to include. Alternatively, models could vary in their choice of the functional form mapping predictor variables to the outcome, as in the choice between a linear and nonlinear model, or the selection of the order of approximation in a sieve estimator. With many possible forecasting models to be considered, it is natural to ask whether a single "best" model can be identified. Model selection, or subset regression methods, attempt to choose such a "best" model, where "best" typically depends on the forecaster's loss function, the underlying data-generating process, the forecaster's information set and the forecast horizon.

To help analyze the problem, suppose there is a finite set of forecasting models, $\mathcal{M}_K$, with each model denoted M_k for $k = 1, \ldots, K$. Each model is used to generate a forecast, $f_k(z_t, \beta_k)$. The model selection problem is related to the classical estimation problem analyzed in chapter 4, the difference being that the minimization of expected loss now involves searching over $\mathcal{M}_K$ to find the best forecasting model. Hence, the problem of searching for the best forecast model is extended beyond merely estimating the parameters of a single model to searching over a restricted set of functions as well.[1]

The list of candidate models could be nested, but does not have to be. If all models are special cases of a "super model" that nests everything else, the distinction between model selection and parameter estimation becomes somewhat blurred. In this case, individual models arise as zero-coefficient constraints on the nesting model's parameters.

Model selection methods can be split into two broad sets: those that use the full data sample to choose the forecasting model (labeled "in-sample" methods) and those that use a "holdout" sample to choose between models ("out-of-sample"

---

[1] In chapter 14 we consider an alternative approach, that of taking a weighted average of the models.

methods).[2] This chapter focuses on in-sample methods as opposed to out-of-sample methods. We make this distinction here mainly because the methods and motivation for the two methods differ, so it is easier to analyze them separately. Out-of-sample methods are examined in chapter 16.

Popular in-sample model selection methods include information criteria (IC), sequential hypothesis testing, and various forms of cross validation. For large-dimensional models the Lasso and variations on this method have gained widespread use. How well the approaches apply to a given situation depends on whether (a) there are few or very many potential predictor variables—in the latter case, methods relying on exhaustive searches will not be feasible; (b) there are few or very many useful predictors among these potential predictor variables. A model is considered sparse if only a few predictors are useful, in which case methods that asymptotically overfit can provide poor forecasts. Leeb and Pötscher (2005) provide a general discussion of issues related to model selection and inference.

Section 6.1 briefly discusses the trade-offs faced by different model selection approaches. Next, we cover specific model selection methods such as sequential hypothesis testing (section 6.2), information criteria (section 6.3), cross validation (section 6.4), the Lasso method (section 6.5), and various hard and soft threshold methods such as Bagging (section 6.6). Section 6.7 provides an empirical application to predictability of stock market returns and section 6.8 covers properties of model selection methods. Monte Carlo methods are used to analyze the risk of a variety of methods in section 6.9, before we conclude in section 6.10. Section 6.11 contains technical derivations used throughout the chapter.

6.1 TRADE-OFFS IN MODEL SELECTION

Model selection involves nontrivial issues because improvements in model fit could either reflect a model's genuine ability to produce better forecasts or, alternatively, be due to the model's tendency to "overfit," i.e., provide a better in-sample fit without offering genuine improvements in predictive accuracy. This can be seen clearly in the case of linear regression as the next example shows.

Example 6.1.1 (Risk for the multivariate regression model). *For the model in Example 3.2.3, the full sample estimate* $\hat{\beta}_T = \left(\sum_{t=0}^{T-1} x_t x_t' \right)^{-1} \left(\sum_{t=0}^{T-1} x_t y_{t+1} \right)$ *leads to a risk estimate*

$$T^{-1} \sum_{t=0}^{T-1} \left(y_{t+1} - \hat{\beta}_T' x_t \right)^2 = T^{-1} \sum_{t=0}^{T-1} \varepsilon_{t+1}^2 - (\hat{\beta}_T - \beta)' \left(T^{-1} \sum_{t=0}^{T-1} x_t x_t' \right) (\hat{\beta}_T - \beta).$$

---

[2] We consider cross validation here since this method averages over multiple holdout samples and so is similar to other methods examined in this chapter.

The first term has mean σ^2; for the second term (estimation-related risk) we have

$$E\left[(\hat{\beta}_T - \beta)'\left(T^{-1}\sum_{t=0}^{T-1} x_t x_t'\right)(\hat{\beta}_T - \beta)\right]$$

$$= T^{-1}E\left[\left(\sum_{t=0}^{T-1} x_t \varepsilon_{t+1}\right)'\left(\sum_{t=0}^{T-1} x_t x_t'\right)^{-1}\left(\sum_{t=1}^{T-1} x_t \varepsilon_{t+1}\right)\right]$$

$$= T^{-1}E\,\mathrm{tr}\left[\left(\sum_{t=0}^{T-1} x_t x_t'\right)^{-1}E\left[\left(\sum_{t=1}^{T-1} x_t \varepsilon_{t+1}\right)\left(\sum_{t=1}^{T-1} x_t \varepsilon_{t+1}\right)'\bigg|x_1,\ldots,x_T\right]\right]$$

$$= T^{-1}E\,\mathrm{tr}\left[\left(\sum_{t=0}^{T-1} x_t x_t'\right)^{-1}\sigma^2\left(\sum_{t=0}^{T-1} x_t x_t'\right)\right]$$

$$= \sigma^2 T^{-1}k.$$

So the risk here is $\sigma^2(1 - T^{-1}k)$. Instead of increasing the expected loss by this term as in (3.19), the in-sample loss estimate subtracts this term from σ^2. Hence, the downward bias in the expected loss estimate can be large in small samples and tends to be greater for more complex models that include more regressors (large K). Even so, estimation effects disappear asymptotically.

In this example the inclusion of additional variables may decrease σ^2, in which case the additional variables help to improve the model. Alternatively, they might reduce only the second (variance) component—the effect is negative because of the added dimensions over which the in-sample risk is minimized as a result of the inclusion of extra variables. Improvement in the in-sample fit does not tell us which of these effects is occurring.

Next, consider a situation with two models, $M_1 = f_1(z_t, \beta_1)$ and $M_2 = f_2(z_t, \beta_2)$, where the second model nests the first.[3] For each model the coefficient estimates are selected such that, for the sample $t = 0, \ldots, T$,

$$\hat{\beta}_i = \arg\min_{\beta_i} T^{-1}\sum_{t=0}^{T-1} L(f_i(z_t, \beta_i), y_{t+1}). \tag{6.1}$$

Because $f_2(z_t, \beta_2)$ nests $f_1(z_t, \beta_1)$, it follows from the properties of minimization that, for a given data sample,

$$T^{-1}\sum_{t=0}^{T-1} L(f_2(z_t, \hat{\beta}_2), y_{t+1}) \leq T^{-1}\sum_{t=0}^{T-1} L(f_1(z_t, \hat{\beta}_1), y_{t+1}). \tag{6.2}$$

---

[3] Assuming linear models, this case can be represented as

$$M_1 : y_{t+1} = \beta_1' x_{1t} + \varepsilon_{1t+1},$$

$$M_2 : y_{t+1} = \beta_1' x_{1t} + \beta_2' x_{2t} + \varepsilon_{2t+1},$$

so M_2 nests M_1, i.e., includes this model as a special case when $\beta_2 = 0$.

Hence the larger model (M_2) always provides at least as good a fit as the smaller model (M_1) and in most cases will provide a strictly better in-sample fit. The key here is that (6.2) compares the in-sample performance of the two models so that the same sample $t = 0, \ldots, T$ is used for parameter estimation and model evaluation. The well-known result that the regression R^2 is (weakly) increasing as additional variables are added to a set of existing regressors is a special case of this result. Indeed, linear regression models with T predictors yield a perfect fit in a sample with T observations even when the predictors are independent of the outcome, assuming that the predictors are not perfectly collinear. Thus the in-sample ranking in (6.2) is always true even if in fact the population expected loss under the first (small) model is smaller than the expected loss under the second (large) model, when evaluated at the respective probability limits of the parameters, β_i^*. Hence, (6.2) could hold simultaneously with

$$E\left[L(f_1(z_t, \beta_1^*), y_{t+1})\right] < E\left[L(f_2(z_t, \beta_2^*), y_{t+1})\right]. \tag{6.3}$$

A superior in-sample fit does *not* by itself lead to the conclusion that a particular forecasting model necessarily produces better forecasts. This special result for nested models gives intuition for the general case: more highly parameterized (or complex) models often perform well in comparisons of in-sample fit even when they produce poor forecasts compared with smaller models that, when applied to new data, may generate a smaller expected loss.

Selection of forecasting models involves a trade-off between the additional estimation error associated with larger models versus the potential for greater model specification error that comes with using more parsimonious models that exclude relevant predictors. This trade-off is very clear for the linear regression model under MSE loss. We saw in Example 3.2.6 that the estimation error effect can be broken into two components: a variance term disappearing at rate T and a bias term which may be of the same order if the coefficients of the omitted variables are close to 0. Alternatively, the bias term could be of a higher order if the model is grossly misspecified. Using the notation and definitions of section 3.2.1, we can write this estimation error term as

$$R_{2k}(\beta) = k\sigma^2 + T\left[(\beta - E(\hat{\beta}_k | Z_{-kT}))' E[x_T x_T' | Z_{-kT}](\beta - E(\hat{\beta}_k | Z_{-kT}))\right],$$

where k is the number of parameters estimated for the kth model.

Let the model be $y_{t+1} = x_t'\beta + \varepsilon_{t+1}$, where some of the elements of β are 0, $x_t'x_t$ is of full rank, and $\dim(\beta) \ll T$. Different submodels, $y_{t+1} = x_t'\beta_k + \varepsilon_{kt+1}$, arise by setting elements of β to 0 by omitting the corresponding covariate(s) from the forecasting model. For any of these submodels, the estimation-related risk term, $R_{2k}(\beta)$, obtained by omitting the common first-order risk component, $\sigma^2 = E[\varepsilon'\varepsilon/T]$, is

$$R_{2k}(\beta) = k\sigma^2 + (\beta - \beta_k)' \sum_{t=0}^{T-1} x_t x_t'(\beta - \beta_k). \tag{6.4}$$

The first term in (6.4) reflects estimation error and is easy to estimate. This increases, the larger the dimension of the model, as measured by n_k. The second term is due to model specification error and is difficult to obtain as it depends on the true model through β which is never known in practice—if it were, there would be no model selection problem. This term will generally decrease as additional variables are included in the model.

The trade-off identified by (6.4) depends on both the true model and on the number of predictors included in the largest model, K. When the dimension of x_t is small, the estimation error term cannot get too large. Many of the traditional model selection methods were developed for this situation. With large-dimensional models (big n_k), the estimation error could potentially become very large. For example, so-called kitchen sink regressions that include all possible predictors often produce very poor forecasts, as $n_k \sigma^2$ is large even though they protect against the misspecification error reflected in the second term in (6.4).

Sparse models are models for which the number of true nonzero elements of β is small relative to the dimension of x_t. The misspecification term for such models is likely to be small relative to the estimation error associated with large models and so methods that remove many covariates are preferable in this situation. Conversely, in situations with many covariates where many elements of β are expected to be nonzero, i.e., $\dim(\beta) < T$ but growing with T, the misspecification term might be large for all parsimonious models. In this case alternative methods that consider many covariates might be more useful although model selection methods are also available for this situation. Chapter 10 on factor models is particular relevant for this case.

Approaches to model section are affected by the size of the set of models to be considered. The number of potential models can quickly become very large, large enough to be a difficulty even with modern computing power. For example consider different forecast models corresponding to different linear regressions involving subsets of variables selected from the list $\{x_1, \ldots, x_K\}$. To conduct a comprehensive search over all possible linear models with K potential predictor variables, $\{x_1, \ldots, x_K\}$ means considering 2^K possible model specifications. For example, with two possible predictors, $\{x_1, x_2\}$, there are four possible constellations, $\{0, 0\}$, $\{1, 0\}$, $\{0, 1\}$, and $\{1, 1\}$, where a 0 indicates that the variable is excluded from the model, while a 1 indicates that it is included. Since the parameters of each model have to be estimated, this can limit comprehensive specification searches to relatively small sets of predictor variables. For example, with $K = 20$, the number of possible models exceeds one million. For this reason, a global search across model specifications is employed only for relatively low-dimensional model sets.

6.2 SEQUENTIAL HYPOTHESIS TESTING

Sequential hypothesis testing is perhaps the most natural approach to building a forecasting model and describes how—at least informally—many researchers construct their model. As a model selection technique the method chooses the "best" submodel from a larger set of available models through a sequence of specification tests that attempt to identify the relevant parts of a model and exclude the remainder. One strategy is to remove variables (or terms) from the model found not to be useful when tested against a smaller model that omits such variables. A great variety of methods have been proposed to this end. For example, t-tests, F-tests, or p-values can be employed to exclude redundant terms. Different orders of the sequence in which variables are tested—forward stepwise and backward stepwise being the most common—can also be considered. Finally, different cross-checks can be employed on the omitted terms in a way that mixes forward and backward stepwise methods.

The two main approaches in the sequential testing literature are general-to-specific and specific-to-general methods. General-to-specific methods include all potential variables in the initial model and then remove variables deemed not to be useful through a sequence of tests. Specific-to-general methods instead begin with a small baseline model, comprising, e.g., the main variables thought to forecast well or simply a constant, and then add further variables if they appear to improve the prediction model. The final selected model will generally depend on the sequence of tests.[4]

Example 6.2.1 (General-to-specific modeling approach). *As an illustration of the general-to-specific approach, consider a linear forecasting model with K potential predictor variables $\{x_1, \ldots, x_K\}$. Suppose least squares is initially used to estimate the "kitchen sink" model with all predictors included:*

$$y_{t+1} = \beta_0 + \beta_1 x_{1t} + \beta_2 x_{2t} + \cdots + \beta_{K-1} x_{K-1,t} + \beta_K x_{Kt} + \varepsilon_{t+1}. \qquad (6.5)$$

We can adopt a unidirectional backward stepwise approach that ranks the predictor variables in terms of the t-statistic of their coefficients in (6.5) or (equivalently) by the p-value of these coefficient estimates. Suppose the smallest absolute value of the t-statistic among all variables falls below some threshold, $\underline{t}$, such as $\underline{t} = 2$:

$$t_{\min} = \min_{k=1,\ldots,K} |t_{\hat{\beta}_k}| < \underline{t}. \qquad (6.6)$$

Then the variable with the smallest t-statistic (or largest p-value) gets eliminated from the model. Assuming for simplicity that x_K is the eliminated variable, the trimmed model with the remaining $K - 1$ variables is next reestimated:

$$y_{t+1} = \beta_0 + \beta_1 x_{1t} + \beta_2 x_{2t} + \cdots + \beta_{K-1} x_{K-1,t} + \epsilon_{t+1}. \qquad (6.7)$$

Once again, we compute the t-statistics for all remaining regressors in this model, check whether $\min_{k=1,\ldots,K-1}\{|t_{\hat{\beta}_k}|\} < \underline{t}$, and drop the variable with the smallest t-statistic if this condition holds. This procedure is repeated until the t-statistics of all variables in the model exceed $\underline{t}$ or until some maximum number of iterations, R, is reached.

For the backward stepwise (general-to-specific) approach, the forecast takes the form (assuming that a constant is always included)

$$f_{t+1|t} = \hat{\beta}_{0k} + \sum_{k=1}^{K} \hat{\beta}_k \mathbb{1}_k(d(|t_{\hat{\beta}_j}^r|), j \in [1, \ldots, K], r \leq R) x_{kt}, \qquad (6.8)$$

where $t_{\hat{\beta}_k}^r$ is the t-statistic for β_k in the rth variable selection round, $r = 1, \ldots, R$, and $k = 1, \ldots, K$. Here $d_k(|t_{\hat{\beta}_j}^r|)$ determines whether the kth variable gets eliminated in

---

[4] For a comprehensive review of model selection, the theory of reduction, and general-to-specific modeling in particular, see Campos, Ericson, and Hendry (2005).

any of the R steps. The indicator variable $\mathbb{1}_k(d_k(|t^r_{\hat{\beta}_j}|), j \in [1, \ldots, K], r \le R)$ equals 1 if the kth variable is included in the final model. Whether a variable gets excluded depends not only on its own t-statistic but also on the t-statistics of all other presently included variables. This means that $\mathbb{1}(d_k(|t^r_{\hat{\beta}_j}|), j \in [1, \ldots, K], r \le R)$ depends on the entire sequence of (absolute values of) t-statistics not only for the kth variable itself but also for all other variables. For example, a variable may not be excluded in a given round even if its test statistic falls below the threshold, provided that the test statistic of another contemporaneously included variable is even lower. This path dependence makes it difficult to establish analytical results for sequential model selection methods.

The so-called "LSE" general-to-specific approach starts with a general model and adds tests for model "congruence" to the sequence of tests. This can include tests for normality, autocorrelation, and conditional heteroskedasticity in the model residuals, but may also involve (out-of-sample) model stability tests; see the discussion in Hoover and Perez (1999). Insignificant predictors are kept in a model if their omission causes the model to fail one or more diagnostic tests. The aim is to ensure that the model residuals are martingale difference sequences with respect to the underlying set of variables considered in the search. A second aim is to obtain a model that is not encompassed by any competing specification, in the sense that no other model adds predictive content beyond the selected model. Hendry (1995) provides a detailed discussion of these issues and references to the literature.

The specific-to-general approach often begins from a simple model that only includes an intercept,[5]

$$y_{t+1} = \beta_0 + \varepsilon_{t+1}.$$

Under the unidirectional forward stepwise approach, each of the K univariate models is next considered separately:

$$y_{t+1} = \beta_{0k} + \beta_k x_{kt} + \varepsilon_{kt+1}, \quad k = 1, \ldots, K. \tag{6.9}$$

Suppose that the highest of these t-statistics exceeds some threshold value $\bar{t}$:

$$t_{\max} = \max_{k=1,\ldots,K} |t_{\hat{\beta}_k}| > \bar{t}. \tag{6.10}$$

Then the variable associated with this t-statistic is included in the model. Next, regressors from the remaining pool are added, one by one, to this univariate model. A new regressor is included provided that its t-statistic exceeds $\bar{t}$, once added to the prediction model. The process continues until the t-statistics of all of the remaining excluded variables fall below the cutoff value, $\bar{t}$, or until a maximum number of iterations is exceeded.

Forecasts from the forward stepwise approach takes the same form as in (6.8), the only difference being how the inclusion indicator $\mathbb{1}_k(d_k(|t^r_{\hat{\beta}_j}|), j \in [1, \ldots, K], r \le R)$ is constructed.

---

[5] Sometimes the specification search starts from a set of "core" variables believed always to be part of a good model. In this case the full set of variables is split into "core" and "potential" predictor variables and the search for a model involves only the latter since the core variables always are included. See Pesaran and Timmermann (2000) for an application of this approach to predictability of stock market returns.

Several variations of sequential tests exist. Blocks of variables instead of individual variables can be considered at each step, using F-tests instead of t-tests to evaluate statistical significance. Such tests might be relevant in the presence of strongly correlated regressors. A bidirectional mixture of forward and backward steps can also be employed. Correlation among regressors mean that the inclusion of a new variable in a forward step could lead some previously significant variables to become insignificant in the extended model. These variables could be eliminated in a backward step. Convergence of such procedures is not guaranteed, however.

The main benefit of the sequential approach is its intuitive appeal: its simplicity and the fact that it is computationally simple to implement—particularly if variables are considered for inclusion or exclusion one at a time. However, the approach does not undertake a comprehensive search across all possible models, its outcome can be path dependent, and so the method suffers from the drawback that there is no guarantee that it finds the globally optimal model, i.e., the best possible model within the feasible model set.

Properties of sequential variable selection approaches have been addressed in many studies. Hoover and Perez (1999) undertake a thorough simulation study of the general-to-specific approach. They find that this approach frequently ends up with overparameterized models that include variables that are spuriously significant in the sense that they are not included in the true model. Insignificant variables are sometimes included to allow the models to pass the residual specification tests. Interestingly, their simulations suggest that these issues can be addressed in part by setting the bar higher for inclusion of variables, using smaller nominal sizes (or higher critical values) in the inclusion tests.

6.3 INFORMATION CRITERIA

Information criteria (IC) choose models by trading off model fit against a penalty for model complexity as measured by the number of free parameters that have to be estimated for the models. Several information criteria have been suggested in the literature, the two most popular of which are the Bayes information criterion (Schwarz BIC, SBIC, or BIC) proposed by Schwarz (1978) and the Akaike information criterion (AIC) due to Akaike (1974). Less often used methods include the Mallows C_p criterion due to Mallows (1973) and the Hannan–Quinn criterion due to Hannan and Quinn (1979). Finally there is a large literature on variations of these methods and on other forms of information criteria. This plethora of criteria arises because of differences in the properties possessed by the information criteria, as we discuss below. BIC, AIC, and the Mallows C_p all attempt to adjust a minimization criterion for the effect of parameter estimation, which tends to make more highly parameterized models appear better in-sample than they really are. The extent to which parameter estimation improves the in-sample fit depends on the true model, so differences across information criteria hinge on how to practically get around our fundamental lack of knowledge of the "true" forecast model.

Information criteria employ different strategies to trade-off fit against parsimony. The Bayesian information criterion selects the model with the highest posterior probability given the data. To choose a single model from the candidate set, the models are ranked according to their posterior probabilities and the model with the highest posterior probability is chosen. The Akaike information criterion seeks to minimize the (Kullback–Leibler) distance between the density of a candidate model and the density of the true (unknown) model.

Consider a set of K parametric models, $\mathcal{M}_k$, where each model $M_k \in \mathcal{M}_K$, $k = 1, \ldots, K$ requires estimating n_k parameters, β_k. The BIC and AIC choose the model (indexed by k) to minimize expressions of the form

$$\text{IC}(k) = -2T^{-1}\ln p(\hat{\beta}_k | z) + h(n_k)g(T), \tag{6.11}$$

over all models, $k = 1, \ldots, K$, where $p(\hat{\beta}_k | z)$ is the likelihood of the data evaluated at the parameter estimates, $h(n_k)$ is an increasing function of the model size, n_k, and $g(T)$ is a decreasing function of the sample size, T. The second term, $h(n_k)g(T)$, penalizes for the estimation of additional parameters (larger n_k), particularly in small sample sizes.

Information criteria differ over their choice of $h(n_k)g(T)$. For BIC and AIC the penalties take the form

$$\text{BIC}: \frac{n_k \ln(T)}{T}, \tag{6.12}$$

$$\text{AIC}: \frac{2n_k}{T}. \tag{6.13}$$

Hence, $h(n_k) = n_k$ for both criteria, while $g(T) = \ln(T)/T$ for the BIC and $g(T) = 2/T$ for the AIC.[6]

The following example illustrates how the information criteria can be applied to the univariate linear prediction model.

Example 6.3.1 (AIC and BIC for linear regressions). *Consider a set of linear prediction models that differ in their chosen predictor variables, x_{kt}:*

$$y_{t+1} = \beta_k' x_{kt} + \varepsilon_{kt+1}, \quad \varepsilon_{kt+1} \sim \text{N}(0, \sigma_k^2).$$

Let $\hat{\sigma}_k^2$ be the MLE estimator of the variance from a regression with n_k regressors. Using the MLE estimates for the kth model, we get (for $Z_T = (y_{t+1}, x_{kt})$, $t = 0, \ldots, T-1$)

$$\ln p_Z(Z_T) = -\frac{T}{2}\ln(2\pi\hat{\sigma}_k^2) - \frac{1}{2\hat{\sigma}_k^2}\sum_{t=0}^{T-1}\hat{\varepsilon}_{kt+1}^2$$

$$= -\frac{T}{2}\ln(2\pi\hat{\sigma}_k^2) - \frac{T\hat{\sigma}_k^2}{2\hat{\sigma}_k^2}$$

$$= -\frac{T}{2}\ln(2\pi\hat{\sigma}_k^2) - \frac{T}{2},$$

---

[6] Refinements to these procedures as well as penalties of a similar form have been proposed. When attention is restricted to subclasses of the models, often the corrected or modified AIC is employed. This approach works better when k is large relative to T, but implies a penalty term that depends on the assumed subclass of models.

and so

$$-2T^{-1}\ln p(\hat{\beta}_k|Z_T) = \ln\hat{\sigma}_k^2 + C,$$

where C is a constant that does not vary across models. Hence, for linear regressions with a univariate outcome variable, the AIC takes the form

$$\mathrm{AIC}(k) = \ln\hat{\sigma}_k^2 + \frac{2n_k}{T} \tag{6.14}$$

and the BIC takes the form

$$\mathrm{BIC} = \ln\hat{\sigma}_k^2 + \frac{n_k\ln(T)}{T}. \tag{6.15}$$

The Mallows C_p criterion proposed by Mallows (1973) is a third criterion that is often used to select a submodel from a set of linear regressions. Consider a model with n_k regressors and associated sum of squared residuals SSR_k, and let $\hat{\sigma}^2$ denote the estimated residual variance for the "super" model that includes all possible (n_K) regressors. Then the Mallows C_p criterion takes the form

$$C_p(k) = \frac{\mathrm{SSR}_k}{\hat{\sigma}^2} - T + 2n_k. \tag{6.16}$$

The preferred model is that with the smallest C_p-value among all possible models. The C_p criterion is an estimator of the expected in-sample MSE applied to a situation where relevant variables have been omitted.

Model selection in linear regressions based on the Mallows C_p is asymptotically equivalent to model selection over the same set of models based on AIC. To see this, multiply (6.14) by T and subtract the common term $\ln(\hat{\sigma}^2)$ to see that the AIC is equivalent to model selection based on $T\ln\left(\hat{\sigma}_k^2/\hat{\sigma}^2\right) + 2n_k$. Applying a first-order Taylor expansion of the natural logarithm around the ratio of the variances set equal to 1, we have

$$T\,(\mathrm{AIC}) - \ln(\hat{\sigma}^2) \approx T\left(\ln(1) + \left(\frac{\hat{\sigma}_k^2}{\hat{\sigma}^2} - 1\right)\right) + 2n_k$$

$$= \frac{T\hat{\sigma}_k^2}{\hat{\sigma}^2} - T + 2n_k,$$

which is the Mallows C_p when $\hat{\sigma}_k^2$ is the MLE estimator. In most cases approximation errors from the Taylor expansion disappear in large samples.

To determine the order of a linear autoregressive model, Hannan and Quinn (1979) suggested the model selection criterion

$$\mathrm{HQIC}(k) = \ln\hat{\sigma}_k^2 + \frac{2k\ln(\ln T)}{T}. \tag{6.17}$$

Their criterion is based on both ensuring consistent estimation of the order of the lag length, k, as well as avoiding overfitting the regression in as far as possible. The penalty term in (6.17) generally falls between that of the AIC and BIC.

The BIC is also often used to choose the lag length in autoregressive or ARMA models; see, e.g., Marcellino, Stock and Watson (2006). Frequently it is imposed that there are no "gaps" in the lag orders—for example excluding a model that includes lags 1, 3, and 7—which greatly simplifies the search over model specifications.

6.4 CROSS VALIDATION

Cross validation is often used for model selection in conjunction with series estimators (see chapter 11) but is also applicable to model selection more generally. The idea of cross validation is to avoid overfitting a model by removing the correlation that causes the estimated in-sample loss to be "small" due to the use of the same observations for both parameter estimation and model evaluation purposes. In contrast to out-of-sample model selection methods discussed in chapter 16, cross validation makes use of the entire data set for both estimation and evaluation. The method averages over all possible combinations (or possibly a subset of these) of estimation and evaluation samples obtainable from a given data set.

The most common cross-validation approach is the "leave-T_v-out" cross-validation estimator developed for independent data. This method holds out $T_v = 2v + 1$ observations for model evaluation, with the remaining observations used for parameter estimation. The loss is calculated solely for each evaluation sample and gets repeated for all possible sets of T_v data points used for model evaluation. In situations where the data are i.i.d., this procedure results in a very large number of possible evaluation sets and can be computationally very costly. For example, there are $T!/((T - T_v)!T_v!)$ possible ways to split T observations into different evaluation (T_v) and estimation ($T - T_v$) samples. For serially dependent time series the holdout samples are often constrained to be contiguous observations, which makes the estimation of average loss far simpler since there are only $T - T_v$ ways to split the sample. For each observation, t, the loss is evaluated on the evaluation sample $[t - v; t + v]$ and averaged across all values of t, omitting ends of the sample where there is no data after removing observations. The cross-validated estimator of MSE loss is

$$ \mathrm{CV}_v = \frac{1}{T - 2v - 1} \sum_{t=v+1}^{T-v} \left\{ \frac{1}{2v + 1} \sum_{s=t-v}^{t+v} (y_{s+1} - f(z_s, \hat{\beta}_{\{t-v:t+v\}}))^2 \right\}, \qquad (6.18) $$

where $\hat{\beta}_{\{a:b\}}$ is the estimator for $\hat{\beta}$ that uses all of the sample apart from the observations from a to b with $0 < a < b < T$. Model selection proceeds by choosing the model, $\hat{M}_k$, that minimizes CV across all models $M_k \in \mathcal{M}_K$.

When data are serially independent, the usefulness of the approach comes from the fact that the parameter estimates will be independent of the evaluation sample. This breaks the connection that leads to overfitting the objective function. In most forecasting situations it is not reasonable to assume serial independence of the forecast errors, perhaps because some of the models are incorrectly specified. In addition, z_t may include lags of y_t which would induce correlation between the estimation and evaluation samples. This necessitates removing enough observations around each estimation date to ensure that the correlation between the estimation and evaluation sample is close to 0. Burman, Chow, and Nolan (1994) and

Racine (2000) propose methods to accomplish this. We briefly describe Racine's $\ell^* v$-block cross-validation approach.

Racine (2000) proposes to omit ℓ^* observations on each side of the validation sample in order to counter any dependence between the estimation and evaluation steps. As with the "leave-n_v-out" cross-validation method, a window of v observations is used before and after time t, resulting in a validation sample of $2v + 1$ observations to average over for each t. This means that the forecast $f(z_t)$ is based on all observations apart from a block of observations running from $s = (t - \ell^* - v)$ to $s = (t + \ell^* + v)$. Under MSE loss, the cross-validated average loss statistic is

$$\text{CV} = \frac{1}{T - 2v - 1 - 2\ell^*}$$
$$\times \sum_{t=\ell^*+v+1}^{T-v-\ell^*} \left\{ \frac{1}{2v+1} \sum_{s=t-v}^{t+v} (y_{s+1} - f(z_s, \hat{\beta}_{\{t-\ell^*-v:t+\ell^*+v\}}))^2 \right\}. \quad (6.19)$$

The method requires choosing two parameters, ℓ^* and v. One rule suggested by Racine is to set $\ell^* = 0.25T$ and use an evaluation sample equal to the integer part of $T^{1/2}$.

Example 6.4.1 (MSE loss for sample estimate of the mean). *Suppose the sample mean, $\bar{y}_T = T^{-1} \sum_{t=1}^{T} y_t$ is used to forecast an i.i.d. time series, y_t, in a sample with T observations. If we use the same data sample to estimate the sample mean and evaluate the average MSE loss, we have*

$$T^{-1} \sum_{t=1}^{T} (y_t - \bar{y}_T)^2 = T^{-1} \sum_{t=1}^{T} ((y_t - \mu) - (\bar{y}_T - \mu))^2$$

$$= T^{-1} \sum_{t=1}^{T} \varepsilon_t^2 + (\bar{y}_T - \mu)^2 - 2(\bar{y}_T - \mu) T^{-1} \sum_{t=1}^{T} (y_t - \mu)$$

$$= T^{-1} \sum_{t=1}^{T} \varepsilon_t^2 - (\bar{y}_T - \mu)^2. \quad (6.20)$$

Hence the squared in-sample estimation error, $(\bar{y}_T - \mu)^2$, gets subtracted from, rather than added to, the average in-sample loss. This happens because of the cross-product term which is expected to equal 0 in the out-of-sample period but is equal to $-(\bar{y}_T - \mu)^2$. Cross validation attempts to remove this cross-product term by breaking the correlation between the forecast error and the estimation error induced in the in-sample period. It does so by separating observations used to estimate the parameters of the prediction model (here the sample mean) from observations used to evaluate the average loss.

In a setting with independently and identically distributed data, the classic cross-validation method is to "leave-one-out." Although this method is not particularly relevant for forecasting, it is helpful for illustrating how the method can be used to remove the cross-product term.

Example 6.4.2 (Cross validation for sample mean). *For each point in time, t, suppose the sample mean $\bar{y}_{\{-t\}}$ is used as the estimate, where $\bar{y}_{\{-t\}} = (T - 1)^{-1} \sum_{s=1, s \neq t}^{T} y_s$,* *i.e., we leave out observation y_t when estimating the sample mean at time t. This term, by virtue of omitting y_t, is now independent of y_t. Specifically, we have*

$$T^{-1}\sum_{t=1}^{T}(y_t - \bar{y}_{\{-t\}})^2 = T^{-1}\sum_{t=1}^{T}\varepsilon_t^2 + \sum_{t=1}^{T}(\bar{y}_{\{-t\}} - \mu)^2 - 2T^{-1}\sum_{t=1}^{T}(\bar{y}_{\{-t\}} - \mu)\varepsilon_t.$$
(6.21)

From the independence assumption, the cross-product term now has zero expectation and tends to be "small." The cost of "leaving-one-out" is that the second term in (6.21) differs from the value we would use in the forecast, $\bar{y}_t$. This results in a slight difference in the expected loss, or, asymptotically, a different second-order term in the expected average loss. To see this, note that if we rearrange (6.21) and ignore terms that are 0 in expectation, we have

$$E\left[T^{-1}\sum_{t=1}^{T}(y_t - \bar{y}_{\{-t\}})^2\right] = T^{-1}\sum_{t=1}^{T}E[\varepsilon_t^2] + \sum_{t=1}^{T}E\left[(\bar{y}_{\{-t\}} - \mu)^2\right].$$
(6.22)

Now,

$$E[(\bar{y}_{\{-t\}} - \mu)^2] = (T-1)^{-2}E\left[\sum_{s=1, s\neq t}^{T}\varepsilon_s^2\right] = \frac{\sigma^2}{T-1},$$
(6.23)

and so

$$E[(\bar{y}_{\{-t\}} - \mu)^2] = \sigma^2\left(1 + \frac{1}{T-1}\right).$$
(6.24)

If instead we used the usual forecast, $\bar{y}_t$, the expected average loss would be $\sigma^2(1 + T^{-1})$, the difference being due to our use of one less observation. This bias increases with the size of the prediction model; for example in a linear regression with n_k regressors the bias of the leave-one-out loss would be $\sigma^2(T - n_k)^{-1}$ instead of $\sigma^2(T-1)^{-1}$. The difference between the estimated loss and the true loss is, however, of a lower order than that for in-sample evaluation.[7]

6.5 LASSO MODEL SELECTION

The Lasso—least absolute shrinkage and selection operator—introduced by Tibshirani (1996) as a shrinkage estimator for least squares regression and briefly discussed in chapter 4, turns out also to have useful model selection properties. The Lasso method estimates linear regression coefficients by minimizing the sum of least squares residuals subject to a penalty function,

$$T^{-1}\sum_{t=0}^{T-1}(y_{t+1} - \beta'x_t)^2 + \lambda\sum_{i=1}^{n_k}|\beta_i|.$$
(6.25)

[7] *To see this, note that the in-sample valuation is off by T^{-1}, whereas the cross validation in (6.24) is off by $(T-1)^{-1} = T^{-1}(T/(T-1)) = T^{-1} + T^{-2}$ and so is off by the lower-order T^{-2}.*

Here $\lambda > 0$ is a tuning parameter that captures the (relative) weight on the penalty function and has the effect of shrinking the parameter estimates towards 0. Since all nonzero parameter values get penalized by the same amount—λ is a scalar as opposed to a vector—it is assumed that all variances of the predictors, x_t, have been scaled to equal 1. There is generally no closed-form solution for minimizing the object in (6.25) and so computational methods are required.

The use of a squared objective function penalized by the absolute value of the parameters means that there are many corner solutions for which the parameter estimates $\hat{\beta}_i$ are 0. This motivates thinking of Lasso as a model selection tool: simply choose the model that remains after removing the x-variables that correspond to β''s whose estimates are equal to 0.

To see why corner solutions arise under the Lasso approach, we follow Tibshirani (1996) and consider the linear regression model in matrix form $Y = X\beta + \varepsilon$ and suppose that the regressors have been orthonormalized so $X'X = I$ and $\hat{\beta}^{\text{ols}} = X'Y$. The least squares forecasts are $\hat{Y} = X\hat{\beta}^{\text{ols}}$ and hence (in matrix form)

$$T^{-1}(Y - X\beta)'(Y - X\beta) + \lambda \sum_{i=1}^{n_k} |\beta_i| \tag{6.26}$$

$$= T^{-1}(Y - \hat{Y} + \hat{Y} - X\beta)'(Y - \hat{Y} + \hat{Y} - X\beta) + \lambda \sum_{i=1}^{n_k} |\beta_i| \tag{6.27}$$

$$= T^{-1}(Y - \hat{Y})'(Y - \hat{Y}) + (\hat{Y} - X\beta)'(\hat{Y} - X\beta) + \lambda \sum_{i=1}^{n_k} |\beta_i|, \tag{6.28}$$

where the cross product drops out since $X'X = I$ and

$$(\hat{Y} - X\beta)'(Y - \hat{Y}) = (\hat{\beta}^{\text{ols}} - \beta)'X'(Y - \hat{Y}) = (\hat{\beta}^{\text{ols}} - \beta)'(X'Y - X'XX'Y) = 0.$$

The first term in (6.28) does not depend on the choice of β, and the second term is

$$(\hat{Y} - X\beta)'(\hat{Y} - X\beta) = (X\hat{\beta}^{\text{ols}} - X\beta)'(X\hat{\beta}^{\text{ols}} - X\beta)$$

$$= (\hat{\beta}^{\text{ols}} - \beta)'(\hat{\beta}^{\text{ols}} - \beta)$$

$$= \sum_{i=1}^{n_k} (\hat{\beta}_i^{\text{ols}} - \beta_i)^2.$$

Minimizing (6.28) over β is therefore the same as minimizing variable by variable, i.e., for each i find

$$\hat{\beta}_{i,\text{lasso}} = \arg\min_{\beta_i} \left[(\hat{\beta}_i^{\text{ols}} - \beta_i)^2 + \lambda |\beta_i| \right]. \tag{6.29}$$

The first-order conditions to this problem give the result $-(\hat{\beta}_i^{\text{ols}} - \beta_i) + (T\lambda/2)\,\text{sign}(\beta_i) = 0$, or, after rearranging, $\beta_i = \hat{\beta}_i^{\text{ols}} - (T\lambda/2)\,\text{sign}(\beta_i)$. This implies that if $|\hat{\beta}_i^{\text{ols}}| < T\lambda/2$, then β_i must be 0. To see this, suppose $\beta_i > 0$ so that $\beta_i = \hat{\beta}_i^{\text{ols}} - T\lambda/2 < 0$ because we assumed that $|\hat{\beta}_i^{\text{ols}}| < T\lambda/2$. Hence β_i cannot

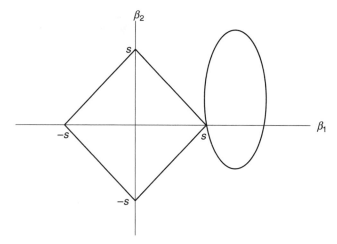

Figure 6.1: Model selection under Lasso.

be positive. But if $\beta_i < 0$, $\beta_i = \hat{\beta}_i^{\text{ols}} + T\lambda/2 > 0$ through the same assumption, which also cannot hold.

Conversely, if $\hat{\beta}_i^{\text{ols}} > T\lambda/2$, then $\beta_i = \hat{\beta}_i^{\text{ols}} - (T\lambda/2)\,\text{sign}(\beta_i) > 0$ and if $\hat{\beta}_i^{\text{ols}} < -T\lambda/2$ then $\beta_i = \hat{\beta}_i^{\text{ols}} - \text{sign}(\beta_i)T\lambda/2 < 0$. These results can be summarized as follows:

$$\hat{\beta}_{\text{lasso},i} = \text{sign}(\hat{\beta}_i^{\text{ols}})(|\hat{\beta}_i^{\text{ols}}| - T\lambda/2)\mathbb{1}(|\hat{\beta}_i^{\text{ols}}| > T\lambda/2). \tag{6.30}$$

Thus, for $|\hat{\beta}_i^{\text{ols}}| < T\lambda/2$ the coefficient estimate is set to 0. The larger is λ, the stronger the penalty and the more coefficients will be set to 0. See Tibshirani (1996) for further analysis and details.

We can also visualize the effect by considering the problem in two dimensions (i.e., only two covariates). To see this, consider the model

$$y_i = \beta_1 x_{1i} + \beta_2 x_{2i} + \varepsilon_i,$$

so we have a bivariate problem and can draw it in (β_1, β_2) space. Assuming quadratic objectives, the objective function has contours $(y_i - \beta_1 x_{1i} - \beta_2 x_{2i})^2 = z$ that are ellipses in the (β_1, β_2) space. Figure 6.1 visualizes this effect.

The LASSO constraints are now of the form $|\beta_1| + |\beta_2| \leq s$, i.e.,

$$\beta_1 + \beta_2 \leq s, \quad \beta_1 > 0, \quad \beta_2 > 0,$$
$$-\beta_1 + \beta_2 \leq s, \quad \beta_1 < 0, \quad \beta_2 > 0,$$
$$\beta_1 - \beta_2 \leq s, \quad \beta_1 > 0, \quad \beta_2 < 0,$$
$$-\beta_1 - \beta_2 \leq s, \quad \beta_1 < 0, \quad \beta_2 < 0,$$

which creates a "diamond" around 0 with coordinates at $(0, s), (0, -s), (s, 0)$, and $(-s, 0)$. Figure 6.1 shows this graphically, where the diamond is the preceding set of constraints and the ellipse is drawn for that value of z that has the constraints binding. The chance that the ellipse intersects the constraints at a corner is high—as pictured in figure 6.1, we have $\beta_1 = 0$ at the constraint.

In practical applications a choice of λ must be made. Choosing $\lambda = 0$ delivers least squares estimates which means that the largest model almost always gets chosen. The larger the choice of λ, the more likely it is that individual β''s are set to 0 and that a more parsimonious model is chosen. Unsurprisingly, the actual choice of λ—or λ_T, since it is generally recommended to let it be a function of the sample size, T—impacts the properties of the method. Typical results provide rate conditions on λ_T rather than pinning down a specific value and are developed in fixed-regressor settings with i.i.d. data. For example, Belloni and Chernozhukov (2011) suggest setting $\lambda_T = 2c\sigma\sqrt{T}\Phi^{-1}(1 - \alpha/2n_k)$ for α near (but below) 1 and $c > 1$, where $\Phi(\cdot)$ is the normal c.d.f., and σ^2 is the variance of the residuals from the true model.

The main difficulty in estimating the Lasso coefficients is that the objective function is nondifferentiable, so standard hill-climbing optimizers will not be useful for solving the minimization problem in (6.25). However, in recent years this estimation problem has been a subject of intense research and there now exist many methods that work well even when the dimension of X is very large.

Having selected a model by Lasso, a post-Lasso step can be added by estimating the parameter of the model using ordinary least squares or similar methods.

The Lasso approach has been extended to a wider group of penalized least squares estimators whose coefficients are estimated by minimizing

$$T^{-1}\sum_{t=0}^{T-1}(y_{t+1} - \beta'z_t)^2 + \sum_{i=1}^{k} p_\lambda(|\beta_i|), \tag{6.31}$$

where p_λ is a penalty function. Bridge estimators set $p_\lambda(|\beta_i|) = |\beta_i|^\gamma$, where $\gamma \geq 0$. As a special case, if $\gamma = 1$, Lasso is obtained, while $\gamma = 2$ yields the Ridge estimator. For $\gamma \leq 1$ this estimator retains the property that some of the estimates for β will be 0 for large enough values of the penalties; see Fan and Li (2001) for theoretical results and Fan, Lv, and Qi (2011) for a review.

6.6 HARD VERSUS SOFT THRESHOLDS: BAGGING

By design, model selection provides hard thresholds for constructing a model in the sense that variables are either included ("in") or excluded ("out"). This makes sense if one is absolutely certain that the β's are 0 or far from 0 so that each variable should be in or out of the model. Better forecasting models might be obtained if variables whose inclusion is uncertain are allowed to have some limited influence. One such approach with this property is shrinkage estimation, which is discussed in chapter 4. A second approach is to combine forecasting models rather than select a single specification. In this case the models can be combined in a way that assigns large weight to models that include variables known to be valuable and assigns lower weight to models using variables whose inclusion is more uncertain. In this sense all variables can be included with weights reflecting how useful we find them to be. Model combination is covered in chapter 14. A third approach is Bagging, which can be viewed as an extension of many of the methods discussed in this chapter.

Bagging, short for bootstrap aggregating, is a general method for estimating a predictor. Introduced by Breiman (1996), the method is included here since the main application of Bagging in the forecasting literature has been to variable selection in prediction models. The method modifies the hard thresholds traditionally used in model selection—corresponding to 0–1 variable selection indicators—to soft thresholds which allow the variable selection indicators to take on a continuum of values. The approach involves three steps for obtaining the estimators $\hat{\beta}$ from the data $\{y_{t+1}, z_t\}_{t=1}^{T-1}$:

1. Draw resamples of the data $\{y_{t+1}, x_t\}_{t=1}^{T-1}$ to obtain a bootstrap sample $\{y_{t+1}^b, x_t^b\}_{t=1}^{T-1}$ of the same length as the original sample.
2. Compute an estimator of β_j, $\hat{\beta}_j^b$, based on the bth resample of the data, $b = 1, \ldots, B$.
3. Compute the final estimator, $\bar{\beta}_j$, as either the mean or some other function of the resampled estimates $\{\hat{\beta}_j^b\}_{b=1}^B$.

Steps (1) and (3) can be tailored to reflect the presumed data-generating process as well as the targeted properties of the final estimator. For example, in Breiman's original formulation, the data are i.i.d. and hence an i.i.d. (empirical) bootstrap is chosen. If the data are dependent, bootstrap methods that retain the dependence are required. For example, Inoue and Kilian (2008) use a block bootstrap that allows for dependent data. Other methods could also be employed, resulting in different estimators and hence different risk functions.

Example 6.6.1 (Bagging used in model selection). *Bagging could be used to determine inclusion of variables to get a predictor:*

$$f_{t+1|t} = B^{-1} \sum_{b=1}^B \left(\hat{\beta}_{0k}^b + \sum_{k=1}^K \hat{\beta}_k^b \mathbb{1}\left(|t_{\hat{\beta}_k}^b| > \bar{t} \right) \right) x_{kt}, \qquad (6.32)$$

where the indicator variable from the bth bootstrap, $\mathbb{1}(|t_{\hat{\beta}_k}^b| > \bar{t})$, equals 1 if the absolute value of the kth t-statistic in the regression model, $t_{\hat{\beta}_k}^b$, exceeds the threshold, $\bar{t}$.

Model selection based on hard thresholding is one area where Bagging can be expected to lead to better results; see, e.g., Bühlmann and Yu (2003) in the context of i.i.d. data. Although hard thresholds are used to select a model in any given resample, Bagging translates this into a soft threshold as a result of choosing different models across different resamples in the second step and then averaging across these choices in the third step.

6.6.1 Generalized Shrinkage Methods

Stock and Watson (2012) show that many of the above methods can be viewed as generalized shrinkage methods in the context of a linear regression model with n_k predictors:

$$Y_{t+1} = \beta' X_t + \varepsilon_{t+1}, \quad t = 0, \ldots, T-1, \qquad (6.33)$$

where the regressors X_t have been orthonormalized, i.e., normalized to have zero mean and unit variance and be uncorrelated so that $X_t' X_t / T = I_{n_k}$. Stock and Watson show that, asymptotically and under assumptions that do not require the predictors to be strictly exogenous, forecasts based on pre-tests, Bagging, and normal Bayes methods can be written in a generalized shrinkage form

$$f_{T+1|T} = \sum_{i=1}^{n_k} \psi(\kappa t_i)\hat{\beta}_i X_{iT} + o_p(1),$$

where $\hat{\beta}_i = T^{-1}\sum_{t=0}^{T} X_{it-1}Y_t$ is the least squares estimator of β_i, $t_i = \sqrt{T}\hat{\beta}_i/\hat{\sigma}_e$, and $\hat{\sigma}_e^2 = \sum_{t=0}^{T-1}(Y_{t+1} - \hat{\beta}'X_t)^2/(T - n_k)$. The scalar κ depends on the forecasting method. For pre-testing methods, the shrinkage function takes the form $\psi(t_i) = \mathbb{1}(|\kappa t_i| > c)$, where c is a threshold. For example, the AIC asymptotically sets $c = \sqrt{2}$.

6.7 EMPIRICAL ILLUSTRATION: FORECASTING STOCK RETURNS

To illustrate the various methods, we next provide an application to predictability of stock market returns. As the dependent variable, y_{t+1}, we use quarterly returns on a value-weighted portfolio of US stocks measured in excess of a three-month T-bill rate.[8] The data sample covers the period 1947Q1–2013Q4. We include 11 variables in the list of predictors: the log dividend–price ratio (dp), the log dividend yield (dy), the log earnings–price ratio (ep), the book-to-market ratio (bm), net equity issues (ntis), the three-month T-bill rate (tbl), long term returns (ltr), term spread (tms), default yield (dfy), inflation (infl) and the investment–capital ratio (ik). Definitions and details of the construction of these variables are provided in Welch and Goyal (2008).

We generate pseudo out-of-sample forecasts using a recursively expanding estimation window. This works as follows. The first forecast uses data from 1947Q1 up to 1969Q4 to estimate a forecast model by least squares and generate a forecast of excess stock returns for 1970Q1. The following quarter we add data for 1970Q1, reestimate the model parameters using the extended data and generate a return forecast for 1970Q2. This procedure continues sequentially up to 2013Q4, for a total of 176 quarterly forecasts.

6.7.1 Statistical Measures of Forecast Performance

We study out-of-sample results even though the methods we use are based on penalized in-sample performance. In part, this is because we wish to see how much the selected forecasting models change over time and across different economic environments. A second reason is that this allows us to simulate the forecasting models' "real-time" performance. The advantages and disadvantages of this approach are discussed in more detail in chapter 17 of the book.

All methods considered here use linear forecasting models. The forward stepwise approach uses a maximum p-value of 0.05 for a predictor to be added to the existing forecasting model. The backward stepwise approach uses a minimum p-value of 0.10 for a predictor to be removed from the existing model.

For the Lasso method, we choose two very small values of the penalty factor, λ. Specifically, we use the formula of Belloni and Chernozhukov (2011), $\lambda = 2c\sigma\sqrt{T}\Phi^{-1}(1 - \alpha/2n_k)$, setting $c = 0.002$ (which we label c_1) and $c = 0.006$ (labeled c_2).[9]

---

[8] The data are available at Amit Goyal's website at http://www.hec.unil.ch/agoyal/.

[9] If we set the value of c closer to 1, as recommended by Belloni and Chernozhukov (2011), the penalty is sufficiently high relative to the degree of return predictability identified by the models that the forecasting models essentially resort to including only a constant and no time-varying predictors.

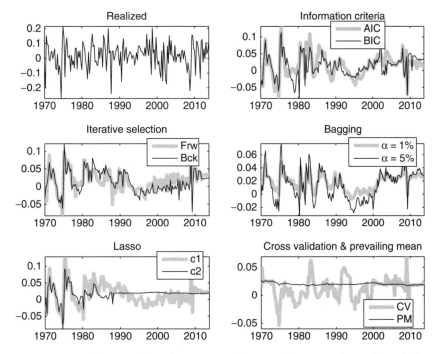

Figure 6.2: Quarterly US stock market returns and recursively generated out-of-sample forecasts based on a variety of forecasting and model selection methods, including the AIC and BIC information criteria, forward (frw) and backward (bck) stepwise selection, Bagging with different significance levels, Lasso with different penalties, cross validation (CV), and the prevailing mean (PM).

Our implementation of the Bagging scheme uses $B = 1,000$ bootstrapped samples of the original data. The data are arranged in $\{y_{t+1:T}, X_{t:T-1}\}$ tuples. Autocorrelation in the predictors is preserved through the circular block bootstrap of Politis and Romano (1994) with block size chosen optimally according to Politis and White (2004). Dependence across observations is preserved by using the same blocks for all variables. For each bootstrapped sample the estimate, $\hat{\beta}^b$, is used to compute forecasts, $\hat{f}_{t+1|t}^b = (x_t' S_t)\hat{\beta}^b$, where S_t is a stochastic selection matrix whose (i, i) element equals the indicator function $\mathbb{1}(|p\text{-val}_i| < \alpha)$. A predictor is added only if its p-value is less than α. Hence, as α grows larger the criterion becomes more liberal and the selected model becomes larger. We consider two different values of α, namely $\alpha = 1\%$, and $\alpha = 5\%$. The final Bagging forecasts are obtained by averaging across the bootstrap draws

$$\hat{f}_{t+1|t}^{\text{BAGG}} = \frac{1}{B} \sum_{b=1}^{B} \hat{f}_{t+1|t}^b. \tag{6.34}$$

The cross-validation scheme uses a validation sample of $v = 0.5(0.5t - \sqrt{t} - 1)$ observations for a sample of size t and discards $0.25t$ observations when constructing the estimation sample.

Figure 6.2 shows the recursively generated forecasts of stock returns for several of the model selection procedures. The realized series, shown in the top left panel, is highly volatile and shows no evidence of autocorrelation. Turning to the forecasts, the first point to note is that many of the forecasts are strongly correlated across the different model selection methods. Even so, there are also important differences on some occasions. For example, the AIC and Lasso method with the smallest penalty (c_1) generate more volatile forecasts than selection methods such as the BIC or the Lasso with a larger penalty term (c_2).

As a benchmark, we follow Welch and Goyal (2008) and use the prevailing mean. This is simply the historical average, and so forecasts y_{t+1} by means of $\sum_{\tau=1}^{t} y_\tau$. As shown in the bottom right window, the prevailing mean forecast is far more stable than the other forecasts.

Table 6.1 shows the extent of the similarity in the forecasts produced by the different methods. Below the diagonal this table shows the correlations between the forecasts, while above the diagonal it shows the correlations between the forecast errors. For most methods—the key exception being the prevailing mean—the correlation between the forecasts is strongly positive. Because of the presence of a large common unexplained component in stock returns, correlations among the forecast errors (shown above the diagonal in table 6.1) are very large and exceed 0.90.

The first two columns of table 6.2 compare the time-series behavior of the forecasts by reporting their volatility and bias. Among the information criteria and the stepwise approaches the forecasts generated by the models selected by the AIC or the backward stepwise approach are more volatile than those generated by models selected by the BIC or the forward stepwise approach. In turn, these methods lead to more volatile forecasts than the forecasts based on the Bagging or cross-validation methods. How we set the parameters of the Bagging or Lasso affects the volatility of the forecast since this influences how many predictors get included by these methods. The lower the penalty for including additional variables, the more variables get included in the forecasting model, and the more volatile the forecasts.

Figure 6.3 plots recursive inclusion frequencies. Specifically, for each variable selection method the plots show which predictors get included, indicated by an asterisk, and which ones get excluded. Such plots provide an informative way to display how different variables enter and exit from the forecasting model. We present results for four variables, namely the dividend–price ratio, the T-bill rate, the term spread, and the default yield. Clearly which variables get included varies a great deal over time and across selection methods. For example, the dividend–price ratio gets included a large proportion of the time by the backward stepwise, Akaike, and 5% Bagging methods but is never selected by the forward stepwise approach, the Lasso method with the highest penalty term, or the cross-validation method. There is also evidence of instability across time in the models being selected. For example, the term spread is selected by many of the criteria in the early-to-midseventies, but rarely afterwards, with the exception of the Lasso method with the smallest penalty factor and the AIC towards the end of the sample.

In light of these differences, it may seem surprising that the forecasts are so strongly correlated. However, many of the predictors are strongly correlated and so can substitute for each other. Different linear combinations of the predictor variables can therefore be strongly correlated.

Forecast evaluation is discussed in detail in part III of the book. However, as an indication of the methods' predictive accuracy, we report root mean squared error (RMSE) values in the third column of table 6.2. By this criterion, the model selection methods associated with the least volatile forecasts perform best, suggesting that the

TABLE 6.1:
Correlations among forecasts (shown below the diagonal) and forecast errors (shown above the diagonal) for different approaches to forecasting quarterly US stock market returns.

	AIC	BIC	Forward step	Backward step	Bagging $\alpha = 1\%$	Bagging $\alpha = 5\%$	Lasso $c = 2$	Lasso $c = 6$	Cross valid	Prevailing mean
AIC	1.0000	0.9689	0.9629	0.9611	0.9594	0.9746	0.9600	0.9505	0.9362	0.9313
BIC	0.7529	1.0000	0.9656	0.9592	0.9608	0.9679	0.9681	0.9640	0.9389	0.9382
Forward step	0.6859	0.6899	1.0000	0.9737	0.9664	0.9711	0.9738	0.9701	0.9468	0.9469
Backward step	0.6870	0.6557	0.7624	1.0000	0.9578	0.9638	0.9834	0.9546	0.9434	0.9383
Bagging $\alpha = 1\%$	0.7135	0.6583	0.6240	0.5739	1.0000	0.9924	0.9583	0.9778	0.9754	0.9897
Bagging $\alpha = 5\%$	0.7915	0.6884	0.6723	0.6349	0.9758	1.0000	0.9662	0.9675	0.9636	0.9662
Lasso $c = 2$	0.6834	0.7343	0.7708	0.8619	0.6281	0.6781	1.0000	0.9615	0.9387	0.9359
Lasso $c = 6$	0.5146	0.6441	0.6481	0.5039	0.3659	0.4254	0.6197	1.0000	0.9716	0.9768
Cross valid	0.3261	0.3038	0.2992	0.3451	0.2581	0.3409	0.3103	0.3772	1.0000	0.9778
Prevailing mean	−0.1019	0.0821	−0.0974	−0.1150	−0.0150	−0.0764	−0.0771	0.1346	0.1167	1.0000

TABLE 6.2:

Out-of-sample forecasting performance for different forecasting methods applied to quarterly US stock market returns. Std and Bias are the standard deviation and bias of the recursive forecasts, while RMSE and R^2 are the root mean squared forecast error and the R^2, the latter measured relative to the prevailing mean model. DM lists the Diebold–Mariano test for equal predictive accuracy. Sign and PT-test give the percentage of correctly predicted signs of quarterly excess returns and the associated value of the Pesaran–Timmermann (1992) test statistic, along with its p-value.

Method	Std(%)	Bias(%)	RMSE(%)	R^2(%)	DM stats	Sign(%)	PT-test	p-val
AIC	3.3089	−0.0324	9.1511	−14.4390	−1.9679	55.1136	−0.0953	0.4620
BIC	3.1860	0.2059	9.1796	−15.1516	−2.4083	54.5455	0.0210	0.4916
Forward step	2.8103	0.0343	8.7978	−5.7728	−1.1157	53.4091	−0.9605	0.1684
Backward step	3.0699	0.2602	8.9566	−9.6253	−1.4700	51.7045	−0.2834	0.3884
Bagging $\alpha = 1\%$	1.2097	−0.1898	8.5683	−0.3265	−0.1366	59.6591	−0.3509	0.3628
Bagging $\alpha = 5\%$	2.2270	0.1921	8.7244	−4.0162	−0.8453	52.2727	−0.6508	0.2576
Lasso c_1	3.1257	0.0511	8.9145	−8.5968	−1.4748	54.5455	0.0210	0.4916
Lasso c_2	1.8825	−0.1747	8.7124	−3.7303	−0.9242	60.2273	0.0304	0.4879
Cross valid	1.8569	0.3547	8.7983	−5.7842	−1.2595	57.3864	0.4494	0.3266
Prevailing mean	0.1944	−0.4041	8.5543	0.0000	0.0000	61.9318	NaN	NaN

predictors are not very powerful and parameter estimation error is important in this application. In fact, the prevailing mean model that does not include any time-varying predictors generates the lowest RMSE value among all the methods.

An alternative measure of predictive accuracy is provided by the out-of-sample R^2 measure shown in the fourth column of table 6.2, measured relative to the prevailing mean model which therefore gets a score of 0.[10] Negative values show underperformance under this metric relative to the simple prevailing mean forecast, while positive values suggest better performance against this benchmark. In this case all models generate negative out-of-sample R^2-values, confirming that the size of the predictable component in stock returns is small.

As we make clear in our discussion of forecast evaluation methods in chapter 17, caution has to be exercised when conducting inference on the sampling distribution of out-of-sample measures of relative forecast precision in situations such as here, where model parameters are estimated using an expanding estimation window and the selected models change over time. With this caveat in mind, as an indication of the statistical significance of the difference in forecasting models, the fifth column of table 6.2 reports Diebold–Mariano tests computed relative to the prevailing mean model which thus gets a value of 0 by this criterion. The Diebold–Mariano test of Diebold and Mariano (1995) is explained in greater detail in chapter 17, but is computed here as a t-test on the differences in two models' mean squared errors. Positive values suggest that the prevailing mean model produces a lower MSE value than the alternative method listed in each row, while negative values suggest

---

[10] The out-of-sample R^2 measure is based on Campbell and Thompson (2008) and is computed as

$$1 - \frac{T^{-1} \sum_{t=0}^{T-1} (y_{t+1} - f_{it+1|t})^2}{T^{-1} \sum_{t=0}^{T-1} (y_{t+1} - \bar{y}_{t+1|t})^2},$$

where $f_{it+1|t}$ is the return forecast for period $t+1$ generated by model i, given information at time t, while $\bar{y}_{t+1|t} = \bar{y}_t$ is the prevailing mean given information at time t.

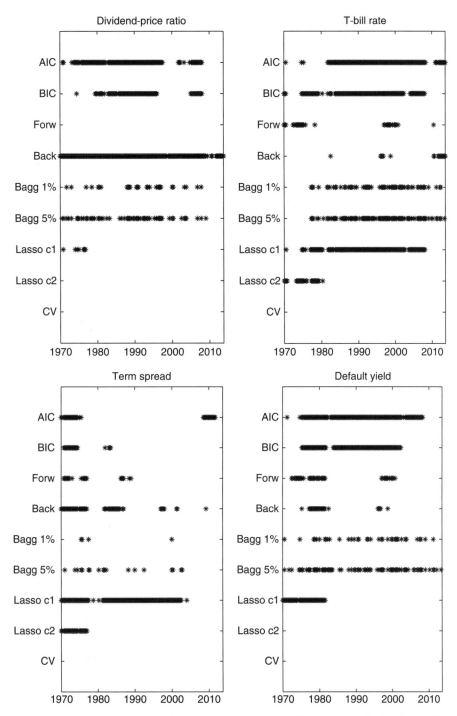

Figure 6.3: Recursive variable inclusion plots for the dividend–price ratio, the T-bill rate, the term spread, and the default yield in models fitted to quarterly US stock market returns. Variable inclusion is marked by an asterisk, while empty spaces indicate that the variable is not selected in a given period.

the opposite. The large negative values of the Diebold–Mariano test statistic obtained here indicate that the performance of the forecasts based on the AIC and BIC model selection criteria is particularly poor.

As argued previously, statistical measures of forecast performance are not necessarily closely aligned with economic measures of forecasting performance. To highlight this, we report two alternative measures of performance. First, we report the percentage of correctly predicted signs of excess returns or the "hit rate." This is shown in column 6 of table 6.2. The numbers range between 51% for the models selected by the backward stepwise approach versus 61% for the prevailing mean and 60% for the Lasso method with the largest penalty term.

The highest hit rate is obtained simply by always predicting a positive mean excess return. This is a so-called "broken clock" forecast that never changes and therefore carries little or no information. A genuine ability to predict the sign of excess returns must entail some ability to forecast both positive and negative signs. The sign test proposed by Pesaran and Timmermann (1992), and explained in more detail in chapter 18, accounts for the forecasts' ability to predict both positive and negative signs. Results for this test, which is asymptotically normally distributed, are shown in the seventh and eighth columns of table 6.2. These reveal no significant ability of any of the forecasting methods to pick models that correctly forecast the direction of the stock market.

6.7.2 Economic Measures of Forecast Performance

We have emphasized the potential for differences between statistical and economic measures of predictive performance. To evaluate this issue in the present context, we consider the portfolio allocation decisions of an investor with mean–variance preferences

$$E[U(y_{t+1})|Z_t] = E[y_{t+1}|Z_t] - \frac{a}{2}\operatorname{Var}(y_{t+1}|Z_t), \tag{6.35}$$

where $E[y_{t+1}|Z_t]$ is the expected portfolio return, $\operatorname{Var}(y_{t+1}|Z_t)$ is the conditional variance of the portfolio return and $a = 5$ captures the investor's risk aversion. The investor chooses between a risk-free asset paying the three-month T-bill rate and the risky stock market portfolio. This investor's portfolio return is given by $y_{t+1} = y_{ft+1} + \omega_t y_{st+1}$, where y_{ft+1} is the risk-free rate, y_{st+1} is the excess returns on stocks, net of the T-bill rate, and ω_t is the weight on stocks selected on the basis of information available at time t, $Z_t = \{y_\tau, x_\tau\}_{\tau=1}^t$. To avoid bankruptcy concerns, we restrict f_t to lie between 0 and 1 and so rule out short selling and leverage. The portfolio weight is then determined from $\omega_t(Z_t) = \max(\min(\hat{\beta}_t' x_t / a\hat{\sigma}_{\varepsilon t}^2, 1), 0)$, where $\hat{\beta}_t$ is the recursively estimated OLS estimate from a linear return regression model and $\hat{\sigma}_{\varepsilon t}^2$ is the recursive estimate of the variance of the residuals from this regression.

Table 6.3 shows the mean return and volatility (standard deviation) of the resulting portfolio, along with the annualized certainty equivalent return (CER) and Sharpe ratio. The CER is defined as the annualized risk-free return which, over the evaluation sample, would have made an investor indifferent between following the benchmark strategy suggested by the prevailing mean model that assumes constant mean returns versus alternative strategies based on time-varying predictors.

TABLE 6.3:

Portfolio performance based on out-of-sample forecasts of quarterly US stock market returns using the forecasting methods listed in the rows. The portfolio performance is reported for a risk-averse mean–variance investor who chooses between stocks and T-bills based on the predicted excess return on stocks. Mean return and Std measure the mean and volatility of the resulting portfolio returns while CER is the certainty equivalent return and Sharpe is the Sharpe ratio. All measures are annualized.

Method	Mean ret(%)	Std ret(%)	CER(%)	Sharpe(%)
AIC	9.2573	23.5458	0.5687	0.3910
BIC	9.5058	22.4110	1.1431	0.4218
Forward step	8.9747	24.2177	0.0855	0.3684
Backward step	9.2020	20.7854	1.2782	0.4402
Bagging $\alpha = 1\%$	9.2130	24.1032	0.3584	0.3801
Bagging $\alpha = 5\%$	9.6601	23.7252	0.9185	0.4050
Lasso c_1	9.7686	23.2203	1.1751	0.4185
Lasso c_2	9.6491	20.9934	1.6710	0.4572
Cross valid	8.3885	19.0016	0.9083	0.4387
Prevailing mean	8.9905	24.5500	0.0000	0.3641

The Sharpe ratio is the mean portfolio return in excess of the T-bill rate divided by the standard deviation of the portfolio return, both estimated over the evaluation sample.

The results suggest that the methods associated with the most volatile return forecasts do not always translate into portfolio strategies with more volatile returns. In fact, the most volatile portfolio returns are associated with the excess return forecasts that are mostly positive, i.e., the Bagging and Lasso methods with the smallest penalty factor, the AIC, and the prevailing mean. These methods do not, however, generate the highest certainty equivalent returns. The BIC, backward stepwise method, and the two Lasso methods generate CER values above 1% and Sharpe ratios somewhat higher than the Sharpe ratio associated with the prevailing mean model.

Figure 6.4 plots the recursively estimated allocation to stocks. This is the fore-caster's choice variable in this setting. A value of 1 corresponds to allocating all money to stocks, while a value of 0 corresponds to holding only T-bills. The portfolio weights fluctuate a great deal and frequently fall on the 0–1 bounds that we impose in our analysis. This is a result of our assumption of no transaction costs and would change if we assumed that large changes to the portfolio weights were costly. The upper bound of 100% invested in stocks is binding more often than the lower bound of zero allocation to stocks. This is a reflection of the equity risk premium, i.e., the higher historical mean of stock returns compared with returns on T-bills, whose average is positive during the sample and so it takes relatively strong evidence to persuade the investor not to allocate any money to stocks.

Figure 6.5 (left) shows a scatterplot of the RMSE versus the hit rate, i.e., the proportion of correctly predicted signs of excess returns, across the nine different model selection methods considered here. There is a negative correlation between the two measures, suggesting that the models with the highest proportion of correctly predicted signs tend to generate the smallest RMSE values.

Figure 6.5 (right) shows the potential disconnect between statistical measures of forecast performance such as RMSE and economic measures such as the CER.

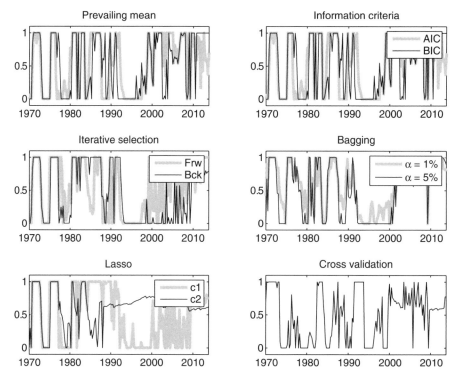

Figure 6.4: Mean–variance investor's allocation to stocks based on recursively generated predictions using different ways to select the forecasting model. A value of 1 on the vertical axis shows a 100% allocation to stocks, while 0 shows a 100% allocation to Treasury bills.

Interestingly, the methods with the highest RMSE values tend to generate the highest CER values. For example, the models selected by the BIC and backward stepwise methods both generate high RMSE values, but also generate mean CER estimates of 1% per year or higher.

These findings suggest that forecasting methods with poor statistical performance can still yield forecasts that are valuable from an economic perspective. The reason is that large forecast errors can be punished more heavily by convex statistical loss functions such as MSE compared with economic loss functions which may put less weight on the large forecast errors.[11]

Figure 6.6 plots the cumulative wealth over time from investing $1 in 1970 and then using the recursively generated forecasts to optimally allocate between the stock market portfolio and three-month T-bills. We show results for the prevailing mean strategy which does not model any time variation in the conditional equity risk premium. This strategy ends up with $35 in 2013. The best performing strategy is the Lasso method using the larger penalty term (c_2) which generates a cumulated wealth above $50 at the end of 2013. Such plots should be interpreted with caution

---

[11] Of course, the use of a cap on the portfolio weights, which are restricted to [0, 1] also affects the results shown here. Thus, economic performance depends both on the forecasts as well as on the action rule translating the raw forecasts into a position in stocks.

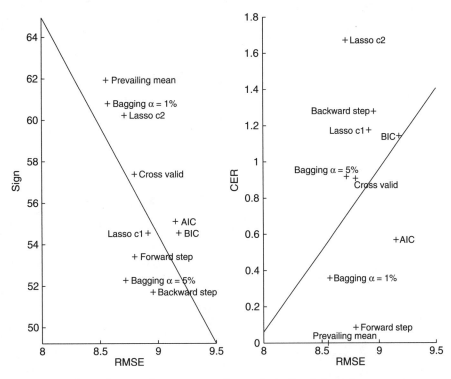

Figure 6.5: Relation between the percentage of correctly predicted signs of excess stock returns versus the root mean squared error (RMSE) (left) and the relation between a mean–variance investor's certainty equivalent return (CER) versus the RMSE (right).

given the wide standard errors that surround the cumulative values. Nevertheless, they do serve as an illustration that economic and statistical measures of forecasting performance can yield quite different results.[12]

6.8 PROPERTIES OF MODEL SELECTION PROCEDURES

Choosing a model selection procedure requires a detailed understanding of how such methods work and the extent to which they possess desirable properties. Different notions of what a "good" selection procedure might achieve exist and, as we shall see, these are not always mutually consistent.

If the true model $M^* = f^*(z_t, \beta)$ mirroring the data-generating process is included in the set of prediction models under consideration, $\mathcal{M}_K = \{M_k = f_k(z_t, \beta_k), k = 1, \ldots, K\}$, the notion of consistent model selection becomes meaningful. Assuming a discrete set of models, consistent model selection means that $P[\hat{M} = M^*] \to 1$ as the sample size gets large, where $\hat{M}$ is the selected model. Methods in common use typically have one of two outcomes by this criterion—either they are consistent model selectors or, alternatively, they imply a positive probability of

---

[12] For example, choosing the penalty term optimally in real time would have been a challenge.

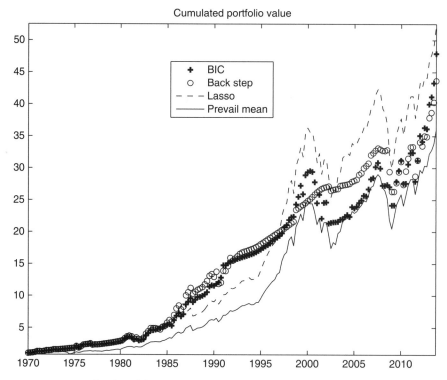

Figure 6.6: Cumulated wealth associated with different forecasting models.

picking too large a model and so are conservative. Selection techniques with a positive asymptotic probability of underfitting the model are rarer.

Standard methods for proving consistency of model selection partition the set of models into three sets, $\mathcal{M}_K = \{M^*, \mathcal{M}_K^u, \mathcal{M}_K^o\}$, where $\mathcal{M}_K^u$ is the set of models that underfit (exclude variables present in the data-generating process, M^*), and $\mathcal{M}_K^o$ is the set of models that overfit (include extraneous variables in addition to those appearing in the true model, M^*). The proof then shows that $P[\hat{M} \in \mathcal{M}_K^u] \to 0$ and $P[\hat{M} \in \mathcal{M}_K^o] \to 0$ as the sample size gets large.

Sequential hypothesis testing is typically not a consistent model selection method and tends to overstate the size of the forecasting model. This can best be demonstrated by considering the choice between two linear regression models, one with n_{k_1} regressors and the other with $n_{k_2} > n_{k_1}$ regressors. The smaller model gets selected if we reject a hypothesis test (e.g., a likelihood ratio test) for the null that the additional coefficients in the larger model are 0. Suppose the larger model is the true model. Then the probability of rejecting the null hypothesis—which equals the probability of selecting the larger (true) model—equals the power of the test. For any consistent test, power goes to 1 asymptotically, and so the probability of underfitting goes to 0. Conversely, if the smaller model is the true model, the probability of rejecting the null hypothesis and hence choosing the smaller (true) model is equal to the size of the test. Standard hypothesis tests control the size to remain nonzero asymptotically, so the probability of overfitting (i.e., choosing the larger model when the smaller one is the true model) is asymptotically equal to the size of the test which is nonzero. Hence, there is a positive probability of overfitting the model, even asymptotically. Computing the extent to which this overfit happens is difficult and method-dependent for more complicated model selection processes, but the basic insight continues to hold.

To gain a heuristic understanding of the types of results that arise for information criteria, we establish model consistency for the general multivariate linear prediction model with n variables:

$$y_{t+1} = Ax_t + \varepsilon_{t+1}. \tag{6.36}$$

Here, y_{t+1} is an $n \times 1$ vector and x_t is an $n \times n_k$ matrix. This setup is not as general as that used in the construction of the information criteria. But, it is general enough to cover the majority of uses of information criteria encountered in practical forecasting situations. Specifically, it covers vector autoregressions (VARs), where x_t captures lagged values of y, in addition to general linear systems of equations which are obtained by inserting 0s into the A matrix. Let n_k denote the total number of variables in the model, e.g., in a VAR there are p lags of n variables and so $n_k = n^2 p$ when all lags are included, $n_k = n^2(p - 1)$ when the pth lag is excluded, and so on. Finally, let $\hat{\Sigma}_k$ denote the covariance matrix of the model's sum of squared residuals.

As we saw in (6.11), ICs choose the model (indexed by k) to minimize $\mathrm{IC}(k) = \ln|\hat{\Sigma}_k| + h(n_k)g(T)$. ICs differ over their choice of $g(T)$ and this term plays a crucial role in determining whether a particular information criterion leads to consistent model choice. To establish when an IC is consistent, note from (6.11),

$$\mathrm{IC}(k) - \mathrm{IC}(k_0) = \ln|\hat{\Sigma}_k| + h(n_k)g(T) - \ln|\hat{\Sigma}_{k_0}| - h(n_{k_0})g(T)$$

$$= \left(\ln|\hat{\Sigma}_k| - \ln|\hat{\Sigma}_{k_0}| \right) + \left(h(n_k) - h(n_{k_0}) \right) g(T). \tag{6.37}$$

Consider first the case with an overfitted model, $n_k > n_{k_0}$, where n_{k_0} is the number of parameters of the true model. In this case the additional model parameters—over and above the n_{k_0} parameters—are 0 in population. Under normality, $-2T \left\{ \ln|\hat{\Sigma}_k| - \ln|\hat{\Sigma}_{k_0}| \right\}$ is the usual likelihood ratio test statistic for testing that these coefficients are 0. Under standard conditions this converges to an $O_p(1)$ random variable, and hence we have

$$P\left(\left(\ln|\hat{\Sigma}_k| - \ln|\hat{\Sigma}_{k_0}| \right) + (h(n_k) - h(n_{k_0}))g(T) > 0 \right)$$

$$= P\left(\left(\ln|\hat{\Sigma}_k| - \ln|\hat{\Sigma}_{k_0}| \right) > (h(n_{k_0}) - h(n_k))g(T) \right)$$

$$= P\left(-2T \left(\ln|\hat{\Sigma}_k| - \ln|\hat{\Sigma}_{k_0}| \right) < 2(h(n_k) - h(n_{k_0}))Tg(T) \right). \tag{6.38}$$

For this to converge to 1, we require that $2(h(n_k) - h(n_{k_0}))Tg(T) \to \infty$. Since $h(n_k) - h(n_{k_0}) > 0$, this means that $Tg(T) \to \infty$ is required.

Next, consider the case with too few model parameters, $n_k < n_{k_0}$. In this case the random variable $\left(\ln|\hat{\Sigma}_k| - \ln|\hat{\Sigma}_{k_0}|\right)$ is positive with probability 1, and we have

$$P\left(\left(\ln|\hat{\Sigma}_k| - \ln|\hat{\Sigma}_{k_0}|\right) + (h(n_k) - h(n_{k_0}))g(T) > 0\right)$$
$$= P\left(\left(\ln|\hat{\Sigma}_k| - \ln|\hat{\Sigma}_{k_0}|\right) > (h(n_{k_0}) - h(n_k))g(T)\right). \qquad (6.39)$$

Since $h(n_{k_0}) - h(n_k) > 0$, we require that $g(T) \to 0$ for the probability in (6.39) to equal 1 in the limit.

Combining these results yields the following conditions for an information criterion to asymptotically choose the correct model:

a. $g(T) \to 0$ as $T \to \infty$;

b. $Tg(T) \to \infty$ as $T \to \infty$.

Checking these conditions for specific information criteria gives a way to verify whether they are consistent model selection criteria. For the AIC in (6.14), $Tg(T) = 2$, and so part (b) does not hold and the AIC does *not* choose the correct model asymptotically. Given the asymptotic equivalence of AIC and the Mallows C_p, this conclusion also holds for Mallows C_p. The AIC is designed with the idea that all models under consideration are subsets of the true model. Hence, lack of consistency should not be viewed as a deficiency of the criterion, but rather as a reflection of the way the method is set up.[13]

We next show what happens when there is a "true" model. As an illustration, consider the univariate case where $n_k = n_{k_0} + 1$. For the AIC, $g(T) = 2/T$, and so (6.37) simplifies to

$$P\left(\left[(\ln|\hat{\sigma}^2_{k_0+1}| - \ln|\hat{\sigma}^2_{k_0}|) + (n_{k_0} + 1 - n_{k_0})\right](2/T) > 0\right) = P\left(U^* < 2T(2/T)\right)$$
$$= P\left(U^* < 4\right), \qquad (6.40)$$

which can easily be computed. In this case, asymptotically $U^* \sim \chi^2_1$ and the correct model gets selected 96% of the time, while the wrong model that includes an additional variable gets chosen 4% of the time. This is similar to the result we would obtain with a t-statistic testing for inclusion of the extra variable with a size of 5%, i.e., a two-sided test with critical values ± 1.96. As with the sequential test procedure discussed above, the issue is that the probability of a type one error does not go to 0 asymptotically.

For the Bayes Information Criterion, $Tg(T) = \ln(T)$, and so $Tg(T) = \ln(T) \to \infty$, while $g(T) \to 0$ as $T \to \infty$. Hence this criterion does asymptotically choose the correct model with probability 1. Repeating the calculations that compare a model

---

[13] Mallows (1973) argues against using C_p as a model selection tool, noting its similarities with sequential pre-test methods.

with one extra parameter to the true model, we now have

$$P\left(\left((\ln|\hat{\sigma}^2_{k_0+1}| - \ln|\hat{\sigma}^2_{k_0}|) + (n_{k_0} + 1 - n_{k_0})\right)(\ln(T)/T) > 0\right)$$
$$= P\left(U^* < 2\ln(T)\right), \tag{6.41}$$

which goes to 1 as the sample size, T, increases, showing that the true model gets selected in large samples.

The Hannan–Quinn criterion also leads to consistent model choice because $g(T) = \ln(\ln(T)) \to \infty$ as $T \to \infty$. However, convergence to the true model is achieved at a much slower rate than for the BIC. The adjustment proposed by Hannan and Quinn was indeed intended to slow the rate at which further variables are added—and hence to minimize overfit—while retaining consistency.

For linear regressions with fixed regressors and i.i.d. errors, Shao (1993) and Shao (1997) show that "leave-T_v-out" cross validation is not a consistent model selection procedure when T_v is fixed. As with the AIC, this method asymptotically never picks too small a model but chooses too large a model with positive probability. Hence, on average the method overfits the data. Shao (1993) shows that if the validation sample dominates the estimation sample, i.e., $T_v/T \to 1$ asymptotically, then the method will consistently estimate the true model. Shao (1997) provides a direct relation between leave-T_v-out cross validation and information criteria which shows the equivalence between these methods in large samples. While the assumptions of these papers are too strong for most forecasting purposes, relaxing them is unlikely to improve upon this result. As a consequence, we expect cross validation to produce models that include too many regressors.

Model consistency can also be considered when the number of parameters in the true model is large relative to T, as can happen when the number of parameters increases with T. In these cases the IC and cross-validation methods, apart from becoming too computationally cumbersome, do not have consistency properties. It is precisely for these situations that methods such as the Lasso and its variations were designed. In a setting with i.i.d. data where the number of nonzero coefficients and their values are fixed, Knight and Fu (2000) show that if $\lambda_T/\sqrt{T}$ converges to a nonnegative constant then the Lasso chooses the correct model with positive probability. This result has been extended to allow the number of included terms to grow with T.[14]

Is model consistency necessarily a desirable property? Consistency is a weak property, in the sense that it neither dramatically reduces the number of model selection approaches nor tells us exactly how to specify the penalty for any particular application. For example, the conditions for consistent selection continue to be satisfied if we modify the BIC, or any other consistent procedure, to have a penalty term $g(T) = c\ln(T)/T$, for an arbitrary constant, $c > 0$. Different values of c can easily lead to different outcomes for which model gets chosen. The same problem arises for the Lasso. Hence, a wide variety of model selection procedures provide consistent model selection. As is common in econometrics, giving a rate condition does not pin down the specific penalty one might want to use in a given application.

---

[14] Results on model consistency have been derived under assumptions that limit the magnitude of the least squares estimates of the zero coefficients in the model (called an irrepresentability condition); see, e.g., Zhao and Yu (2006).

Shibata (1980, 1981) argue against choosing model selection procedures based on the consistency results above. If the model is not sparse in the sense that there are many coefficients that are close to but not exactly equal to 0, the asymptotic experiment used to examine consistency properties would not be informative. Consistent methods do not underfit because the power of exclusion tests goes to 1 for a fixed set of larger alternatives. However, if the additional coefficients in the larger model are near 0 and so are not large asymptotically, consistent methods can easily underfit. In more complicated experiments where all models are smaller approximations, the assumptions underpinning the consistent model selection results might not be appropriate. Indeed, Akaike (1974) developed the AIC for precisely this type of situation. Furthermore, the available sample size may not be large enough for asymptotic properties to provide reasonable guidance. We also are not necessarily interested in choosing the correct variables but instead in selecting models that lead to good predictions.

For linear regression models with a large or even infinite number of nonzero coefficients, Shibata (1980, 1981) introduce the notion of asymptotic efficiency of the model selection criterion when none of the models are correctly specified. The idea is that some model, $M_k^* \in \mathcal{M}_K$, provides a lower bound for estimation-related risk, denoted R_{2k}^*. Since no model is correct, the "best" model in $\mathcal{M}_K$ replaces the correct model. A model selection procedure is considered to be asymptotically efficient if, in the limit as $T \to \infty$, the (estimation-related) risk of the selected model, $\hat{M}_k^*$, has the property that

$$\hat{R}_2(\hat{M}_k^*)/R_{2k}^* \to 1. \tag{6.42}$$

Here it is assumed that the risks of all models diverge asymptotically. This implies that all models underfit the true model and rules out that the true model is contained in $\mathcal{M}_K$.

Shibata (1981) shows that the AIC and Mallows C_p are asymptotically efficient under this criterion, whereas the BIC fails to be asymptotically efficient. Indeed, for information criteria with deterministic penalties ($h(n_k)g(T)$ is nonrandom) Yang (2005) and Shao (1997) show that criteria that are consistent cannot be asymptotically efficient in the Shibata sense, and so there is no information criterion that has both properties.

To establish these results, usually the number of models is assumed to be small relative to the sample size. This assumption is required to obtain statistics for which the asymptotic representations are reasonable. In the literature on asymptotic efficiency the true model can get large asymptotically, but the number of models examined remains small relative to the sample size. More recently, attention has shifted to properties of model selection methods when the number of models is large—perhaps even larger than the sample size. As noted above, information criteria cannot be examined in these cases because they are too computationally demanding and require evaluating all possible models, which becomes impossible in practice. However, useful results for the Lasso and its variants have been established for this case. Leng, Lin, and Wahba (2006) show a result that is similar to the asymptotic efficiency property established for information criteria. Specifically, choices of the Lasso penalty factor, λ_T, that lead to good model selection properties differ from choices of λ_T that ensure the best in-sample predictive accuracy. The in-sample predictive accuracy criterion generally allows the inclusion of additional variables over and above those in the true model, albeit in a constrained way. All of these results are for i.i.d. models, and include additional restrictions on the regressors and on the behavior of β. However, it is likely that the intuition generated from these results carries over to forecasting situations with non-i.i.d. data.

6.9 RISK FOR MODEL SELECTION METHODS: MONTE CARLO SIMULATIONS

Model selection methods should be considered part of the estimation process. This leads us to focus on the risk of the forecast method as a function of the selection rule, the set of models under consideration, the data, and the true model parameters. For example, with two models and a statistic $\varphi(z) = \{0, 1\}$, where 0 indicates choosing the first model and 1 indicates choosing the second model, the forecast generated by a model selection method can be written as

$$f^{\mathrm{MS}}(z) = f_1(z_t, \hat{\beta}_1)(1 - \varphi(z)) + f_2(z_t, \hat{\beta}_2)\varphi(z). \tag{6.43}$$

The forecast associated with a model selection procedure is simply a more complicated function of the data than either of the individual models. However, it remains a function of the data and hence has a risk function that depends on the parameters of the true model, θ. A good model selection procedure delivers tolerable risk over reasonable models that are not obviously misspecified. The consistency criterion examines risk in the sense that it focuses on minimizing pointwise asymptotic risk when the true model lies in the set of candidate models. Asymptotic efficiency focuses on the limit of relative risk when the true model is larger than any of the candidate models. Each of these properties is asymptotic. Small sample evaluations of risk show that consistent model selection methods will not generally choose the correct model with probability 1. Methods that asymptotically are as good as the best model will not always be as good as the best model in small samples. Because of this, it is constructive to examine the risk functions of some popular methods in a Monte Carlo setting.

Another reason for considering Monte Carlo experiments is that risk functions associated with forecasts based on the model selection methods covered in this chapter are generally very difficult to characterize analytically. The reason is that the selected forecasts are not smooth functions of the underlying data, as is clear from (6.43), and risk depends heavily on the parameters of the forecasting model.

The first Monte Carlo simulation examines estimation of the mean for i.i.d. data generated as

$$y_t = \mu + \varepsilon_t, \quad \varepsilon_t \sim \mathrm{ind}\ N(0, 1). \tag{6.44}$$

Under MSE loss the best possible—but infeasible—estimator is to know the mean, μ, which results in a risk of 1, i.e., the variance of the unpredictable component, ε_t. Estimation of the mean, based on the sample average, results in a risk equal to $(1 + T^{-1})$, where T is the sample size. In addition to simply using the sample mean, we can employ the model selection methods discussed above to choose between the model that either fixes the mean at $\mu = 0$ (and hence involves no estimation error) or instead uses the sample mean, $\bar{y}_t$, as the forecast. The methods we employ are

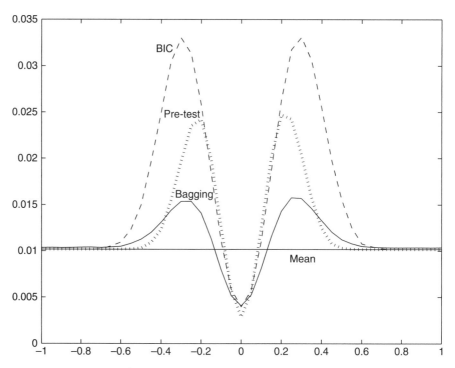

Figure 6.7: Estimation-related risk under different model selection methods for the model with a constant mean, μ, and no time-varying predictors. The horizontal axis shows the magnitude of the mean, μ, while the vertical axis shows the estimation-related risk.

(i) AIC; (ii) BIC; (iii) a pre-test method based on a t-test with a two-sided alternative and a size of 5%; (iv) Bagging of the loss minimization method in (iii), using an i.i.d. bootstrap that samples with replacement from the demeaned data.

Figure 6.7 shows the approximate estimation-related risk for four of these methods using a sample size of $T = 100$. The estimation-related risk removes first-order uncertainty by removing the unpredictable component. Here this amounts to subtracting 1 from the risk. When the true mean is near 0, in this example each of the model selection methods has a lower risk than that of simply estimating the mean. This happens because the model selection methods have a nonzero probability of choosing the forecast that imposes a zero mean. They do not always choose the correct model with $\mu = 0$, however, which is why none of the methods attain a zero estimation-related risk. The different values of risk at $\mu = 0$ reflect the probability that the model with no mean is chosen.

Such gains from applying model selection methods when the true model has $\mu = 0$ come at a cost, though, since all model selection methods have risk well above that of simply using the sample mean to forecast y when μ is "small," i.e., close but not exactly equal to 0. In this neighborhood the risk rises above that of simply using the sample mean because the probability of choosing the (incorrect) model that imposes $\mu = 0$ is nontrivial, which adversely impacts the MSE. This region of the parameter space is exactly where the tests have difficulties distinguishing between the two models. Eventually, though, as the true mean gets larger, each of the model selection methods chooses the model with a nonzero mean with probability 1 and the risk again declines to that of simply estimating the sample mean.

This "hump" in the risk function is ignored by the pointwise proofs discussed earlier—asymptotically at any point where $\mu \neq 0$, the risk function converges to 0 pointwise. The hump never disappears, however, and there will always be a region near $\mu = 0$, where the model selection methods do not choose either model with probability 1, and hence there is always the chance that the risk induced by model selection will be higher than when the larger model is used. Hence, the uniform convergence results are not just of theoretical interest but also have practical value.

When more models are included in the search and coefficients are local to 0,[15] analogous results can be obtained. Consider forecasting an outcome variable with $n_K = 8$ possible regressors. The regressors are assumed to be independent of each other and are linked to the dependent variable through a linear model with coefficient vector β_0. Let n_{k_0} coefficients be equal to $\mu/\sqrt{n_{k_0} T}$, where T is the length of the estimation sample, which we again set to 100. The remaining coefficients are set to 0, so the data-generating process is

$$y_{t+1} = \sum_{i=1}^{n_{k_0}} \frac{\mu}{\sqrt{n_{k_0} T}} x_{it} + \varepsilon_{t+1}, \quad \varepsilon_{t+1} \sim \text{ind } N(0, 1).$$

The full model uses all eight regressors. When $\mu \neq 0$, the correctly specified regression includes only those variables that correspond to the n_{k_0} nonzero coefficients. We consider sequential hypothesis tests, removing all variables with t-statistics that fail to reject a two-sided significance test at the 5% level, along with the BIC and AIC. Figure 6.8 reports results when $n_{k_0} = 3$, so the majority of variables should be excluded, while figure 6.9 repeats the same exercise with $n_{k_0} = 7$, so only one variable needs to be excluded.

Figure 6.8 shows that the "hump" near 0 carries over to more complicated situations. Indeed, the only question is how big the hump is. Model selection methods can now perform worse than the kitchen sink approach that includes all—useful and useless—regressors. Even so, for most of the parameter space, the model selection methods outperform the kitchen sink approach which explains why model selection techniques are popular in practice. Moreover, the model selection procedures do even better than the correct specification when μ is sufficiently close to 0. This happens because model selection procedures are essentially shrinkage estimators, so when μ is close to 0, shrinkage becomes a useful approach.

In this example the AIC has very different properties to the BIC and the sequential testing approach. AIC does not perform so well when the other approaches do well, and does not do as poorly when the other approaches are poor. This is a consequence of the overfitting described above. When too many variables are included, the coefficient estimates do not get shrunk as much, and we are closer to the solution that includes all regressors and has a flat risk function. As μ gets larger, none of the methods are as good as including only the correct regressors. Despite the BIC's property of correct asymptotic model selection, in small samples this method still

---

[15] This means that the coefficients take the form $b/\sqrt{T}$, where $b \neq 0$ and T is the sample size. For such regressors the power of tests that their coefficients equal 0 will not asymptote to 1 as the sample size gets large.

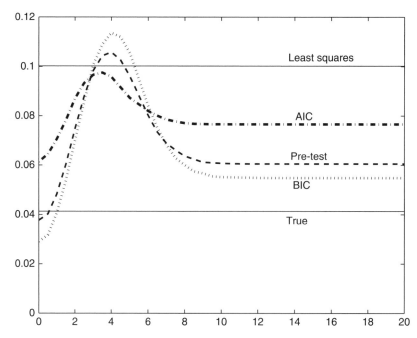

Figure 6.8: Estimation-related risk under different model selection methods for the model with eight time-varying predictors, three of which have nonzero coefficients. The horizontal axis shows the magnitude of the nonzero coefficients for the three predictor variables, while the vertical axis shows the estimation-related risk.

appears to overfit somewhat. The overfitting is not as severe as that of the AIC, which also overfits asymptotically. In this experiment the sequential hypothesis test procedure is close to the BIC, but in larger samples the loss function of the BIC will get closer to that of the correct specification.

When nearly all the variables are to be included, the difference between the true model and the model that includes all variables is obviously small, as shown in figure 6.9. The effect of not needing to exclude many variables is threefold. First, the gains from model selection get larger when the coefficients are very close to 0. Second, the size of the hump in expected loss is larger for coefficients further away from 0. Third, when the coefficients are sufficiently far from 0, all of the methods perform similarly since the range of possibilities is small. The ordering of the size of the hump and the eventual point at which the methods settle down as μ gets larger is the same across all methods, however.

Despite these results, pre-test methods do have some valuable properties compared to simply using the underlying models. For large enough values of the nonzero parameters, asymptotically the pre-test estimator has the same risk as the largest model included in the set of models over which the search is conducted. This follows directly from the property that pre-tests are consistent, and hence the model preferred by the sequential search will be the largest model and so they have the same risk function. This prevents the risk function from increasing beyond bounds due to wrong exclusion of variables whose parameters are far away from 0. Contrast this with shrinkage methods which do not have such a property. This might not be as comforting as it seems, however, as it guarantees only that pre-testing performs well

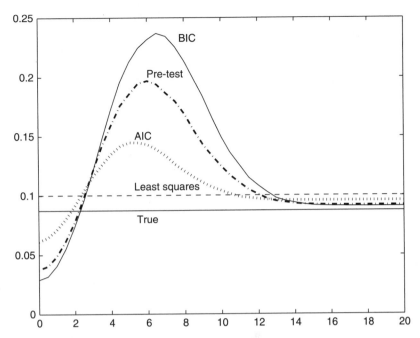

Figure 6.9: Estimation-related risk under different model selection methods for the model with eight time-varying predictors, seven of which have nonzero coefficients. The horizontal axis shows the magnitude of the nonzero coefficients for the seven predictor variables, while the vertical axis shows the estimation-related risk.

when it is obvious that some parameters are nonzero—a situation where shrinkage towards 0 is unlikely to be a sensible approach anyway.

The results here are consistent with the findings in Ng (2013) that neither of the BIC or AIC criteria systematically dominate the other when it comes to evaluating the finite-sample risk of the associated forecasts. Using Monte Carlo simulations, Ng (2013) find that small models (models with few parameters to estimate) are not necessarily better than large models even if the data are generated by a model with a finite number of parameters. There is no way of getting around the problem that the best procedure will depend on the true data-generating process which in practice remains unknown.

6.10 CONCLUSION

When applied to forecasting problems, model selection procedures are best thought of as more complicated estimators rather than as a separate step in the construction of the prediction model. Model selection simply increases the set of functions over which the search for the best forecasting model is conducted.

This view contrasts with how model selection methods are often portrayed in the forecasting literature. In many instances a particular set of models might be chosen as providing the "best" forecasts, and model selection is introduced as if it has no effect on the original analysis. Such an approach has its roots in consistent model selection, the notion that the model selection step can be ignored since asymptotically the correct model is chosen with probability 1. This argument can be very misleading, however. First, it relies on a pointwise argument and does not hold uniformly, i.e., for values of the unknown "true" parameters that are close to the dominant model. Second, such results rely on the—frequently invalid—assumption that a correct true or pseudo-true model is included in the set over which the model specification search is conducted.

The effects of model selection on the risk function are typically of the same order as that of parameter estimation. Risk functions, though, are generally very hard to examine analytically. Viewed as estimators, risk functions are often very complicated functions of the underlying data, and generally nonsmooth due to the presence of data-dependent indicator functions.

We use Monte Carlo methods to examine the general effect of model selection on the risk function. When one model is clearly superior it will nearly always be selected and hence the risk function for the model selection method is equivalent to that for the superior model as if this model were known to be valid. This explains the popularity of model selection methods in applied work. However, there is no free lunch—when a single model is not obviously superior to all other models, model selection methods result in a risk function that is a probability weighted average across all models. In such cases, there is typically a region of the parameter space where the risk associated with the forecasts based on model selection procedures is greater than the risk of any of the models near the optimal model. Such a situation is often highly empirically relevant since statistical techniques for model selection are employed precisely because models are hard to tell apart, and not because one model is obviously superior.

6.11 APPENDIX: DERIVATION OF INFORMATION CRITERIA

This appendix provides a derivation of the Schwarz and Akaike information criteria.

6.11.1 Schwarz Information Criterion

The Schwarz Bayesian information criterion (BIC) ranks models by their posterior probabilities. To make this idea operational, we require model priors, $\pi(M_k)$, that sum to 1 across all models: $\sum_{M_k \in \mathcal{M}_K} \pi(M_k) = 1$. We also need priors over the parameters of each model, $\pi(\beta_k)$. With these in place, the posterior probability of each model, M_k, is given by

$$\pi(M_k, \beta_k | Z) = \frac{p(\beta_k | Z, M_k)\pi(\beta_k)}{p_Z(Z)}\pi(M_k), \tag{6.45}$$

where $p(\beta_k | Z, M_k)$ is the likelihood for model k, and $p_Z(Z)$ is the marginal density for the data, Z. For notational convenience we use Z to denote the entire data set used to construct the forecasting model, e.g., $\{y_t, z_t\}_{t=1}^{T}$. To obtain the model posterior given the data, β_k must be integrated out. To do this we employ an approximation that allows the normal prior to be used as an approximate conjugate for any distribution.

Using a two-term expansion for the likelihood around the maximum likelihood estimate $\hat{\beta}_k$, we have

$$\ln p(\beta_k|Z) \approx \ln p(\hat{\beta}_k|Z) + \tfrac{1}{2}(\hat{\beta}_k - \beta_k)'(T\,\mathrm{I}(\hat{\beta}_k))(\hat{\beta}_k - \beta_k), \qquad (6.46)$$

where $T\,\mathrm{I}(\hat{\beta}_k)$ is the average Fisher information evaluated at the sample estimate scaled by the sample size T, which is an $O_p(1)$ term. Exponentiating (6.46) and integrating over β_k we get

$$\int p(\beta_k|Z)\pi(\beta_k)d\beta_k$$

$$\approx \int p(\hat{\beta}_k|Z) \exp\left\{-\tfrac{1}{2}(\hat{\beta}_k - \beta_k)'(T\,\mathrm{I}(\hat{\beta}_k))(\hat{\beta}_k - \beta_k)\right\} \pi(\beta_k)d\beta_k$$

$$= p(\hat{\beta}_k|Z) \int \exp\left\{-\tfrac{1}{2}(\hat{\beta}_k - \beta_k)'(T\,\mathrm{I}(\hat{\beta}_k))(\hat{\beta}_k - \beta_k)\right\} \pi(\beta_k)d\beta_k. \qquad (6.47)$$

This approximate result allows the normal distribution to become a conjugate. Setting the prior over the coefficients to $\pi(\beta_k) = 1$ and evaluating the integral in (6.47) yields

$$\int p(\beta_k|Z)\pi(\beta_k)d\beta_k \approx p(\hat{\beta}_k|Z)(2\pi)^{n_k/2}|T\,\mathrm{I}(\hat{\beta}_k)|^{-1/2}.$$

Using this result in the expression for the posterior probability in (6.45), we have

$$\int \pi(M_k, \beta_k)d\beta_k \approx \pi(M_k)\frac{p(\hat{\beta}_k|Z)(2\pi)^{n_k/2}|T\,\mathrm{I}(\hat{\beta}_k)|^{-1/2}}{p_Z(Z)}$$

$$= \pi(M_k)\frac{p(\hat{\beta}_k|Z)(2\pi/T)^{n_k/2}|\mathrm{I}(\hat{\beta}_k)|^{-1/2}}{p_Z(Z)}. \qquad (6.48)$$

Taking logarithms in (6.48),

$$\ln \int \pi(M_k, \beta_k)d\beta_k$$

$$\approx \ln \pi(M_k) - \ln(p_Z(Z)) + \ln(p(\hat{\beta}_k|Z)) + \frac{n_k}{2}\ln(2\pi/T) - \frac{1}{2}\ln|\mathrm{I}(\hat{\beta}_k)|. \qquad (6.49)$$

The logarithm of the marginal distribution of Z is the same for each model and so can be ignored in model rankings. Maximizing (6.49) is therefore the same as minimizing

$$-2\ln \pi(M_k) - 2\ln(p(\hat{\beta}_k|Z)) + n_k \ln(T/2\pi) + \ln|\mathrm{I}(\hat{\beta}_k)|. \qquad (6.50)$$

As the sample size, T, gets large, the first and last terms in (6.50) are bounded and so remain "small" and can be ignored, while the second and third terms get larger.[16]

---

[16] Note that nontrivial priors are required for the first term in equation (6.50) not to dominate.

This suggests choosing the model that minimizes the following criterion:

$$-2\ln(p(\hat{\beta}_k|Z)) + n_k \ln(T), \tag{6.51}$$

or, as is more common in practice, minimizing (6.51) divided by the sample size,

$$\text{BIC}(k) = -2T^{-1}\ln(p(\hat{\beta}_k|Z)) + n_k \ln(T)/T. \tag{6.52}$$

Choosing the model that minimizes the expression in (6.51) or (6.52) is thus equivalent, in large samples, to selecting the model with the highest posterior probability.

6.11.2 Akaike Information Criterion

An alternative approach to model selection is to consider a measure of the distance between the true model and the models in some approximating class. One such distance measure is the Kullback–Leibler distance or entropy. For a true density $p_0(y, x, \beta)$ and an approximating density $p(y, x, \beta_k)$ this is defined as

$$\text{KL}(p_0, p) = E_{p_0}\left[\ln \frac{p_0}{p}\right]$$
$$= E_{p_0} \ln p_0 - E_{p_0} \ln p, \tag{6.53}$$

where E_{p_0} computes the expected value under the true probability. Since the first term is constant across models and depends only on the true model, minimizing the distance between the true and approximating models in (6.53) is equivalent to making the second term as large as possible. The distance can be shown to be nonnegative and is 0 only when $p = p_0$, almost surely. Unfortunately the true density is unknown so we need to find a way of making this idea operational without reducing the problem a great deal.

One approach is to think of all models as being misspecified in the sense that they are underparameterized relative to some unknown true model with parameters, β_K. For each model, β_k is then a subset of β_K, i.e., model M_k has fewer parameters than M_K, $n_k < n_K$. Consider maximum likelihood estimates of β_k, stacked into a $(K \times 1)$ vector $\hat{\beta}_k$ with 0s where a variable is omitted and 1s elsewhere. Once again, we can approximate the log density through a second-order expansion around β_K evaluated at the MLE values:

$$\ln p(\beta_K) \approx \ln p(\hat{\beta}_k) + \tfrac{1}{2}(\beta_K - \hat{\beta}_k)'(T\,\text{I}(\hat{\beta}_k))(\beta_K - \hat{\beta}_k).$$

Multiplying by -2,

$$-2\ln p(\hat{\beta}_k) \approx -2\ln p(\beta_K) + (\beta_K - \hat{\beta}_k)'(T\,\text{I}(\hat{\beta}_k))(\beta_K - \hat{\beta}_k).$$

Ignoring terms that are independent of $\hat{\beta}_k$, the approximation of $-2E_{p_0}\ln p$ based on the MLE values becomes

$$-2E_{p_0}\ln p_k \approx E_{p_0}(\beta_K - \hat{\beta}_k)'(T\,\text{I}(\beta_k))(\beta_K - \hat{\beta}_k). \tag{6.54}$$

Without loss of generality, assume that the coefficients in $\hat{\beta}_k$ appear in the first k rows of β_K. Partition $\beta_K = (\beta_{1k}', \beta_{2k}')$ (along with the information matrix) corresponding to the dimension of the estimated parameters, and partition the information matrix accordingly. We then have[17]

$$E_{p_0}(\beta_K - \hat{\beta}_k)' T \times \mathrm{I}(\beta_k)(\beta_K - \hat{\beta}_k) = E_{p_0}(\beta_{1K} - \hat{\beta}_{1k})' T \, \mathrm{I}_{11}(\hat{\beta}_k)(\beta_{1K} - \hat{\beta}_{1k})$$
$$+ E_{p_0}\beta_{2K}' T \, \mathrm{I}_{22}(\hat{\beta}_k)\beta_{2K}. \tag{6.55}$$

This expression breaks the problem into two pieces, namely the estimated part, which introduces a variance term, and a squared bias term involving the parameters of the true model that are omitted. Dealing with the variance term is relatively simple. This term, scaled appropriately by the information matrix, resembles a Wald statistic:

$$T(\beta_{1K} - \hat{\beta}_{1k})'(T \, \mathrm{I}_{11}(\hat{\beta}_k))(\beta_{1K} - \hat{\beta}_{1k}) \sim \chi^2_{n_k}. \tag{6.56}$$

The expected value of this term is approximately n_k / T.

The squared bias term is simply a nonrandom number that depends on the size of the omitted coefficients, β_{2K}. Akaike's approach is to note that this term resembles a likelihood ratio test $-2\ln(p(\hat{\beta}_k|Z) - p(\hat{\beta}_K|Z))$ testing that the omitted terms are 0 under the alternative, where $p(\hat{\beta}_K|Z)$ is the likelihood based on the full model and so is invariant across different models, k. This test resembles estimating β_{2K} with zero restrictions and so converges to a noncentral χ^2-variable. In sufficiently large samples a test statistic that these parameters equal 0 is distributed as $\chi^2_{n_K - n_k}(\delta)$, where δ is the noncentrality parameter $\beta_{2K}' T \, \mathrm{I}_{22}(\beta_k)\beta_{2K}$. Now $E_{p_0}(-2\ln(p(\hat{\beta}_k|Z) - p(\hat{\beta}_K|Z))) = \delta + (n_K - n_k)$ and hence the noncentrality parameter $\delta = E_{p_0}(-2\ln(p(\hat{\beta}_k|Z) - p(\hat{\beta}_K|Z))) - (n_K - n_k)$. Combining these results, we obtain

$$-2E_{p_0}\ln p \approx E_{p_0}(\beta_K - \hat{\beta}_k)'(T \, \mathrm{I}(\hat{\beta}_k))(\beta_K - \hat{\beta}_k)$$
$$\approx n_k + E_{p_0}(-2\ln p(\hat{\beta}_k|Z) - p(\hat{\beta}_K|Z)) - (n_K - n_k)$$
$$= E_{p_0}(-2\ln p(\hat{\beta}_k|Z)) + 2n_k - (\ln p(\hat{\beta}_K|Z) + n_K). \tag{6.57}$$

When minimizing this criterion, $\ln p(\hat{\beta}_K|Z) + K$ can be ignored since it is the same for each model, and so the AIC seeks to minimize

$$\mathrm{AIC}(k) = E_{p_0}(-2\ln p(\hat{\beta}_k|Z)) + 2n_k. \tag{6.58}$$

The preferred model is that which minimizes the distance between the true density and the model-implied density and thus has the smallest value of $\mathrm{AIC}(k)$ across all models under consideration.

---

[17] Cross products involving expressions such as $E_{p_0}(\beta_{1K} - \hat{\beta}_{1k}) = 0$ drop out.

II
Forecast Methods

7

◇◇

Univariate Linear Prediction Models

When building a forecasting model for an economic variable, the variable's own past time series is often the first thing that comes to mind. Using only this predictor has given rise to a surprisingly successful class of time-series specifications known as autoregressive moving average (ARMA) models. Dating back to the seminal work by Box and Jenkins (1970), these models have become the workhorse of the forecast profession and an extensive literature covers estimation and forecasting with ARMA models. Indeed, ARMA models form the backbone of many commercial forecasts and remain the centerpiece of many applied forecasting courses.

The popularity and success of ARMA models can be explained by several phenomena. First and foremost, these models pose a very minimalist demand on the forecaster's information set. The only information required by these models is the history of the variable of interest, $Z_t = \{Y_1, Y_2, \ldots, Y_{t-1}, Y_t\}$. This information can be used to construct an ARMA forecast even in situations where the forecaster has no real idea of a model for Y and hence does not know which other variables to obtain data on. For example, an inventory manager will often have information on past inventories, but may not have information, let alone a fully specified model, to suggest why there are fluctuations in the demand for a product. Even if a sales model were available, it might be too expensive to collect the data required for estimation of the model's parameters.

Second, because of their minimal information requirements, ARMA forecasts make for an excellent "baseline" against which the forecasts from more complicated methods can be compared. By excluding other variables, ARMA forecasts show how useful the past of a time series is for predicting its future. The value added by using more complicated forecasting methods or including additional predictor variables can then be measured by the extent to which such forecasts reduce the average loss relative to the loss associated with the best ARMA model.

Third, the use of ARMA models is underpinned by theoretical arguments. Specifically, the Wold representation theorem shows that all covariance stationary processes can be represented by a (possibly infinite-order) moving average representation. ARMA models form an exhaustive set for such processes and have certain optimality properties among linear projections of a variable on its own past and past shocks to the series. This result does *not* say that ARMA models are optimal in a global sense. For example, it may be better to use nonlinear transformations of past values of the series in the prediction model or to condition on a wider information set. However, if attention is restricted to linear functions of past values of the series, then it is natural to start with ARMA prediction models.

Fourth, despite—or, maybe because of—their simplicity, ARMA models have proved surprisingly difficult to beat in empirical work. Provided that the lag order of ARMA models is sensibly determined, they rarely produce extreme forecasts and are good at capturing persistence in economic variables through low-order autoregressive or moving average components.

Full expositions of the material covered in this chapter are available in many textbooks, including Brockwell and Davis (1996) at the more technical end and Diebold (2007) at a level that is easier to access. The purpose of this chapter is to provide a brief survey of an area that is part of classical work in forecasting and thus provides foundations for material covered in subsequent chapters, most notably chapter 8 on univariate nonlinear forecasting models and chapter 9 on multivariate forecasting with vector autoregressions.

The chapter proceeds as follows. Section 7.1 offers a brief review of the basic properties of ARMA models. Section 7.2 discusses parameter estimation and lag length selection for these models. Section 7.3 introduces forecasting schemes for ARMA models. Section 7.4 covers extensions to deterministic and seasonal components. Section 7.5 introduces exponential smoothing and unobserved components models and section 7.6 concludes.

7.1 ARMA MODELS AS APPROXIMATIONS

We first introduce some basic concepts from time-series analysis required for understanding the forecasting models. Next, we introduce the basic autoregressive (AR) and moving average (MA) models.

7.1.1 Covariance Stationarity

Consider a time series, or stochastic process, of infinite length, $\{y_t\}_{t=-\infty}^{\infty}$, observed at discrete points in time, t. The mean of y_t, denoted by $\mu_t = E[y_t]$, is assumed to be a deterministic process. A deterministic process is perfectly predictable infinitely far into the future. Examples include a constant term, a linear time trend, or even a sinusoid with known periodicity. Of special interest is the case where μ_t is the same for all values of t:

$$\mu_t = E[y_t] = \mu \quad \text{for all } t.$$

In what follows we simplify matters by assuming that $\mu = 0$. This assumption is without loss of generality since we can just subtract the common (constant) mean from the process if it were not true and study the demeaned series.

For any integer, j, define the autocovariance of the zero-mean process as the unconditional expectation

$$\gamma(j, t) \equiv E[y_t y_{t-j}].$$

Further, assume that this does not depend on t, but only on the distance, j, i.e., $\gamma(j, t) = \gamma(j)$ for all t. Under these conditions the process $\{y_t\}_{t=-\infty}^{\infty}$ is said to be covariance stationary—sometimes called wide sense stationary or second-order stationary.

Covariance stationary processes can be built from white noise. A white noise process has zero unconditional mean, constant variance, and zero autocovariance at all leads and lags:

Definition 7.1. *A stochastic process, ε_t, is called white noise if it has zero mean, constant unconditional variance, and is serially uncorrelated:*

$$E[\varepsilon_t] = 0,$$

$$\text{Var}(\varepsilon_t) = \sigma^2,$$

$$E[\varepsilon_t \varepsilon_s] = 0, \quad \textit{for all } t \neq s.$$

For such processes we write $\varepsilon_t \sim \text{WN}(0, \sigma^2)$. A result known as the Wold representation theorem establishes that any covariance stationary process can be written as an infinite sum of current and past white noise terms—also known as an infinite-order moving average MA(∞)—with weights, θ_i, that are independent of t:

Theorem 7.2 (Wold representation theorem). *Any covariance stationary stochastic process $\{y_t\}$ can be represented as a linear combination of serially uncorrelated white noise terms $\varepsilon_{t-j} \in Z_t$, $j = 0, \ldots, \infty$ and a linearly deterministic component, μ_t:*

$$y_t = \sum_{j=0}^{\infty} \theta_j \varepsilon_{t-j} + \mu_t,$$

where $\{\theta_j\}$ are independent of time and $\sum_{j=0}^{\infty} \theta_j^2 < \infty$.

We sketch a short proof of the representation of the stochastic component in the Wold representation theorem that follows Sargent (1987, pages 285–290). Let ε_t be projection errors from a regression of y_t on its own past values:

$$\varepsilon_t = y_t - \text{Proj}[y_t | y_{t-1}, y_{t-2}, \ldots]. \tag{7.1}$$

Here $\text{Proj}[y_t | y_{t-1}, y_{t-2}, \ldots]$ is the projection value from a linear least squares regression of y_t on past values of y:

$$\text{Proj}[y_t | y_{t-1}, y_{t-2}, \ldots] = \sum_{i=1}^{\infty} \beta_i y_{t-i}, \tag{7.2}$$

and β_i are projection coefficients. From (7.1), ε_t is a linear combination of current and past values of y constructed in such a way that ε_t is orthogonal to all past values of the series $\{y_{t-1}, y_{t-2}, \ldots\}$.

Previous projection errors ε_{t-s} ($s > 0$) can similarly be written as a linear function of past y-values:

$$\varepsilon_{t-s} = y_{t-s} - \text{Proj}[y_{t-s} | y_{t-s-1}, y_{t-s-2}, \ldots].$$

These errors are again linear functions of $y_{t-j}, y_{t-j-1}, \ldots$, and so it follows from the definition of ε_t in (7.1), that $E[\varepsilon_t \varepsilon_{t-s}] = 0$ for all $s \neq 0$, i.e., ε_t is serially uncorrelated.

Projecting the current value, y_t, on $\{\varepsilon_t, \varepsilon_{t-1}, \ldots, \varepsilon_{t-m}\}$, $m > 0$ we get the population forecast

$$\hat{y}_t^m = \sum_{j=0}^{m} \theta_j \varepsilon_{t-j}, \qquad (7.3)$$

where $\theta_j = E[y_t \varepsilon_{t-j}]/E[\varepsilon_t^2]$ because the ε-values are orthogonal to each other. Moreover, the weights θ_j will be constant because of the assumed covariance stationarity of y_t. From (7.1), we have $E[\varepsilon_t^2] = E[y_t \varepsilon_t] - E[\varepsilon_t \, \mathrm{Proj}[y_t | y_{t-1}, y_{t-2}, \ldots, y_{t-m}]] = E[y_t \varepsilon_t] = \sigma^2$ because ε_t is orthogonal to all past values, $y_{t-1}, \ldots, y_{t-m}$. It follows that $\theta_0 = E[y_t \varepsilon_t]/E[\varepsilon_t^2] = 1$ in (7.3) and so the mean squared error is given by

$$E\left[\left(y_t - \sum_{j=0}^{m} \theta_j \varepsilon_{t-j}\right)^2\right] = E[y_t^2] - 2\sum_{j=0}^{m} \theta_j E[y_t \varepsilon_{t-j}] + E\left[\sum_{j=0}^{m} \theta_j^2 \varepsilon_{t-j}^2\right]$$

$$= E[y_t^2] - 2\sigma^2 \sum_{j=0}^{m} \theta_j^2 + \sum_{j=0}^{m} \theta_j^2 \sigma^2$$

$$= E[y_t^2] - \sigma^2 \sum_{j=0}^{m} \theta_j^2 \geq 0.$$

It follows that

$$\sigma^2 \sum_{j=0}^{m} \theta_j^2 \leq E[y_t^2].$$

Letting $m \to \infty$, we have $\sum_{j=0}^{\infty} \theta_j^2 < E[y_t^2] < \infty$, and hence the forecast based on the infinite-order projection in (7.2) converges in mean square.

Note that any nonzero mean is captured by the deterministic component, μ_t. From the definition of white noise it follows that ε_t is not predictable using linear models of past data. Usually $\theta_0 = 1$ is taken as a normalization. The fact that the moving average coefficients θ_i are time invariant will be important for estimating forecasting models. If the parameters changed over time there would be less reason to use past data to forecast the future. The result that $\sum_{j=0}^{\infty} \theta_j^2 < \infty$, tells us that the sum of squared moving average parameters θ_j^2 converges and in practice implies that shocks in the distant past have a limited effect on the current value.

Example 7.1.1 (MA representation of random walk model). *The random walk model has*

$$y_t = y_{t-1} + \varepsilon_t$$

$$= y_0 + \sum_{j=1}^{t} \varepsilon_{t-j},$$

where ε_t is white noise and so $\theta_j = 1$ for all j, $E[y_t] = y_0$ and $\mathrm{Var}(y_t) = t\sigma^2$. Since the variance is not constant and depends on time, t, this process does not satisfy the assumptions for stationarity.

Example 7.1.2 (Break model). *A second example is a model that has a break in the weight on the past innovation:*

$$y_t = \begin{cases} \varepsilon_t + \theta_1 \varepsilon_{t-1} & \text{for } t \leq t_0, \\ \varepsilon_t + \theta_2 \varepsilon_{t-1} & \text{for } t > t_0, \end{cases}$$

where $\theta_1 \neq \theta_2$ and ε_t is white noise. The break in the weight on ε_{t-1} occurs at time t_0 and so covariances depend on t and the assumption of time-invariant weights is violated.

The Wold representation theorem shows that the moving average representation holds apart from a possible deterministic term, μ_t. Conversely, the MA(∞) process captures stochastic movements in y_t.

The Wold representation theorem makes clear the sense in which an MA model captures the entire set of linear models for covariance stationary processes. A practical concern is that the moving average order is potentially infinite. The construction of ε_t as $\varepsilon_t = y_t - \text{Proj}(y_t | y_{t-1}, y_{t-2}, \ldots)$, where $\text{Proj}(\cdot)$ is the linear projection operator, also means that we potentially need data going back to the infinite past. However, as we show below, even a stationary first-order AR model can be inverted to obtain an MA model of infinite order. Hence, a popular modeling strategy is to approximate the general moving average representation implied by the Wold representation with an ARMA(p, q) model where both p and q are of low order. We next turn to such models.

7.1.2 ARMA Models

As suggested by their name, autoregressive models specify Y as a function of its own lags, while moving average models specify Y as a function of an average of past shocks (innovations) to the series. Specifically, an ARMA(p, q) specification for a stationary variable y_t is a model whose highest-order autoregressive term is of pth order while the highest-order moving average term is of qth order so the model takes the following form:[1]

$$y_t = \phi_1 y_{t-1} + \cdots + \phi_p y_{t-p} + \varepsilon_t + \theta_1 \varepsilon_{t-1} + \cdots + \theta_q \varepsilon_{t-q}. \tag{7.4}$$

Equivalently, in power series notation,

$$\phi(L) y_t = \theta(L) \varepsilon_t, \tag{7.5}$$

where the lag polynomials take the form

$$\phi(L) = 1 - \sum_{j=1}^{p} \phi_i L^i, \tag{7.6}$$

$$\theta(L) = \sum_{j=0}^{q} \theta_i L^i, \tag{7.7}$$

---

[1] It is common to use the normalization $\theta_0 = 1$, as we do here.

and L is the lag operator, i.e., $L^j y_t = y_{t-j}$ for positive integers j. The innovation term ε_t in (7.4) or (7.5) is assumed to be a white noise process.

Example 7.1.3 (Forecast errors for the AR(1) model). *Pure AR or MA models arise through simple restrictions on the ARMA parameters in (7.4). The simplest and most common ARMA process is the ARMA(1,0) or AR(1) model which has no moving average terms:*

$$y_t = \phi_1 y_{t-1} + \varepsilon_t, \tag{7.8}$$

or, in lag polynomial notation, $(1 - \phi_1 L)y_t = \varepsilon_t, \theta(L) = 1$.
By backward substitution,

$$y_t = \phi_1 \underbrace{(\phi_1 y_{t-2} + \varepsilon_{t-1})}_{y_{t-1}} + \varepsilon_t = \phi_1^2 y_{t-2} + \varepsilon_t + \phi_1 \varepsilon_{t-1}.$$

Iterating further backwards, we have, for $h \geq 1$,

$$y_t = \phi_1^h y_{t-h} + \sum_{s=0}^{h-1} \phi_1^s \varepsilon_{t-s}$$

$$= \phi_1^h y_{t-h} + \theta(L)\varepsilon_t, \tag{7.9}$$

where the elements of the lag polynomial $\theta(L)$ are $\theta_i = \phi_1^i$. Further iterations result in the order of the polynomial $\theta(L)$ becoming larger and larger and so the AR(1) model is equivalent to an MA(∞) model as long as $\phi_1^k y_{t-k}$ becomes "small" in a mean squared sense. To see what this implies for the AR(1) model, note that

$$E\left[y_t - \sum_{s=0}^{h-1} \phi_1^s \varepsilon_{t-s}\right]^2 = E\left[\phi_1^h y_{t-h}\right]^2 \leq \phi_1^{2h} \gamma_y(0) \to 0 \tag{7.10}$$

as $h \to \infty$, provided that $\phi_1^{2h} \to 0$. This condition is satisfied if $|\phi_1| < 1$ holds. Hence, the AR(1) process has an equivalent MA(∞) representation provided that $\phi_1^{2h} \to 0$, which is thus the stationarity condition for this process.

Example 7.1.4 (AR representation of the MA(1) process). *A second example is the ARMA(0,1) or MA(1) model*

$$y_t = \varepsilon_t + \theta_1 \varepsilon_{t-1}, \tag{7.11}$$

where now $\phi(L) = 1, \theta(L) = 1 + \theta_1 L$. Again we can construct an infinite-order AR process from this MA(1) process. Backwards substitution in (7.11) yields

$$\varepsilon_t = \sum_{s=0}^{h} (-\theta_1)^s y_{t-s} + (-\theta_1)^{h+1} \varepsilon_{t-h-1}. \tag{7.12}$$

Once again, in a mean squared sense y_t becomes equivalent to an AR(h) process with coefficients $\phi_s = (-\theta_1)^s$ provided that $E\left[(-\theta_1)^h \varepsilon_{t-h}\right]$ gets small as h increases. Letting

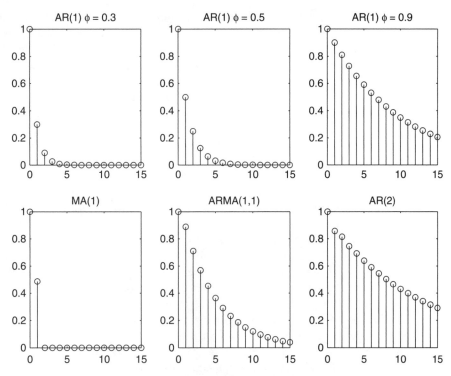

Figure 7.1: Population values of autocorrelations for different ARMA processes.

$h \to \infty$, $E[(-\theta_1)^h \varepsilon_{t-h}]^2 = (-\theta_1)^h \sigma^2 \to 0$ *provided that* $|\theta_1| < 1$. *This condition,* $|\theta_1| < 1$, *is known as invertibility. Hence, an invertible MA(1) process is equivalent to an infinite-order AR process.*

The stationarity condition for the AR(1) process $|\phi_1| < 1$ can be thought of in terms of the roots of the power series for the polynomial $\phi(z) = 1 - \phi_1 z$. The root of this polynomial is ϕ_1^{-1} and so $|\phi_1| < 1$ means that the root is greater than 1. This is a necessary and sufficient condition for stationarity of an AR(1) process. More generally, stationarity of an AR(p) model requires that all roots of the polynomial $\phi(z)$ fall outside the unit circle.[2] The invertibility condition for $\theta(z)$ is similar. For the MA(1) case $|\theta_1| < 1$ is equivalent to the condition that the root of the polynomial $\theta(z) = 1 + \theta_1 z$ is greater than 1. More generally for an MA(q) model the roots of $\theta(z)$ must be outside the unit circle for invertibility to be satisfied. Thus, an ARMA(p, q) process that is stationary and invertible can be written either as an AR model or as an MA model, typically of infinite order. In power series notation, we have either $y_t = \phi(L)^{-1}\theta(L)\varepsilon_t$ or $\theta(L)^{-1}\phi(L)y_t = \varepsilon_t$.

To obtain intuition for the ARMA models, it is useful to consider the autocorrelations for some specific models. Figure 7.1 plots the population autocorrelations, $\gamma(j)$, for AR(1) processes with $\phi_1 = 0.3, 0.5, 0.9$, an MA(1) process with $\theta_1 = 0.8$, an ARMA(1, 1) process with $(\phi_1, \theta_1) = (0.8, 0.5)$, and an AR(2) process with $(\phi_1, \phi_2) = (0.6, 0.3)$. In all cases the autocorrelations taper off as the horizon gets extended. This

[2] The condition that the root of the AR(1) model is greater than 1 is equivalent to the condition for $p > 1$ that all roots lie outside the unit circle since some of these roots may be complex.

is a consequence of stationarity. For stationary processes, as $h \rightarrow \infty$, the forecast $f_{T+h|T} \rightarrow E[y_{T+h}]$ converges to the unconditional mean (assumed to be 0 here) and so the MSE converges to the unconditional variance, $\text{Var}(y_T)$. This mean-reverting property is important to bear in mind when considering the limitations of ARMA forecasts. These models will never generate expected values that are further away from the long-run (steady-state) mean than the current value.

There are large differences in the autocorrelation patterns shown in figure 7.1. Since the autocorrelations of the AR(1) processes are ϕ_1^h, these processes display stronger autocorrelations, the larger is ϕ_1. The autocorrelation of the AR(2) process is quite similar to the AR(1) process with $\phi_1 = 0.9$. Conversely, the MA(1) process has very short memory. Compared with the AR(1) process, the autocorrelations of the ARMA(1,1) process get an extra "bump" in the first-order autocorrelation, but decay exponentially for higher-order autocorrelations.

One way to identify a forecasting model for a given time series is by comparing its autocorrelations with plots of known processes such as those shown in figure 7.1. To illustrate how this works, consider four variables, namely the rate of inflation, stock returns, the unemployment rate, and the three-month T-bill rate, all measured at a quarterly horizon. The inflation rate is defined as $\Delta \log(\text{CPIAUCSL}_{t+1}/\text{CPIAUCSL}_t)$, where CPIAUCSL is the Consumer Price Index for All Urban Consumers: All Items, available from the FRED database maintained by the Federal Reserve Bank of St. Louis. Stock returns are measured as the value-weighted return (including dividends) on stocks traded on the NYSE, AMEX, and NASDAQ exchanges and are obtained from Welch and Goyal (2008). The unemployment rate is taken from FRED. The interest rate is the three-month Treasury Bill rate (secondary market, TB3MS) and is also available from the FRED database. Our data sample runs from 1947Q1 through 2014Q4.

Figure 7.2 provides time-series plots of these four variables, while figure 7.3 shows the sample estimates of their autocorrelations along with standard error bands. The interest rate series in particular, but also the unemployment rate, is highly persistent with autocorrelations that decay very slowly. The inflation rate is modestly persistent with a first-order autocorrelation estimate around 0.6, followed by a gradual decay in higher-order autocorrelations. Unemployment rates and, especially, interest rates have low-order autocorrelations that exceed 0.9 and the autocorrelations of the interest rate series exceed 0.2 even after 40 quarters. Stock returns, on the other hand, are not serially correlated at all with autocorrelations fluctuating around 0 and no systematic patterns in signs or magnitudes.

The Wold representation theorem states that MA(∞) processes can be used to represent the first two moments of any covariance stationary process. In practice, we cannot estimate an infinite set of MA coefficients and so instead use finite order ARMA models. These can be viewed as approximations to such MA(∞) processes. ARMA models are based on linear projections which provide reasonable forecasts of linear processes under MSE loss. AR models are particularly popular in forecasting in part because, for any forecast horizon, $h > 0$, they can be estimated by least squares by projecting Y_{t+h} on $\{Y_{t-j}\}_{j=0}^{\infty}$, regardless of stationarity of the data-generating process. This does not ensure, however, that the coefficients on the AR model remain constant over time, nor does it suggest that a finite-order AR or ARMA approximation is appropriate. This matters since we never observe the infinite past.

Second, the Wold representation theorem establishes that we can write any covariance stationary process as an MA process, possibly of infinite order. ARMA

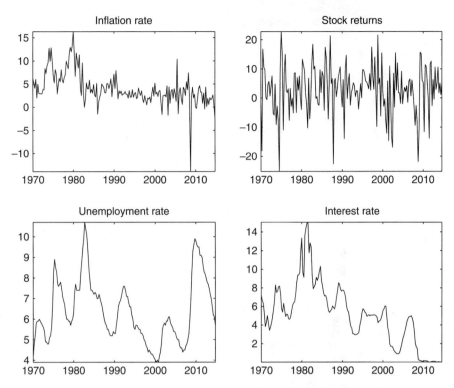

Figure 7.2: Time-series plots of the quarterly inflation rate, stock returns, unemployment rate, and interest rate.

models fill out or exhaust the set of all possible linear models that capture the first two moments (mean and covariances) of a covariance stationary process. Further, from the Wold representation theorem, we are guaranteed that the coefficients on the lagged values of y_t and ε_t are constant. This result, along with their appealing simplicity, suggest that ARMA models will be practically useful for forecasting many economic time series.

None of this excludes the possibility that there is a nonlinear model of past data that provides a better predictor. Under MSE loss the best predictor is the conditional mean, which need not be a linear function of the past. We cover nonlinear models in more detail in chapter 8 but illustrate the point here through a simple example.

Example 7.1.5 (Bilinear process). *Consider the bilinear process studied by Granger and Andersen (1978):*

$$y_{t+1} = \beta \varepsilon_t y_{t-1} + \varepsilon_{t+1}, \quad \varepsilon_{t+1} \sim iid(0, \sigma^2).$$

The autocorrelations of this process are 0 at all lags:

$$E[y_{t+1} y_t] = E[(\beta \varepsilon_t y_{t-1} + \varepsilon_{t+1})(\beta \varepsilon_{t-1} y_{t-2} + \varepsilon_t)]$$

$$= \beta E[\varepsilon_t^2 y_{t-1}] = \beta \sigma^2 E[y_{t-1}] = 0,$$

$$E[y_{t+1} y_{t-1}] = E[(\beta \varepsilon_t y_{t-1} + \varepsilon_{t+1})(\beta \varepsilon_{t-2} y_{t-3} + \varepsilon_{t-1})] = 0.$$

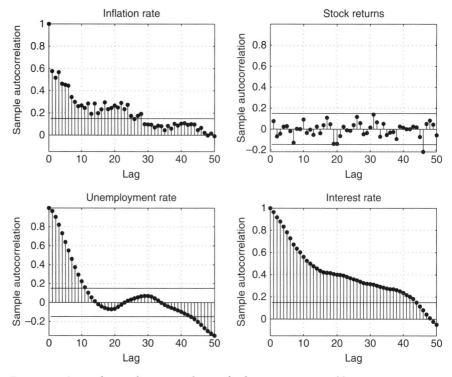

Figure 7.3: Quarterly sample autocorrelations for four economic variables.

Here we used that $E[\varepsilon_t\varepsilon_{t-j}] = 0$ for all $j \neq 0$. This means that the series cannot be predicted by means of linear forecasting models. Assuming that current and past values of y and ε are in the forecaster's information set, so $Z_t = \{y_t, \varepsilon_t, y_{t-1}, \varepsilon_{t-1}, \ldots\}$, however, a nonlinear model will be able to forecast y_{t+1} since

$$E[y_{t+1}|Z_t] = \beta\varepsilon_t y_{t-1}, \qquad (7.13)$$

which is generally nonzero.

7.2 ESTIMATION AND LAG SELECTION FOR ARMA MODELS

The forecasting methods discussed in the previous section assume that the ARMA model and its parameters are known. In practice these need to be estimated from the data. To construct forecasts we require (i) the order of the ARMA(p, q) model; (ii) estimates of the parameters $\phi_1, \ldots, \phi_p, \theta_1, \ldots, \theta_q$; and (iii) estimates of past shocks, $\varepsilon_t, \ldots, \varepsilon_{t-q}$ if $q \geq 1$. This section discusses how to obtain parameter estimates, select the order of the lag polynomials, p, q, and obtain filtered estimates of current and lagged innovations for ARMA(p, q) models.

7.2.1 State-Space Representations of ARMA Models

ARMA models can be estimated using state-space techniques. Writing forecasting models in their state-space representation has a number of advantages. First, if the model has a moving average component, often the state-space form and the Kalman filter provide an easy estimation strategy, i.e., one that is employed in many standard computer packages. Second, the state-space representation provides a convenient representation of the model for constructing multistep forecasts.

The state-space representation of a model consists of two equations, known as the state equation and the measurement equation. The state equation is written in the form of a (typically multivariate) first-order autoregression in "states" ξ_t,

$$\xi_t = F\xi_{t-1} + v_t. \tag{7.14}$$

Similarly, a typical form for the measurement equation is

$$y_t = H\xi_t + w_t, \tag{7.15}$$

where the error terms $(v_t, \omega_t)'$ are white noise and mutually uncorrelated:

$$E\left[\begin{pmatrix} v_t \\ w_t \end{pmatrix} \begin{pmatrix} v_t' & w_t' \end{pmatrix}\right] = \begin{pmatrix} Q & 0 \\ 0 & R \end{pmatrix}.$$

Here y_t denotes observed values while the states ξ_t may or may not be observed. The parameters of the model F, H, Q, and R can be allowed to vary with time. Often either Q or R is 0, which presents no difficulties.

As an example of how ARMA models can be written in state-space form, consider the ARMA(1,1) model,

$$y_t = \rho y_{t-1} + \varepsilon_t + \theta\varepsilon_{t-1}.$$

This model can be written in state-space form as

$$\begin{pmatrix} \xi_{1t} \\ \xi_{2t} \end{pmatrix} = \begin{pmatrix} \rho & 1 \\ 0 & 0 \end{pmatrix} \begin{pmatrix} \xi_{1t-1} \\ \xi_{2t-1} \end{pmatrix} + \begin{pmatrix} 1 \\ \theta \end{pmatrix} \varepsilon_t,$$

$$y_t = \xi_{1t},$$

which yields the ARMA(1,1) model since $\xi_{2t} = \theta\varepsilon_t$ and $y_t = \xi_{1t} = \rho\xi_{1t-1} + \varepsilon_t + \xi_{2t-1} = \rho\xi_{1t-1} + \varepsilon_t + \theta\varepsilon_{t-1}$. The appendix at the end of the book contains additional examples.

When moving average terms are involved $(q > 0)$, plug-in forecasts require estimates of the MA parameters and of the underlying shocks $\{\varepsilon_t\}$. The most common approach is to use maximum likelihood estimation under the assumption of normal errors. Hamilton (1994, chapters 3 and 5) provides an excellent overview of the precise formulas for the likelihood and methods for maximizing it. Typically the Kalman filter is employed to construct the likelihood. Kalman filter recursions also provide estimates of the shocks and the forecast directly from the updating and prediction equations for the state variables, respectively.[3] An appendix shows how the state-space form can be used for constructing maximum likelihood estimates and estimating parameters.

Taking advantage of the first-order recursive structure, state-space representations are useful for forecasting multiple periods ahead. Since $\xi_t = F\xi_{t-1} + v_t$, it follows that $E[\xi_{t+h}|\xi_t] = F^h\xi_t$. Moreover, from (7.15), we have $E[y_{t+h}|\xi_t] = H[\xi_{t+h}|\xi_t] = HF^h\xi_t$. This is often a much simpler approach to computing the forecast than working with the original model.

7.2.2 Choice of Lag Orders

So far we have assumed that the lag orders, p and q, were known. In some financial forecasting problems, appeals to market efficiency may lead one to choose zero lags or a low-order moving average process, to reflect market microstructure effects on the dynamics of security prices. For quarterly data one might want at least four lags to account for a seasonal component. In most situations, forecasters do not have a great deal of knowledge about these parameters, however, other than the broad notion under stationarity that shocks in the distant past have less of an impact on today's value than more recent shocks. This, combined with the finding that estimating a large number of parameters relative to the sample size is likely to result in imprecise estimates, suggests working with parsimonious ARMA models that include relatively few lags.

Different methods can be used to empirically determine the values for p and q or, if noncontiguous lags are considered, which specific lags to include. Box and Jenkins (1970) originally suggested a judgemental approach based on examining the autocorrelations and partial autocorrelations of the data. However, automated methods for lag selection in general specifications are now more commonly used.

A widely used approach is to employ model selection criteria such as those discussed in chapter 6. Each of these defines a family of methods distinguished by its own trade-off between goodness of fit, which improves as more lags get included, versus a penalty term that grows as an increasing number of parameters are used. Varying the choice of ARMA order (p, q) results in different models, and we can define the set of such models as $\{M_k\}_{k=1}^{K}$, where M_k represents model k and the search is conducted over K different combinations of p and q. Define the squared standard deviation of the residuals from model k as $\hat{\sigma}_k^2 = T^{-1}\sum_{\tau=1}^{T}\hat{\varepsilon}_\tau^2$. For linear ARMA specifications, information criteria take the form

$$\text{IC}_k = \ln\hat{\sigma}_k^2 + n_k g(T). \qquad (7.16)$$

Here n_k counts the number of estimated parameters for model k, so $n_k = p_k + q_k$ if there is no constant term, while $n_k = p_k + q_k + 1$ if a constant is included. Here $g(T)$ is a penalty term that is a function of the sample size, T. The objective is to choose a model that minimizes (7.16). As discussed in section 6.3, popular information criteria

---

[3] It is possible to come up with multiple state-space representations for some models. However, the results will be the same up to a normalization.

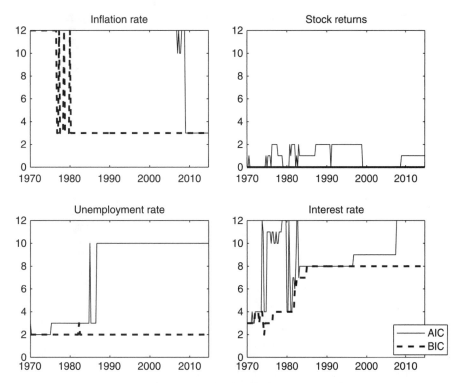

Figure 7.4: Recursive lag length selections for the Akaike and Bayes information criteria (AIC, BIC) applied to AR(p) models with up to 12 autoregressive lags.

routinely reported in regression packages use the following penalty terms:

Criterion	$g(T)$
AIC (Akaike, 1974)	$2T^{-1}$
BIC (Schwarz, 1978)	$\ln(T)/T$
Hannan Quinn (1979)	$2\ln(\ln(T))/T$.

Since the penalty terms differ but the measure of fit, $\hat{\sigma}_k^2$, is the same across the various methods, different information criteria often favor different models. For example, the penalty term for the BIC is greater than that for the AIC provided that $\ln(T) > 2$, which holds whenever the sample size is greater than seven observations. The BIC therefore tends to choose more parsimonious models with fewer parameters than the AIC.

Figure 7.4 shows selection of the lag order for autoregressive models fitted to the four series introduced earlier. To select the lag order we use an expanding estimation window starting in 1970 and ending in 2014. For simplicity we compare only lag orders selected by the AIC and BIC. A maximum of 12 lags is considered, and we assume contiguous lags, i.e., we cannot include lag k without also including lags $1, \ldots, k-1$. For the inflation rate series, the AIC selects 12 lags most of the

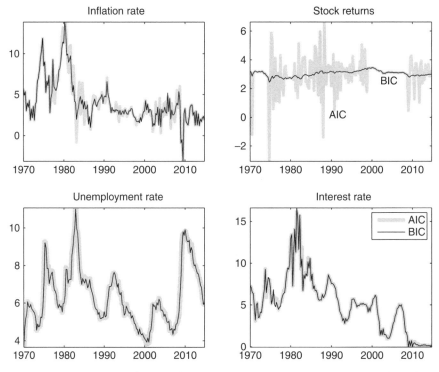

Figure 7.5: Recursive out-of-sample forecasts generated by autoregressive models with lag
length selected by the AIC or BIC.

time, while the BIC selects 3 lags most of the time, at least after 1980. For the less
persistent stock return series, BIC selects no lags, while the AIC selects 1 or 2 lags.
The difference between the lag length selection of the AIC and BIC is even more
pronounced for the unemployment rate series for which the AIC initially selects
2–3 lags, followed by 10 lags after the mideighties. In contrast, the BIC selects only
2 lags most of the time. Finally, for the interest rate series, the lag length selection is
quite unstable during the first decade, albeit with the AIC choosing more lags than
the BIC, only for the two criteria to settle on 12 (AIC) and 8 (BIC) lags towards the
end of the sample.

How important are such differences in lag length selection to forecasting performance? To address this issue, we plot the forecasts from the models selected by
the AIC and BIC in figure 7.5. While there are some minor differences between
the forecasts, the series are clearly very similar, with correlations ranging from
0.27 between the two forecasts of stock returns to 0.95 (inflation rate) and 0.99
(unemployment and interest rate forecasts).

The reason the differences in predicted values are so small, despite large differences in model specification, is that many of the series are highly persistent. For
such variables, neighboring lags y_{t-j} and y_{t-j-1} will be close substitutes. The one
variable considered here for which this is not true—stock returns—is also the variable
for which we observe the greatest difference between the forecasts generated by the
models selected by AIC versus BIC.

7.3 FORECASTING WITH ARMA MODELS

We next cover the classical theory for forecasting with ARMA models. This area is well understood, so we provide only a few key results and formulas which will prove useful in the subsequent analysis. Next, we discuss properties of forecasts using AR models with estimated parameters, direct versus iterated procedures for generating multiperiod forecasts, and forecasts of variables that have unit roots.

7.3.1 Classical Theory of Forecasting with ARMA Models

Simple and well-understood procedures exist for using ARMA models to generate forecasts of future outcomes. Prediction is particularly straightforward for purely autoregressive, AR(p), models, i.e., models without moving average terms:

$$y_{t+1} = \phi_1 y_t + \cdots + \phi_p y_{t-p+1} + \varepsilon_{t+1}, \quad \varepsilon_{t+1} \sim \text{WN}(0, \sigma^2). \tag{7.17}$$

To introduce the mechanics of how ARMA forecasts are generated, we initially treat the parameters as known and thus ignore estimation error. Using that $P[\varepsilon_{t+1}|Z_t] = 0$ and $\{y_{t-p+1}, \ldots, y_t\} \in Z_t$, the linear forecast of y_{t+1} given Z_t becomes

$$f_{t+1|t}(Z_t, \beta) = \phi_1 y_t + \cdots + \phi_p y_{t-p+1}, \tag{7.18}$$

with $\beta = (\phi_1, \ldots, \phi_p)$ and $Z_t = \{y_1, \ldots, y_t\}$. When generating forecasts multiple steps ahead, unknown values of y_{t+i} ($i \geq 1$) can be replaced with their forecasts, $f_{t+i|t}$, setting up a recursive system:

$$f_{t+2|t}(z_t, \beta) = \phi_1 f_{t+1|t}(z_t, \beta) + \phi_2 y_t + \cdots + \phi_p y_{t-p+2},$$

$$f_{t+3|t}(z_t, \beta) = \phi_1 f_{t+2|t}(z_t, \beta) + \phi_2 f_{t+1|t}(z_t, \beta) + \phi_3 y_t + \cdots + \phi_p y_{t-p+3},$$

$$\vdots \tag{7.19}$$

$$f_{t+p+1|t}(z_t, \beta) = \phi_1 f_{t+p|t}(z_t, \beta) + \phi_2 f_{t+p-1|t}(z_t, \beta) + \phi_3 f_{t+p-2|t} + \cdots$$
$$+ \phi_p f_{t+1|t},$$

and so forth, out to f_{t+h}. This "chain rule" provides a computationally simple approach and is equivalent to recursively expressing unknown future values y_{t+i} as functions of y_t and its past. Known values of y affect the forecasts up to horizon $t + p$, while forecasts further ahead depend on forecasts recorded at shorter horizons.

Example 7.3.1 (Forecasts generated by the AR(1) model). *For the AR(1) model* $y_{t+1} = \phi_1 y_t + \varepsilon_{t+1}$, *the chain rule forecasts are*

$$f_{t+1|t}(y_t, \phi_1) = \phi_1 y_t,$$

$$f_{t+2|t}(y_t, \phi_1) = \phi_1^2 y_t,$$

$$\vdots$$

$$f_{t+h|t}(y_t, \phi_1) = \phi_1^h y_t.$$

Next, consider the MA(q) model,

$$y_{t+1} = \varepsilon_{t+1} + \theta_1 \varepsilon_t + \cdots + \theta_q \varepsilon_{t-q+1}. \tag{7.20}$$

Assuming again that $\theta_1, \ldots, \theta_q$ are known and $Z_t = (\varepsilon_t, \varepsilon_{t-1}, \ldots, \varepsilon_0)$, the one-step-ahead forecast becomes

$$f_{t+1|t}(z, \beta) = \theta_1 \varepsilon_t + \cdots + \theta_q \varepsilon_{t-q+1},$$

$$f_{t+2|t}(z, \beta) = \theta_2 \varepsilon_t + \cdots + \theta_q \varepsilon_{t-q+2},$$

$$\vdots$$

$$f_{t+q|t}(z, \beta) = \theta_q \varepsilon_t,$$

$$f_{t+q|t}(z, \beta) = 0.$$

The MA(q) model has limited memory: values of an MA(q) process more than q periods into the future are not predictable. In contrast, whereas the degree of predictability eventually decays for a stationary AR(p) process, there is not the same sharp drop off in predictability for this process.

While the sequence of shocks $\{\varepsilon_t\}$ are not directly observable, they can be computed recursively given the model. Or, depending on the estimation procedure, they can be estimated given a set of assumptions on the initial values for ε_t, $t = 0$, $\ldots, q - 1$.

Example 7.3.2 (Forecasts generated by the MA(1) model). *For the MA(1) model, we can use $\varepsilon_0 = 0$ and set up the recursion*

$$\varepsilon_1 = y_1,$$

$$\varepsilon_2 = y_2 - \theta_1 \varepsilon_1 = y_2 - \theta_1 y_1,$$

$$\varepsilon_3 = y_3 - \theta_1 \varepsilon_2 = y_3 - \theta_1(y_2 - \theta y_1),$$

and so forth. Unobserved shocks can be written entirely as functions of the parameter value, θ_1, and current and past values of y. Simple recursions using past forecasts can also be employed to update the forecasts. This follows since $\varepsilon_t = y_t - P[y_t|Z_{t-1}] = y_t - f_{t|t-1}$. For the MA(1) model we have

$$f_{t+1|t} = \theta_1 \varepsilon_t = \theta_1(y_t - f_{t|t-1}). \tag{7.21}$$

For a general MA(q) process the updating formula again involves only past observations of y and past forecasts.

Next, consider MA processes of infinite order. Using that the MA coefficients are time invariant according to the Wold representation theorem, the infinite-order MA model for y_{t+h} for $h \geq 1$ is

$$
\begin{aligned}
y_{t+h} &= \sum_{i=0}^{\infty} \theta_i \varepsilon_{t+h-i} \\
&= \underbrace{(\varepsilon_{t+h} + \theta_1 \varepsilon_{t+h-1} + \cdots + \theta_{h-1} \varepsilon_{t+1}}_{\text{future shocks}} + \underbrace{\theta_h \varepsilon_t + \theta_{h+1} \varepsilon_{t-1} + \cdots,}_{\text{current and past shocks}}
\end{aligned}
$$

where the last line assumes $h \geq 1$. Using the lack of serial correlation in ε, this allows us to decompose y_{t+h} into predictable and unpredictable parts. Hence if ε_t were observed, the forecast would be

$$
\begin{aligned}
f_{t+h|t}(z_t, \beta) &= \theta_h \varepsilon_t + \theta_{h+1} \varepsilon_{t-1} + \cdots \\
&= \sum_{j=h}^{\infty} \theta_j \varepsilon_{t+h-j}.
\end{aligned} \tag{7.22}
$$

Example 7.3.3 (Wiener–Kolmogorov prediction formulas). *For a process with MA representation $y_t = \theta(L)\varepsilon_t$, the Wiener–Kolmogorov prediction formula for linear projections $P(y_{t+h}|Z_t)$ takes the form*

$$
P(y_{t+h}|Z_t) = \left[\frac{\theta(L)}{L^h}\right]_+ \frac{y_t}{\theta(L)}, \tag{7.23}
$$

where the $[.]_+$ operator excludes negative exponents of the lag operator, L. For example, for the invertible AR(1) model in (7.8), $\theta(L) = (1 - \phi_1 L)^{-1}$, so (7.23) yields

$$
\begin{aligned}
P(y_{t+h}|Z_t) &= \frac{\phi_1^h}{1 - \phi_1 L}(1 - \phi_1 L)y_t \\
&= \phi_1^h y_t.
\end{aligned}
$$

Similarly, for the MA(q) process in (7.20),

$$
\left[\frac{1 + \theta_1 L + \theta_2 L^2 + \cdots + \theta_q L^q}{L^h}\right]_+ = \begin{cases} \sum_{j=h}^{q} \theta_j L^{q-h} & \text{if } h \leq q, \\ 0 & \text{if } h > q, \end{cases}
$$

and so the h-step-ahead linear prediction becomes

$$
P(y_{t+h}|Z_t) = \begin{cases} \sum_{j=h}^{q} \theta_j L^{q-h} \varepsilon_t & \text{if } h \leq q, \\ 0 & \text{if } h > q. \end{cases}
$$

For mixed ARMA(p, q) models

$$
y_{t+1} = \phi_1 y_t + \phi_2 y_{t-1} + \cdots + \phi_p y_{t-p+1} + \varepsilon_{t+1} + \theta_1 \varepsilon_t + \cdots + \theta_q \varepsilon_{t-q+1}, \tag{7.24}
$$

the separate AR and MA prediction steps can be combined by recursively replacing future values of y_{t+i} with their predicted values and setting $E[\varepsilon_{t+j}|Z_t] = 0$ for $j \geq 1$. This works as follows:

$$f_{t+1|t} = \phi_1 y_t + \phi_2 y_{t-1} + \cdots + \phi_p y_{t-p+1} + \theta_1 \varepsilon_t + \cdots + \theta_q \varepsilon_{t-q+1},$$

$$f_{t+2|t} = \phi_1 f_{t+1|t} + \phi_2 y_t + \cdots + \phi_p y_{t-p+2} + \theta_2 \varepsilon_t + \cdots + \theta_q \varepsilon_{t-q+2},$$

$$\vdots \qquad\qquad (7.25)$$

$$f_{t+h|t} = \phi_1 f_{t+h-1|t} + \phi_2 f_{t+h-2|t} + \cdots + \phi_p f_{t-p+h|t} + \theta_h \varepsilon_t + \cdots + \theta_q \varepsilon_{t-q+h},$$

where $f_{t-j+h|t} = y_{t-j+h}$ if $j \geq h$, and $\theta_h = 0$ for $h > q$.

Having characterized the forecasts, we next turn to the forecast errors. By the Wold representation theorem, each stationary ARMA process can be written as an MA process, possibly of infinite order. From (7.22), the forecast error of such a process is

$$y_{t+h} - f_{t+h|t}(z_t, \beta) = \varepsilon_{t+h} + \theta_1 \varepsilon_{t+h-1} + \cdots + \theta_{h-1} \varepsilon_{t+1},$$

and so the mean squared forecast error is

$$E\left[(y_{t+h} - f_{t+h|t}(z_t, \beta))^2\right] = E[\varepsilon_{t+h} + \theta_1 \varepsilon_{t+h-1} + \cdots + \theta_{h-1} \varepsilon_{t+1}]^2$$

$$= \sigma^2 (1 + \theta_1 + \cdots + \theta_{h-1})^2. \qquad (7.26)$$

This can be calculated for various ARMA(p, q) models. The chief difficulty stems from the MA coefficients being nonlinear functions of the original ARMA(p, q) coefficients in (7.26).

Example 7.3.4 (MSE for the AR(1) process). *For the AR(1) model, $\theta_i = \phi_1^i$ and so*

$$E[(y_{t+h} - f_{t+h|t}(z_t, \beta))^2] = \sigma^2 (1 + \theta_1 + \cdots + \theta_{h-1})^2$$

$$= \sigma^2 \sum_{j=0}^{h-1} \phi_1^j$$

$$= \frac{\sigma^2 (1 - \phi_1^{2h})}{1 - \phi_1^2}. \qquad (7.27)$$

This result could as easily have been obtained using the backward recursion in (7.9):

$$f_{t+h|t} = \phi_1^h y_t + \sum_{s=0}^{h-1} \phi_1^s \varepsilon_{t+h-s}.$$

The forecast is $f_{t+h|t}(z_t, \beta) = \phi_1^h y_t$ and the MSE is again $\sigma^2 \sum_{j=0}^{h-1} \phi_1^j = \sigma^2 (1 - \phi_1^{2h})/(1 - \phi_1^2)$. As $h \to \infty$, this converges to $\sigma^2/(1 - \phi_1^2)$ which is the unconditional variance of the process. This makes sense since, at very long horizons, predictions of a stationary AR process are simply the unconditional mean of the process.

7.3.2 Finite-Sample Properties of Forecasts from AR(1) Models

Consider the AR(p) model where p is assumed to be known and greater than 0. Since there are no MA terms ($q = 0$), only p autoregressive parameters have to be estimated. This involves projecting y_t on a fixed number of its own lagged values, all of which are observed, and so lends itself to least squares estimation. The regressor matrix can be constructed by dropping the first p observations. For example, for an AR(1) model we regress the vector $\{y_1, \ldots, y_T\}$ on any deterministic terms and the regressor $\{y_0, \ldots, y_{T-1}\}$, where T is the sample size. Assuming the data are covariance stationary, least squares estimates of the coefficients $\phi_1, \ldots, \phi_p$ are consistent and asymptotically normal.

Provided the model is correctly specified, such estimates are also asymptotically efficient. However, even if the model is correctly specified, least squares estimates do not have optimality properties in finite samples and will be biased (e.g., Kendall (1954), Kendall and Stuart (1961), Marriott and Pope (1954)). For the AR(1) model, the OLS estimate $\hat{\phi}_1$ is biased towards 0. Specifically, Kendall (1954) shows that $\hat{\phi}_1$ has a downward bias of $(1 + 3\phi_1)/T$, so $E[\hat{\phi}_1] = \phi_1 - ((1 + 3\phi_1)/T$ in an AR(1) model with a constant. For higher-order models, the biases are complicated and can go in either direction (e.g., Shaman and Stine (1988)).

This lack of small sample optimality for least squares estimates has led to a number of alternative estimation methods being used, the most popular of which is maximum likelihood estimation.[4] This method differs from least squares in its treatment of the first p observations. These are dropped under least squares estimation but can be considered as draws from their unconditional distributions in the construction of the likelihood for the data.

Regardless of the estimation technique, the estimated parameters are likely to be biased. Forecasters are not, however, interested in properties of the coefficient estimates themselves but rather in the overall forecast error or loss. For example, the forecast error for the AR(1) model is given by

$$y_{t+h} - f_{t+h|t} = \left(\phi_1^h - \hat{\phi}_1^h\right) y_t + \sum_{s=0}^{h-1} \phi_1^s \varepsilon_{t+h-s},$$

where ϕ_1 and $\hat{\phi}_1$ are the true and estimated AR(1) coefficients, respectively. The key observation is that the bias in the parameter estimate $\left(\phi_1^h - \hat{\phi}_1^h\right)$ interacts with the data $\{y_t, y_{t-1}, \ldots, y_1\}$ used to construct the forecast. Interestingly, in a wide range of situations, the forecast errors are unconditionally unbiased, i.e., $E[y_{t+h} - f_{t+h|t}] = 0$, so that a sequence of forecasts are unbiased "on average," i.e., across realizations of a sequence of forecasts, provided that the innovations, ε, have a symmetric distribution.[5] The result is surprising since neither of the estimates, $\hat{\mu}_t$, $\hat{\phi}_t$, is unbiased, but the two biases may cancel out.

In practice, this result may not be of too great interest to forecasters. A forecaster knows precisely which set of data $\{y_t, y_{t-1}, \ldots, y_{t-p}\}$ is employed to construct the forecast and is therefore more likely to be interested in the bias conditional on

---

[4] A second alternative is the Yule–Walker approach which involves method of moments estimation.

[5] This result was shown for the AR(1) model by Malinvaud (1970) and Fuller and Hasza (1980) and for more general models by Dufour (1984).

these values. Unfortunately, forecast errors are generally not conditionally unbiased. Phillips (1979) constructs exact results for the distribution of one-step-ahead ($h = 1$) forecast errors from an AR(1) model estimated by OLS.[6] Consider an AR(1) model without an intercept,

$$y_t = \phi_1 y_{t-1} + \varepsilon_t, \ \varepsilon_t \sim \text{iid}(0, \sigma^2).$$

Phillips shows that the forecast of y_{T+1} conditional on y_T is biased with a bias that depends on ϕ_1 and y_T:

$$E[y_{T+1} - f_{T+1|T}|y_T] = \frac{2\phi_1}{T} y_T + O(T^{-2}).$$

Note that the direction of the bias in the forecast error depends on the sign of y_T, with the bias being positive if the final observation of y is positive, $y_T > 0$. Accounting for the statistical dependence between $\hat{\phi}_{1T}$ and y_T, Phillips characterizes the effect of estimation error on the approximate conditional distribution of the one-period forecast $f_{T+1|T}$ given y_T in a sample with T observations. Let $f^*_{T+1|T} = \phi_1 y_T$ be the infeasible population forecast, i.e., the forecast without estimation error, while $f_{T+1|T} = \hat{\phi}_{1T} y_T$ is the feasible forecast based on the estimated AR(1) coefficient $\hat{\phi}_{1T} = \left(\sum_{\tau=1}^{T} y_{\tau-1}^2\right)^{-1} \left(\sum_{\tau=1}^{T} y_{\tau-1} y_\tau\right)$. Further, let Φ be the normal c.d.f., while Φ' is the normal density. Phillips shows that when $y_T > 0$, as an approximation, the scaled difference between the feasible and infeasible one-step-ahead forecast follows the distribution

$$P(\sqrt{T}(f_{T+1|T} - f^*_{T+1|T}) \leq x|y_T) \tag{7.28}$$

$$= \Phi\left(\frac{x}{y_T\sqrt{1-\phi_1^2}}\right)$$

$$+ \frac{\phi_1}{\sqrt{T(1-\phi_1^2)}} \Phi'\left(\frac{x}{y_T\sqrt{1-\phi_1^2}}\right) \left(2 + \frac{x^2}{y_T^2(1-\phi_1^2)} - \left(\frac{y_T}{\sigma_y}\right)^2\right) + O(T^{-1}),$$

where $\sigma_y = \sigma/\sqrt{1-\phi_1^2}$. When $y_T < 0$,

$$P(\sqrt{T}(f_{T+1|T} - f^*_{T+1|T}) \leq x|y_T) \tag{7.29}$$

$$= \Phi\left(\frac{-x}{y_T\sqrt{1-\phi_1^2}}\right)$$

$$- \frac{\phi}{\sqrt{T(1-\phi_1^2)}} \Phi'\left(\frac{x}{y_T\sqrt{1-\phi_1^2}}\right) \left(2 + \frac{x^2}{y_T^2(1-\phi_1^2)} - \left(\frac{y_T}{\sigma_y}\right)^2\right) + O(T^{-1}).$$

Notice from (7.28) and (7.29) that, assuming $\phi_1 > 0$, the distribution of forecasts has a negative skew when $y_T > 0$, whereas it has a positive skew when $y_T < 0$, so

---

[6] Maekawa (1987) provides asymptotic expansions for h-step-ahead forecast errors and MSE values for an AR(p) model.

that there is a skewness towards the origin (0) which is the mean of the process. The dependence between the least squares estimate of ϕ_1, $\hat{\phi}_{1T} = \sum_{t=1}^{T} y_t y_{t-1} / \sum_{t=1}^{T} y_{t-1}^2$, and y_T deepens the skewness towards the origin that is also present when $\hat{\phi}_{1T}$ is based on data that are independently distributed of y_T.

Phillips (1979) (Theorem 3) also shows that the distribution of the forecast error conditional on y_T can be approximated by

$$P(y_{T+1} - f_{T+1|T} \geq -x|y_T) \tag{7.30}$$

$$= \Phi\left(\frac{x}{\sigma}\right)$$

$$+ \Phi'\left(\frac{x}{\sigma}\right)\left(\frac{1}{T}\left[\frac{\phi_1}{\sqrt{1-\phi_1^2}}\right]\left(\frac{y_T}{\sigma_y}\right)\left(3 - \frac{y_T^2}{\sigma_y^2}\right) - \frac{y_T^2}{2T\sigma_y^2}\left(\frac{x}{\sigma}\right)\right) + O(T^{-2}).$$

Hence, the approximate conditional distribution of the forecast error $y_{T+1} - f_{T+1|T}$ is positively skewed when $y_T > 0$ and negatively skewed when $y_T < 0$. This is consistent with the reverse direction of the skew in $f_{T+1|T}$ discussed above.

7.3.3 Direct versus Iterated Multiperiod Forecasts

In many situations, multiperiod forecasts ($h > 1$) may be of interest and so there is a question of whether an iterated or a direct forecasting approach should be used. Under the iterated approach the forecasting model is estimated at a frequency higher than the forecast horizon and iterated upon to obtain multistep forecasts. For example, monthly data could be used to estimate a model used to provide quarterly forecasts. Under the direct approach, the forecasting model is matched with the desired forecast horizon. Hence, the dependent variable is dated period $t + h$, while all predictor variables are dated period t.

It is common to simply plug in the parameter estimates of the single-period model and iterate forward to the desired horizon using chain rules such as (7.25). For the AR(1) model this entails using the estimated value, $\hat{\phi}_1$, to obtain a forecast $f_{t+1|t} = \hat{\phi}_1 y_t$, $f_{t+2|t} = \hat{\phi}_1^2 y_t$, or, more generally, $f_{t+h|t} = \hat{\phi}_1^h y_t$.

An alternative approach is to estimate the parameters directly by projecting y on information lagged by h or more periods, using the recursively substituted model. Returning to the AR(1) example, by recursive substitution,

$$y_{t+h} = \phi_1^h y_t + \sum_{s=0}^{h-1} \phi_1^s \varepsilon_{t+h-s}.$$

The direct forecasting method entails regressing y_t on y_{t-h} to obtain an estimate of ϕ_1^h, which can then be used to construct the forecast. Note that if overlapping data are used and a model is fitted to every data point, then the error term will follow an MA($h-1$) process even if the underlying innovations ε_t are serially uncorrelated. This can potentially be exploited for efficiency gains in the estimation. Alternatively, if nonoverlapping data are used, i.e., if the data are sampled every h periods, then the errors in this regression are serially uncorrelated provided that ε_t is serially uncorrelated. More generally, for an AR(p) regression model,

$y_t = \sum_{s=1}^{p} \phi_s y_{t-s} + \varepsilon_t$, we have

$$y_{t+h} = \phi_h(L)y_t + \theta_h(L)\varepsilon_{t+h} = \sum_{s=1}^{p} \phi_s^h y_t + \sum_{s=0}^{h-1} \theta_s \varepsilon_{t+h-s}, \qquad (7.31)$$

where $\phi_s^h(L)$ and θ_s are nonlinear functions of the original AR(p) coefficients ϕ_s. Equation (7.31) suggests regressing y_t on $\{y_{t-h}, y_{t-h-1}, \ldots, y_{t-h-p+1}\}$ to directly obtain a forecasting model.[7]

A large theoretical and empirical literature compares the predictive accuracy of the iterated and direct forecasting methods.[8] Theoretical analysis suggests a basic trade-off. When the autoregressive model is correctly specified, the iterated approach makes more efficient use of the data and so tends to produce good forecasts.[9] Conversely, by virtue of being a linear projection, the direct approach tends to be more robust towards misspecification. Which approach performs best will therefore depend on the true data-generating process, the degree of model misspecification, both of which are unknown, as well as on the extent of parameter estimation error which reflects the sample size. Iterating on the parameters to obtain a multistep forecast generally leads to good forecasts when the model is not grossly misspecified. However, when the model is misspecified, iteration on the misspecified model can exacerbate biases and may result in a larger MSE, although the effects appear to be small in the Monte Carlo study in Bhansali (2002). Empirical evidence presented in Marcellino, Stock, and Watson (2006) suggests that the iterated approach typically works best across a range of variables and improves at longer horizons, although the results can depend on how the lag length of the AR polynomial is selected.

7.3.4 Forecasting Variables with Unit Roots

This chapter focuses on stationary ARMA processes, but we briefly explain how to proceed if not all of the roots of the autoregressive polynomial $\phi(L)$ fall outside the unit circle. The most common case is when one or more of the roots equals unity, while the remaining roots fall outside the unit circle. Suppose that d roots of $\phi(L)$ lie on the unit circle for some integer d while the remaining ones lie outside the unit circle and consider the factorization $\phi(L) = \tilde{\phi}(L)(1-L)^d$. Factoring the polynomial in this way, $\phi(L)y_t = \theta(L)\varepsilon_t$ can be written as $\tilde{\phi}(L)\tilde{y}_t = \theta(L)\varepsilon_t$, where $\tilde{y}_t = (1-L)^d y_t$ is called the dth difference of y_t. By assumption, the roots of $\tilde{\phi}(L)$ lie outside the unit circle so the differenced process, $\tilde{y}_t$, will be stationary and can be studied instead of y_t. This is known as differencing y_t to stationarity and is a commonly applied method. Processes with $d \neq 0$ need to be differenced to achieve stationarity and are called ARIMA(p, d, q) processes, where the "I" stands for "integrated," i.e., the opposite of differencing. There are many practical difficulties involved with determining d as well as with handling the discreteness of the properties of the model as the roots move from being close to 1 to being equal to 1. These are addressed more generally in chapter 20.

---

[7] This approach is discussed by Shibata (1980).

[8] A review of the theoretical results is available in Bhansali (2002).

[9] This is only true if the direct approach does not make use of the correlation in the partially overlapping forecast errors in estimating the covariance matrix of the forecast errors. Exploring this information will, however, lead to a highly nonlinear estimation problem.

The common practice of transforming variables by differencing them a suitable number of times to ensure that they are stationary is important for estimation and model selection. Forecasts of the differenced variables can then be transformed back to levels and compared to outcomes in levels, if desired. We briefly illustrate how this works.

Suppose we are interested in forecasting the future level of y, denoted y_{t+h}, but that y may be integrated of first or second order, which we denote by I(1) or I(2), so that Δy_t is stationary if y is I(1), while $\Delta^2 y$ is stationary if y is I(2). When y is I(1), we model the first-differenced series and so predict $\Delta y_{t+h} = y_{t+h} - y_{t+h-1}$. We denote this forecast by $\Delta f_{t+h|t}$. When y is I(2), we model the second-differenced series and so predict $\Delta^2 y_{t+h} = (y_{t+h} - y_{t+h-1}) - (y_{t+h-1} - y_{t+h-2}) = y_{t+h} - 2y_{t+h-1} + y_{t+h-2}$. We denote this forecast by $\Delta^2 f_{t+h|t}$.

Forecasts of the level of y_{t+h} can be constructed from the forecast of y_{t+h}, Δy_{t+h}, and $\Delta^2 y_{t+h}$ as follows:

$$
f_{t+h|t} = \begin{cases}
f_{t+h|t} & \text{if } y_t \text{ is I(0),} \\
y_t + \sum_{i=1}^{h} \Delta f_{t+i|t} & \text{if } y_t \text{ is I(1),} \\
y_t + h\Delta y_t + \sum_{i=1}^{h} \sum_{j=1}^{i} \Delta^2 f_{t+j|t} & \text{if } y_t \text{ is I(2).}
\end{cases}
$$

7.4 DETERMINISTIC AND SEASONAL COMPONENTS

Many economic time series follow a seasonal pattern. For example, retail sales, employment numbers, and housing starts are linked to weather patterns and holidays as workers are temporarily laid off due to bad weather or hired because of busier seasons in retail and services. It is common to filter out the seasonal component and report economic activity numbers on a seasonally adjusted basis. However, the raw, unfiltered number can be of separate interest, in which case a good prediction model must account for seasonal variation.[10]

7.4.1 Forecasting Models with Seasonal Components

Seasonal patterns can be modeled either as deterministic or stochastic variations, or some combination thereof. The stochastic modeling approach uses differencing to incorporate seasonal components. Intuition for this is that if a variable varies strongly at the seasonal frequency, one way to model its dynamics is to consider year-on-year changes in the variable. For example, corporate earnings or dividends are often compared with the figure in the same quarter during the previous year.

Box and Jenkins (1970) considered seasonal ARIMA, or SARIMA, models of the form

$$
\phi(L)(1 - L^S)y_t = \theta(L)\varepsilon_t. \tag{7.32}
$$

Here S denotes the seasonal frequency. With quarterly data, $S = 4$, with monthly data $S = 12$, with weekly data $S = 52$, and so forth, so that applying the seasonal differencing operator $(1 - L^S)$ means that the dynamics in year-on-year changes are

---

[10] See Hylleberg (1992) for a comprehensive treatment of seasonal modeling techniques in economics and Ghysels, Osborn, and Rodrigues (2006) for their use in forecasting.

being modeled in (7.32). Other than this, the mechanics of computing forecasts does not change.

Another way to write seasonal models is to convert the linear time indicator $t = 1, \ldots, T$ into a seasonal indicator such as 2000:01, 2000:02, ..., 2000:04, 2001:01, etc., in the quarterly case:

$$\phi(L)(1 - L^S)y_{S\tau+s} = \theta(L)\varepsilon_{S\tau+s}. \tag{7.33}$$

Here $\tau = 0, \ldots, T - 1$ counts years, while $s = 1, \ldots, S$ counts seasons, and $t = S\tau + s$. For example, if $S = 4$, corresponding to quarterly data, and $s = 1$, then as τ varies from $0, 1, 2, \ldots, T - 1$, first-quarter observations $y_1, y_5, y_9, \ldots, y_{(T-1)S+1}$ are selected.

The model in (7.32) has a unit root, but the year-on-year changes will be stationary provided that the roots of $\phi(L)$ lie outside the unit circle and the sum of squared coefficients of $\theta(L)$ is bounded. The autoregressive polynomial $\phi(L)$ could have additional unit roots, although this is usually found only empirically in strongly trending series. For example, the so-called airline model of Box and Jenkins (1970) takes the form

$$(1 - L)(1 - L^S)y_t = (1 - \theta_1 L)(1 - \theta_S L^S)\varepsilon_t. \tag{7.34}$$

This model allows for seasonal variation in both the AR and the MA part.

Deterministic seasonal components can easily be incorporated by assuming that once a seasonal deterministic component, $\mu_{S\tau+s}$, has been taken out of $y_{S\tau+s}$, the remaining stochastic component $\tilde{y}_{S\tau+s} = y_{S\tau+s} - \mu_{S\tau+s}$, follows an ARMA process:

$$y_t = \mu_t + \tilde{y}_t,$$
$$\phi(L)\tilde{y}_t = \theta(L)\varepsilon_t, \tag{7.35}$$

where $\varepsilon_t \sim \text{WN}(0, \sigma^2)$. The simplest approach for modeling seasonal variation in the mean, μ_t, is to apply S seasonal dummies, each of which equals 1 in season s and is 0 otherwise:

$$D_{1t} = \begin{cases} 1 & \text{if } s = 1 \text{ at time } t, \\ 0 & \text{otherwise.} \end{cases}$$

For example, with quarterly data there will be four seasonal dummies of the form (assuming the initial point occurs in the first quarter)

$$D_{1t} = \begin{pmatrix} 1 & 0 & 0 & 0 & 1 & 0 & 0 & 0 & 1 & 0 & 0 & 0 \end{pmatrix},$$
$$D_{2t} = \begin{pmatrix} 0 & 1 & 0 & 0 & 0 & 1 & 0 & 0 & 0 & 1 & 0 & 0 \end{pmatrix},$$
$$D_{3t} = \begin{pmatrix} 0 & 0 & 1 & 0 & 0 & 0 & 1 & 0 & 0 & 0 & 1 & 0 \end{pmatrix},$$
$$D_{4t} = \begin{pmatrix} 0 & 0 & 0 & 1 & 0 & 0 & 0 & 1 & 0 & 0 & 0 & 1 \end{pmatrix}.$$

The ARMA model with seasonal dummies takes the form

$$\phi(L)\left(y_t - \sum_{s=1}^{S} \delta_s D_{st}\right) = \theta(L)\varepsilon_t. \qquad (7.36)$$

Application of such seasonal dummies can sometimes yield large improvements in predictive accuracy.

Seasonal patterns are examples of regularly occurring patterns linked to the calendar. These can induce patterns in the mean or volatility of the distribution of economic variables such as volume on the stock exchange during the day (volume tends to be highest during the first and last few minutes of the day), credit card transactions, road congestion, and energy usage.

Example 7.4.1 (Modeling seasonal components). *Day-of-the-week dummies, month-of-the-year dummies, and dummies for holidays tend to be very important when modeling electricity demand. Following Diebold (2007), this suggests a deterministic component of the form*

$$\mu_t = \sum_{\text{day}=1}^{7} \beta_{\text{day}} D_{\text{day},t} + \sum_{\text{holiday}=1}^{H} \beta_{\text{holiday}} D_{\text{holiday},t} + \sum_{\text{month}=1}^{12} \beta_{\text{month}} D_{\text{month},t}, \qquad (7.37)$$

where H is the number of holidays. Holiday dummies could include a Christmas dummy that equals 1 on December 25, otherwise is 0, a Thanksgiving dummy that equals 1 on Thanksgiving, otherwise equals 0, etc. Such dummies can be used to capture the typical (average) electricity consumption on a given day. We have included daily and monthly dummies in addition to a holiday dummy since electricity consumption typically is very different on public holidays such as Christmas or Thanksgiving. Interaction terms such as $\sum_{\text{day}=1}^{7} \beta_{\text{day,holiday}} D_{\text{day},t} D_{\text{holiday},t}$ can also be included to account for differences in electricity consumption patterns for holidays occurring on different weekdays. Subtracting the deterministic seasonal term from the ARMA model, future demand at time $t+h$ can be predicted using a model of the form

$$\phi(L)(y_{t+h} - \mu_{t+h}) = \theta(L)\varepsilon_{t+h}, \qquad (7.38)$$

so that the deseasonalized component $y_{t+h} - \mu_{t+h}$ follows an ARMA process. Assuming that we have estimates of $\{\beta_{\text{day}}, \beta_{\text{holiday}}, \beta_{\text{month}}\}$, it is straightforward to compute an estimate of the deterministic component of y_{t+h}. This can then be added to the ARMA forecast of $\tilde{y}_{t+h}$ given the available information at time t. See Diebold (2007) and Ghysels, Osborn, and Rodrigues (2006) for further discussion of forecasting models with seasonal components.

7.4.2 Deterministic Time Trends

Sometimes a deterministic trend component is used to predict the level of a variable. For example, linear, quadratic, and exponential trends take the forms

$$\mu_t = \mu_0 + \beta_0 t,$$

$$\mu_t = \mu_0 + \beta_0 t + \beta_1 t^2, \tag{7.39}$$

$$\mu_t = \exp(\mu_0 + \beta_0 t).$$

These are global trends and so are unlikely to provide accurate descriptions of the future value of most time series at long forecast horizons. Even if a variable's past can be well approximated by one of these trend models, it is common to find that the dynamics changes as the variable reaches a saturation point or other dynamics start to dominate at future points in time.

7.4.3 Holt–Winters Procedure

The Holt–Winters procedure is commonly used to forecast time series that could contain both a deterministic trend and a seasonal component. The additive version of this approach models the outcome variable as the sum of a local mean, a seasonal factor, and an error term. The multiplicative version factors the outcome into the product of a local mean, and a seasonal component and adds an error term. In both cases the local mean at time t is updated from the the local mean at time $t-1$ plus a local trend.

Following Chatfield (1978), let m_t be an estimate of the deseasonalized local mean at time t, while seas_t is an estimate of the seasonal component at time t, and trend_t is the estimated trend term for period t (the amount by which the deseasonalized mean is expected to change from $t-1$ to t). Here S is again the seasonal frequency, i.e., 4 for quarterly data, 12 for monthly data, etc. Given a set of estimates for period $t-1$, m_{t-1}, seas_{t-1}, trend_{t-1}, the updating equations for the multiplicative Holt–Winters procedure take the form

$$m_t = \alpha \frac{y_t}{\text{seas}_{t-S}} + (1-\alpha)(m_{t-1} + \text{trend}_{t-1}),$$

$$\text{seas}_t = \beta \frac{y_t}{m_t} + (1-\beta)\text{seas}_{t-S}, \tag{7.40}$$

$$\text{trend}_t = \gamma(m_t - m_{t-1}) + (1-\gamma)\text{trend}_{t-1}.$$

Here α, β, γ are a set of smoothing coefficients that can either be estimated or set in advance. Multistep forecasts from this model can now be generated from (7.40) as (for $h = 1, 2, \ldots$)

$$f_{t+h|t} = (m_t + h \times \text{trend}_t)\text{seas}_{t+h-S}. \tag{7.41}$$

The additive Holt–Winters model leaves the trend equation unchanged, but alters the first two equations to

$$m_t = \alpha(y_t - \text{seas}_{t-S}) + (1-\alpha)(m_{t-1} + \text{trend}_{t-1}),$$

$$\text{seas}_t = \beta(y_t - m_t) + (1-\beta)\text{seas}_{t-S}, \tag{7.42}$$

with forecasts generated as

$$f_{t+h|t} = m_t + h \times \text{trend}_t + \text{seas}_{t+h-s}. \tag{7.43}$$

How well this method works will of course depend on the extent to which the assumed form of the trend and seasonality is aligned with the data and also on how well the smoothing parameters α, β, γ can be estimated. See Chatfield (1978) for further discussion.

7.5 EXPONENTIAL SMOOTHING AND UNOBSERVED COMPONENTS

Exponential smoothing methods provide an alternative approach to ARMA models for predicting a variable using only its own past values. These methods are essentially automated rules for updating forecasts based on the arrival of a new observation and a forecast error each period. The simplest and most common example of such an updating rule is

$$f_{t+1|t} = f_{t|t-1} + (1-\delta)(y_t - f_{t|t-1}), \tag{7.44}$$

where $0 < \delta < 1$ is a constant and the process is initialized at f_0. Here the previous forecast, $f_{t|t-1}$, is updated with some portion $(1-\delta)$ of the previous period's forecast error, $e_{t|t-1} = y_t - f_{t|t-1}$. For a book length examination of forecasting with exponential smoothing, see Hyndman et al. (2008).

7.5.1 Exponentially Weighted Moving Average

The exponentially weighted moving average (EWMA) model computes a moving average of y_t using exponentially declining weights over the entire history of the data. The forecast, or "trend," is

$$f_{t+1|t} = \frac{(1-\delta)}{(1-\delta^t)} \sum_{s=0}^{t-1} \delta^s y_{t-s}. \tag{7.45}$$

We can motivate this as a weighted average, $f_{t+1|t} = c_t \sum_{s=0}^{t-1} \delta^s y_{t-s}$, where the scaling factor c_t is chosen to ensure that the weights sum to 1 (Abraham and Ledolter, 1983). The sequence of forecasts $\{f_{t+1|t}\}$ is $\{y_1, (1+\delta)^{-1}(y_2 + \delta y_1), (1+\delta+\delta^2)^{-1}(y_3 + \delta y_2 + \delta^2 y_1, \ldots), \ldots\}$.

The EWMA model in (7.45) relates to the simple smoothing method (7.44) in the sense that they are equivalent in the limit as $t \to \infty$.[11] To see this, note that

$$f_{t+1|t} - \delta f_{t|t-1} = \frac{(1-\delta)}{(1-\delta^t)} \sum_{s=0}^{t-1} \delta^s y_{t-s} - \frac{(1-\delta)}{(1-\delta^{t-1})} \delta \sum_{s=0}^{t-2} \delta^s y_{t-1-s} \tag{7.46}$$

$$= \frac{(1-\delta)}{(1-\delta^t)} y_t + \left(\frac{(1-\delta)}{(1-\delta^t)} - \frac{(1-\delta)}{(1-\delta^{t-1})} \right) \sum_{s=1}^{t-1} \delta^s y_{t-s}.$$

[11] See Fan, Farmen, and Gijbels (1998) for a discussion of exponentially weighted estimators and local maximum likelihood estimation.

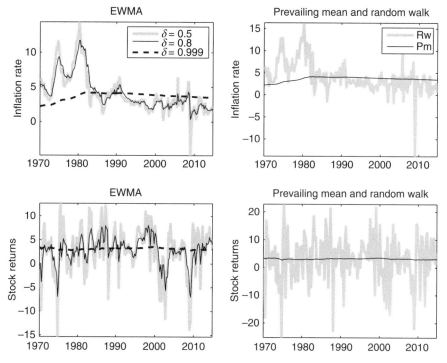

Figure 7.6: Forecasts of the inflation rate and stock returns generated by exponentially weighted moving average (EWMA) models with different smoothing factors (δ).

Since $0 < \delta < 1$, $\lim_{j \to \infty} \delta^j = 0$, and so we have, approximately,

$$f_{t+1|t} - \delta f_{t|t-1} = (1 - \delta) y_t,$$

which is identical to (7.44).

Figure 7.6 shows forecasts of the quarterly rate of inflation and quarterly stock returns generated by three EWMA models with $\delta = 0.5, 0.8$, and 0.999. The bigger is δ, the smoother the forecast as the weights are spread out more evenly on past observations. In fact, comparing these forecasts with the random walk forecast ($f_{t+1|t} = y_t$) and the prevailing mean ($f_{t+1|t} = t^{-1} \sum_{\tau=1}^{t} y_\tau$) shown in the right window of the figure, it is clear that the EWMA forecasts get increasingly similar to a random walk forecast, the smaller is δ, while the EWMA forecasts increasingly resemble the prevailing mean forecast, the closer is δ to unity.[12] Given the importance of δ to the forecast, one might use methods such as cross validation to select this parameter optimally, i.e., to generate the smallest average loss, given the loss function. We consider this in an empirical application in chapter 8.

---

[12] RiskMetrics, a product of J.P. Morgan, uses an exponentially weighted moving average model to estimate volatility. Here the idea is that volatility is unobserved, but can be proxied by squared changes in returns which play the role of Y_t.

7.5.2 Discounted Least Squares

Brown (1962) considered the discounted least squares loss function,

$$L(y_1, \ldots, y_t, \mu) = \sum_{s=0}^{t-1} \delta^s (y_{t-s} - \mu)^2,$$

as an estimator for the mean of a series. The first-order condition for μ, computed at time t, is

$$\sum_{s=0}^{t-1} \delta^s (y_{t-s} - \hat{\mu}) = 0,$$

which can be rearranged to give

$$\hat{\mu} = \left(\sum_{s=0}^{t-1} \delta^s \right)^{-1} \sum_{s=0}^{t-1} \delta^s y_{t-s}$$

$$= \frac{(1-\delta)}{(1-\delta^t)} \sum_{s=0}^{t-1} \delta^s y_{t-s}.$$

This is identical to the EWMA model in (7.45).

Hence the discounted least squares path for the means (which can be employed as the forecasts) is the same as that for the EWMA and hence approximately the same as the simple updating formula (7.44).

7.5.3 Unobserved Components

The unobserved components model consists of two equations,

$$y_t = \xi_t + \varepsilon_t,$$
$$\xi_t = \xi_{t-1} + v_t, \qquad (7.47)$$

where the process is initialized by ξ_0. The idea is that the observed process, y_t, is a noisy version of the process of interest, ξ_t. In this sense the unobserved sequence $\{\xi_t\}$ can be seen as a smoothed version of the data y_t.

From a forecasting perspective we are interested in predicting ξ_{T+1} given the observed data $\{y_t\}_{t=1}^T$. It is typically assumed that the innovations are serially uncorrelated and

$$\begin{pmatrix} \varepsilon_t \\ v_t \end{pmatrix} \sim N \left[\begin{pmatrix} 0 \\ 0 \end{pmatrix}, \begin{pmatrix} \sigma^2 & 0 \\ 0 & \tau^2 \end{pmatrix} \right], \qquad (7.48)$$

where the lack of contemporaneous correlation between the innovations is imposed for identification. The normality assumption in (7.48) makes it easy to write down the likelihood function used in estimation of the model.

Typically estimates of the model in (7.47)–(7.48) employ the Kalman filter (Kalman, 1960). The appendix explains the Kalman filter equations and operation. The Kalman filter was introduced for engineering applications and has subsequently found great use in many situations. For normally distributed variables it can be used to write down a likelihood function, or more generally a pseudo likelihood. Many models can be rewritten in the state-space form required by this method, but the approach is particularly convenient for estimating ARMA models with a nontrivial MA component.

The unobserved components model is in state-space form (see the appendix for the equations of the filter). Define $\xi_{t|t-1}$ and $\xi_{t|t}$ as the best prediction of ξ_t given information at time $t-1$ and t, respectively; define $y_{t|t-1}$ and $y_{t|t}$ correspondingly, and let $P_{t|t-1} = E[(\xi_t - \xi_{t|t-1})(\xi_t - \xi_{t|t-1})']$, $G_{t|t-1} = E[(y_t - y_{t|t-1})(y_t - y_{t|t-1})']$ be MSE matrices. Then we can write the updating equation for the unobserved "mean" ξ_t as

$$\xi_{t|t} = \xi_{t|t-1} + P_{t|t-1} G_{t|t-1}^{-1} (y_t - y_{t|t-1})$$

$$= \xi_{t-1|t-1} + P_{t|t-1} G_{t|t-1}^{-1} (y_t - \xi_{t-1|t-1}). \qquad (7.49)$$

This again simplifies to (7.44) if $P_{t|t-1} G_{t|t-1}^{-1} = 1 - \delta$. Moreover, for the unobserved components model we have

$$P_{t|t-1} G_{t|t-1}^{-1} = \frac{P_{t-1|t-1} + \tau^2}{P_{t-1|t-1} + \tau^2 + \sigma^2}. \qquad (7.50)$$

This is simply $\delta = \sigma^2/(\tau^2 + \sigma^2)$ when the variances are not time varying for a filter with $P_{t-1|t-1}$ set to 0. This gives another insight into the choice of (or method for estimating) the discount parameter δ. When there is little variation in the mean relative to the variation in the observed data (so τ^2 is small relative to σ^2), δ will be large and it becomes optimal to put more weight on "old" data that remains relevant for estimating the mean. When variation in the innovations to the unobserved mean is large relative to σ^2, δ will be closer to 0.

7.5.4 Equivalence with ARMA Models

Exponential smoothing models have been shown to be equivalent to a restricted class of ARMA models (Abraham and Ledolter, 1983). Suppose the data have been differenced to obtain a covariance stationary process. Then we know from the Wold representation theorem that there exists a linear MA model for the data. Since exponential smoothing rules are also linear, it seems reasonable to expect the two representations to be related.

An example is the unobserved components model in (7.47). Consider the change in Y_t, i.e.,

$$\Delta Y_t \equiv (1 - L)Y_t = (1 - L)\mu_t + (1 - L)\varepsilon_t$$

$$= v_t + \varepsilon_t - \varepsilon_{t-1}. \qquad (7.51)$$

To find the equivalent MA representation, consider the autocorrelation function for ΔY_t:

$$\gamma(0) = E[\Delta Y_t]^2 = E[(v_t + \varepsilon_t - \varepsilon_{t-1})^2] = \sigma_v^2 + 2\sigma_\varepsilon^2,$$

$$\gamma(1) = E[\Delta Y_t \Delta Y_{t-1}] = E[(v_t + \varepsilon_t - \varepsilon_{t-1})(v_{t-1} + \varepsilon_t - \varepsilon_{t-1})] = -\sigma_\varepsilon^2,$$

$$\gamma(k) = 0 \quad \text{for } k \geq 2.$$

Next consider an ARIMA(0,1,1) model for Y_t,

$$(1 - L)y_t = \eta_t + \theta\eta_{t-1} \equiv \eta_t - \tilde{\theta}\eta_{t-1}, \tag{7.52}$$

where $\tilde{\theta} = -\theta$. The variance and covariances of ΔY_t are given by

$$\gamma(0) = \sigma_\eta^2(1 + \theta^2),$$

$$\gamma(1) = -\tilde{\theta}\sigma_\eta^2,$$

$$\gamma(k) = 0 \quad \text{for } k \geq 2.$$

Hence if $\sigma_\eta^2(1 + \tilde{\theta}^2) = (\sigma_v^2 + 2\sigma_\varepsilon^2)$ and $\sigma_\eta^2\tilde{\theta} = \sigma_\varepsilon^2$, the two representations will be identical.[13] To see this, write the ARIMA(0,1,1) model in (7.52) as an infinite AR recursion:

$$\eta_t = \sum_{j=0}^{\infty} \tilde{\theta}^j (y_{t-j} - y_{t-j-1})$$

$$= y_t - (1 - \tilde{\theta}) \sum_{j=1}^{\infty} \tilde{\theta}^{j-1} y_{t-j}.$$

Rearranging, we can express the forecast as an infinite sum of the past:

$$f_{t+1|t} = (1 - \tilde{\theta}) \sum_{j=1}^{\infty} \tilde{\theta}^{j-1} y_{t+1-j}.$$

Noting that we can write

$$f_{t+1|t} = (1 - \tilde{\theta})[y_t + \tilde{\theta}y_{t-1} + \tilde{\theta}^2 y_{t-2} + \cdots],$$

$$\tilde{\theta} f_{t|t-1} = (1 - \tilde{\theta})[\quad \tilde{\theta}y_{t-1} + \tilde{\theta}^2 y_{t-2} + \cdots],$$

it follows that

$$f_{t+1|t} - \tilde{\theta} f_{t|t-1} = (1 - \tilde{\theta})y_t,$$

---

[13] See Fan and Yao (2003) for an alternative explanation.

or, after rearranging,

$$f_{t+1|t} = f_{t|t-1} + (1 - \tilde{\theta})(y_t - f_{t|t-1}),$$

which is the same as the exponential smoothing model with $\delta = \tilde{\theta}$. Hence, the choice of the smoothing parameter, δ, is directly related to the MA coefficient, $\tilde{\theta}$, which is suggestive of a method for estimating the smoothing coefficient.

7.5.5 Extensions of the Exponential Smoother

The ARIMA, unobserved component, and exponential smoothing methods described above are equivalent in the sense that they model time variation in the mean $y_t = \mu_t + \varepsilon_t$ and attempt to predict μ_{t+1} given information at time t. This turns out to be equivalent to parameterizing the mean as is done in the unobserved components model. Alternatively, we could construct a more complicated model for the forecast. Suppose such a model is

$$y_t = \mu_t + \beta_t' x_t + \varepsilon_t, \tag{7.53}$$

for a known p-dimensional vector of predictors, x_t, and a p-dimensional vector of time-varying coefficients, β_t. This setup generalizes the earlier methods. Most filtering methods set x_t to be some nonstochastic process. Examples include

a. double exponential smoothing models, $x_t = t$;
b. triple exponential smoothing models, $x_t = (t, t^2/2)'$;
c. trigonometric models, $x_t = (\sin(2\pi t/S), \cos(2\pi t/S))'$, where S is the number of observations in a cycle ($S = 4$ for quarterly data, $S = 12$ for monthly data, etc.).

In each case, discounted least squares can be used to obtain estimates for μ_t and β_t and hence generate the forecast $f_{t+1|t} = \mu_{t+1|t} + \beta_{t+1|t}(t + 1)$. The updating equations that use the discount factor δ for the coefficients are

$$\mu_{t+1|t} = (1 - \delta^2) \sum_{j=0}^{t} \delta^j y_{t-j} - (1 - \delta)^2 \sum_{j=0}^{t} \delta^j j y_{t-j},$$

$$\beta_{t+1|t} = (1 - \delta)^2 \sum_{j=0}^{t} \delta^j y_{t-j} - \delta^{-1}(1 - \delta)^3 \sum_{j=0}^{t} \delta^j j y_{t-j}, \tag{7.54}$$

see, e.g., Abraham and Ledolter (1983, page 105).

7.6 CONCLUSION

Univariate ARIMA models have long been the workhorse in applied forecasting. ARIMA models tend to work best for time series with a clearly defined and stable persistent component such as the unemployment rate or the rate of inflation. However, they do not work so well for series such as stock returns for which the evidence of a sizable persistent component in the conditional mean is much weaker.

Provided that the lag length is chosen in a reasonable way, ARMA forecasts are often difficult to outperform empirically for many macroeconomic variables that contain a persistent component. Alternatives such as exponential smoothing and unobserved components models have been proposed and are used extensively to model and predict time series with strong seasonal components such as company sales or corporate dividends.

The success of ARIMA models owes much to their simplicity of use; these models are easy to estimate and impose minimal requirements on the information set used by the forecaster. We consider the main limitations to these models—the restriction to linear models and the use of a univariate information set (the past history of the variable being predicted)—in the following two chapters.

8

◇◇

Univariate Nonlinear Prediction Models

Linear models have many useful properties and are a natural starting point for forecasting analysis given that they are generally easy to estimate and analyze as we saw in chapter 7. However, unless the data are jointly Gaussian, it could well be that there are better-performing nonlinear forecasting models. Indeed, we would expect that linear prediction models are misspecified for many economic variables. For example, recessions tend to be shorter than expansions, and economic recoveries can have very different dynamics from recessions; see, e.g., Pesaran and Potter (1997). Large increases in oil prices have been found to affect GDP growth differently from declines of a similar magnitude (Hamilton, 1996). Asset prices such as exchange rates are a third example in which crashes and recoveries can have very different dynamics as a result of the unwinding of carry trades in periods with waning appetite for risk among investors (e.g., Brunnermeier, Nagel, and Pedersen (2008)). See also Clements, Franses, and Swanson (2004) for further discussion and examples.

If economic (or scientific) theory does not provide guidance on the functional form of the forecasting model, we could posit the forecasting problem in its most general form,

$$f^*(z) = \arg \min_{f(\cdot) \in \mathcal{F}} E_Y \left[L(f(Z), Y) \right], \tag{8.1}$$

where $\mathcal{F}$ is the set of all possible functions of the conditioning variables, Z. Faced with such a general model it is natural to use a nonparametric estimation approach. Nonparametric forecasting models are covered in more depth in chapter 11.

In practice, we often restrict $\mathcal{F}$ to a subset of all possible models. Linear models restrict the models to be linear functions of Z with an additive error term. Nonlinear models could take the form

$$y_{t+1} = f(z_t) + \varepsilon_{t+1}, \tag{8.2}$$

where the linear additive term captures the unpredictable component and $f(z_t)$ could be limited to a set of models, $\mathcal{F}$, where the set of models is restricted to a parametric subset of all possible models that could be considered, $\mathcal{F}^R$. Limiting Z to past values of Y suggests models of the form $y_{t+1} = f(y_t) + \varepsilon_{t+1}$. We next examine such models, noting that different methods make different assumptions on $\mathcal{F}^R$. We focus on parametric models, where $\mathcal{F}^R$ is limited to sets of nonlinear models that are known up to a set of parameters.

A large literature seeks to improve on ARMA models by allowing for parametric deviations from linearity. Typically the models employed have heuristic rather than theoretical motivations—e.g., there might be two or more regimes rather than a single one, which leads to switching regressions or smooth transition models for the data. Alternatively, the linear relation between current and past values of a series may break down as the data varies, which leads to threshold autoregression models. The models differ in their choice of exact functional form but all nest the linear model as a special case. While nonlinear least squares can be used to estimate model parameters, tests for nonlinear effects are difficult to interpret.

One limitation of these models is that they provide an inflexible approximation to unknown forms of nonlinearity. This should be contrasted with more general approaches to capture nonlinearity (such as series expansions) which provide more flexible approximations. These approaches are covered in chapter 11.

We first review some of the more popular models that have been applied to forecasting problems, including threshold autoregressive models (section 8.1), smooth transition autoregressive models (section 8.2), regime switching models (section 8.3), before briefly discussing tests for nonlinearities in section 8.4 and covering general procedures for forecasting with nonlinear models in section 8.5. Section 8.6 concludes.

8.1 THRESHOLD AUTOREGRESSIVE MODELS

Consider an extension of the $AR(p)$ model,

$$y_{t+1} = \phi_1 y_t + \cdots + \phi_p y_{t-p+1} + \sigma \varepsilon_{t+1}, \quad \varepsilon_{t+1} \sim (0, 1),$$

where the coefficients, including the variance of the residuals, can vary across different ranges of y_{t-d}, for some $d \geq 0$:

$$y_{t+1} = \begin{cases} \phi_{11} y_t + \cdots + \phi_{1p} y_{t-p+1} + \sigma_1 \varepsilon_{t+1} & \text{if } y_{t-d} \in S_1, \\ \vdots & \vdots \\ \phi_{k1} y_t + \cdots + \phi_{kp} y_{t-p+1} + \sigma_k \varepsilon_{t+1} & \text{if } y_{t-d} \in S_k. \end{cases} \quad (8.3)$$

Here the states S_i cover all possible values for y_{t-d}, the endpoints of which are known as thresholds. For example, for $k = 2$ we might have $S_1 = (-\infty, s]$ and $S_2 = (s, \infty)$ so the threshold is s. Models such as (8.3) are called threshold autoregressive (TAR) or "self-exciting TAR" (SETAR) since the threshold depends on y_{t-d} as opposed to some exogenous variable.

When the thresholds, $S_1, \ldots, S_k$, and d are known, the extension over the standard linear model is to simply split the sample into k fully defined groups. Parameter estimation is then straightforward, since least squares estimation can be applied separately to each group. Alternatively, if the errors are assumed to be normally distributed, one can use maximum likelihood estimation, which would lead to efficiency gains especially if there are parameter restrictions across the states, e.g., if $\sigma_i = \sigma$ for $i = 1, \ldots, k$.

If the thresholds are unknown, this widens the class of models to search over. However, the thresholds can be and often are estimated. In a model with $k = 2$ and $p_1 = p_2$, Chan (1993) showed that the threshold value, s, and the coefficients in each state can be consistently estimated when y_t is ergodic and strictly stationary. Moreover, the threshold estimate converges at rate T.

One-step-ahead forecasts are easily computed from the TAR model. Suppose $k = 2$, $p = 1$, and $d = 0$. Then, from (8.3) we have

$$f_{t+1|t} = [(\phi_{11} - \phi_{21}) \mathbb{1}(y_t \leq s) + \phi_2] y_t, \qquad (8.4)$$

where $\mathbb{1}(y_t \leq s)$ is an indicator variable that is known at time t, and so the forecast is conditionally linear in y_t.

Multistep forecasts are not as easily computed since they depend on future values taken by Y. Continuing with our earlier example, the two-step-ahead forecast depends on whether $y_{t+1} \leq s$:

$$y_{t+2} = \begin{cases} \phi_{11} y_{t+1} + \sigma_1 \varepsilon_{t+2} & \text{if } y_{t+1} \leq s, \\ \phi_{21} y_{t+1} + \sigma_2 \varepsilon_{t+2} & \text{if } y_{t+1} > s. \end{cases} \qquad (8.5)$$

This means that

$$f_{t+2|t} = E\left[[(\phi_{11} - \phi_{21}) \mathbb{1}(y_{t+1} \leq s) + \phi_{21}] y_{t+1} | Z_t\right], \qquad (8.6)$$

where $Z_t = \{y_1, \ldots, y_t\}$. This expression depends on the future innovation, ε_{t+1}, which affects both the indicator function $\mathbb{1}(y_{t+1} \leq s)$ and y_{t+1} and so $f_{t+2|t}$ is a nonlinear function of y_{t+1}. To evaluate the expectation in (8.6) we need the distribution of the innovation, ε_t. Popular methods include Monte Carlo simulation or the bootstrap. The former can be used if the distribution of ε is known up to a set of estimated parameters, while the latter involves redrawing with replacement from the sample of residuals, $\{\hat{\varepsilon}_1, \ldots, \hat{\varepsilon}_t\}$. Either method seeks to numerically evaluate the integral

$$\int [(\phi_{11} - \phi_{21}) \mathbb{1}(y_{t+1} \leq s) + \phi_{21}] y_{t+1} P(y_{t+1} | Z_t) dy_{t+1} \qquad (8.7)$$

through some average

$$\frac{1}{B} \sum_{b=1}^{B} [(\phi_{11} - \phi_{21}) \mathbb{1}(y_{t+1}^b \leq s) + \phi_{21}] y_{t+1}^b, \qquad (8.8)$$

where y_{t+1}^b is the bth draw of y_{t+1} generated by drawing a new innovation, ε_{t+1}^b, and computing

$$y_{t+1}^b = [(\phi_{11} - \phi_{21}) \mathbb{1}(y_t \leq s) + \phi_{21}] y_t + [(\sigma_1 - \sigma_2) \mathbb{1}(y_t \leq s) + \sigma_2] \varepsilon_{t+1}^b.$$

Similarly, if a sequence of draws $\{\varepsilon_{t+1}^b, \varepsilon_{t+2}^b, \ldots, \varepsilon_{t+h-1}^b\}_{b=1}^{B}$ are available, we can recursively generate values of y_{t+h}^b from y_{t+h-1}^b,

$$y_{t+h}^b = [(\phi_{11} - \phi_{21}) \mathbb{1}(y_{t+h-1}^b \leq s) + \phi_{21}] y_{t+h-1}^b + [(\sigma_1 - \sigma_2) \mathbb{1}(y_{t+h-1}^b \leq s) + \sigma_2] \varepsilon_{t+h-1}^b.$$

Finally, the forecast of y_{t+h} can be computed as

$$\bar{f}_{t+h|t} = \frac{1}{B} \sum_{b=1}^{B} y_{t+h}^{b}. \tag{8.9}$$

Setting the number of draws, B, to some large number should generally give a good approximation to the forecast.

8.2 SMOOTH TRANSITION AUTOREGRESSIVE MODELS

The smooth transition autoregressive (STAR) model is similar to the threshold autoregressive model, the key difference being that it allows a smoother transition between the states. To see the relation between the two models, consider the two-state TAR model:

$$y_{t+1} = \left(\phi_{11} y_t + \cdots + \phi_{1p} y_{t-p+1} + \sigma_1 \varepsilon_{t+1}\right) \mathbb{1}(y_{t-d} \in S_1)$$
$$+ \left(\phi_{21} y_t + \cdots + \phi_{2p} y_{t-p+1} + \sigma_2 \varepsilon_{t+1}\right) (1 - \mathbb{1}(y_{t-d} \in S_1)). \tag{8.10}$$

The transition between the states can be smoothed by replacing the indicator function $\mathbb{1}(\cdot)$ with a function $F(s_t; \gamma, c) \in (0, 1)$ that smoothly moves between 0 and 1, where s_t is data dependent—e.g., $s_t = y_{t-d}$—and $\gamma > 0$ and c are parameters affecting the transition across states:

$$y_{t+1} = \left(\phi_{11} y_t + \cdots + \phi_{1p} y_{t-p+1} + \sigma_1 \varepsilon_{t+1}\right) F(s_t; \gamma, c)$$
$$+ \left(\phi_{21} y_t + \cdots + \phi_{2p} y_{t-p+1} + \sigma_2 \varepsilon_{t+1}\right) (1 - F(s_t; \gamma, c)). \tag{8.11}$$

The main STAR models are the logistic STAR (LSTAR) and exponential STAR (ESTAR) models, summarized below, where in each case, $\gamma > 0$.

Model	$F(s_t; \gamma, c)$	
Logistic STAR (LSTAR)	$(1 + \exp\{-\gamma(s_t - c)\})^{-1}$	(8.12)
Exponential STAR (ESTAR)	$1 - \exp\{-\gamma(s_t - c)^2\}$	

For the LSTAR model, the weight on the first model exceeds 0.5 when $s_t > c$ and is otherwise smaller. When $\gamma \to \infty$ the LSTAR model approaches the TAR model, while for $\gamma \to 0$ it approaches a linear AR model.

The ESTAR model does not nest the TAR model. It is close to the TAR model in the second state, provided s_t is near c and is otherwise close to the TAR model in the first state. The ESTAR model converges to a linear model when $\gamma \to \infty$ or when $\gamma \to 0$.

When s_t equals the time index, these models become time-varying STAR models, and are akin to a permanent break model with smooth transitions between breaks and no mean reversion. Multiple regimes can also be handled. Surveys of the models are provided by van Dijk, Teräsvirta, and Franses (2002) and Teräsvirta (2006). For a book length treatment, see Franses and van Dijk (2000).

Assuming quadratic loss, the model parameters can be obtained through M-estimation using the objective function

$$\text{SSR}_T(z, \beta) = \frac{1}{T} \sum_{t=1}^{T} (y_t - \phi_1(L) F(s_t; \gamma, c) - \phi_2(L)(1 - F(s_t; \gamma, c)))^2. \quad (8.13)$$

Here the M-estimator amounts to nonlinear least squares and the parameters are $\beta = (\phi_{11}, \ldots, \phi_{1p}, \phi_{21}, \ldots, \phi_{2p}, \gamma, c)$. We could also assume that the errors are normal and employ maximum likelihood. The model is partially nonlinear with nonlinearities arising only through F. For given values of (γ, c) the optimization problem is linear, which enables the search problem to be reduced to a maximum of two dimensions.

Forecasts from STAR models can be computed in the same way as for the TAR models. For example, given a set of parameter estimates, $\hat{\beta}$, the one-step-ahead plug-in forecasts reduce to

$$f_{t+1|t}(z) = \left(\hat{\phi}_{11} y_t + \cdots + \hat{\phi}_{1p} y_{t-p+1} \right) F(s_t; \hat{\gamma}, \hat{c})$$
$$+ \left(\hat{\phi}_{21} y_t + \cdots + \hat{\phi}_{2p} y_{t-p+1} \right) (1 - F(s_t; \hat{\gamma}, \hat{c})).$$

These forecasts are computed as a weighted average of the forecasts in each of the states, with weights dependent on $F(s_T; \hat{\gamma}, \hat{c})$. Multistep forecasts must again be handled by numerical methods that account for the nonlinear effect of future innovations.

Smooth transition methods can also be used to model the local dynamics of a time series around exogenous variables such as a deterministic trend. For example, González, Hubrich, and Teräsvirta (2011) propose a local deterministic trend of the form

$$\mu(t) = \mu_0 + \sum_{i=1}^{g} \delta_i g(\gamma_i, c_i, t/T),$$

where t/T is the local point in time, measured as a fraction of the total sample, T, μ_i, and $\gamma_i > 0$ are parameters, and g is a logistic transition function,

$$g(\gamma_i, c_i, t/T) = (1 + \exp(-\gamma_i(t/T - c_i)))^{-1}. \quad (8.14)$$

Here $c_1 < \cdots < c_q$ are the points in time (as a fraction of the full sample) at which the deterministic component transitions from one level, $\mu_0 + \mu_1 + \cdots + \mu_{i-1}$ to the next, $\mu_0 + \mu_1 + \cdots + \mu_{i-1} + \mu_i$, $i \leq q$. When γ_i is close to 0, the transition will be smooth and gradual, while a large value of γ_i gives rise to a sudden shift, akin to a step function.

8.2.1 Empirical Evidence

Empirical evidence generally does not suggest that these nonlinear univariate models systematically produce better forecasts than linear alternatives. In the forecasting experiment for US macroeconomic data conducted by Stock and Watson (1999), STAR models did not generally outperform linear models. Sarantis (1999) comes to

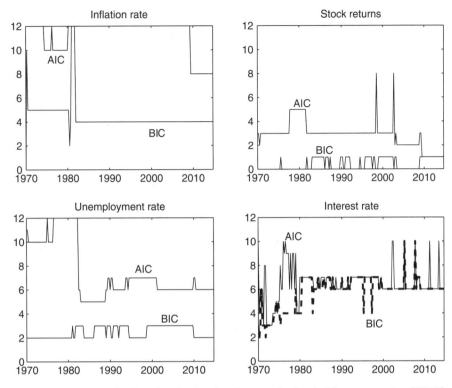

Figure 8.1: Recursive lag length selection for the smooth threshold autoregressive (STAR) model with two states.

the same conclusion in analyzing predictability of real exchange rates, while Kilian and Taylor (2003) find some evidence that exponential STAR models can predict exchange rates at 2–3 year horizons, though not at shorter horizons. Teräsvirta (2006) also concludes that there is relatively weak evidence that these models generate better point forecasts than competing methods, although he also concludes that these models have greater promise in density forecasting and can be useful as part of forecast combinations.

Part of the reason for these findings is that these nonlinear models can be more sensitive to outliers in the data and so parameter estimation error is an important consideration, especially in small samples.

As an empirical illustration, using the quarterly data on inflation, stock returns, unemployment and interest rates from chapter 7, figure 8.1 plots the number of terms in the STAR model selected recursively from 1970 to 2010 using the AIC or BIC methods. For most of these series, once again, the AIC selects considerably more lags than the BIC. For example, for the inflation rate the AIC selects 12 lags most of the time, although this declines to 8 lags at the end of the sample. The BIC, meanwhile, selects 4 or 5 lags during most of the sample.

Figure 8.2 shows recursively generated forecasts generated by the STAR models with lag length selected by the AIC or BIC methods. The forecasts are mostly similar to those generated by the linear AR model although on some occasions these nonlinear models can generate quite extreme forecasts, as in the case of the

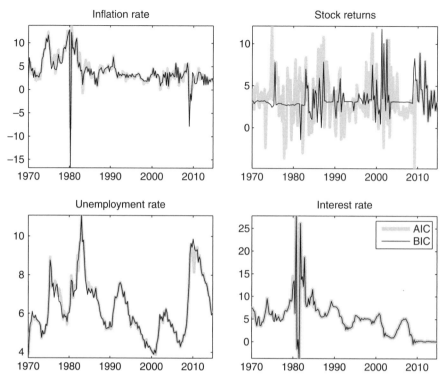

Figure 8.2: Recursive out-of-sample forecasts generated by smooth threshold autoregressive (STAR) models selected by the AIC or BIC.

inflation rate for which an extremely large negative forecast is generated in 1980 or for the T-bill rate where large negative forecasts are generated in the early eighties. The forecasts of stock returns generated by the models selected by the AIC are also notably more volatile than their linear counterparts in chapter 7 due in part to the inclusion of a larger number of terms by the STAR model.

8.3 REGIME SWITCHING MODELS

Since their introduction into economics by Hamilton (1989), Markov switching or regime switching models have become a popular class of models in economics and finance. Regime switching models share similarities with both TAR and STAR models. In common with these models, they introduce a number of regimes linked by a function that determines which regime occurs at a particular point in time. An example of a simple regime switching process with regime-dependent mean and variance is

$$y_{t+1} = \mu_{s_{t+1}} + \sigma_{s_{t+1}} \varepsilon_{t+1}, \quad \varepsilon_{t+1} \sim N(0, 1), \tag{8.15}$$

where $s_{t+1} \in \{1, \ldots, K\}$ indicates the current regime. For example, with two regimes, y is normally distributed $N(\mu_1, \sigma_1^2)$ in regime 1 and normally distributed

$N(\mu_2, \sigma_2^2)$ in regime 2. The difference between TAR or STAR models versus Markov switching models lies in how they determine the regime.

The Markov switching model assumes that the regime indicator is driven by an underlying Markov process. It is common to assume that the transition probabilities are constant through time and that transitions between regimes depend only on the previous regime and so are first-order Markov:

$$p_{ij} = P(S_t = i | S_{t-1} = j). \tag{8.16}$$

Since probabilities sum to 1 we need only define parameters for a subset of the probabilities. For the model with two regimes we can write the transition probability matrix $P = [p_{ij}]$ as

$$P = \begin{pmatrix} p_{11} & 1 - p_{22} \\ 1 - p_{11} & p_{22} \end{pmatrix}.$$

Hence there are only two transition probabilities to model, equivalent to the probabilities of remaining within the same regime. The first-order homogenous Markov chain assumes that the transition probabilities do not depend on the data. For example if regime 1 is expansion and regime 2 is recession, the model has a constant probability of transiting from a recession to an expansion no matter how long the recession has been going on.

8.3.1 Forecasting with Regime Switching Models

Forecasting the first-order Markov chain is straightforward. Following Hamilton (1994) let the $(K \times 1)$ vector ξ_t be a random indicator variable that tracks the current regime, i.e.,

$$\xi_t = (1, 0, 0, \ldots, 0)' \quad \text{if } s_t = 1,$$
$$\xi_t = (0, 1, 0, \ldots, 0)' \quad \text{if } s_t = 2,$$
$$\vdots \qquad\qquad \vdots$$
$$\xi_t = (0, 0, \ldots, 0, 1)' \quad \text{if } s_t = K.$$

Under the assumption of constant transition probabilities in (8.16), ξ_{t+1} can be written as a VAR(1) in state space form:

$$\xi_{t+1} = P\xi_t + v_{t+1}, \tag{8.17}$$

where $v_{t+1} = \xi_{t+1} - E[\xi_{t+1} | \xi_t, \xi_{t-1}, \ldots]$ is a martingale difference sequence, i.e.,

$$E[v_{t+1} | v_t, v_{t-1}, \ldots] = 0.$$

Iterating on (8.17), we have

$$\xi_{t+h} = P\xi_{t+h-1} + v_{t+h}$$

$$= P(P\xi_{t+h-2} + v_{t+h-1}) + v_{t+h}$$

$$= (P \times P)\xi_{t+h-2} + Pv_{t+h-1} + v_{t+h}$$

$$= P^h\xi_t + v_{t+h} + Pv_{t+h-1} + \cdots + P^{h-1}v_{t+1},$$

so $\quad E[\xi_{t+h}|\xi_t] = P^h\xi_t.$ \hfill (8.18)

Here $P^h = \prod_{t=1}^{h} P$ is P multiplied by itself h times. The h-period-ahead transition probabilities are thus obtained by multiplying P by itself h times and the probability that an observation from regime i is followed h periods later by an observation from regime j, $P(S_{t+h} = j|S_t = i)$ is given by the row i, column j element of the matrix P^h.

For the two-state model ($K = 2$), forecasts of future regime probabilities take the simple form (see Hamilton, 1994)

$$P^h = \begin{bmatrix} \frac{(1-p_{22})+(p_{11}+p_{22}-1)^h(1-p_{11})}{2-p_{11}-p_{22}} & \frac{(1-p_{22})-(p_{11}+p_{22}-1)^h(1-p_{22})}{2-p_{11}-p_{22}} \\ \frac{(1-p_{11})-(p_{11}+p_{22}-1)^h(1-p_{11})}{2-p_{11}-p_{22}} & \frac{(1-p_{11})+(p_{11}+p_{22}-1)^h(1-p_{22})}{2-p_{11}-p_{22}} \end{bmatrix}. \quad (8.19)$$

From this we can see that the key to the long-term regime forecasts is the "overall" persistence measure $(p_{11} + p_{22} - 1)$. The two-state process is in fact positively autocorrelated if $p_{11} + p_{22} > 1$ and the bigger is $p_{11} + p_{22} - 1$, the more persistent the process.

In practice, the underlying states are unobserved and so regime switching forecasts rely on estimated state probabilities. Once again, the forecast becomes a weighted average of forecasts conditional on the respective regimes with weights reflecting the predicted state probabilities. In the case with two states, we have from (8.15),

$$f_{t+1|t}(z) = \mu_1 \left[\hat{p}_{1t} p_{11} + (1 - \hat{p}_{1t})(1 - p_{22}) \right]$$

$$+ \mu_2 \left[\hat{p}_{1t}(1 - p_{11}) + (1 - \hat{p}_{1t})p_{22} \right], \quad (8.20)$$

where $\hat{p}_{1t}$ is the estimated probability of being in regime 1 at time t using data up to time t and so itself depends on the entire data set up to time t.

Recursive updates to the state probabilities will affect the forecasts even if the parameters are known, as the next example shows.

Example 8.3.1 (Recursive updates of state probabilities). *If the model parameters* $\theta = (\mu_1, \mu_2, \sigma^2, p_1, p_2)'$ *are known and* $\varepsilon_t \sim ind$ $N(0, \sigma^2)$*, the state probabilities can be derived recursively as shown by Hamilton (1994, page 692). Let* $p_{t|t} \equiv (p_{1t|t} \ p_{2t|t}) = (\Pr(S_t = 1|y_t, y_{t-1}, \ldots), \Pr(S_t = 2|y_t, y_{t-1}, \ldots))'$*, while* $p_{t+1|t} \equiv (p_{1t+1|t} \ p_{2t+1|t}) = (\Pr(S_{t+1} = 1|y_t, y_{t-1}, \ldots), \Pr(S_{t+1} = 2|y_t, y_{t-1}, \ldots))'$ *be the conditional probabilities for the current and future state given the observed history of realizations. These evolve* *according to the equations*

$$p_{t|t} = \frac{p_{t|t-1} \odot \begin{pmatrix} \exp(-\frac{(y_t-\mu_1)^2}{2\sigma^2})/\sqrt{2\pi\sigma^2} \\ \exp(-\frac{(y_t-\mu_2)^2}{2\sigma^2})/\sqrt{2\pi\sigma^2} \end{pmatrix}}{p_{1t|t-1}\exp(-\frac{(y_t-\mu_1)^2}{2\sigma^2})/\sqrt{2\pi\sigma^2} + p_{2t|t-1}\exp(-\frac{(y_t-\mu_2)^2}{2\sigma^2})/\sqrt{2\pi\sigma^2}}, \quad (8.21)$$

$$p_{t+1|t} = \begin{pmatrix} p_1 & 1-p_2 \\ 1-p_1 & p_2 \end{pmatrix} p_{t|t}. \quad (8.22)$$

where $\odot$ is the Hadamard product. The recursions can be started using initial values such as $p_{0|0} = \pi$.

Estimation of regime switching models is typically based on either maximum likelihood or Bayesian methods and assumes that the likelihood is Gaussian within each regime. The likelihood itself is quite complicated but can be written in state-space form and hence a recursive algorithm similar to the Kalman filter can be used to construct the sequences of probability forecasts and forecasts of y_t as well.

Example 8.3.2 (Multistep forecasts for the two-state Markov switching process). *For many Markov switching models, multistep forecasts can be derived in closed form, at least when parameter estimation uncertainty is ignored. For example, Clements and Krolzig (1998) analyze the following two-state model with first-order autoregressive dynamics:*

$$\Delta y_{t+1} - \mu_{s_{t+1}} = \alpha(\Delta y_t - \mu_{s_t}) + u_{t+1}, \quad u_{t+1} \sim ind \ N(0, \sigma_u^2). \quad (8.23)$$

Define the variable $\zeta_t = 1 - \Pr(s_t = 2)$, if $s_t = 2$, otherwise $\zeta_t = -\Pr(s_t = 2)$ which tracks the state of the hidden Markov chain. The forecast of ζ_{t+h} given information at time t takes the form

$$\hat{\zeta}_{t+h|t} = (p_{11} + p_{22} - 1)^h \hat{\zeta}_{t|t}.$$

Clements and Krolzig use this to show that the forecast of Δy_{t+h} above its unconditional mean, μ_y, is given by

$$\Delta y_{t+h} - \mu_y = \alpha^h(\Delta y_t - \mu_y) + (\mu_2 - \mu_1)[(p_{11} + p_{22} - 1)^h - \alpha^h]\hat{\zeta}_{t|t}. \quad (8.24)$$

The expression in (8.24) is helpful for understanding when forecasts from a Markov switching process such as that in (8.23) can be expected to improve upon forecasts from a simple AR model and when they cannot. First notice that the first term in (8.24) is identical to that from a regular AR(1) model. Only the second term differentiates the Markov switching forecast from the regular AR(1) prediction. This second term will tend to be small if $|\mu_2 - \mu_1|$ is small, i.e., if the means in the two states are similar, or if the persistence of the underlying states as measured by $p_{11} + p_{22} - 1$ is not very different from α.[1] A third reason for the two forecasts to be similar arises if the states are not well identified so that $\hat{\zeta}_{t|t}$ is mostly constant over time. In this case, the

---

[1] Using data on quarterly US real GNP growth, Clements and Krolzig (1998) obtain estimates $\hat{p}_{11} + \hat{p}_{22} - 1$ that are very close to their estimate of α, and so the second term in (8.24) nearly vanishes in their empirical application.

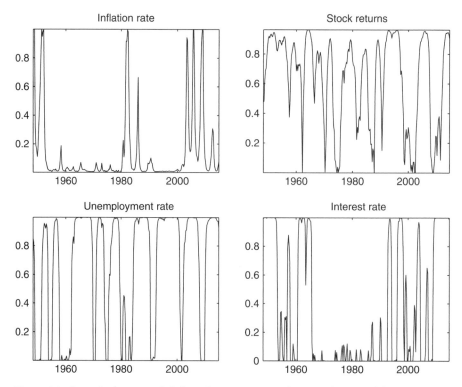

Figure 8.3: Smoothed-state probabilities for two-state Markov switching models.

second term in (8.24) can be picked up through a constant. Conversely, for the Markov switching process to produce better forecasts, μ_2 and μ_1 should be quite different, the persistence of the regime switching process should differ from α and the conditional state probabilities should be well identified by the filter.

8.3.2 Empirical Example: Two-State Regime Switching Models

As an empirical illustration, we fitted two-state regime switching models to the four variables studied previously, i.e., inflation, stock returns, unemployment and interest rates, using a simple model with state-dependent intercepts, first-order autoregressive terms and volatilities:

$$y_{t+1} = \mu_{s_{t+1}} + \phi_{s_{t+1}} y_t + \sigma_{s_{t+1}} \varepsilon_{t+1}, \quad \varepsilon_{t+1} \sim N(0, 1). \tag{8.25}$$

Figure 8.3 plots the smoothed-state probabilities, i.e., the states inferred from the full data sample. Two highly persistent states are identified for both the inflation and the interest rate series—for the latter variable, one state picks up the changes to the Fed's monetary policy during 1979–82. For stock returns, shorter-lived regimes with high and low volatility are identified by the two-state models.

Table 8.1 reports full-sample coefficient estimates for the Markov switching model (8.25) fitted to the four series. For the inflation rate, outcomes in the first state are largely serially uncorrelated, whereas the second state sees strongly autocorrelated outcomes. Both states have high persistence, with "stayer" probabilities of 0.75

TABLE 8.1:
Maximum likelihood estimates of the parameters of two-state regime switching models: σ_1 and σ_2 measure the volatility parameters in states 1 and 2; μ_1 and μ_2 measure the intercept in states 1 and 2; ρ_1 and ρ_2 measure the autoregressive coefficient in the two states. Finally, p_{11} and p_{22} are the probabilities of remaining in states 1 and 2, respectively.

Parameters	Inflation rate	Stock returns	Unemployment rate	Interest rate
$\sigma_1(\%)$	4.9324	5.4268	0.1534	0.0871
$\sigma_2(\%)$	1.9049	10.3857	0.5772	0.8427
$\mu_1(\%)$	2.6561	4.0226	0.0901	0.0091
$\mu_2(\%)$	0.8200	1.1493	0.6442	0.1712
ρ_1	0.0946	0.0227	0.9667	1.0114
ρ_2	0.7897	0.0957	0.9302	0.9648
p_{11}	0.7549	0.9084	0.9385	0.8843
p_{22}	0.9633	0.8413	0.8797	0.9363

and 0.96, respectively. This means that the expected duration of the second state exceeds 20 quarters. The first state has a large intercept, while the second state has a small intercept, suggesting that the predicted inflation rate will vary substantially depending on the initial state. Inflation rate uncertainty also varies considerably across the two states, with the volatility parameter in the first state (σ_1) being two and a half times greater than that in the second state (σ_2).

For stock returns, the model identifies a low volatility state with a high mean (state 1) and a high volatility state with a low mean (state 2), with no evidence of serial correlation in either state. These states are only moderately persistent, and so we observe many regime switches for this series.

The regimes identified for the unemployment rate series suggest the presence of two moderately persistent states, one of which (state 1) has a small intercept and low volatility, while the other (state 2) has a higher intercept and high volatility. Both states have stayer probabilities around 0.90.

The interest rate process is mildly explosive in the first state and highly persistent but stationary in the second state. Again, both states have stayer probabilities close to 0.90. As shown in figure 8.3, the mildly explosive behavior in the interest rate is associated with the sharp reduction in interest rates following the Fed's policy actions during 1979–82.

Recursively generated one-step-ahead forecasts from the two-state Markov switching models are shown in figure 8.4. Despite the very different functional form of the regime switching model in (8.25) versus the simple autoregressive model, the point forecasts for the three persistent variables (inflation, unemployment and interest rates) are quite similar to the ones generated by the linear AR models.

8.3.3 Refinements to the Markov Switching Model

So far we assumed that transition probabilities were constant. However, this may not be a good assumption in some empirical applications. Fortunately it is straightforward to relax this assumption. One approach is to use probit or logit specifications to

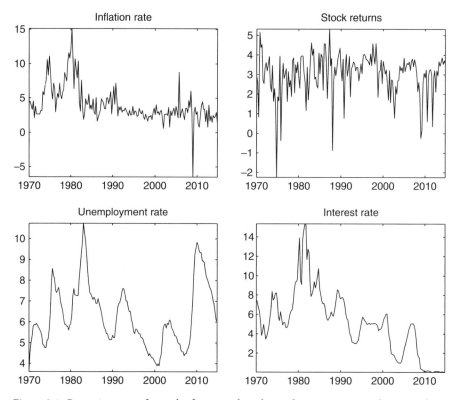

Figure 8.4: Recursive out-of-sample forecasts based on the two-state Markov switching models.

capture time-varying transitions,

$$P(S_{t+1} = k | S_t = i, z_t) = \Phi(c_{ik} + \beta'_{ik} z_t),$$

$$P(s_{t+1} = k | S_t = i, z_t) = \frac{\exp(c_{ik} + \beta'_{ik} z_t)}{1 + \exp(c_{ik} + \beta'_{ik} z_t)},$$

for some $z_t \in Z_t$. Such time-varying transition probabilities allow the Markov switching model to adjust its persistence to the state of the economy. If multistep forecasts are warranted, then the dynamics in z_t must also be modeled. See also Diebold, Lee, and Weinbach (1994) and Filardo (1994) for work on regime switching models with time-varying transitions.

A second approach, suggested by Durland and McCurdy (1994) is to let the state transition probabilities depend on the duration of the current state. Define the duration variable,

$$D(S_t) = \begin{cases} D(S_{t-1}) + 1 & \text{if } S_t = S_{t-1}, \\ 1 & \text{if } S_t \neq S_{t-1}. \end{cases}$$

Then state-dependent transitions can be modeled as follows (see Durland and McCurdy (1994)):

$$P(S_t = k | S_{t-1} = k, D(S_{t-1}) = d) = \begin{cases} \dfrac{\exp(c_k + \beta_k d)}{1 + \exp(c_k + \beta_k d)}, & d \le \tau, \\[2ex] \dfrac{\exp(c_k + \beta_k \tau)}{1 + \exp(c_k + \beta_k \tau)}, & d > \tau. \end{cases}$$

This model keeps track of durations up to length τ. For example, the probability of remaining in a recession could be a declining function of how long the recession has lasted if $\beta_k < 0$ for this state.

The idea of Markov switching is quite general in the sense that it can be applied to all or a subset of the parameters of most time-series models. For example, one can allow for regime switching models in the dynamic specification of an ARMA model, in the variance of the innovations, or in the effect of other predictors on the outcome. For example, Haldrup and Nielsen (2006) introduce regime switching in the parameters of an autoregressive fractionally integrated model for electricity prices in the Nordic countries, a special case of which is

$$A_{s_t}(1 - L)^{d_{s_t}}(y_t - \mu_{s_t}) = \sigma_{s_t}\epsilon_t,$$

where $\epsilon \sim$ ind $N(0, 1)$, A_{s_t} is a regime-dependent lag polynomial with roots outside the unit circle, and d_{s_t} is a regime-dependent fractional integration parameter. Fractional integration allows for a slower decay in the model's autocorrelation pattern as compared to a stationary model.

Empirically, Markov switching models have been used extensively in economics and finance to model variables such as exchange rates, stock returns, bond prices, GDP growth, inflation, and unemployment dynamics. In applications to returns on equities or currencies it is often found that the regimes are mostly identified by volatility differentials, although studies such as Guidolin and Timmermann (2006) and Guidolin and Timmermann (2008) that use multiple asset classes and multiple states have found sufficient power to reject that mean returns are the same across different regimes. Applications to interest rates have found evidence of regimes in the dynamics of real rates, inflation expectations, and the inflation risk premium; see, e.g., Ang, Bekaert, and Wei (2008). In the context of exchange rate forecasting, Dacco and Satchell (1999) provide a discussion of why Markov switching models can fit the data well, but sometimes perform poorly when used to forecast out-of-sample. Gray (1996) and Marcucci (2005) develop Markov switching models that can accommodate GARCH effects within the regimes to predict interest rate dynamics and stock market volatility, respectively. For a recent summary of regime switching models, see Ang and Timmermann (2012).

8.4 TESTING FOR NONLINEARITY

Nonlinear models typically nest linear models as special cases and therefore can be expected to provide better in-sample fits of the data simply because they adopt a more flexible functional form. Most applied studies using nonlinear forecasting models examine tests of the null of nonlinearity to motivate their use of such models, so it is helpful to briefly review such tests.

Tests of the null of a linear model against a nonlinear alternative that nests the linear specification often result in nonstandard problems since most nonlinear models have parameters that are not identified under the null hypothesis of a linear model. This problem can be illustrated using the nonlinear models introduced above. For the TAR model in (8.5), the threshold, s, is not identified since the model is the same for all s under the null that the parameters do not differ across regimes. The STAR models in (8.12) are linear if $\gamma = 0$, in which case c is unidentified since the model is the same for all possible values for c. Similarly, for the Markov switching model, if the linear specifications are the same in each regime, the transition probabilities p_{ij} are not identified.

This problem—illuminated in Davies (1977) and Davies (1987) and discussed extensively in the statistical and econometric literature since then—has three implications. First, Likelihood Ratio (LR), Wald and Lagrange Multiplier (LM) tests are typically not asymptotically equivalent under the null and alternative hypotheses; second, these tests are often no longer well approximated by the usual χ^2 distributions; third, the LR statistic is no longer necessarily an optimal test.

The approach favored in the literature on STAR models is to take a first-order expansion around the model under the null ($\gamma = 0$) and test whether the additional terms that arise from the expansion, over and above the linear model, are significant. See Teräsvirta (2006) for further discussion.

One issue with this approach is that if the tests are rejected, it does not follow directly that a particular nonlinear model is appropriate. The tests that are usually employed have power against many forms of nonlinearity, and so a rejection does not imply a particular parametric form for the apparent nonlinearity and the forecaster does not know which of the above models, if any, would provide the best forecasts.

8.5 FORECASTING WITH NONLINEAR UNIVARIATE MODELS

As is clear from the discussion of the nonlinear models above, forecasting with univariate nonlinear models generally relies on numerical methods—at least in so far that multi-step-ahead forecasts are of interest. To see this, consider the general nonlinear model with additive innovations:

$$y_{t+1} = f(y_t) + \varepsilon_{t+1}, \quad \varepsilon_{t+1} \sim (0, \sigma_\varepsilon^2).$$

Multi-step-ahead values for y depend on $\varepsilon_{t+1}, \varepsilon_{t+2}, \ldots, \varepsilon_{t+h}$:

$$y_{t+2} = f(f(y_t) + \varepsilon_{t+1}) + \varepsilon_{t+2},$$
$$y_{t+3} = f(f(f(y_t) + \varepsilon_{t+1}) + \varepsilon_{t+2}) + \varepsilon_{t+3},$$
$$y_{t+h} = f(f(y_{t+h-1}) + \varepsilon_{t+h-1}) + \varepsilon_{t+h}. \tag{8.26}$$

If f is a nonlinear function, then in general we have $E[y_{t+h}|Z_t] \neq E[f^h(y_t)]$ even if $E[\varepsilon_{t+j}|Z_t] = 0$. This means that the full density of ε matters even under MSE loss where the focus is on computing the expectation of y_{t+h}. Brown and Mariano (1989) discuss the behavior of predictors in nonlinear dynamic models.

There are three strategies for dealing with this issue. First, if the density for ε is known or can be estimated, we can use Monte Carlo simulation to draw future values

$\{\varepsilon_{t+1}, \ldots, \varepsilon_{t+h}\}$ and compute y_{t+h} iteratively. Letting $b = 1, \ldots, B$, we can compute

$$y_{t+1}^b = f(y_t) + \varepsilon_{t+1}^b, \qquad\qquad (8.27)$$

$$\vdots$$

$$y_{t+h}^b = f(f(y_{t+h-1}^b) + \varepsilon_{t+h-1}^b) + \varepsilon_{t+h}^b.$$

Finally, the forecast can be based on the simulated density for y_{t+h}. For example, under MSE loss, the forecast would be the conditional mean

$$f_{t+h|t} = \frac{1}{B} \sum_{b=1}^{B} y_{t+h}^b,$$

whereas under lin-lin loss, the forecast would be a quantile of the simulated distribution for y_{t+h}.

The second approach is to use a nonparametric bootstrap rather than assuming some parametric distribution for ε. The bootstrap repeatedly draws $(\hat{\varepsilon}_{t+1}, \hat{\varepsilon}_{t+2}, \ldots, \hat{\varepsilon}_{t+h})$ with replacement from the empirical c.d.f. of the fitted model for $b = 1, \ldots, B$:

$$y_{t+1}^b = f(y_t) + \hat{\varepsilon}_{t+1}^b,$$

$$\vdots \qquad\qquad (8.28)$$

$$y_{t+h}^b = f(f(y_{t+h-1}^b) + \hat{\varepsilon}_{t+h-1}^b) + \hat{\varepsilon}_{t+h}^b.$$

As for the Monte Carlo simulation approach, these draws can be used to compute expected loss. Several different bootstrap methods can be used here, including the block bootstrap, the stationary bootstrap, or even semiparametric bootstraps that allow for dynamics in the second moment of the residuals.

The third and final approach is to use the direct forecast approach and model y_{t+h} directly as a function of y_t:

$$y_{t+h} = f_h(y_t) + \varepsilon_{t+h}. \qquad\qquad (8.29)$$

Under this approach, we use the nonlinear model to relate y_{t+h} directly to y_t and so there is no need to iterate on the forecasts to obtain multi-step-ahead predictions. Conversely, each forecast horizon requires its own separate forecasting model, f_h, and there is no attempt to make sure that multi-step-ahead forecasts are consistent across different horizons. This is important since the functional form of nonlinear models typically is not preserved at multi-step-ahead horizons as can easily be verified from the iteration in (8.26).

Once again, there will be a trade-off between the efficiency gains that can be obtained by using a model-consistent approach that iterates on a model fitted to the highest frequency at which data are available to obtain a multi-step-ahead forecast versus using the direct approach which is likely to be less sensitive to misspecification.

The Markov switching model can be used to illustrate the potential gains from using nonlinear as opposed to linear forecasts as we next show using an example from Hamilton (1989).

Example 8.5.1 (Forecasting with linear versus nonlinear models). *Following Hamilton (1989), consider a simple version of the Markov switching model:*

$$y_t = s_t + \varepsilon_t, \tag{8.30}$$

where $\varepsilon_t \sim iid(0, \sigma^2)$, and s_t is a two-state binary variable that follows the first-order Markov process[2]

$$\Pr(s_t = 0 | s_{t-1} = 0) = p_0,$$
$$\Pr(s_t = 1 | s_{t-1} = 1) = p_1. \tag{8.31}$$

Even though this is a nonlinear process, it can be represented through an AR(1) model with an unusual error distribution:

$$s_t = (1 - p_0) + \lambda s_{t-1} - v_t, \tag{8.32}$$
$$\lambda = p_0 + p_1 - 1,$$

where the innovation term v_t is conditionally binomially distributed. Conditional on $s_{t-1} = 0$, v_t follows the distribution

$$v_t = \begin{cases} 1 - p_0 & \text{with probability } p_0, \\ -p_0 & \text{with probability } 1 - p_0, \end{cases}$$

while, conditional on $s_{t-1} = 1$,

$$v_t = \begin{cases} -(1 - p_1) & \text{with probability } p_1, \\ p_1 & \text{with probability } 1 - p_1. \end{cases}$$

These properties mean that, conditional on s_{t-1}, v_t is a martingale difference sequence and so has zero conditional mean in both states:

$$E[v_t | s_{t-1} = 0] = p_0(1 - p_0) - p_0(1 - p_0) = 0, \tag{8.33}$$
$$E[v_t | s_{t-1} = 1] = -p_1(1 - p_1) + p_1(1 - p_1) = 0.$$

However, v_t is clearly not independent of s_{t-1}. For example, its conditional variance is

$$E[v_t^2 | s_{t-1} = 0] = p_0(1 - p_0)^2 + p_0^2(1 - p_0) = p_0(1 - p_0),$$
$$E[v_t^2 | s_{t-1} = 1] = p_1(1 - p_1)^2 + p_1^2(1 - p_1) = p_1(1 - p_1).$$

Using (8.30) and (8.32), notice that

$$y_t - \lambda y_{t-1} = s_t - \lambda s_{t-1} + \varepsilon_t - \lambda \varepsilon_{t-1}$$
$$= (1 - p_0) - v_t + \varepsilon_t - \lambda \varepsilon_{t-1}.$$

---

[2] Note that the states here are labeled "0" and "1"; this helps to simplify the derivations in the example.

As shown by Hamilton, the error term on the right-hand side of this equation follows an MA(1) process:

$$-v_t + \varepsilon_t - \lambda \varepsilon_{t-1} = u_t - \theta u_{t-1},$$

where $u_t \sim \mathrm{WN}(0, \sigma_u^2)$ and θ and σ_u^2 are parameters determined by the equations

$$(1+\theta^2)\sigma_u^2 = (1+\lambda^2)\sigma_\varepsilon^2 + \sigma_v^2,$$
$$\theta \sigma_u^2 = \lambda \sigma_\varepsilon^2,$$

and

$$\sigma_v^2 = (1-\pi)p_0(1-p_0) + \pi p_1(1-p_1)$$

is the unconditional variance of v_t. Here $\pi = (1-p_0)/(2-p_0-p_1)$ is the steady-state (unconditional) probability of state 1. This suggests using the ARMA(1,1) linear model,

$$y_{t+1} = \lambda y_t + (1-p_0) + u_{t+1} - \theta u_t,$$

to predict y_{t+1} or, more generally, y_{t+h}. However, such a forecasting scheme is not optimal: although u_t is uncorrelated with $u_{t-1}, u_{t-2}, \ldots$, it is not independently distributed of earlier values. The optimal forecast is in fact

$$E[y_{t+h}|y_t, y_{t-1}, \ldots] = \pi + \lambda^h (\Pr(S_t = 1|y_t, y_{t-1}, \ldots) - \pi). \qquad (8.34)$$

The state probability $\Pr(S_t = 1|y_t, y_{t-1}, \ldots)$ is a highly nonlinear function of y_t which makes the optimal forecast a nonlinear function of current and past values of y. See Hamilton (1989) for further details.

8.5.1 Empirical Comparisons

Table 8.2 reports out-of-sample root mean squared forecast errors for a subset of the models considered here and in the previous chapter, including random walk, prevailing mean, EWMA, AR, STAR, and Markov switching models. For the inflation series, the EWMA model with $\delta = 0.8$ or δ chosen optimally (labeled δ^*) by recursively minimizing the MSE as well as the AR model with lag length selected by the BIC, produce the lowest RMSE values while the STAR and prevailing mean model perform very poorly. The poor performance of the prevailing mean is perhaps to be expected since this model fails to capture the persistence of the underlying variable. This is not a concern for stock returns where the prevailing mean model comes out on top, along with the AR model selected by BIC which, as we have seen, rarely includes any lags.

While the nonlinear models do not perform well for the inflation and stock return series, they produce quite accurate predictions for the unemployment rate series, although even here they are bettered by the AR models. In the case of the interest rate series, we would expect the regime switching model to perform quite well because of the presence of periods with very different dynamics such as the Federal Reserve's monetarist experiment during 1979–1982 and the period with zero lower bound on

TABLE 8.2:
Out-of-sample root mean squared forecast errors for different forecasting methods. For methods with estimated parameters, the parameters are estimated using a recursively expanding window. The sample evaluation period is 1970–2014.

Method	Inflation	Stock	Unemployment	Interest rate
Random walk	3.1462	11.3614	0.3541	0.7914
Prevailing mean	3.6420	8.3953	1.8370	3.5627
EWMA $\delta = 0.999$	3.6304	8.3965	1.8220	3.5389
EWMA $\delta = 0.8$	2.6567	8.8307	0.9459	1.4521
EWMA $\delta = \delta^*$	2.6492	8.4570	0.3543	0.7916
AR(AIC)	2.8053	8.5715	0.2672	0.8580
AR(BIC)	2.6528	8.3951	0.2689	0.8226
STAR(AIC)	3.1102	8.7316	0.3248	2.8356
STAR(BIC)	3.4488	8.5555	0.2911	2.8337
Markov switching	2.7666	8.5096	0.3387	0.8183

TABLE 8.3:
Diebold–Mariano tests comparing the mean squared error performance of different forecasting methods to the benchmark random walk model (for inflation, unemployment and interest rates) or the prevailing mean model (for stock returns). Positive values indicate that a model produces lower mean squared errors than its benchmark.

Method	Inflation	Stock	Unemployment	Interest rate
Random walk	0.0000	−4.7529	0.0000	0.0000
Prevailing mean	−1.1296	0.0000	−5.0621	−5.3658
EWMA $\delta = 0.999$	−1.1140	−0.4951	−5.0585	−5.3922
EWMA $\delta = 0.8$	1.8218	−1.5694	−4.5412	−5.3357
EWMA $\delta = \delta^*$	2.4482	−1.0482	−3.5771	−2.6736
AR(AIC)	1.6042	−2.4535	2.9477	−0.8611
AR(BIC)	2.0996	0.0276	2.8725	−0.4660
STAR(AIC)	0.0905	−1.4695	0.7963	−1.5703
STAR(BIC)	−0.4402	−1.0680	2.1382	−1.5681
Markov switching	2.0560	−1.3690	1.2356	−1.5420

the short interest rate following the global financial crisis. This is indeed what we find as this model produces more accurate point forecasts than the linear models, although the random walk model performs even better for this variable.

Table 8.3 shows Diebold–Mariano tests for different models' mean squared error performance measured against the performance of a benchmark which, for the persistent inflation, unemployment and interest rate series is the random walk model, while the benchmark is the prevailing mean for the stock return series. Positive values indicate superior performance relative to the benchmark and the Diebold–Mariano test, discussed in detail in chapter 17, gives some indication of the significance of differences in forecasting performance. By this measure, the EWMA approach with optimal choice of δ, the AR model with lag length selected by BIC, and the Markov switching model perform somewhat better than the random walk benchmark for the inflation rate. For the unemployment rate series, linear autoregressive models perform quite well as does the STAR model with lag length selected by BIC. Conversely, none of the models produce accurate forecasts, and many produce distinctly worse forecasts than their benchmark, for stock returns and the interest rate series.

The stock return series is quite different from the other series considered here. This variable is not persistent at all and so it is perhaps unsurprising that the random walk model (using the past quarter's stock return to forecast next quarter's stock return) does extremely poorly. Interestingly, the STAR models also perform very poorly for this series, and only the AR(BIC) method applied to stock returns produces lower RMSE values than the prevailing mean.

8.6 CONCLUSION

Univariate models such as threshold autoregressions or smooth threshold autore-gressions have been motivated as nonlinear extensions to the linear AR specification. While such models can sometimes capture nonlinear dynamics, their parameters are often poorly estimated and effectively fitted to very few episodes in the data. This means that forecasts from such models sometimes become quite extreme, rendering estimation error particularly important.[3]

Another class of models, Markov switching models, have the potential to be more robust to this limitation of the nonlinear models as they limit the range of forecasts based on the regimes identified in the historical sample. Moreover, these models have proved easy to use to generate multiperiod forecasts under the assumption that state transitions are driven by a first-order homogeneous Markov chain. The general evidence, consistent with what we find here, is that Markov switching models can be quite successful for variables that display clear regime switching behavior such as interest rates, but produce less accurate forecasts for variables whose regimes are either historically unique, and thus do not repeat over time, or have fewer regime shifts so that the regime-specific parameters cannot be estimated with sufficient precision.

Some authors (e.g., Teräsvirta, 2006) argue that forecasts from individual non-linear models can be combined with forecasts from other nonlinear models or with forecasts from simple, linear models. This is a promising way to handle the robustness issues arising due to the effect that estimation error has on nonlinear models in particular. We discuss this point further in chapter 14. Density forecasting is another area for which nonlinear univariate models have shown some promise. We discuss this in chapter 13.

[3] See Teräsvirta, Tjøstheim, and Granger (2010) for a comprehensive treatment of estimation of nonlinear time series models.

9

⬦⬦

Vector Autoregressions

Since their introduction to econometrics by Sims (1980), vector autoregressions (VARs) have become a workhorse for forecasting macroeconomic and financial time series. VARs generate dynamic forecasts in a way that ensures consistency across different equations and forecast horizons. They are frequently used to forecast macroeconomic variables such as inflation and GDP growth and are integral to the calculation of stock prices in the log-linearized present value model of Campbell and Shiller (1988).

Sims (1980) argued that the large-scale macroeconomic forecasting models used at the time of his study were built on shaky foundations, including identifying restrictions that were difficult to justify. Instead he proposed to use unrestricted VARs of much lower dimension, the idea being that the data would help identify any patterns that might be helpful for prediction purposes.

Section 9.1 introduces vector autoregressions. Section 9.2 discusses classical estimation of VARs and their use in forecasting. We cover Bayesian approaches to estimation and forecasting with VARs, including models with time-varying parameters and large-dimensional VARs, in section 9.3. Section 9.4 discusses dynamic stochastic general equilibrium (DSGE) models which embed VARs in the context of a macroeconomic model that imposes restrictions from agents' optimizing and forward-looking behavior. Section 9.5 covers the use of conditional forecasts, while section 9.6 provides empirical examples and Section 9.7 concludes.

9.1 SPECIFICATION OF VECTOR AUTOREGRESSIONS

Vector autoregressions generalize the simple univariate autoregressions to the multivariate case where y_t becomes an $(n \times 1)$ vector and so extend the information set to $Z_t = \{y_{it}, y_{it-1}, \ldots\}_{i=1}^{n}$. As with univariate data, nearly all the work on forecasting with VARs assumes MSE loss and uses VARs to approximate the conditional mean of the outcome variable of interest. Many of the properties of VARs are simple multivariate generalizations of the results for the univariate models covered in chapter 7. For example, just as an autoregression summarizes the first and second moments of a univariate time series, we can think of the VAR as a summary of the first and second moments of the vector y_t. The Wold representation theorem also extends to the multivariate case and hence VARs can be used to approximate covariance stationary multivariate processes. Indeed, some papers extend VARs to include moving average terms so as to better approximate the underlying process by means of a parsimonious representation.[1]

The pth order VAR for an $(n \times 1)$ vector y_t takes the following form:

$$y_t = c + \sum_{i=1}^{p} A_i y_{t-i} + u_t, \tag{9.1}$$

where A_i is an $(n \times n)$ matrix of autoregressive coefficients for $i = 1, \ldots, p$, and $E[u_t u_t'] = \Sigma$. The $(n \times 1)$ vector of intercepts c can easily be extended to contain a set of deterministic variables such as seasonals or trends.

Model (9.1) is a system of equations with the same regressors appearing in each equation. The innovations of u_t, u_{it}, can be correlated across individual equations with general covariance matrix Σ, but the lag length, p, is typically chosen to be large enough so u_t is serially uncorrelated for all variables in the VAR.

Equation (9.1) is convenient shorthand but buries a lot of notation that is needed to examine these models. Letting a_{1ij} be the coefficient capturing the effect of the jth lag of y_{1t} on y_{it}, we can write

$$y_{it} = c_i + \sum_{j=1}^{p} a_{1ij} y_{1t-j} + \cdots + \sum_{j=1}^{p} a_{nij} y_{nt-j} + u_{it}, \quad i = 1, \ldots, n. \tag{9.2}$$

Here the first p terms show how y_{it} is affected by $y_{1t-1}, \ldots, y_{1t-p}$, while the last p terms show how y_{it} is affected by lags of y_n.

Defining $z_t = (1, y_{t-1}', \ldots, y_{t-p}')'$ and $\beta = (c, A_1, \ldots, A_p)'$, (9.1) can conveniently be written as a set of stacked equations for the $(T \times n)$ matrices $Y = (y_1, \ldots, y_T)'$ and $U = (u_1, \ldots, u_T)'$ and a $(T \times (np + 1))$ matrix $Z = (z_1, \ldots, z_T)'$,

$$Y = Z\beta + U, \tag{9.3}$$

where β is $(np + 1) \times n$.

VARs initially became a popular forecasting tool because of their relative simplicity in terms of which choices need to be made by the forecaster. When estimating a VAR by classical methods, only two choices need to be made to construct forecasts: which variables to include (selection of $(y_1, \ldots, y_n)$), and how many lags of the variables to include (selection of p). However, the risk of overparameterization of VARs is high given that the inclusion of just a few variables with a few lags requires a large number of parameters to be estimated, often from relatively short data spans. For example, the model in (9.1) has $n(np + 1)$ mean parameters, β, plus another $n(n + 1)/2$ covariance parameters, Σ. To deal with parameter estimation error, very quickly forecasters turned to methods such as Granger causality tests which can help remove regressors that do not appear to be useful and hence reduce the size of the model. Bayesian procedures which reduce parameter estimation error by

[1] Lütkepohl (2006, 2007) provide an extensive coverage of VARMA models and their use in forecasting. Athanasopoulos and Vahid (2008) report on a variety of empirical applications of VARMA models. They find that VARMA models produce better out-of-sample forecasts than VAR models for a range of macroeconomic variables.

shrinking the parameter estimates towards some target value are also popular. The move towards Bayesian methods has, however, complicated the formulation of the models as they require choices on priors and algorithms for estimation. A large and sophisticated literature makes use of improvements in computational algorithms to address such issues.

Example 9.1.1 (Modeling the term structure of interest rates). *Affine term structure models make extensive use of vector autoregressive dynamics to derive the complete term structure of interest rates under no-arbitrage restrictions. To see how this works, let P_t^n be the price at time t of a zero-coupon bond that expires in period $t + n$, so that n is the bond's maturity. To account for risk, let M_{t+1} be the stochastic discount factor, or so-called pricing kernel, used to price nominal payoffs at time $t + 1$. Under no-arbitrage, the current price of an n-period bond that pays one dollar at time $t + n$ is*

$$P_t^n = E_t \left[\prod_{j=1}^{n} M_{t+j} \right]. \tag{9.4}$$

To derive pricing restrictions from this equation, suppose that the pricing kernel takes the form

$$M_{t+1} = \exp\left(-r_t - \tfrac{1}{2}\lambda_t'\lambda_t - \lambda_t'\varepsilon_{t+1}\right), \quad \varepsilon_{t+1} \sim i.i.d. \, N(0, I), \tag{9.5}$$

where $\lambda_t = \lambda_0 + \lambda_1'X_t$ and r_t is the short rate. Thus, the coefficients, λ_t, are assumed to be affine functions of a vector of state variables, X_t. Assuming that the short interest rate, r_t, is also an affine function of X_t, i.e., $r_t = \delta_0 + \delta_1'X_t$, the entire term structure will be driven by the vector of state variables X_t. Suppose these follow a VAR(1) process,

$$X_{t+1} = \mu + AX_t + \Sigma\varepsilon_{t+1}, \tag{9.6}$$

and so are affected by the same shocks as the pricing kernel in (9.5). Conjecturing a solution of the form

$$P_t^n = \exp(a_n + b_n'X_t),$$

it can easily be verified from (9.4)–(9.6) that a_n and b_n must satisfy the recursive relations

$$a_{n+1} = -\delta_0 + a_n + b_n'(\mu - \Sigma\lambda_0) + \tfrac{1}{2}b_n'\Sigma\Sigma'b_n, \tag{9.7}$$

$$b_{n+1} = (A - \Sigma\lambda_1)'b_n - \delta_1,$$

with $a_1 = -\delta_0$, $b_1 = -\delta_1$ as initial conditions. Given a set of estimates for the VAR coefficients μ, A, Σ in (9.6) and for the remaining parameters δ_0, λ_0, λ_1, δ_1, we can compute the entire term structure of zero-coupon bond prices from (9.7); see Wright (2011) for further discussion of how this model can be estimated.

9.2 CLASSICAL ESTIMATION OF VARS

After determining the n variables to include in the VAR, we must decide how many lags to use. Rather than keeping the same number of lags for all variables, refinements that eliminate some variables in some of the equations can be used. Classical estimation also requires settling on an estimation technique for the model. We first assume that the lag length, p, has been chosen and consider parameter estimation before we address the choice of model specification.

9.2.1 Estimation of VAR(p) Models

From an econometric perspective VARs are seemingly unrelated regressions (SUR) whose equations are related through the covariances of the residual terms (Zellner, 1962). In its unconstrained form where each equation includes the same lags of each of the same regressors (and the same exogenous variables as well), SUR estimation simplifies to be numerically identical to OLS estimation equation by equation, which therefore offers the easiest estimation method.[2] Conversely, for constrained VARs with different regressors in each equation, typically SUR methods will result in more efficient estimates.

In sufficiently large samples and under conventional assumptions, the centered and standardized least squares estimators for the coefficients β in (9.3) will be distributed according to

$$T^{1/2}(\hat{\beta} - \beta_0) \overset{a}{\sim} \mathrm{N}(0, \Sigma \otimes (Z'Z)^{-1}), \tag{9.8}$$

where β_0 is the true parameter value. Standard errors for each regression are computed using the OLS estimates equation by equation. Tests of cross-equation restrictions must, however, account for the full covariance matrix of the residuals, Σ.

While OLS estimation is asymptotically efficient in the unconstrained case, there are many other estimators with the same first-order asymptotic properties. Hence, asymptotic efficiency alone does not eliminate interest in alternative estimators. Moreover, other properties familiar from OLS estimation may fail. For example, consider the OLS estimator $\hat{\beta}_i = (Z'Z)^{-1}Z'y_i$ from the ith column of (9.3), $y_i = Z\beta_i + u_i$. The bias of $\hat{\beta}_i$ is given by

$$E[\hat{\beta}_i - \beta_i] = E[(Z'Z)^{-1}Z'u_i]$$
$$= E[E[(Z'Z)^{-1}Z'u_i | Z]]. \tag{9.9}$$

When $E[u_i|Z] = 0$, this bias is 0 and the OLS estimator is unbiased. However it is impossible for this to hold here, since the shocks u_{is} affect y_{jt} for $t > s$, i.e., current shocks affect future values of the regressors. Since u determines the path of y and hence appears inside Z, in general $E[u_i|Z] \neq 0$ and the OLS estimator is not unbiased.[3]

The claim that OLS is asymptotically efficient may also not be very comforting from a forecasting perspective. It only means that in large samples the distribution

---

[2] We will refer to these as the conventional assumptions.

[3] This is of course similar to the result for univariate AR(p) models discussed in chapter 7.

of the parameters is well approximated by a normal distribution with a variance–covariance matrix that is as small as possible. In practice, however, we often do not have a great amount of data at hand and need to estimate many parameters. In such situations it is not obvious that the number of degrees of freedom is large enough to ensure that the asymptotic approximation is reasonable. If the asymptotic approximation is not reasonable, efficiency calculations based on it are clearly not relevant. Alternatively, a wide range of analytical and bootstrap methods for bias correction have been suggested; see, e.g., Bauer, Rudebusch, and Wu (2012) for an application to the term structure of interest rates.

After determining which variables to include in the VAR, we need to choose the lag length of the VAR. Often the choice uses the methods for model selection discussed in chapter 6 which readily apply to this problem. Beyond this, some researchers also employ Granger causality tests to remove individual variables from some of the equations. The idea is to remove predictors from the model if there is insufficient evidence that such predictors are useful.

9.2.2 Choice of Lag Length

The standard approach for choosing the lag length for a VAR is to treat this as a model selection problem and use information criteria. Popular methods in the literature on VARs are the BIC and AIC. As we have seen, SUR estimation simplifies to OLS estimation equation by equation in a system with the same variables appearing in each regression. This explains why it is common practice to search over different values for p and hence exclude the same regressors from each equation. Here the search is not over all possible models but instead involves a sequence of models corresponding to each lag length, i.e., either setting all elements of A_p to 0 or leaving all of them unrestricted. With n variables, p lags, and T observations, and assuming that a constant term is included in each equation of the VAR, the BIC and AIC information criteria take the forms

$$\text{BIC}(p) = \ln|\hat{\Sigma}_p| + n(np + 1)\frac{\ln(T)}{T}, \tag{9.10}$$

$$\text{AIC}(p) = \ln|\hat{\Sigma}_p| + n(np + 1)\frac{2}{T}, \tag{9.11}$$

where $\hat{\Sigma}_p = T^{-1}\sum_{t=t}^{T}\hat{u}_t\hat{u}_t'$. In each case the objective is to identify the model (indexed by p) that minimizes the information criterion. In practice the search is sometimes not conducted over all possible values of p but restricted to include a minimum value of p that reflects the periodicity of the data. For example a minimum of four lags is sometimes chosen when the data are quarterly. Such restrictions reflect seasonality patterns believed to be present in the data. Moreover, it is common practice not to allow for gaps in the lags, i.e., all lags up to the pth order are included as opposed to, for example, dropping lag $p - 1$.

9.2.3 Granger Causality Tests

Each variable predicts every other variable in the general VAR. However, in VARs that include many variables, it is quite likely that some individual variables are not particularly useful for forecasting all the other variables. Granger (1969a) used a variable's predictive content and notions of causality to develop a definition of causality that depends on the conditional distribution of the predicted variable. Consider the conditional density of a random variable y_{it} given its own past history and that of a set of other random variables, $p_{y_{it}}(y_{it}|y_{1t-1}, \ldots, y_{1t-p}, \ldots, y_{nt-1}, \ldots, y_{nt-p})$. Suppose that this density is independent of the past history of the rth random variable, y_{rt}, i.e.,

$$p_{y_{it}}(y_{it}|\cup_{j=1}^{n} y_{jt-k}, k = 1, \ldots, p) = p_{y_{it}}(y_{it}|\cup_{j\neq r} y_{jt-k}, k = 1, \ldots, p), \quad (9.12)$$

so the ith density does not depend on $y_{rt-1}, \ldots, y_{rt-p}$. When this holds, y_{rt} is said not to Granger-cause y_{it} in the universe of variables $y_{1t}, \ldots, y_{nt}$. If such a statement were true, the past of y_{rt} would not be useful for forecasting y_{it} one step ahead regardless of the loss function. The proviso "in the universe of variables $y_{1t}, \ldots, y_{nt}$" is important. It is entirely possible that a finding of Granger causality can be overturned by adding more variables to the system — y_{rt} may simply have nonzero coefficients because of omitted variable bias.

In practice, the condition in (9.12) is not what is usually examined to see whether a variable adds value from a predictive perspective. Part of the problem is that testing independence for the conditional density is not straightforward. Instead, it is common to test for lack of linear predictability rather than independence, and thus focus on the weaker notion that the lags $y_{rt-1}, \ldots, y_{rt-p}$ do not enter the equation for y_{it} for the linear VAR. This is a test for exclusion in a VAR, and is thus simple to undertake. Consider the bivariate VAR,

$$\begin{pmatrix} y_{1t} \\ y_{2t} \end{pmatrix} = \begin{pmatrix} a_{11}(L) & a_{12}(L) \\ a_{21}(L) & a_{22}(L) \end{pmatrix} \begin{pmatrix} y_{1t-1} \\ y_{2t-1} \end{pmatrix} + \begin{pmatrix} u_{1t} \\ u_{2t} \end{pmatrix}. \quad (9.13)$$

The test is simply that $a_{12}(L) = 0$ for y_{1t} not to be Granger-caused by y_{2t}. This more limited notion of predictability is really a statement that past information in y_{2t} is not useful in predicting the mean of y_{1t} and so this concept is most relevant under MSE loss.

Under MSE loss, Granger causality tests examine whether all lags of some variable can be removed from the forecasting equation. If lags of a variable are constrained to have zero coefficients, the same variables will no longer appear in each equation and hence OLS estimation equation by equation is no longer asymptotically efficient. In such cases either full information maximum likelihood (FIML) or minimum distance methods can be used to estimate the coefficients. For further discussion, see Hamilton (1994, chapter 11).

9.2.4 Multiperiod Forecasts with VARs

VARs are ideally designed for generating multiperiod forecasts. For the VAR(1) specification,

$$y_{t+1} = c + Ay_t + u_{t+1}, \quad u_{t+1} \sim (0, \Sigma), \quad (9.14)$$

with serially uncorrelated innovations u_{t+1}, the h-step-ahead value can be written

$$y_{t+h} = (I - A^h)(I - A)^{-1}c + A^h y_t + \sum_{i=1}^{h} A^{h-i} u_{t+i}, \tag{9.15}$$

and so the forecast under MSE loss becomes

$$f_{t+h|t} = (I - A^h)(I - A)^{-1}c + A^h y_t. \tag{9.16}$$

Higher-order dynamics can easily be handled in this setup by writing the VAR in companion form. For example, the VAR(2) model,

$$y_{t+1} = c + A_1 y_t + A_2 y_{t-1} + u_{t+1},$$

can be rewritten as a VAR(1) for $\tilde{y}_{t+1} = (y'_{t+1}, y'_t)'$:

$$\tilde{y}_{t+1} = \begin{pmatrix} y_{t+1} \\ y_t \end{pmatrix} = \begin{pmatrix} A_1 & A_2 \\ I & 0 \end{pmatrix} \begin{pmatrix} y_t \\ y_{t-1} \end{pmatrix} + \begin{pmatrix} u_{t+1} \\ 0 \end{pmatrix}.$$

When we are interested in forecasting y multiple periods ahead, an important issue is whether it is best to estimate the model at the highest frequency (corresponding to a one-period horizon) and then iterate the model h steps ahead as in (9.16), or whether it is better to use a loss function defined directly on the h-step forecast error. The latter entails estimating a VAR with the variables lagged h periods, i.e., in the VAR(p) case,

$$y_{t+h} = c + \sum_{i=1}^{p} A_{hi} y_{t+1-i} + u_{t+h}. \tag{9.17}$$

Using maximum likelihood estimation on data at the highest available frequency tends to generate less sampling variation and so is more efficient if the model is correctly specified than the loss-function-based approach (9.17) that fits the VAR to observations h periods ahead. Conversely, if the VAR is misspecified, the direct forecasting approach based on (9.17) is potentially more robust as it is simply a linear projection model that avoids the cumulated effect of iterating multiple periods ahead on a misspecified model as in (9.16).

A particular source of misspecification for the VAR is the choice of lag order. Schorfheide (2005) develops a model selection criterion that can be used to select both the lag order of the VAR and the parameter estimation method—maximum likelihood or loss based.

Pesaran, Pick, and Timmermann (2011) propose SUR (seemingly unrelated) estimation methods and a modified AIC for model selection that accounts for serial correlation in the residuals from multistep direct forecasts induced by the resulting overlaps. When applied to 170 macroeconomic and financial variables, they find empirically that both SUR estimation and their modifications to the AIC can help improve the predictive accuracy of direct multistep forecasts. Moreover, they find that forecasts from a factor-augmented VAR tend to outperform univariate forecasts (with the exception of variables such as prices and wages), suggesting that multivariate (factor) information helps improve the benchmark autoregressive forecasts.

Example 9.2.1 (Log-linearized present value model for stock prices). *Campbell and Shiller (1988) use a first-order Taylor expansion to express the continuously compounded stock return in period $t+1$, r_{t+1}, as an approximate linear function of the logarithms of current and future stock prices, p_t, p_{t+1}, and the future log-dividend, d_{t+1}:*

$$r_{t+1} \approx k + \rho p_{t+1} + (1-\rho)d_{t+1} - p_t, \tag{9.18}$$

where ρ is some parameter close to (but below) 1, and k is a constant. Rearranging, we get a recursive equation for log-prices:

$$p_t = k + \rho p_{t+1} + (1-\rho)d_{t+1} - r_{t+1}.$$

Iterating forward under the transversality condition that $\lim_{j \to \infty} \rho^j E_t[p_{t+j}] = 0$ and taking expectations conditional on current information, we have

$$p_t = \frac{k}{1-\rho} + (1-\rho)E_t\left[\sum_{j=0}^{\infty} \rho^j d_{t+1+j}\right] - E_t\left[\sum_{j=0}^{\infty} \rho^j r_{t+1+j}\right]. \tag{9.19}$$

According to this expression, stock prices depend on an infinite sum of expected future dividends and returns and will be higher, the higher the expected future dividends and the lower the expected future returns. Key to the present value model is therefore how such expectations are formed. VARs are ideally suited to address this question since they provide a framework for iteratively generating multiperiod forecasts.

To illustrate this point, let z_{t+1} be a vector of state variables with $z_{1t} = p_t$, $z_{2t} = d_t$, $z_{3t} = r_t$ and assume that

$$z_{t+1} = Az_t + \varepsilon_{t+1},$$

so that

$$E_t[z_{t+1+j}] = A^{j+1} z_t.$$

Further, define selection vectors $e_1 = (1\ 0\ 0\ 0 \ldots 0)'$, $e_2 = (0\ 1\ 0\ 0 \ldots 0)'$, $e_3 = (0\ 0\ 1\ 0 \ldots 0)'$ so $p_t = e_1' z_t$, $d_t = e_2' z_t$, $r_t = e_3' z_t$. Assuming that $(\rho A)^{-1}$ exists, we have (up to a constant) from (9.19),

$$p_t = (1-\rho)\sum_{j=0}^{\infty} \rho^j e_2' A^{j+1} z_t - \sum_{j=0}^{\infty} \rho^j e_3' A^{j+1} z_t$$

$$= \left[(1-\rho)e_2' A(I - \rho A)^{-1} - e_3' A(I - \rho A)^{-1}\right] z_t.$$

This example illustrates how useful VARs are for generating an infinite sequence of internally consistent forecasts.

9.2.5 Factor-Augmented VARs

If the number of predictor variables is very large, unrestricted VARs may not be well suited for constructing prediction models as they would involve the estimation of a very large number of coefficients. One approach that can be used to address this is to keep the key variables of interest in the VAR and then augment the VAR with a small set of common factors, F_t, that summarize the information from a potentially very large set of conditioning variables. Letting $\tilde{y}_t = (y_t', F_t')'$, the factor-augmented VAR (FAVAR) model proposed by Bernanke, Boivin, and Eliasz (2005) takes the form

$$\tilde{y}_t = c + \sum_{i=1}^{p} A_i \tilde{y}_{t-i} + \tilde{u}_t.$$

The key to the FAVAR model is that the dimension of F_t is far smaller than that of an original set of conditioning variables. In practice F_t will be extracted from a set of factors. Pesaran, Pick, and Timmermann (2011) suggest treating y_t and F_t asymmetrically so that lagged values of y are used to predict F, but not the other way round. This means that fewer parameters have to be estimated, although this constraint can be relaxed. Forecasting with factors is covered more extensively in chapter 10.

9.3 BAYESIAN VARS

The Bayesian approach complicates the problem of estimating a VAR in two ways: first, a prior for the model must be specified; second, estimation is no longer undertaken by OLS, apart from in very simple cases. Despite these complications, Bayesian VAR (BVAR) methods are popular for a number of reasons. First, even from a classical perspective, BVARs often provide better forecasts than those from an unrestricted OLS estimation of VARs. Second, BVARs can facilitate a closer relationship between the underlying economics of the forecast problem and the estimation, for instance by imposing economic theory through the prior. Such theory-based information can sometimes be used to improve estimation. Early Bayesian methods made assumptions not only to follow economic theory but also to address computational difficulties. Subsequent methods, developed when computational limitations were less binding, focus less on assumptions that ease computation.[4]

Bayesian forecasts can often be thought of as shrinkage methods that reduce the effect of estimation errors. Bayesian methods have the additional advantage that a by-product is the construction of a posterior density for the outcome. Hence, unlike some of the classical methods, Bayesian methods are not tied to MSE loss in particular.

Under the assumption that the innovations are normally distributed, the likelihood of the VAR is fully specified and has a well-known form. Combined with a set of priors, one can construct posteriors and the desired forecasts. How complicated this process gets depends both on distributional assumptions and on the form of the model.

We provide here a general overview of the literature. A number of sources give details of the precise methods for construction of forecasts from Bayesian VARs. Koop and Korobilis (2010) provide an overview from an estimation perspective. Karlsson (2013) is an excellent and detailed reference on the assumptions of different

---

[4] For more extensive coverage of Bayesian methods, see Geweke and Whiteman (2006), Robert (2001), and Zellner (1971).

models and also provides algorithms that can be used to estimate and generate forecasts from VARs.

9.3.1 Bayesian Estimation

Assuming that $u_t \sim \text{ind } N(0, \Sigma)$, then y_t has a density $f(y_t|Y_{t-1}, \theta) = N(y_t; z'_{t-1}\beta, \Sigma)$, where $\beta = (c, A_1, \ldots, A_p)'$, $z_{t-1} = (1, y'_{t-1}, \ldots, y'_{t-p})'$, and $Y_{t-1} = \{y_\tau\}$, $\tau = 1, \ldots, t-1$. The likelihood function for Y can then be written as

$$L(Y|\beta, \Sigma) = \frac{1}{(2\pi)^{nT/2}} |\Sigma|^{-T/2} \exp\left(\frac{-1}{2} \text{tr}\left[\Sigma^{-1}(Y - Z\beta)'(Y - Z\beta)\right]\right), \quad (9.20)$$

where Y and Z are defined above equation (9.3). Assuming uninformative (diffuse) priors with a uniform prior on β and a Jeffrey's prior on Σ, we have

$$p(\beta, \Sigma) \propto |\Sigma|^{-(n+1)/2}. \quad (9.21)$$

Conditional on the data up to time T,

$$\Sigma|Y_T \sim \text{iW}_n(S, T - np - 1), \quad (9.22)$$

where iW_n denotes the inverse Wishart distribution, $S = (Y - Z\hat{\beta})'(Y - Z\hat{\beta})$, and $\hat{\beta} = (Z'Z)^{-1}Z'Y$ is the OLS estimate.

Conditional on Σ and Y_T, β follows a normal distribution,[5]

$$\text{vec}(\beta)|Y_T, \Sigma \sim N(\hat{\beta}, \Sigma \otimes (Z'Z)^{-1}). \quad (9.23)$$

Combining the prior in (9.21) with the likelihood in (9.20), the posterior $\beta|Y_T$ has a t-distribution with mean $\text{vec}(\hat{\beta})$, variance proportional to $S \otimes (Z'Z)^{-1}$, and degrees of freedom $T - np - 1$. Hence, the marginal posterior of β conditioned only on the data has a t-distribution.

What do these results imply for the predictive distribution? At the one-period forecast horizon, $h = 1$, we have

$$y_{T+1} = c + A_1 y_T + A_2 y_{T-1} + \cdots + A_p y_{T-p+1} + u_{T+1},$$

which again follows a t-distribution. For $h = 2$, we have

$$y_{T+2} = (A_1^2 + A_2)y_T + (A_2 A_1 + A_3)y_{T-1} + \cdots + (A_{p-1}A_1 + A_p)y_{T-p+2}$$
$$+ A_p A_1 y_{T-p+1} + A_1 c + c + A_1 u_{T+1} + u_{T+2}.$$

This is a nonlinear function of the parameters and so there is no closed-form expression for the density of y_{T+h} for $h \geq 2$. Fortunately the model easily lends itself to generate out-of-sample forecasts. Following (Karlsson, 2013, algorithm 1), this works as follows. To make the jth draw, first a value of $\Sigma^j|Y_T$ is generated from the inverse Wishart distribution using (9.22). Second, conditional on Y_T and Σ^j, β^j

---

[5] For derivations and further details, see Karlsson (2013).

is drawn from the normal distribution using (9.23). Third, $u^j_{T+1}, \ldots, u^j_{T+h}$ are drawn from independent distributions $u^j_{t+i} \sim N(0, \Sigma^j)$. These draws, along with the parameter draws Σ^j, β^j are then used to iteratively generate a single draw of the out-of-sample value of y,

$$y^j_{T+h} = c^j + \sum_{i=1}^{p} A^j_i y^j_{T+h-i} + u^j_{T+h},$$

where $y^j_{T+h-i} = y_{T+h-i}$ for $i \geq h$. Repeating these steps J times yields a sample of draws from the posterior predictive distribution $\left\{ y^j_{T+1}, \ldots, y^j_{T+h} \right\}$, $j = 1, \ldots, J$. These can in turn be used to compute statistics such as the mean forecast,

$$\bar{y}_{T+h} = J^{-1} \sum_{j=1}^{J} y^j_{T+h},$$

which minimizes a quadratic loss function. Using this approach we can also construct statistics for the posterior predictive distribution such as the posterior predictive variance or $(1 - \alpha)\%$ interval forecasts.

9.3.2 Minnesota Prior

Forecasts generated by the unrestricted (so-called reduced-form) VAR in (9.1) can quickly become imprecise as the dimension of the VAR increases due to the effects of parameter estimation error. This becomes a particular issue in cases where a high lag order, p, is required to account for serial correlation in the variables included in the y vector. If some of the components in y are highly persistent (e.g., interest rates or inflation), while others are not, this could lead to the inclusion of many redundant terms in the model and a large number of unknown parameters. For example, with five variables ($n = 5$) and four lags ($p = 4$), we would need to estimate $n(np + 1) = 105$ mean parameters.

Allowing the data to inform the model estimates, yet not overwhelm the forecasts due to estimation error, requires a balancing act. To address this issue, Litterman (1979, 1986), and Doan, Litterman, and Sims (1984) introduced what is known as the "Minnesota" priors on the parameters of a VAR. Constructing forecast models with macroeconomic variables modeled in levels, Litterman proceeded to use a random walk as the prior model for each of the equations in the VAR. Hence, the prior for A_1 is the identity matrix, while for A_j, $j > 1$, the prior is that the coefficients of the matrix are 0. Denoting priors by $\underline{A}$, the mean of the prior on the regression coefficients β is specified as

$$(\underline{A}_1)_{ij} = \begin{cases} 1 & \text{for } i = j, \\ 0 & \text{for } i \neq j, \end{cases}$$

$$(\underline{A}_2)_{ij} = \cdots = (\underline{A}_p)_{ij} = 0. \tag{9.24}$$

The strength of the prior varies with the horizon and also depends on cross-variable effects, with greater shrinkage applied to other variables and their lags.

Specifically, a common variant of the Minnesota prior constructs the prior variance–covariance matrix for the ith equation by setting the variance of the prior on the own lags equal to π_1^2/l^2, where l is the lag length, so the prior gets tighter and tighter as the lag length increases. For lags of other variables in the VAR ($j = 1, \ldots, n, \ j \neq i$), the variance of the prior is set to $\pi_1^2\pi_2\sigma_i^2/(\sigma_j^2 l^2)$, where σ_j is the standard deviation of the errors of the jth equation. The factor σ_i/σ_j ensures that variables are standardized to have the same scale, as measured by their variance. The hyperparameter π_1 measures how tight the prior distribution is around the random walk, with $\pi_1 = 0$ denoting the dogmatic random walk prior that disregards all data, while $\pi_1 = \infty$ denotes a diffuse prior corresponding to OLS estimation; π_2 measures the relative tightness of priors on cross-variable effects versus own-variable effects.[6] Finally, $\mathrm{Var}(\underline{c}) = \infty$, corresponding to a diffuse prior for the intercept, i.e., $\underline{c} \sim \mathrm{N}(0, \kappa I)$, for a very large value of κ.

In summary, denoting the prior variance of element i, j of A_l by $\underline{\mathrm{Var}}(A_l)_{ij}$, we have

$$
\underline{\mathrm{Var}}(A_l)_{ij} =
\begin{cases}
\frac{\pi_1^2}{l^2} & \text{for } i = j, \\
\frac{\pi_1^2\pi_2}{l^2}\left(\frac{\sigma_i}{\sigma_j}\right)^2 & \text{for } i \neq j.
\end{cases}
\tag{9.25}
$$

These define the variance covariance Ω of the prior on β. Finally, for the variance–covariance matrix Σ it is assumed that the residuals of the VAR equations are contemporaneously uncorrelated with known variances. In practical applications the "known" variances are replaced with their OLS estimates and so $\Sigma = \mathrm{diag}(\hat{\sigma}_1^2, \ldots, \hat{\sigma}_n^2)$. Taken together, these are known as the Litterman priors. Because of the independence between parameters in the prior and the diagonal form of Σ, the posteriors for each of the equations are also unrelated. Hence the VAR can be estimated equation by equation as in the OLS case.

As noted by Karlsson (2013, page 804), the priors $\beta_{ij} \sim \mathrm{N}(\underline{\beta}_{ij}, \tau_{ij}^2)$ can usefully be thought of in the context of an augmented regression model,

$$
\begin{pmatrix} y_j \\ r_j \end{pmatrix} = \begin{pmatrix} Z \\ R_j \end{pmatrix} \beta_j + \begin{pmatrix} u_j \\ \tilde{u}_j \end{pmatrix},
$$

where $r_j = R_j\beta_j + \tilde{u}_j$ is a set of pseudo data whose ith element is $\underline{\beta}_{ij}\hat{\sigma}_j/\tau_j$, where $\tilde{u}_j \sim \mathrm{N}(0, \hat{\sigma}_j^2)$ and the off-diagonal elements of R_j are 0, while the diagonal elements are $\hat{\sigma}_j/\tau_{ij}$, for $i, j = 1, \ldots, np$. Using this representation, the posterior distribution becomes $\beta_j | Y_T \sim \mathrm{N}(\bar{\beta}_j, \bar{\Sigma}_j)$ with mean and variance,

$$
\bar{\beta}_j = (Z'Z + R_j'R_j)^{-1}(Z'y + R_j'r),
$$

$$
\bar{\Sigma}_j = \hat{\sigma}_j^2(Z'Z + R_j'R_j)^{-1}.
$$

In practice, this means that we can use OLS estimation on the augmented regression to compute the posterior mean and variance.

---

[6] Litterman suggests setting the prior hyperparameters to $\pi_1 = 0.04$ and $\pi_2 = 0.0004$.

9.3.3 Alternative Priors

The Litterman priors are quite restrictive and so are often relaxed. Extensions allow for a nondiagonal prior variance–covariance matrix Σ, and also allow the priors on β and Σ to be correlated. Bayesian posterior computation can be handled by methods such as the Gibbs sampler. The conjugate combination of a normal prior distribution on β and an independent Wishart distribution on Σ does not give a closed-form solution for the means of the posterior but yields a posterior distribution that is easy to simulate from. Karlsson (2013) and Kadiyala and Karlsson (1997) examine and extend conventional priors by introducing a more general prior which they call the Extended Natural Conjugate (ENC) prior which relaxes the requirements on the prior on β. In evaluations, there seem to be modest gains from this relaxation of the restrictions on prior distributions. While most of these methods can be thought of as shrinkage methods, they do not differentiate between parameters by removing some while keeping others. To remedy this, George, Sun, and Ni (2008) use a mixture prior with mixture weights estimated from the data. The mixture is between a very tight prior and a less tight prior, so if the estimation method gives a large weight to the tight prior the coefficient is effectively set to 0.

A number of improvements to the specification of the priors on β appear to have been useful in empirical work. In the context of macroeconomic forecasting, rather than employing the random walk or ad hoc priors, Ingram and Whiteman (1994) and Del Negro and Schorfheide (2004) suggest setting priors in a manner that implies shrinking towards the coefficients that arise from a linearized general equilibrium model of the macroeconomy. The idea is that a real business cycle (RBC) model can be used to generate implied variances and covariances of the data. These can be combined to obtain implied VAR parameter values, which form the priors for the OLS coefficients. The methods then shrink the OLS estimates towards the implied values. Ingram and Whiteman (1994) develop a model that implies a VAR with one lag, while priors on lags of higher order are set to 0. This is not strictly a fully Bayesian approach since the priors are applied to the reduced-form regression rather than to the likelihood for the data. Ingram and Whiteman call it a "limited information Bayesian" approach and find that their method results in forecasts comparable to those based on a Litterman prior but better than those from an unrestricted VAR.

Villani (2009) suggests an alternative approach to eliciting priors. Motivated by economic models, Villani places informative priors directly on the steady state of the model rather than on the coefficients of the VAR. Villani uses the unconditional means of the variables in the VAR to model the steady state.

Wright (2013) instead suggests using long-run forecasts from survey data to pin down the steady state. Using the reparameterized VAR,

$$(y_t - \mu) = A_1(y_{t-1} - \mu) + \cdots + A_p(y_{t-p} - \mu) + u_t,$$

where $E[u_t u_t' = \Sigma]$, Wright suggests using the priors

$$\text{vec}(A'_{1t}, \ldots, A'_{pt}) \sim N(\theta_{At}, \Omega_A),$$

$$\mu_t \sim N(\theta_{\mu t}, \Omega_{\mu t}),$$

$$\Sigma_t \sim |\Sigma_t|^{-(n+1)/2}.$$

Notice that the parameters are allowed to vary with t, the point in time where the model is estimated and the forecast is generated. Specifically, Wright (2011) proposes to set the prior mean $\theta_{\mu t}$ at the mean of the most recent long-run forecasts obtained from the Blue Chip survey. For variables such as CPI inflation, growth in industrial production, and T-bill yields, Wright reports notable gains in out-of-sample forecast performance from using this approach relative to both VARs estimated by least squares or Bayesian VARs based on the Minnesota prior.

9.3.4 Time-Varying Parameter VARs

Following empirical evidence on model instability related to the Great Moderation or the global financial crisis, a number of recent papers have modeled VARs with time-varying parameters.[7] The simplest version of these models assumes that the parameters of the mean equation, β_t, follow a random walk, i.e.,

$$y_t = (I_n \otimes z_t')\beta_t + u_t, \tag{9.26}$$

$$\beta_t = \beta_{t-1} + \varepsilon_t,$$

$$\varepsilon_t \sim N(0, Q), \quad u_t \sim N(0, \Sigma),$$

where the innovations ε_t and u_t are uncorrelated. Conventionally it is assumed that the initial state is normally distributed $\beta_1 \sim N(s_{1|0}, P_{1|0})$ and $\beta_{t+1}|\beta_t, Q \sim N(\beta_t, Q)$ is obtained iteratively.

Primiceri (2005) and Karlsson (2013) discuss implementation of a Gibbs sampler for this model. Since β_t is an unobserved state variable, estimation and forecasting with the model involves the Kalman filter. The Gibbs sampler for the time-varying parameter (TVP) model first draws β_T from its full conditional posterior given the full data set and initial values for Σ and Q, using the Kalman filter and simulation smoother. In turn, Q and Σ are updated given the states $\beta_1, \ldots, \beta_T$. Finally, using these updated parameter values, draws from the posterior distribution $y_{T+1}, \ldots, y_{T+h}$ are generated by drawing $u_{T+1}, \ldots, u_{T+h}$ and iterating on (9.26)

Stochastic volatility models allow for time-varying second moments in the data. There is strong empirical evidence in economics and finance of such features. One way to incorporate time-varying volatility is by assuming that the variance–covariance matrix for the innovations in the VAR, u_t, rather than being constant at Σ, takes the form

$$\Sigma_t = L_t^{-1} D_t \left(L_t^{-1}\right)', \tag{9.27}$$

where the diagonal matrix $D_t = \text{diag}(d_{1t}, \ldots, d_{nt})$ has dynamics (see Karlsson, 2013)

$$d_{it} = \exp(\tfrac{1}{2}h_{it}),$$

$$h_{it+1} = \mu_i + \phi_i(h_{it} - \mu_i) + \eta_{it}, \tag{9.28}$$

$$\eta_t = (\eta_{1t}, \ldots, \eta_{nt}) \sim \text{ind } N(0, V_\eta).$$

---

[7] Sims (1993) allows for time variation as well as heteroskedasticity and nonnormal errors in VARs.

Hence the log-volatility of the n individual series, h_{it+1}, is assumed to follow either a mean-reverting process (if $|\phi_i| < 1$) or a random walk specification (if $\phi_i = 1$, in which case typically μ_i is set to 0); see Primiceri (2005).

The matrix L_t can be specified as lower triangular with 1s on the diagonal:

$$L_t = \begin{pmatrix} 1 & 0 & 0 & \cdots & 0 \\ l_{21t} & 1 & 0 & \cdots & \vdots \\ l_{31t} & l_{32_t} & \ddots & & \\ \vdots & \vdots & & 1 & 0 \\ l_{n1t} & l_{n2t} & & l_{n(n-1)t} & 1 \end{pmatrix},$$

$$l_{ijt} = l_{ijt-1} + \vartheta_{ijt}, \quad (\vartheta_{11t}, \dots, \vartheta_{n(n-1)t})' \sim \text{ind N}(0, V_\vartheta), \; i > j.$$

The autoregressive parameters can be restricted to imply a stationary volatility process by using truncated distributions, i.e., $\phi_{ii} \sim \text{N}(\phi_0, V_\phi)\mathbb{1}(|\phi_{ii}| < 1)$, where $\mathbb{1}(\cdot)$ is an indicator function. As discussed in Karlsson (2013, algorithm 13), estimation and forecasting with the model involves a Gibbs sampler with Kalman filter steps to account for the latent state variables in Σ_t.

These types of models have been used extensively in recent work and there is much evidence to suggest that allowing for time-varying volatility can improve model performance considerably. Clark (2011) applies stochastic volatility models to density forecasting of a four-variable model with GDP growth, unemployment, inflation, and the Federal funds rate, while Primiceri (2005) uses stochastic volatility models to analyze monetary policy. Clark and Ravazzolo (2014) compare different volatility models' ability to predict macroeconomic outcomes. Pettenuzzo and Timmermann (2015) consider different models' ability to forecast US GDP growth and inflation and find that stochastic volatility models generate better density forecasts than Markov switching or change point models. See also Koop and Korobilis (2010).

A closely related literature studies Bayesian Markov switching VAR models, see, e.g., Sims and Zha (2006), Hartmann et al. (2014), and Hubrich and Tetlow (2015). Sims and Zha (2006) use a multivariate regime switching model to analyze US monetary policy. Hartmann et al. (2014) study the effect of systemic stress and lending on the European economy while Hubrich and Tetlow (2015) study the interaction between economic growth and financial distress. These models are mostly used for analyzing economic policy, but can also be used for forecasting.

9.3.5 Large-Dimensional Bayesian VARs

VARs have traditionally been used to model and predict low-dimensional vectors. Extending the VAR to include large-dimensional vectors poses problems in so far as it is likely to lead to greater parameter estimation errors—recall that $n(np + 1)$ mean parameters have to be estimated for an unconstrained VAR(p) model.

Banbura, Giannone, and Reichlin (2010) apply Bayesian shrinkage methods to large-dimensional unrestricted VARs in such a way that the degree of shrinkage is allowed to depend on the number of variables included in the VAR. Specifically, the tightness of the priors increases as more variables are added to the model. This approach can be viewed as an alternative to the type of factor models covered in chapter 10 and deals directly with the challenge that estimation error can be expected to increase with the dimension of the VAR, n.

Writing the BVAR as a $T \times n$ multivariate regression,

$$Y = Z\beta + U, \tag{9.29}$$

where, again, $Y = (y_1, \ldots, y_T)'$, $Z = (z_1, \ldots, z_T)'$, for $z_t = (1, y'_{t-1}, \ldots, y'_{t-p})'$, $U = (u_1, \ldots, u_T)$, and $\beta = (c', A'_1, \ldots, A'_p)$, Banbura, Giannone, and Reichlin (2010) assume standard normal-inverted Wishart priors,

$$\text{vec}(\beta)|\Sigma \sim N(\text{vec}(\beta_0), \Sigma \otimes \Omega_0),$$

$$\Sigma \sim \text{iW}(S_0, \alpha_0),$$

where $E[u_t u'_t] = \Sigma = \text{diag}(\sigma_1^2, \ldots, \sigma_n^2)$ and the prior parameters $\beta_0, \Omega_0, S_0, \alpha_0$ are chosen in accordance with what amounts to a set of modified Minnesota priors. To understand the key difference from (9.24), let $E[(A_k)_{ij}] = \delta_i$ when $j = i$. When the data are stationary, a prior with $\delta_i < 1$ is more appropriate than the original Minnesota prior which sets $\delta_i = 1$ and so assumes a random walk. This prior may seem difficult to implement, but Banbura, Giannone, and Reichlin (2010) suggest a simple strategy based on augmenting the model (9.29) with T_d dummy observations Y_d and Z_d given by

$$Y_d = \begin{pmatrix} \text{diag}(\delta_1\sigma_1, \ldots, \delta_n\sigma_n)/\lambda \\ 0_{n(p-1) \times n} \\ \cdots \\ \text{diag}(\sigma_1, \ldots, \sigma_n) \\ \cdots \\ 0_{1 \times n} \end{pmatrix},$$

$$Z_d = \begin{pmatrix} \text{diag}(1, 2, \ldots, p) \otimes \text{diag}(\sigma_1, \ldots, \sigma_n)/\lambda & 0_{np \times 1} \\ \cdots & \cdots \\ 0_{n \times np} & 0_{n \times 1} \\ \cdots & \cdots \\ 0_{1 \times np} & \varepsilon \end{pmatrix},$$

where ε is a very small number and the hyperparameter λ controls the tightness of the prior variance of A_k and thus can be thought of as a shrinkage parameter.

Consider OLS estimation of the augmented $T_* \times N_*$ regression model,

$$Y_* = Z_*\beta + U_*, \tag{9.30}$$

where

$$T_* = T + T_d,$$

$$Y_* = (Y', Y'_d)', \quad Z_* = (Z', Z'_d), \quad U_* = (U', U'_d)'.$$

Banbura, Giannone, and Reichlin (2010) show that these OLS estimates have the same posterior mean as the posterior of β based on a set of normal-inverted Wishart priors with

$$\beta_0 = (Z_d' Z_d)^{-1} Z_d' Y_d,$$

$$\Omega_0 = (Z_d' Z_d)^{-1},$$

$$S_0 = (Y_d - Z_d \beta_0)'(Y_d - Z_d \beta_0),$$

$$\alpha_0 = T_d - np - 1.$$

Specifically, under an improper prior, $\Sigma \sim |\Sigma|^{-(n+3)/2}$, the posterior becomes

$$\text{vec}(\beta)|\Sigma, Y \sim \text{N}(\text{vec}(\tilde{\beta}), \Sigma \otimes (Z_*' Z_*)^{-1}),$$

$$\Sigma|Y \sim \text{iW}(\tilde{\Sigma}, T_d + 2 + T - np - 1),$$

where $\tilde{\beta} = (Z_*' Z_*)^{-1} Z_*' Y$ and $\tilde{\Sigma} = (Y_* - Z_* \tilde{\beta})'(Y_* - Z_* \tilde{\beta})$ are the least squares estimates from the augmented model (9.30). The matrix that needs to be inverted in the OLS estimation of the augmented model has dimension $(np + 1)$ and so this is feasible even for large values of n and p.

Banbura, Giannone, and Reichlin (2010) apply this approach to a data set used by Stock and Watson which has 131 monthly macro variables. In practice, they set $\delta_i = 1$ for variables deemed to be nonstationary while $\delta_i = 0$ for variables deemed to be stationary. The shrinkage parameter, λ, is clearly important in this setup. Banbura, Giannone, and Reichlin (2010) set λ so that it matches the in-sample one-step-ahead MSE of a three-variable VAR with 13 monthly lags. Moreover, they consider three different values for the dimension of the VAR, $n = 3$, $n = 20$, and $n = 131$. Their empirical results look at out-of-sample MSE performance for employment, CPI inflation, and the Federal funds rate. For these variables, the medium- and large-scale models perform well compared to both a benchmark random walk with drift model and also compared to the small-scale model that includes only three variables. Interestingly, whereas the gains from going from $n = 3$ to $n = 20$ are very large, the gains from further extending to include $n = 131$ variables are more modest.

Similar empirical evidence by Carriero, Kapetanios, and Marcellino (2009, 2012) suggests that large-scale Bayesian VARs can produce accurate forecasts of exchange rates and government bond yields whose performance is comparable to the best univariate benchmarks (e.g., random walks). Such benchmarks are often found to be hard to beat for these types of variables.

9.3.6 Empirical Performance of Bayesian VARs

Ni and Sun (2005) provide a broad comparison of frequentist risks for Bayesian VAR estimates of regression coefficients and the variance–covariance matrix for VARs. In a Monte Carlo study they consider different priors, loss functions, and data distributions. Their results suggest that the choice of priors affects the Bayesian estimates more strongly than the choice of loss function. Interestingly, however, they find that the estimator of the slope coefficients based on an asymmetric Linex loss function performs better than the estimator based on quadratic loss.

Estimation error can make a very large difference in empirical studies. In the context of Federal funds rate forecasts, Rudebusch (1998) and others have found that structural VARs produce much greater forecast errors than the errors associated with forecasts based on prices in the Federal funds futures markets. Robertson and Tallman (2001) examine whether this finding could be due to parameter estimation error. They study the forecasting performance of flat prior VARs, i.e., the usual OLS estimates, and Bayesian methods based on more informative priors. Their model includes many highly persistent variables in levels and requires many lags and thus the estimation of a large number of coefficients. Empirically, they find that VAR models based on OLS estimates generate one-month-ahead MSE values nearly three times greater than the Federal funds futures benchmark. Shrinkage VAR models perform much better than VARs using OLS estimates, although they produce MSE values that are still between $\frac{1}{3}$ and 60% higher than their benchmark. Interestingly, a simple first-order autoregressive model for the change in the Federal funds rate produces forecasts comparable to the best forecasts from the multivariate models in levels.

In regional forecasting, VAR models have also been used to generate growth forecasts. Kinal and Ratner (1986) generate forecasts for New York state employment, output, retail sales, and consumer prices using both state-specific and national variables. They find relatively poor forecasting performance for the VARs which they attribute to overparameterization. Consistent with this, Bayesian VARs perform better.

9.3.7 Empirical Example: Asset Allocation with Return Predictability

To illustrate the use of Bayesian VAR methods, we next return to the empirical asset allocation example from section 3.5 but in a setting that, following Barberis (2000), allows for return predictability and so introduces a market timing component in the investor's decision process. Specifically, suppose that the continuously compounded stock returns, r_t, measured in excess of a risk-free asset paying r_f, contain a predictable component which is captured through a single predictor variable, x_t, and assume that $y_t' = (r_t, x_t)$ follows a first-order VAR:

$$y_t = c + A_1 y_{t-1} + \varepsilon_t, \quad \varepsilon_t \sim \text{ind } N(0, \Sigma). \tag{9.31}$$

Under the classical approach the VAR parameters $\theta = (c, A_1, \Sigma)$ can be estimated and the VAR in (9.31) can be iterated forward conditional on these parameter estimates. This generates a distribution of future cumulative stock returns conditional on the parameter values, $p_Y(\sum_{\tau=1}^h y_\tau | Z_T, \hat{\theta})$, where $Z_T = (y_1, \ldots, y_T)$ is the observed data vector. Specifically,

$$y_{T+h} = c + A_1 c + A_1^2 c + \cdots + A_1^{h-1} c \tag{9.32}$$
$$+ A_1^h y_T + \varepsilon_{T+h} + A_1 \varepsilon_{T+h-1} + A_1^2 \varepsilon_{T+h-2} + \cdots + A_1^{h-1} \varepsilon_{T+1}.$$

Conditional on c, A_1, Σ, from (9.32) the sum $y_{T+1:T+h} \equiv y_{T+1} + y_{T+2} + \cdots + y_{T+h}$ is normally distributed with mean and variance (see Barberis (2000))

$$E[y_{T+1:T+h}|\theta] = hc + (h-1)A_1 c + (h-2)A_1^2 c + \cdots + A_1^{h-1}c$$
$$+ (A_1 + A_1^2 + \cdots + A_1^h)z_T,$$

$$\mathrm{Var}[y_{T+1:T+h}|\theta] = \Sigma \tag{9.33}$$
$$+ (I + A_1)\Sigma(I + A_1)'$$
$$+ (I + A_1 + A_1^2)\Sigma(I + A_1 + A_1^2)'$$
$$\vdots$$
$$+ (I + A_1 + A_1^2 + \cdots + A_1^{h-1})\Sigma(I + A_1 + A_1^2 + \cdots + A_1^{h-1})'.$$

Using these expressions and plugging in parameter estimates $\hat{\theta} = (\hat{c}, \hat{A}_1, \hat{\Sigma})$, the classical investor maximizes the expected utility of future wealth $u(W_{T+h})$, where

$$\max_{\omega \in [0,1)} \int \cdots \int u(W_{T+h}) p_Y \left(\sum_{\tau=1}^h y_{T+\tau} | Z_T, \hat{\theta} \right) dy_{1,T+1} \ldots dy_{1,T+h}, \tag{9.34}$$

where $y_{1,T+\tau} = e_1' y_{T+\tau}$ selects the first element of $y_{T+\tau}$ and where future wealth is given by

$$W_{T+h} = (1 - \omega(z)) \exp(r_f h) + \omega(z) \exp\left(r_f h + \sum_{\tau=1}^h y_{T+\tau} \right). \tag{9.35}$$

The Bayesian approach conditions only on the data and so uses the following posterior density to compute expected utility:

$$p_Y \left(\sum_{\tau=1}^h y_{1,T+\tau} | Z_T \right) = \int p_Y \left(\sum_{\tau=1}^h y_{T+\tau} | Z_T, \theta \right) p(\theta | Z_T) d\theta. \tag{9.36}$$

To draw from the posterior return distribution, $p(c, A_1, \Sigma | Z_T)$, write the model as

$$\begin{pmatrix} y_2' \\ \vdots \\ y_T' \end{pmatrix} = \begin{pmatrix} 1 & y_1' \\ \vdots & \vdots \\ 1 & y_{T-1}' \end{pmatrix} \begin{pmatrix} c' \\ A_1' \end{pmatrix} + \begin{pmatrix} \varepsilon_2' \\ \vdots \\ \varepsilon_T' \end{pmatrix},$$

or, in more compact form,

$$Y = Z\beta + U,$$

where Y is a $((T-1) \times 2)$ matrix with the vectors $y_2', \ldots, y_T'$ as rows. Assuming a single predictor variable, Z is a $((T-1) \times 2)$ matrix with the vectors $(1, y_1'), \ldots, (1, y_{T-1}')$ as rows; and U is a $((T-1) \times (n+1))$ matrix with the vectors $\varepsilon_2', \ldots, \varepsilon_T'$ as rows. The matrix β is (2×2) with top row c' and the matrix A_1' below that.

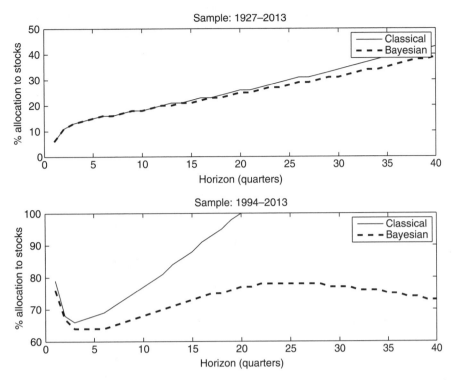

Figure 9.1: Percentage allocation to stocks for different holding periods in the presence of return predictability from the dividend yield.

To sample from the Bayesian predictive distribution, we first generate a sample of size I from the posterior distribution for the parameters, $p(c, A_1, \Sigma | Z_T)$. For each set of parameter values drawn, $\theta^i = \{c^i, A_1^i, \Sigma^i\}$, we sample from the distribution of returns conditional on Z and θ^i. Assuming uninformative priors, Barberis (2000) shows that the posterior of the parameters are given by

$$p(\Sigma^{-1} | Z_T) \sim \text{Wishart}(T - n - 2, S^{-1}),$$

$$p(\text{vec}(\beta) | \Sigma, Z_T) \sim \text{N}(\text{vec}(\hat{\beta}), \Sigma \otimes (Z'Z)^{-1}),$$

where $S = (Y - Z\hat{\beta})'(Y - Z\hat{\beta})$ with $\hat{\beta} = (Z'Z)^{-1}Z'Y$. Samples from the posterior return distribution are generated by first drawing from the marginal distribution, $p(\Sigma^{-1} | Z_T)$, then drawing from the conditional distribution $p(C | \Sigma, Z_T)$. For each draw of parameters from the posterior $p(c, A_1, \Sigma | Z_T)$, we generate a single draw from the normal distribution with mean and variance given by (9.33). Repeating this many times gives a large sample from the predictive return distribution.

Empirical results for the case with return predictability from the dividend yield—the predictor variable used by Barberis (2000)—are presented in figure 9.1. To show the importance of the length of the estimation sample, the top figure uses quarterly returns data over the sample 1927–2013, while the bottom window uses a shorter 20-year data sample from 1994–2013. The results assume a coefficient of relative risk aversion of 5 and power utility, i.e., the objective function in equation (3.33). We set the risk-free rate and the dividend yield at their values as of the end of the sample.

First consider the long estimation sample (top). Since a lot of data are available to estimate model parameters, we observe only small differences in the allocations under the classical and Bayesian approaches. In both cases the allocation to stocks increases as the forecast horizon grows longer. In contrast, the two allocations are very different under the classical and Bayesian approaches when the 20-year estimation sample is used (bottom). In this case, long-run investors will allocate a considerably smaller amount to stocks under the Bayesian approach (which accounts for parameter estimation uncertainty) than under the classical approach (which ignores such uncertainty).

The nonmonotonic pattern seen in the shorter sample (1994–2013) reflects two distinct effects. First, the value of the dividend yield that the model conditions on at the point of the investment decision is quite low relative to the sample mean of the predictor. Given the positive relation between the dividend yield and predicted stock returns, this reduces expected returns, particularly at short to medium horizons. On the other hand, the dividend yield captures a slowly, mean-reverting component in stock returns which makes stock returns less risky particularly at the longer horizons where this effect dominates.

A very different pattern is observed for the Bayesian investor whose allocation to stocks falls uniformly from close to 70% at the one-month horizon to less than 40% at the longest five-year horizon. For this investor, the effect of estimation error clearly does not get reduced as the investment horizon gets extended.

9.4 DSGE MODELS

DSGE—dynamic stochastic general equilibrium—models provide a way to generate internally consistent forecasts in a way that links the current state of the economy with agents' forward-looking expectations of outcomes that may depend on economic policy decisions. Due to their ability to condition forecasts on future policy actions, DSGE models are well suited for conditional forecasting exercises such as scenario analysis. They can also be used to decompose forecasts in a way that improves economic interpretation—e.g., an optimistic output growth forecast may be predicated on planned future fiscal stimulus.

DSGE models start from intertemporally optimizing agents' decisions given a set of assumptions about household preferences and firms' production function. These are augmented with monetary and fiscal policy decision rules as well as assumptions about drivers such as shocks to technology, monetary, and fiscal policy. The models make use of macroeconomic equilibrium specifications which usually can be grouped into either neoclassical growth models or New Keynesian models that incorporate nominal and real frictions and adjustment costs.

The chief determinant of the size of a DSGE model is the extent to which the model accounts for dynamic capital accumulation effects, wage stickiness, households' habit formation, and financial frictions.

For an exhaustive coverage of DSGE models, we refer to Del Negro and Schorfheide (2013) who describe large-, medium-, and small-scale DSGE models. As an illustration, we briefly describe their "small" DSGE model which is a special case of a model by Smets and Wouters (2003) and ignores capital accumulation, wage stickiness, habit formation, and financial frictions.

This model includes an Euler equation that links current consumption, c_t, to expected future consumption, c_{t+1}, and total output, z_{t+1}, as well as the expected real interest rate which is given by the current nominal interest rate, R_t, minus the expected rate of inflation, $E_t[\pi_{t+1}]$:

$$c_t = E_t[c_{t+1} + z_{t+1}] - \frac{1}{A_c}(R_t - E_t[\pi_{t+1}]). \qquad (9.37)$$

Here A_c measures households' risk aversion. Households supply labor to the point where their marginal rate of substitution between consumption and leisure equals their wage which, in turn, is linked to companies' marginal cost, mc_t. In this simple model without capital the detrended output, y_t, is equal to the labor input, L_t, and so, in equilibrium,

$$mc_t = c_t + \nu L_t, \qquad (9.38)$$

where ν is a parameter that measures the curvature of households' disutility of supplying labor.

Del Negro and Schorfheide (2013) show that an expectation-augmented Phillips curve can be derived to capture the trade-off between inflation and employment costs,

$$\pi_t = b_1(\lambda)mc_t + b_2(\lambda)E_t[\pi_{t+1}] + b_3(\lambda)\pi_{t-1}, \qquad (9.39)$$

where λ is a set of parameters capturing price rigidity, households' intertemporal discount rate, and the economy's degree of price indexation.

Three types of "shocks" drive this model, namely, monetary policy shocks (or interest rate shocks), ε_{Rt}; shocks to government policy (fiscal policy shocks), ε_{gt}; and shocks to the trend process for output (technology shocks), ε_{zt}. These shocks are embedded in three equations that show how interest rates, government spending, and economic growth evolve.

Specifically, the central bank sets its monetary policy such that the nominal interest rate, R_t, is higher the higher are past interest rates, current inflation, and output growth in relation to the trend:

$$R_t = \rho_R R_{t-1} + (1 - \rho_R)[\psi_1 \pi_t + \psi_2(y_t - y_{t-1} + z_t)] + \sigma_R \varepsilon_{Rt}, \qquad (9.40)$$

where ρ_R, ψ_1, and ψ_2 are parameters of the monetary policy rule. Government spending, g_t, is assumed to follow an AR(1) process,

$$g_t = \rho_g g_{t-1} + \sigma_g \varepsilon_{gt}. \qquad (9.41)$$

Finally, the growth rate in the economy's trend process, z_t, is given by

$$z_t = (\rho_z - 1)(1 - \varphi)\tilde{z}_{t-1} - \varphi(\tilde{z}_{t-1} - \tilde{z}_{t-2}) + \sigma_z \epsilon_{zt}, \qquad (9.42)$$

$$\tilde{z}_t = \rho_z(1 - \varphi)\tilde{z}_{t-1} + \varphi\tilde{z}_{t-2} + \sigma_z \epsilon_{zt},$$

where the AR(2) process $\tilde{z}_t$ affects the total factor process and so captures changes to technology. Naturally, this model can be amended in several ways, e.g., by changing the dynamics in (9.40), (9.41), or (9.42), or by introducing capital buildup or financial market frictions. See Del Negro and Schorfheide (2013) for further discussion and details.

9.4.1 Estimation and Computation of Forecasts for DSGE Models

Estimation of DSGE models can proceed using a state-space representation for the linearized DSGE model given assumptions such as normally distributed innovations. Letting s_t denote the vector of state variables, suppose we can approximate the solution to the DSGE model through a log-linearized first-order VAR,

$$s_t = \Phi_1(\theta)s_{t-1} + \Phi_\epsilon(\theta)\varepsilon_t, \tag{9.43}$$

where the vector ε_t collects structural shocks (innovations) to the model, i.e., $\varepsilon_t = (\varepsilon_{Rt}, \varepsilon_{gt}, \varepsilon_{zt})'$ in the small-scale model described above. The matrices Φ_1 and Φ_ϵ depend on the parameters of the DSGE model, θ. Given this representation, the measurement equation for the aggregate output, y_t, can be written as

$$y_t = \Psi_0(\theta) + \Psi_1(\theta)t + \Psi_2(\theta)s_t. \tag{9.44}$$

Under these assumptions, the Kalman filter can be used to evaluate the likelihood function and estimate the parameters.

A key complication arising from (9.43) and (9.44) is that the parameters of the linearized state and measurement equations, Φ_1, Φ_ϵ, Ψ_0, Ψ_1, Ψ_2 are nonlinearly related to the parameters underlying the DSGE model, θ. Standard sampling algorithms can therefore typically not be used since the conditional probability distribution of θ is not easily available. To address this issue, one can use algorithms such as the random walk metropolis algorithm; see Del Negro and Schorfheide (2013) for details and references.

Using Bayesian methods, draws from the posterior predictive distribution of the dependent variables in the DSGE model can be based on the following useful decomposition (see Del Negro and Schorfheide, 2013):

$$p_Y(y_{T+1}|y_1, \ldots, y_T) = \int_{s_T, \theta} \left[\int_{s_{T+1}} p_Y(y_{T+1}|s_{T+1})p(s_{T+1}|s_T, \theta, y_1, \ldots, y_T)ds_{T+1} \right]$$

$$\times p(s_T|\theta, y_1, \ldots, y_T)p(\theta|y_1, \ldots, y_T)d(s_T, \theta). \tag{9.45}$$

Such draws are generated using the same sorts of steps described earlier in this chapter. First, suppose that an algorithm is in place to generate draws θ^j from the posterior parameter distribution $p(\theta|y_1, \ldots, y_T)$. Next, use the Kalman filter to generate draws s_T^j from the conditional posterior distribution $p(s_T|\theta^j, y_1, \ldots, y_T)$. Using these draws, we can obtain draws from $p(s_{T+1}|s_T^j, \theta^j, y_1, \ldots, y_T)$ by using (9.43) along with draws of ε_{T+1}^j. Finally, using (9.44), we can generate draws from y_{T+1}^j:

$$y_t^j = \Psi_0(\theta^j) + \Psi_1(\theta^j)t + \Psi_2(\theta^j)s_t^j. \tag{9.46}$$

Given a sufficient number of draws, we can compute the mean forecast, forecast intervals, and even a predictive distribution in a manner that has the advantage of not conditioning on plug-in parameter estimates, $\hat{\theta}$. Rather, the forecasts will reflect uncertainty about the underlying parameters, θ, the current state, s_T, and future shocks, ε_t. For further details, see (Del Negro and Schorfheide, 2013, algorithm 2).

9.4.2 Empirical Evidence on DSGE Models

The key strength of DSGE models is their use of internally consistent model forecasts that facilitates inclusion of conditioning information such as current and future policy decisions. The jury is still out, however, on how helpful DSGE models are in terms of their ability to improve the accuracy of more ad hoc economic forecasts. In part this reflects the DSGE models' disadvantages due to their use of representations of the economy that inevitably are highly simplified. If cross-equation restrictions imposed by DSGE models are rejected by the data, this will bias the forecasts. Countering such biases, DSGE models have the potential to reduce the effect of parameter estimation error.

In their empirical analysis, Del Negro and Schorfheide (2013) find that short-run forecasts of output growth and inflation from the Blue Chip survey are more precise than DSGE forecasts generated by a Smets and Wouters (2003) type model. At longer horizons between five and eight quarters, however, the DSGE forecasts of output growth are more precise than the corresponding survey forecasts. In turn Blue Chip interest rate forecasts are better than DSGE forecasts at horizons between one and eight quarters.

Ghent (2009) examines different DSGE models and their implied prior distributions in a forecasting exercise involving US output, investment, hours worked, and consumption. Despite considering a wide variety of models with different implications for the relationships between the variables, Ghent finds that the models yield Bayesian VARs with very similar forecast performance, although with improvements over an unconstrained VAR model as well as a simple BVAR with Minnesota priors.

Edge and Gürkaynak (2010) use Mincer–Zarnowitz regressions of outcomes on an intercept and the DSGE forecasts. If forecasts are unbiased, the intercept should equal 0 and the slope should equal 1; see chapter 15 for more details. For inflation forecasts they find that the intercept (α) is significantly positive, while the slope coefficient on the DSGE forecast (β) is significantly smaller than 1, indicating that the forecasts are biased. A similar pattern emerges for output growth forecasts although here the evidence of bias is weaker in a statistical sense. For interest rate forecasts, the slope coefficient on the DSGE inflation forecasts exceeds 1 at one through six quarter forecast horizons and the intercept is negative and significantly different from 0 for the shortest horizons.

Summarizing the broader literature, Del Negro and Schorfheide (2013) conclude that "the empirical evidence in the literature suggests that DSGE model forecasts are comparable to standard autoregressive or vector autoregressive models but can be dominated by more sophisticated univariate or multivariate time-series models."

Del Negro and Schorfheide (2013) argue that some of the inferior short-run predictive performance of the DSGE models may be due to their use of a narrow information set compared with survey forecasts which can make use of a larger set of variables and more updated information. They point at several ways for improving DSGE forecasts by better incorporating external information. To deal with the informational disadvantage that these models have vis-à-vis survey forecasts, Del Negro and Schorfheide suggest using observable long-run expectations data when estimating the model parameters. Such long-run inflation expectations can be used to determine the target inflation rate by modifying the central bank's interest rate feedback rule and augmenting the model with a stationary time-varying inflation target.

An alternative strategy is to use external nowcasts from survey data to improve the model's estimates of current and future states as well as to estimate model parameters. Nowcasts from surveys embed substantial amounts of information and so can be used to summarize broad sets of information.[8] Specifically, at the one-period forecast horizon Del Negro and Schorfheide propose to modify $p(s_T, s_{T+1}|\theta, y_1, \ldots, y_T)$ in (9.45) by $p(s_T, s_{T+1}|\theta, y_1, \ldots, y_T, z_{T+1})$, where z_{T+1} is the one-period Blue Chip nowcasts which are available prior to the publication of y_{T+1}.

Forecasting with DSGE models remains a highly active and promising area of research with the potential for coming up with ways to improve how these models incorporate extraneous information while simultaneously incorporating constraints from economic theory in a way that can help reduce estimation error and guide the use of these models in providing feedback for policy advice.

9.5 CONDITIONAL FORECASTS

Scenario forecasting offers a way to compute forecasts conditional on the future values taken by some of the variables in a forecasting model. Fixing the future values of a subset of the variables has two effects on the forecasts. First, and most obviously, the fixed variables no longer have to be predicted, but are assumed known (conditioned on). Second, because these variables have a joint distribution under the forecasting model, the conditional distribution of the remaining variables given the fixed variables will typically change.

Waggoner and Zha (1999) consider conditional forecasts in situations where restrictions are imposed on the future values of a set of endogenous variables which are part of a VAR(p) model for an ($n \times 1$) vector, y. For the special case where y follows a VAR(1) process, their setup reduces to

$$A_0 y_t + A_1 y_{t-1} = d + \varepsilon_t, \quad t = 1, \ldots, T, \tag{9.47}$$

where, for $s > 0$,

$$E[\varepsilon_t \varepsilon_t'|y_{t-s}] = I,$$
$$E[\varepsilon_t|y_{t-s}] = 0.$$

Forecasts from (9.47) are most easily generated by rewriting the model as

$$y_t = c + B_1 y_{t-1} + A_0^{-1}\varepsilon_t,$$

$$\text{where} \quad c = A_0^{-1}d, \quad B_1 = -A_0^{-1}A_1.$$

---

[8] The alternative approach of extending the model to include much larger information sets, while seemingly attractive, appears more involved and poses questions on how to relate additional information variables to the underlying economic model. See Boivin and Giannoni (2006) for an approach that addresses these issues.

Waggoner and Zha show that out-of-sample forecasts for period $T + h$ given information at time T, take the form

$$y_{T+h} = K_{h-1}c + B_1^h y_T + \sum_{j=1}^{h} M_{h-j}\varepsilon_{t+j}, \tag{9.48}$$

where K and M can be characterized in recursive form:

$$K_h = \sum_{j=0}^{h} B_1^j,$$

$$M_i = A_0^{-1} B_1^i,$$

with $B_1^0 = I$. The first two terms in (9.48) capture the usual predictive dynamics from a VAR(1) model. For unconditional forecasts, the third term involving the impulse response matrices, M_i, would be 0. For forecasts that condition on future values of y_{T+h}, this condition need not hold. For example, if we constrain the jth element of y_{T+h} to some range $y_{T+h}(j) \in \left[\underline{y}(j); \bar{y}(j)\right]$, it follows from (9.48) that this amounts to constraining the sum of weighted shocks so that

$$\sum_{j=1}^{h} M_{h-j}\varepsilon_{T+j} \in \left[\underline{y}(j) - K_{h-1}c - B_1^h(j)y_T; \bar{y}(j) - K_{h-1}c - B_1^h(j)y_T\right],$$

and hence the expectation of future values of ε, conditional on this range information, is no longer 0.

Alternatively, we can consider hard conditions which restrict q elements of y'_{T+h} to single values $r(a)$,

$$R(a)'\varepsilon = r(a), \tag{9.49}$$

where $a = (\text{vec}(A_0)' \ \text{vec}(-A_1, d)')'$, $R(a)$ is a $(q \times k)$ weighting matrix that stacks the impulse responses, and $k = hm$ is the number of future shocks, ε. Under the restrictions in (9.49), Waggoner and Zha (1999, Proposition 2) establishes that the one-step conditional distribution of y_{T+h} given the vector of parameters, a; all observed data up to time $T + h - 1$, Z_{T+h-1}; and assuming Gaussian shocks, ε, denoted by $p_R(y_{T+h}|a, ZY_{T+h-1})$; is Gaussian:

$$p_R(y'_{T+h}|a, Z_{T+h-1}) = \mathrm{N}\left(c + B_1 y_{T+h-1} + A_0^{-1} E_R[\varepsilon_{T+h}], A_0^{-1'} V_R(\varepsilon'_{T+h})A_0^{-1}\right), \tag{9.50}$$

where $E_R[\varepsilon'_{T+h}]$ and $V_R[\varepsilon'_{T+h}]$ are the restricted (conditional) mean and variance of ε_{T+h}, i.e.,

$$\varepsilon'_{T+h} \sim \mathrm{N}(E_R[\varepsilon'_{T+h}], V_R(\varepsilon'_{T+h})), \tag{9.51}$$

$$E_R[\varepsilon'_{T+h}] = R(a)\left[R(a)'R(a)\right]^{-1} r(a),$$

$$V_R(\varepsilon'_{T+h}) = I - R(a)\left[R(a)'R(a)\right]^{-1} R(a)'.$$

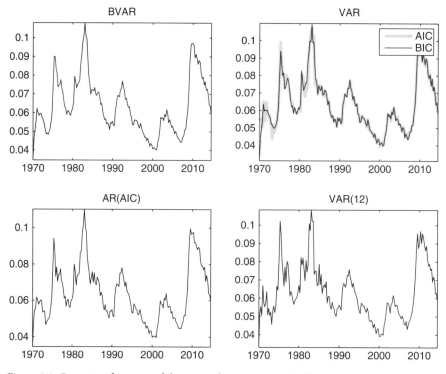

Figure 9.2: Recursive forecasts of the unemployment rate. The figure shows forecasts of the unemployment rate generated by a Bayesian VAR (BVAR), VARs with lag length selected by the AIC or BIC information criteria, a univariate AR with lag length selected by the AIC, and a VAR with 16 lags.

Waggoner and Zha propose a Gibbs sampler that can account for parameter estimation errors in generating these conditional forecasts. Given a starting value for the parameters, $a^{(0)}$, the procedure first uses (9.50) and (9.51) to generate values $y^{(i)}_{T+1}, \ldots, y^{(i)}_{T+h}$ given $a^{(i-1)}$. Using these values, it then generates draws $a^{(i)}$ from $p(a|y^{(i)}_{T+1}, \ldots, y^{(i)}_{T+h}, y_T, \ldots, y_1)$. This is repeated a large number of times to obtain a set of out-of-sample forecasts that account for estimation error.

9.6 EMPIRICAL EXAMPLE

We next consider an empirical example based on a three-variable system comprising the CPI inflation rate, the unemployment rate, and the three-month T-bill rate. This small-scale VAR serves to illustrate some of the issues that arise in empirical forecasting with VAR models. Our analysis uses quarterly data over the period 1954Q1–2014Q4.

Figure 9.2 shows recursively generated forecasts of the US unemployment rate over the period 1970–2014. The graphs show forecasts from a BVAR with Minnesota priors, a VAR with lag length selected by AIC or BIC, a univariate autoregressive (AR) model with lag length selected by the AIC, and forecasts from a fixed-lag

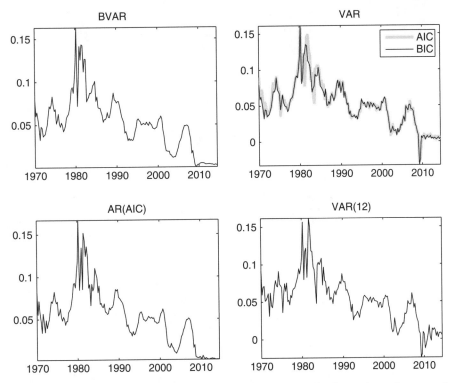

Figure 9.3: Recursive forecasts of the three-month T-bill rate. The figure shows forecasts of the three-month T-bill rate generated by a Bayesian VAR (BVAR), VARs with lag length selected by the AIC or BIC, a univariate AR with lag length selected by the AIC, and a VAR with 12 lags.

VAR(12).[9] The forecasts are very similar with correlations ranging from 0.97 to 0.998, suggesting that for this variable how the lags are selected in the VAR makes little difference for the forecasts. Moreover, the similarity of the BVAR and AR forecasts suggests that past unemployment captures most of the predictability of future unemployment.

Similar conclusions emerge for the T-bill rate forecasts shown in figure 9.3. The forecasts from the BVAR, VAR, and AR models share a very similar trend although the individual forecasts differ on occasion, particularly towards the end of the sample where the extremely low interest rates result in near-zero forecasts for the BVAR and AR models, whereas the VAR models produce negative and more volatile forecasts during this period. Again the forecasts are very similar, with correlations ranging from 0.96 to 0.99.

Larger differences in forecasts are found for the inflation rate shown in figure 9.4. For example, notable differences emerge during 1980, which reflect the highly volatile interest rates, information on which is of course ignored by a purely autoregressive model for inflation. Only the VAR(12) model forecasts a sharp, but short-lived, decline in the inflation rate around 1983. Correlations across the various forecasts are now much smaller and range from 0.71 to 0.89.

---

[9] The Minnesota priors use a tightness parameter of 0.1, a decay parameter of 1 and eight lags.

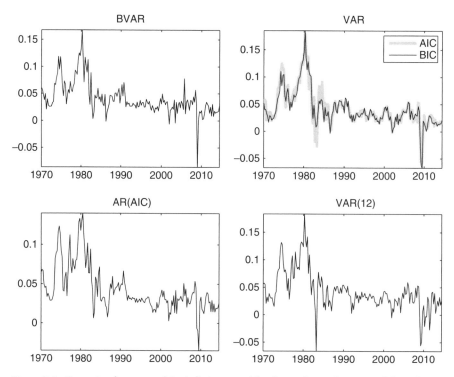

Figure 9.4: Recursive forecasts of the inflation rate. The figure shows forecasts of the inflation rate generated by a Bayesian VAR (BVAR), VARs with lag length selected by the AIC or BIC, a univariate autoregressive (AR) model with lag length selected by the AIC, and a VAR with 16 lags.

A key reason for the popularity of VARs is that they can be used to generate multistep forecasts. For a stationary VAR, the forecasts should converge to the steady-state value, the longer the forecast horizon, which will tend to smooth the forecasts. Figure 9.5 illustrates this effect at two separate points, namely for an initial value below the mean and an initial value above the mean. In both cases the forecast converges to the mean as the horizon is extended.

Figure 9.6 plots recursively generated one-, two-, four-, and eight-quarter-ahead forecasts of the unemployment rate generated by VAR(4) and VAR(12) models. Mean reversion in the long-horizon forecasts is clearly seen at the two longest horizons, although the persistence of the variables means that substantial time variation remains in the forecasts even at the eight-quarter horizon. The VAR(4) model generates smoother forecasts than the VAR(12) model, particularly at the four- and eight-quarter horizons.

Table 9.1 reports out-of-sample RMSE values for the various VAR models, using 1970–2014 as the evaluation period. For the unemployment rate, the best forecasts are generated by the BVAR model followed by the univariate autoregressive model with lag length selected by the AIC. The VAR(12) model generates particularly poor forecasts as does the random walk model (particularly at long horizons) which ignores mean reversion in the unemployment rate. Conversely, for the interest rates series the random walk forecasts are best, followed by the BVAR forecasts and the VAR forecasts with lag length selected by the BIC. Once again, methods that include

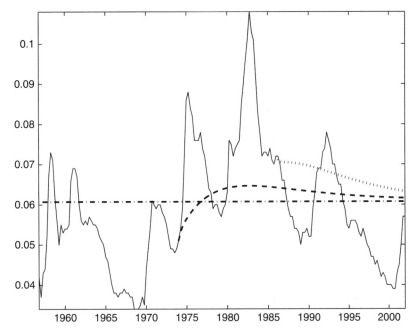

Figure 9.5: Mean reversion of multi-step-ahead forecasts of the unemployment rate generated at values above and below the average unemployment rate.

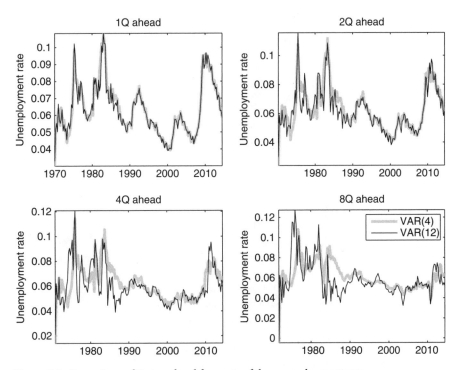

Figure 9.6: Recursive multi-step-ahead forecasts of the unemployment rate.

TABLE 9.1:
Root mean squared forecast errors from various VAR models fitted to a model comprising the quarterly unemployment rate, interest rate, and inflation rate.

Steps	BVAR	VAR(AIC)	VAR(BIC)	VAR(4)	VAR(12)	AR(AIC)	RW
Unemployment rate							
1Q	0.3322	0.4133	0.3543	0.3677	0.4772	0.3326	0.3799
2Q	0.5750	0.7187	0.6097	0.6417	0.8295	0.5817	0.6635
4Q	0.9941	1.2745	1.0644	1.1540	1.4694	1.0610	1.1423
8Q	1.4114	1.7281	1.4693	1.6122	1.9049	1.5614	1.7617
Interest rate							
1Q	1.1489	1.3717	1.2117	1.2298	1.4554	1.2490	1.1038
2Q	1.4845	1.6204	1.5309	1.5269	1.8346	1.5110	1.4045
4Q	1.9263	2.2775	1.9702	2.0441	2.5018	2.0024	1.8264
8Q	2.8213	3.5367	2.7966	3.1453	3.6461	2.9525	2.6779
Inflation rate							
1Q	2.7894	2.8939	2.7982	2.7417	2.9751	2.7221	3.1377
2Q	2.9455	3.1772	3.1455	3.0765	3.3546	2.8400	3.3567
4Q	3.1777	3.6610	3.3607	3.4140	3.8364	3.1344	3.5600
8Q	4.1238	5.5776	4.5494	5.1039	4.9918	3.7780	4.1143

TABLE 9.2:
Diebold–Mariano test statistics for one-quarter-ahead squared error forecasting performance measured relative to the random walk benchmark.

Method	Unemployment	Interest rate	Inflation rate
BVAR	3.6023	−1.3997	−0.0579
VAR(AIC)	−0.1369	−3.0321	−2.4497
VAR(BIC)	1.9550	−0.7372	−1.0005
VAR(4)	0.7274	−2.2550	−1.8303
VAR(12)	−1.2952	−3.2039	−2.3156
AR(AIC)	1.7936	−2.1504	0.8370
Random walk	0.0000	0.0000	0.0000

the most lags and thus are most prone to estimation error such as the VAR(12) and the VAR with lag length selected by AIC, produce the least accurate forecasts. Finally, for the inflation series the univariate forecasts are best, followed by the BVAR forecasts. Again the least accurate forecasts are generated by the VAR(12) model.

Table 9.2 reports values of the Diebold–Mariano test for equal MSE performance using the random walk forecasts as benchmark. The t-tests are set up so that positive values of the test statistic indicate that a particular forecasting method beats the random walk forecast, whereas negative values suggest that the benchmark is best. Only for the unemployment series do we find some evidence that the BVAR, VAR with AIC lag length selection, and the univariate autoregressive model outperforms the random walk.

These findings suggest that using an overparameterized model such as the VAR(12) specification can yield poor results. More parsimonious VAR models tend to do better—as witnessed by the tendency of VARs selected by the BIC to perform better than VARs selected by the AIC, and for some variables the parsimonious univariate autoregressive model performs well. Although the BVAR forecasts generally perform well, no single approach appears to be dominant across variables and forecast horizons, illustrating the need to adopt different approaches to different situations and perhaps also consider forecast combinations; see chapter 15.

9.7 CONCLUSION

Vector autoregressions provide a coherent way to generate internally consistent multiperiod forecasts that account for concurrent and dynamic correlations across the included variables. While the basic VAR model is a powerful tool in the forecasting literature, once more than a handful of variables are included, the number of parameters that require estimation increases rapidly. This can sometimes cause parameter estimation error to become larger. Different methodologies have evolved to handle issues related to such estimation errors, most notably Bayesian estimation methods. Baillie (1979) derives expressions for the asymptotic mean squared error of multistep forecasts generated by VARs and ongoing research continues to address the importance of controlling the risk of multivariate prediction models.

Important progress has been made in recent years in the areas of computational methods and estimation techniques. Bayesian methods as well as factor augmentation methods are now available to handle large conditioning information sets. The use of economically motivated constraints through DSGE models is another area where important progress has been made which can facilitate the use of economic theory. Such models can be used to conduct conditional forecast evaluation experiments and also have the potential for reducing the effect of estimation error.

10

<<<<<<<<<<<<<<<<<<<<<<<<<<<<<<<<<<<<<<<<<<<<<<<<<<<<<<<<<<<<<<<<<<<<<<<<<<<<<<

Forecasting in a Data-Rich Environment

In many forecasting exercises, the forecaster has access to a wealth of potentially relevant variables that could be used for constructing a forecasting model. Just as often the forecaster has no strong theoretical reasons for excluding many of these variables from the model. This plethora of information is the result of different ways of measuring particular variables as well as different levels of information aggregation. Many economic variables, e.g., interest rates, output, or employment, lend themselves to numerous ways of measurement and reporting. For example, as a measure of interest rates one could use overnight bank rates, three-month Libor, T-bill rates at various points of the term structure, commercial paper rates, forward or swap rates. We often have no particular reason for choosing one measure over another. Turning to the question of aggregation, one could use a single measure for aggregate output such as real GDP or decompose this into sectors, subsectors, or geographical regions to obtain a finer-grained measure of output. The result is that often the dimension of reasonable predictor variables to include can be very large, even outstripping the sample size available for constructing the forecasting model.

When the dimension of the conditioning information variables x_t is large relative to the sample size, most of the methods from previous chapters cannot be directly applied. Linear regression, VAR, or VARMA models and conventional covariance-based estimation methods are not feasible when there are more parameters to be estimated than observations available. Less parametric approaches are even less viable. And even if this constraint does not bind, when the number of estimated parameters is large relative to the sample size (but still smaller) the parameters are likely to be estimated too imprecisely for the construction of forecasting models that perform well. Many of the model selection methods also become infeasible to implement, as there are so many potential models to be considered.

Faced with these challenges, we need methods for constructing more parsimonious models. In situations where a linear model is entertained and it is expected that the best forecasting model is sparse—by which we mean that most of the variables are not useful for forecasting—methods such as the Lasso (chapter 6) can be used. These methods work best when the variables are not highly correlated, which in practice rules out many economic applications. Another approach attempts, on a variable-by-variable basis, to select a subset of predictor variables deemed to be of particular relevance to the target variable, usually by searching over a subset of the potentially relevant variables. This is part of the broader area of regularization methods surveyed by Ng (2013).

The factor methods described in this chapter take a different approach, one that attempts to extract the salient information in x_t using dimensionality reduction techniques. Such methods are particularly useful when the variables in x_t are collinear. Factor models take linear combinations of the original x_t, choosing a small set of linear combinations that capture most of the variation in x_t. Such linear combinations, or factors, are then employed to forecast y_{t+1}. Specifically, suppose the individual x-variables are linearly related to a set of common factors, F_t, so that

$$x_{it} = \Lambda_i' F_t + \varepsilon_{it}, \quad i = 1, \ldots, N, \tag{10.1}$$

where Λ_i is a $(q \times 1)$ vector of factor loadings (constants), F_t is a $(q \times 1)$ vector of factors, and ε_{it} are idiosyncratic shocks. Each of the right-hand-side objects $\{\Lambda_i, F_t, \varepsilon_{it}\}$ is unobserved and the two stochastic components are uncorrelated so they represent a decomposition of x_{it}. Taking the expectation of the square of each side (after removing means) results in the variation in x_t being decomposed into a factor component and an idiosyncratic component. The hope in using factor analysis for forecasting is that there exists a decomposition with q small enough that the F_t factors explain a large amount of the variation in $x_t = (x_{1t}, \ldots, x_{Nt})'$, but with far fewer variables when the factors are used in the forecasting equation rather that the original data.

Factor modeling in macroeconomic analysis dates back to Geweke (1976) and Sargent and Sims (1977). Early work on latent factor dynamics includes Sargent and Sims (1977), Engle and Watson (1981), Sargent (1989), Stock and Watson (1989, 1991), and Quah and Sargent (1993). Many studies in the early literature keep N fixed and let $T \to \infty$. There is also a closely related literature in finance that investigates the presence of common factors in cross sections of stock returns; see Chamberlain and Rothschild (1983) and Connor and Korajczyk (1986). This setting is better represented by fixing T and letting $N \to \infty$. More recent studies on dynamic factor models, such as Stock and Watson (2002a) and Bai and Ng (2002, 2006), let both N and T go to infinity.

The literature varies in the strictness of the assumptions imposed on the factor structure. Assuming that a small number of factors account for most of the common variation across economic variables, the remaining idiosyncratic variation is either uncorrelated—the case of an exact factor structure (Chamberlain and Rothschild, 1983)—or display substantially weaker correlation cross-sectionally than in the original data, which gives rise to an approximate factor structure.

From a forecasting perspective, factor analysis is a relatively model-free approach that does not require making strong assumptions about which variables matter; see, e.g., Breitung and Eickmeier (2006). Indeed, the researcher can take a relatively agnostic view on which variables to include, although in practice the design of the initial set of predictor variables from which the common factors are extracted can be quite important. The approach can be expected to perform well if the predictive content of "most" variables is captured by the common factor whereas the variable-specific information has predictive value only for a few select variables, most notably lags of the predicted variable itself.

This chapter goes through methods for incorporating common factors in prediction models. Section 10.1 discusses dynamic and static factor models along with the role played by factors in prediction models (as conditioning information) before section 10.2 turns to estimation of factor models and section 10.3 discusses methods for determining the number of factors required to characterize a large-dimensional data set. Section 10.4 discusses practical issues in factor construction and interpretation of factors while section 10.5 discusses empirical evidence. Finally, section 10.6 briefly covers how panel methods can be used to construct forecasts for data with a large cross-sectional dimension. Section 10.7 concludes.

10.1 FORECASTING WITH FACTOR MODELS

When presented with the information embedded in a large set of potentially relevant predictor variables, x_{it}, $i = 1, \ldots, N$, the simplest forecasting approach would be to consider a linear model of the form

$$y_{t+1} = \alpha + \sum_{i=1}^{N} \beta_i(L)x_{it} + \gamma(L)y_t + \varepsilon_{yt+1}, \tag{10.2}$$

where $\beta_i(L) = \sum_{j=0}^{p_x} \beta_{ij} L^j$ is a lag polynomial of order p_x which contains the regression coefficients for the ith variable, and $\gamma(L) = \sum_{j=0}^{p_y} \gamma_j L^j$ is a lag polynomial of order p_y. While we assume a one-period forecast horizon, the model can easily accommodate arbitrary forecast horizons h by projecting y_{t+h} on variables observed at time t. Ignoring potential serial correlation in ε_y, this model can be estimated by OLS, assuming that the total number of mean parameters, $N_\beta = N \times p_x + p_y + 1$, is small relative to the length of the time series, T. Often, however, $N_\beta > T$ and so conventional estimation methods are not feasible. Instead it is common practice to assume that, while a few (n_{x^*}) key predictor variables, x^*, directly affect y, most of the x-variables affect y only through a set of q common components, F, where q is much smaller than N.

Focusing our attention on linear models, this suggests using a model of the form

$$y_{t+1} = \alpha + \beta_f(L)'F_t + \gamma(L)y_t + \phi'(L)x_t^* + \varepsilon_{yt+1}, \tag{10.3}$$

where $F_t = (F_{1t}, \ldots, F_{qt})'$ is a set of q common factors extracted from the list of N original predictors, x_t. Here $\beta_f(L)$, $\gamma(L)$, and $\phi(L)$ are vector lag polynomials of order p_f, p_y, and p_{x^*}, respectively, so that this model has $p_f \times q + p_y + p_{x^*} \times n_{x^*} + 1$ parameters. Economic theory could justify inclusion of certain x^*-variables—e.g., the Phillips curve suggests including current and lagged unemployment rates in a model for the inflation rate. If idiosyncratic variation in these variables matters to y, they should be included since the common factors suppress this information. Typically it is assumed that the identity of such variables is known ex ante since otherwise the search for such variables could quickly become infeasible.

To see how this matters in practice, suppose that all lag polynomials contain two lags ($p_y = p_x = p_f = p_{x^*} = 2$) and $N = 200$, while $q = 4$ and $n_{x^*} = 2$. Then the forecasting model in (10.2) requires fitting 403 parameters, while the model in (10.3) requires estimating only 15 parameters. Of course the representation in (10.3) offers parsimony only when the number of factors, q, and sources of "direct" influence, n_{x^*}, represent a significant reduction from the N original variables x_t.[1]

Forecasters are interested in the common factors only to the extent that they help improve predictions of the target variable, y_{t+1}. If the factors were known, forecasting with (10.3) would simply amount to choosing the right number of lags for F, x^*, and y and estimating their coefficients. Provided that the variables have all been transformed so that they are stationary, OLS estimation and model selection criteria such as BIC could be used to select the lag orders.

In practice, the common factors are usually unknown and so must be extracted from the data. Forecasting with common factor models can therefore be thought of as a two-step process. In the first step, estimates of the common factors are extracted. In the second step, the factors, along with past values of the predicted variable and possibly other relevant variables are used to select and estimate a forecasting model.

To operationalize the forecast, suppose that a set of factor estimates, $\hat{F}_t$, have been extracted. These are then used in (10.3) along with current and past values of y and x^* to select and estimate a forecasting model. The actual forecasts thus take the form

$$\hat{f}_{t+1|t} = \hat{\alpha} + \sum_{j=1}^{p_f} \hat{\beta}_j' \hat{F}_{t+1-j} + \sum_{j=1}^{p_y} \hat{\gamma}_j y_{t+1-j} + \sum_{j=1}^{p_{x^*}} \hat{\phi}_j' x_{t+1-j}^*, \tag{10.4}$$

where $\{\hat{\alpha}, \hat{\beta}_j, \hat{\gamma}_j, \hat{\phi}_j\}$ are obtained from a regression of the predicted variable on a constant and lagged values of the extracted factors, the predicted variable, and the x^*-variables.

10.1.1 Dynamic Factor Models

As shown by Stock and Watson (2006), the forecasting model in (10.3) is implied by quite general procedures for the dynamics in x and y. This section follows their analysis and lays out the framework leading to the forecasting model (10.3).

Suppose that a panel of data $\{x_{it}\}$, $i = 1, \ldots, N$, $t = 1, \ldots, T$ is available and that the variation in each of the observed variables, x_{it}, can be decomposed into the effects of past and current values of a common component, F_t, and an idiosyncratic component, ε_{xit}:

$$x_{it} = \lambda_i(L)' F_t + \varepsilon_{xit}, \tag{10.5}$$

where x_{it} and ε_{xit} are scalars, F_t is a $(q \times 1)$ vector of unobserved common factors, while $\lambda_i(L) = (\lambda_{i1}(L) \; \lambda_{i2}(L) \; \ldots \; \lambda_{iq}(L))'$ is a vector lag polynomial containing the dynamic factor loadings. Moreover, the idiosyncratic shocks are usually assumed to be uncorrelated with the factors at all leads and lags, i.e., $E[F_t \varepsilon_{xis}] = 0$ for all i, t, and s. Because current and past values of the factors can affect the current value of the x-variables, this model is clearly dynamic.[2] Dynamics may also arise through

---

[1] In the context of macroeconomic forecasting Stock and Watson (2002b) refer to the extracted factors as diffusion indexes.

[2] How the x-variables are transformed can be important in practice. For example, if most variables under consideration are close to being serially uncorrelated whereas a few variables are highly persistent, the first factors will tend to be dominated by the persistent variables, whose past values have more power in predicting future variation in the x-variables. This is not a weakness of the dynamic factor approach which is set up to identify predictability, but it is an important consideration when interpreting the identity of the factors.

serial correlation in the idiosyncratic shocks, ε_{xit}:

$$\delta_i(L)\varepsilon_{xit} = v_{xit}, \tag{10.6}$$

where v_{xit} is unpredictable given past information, i.e., $E[v_{xit}|F_{t-1}, x_{t-1}, F_{t-2}, x_{t-2}, \ldots] = 0$ and $x_{t-1} = (x_{1t-1}, \ldots, x_{Nt-1})'$ contains the complete set of variables.

Suppose dynamics in the common factors can be captured through an autoregressive process of the form

$$\Gamma(L)F_t = v_{ft}, \tag{10.7}$$

where $\Gamma(L)$ is a matrix lag polynomial and v_{ft} is a vector of unpredictable innovations.

The common factor structure in (10.5) is assumed to also carry over to y, the variable we are interested in forecasting:

$$y_t = \lambda_y(L)'F_t + \varepsilon_{yt}, \tag{10.8}$$

where ε_y may be serially correlated as captured through an autoregressive process:

$$\delta_y(L)\varepsilon_{yt} = v_{yt}, \tag{10.9}$$

and v_{yt} is assumed to be unpredictable given current information, $E[v_{yt+1}|F_t, x_t, y_t, F_{t-1}, x_{t-1}, y_{t-1}, \ldots] = 0$.

Stock and Watson (2006) show that (10.8) and (10.9) are consistent with the factor model in (10.3). Specifically, if we pre-multiply equation (10.8) by $\delta_y(L)$ and use (10.9), we have

$$\delta_y(L)y_{t+1} = \delta_y(L)\lambda_y(L)'F_{t+1} + v_{yt+1},$$

or, equivalently,

$$y_{t+1} = \delta_y(L)\lambda_y(L)'F_{t+1} + L^{-1}(1 - \delta_y(L))y_t + v_{yt+1}. \tag{10.10}$$

Defining $\beta_f(L)F_t = E[\delta_y(L)\lambda_y(L)'F_{t+1}|F_t, F_{t-1}, \ldots]$ and $\gamma(L) = L^{-1}(1 - \delta_y(L))$, we can rewrite (10.10) as

$$y_{t+1} = \beta(L)F_t + \gamma(L)y_t + u_{yt+1}, \tag{10.11}$$

where $u_{yt+1} = v_{yt+1} + \{\delta_y(L)\lambda_y(L)'F_{t+1} - E[\delta_y(L)\lambda_Y(L)'F_{t+1}|F_t, F_{t-1}, \ldots]\}$ comprises both idiosyncratic shocks that are specific to y (v_{yt+1}) as well as shocks to the common factors, v_{ft+1}. This equation thus expresses the future value of y in terms of past values of the common factors, past values of y itself, and future shocks, u_{yt+1}, whose mean is unpredictable given current information. This is consistent with (10.3), the only difference being the x^*-variables which, for simplicity, we ignore here.

In cases where N is large, it is convenient to recast the dynamic factor model using the following static representation:

$$X_t = \Lambda F_t^p + \varepsilon_{xt}, \tag{10.12}$$

where now $F_t^p = (F_t', F_{t-1}', \ldots, F_{t-p+1}')'$ is an $(r \times 1)$ vector that stacks current and lagged values of the common components (with $r = p \times q$) and ε_{xt} again represents the idiosyncratic components. Supplementing (10.12) with an autoregressive model for the factor dynamics gives a state-space equation with F_t^p as the latent state and (10.12) as the observation equation.[3]

The factor representation in (10.12) gives rise to a forecasting model of the form

$$y_{t+1} = \beta' F_t^p + \gamma(L)y_t + \varepsilon_{yt+1}, \tag{10.13}$$

where the effects of current and lagged values of the factors come through the β-coefficients.

10.2 ESTIMATION OF FACTORS

So far we have assumed that a set of factor estimates are available. In practice the factors are almost always unobserved and so have to be estimated. The two main methods for extracting factors are the parametric approach which makes use of assumptions about the dynamics and distributions of innovations in the model and nonparametric methods such as principal components which make weaker assumptions to identify the factors.

10.2.1 Maximum Likelihood Estimation (Small N)

When the number of variables, N, is small, a three-step parametric estimation approach can be followed to obtain an exact dynamic factor model. The first step uses the Kalman filter to estimate the parameters of a Gaussian likelihood function for $\{y_{t+1}, x_t\}$. In the second step, the Kalman filter and smoother is used to extract estimates of the unknown factor realizations, $\{F_t\}_{t=1}^T$. In a third and final step, the forecast is computed by projecting the dependent variable on the factor estimates and any observable variables, x_t^*, deemed relevant. The approach involves nonlinear optimization which in practice limits the dimension of the problem.

Stock and Watson (2006) discuss conditions under which a well-identified Gaussian likelihood function exists for data-generating processes represented by equations (10.5)–(10.9). First, it is required that the idiosyncratic components can be represented by finite-order AR processes $\delta_i(L)\varepsilon_{xit} = v_{xit}$ and $\delta_y(L)\varepsilon_{yt} = v_{yt}$ as in equations (10.6) and (10.9). Second, it is required that the factor dynamics can be captured through a finite-order AR process, $\Gamma(L)F_t = v_{ft}$ as in (10.7), where the innovations $(v_{x1t}, \ldots, v_{xNt}, v_{yt}, v_{f1t}, \ldots, v_{frt})$ are mutually uncorrelated, i.i.d., and normally distributed. Finally, $\lambda_i(L)$ and $\lambda_y(L)$ in (10.5) and (10.8) should be finite-order lag polynomials.

Under these assumptions, the Kalman filter can be used to compute the likelihood function for the dynamic system comprised of (10.5), (10.7), and (10.11). The resulting likelihood function can be maximized by means of the EM algorithm to obtain maximum likelihood estimates while the Kalman smoother can be used to provide estimates of the factors, $\hat{F}_t$. With these in place, a forecast can be computed

---

[3] The static representation relies on the assumption that the lag polynomials are of finite order.

from an OLS regression using data up to time T:

$$y_{T+1} = \beta(L)\hat{F}_T + \gamma(L)y_T + \varepsilon_{T+1}. \tag{10.14}$$

Estimates of $\beta(L)$ and $\gamma(L)$ will be consistent because errors in the factor estimates, $F_T - \hat{F}_T$, are uncorrelated with current and past values of $\hat{F}$ and y.

In an interesting application of the Kalman filter, Aruoba, Diebold, and Scotti (2009) use a single factor approach to extract a daily summary measure of the state of the business cycle based on data measured at weekly, monthly, and quarterly frequencies. This application makes use of the ability of the Kalman filter to allow the underlying state variable to evolve at a different frequency than the observables. Although Aruoba, Diebold, and Scotti do not use the extracted factor for prediction, clearly their factor could be used for such purposes. We further discuss this approach in chapter 21.

10.2.2 Principal Components Estimation (Large N)

Maximum likelihood estimation is not feasible when N is large. In such cases a nonparametric principal components approach can be used instead. Under the assumption in the static representation (10.12) that F_t^p and ε_{xt} are uncorrelated at all leads and lags, we can express the covariance matrix of the observed variables, X_t, as the weighted sum of the covariance matrix of the common factors, $\Sigma_{FF} = E[(F_t^p - \bar{F}^p)(F_t^p - \bar{F}^p)']$, where $\bar{F}^p$ is the time-series average of F_t^p, and the covariance matrix of the idiosyncratic terms, $\Sigma_{\varepsilon\varepsilon} = E[\varepsilon_t\varepsilon_t']$:

$$\Sigma_{XX} = \Lambda \Sigma_{FF} \Lambda' + \Sigma_{\varepsilon\varepsilon}. \tag{10.15}$$

Given this expression, estimation proceeds by minimizing a nonlinear least squares objective that treats both Λ and F_t^p, for $t = 1, \ldots, T$, as unknown fixed parameters:

$$\min_{F_1^p, \ldots, F_T^p, \Lambda} (NT)^{-1} \sum_{t=1}^{T} (X_t - \Lambda F_t^p)'(X_t - \Lambda F_t^p), \tag{10.16}$$

subject to the normalizing constraint that $\Lambda'\Lambda = I_r$. Given an estimate of the factor loadings, $\hat{\Lambda}$, it follows from (10.12) that an estimator of the factors can be obtained from a cross-sectional regression of X_t on $\hat{\Lambda}$:

$$\hat{F}_t^p = (\hat{\Lambda}'\hat{\Lambda})^{-1}\hat{\Lambda}'X_t = \hat{\Lambda}'X_t. \tag{10.17}$$

Substituting this expression back into the objective function (10.16) and minimizing the resulting expression is equivalent to maximizing $\Lambda'\hat{\Sigma}_{XX}\Lambda$ subject to the constraint $\Lambda'\Lambda = I_r$. Setting $\hat{\Lambda}$ equal to the r eigenvectors of $\hat{\Sigma}_{XX} = T^{-1}\sum_{t=1}^{T}X_t X_t'$ corresponding to the first r eigenvalues of this matrix provides the solution to this problem. This in turn means that the common factors (10.17) take the form $\hat{F}_t^p = \hat{\Lambda}'X_t$, i.e., they are the largest r principal components of X_t. By construction these principal components will be mutually orthogonal.

If $\varepsilon_{xt} = (\varepsilon_{x1t} \ \ldots \ \varepsilon_{xNt})'$ are independently and identically distributed (i.i.d.) and Gaussian with homogenous variances, $N(0, \sigma^2 I_N)$, the principal components estimator and the maximum likelihood estimator are identical. On the other hand, if $\varepsilon_{xt} = (\varepsilon_{x1t} \; \ldots \; \varepsilon_{xNt})' \sim \text{ind } N(0, \Sigma_{\varepsilon\varepsilon})$ with known covariance matrix, a more efficient estimator could be obtained by solving the nonlinear least squares problem

$$\min_{F_1^p, \ldots, F_T^p, \Lambda} T^{-1} \sum_{t=1}^{T} (X_t - \Lambda F_t^p)' \Sigma_{\varepsilon\varepsilon}^{-1} (X_t - \Lambda F_t^p). \tag{10.18}$$

In practice $\Sigma_{\varepsilon\varepsilon}$ is unknown and so solving this problem is infeasible. Weighted principal components estimators that are feasible have been proposed by Boivin and Ng (2006). Boivin and Ng suggest estimating the diagonal elements of $\Sigma_{\varepsilon\varepsilon}$ using the residuals from a first-stage regression of X_t on the factors obtained through (unweighted) principal components. Other refinements of the simple principal components problem in (10.16) entail accounting for serial correlation in ε_{xt}; see Stock and Watson (2005).

While principal components methods do not rely on any particular model for the data-generating process, it has been argued by authors such as Tipping and Bishop (1999) that this method can be given a Gaussian latent variable interpretation and as such is related to more structured factor models. Moreover, in a setting where the predicted variable is included among the variables from which the principal components are extracted, it is easily demonstrated that principal components and factor augmented forecasts become equivalent.

More informally, in situations where a few unobserved factors account for the common variation among the predictors while the remaining idiosyncratic variation in the variables is only weakly correlated, the principal components can be expected to provide a good approximation of the information contained in "most" of the predictors. This information can then be topped up with variable-specific information from a few select predictors, such as autoregressive lags, in the prediction model.

10.2.3 Consistency and Efficiency

Stock and Watson (2002a) provide conditions under which the unobserved common factors can be consistently estimated and principal components analysis consistently estimates the space spanned by the common factors. Equally important, they establish when the feasible forecasts based on factor estimates and estimated coefficients of the forecasting relation (10.13) are asymptotically efficient in the sense that, at least up to first order, nothing is lost by using the extracted as opposed to the true factors. Their conditions are quite general and allow for serial correlation in the errors as well as "weak" temporal instability.

Specifically, Stock and Watson (2002a) assume that the factors and factor loadings in representations such as (10.12) satisfy (a) $(\Lambda'\Lambda/N) \to I_r$; (b) $E[F_t^p F_t^{p'}] = \Sigma_{FF}$, with Σ_{FF} being a diagonal matrix for which $\sigma_{ii} > \sigma_{jj}$ for $i < j$; (c) $|\lambda_{i,m}| \le \bar{\lambda} < \infty$; and (d) $T^{-1} \sum_t F_t^p F_t^{p'} \to^P \Sigma_{FF}$, where $\lambda_{i,m}$ are the elements of the factor loadings, Λ.

Assumptions (a) and (d) ensure that each of the factors contributes a nonvanishing amount to the variation in each of the observed variables (X_t). The requirement that the matrix $N^{-1}\Lambda'\Lambda$ converges to a positive-definite limit means that, on average, factors affect all variables in a similar way. For example, some factors cannot affect only the first few variables but have a zero impact (loading) on a large set of additional variables.

Assumptions (a) and (b) together identify the factors up to a diagonal matrix with elements ± 1. The assumptions do not rule out serial correlation in the factors, nor do they rule out conditional dynamics in the second moments of the factors. Temporal variations such as trends or structural breaks in the variance of the factors are ruled out, however.

Stock and Watson allow the innovations in the factor model ε_{xt} to be serially correlated and weakly cross-sectionally correlated. Although no specific distributional assumptions such as normality are made, their assumption on the fourth moments of the innovations rules out some error distributions.

These assumptions are related to the distinction between strict and approximate factor models. Strict factor models assume that the elements of the vector of innovations ε_{xt} are mutually uncorrelated so that $E[\varepsilon_{xt}] = 0$, $E[\varepsilon_{xt}\varepsilon_{xt}'] = \text{diag}(\sigma_1^2, \ldots, \sigma_N^2)]$, and $E[F_t\varepsilon_{xt}'] = 0$. Approximate factor models relax these strong assumptions in two ways. First, they allow for weak serial correlation in the idiosyncratic errors. It turns out that as long as the idiosyncratic errors follow stationary ARMA processes, the principal component estimator will still be consistent as N tends to infinity. Second, the idiosyncratic errors can be weakly cross-sectionally correlated and heteroskedastic. This may be relevant if certain variables form clusters. The idiosyncratic errors and factors can also be weakly correlated.[4]

Under these assumptions, Stock and Watson (2002a) show that the true factors can be consistently estimated and are identified up to a sign transformation. Specifically, letting $N, T \to \infty$ for a model with k estimated factors, a set of indicator variables $S_i \in \{-1, +1\}$ can be selected such that, from Stock and Watson (2002a, Theorem 1),

$$T^{-1} \sum_{t=1}^{T} (S_i \hat{F}_{it}^p - F_{it}^p)^2 \to^p 0 \quad \text{for } i = 1, \ldots, r,$$

$$S_i \hat{F}_{it}^p \to^p F_{it}^p \quad \text{for } i = 1, \ldots, r,$$

$$T^{-1} \sum_{t=1}^{T} (\hat{F}_{it}^p)^2 \to^p 0 \quad \text{for } i = r+1, \ldots, k.$$

Returning to the general forecasting equation based on the static factor representation,

$$y_{t+1} = \beta_F' F_t^p + \beta_w' w_t + \varepsilon_{yt+1}, \tag{10.19}$$

where w_t contains observable predictor variables, including lagged values of y. Perhaps the most important result proved by Stock and Watson is that the feasible forecast (which is based on extracted factors and estimates of the parameters of the forecasting model) converges asymptotically to the optimal infeasible forecast which assumes that F_t^p and $(\beta_F' \, \beta_w')'$ are known, thus ensuring that the feasible coefficient estimates are consistent. To prove this, Stock and Watson use standard assumptions on the forecasting equation that ensure consistency of the parameter estimates, but add extra assumptions to deal with the fact that an estimate, $\hat{F}_t^p$, is used in place of F_t^p.

---

[4] Specifically, approximate factor models assume that $N^{-1} \sum_{i=1}^{N} \sum_{j=1}^{N} |\varepsilon_{xit}\varepsilon_{xjt}|$ is bounded for large N.

Defining $z_t = (F_t^{p'} \ w_t')'$ and $\beta = (\beta_F' \ \beta_\omega')'$ with $|\beta| < \infty$, Stock and Watson (2002a) assume that $E[z_t z_t'] = \Sigma_{zz}$ is a positive-definite matrix. Moreover,

$$T^{-1} \sum_t z_t z_t' \to^P \Sigma_{zz},$$

$$T^{-1} \sum_t z_t \varepsilon_{yt+1} \to^P 0,$$

$$T^{-1} \sum_t \varepsilon_{yt+1}^2 \to^P \sigma^2.$$

Using these assumptions along with the earlier factor and error moment assumptions, Stock and Watson (2002a) establish results for the OLS estimates $(\hat{\beta}_F' \ \hat{\beta}_{x^*}')'$ obtained from regressions of $\{y_{t+1}\}_{t=1}^{T-1}$ on $\{\hat{F}_t^p, x_t^*\}_{t=1}^{T-1}$. Specifically, they show that

$$(\hat{\beta}_F' \hat{F}_T^p + \hat{\beta}_w' w_T) - (\beta_F' F_T^p + \beta_w' w_T) \to^P 0.$$

Moreover, $\hat{\beta}_\omega - \beta_\omega \to^P 0$ and there exists an $S_i \in \{-1, +1\}$ such that $S_i \hat{\beta}_{iF} - \beta_{iF} \to^P 0$ for $i = 1, \ldots, r.$[5]

To summarize, even under an approximate factor structure entailing weak serial and cross-sectional correlation in the idiosyncratic shocks, common factors can be consistently estimated under fairly mild rate and moment conditions. In turn, such factor estimates can be treated as if they were the true factors in the forecast model that projects future realizations on the factors in the sense that the asymptotic properties of the regression coefficients will not be affected by estimation error in the factors.

Despite the elegance and generality of these theoretical results, one should also bear in mind that, as emphasized by Ng (2013) as well as our discussion in chapter 6, there is an inevitable tension between selecting the true model (consistent model selection) versus generating accurate forecasts. Hence, it is not necessarily the case that methods that succeed in (asymptotically) identifying the correct factor structure and consistently estimate the model parameters lead to the best forecasts.

10.2.4 Extracting Factors from the Frequency Domain

Forni et al. (2000) propose an alternative method for factor extraction that does not require a rational lag distribution or autoregressive representation for the dynamics in the factors. Their model starts from the moving average representation

$$x_{it} = b_{i1}(L)u_{1t} + b_{i2}(L)u_{2t} + \cdots + b_{iq}(L)u_{qt} + \xi_{it}, \quad i = 1, \ldots, N, \quad (10.20)$$

where each of the common shock processes u_{jt} $(i = 1, \ldots, q)$ are uncorrelated white noise with zero mean and unit variance, $(\xi_{1t}, \ldots, \xi_{Nt})$ is a stationary process that is orthogonal to the u_{jt} processes, and the coefficients of the lag polynomials $b_{ij}(L)$

---

[5] For the case where $N, T \to \infty$ and $\sqrt{T/N} \to 0$, Bai and Ng (2006) show that the estimated least squares coefficients in a projection of y_{t+1} on an intercept and the estimated factors are $\sqrt{T}$ consistent and asymptotically normally distributed. Thus, we can ignore that we are using estimated rather than true factors in the prediction model.

are square-summable. Moreover, the idiosyncratic components ξ_{it} may be cross-sectionally correlated. These assumptions imply that $(x_{1t}, \ldots, x_{nt})'$ is a stationary process. In this representation, the contribution of the common component to the ith observable variable, x_{it}, is captured through the linear combination of the q factors $\chi_{it} = b_{i1}(L)u_{1t} + b_{i2}(L)u_{2t} + \cdots + b_{iq}(L)u_{qt}$.

Let $\Sigma_n(\theta)$ be the spectral density matrix of x_t, where $\theta \in [-\pi, \pi]$. Define λ_{nj} as the real nonnegative jth eigenvalue of $\Sigma_n(\theta)$ organized in descending order of magnitude or, equivalently, the jth dynamic eigenvalue of $\Sigma_n(\theta)$. Similarly, let λ_{nj}^χ be the dynamic eigenvalues associated with the covariance matrix of the common components, Σ_n^χ, and let λ_{nj}^ξ be the eigenvalues of the covariance matrix of the idiosyncratic components, Σ_n^ξ. A key assumption in Forni et al. (2000) is that the first idiosyncratic dynamic eigenvalue ψ_{n1}^ξ is uniformly bounded, i.e., $\lambda_{n1}^\xi(\theta) \leq \bar{\lambda}$ for any $\theta \in [0, 2\pi]$, while conversely the first q common dynamic eigenvalues diverge, i.e., $\lim_{n \to \infty} \lambda_{nj}^\chi(\theta) = \infty$ for $j \leq q$ and $\theta \in [0, 2\pi]$ almost everywhere.

The common components can be recovered from a sequence of filters $K_{ni}(L)(x_{1t}, \ldots, x_{nt})'$ which are functions of the unknown spectral density matrices $\Sigma_n(\theta)$. Estimation of these can proceed using a discrete Fourier transform of a truncated two-sided sequence of covariance matrices of x_{nt},

$$\Sigma_n^T(\theta_m) = \sum_{k=-M}^{M} \Gamma_{nk}^T \omega_k e^{-ik\theta_m},$$

where $i = \sqrt{-1}$, $\theta_m = 2\pi m/(2M+1)$, $m = 0, 1, \ldots, 2M$, and Γ_{nk}^T is the sample covariance matrix of $(x_{1t}, \ldots, x_{nt})'$ and $(x_{1t-k}, \ldots, x_{nt-k})'$, and the weights, ω_k, follow a Bartlett window of size M, i.e., $\omega_k = 1 - [|k|/(M+1)]$. Denote the first q eigenvectors of $\Sigma_n^T(\theta_m)$ by $p_{nj}^T(\theta_m)$, for $j = 1, \ldots, q$, and $m = 0, 1, \ldots, 2M$, while $\tilde{p}_{nj}^T(\theta_m)$ is its adjoint (transposed, complex conjugate). Then we can compute

$$K_{ni}^T(\theta_m) = \tilde{p}_{n1,i}^T(\theta_m) p_{n1}^T(\theta_m) + \cdots + \tilde{p}_{nq,i}^T(\theta_m) p_{nq}^T(\theta_m).$$

The filter $\underline{K}_{nj}(L)$ can be estimated from the inverse Fourier transform of the vector $(K_{ni}^T(\theta_0), \ldots, K_{ni}^T(\theta_{2M}))'$ as follows:

$$\underline{K}_{ni,k}^T = \frac{1}{2M+1} \sum_{m=0}^{2M} K_{ni}^T(\theta_m) e^{ik\theta_m}.$$

Finally, the common components can be obtained from the relation $\varkappa_{it,n} = \underline{K}_{ni}^T(L)(x_{1t}, \ldots, x_{nt})'$, where the estimated two-sided filter is given by

$$\underline{K}_{ni,k}^T(L) = \sum_{k=-M}^{M} \underline{K}_{ni,k}^T L^k.$$

To the extent that the estimation of the factors relies on two-sided filters, this approach is not well suited for forecasting since estimates of the current values of the factors are not available and so cannot be used to condition on when forecasting future values of the dependent variable.

10.2.5 Bayesian Methods

De Mol, Giannone, and Reichlin (2008) compare the performance of principal components methods to that of Bayesian linear regression models with Gaussian or double exponential priors. Bayesian regressions with a Gaussian prior result in nonzero coefficients on all variables under consideration, although the coefficients are shrunk compared with their OLS equivalents. In fact, assuming i.i.d. regression coefficients, Bayesian prediction with a Gaussian prior amounts to Ridge regression. To see this, consider the linear regression model with Gaussian prior $\beta \sim N(\beta_0, \Sigma_0)$ and normally distributed i.i.d. residuals, $y_{t+1} = \beta' x_t + u_{t+1}$, $u \sim$ ind $N(0, \sigma_u^2)$.

If we restrict the prior parameters to be independent, $\Sigma_0 = \sigma_\beta^2 I$, as noted by De Mol, Giannone, and Reichlin (2008), the Bayesian estimation problem reduces to Ridge regression,

$$\hat{\beta}^{\text{Bayes}} = \arg\min_{\beta}\{||y - X\beta||^2 + (\sigma_u^2/\sigma_\beta^2)||\beta||^2\}, \qquad (10.21)$$

where $||.||$ denotes the Euclidean norm and X and y stack the sample observations of $y_{\tau+1}$ and x_τ.

Assuming shrinkage towards 0 ($\beta_0 = 0$), and a known variance, σ_u^2, the Bayesian estimator and forecasts take the form

$$\hat{\beta}^{\text{Bayes}} = (X'X + \sigma_u^2 \Sigma_0^{-1})^{-1} X'y, \qquad (10.22)$$

$$\hat{f}_{t+1|t} = x_t' \hat{\beta}^{\text{Bayes}}.$$

Unlike the case with Gaussian priors, double exponential priors tend to put either large or zero weights on the individual regressors and so give rise to sparse prediction models. There is no closed-form solution to the coefficients under double exponential priors, but optimization reduces to the penalized least absolute deviation problem and so can be solved using the Lasso algorithm.

Using the data of Stock and Watson (2005) to forecast growth in industrial production and inflation, De Mol, Giannone, and Reichlin (2008) find empirically that, despite their very different implications for model selection, Bayesian linear regression forecasts generated under either Gaussian or double exponential priors tend to be strongly correlated and produce very similar mean squared forecast errors. In turn, the two sets of forecasts are similar to those generated by principal components regression. The reason why two seemingly very different approaches—one that favors sparse models that typically select just a few predictors versus another that puts nonzero weights on most predictors—yield similar forecasts and predictive accuracy is of course that the underlying X-variables are strongly collinear. In this situation, many variables will be close substitutes and it does not matter a great deal which specific variables—or how many—get selected.

10.3 DETERMINING THE NUMBER OF COMMON FACTORS

A key issue when forecasting with common factors is how many factors to include in the model. Two separate issues must be considered in constructing a forecasting model: first, how many factors are required to characterize the variation in the x-variables through the dynamics in (10.7) and (10.12), and second, how many factors should be included in a forecasting model such as (10.13).

Consider the first of these problems—how many factors should be chosen to replace the large-dimensional X_t with a smaller set of factors. Let the number of factors be r and consider the static factor representation

$$X_{it} = \lambda_i' F_t^p + \varepsilon_{xit}, \quad i = 1, \ldots, N. \tag{10.23}$$

Inspection of the eigenvalues of the sample correlation matrix, $\hat{\Sigma}_{XX} = T^{-1} \sum_{t=1}^{T} X_t X_t'$, provides a first informal way to select the number of factors, r. Letting μ_i be the i'th eigenvalue of the covariance matrix arranged in descending order, the fraction of the total variance of X explained by the first r common factors is equal to $\sum_{i=1}^{r} \mu_i / N$. Hence, factors with an eigenvalue exceeding 1 contribute more than the average factor. Eigenvalues close to 0 suggest that very little variation is explained by the accompanying factor. In any sample, the ordered eigenvalues will typically tail off towards 0 with no obvious "separation" between those that are nonzero in the limit and those that might be 0. This is entirely analogous to the usual model selection problem where coefficients that are truly nonzero and those that are truly 0 do not reveal themselves in a sample. There may not be an obvious threshold or cutoff point for determining the optimal value of r in any sample. Mirroring the general model selection problem, formal methods have been developed to address this point.

For consistent estimation of r, formal methods require assumptions on the eigenvalues of the variance–covariance matrix of X_t. What is required for the r factors to continue to account for the majority of the variation in X_t as N becomes large is that the rth largest eigenvalue diverges to infinity. This ensures that the rth largest eigenvalue becomes separated from the remaining eigenvalues (asymptotically in N). Thus methods that consistently select the correct number of factors become available. Again, notice that this is analogous to the usual consistent model selection procedures outlined in chapter 6 where estimates of nonzero parameters and zero parameters asymptotically become far apart, enabling consistent model selection procedures such as BIC to pick the right model.

Differences across estimation procedures reflect the assumptions made on the speed at which the rth largest eigenvalue diverges. Additional differences center on the precise correlation structure of the idiosyncratic component ε_{xit}, particularly the allowance for temporal and cross-sectional dependence.

Bai and Ng (2002) develop methods for consistently selecting the number of factors in the context of approximate factor models. Their analysis allows for time series and cross-sectional heteroskedasticity as well as weak dependencies in ε_{xit}. Bai and Ng (2002) characterize the conditions under which a class of selection criteria consistently identify the correct number of factors, r. Let $\hat{F}_k^p$ be a matrix of k factors obtained through principal components so the sum of squared residuals from the associated model is given by

$$V(k, \hat{F}_k^p) = \frac{1}{NT} \sum_{i=1}^{N} \sum_{t=1}^{T} (X_{it} - \lambda_i^{k'} \hat{F}_{kt}^p)^2.$$

The three information criteria proposed by Bai and Ng take the following form:

$$\mathrm{IC}_{p1}(k) = \ln(V(k, \hat{F}_k^p)) + k \left(\frac{N+T}{NT}\right) \ln\left(\frac{NT}{N+T}\right),$$

$$\mathrm{IC}_{p2}(k) = \ln(V(k, \hat{F}_k^p)) + k \left(\frac{N+T}{NT}\right) \ln\left(\min(N, T)\right),$$

$$\mathrm{IC}_{p3}(k) = \ln(V(k, \hat{F}_k^p)) + k \frac{\ln\left(\min(N, T)\right)}{\min(N, T)}. \tag{10.24}$$

In each case the first term is a measure of fit while the second is a penalty term that increases as a function of $\min(N, T)$ and the number of factors, k. Different values of $k = 0, \ldots, \bar{k}$ can be tried and the value of k that minimizes (10.24) gives the number of selected factors. The penalty terms in (10.24) depend on both N and T. Conventional criteria that depend only on T or N generally choose too many factors. Bai and Ng establish conditions under which these criteria are consistent in the sense that when N and T both go to infinity, the selected number of factors, $\hat{k}$, tends to the true number of factors, r. For small values of N or T, Bai and Ng report that the criteria proposed in (10.24) fail to select the right number of factors, while for $\min(N, T) \geq 40$, the criteria are found to work well in a set of Monte Carlo simulations.

Results are also available under weaker assumptions on the rate of divergence of the rth largest eigenvalue. Under weaker assumptions, the separation is not as clear, even asymptotically; the smaller eigenvalues converge to a distribution and so the separation between the rth largest eigenvalue and the remaining ones is less clear. This analysis is intended to provide a better asymptotic approximation to the empirical sample distribution of the eigenvalues, which as noted above typically do not show such a large separation. The weaker assumption in this direction is often accompanied by stronger assumptions on the correlation structure of ε_{xit}, although Monte Carlo evidence suggests that the effect of misspecifying the assumptions on the errors is small for reasonable models.

Onatski (2010) suggests a method based on these weaker assumptions on the rate of divergence of the eigenvalues. Under the weaker assumptions, the distribution of the eigenvalues smaller than the rth largest eigenvalue can be determined and the maximum point of this distribution can be employed as a cutoff value. The method involves estimating this cutoff value and then estimating the number of factors as the number of eigenvalues above the cutoff. The steps in the method of Onatski (2010, see page 1008) to estimate this cutoff are as follows in our notation:

Step 1: Compute the N eigenvalues of $\hat{\Sigma}_{XX}$ and denote them by μ_i, $i = \{1, 2, \ldots, N\}$, listed in descending order. Let $r_{\max}$ be the largest number of factors to be considered, and set $j = r_{\max} + 1$.

Step 2: Run a regression of $\{\mu_j, \ldots, \mu_{j+4}\}$ on $\{(j-1)^{2/3}, (j)^{2/3}, \ldots, (j+3)^{2/3}\}$ and set δ equal to 2 times the absolute value of the coefficient from this regression.

Step 3: Compute $\hat{r}(\delta) = \max\{i \leq r_{\max} : \mu_i - \mu_{i+1} \geq \delta\}$. If $\mu_i - \mu_{i+1} < \delta$, set $\hat{r}(\delta) = 0$.

Step 4: Set $j = \hat{r}(\delta) + 1$ and repeat steps (2) and (3) until convergence.

Here $r_{\max}$ is set to the largest number of factors to be considered.

Technically, $r_{\max} = r_{\max}^N$ should be chosen to be a sequence in N such that $r_{\max}^N/N \to 0$ as $N \to \infty$, although rate conditions offer no specific insights for particular applications. This is standard when relying on as weak a concept as consistency and is similar to consistent model selection for information criteria discussed in chapter 6.

As always, there is a trade-off between parsimony and model fit. If too many factors are included in the forecast equation, this is likely to adversely affect the precision of the parameter estimates. Conversely, including too few factors means that potentially relevant information is not being used and leads to a loss of efficiency.

10.4 PRACTICAL ISSUES ARISING WITH FACTOR MODELS

Several practical issues arise in the use of common factor models in economic forecasting. This section discusses identification of the factors, parameter instability, missing observations, factor-augmented VARs, and partial least squares methods.

10.4.1 Identification and Economic Interpretation of Factors

The unobserved common factors are fundamentally unidentified. For practical purposes, it is commonly found to be empirically important to standardize the underlying x-variables prior to the analysis, e.g., by subtracting the mean and dividing by the standard deviation of each series. However, without further identifying assumptions, it makes little sense to inquire into the sign and magnitude of the coefficients of $\lambda_i(L)$ and $\lambda_y(L)$ in the dynamic factor model (10.5), (10.8), or the static factor loadings Λ in (10.12). To see this, rewrite the contribution from the factors in the static model (10.12) as $\Lambda F_t^p = \Lambda R R^{-1} F_t^p$ for any nonsingular $r \times r$ "rotation" matrix, R. Hence, data generated from a model with loading matrix Λ and factors F_t^p will be identical to data from a rotated model with loading matrix $\tilde{\Lambda} = \Lambda R$ and factors $\tilde{F}_t^p = R^{-1}F_t^p$. If interest lies purely in mechanically computing a forecast, this is not a problem, of course, since all forecasts are identical under nonsingular rotations of the factors.

A forecast user may nevertheless be skeptical about a purely statistical "black-box" approach that does not allow economic interpretation of the factors. To facilitate interpretation of the factors, one can project the extracted factors on economic variables identified in advance. For example, the first principal component may be strongly correlated with nominal interest rates while the second principal component is strongly correlated with real output growth. Alternatively, one can first group economic variables into clusters such as interest rate or term structure variables, real growth variables, wages, and prices and extract common factors from each of these groups which are in turn used to predict the variable of interest. This would result in "interest rate" and "output" factors that are easier to interpret, although there is no guarantee that such factors closely mimic the factors obtained from a "global" factor extraction method that does not rely on bins.

10.4.2 Instability

Instability in the processes driving the observed variables can be an important issue. Estimates of the dynamic factors reflect the covariance structure embedded in Σ_{XX} and also depend on the dynamic processes driving ε_{xt}. If these are not stable over time, this can lead to inconsistent estimates of the factors used in the forecasting model. A limited amount of instability is permitted, however, provided that this is sufficiently idiosyncratic across the individual series so that it washes out in the cross section and can be diversified away in the aggregate.

Specifically, Stock and Watson (2002a) allow for a stochastic drift in the factor loadings of the form

$$x_{it} = \lambda'_{it} F_t + \varepsilon_{xit},$$

$$\lambda_{it} = \lambda_{it-1} + g_{iT} \varepsilon_{\lambda it}, \tag{10.25}$$

where $\varepsilon_{\lambda it}$ is an $(r \times 1)$ vector of random variables, while g_{iT} is a scalar. The random walk evolution in the factor loadings captures the tendency of many economic relations to gradually change over time. Under this type of temporal instability, we can rewrite the model in (10.25) as

$$x_{it} = \lambda_{i0} F_t + a_{it},$$

$$a_{it} = \varepsilon_{xit} + (\lambda_{it} - \lambda_{i0}) F_t = \varepsilon_{xit} + g_{iT} \sum_{s=1}^{t} \varepsilon'_{\lambda is} F_t. \tag{10.26}$$

Provided that the time-series variation in the parameter values is "small," sufficiently idiosyncratic in a cross-sectional sense, and g_{iT} is independent of F_t, ε_{xjt}, and $\varepsilon_{\lambda jt}$ for all i, j, and t, Stock and Watson show that the underlying factors can still be consistently estimated from the cross section of X-variables and the forecast based on estimated factors will converge to the forecast given the true factors.

In subsequent work, Stock and Watson (2009) show that when the factor structure is subject to a single large break, full-sample principal component estimates still span the space of pre- and post-break factors, the only difference being that the pre- and post-break factor estimates use different linear combinations of the full-sample principal components.

10.4.3 Missing Observations

Incomplete data and missing observations are important practical concerns for economic forecasters. Far from being a balanced panel of $T \times N$ observations, the typical data set encountered in practice involves variables whose samples are of different length and may even be measured at different frequencies. To address this problem, Stock and Watson (2002b) propose using a simple expectation-maximization (EM) algorithm that fills in missing observations. Consider the objective function

$$V(F^P, \Lambda) = \sum_{i=1}^{N} \sum_{t=1}^{T} \mathbb{1}_{it} (X_{it} - \lambda'_i F_t)^2, \tag{10.27}$$

where λ_i is the ith row of Λ and $\mathbb{1}_{it}$ is an indicator function defined as follows:

$$\mathbb{1}_{it} = \begin{cases} 1 & \text{if } x_{it} \text{ is observed,} \\ 0 & \text{if } x_{it} \text{ is missing.} \end{cases}$$

Stock and Watson propose an iterative procedure for obtaining an initial set of estimates, $\hat{\lambda}_i$, and the accompanying factors, $\hat{F}_t$. These are then used to fill out the missing values, i.e., $\hat{X}_{it} = \mathbb{1}_{it} X_{it} + (1 - \mathbb{1}_{it})\hat{\lambda}'_i \hat{F}_t$. Using the rebalanced data set, a new set of factor estimates, $\hat{F}_t$, is extracted from the largest eigenvalues of the sample covariance matrix, $N^{-1} \sum_{i=1}^{N} \hat{X}_i \hat{X}'_i$, where $\hat{X}_i = (\hat{X}_{i1}, \ldots, \hat{X}_{iT})'$. These factor estimates are in turn used to obtain new estimates of $\hat{\lambda}_i$ by regressing $\hat{X}$ on the updated factor estimates and updating the missing observations. The process continues until convergence. For further details, see Stock and Watson (2002b, Appendix A).

In addition to missing data points, outliers can be a real problem when dealing with large data sets for which every series cannot be guaranteed to be of the same quality as when only a few series are used. A filter that replaces outliers with an estimate can be adopted in such situations.

10.4.4 Partial Least Squares

Principal components methods ignore information on the outcome variable, y, in constructing linear combinations of the N predictors, X. The partial least squares (PLS) method accounts for such correlations in constructing linear combinations of the predictors. The method first standardizes each x-variable to have zero mean and unit variance, i.e., $\tilde{x}_i = (x_i - \bar{x}_i)/\hat{\sigma}_i$, where $\bar{x}_i, \hat{\sigma}_i$ are the sample mean and sample standard deviation of x_i, respectively. The method then proceeds iteratively through the following algorithm as described by Hastie, Tibshirani, and Friedman (2009, page 81). First, initiate the algorithm by setting $f^0 = \bar{y} \iota_T$, where $\bar{y} = T^{-1} \sum_{t=1}^{T} y_t$, and $\tilde{x}_i^0 = \tilde{x}_i$. Then, for $m = 1, \ldots, \bar{m} \leq N$ repeat the following steps: (i) form the linear combination of x-variables $z_m = \sum_{j=1}^{N} \hat{\beta}_{jm} \tilde{x}_j^{m-1}$, where $\hat{\beta}_{jm} = \text{Cov}(\tilde{x}_j^{m-1}, y)$; (ii) update the forecast to $f^m = f^{m-1} + \hat{\theta}_m z_m$, where $\hat{\theta}_m = \widehat{\text{Cov}}(z^m, y)/\widehat{\text{Var}}(z^m)$; (iii) orthogonalize $\tilde{x}_j^{m-1}$ with respect to z_m by setting $\tilde{x}_j^m = \tilde{x}_j^{m-1} - \hat{\gamma}_j^m z_m$, where $\hat{\gamma}_j^m = \widehat{\text{Cov}}(z_m, x_j^{m-1})/\widehat{\text{Var}}(z_m)$. Then repeat step (i).

Here z_m are linear combinations of the $\tilde{x}$-variables and are often referred to as directions. Notice how the partial least squares method weights the individual $\tilde{x}$-variables by the strength of their (univariate) correlations with the outcome. If the algorithm continues until $m = N$, it becomes similar to OLS regression on the full set of original predictors.

Despite explicitly accounting for the correlation between the outcome and the linear combinations of x-variables, in practice, often the PLS method acts similarly to Ridge regressions and principal components methods; for further discussion, see Hastie, Tibshirani, and Friedman (2009).

10.5 EMPIRICAL EVIDENCE

We finally review the empirical evidence on forecasting with factor models and present an empirical application. Spurred by the important progress made in our theoretical understanding of the properties of factor models accompanied by easier access to vast data sets, recent years have seen a rapid rise in the number of empirical forecasting studies that use factor models.

Before including factors in a prediction model, it is important to ask whether the factors summarize the essence of the common variation in a given set of variables. In most empirical applications, a small number of factors seem to summarize the common factors well. For example, Giannone, Reichlin, and Sala (2005) report that a small number of factors account for a large part of the variance of most macroeconomic variables. To the extent that the role of the factors is to capture common fluctuations, this suggests as a general rule to keep the number of factors small. However, it should also be kept in mind that the ability of a common factor to explain the common variation in the conditioning variables need not be a good measure of its importance as a predictor for any one particular series.

The empirical success of factor models seems to vary significantly across different types of economic variables and it is a common finding that gains in out-of-sample predictive accuracy for factor models are stronger for real as opposed to nominal variables; see Stock and Watson (2011). For example, for real variables such as growth in industrial production, personal income, trade, or employment, Stock and Watson (2002a) find that using two common factors results in considerable improvements in predictive accuracy over simply using a univariate autoregressive specification with lag length selected by the BIC. Since the difference between real and nominal variables is the rate of inflation, this suggests that factor models have less to offer when it comes to forecasting inflation.

Pesaran, Pick, and Timmermann (2011) find that factor-augmented VAR forecasts outperform univariate forecasts at short horizons of one and three months and across both short and long horizons for four out of the five categories of economic variables studied by Marcellino, Stock, and Watson (2006). This suggests that, for most economic variables and particularly at short horizons, information beyond what is contained in the past history of the variables themselves can be helpful in producing better forecasts.

While factor models can count some important empirical successes, an important and related issue is whether there are systematic gains in predictive accuracy from using more sophisticated factor approaches. For example, given the choice between static and dynamic factor models, which approach should a researcher adopt? Empirically, Boivin and Ng (2005) find that the two approaches yield very similar forecasts and that no single approach is obviously dominant provided that the parameters are appropriately determined. Pragmatic reasons would seem to argue in favor of the approach that is easiest to implement, i.e., the static factor approach. Along similar lines, Boivin and Ng (2005) and D'Agostino and Giannone (2006) find empirically that different factor estimates lead to similar forecasts with comparable out-of-sample forecasting performance.

Stock and Watson (2012) compare forecasts from a model with five principal components to forecasts based on pre-tests, Bagging and Bayesian model averaging methods, all of which they show can be viewed as generalized shrinkage methods. Comparing forecasts across 143 macroeconomic series over the period 1985–2008, they find little evidence that the generalized shrinkage methods improve in notable ways over the dynamic factor models. Interestingly, they also find that the dynamic factor models fail to improve on a simple AR(4) model for more than half of the time series, although there is evidence of stronger forecasting performance of the dynamic forecasting model relative to this univariate benchmark in a longer sample 1960–2008 that includes the period prior to the Great Moderation which starts around 1984.

Dobrev and Schaumburg (2013) consider robust forecasting methods that use regularization and reduced rank regression methods. They find that their method performs well relative to the five-factor principal components regression method of Stock and Watson (2012) and also relative to partial least squares methods.

10.5.1 Factor Models versus Bayesian VARs

In settings with large sets of predictor variables, empirical researchers have traditionally used factor models to generate forecasts. However, as we discussed in chapter 9, studies such as Banbura, Giannone, and Reichlin (2010) develop Bayesian VAR methods that work even with large sets of conditioning variables, e.g., more than 100. Empirically, they find that their Bayesian VARs produce better forecasts than factor-based approaches. Consistent with this, Koop (2013) finds that a common factor approach often produces worse forecasts than Bayesian VARs although the ranking depends on how the trade-off between incorporating more information and dampening the effect of estimation error is implemented across different Bayesian methods.

This highlights important trade-offs between factor models and Bayesian VARs. The performance of the Bayesian VARs can be quite sensitive to the choice of prior and it is clear that the same prior, and thus the degree of shrinkage, does not work well across different economic variables. For some dependent variables, small-scale BVARs work well, corresponding to ignoring the information contained in a large set of predictors. For other dependent variables, it can be important to condition on a larger set of predictors. One important advantage of Bayesian VARs is that they are set up to produce density forecasts as opposed to simple point forecasts. While density forecasts can also be generated from factor models, they require additional assumptions and will typically not account for parameter estimation error in the same way as the Bayesian approach does.

10.5.2 Application

To illustrate the factor approach empirically, we constructed a data set containing 65 variables capturing different aspects of the US economy. The variables include several categories such as industrial production growth, capacity utilization, personal consumption expenditures, retail sales, unemployment and payroll data, housing starts, inventories, inflation, average hourly earnings, commodity and stock price indexes, interest rates, and money supply. In each case we transform the series so it is stationary. The data are monthly and run from 1948:1 to 2010:12.

Figure 10.1 plots time series of the first four principal components extracted from this data set. The first three factors are quite persistent with occasional large shifts in levels, particularly for the second and third factor, while the fourth factor is far less persistent.

We next consider the stability of the factor approach when applied recursively through time. To this end, we report both the proportion of the total variation in the panel of predictor variables that can be explained by the first four factors, the number of factors selected by the forecasting models, along with the forecasts based on the factor models, and their resulting out-of-sample performance.

Figure 10.2 plots the fraction of the explained variance over time. The first factor accounts for close to 50% of the variance, while factor two accounts for between 20 and 25%. The third factor accounts for between 15 and 20% of the variation,

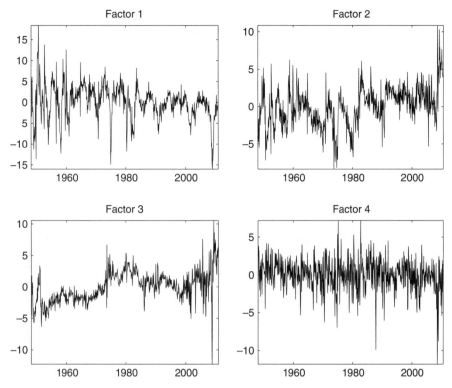

Figure 10.1: First four common factors extracted from a sample of macroeconomic and financial variables.

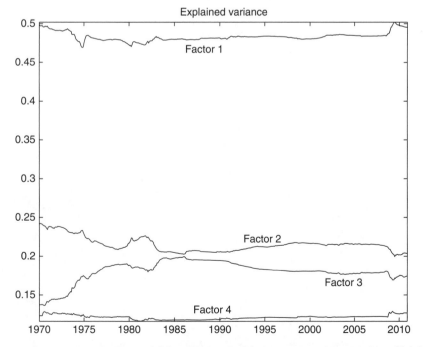

Figure 10.2: Recursive estimates of the proportion of the common variation explained by the first four factors.

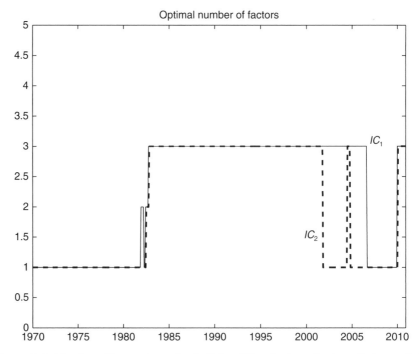

Figure 10.3: Number of factors chosen by the Bai and Ng selection criteria applied recursively through time.

while the fourth factor accounts for close to 12%. Thus, while the proportion of the variance explained by the first and fourth factors is quite stable through time, it is less stable for the second and third factors, although the total variation explained jointly by these two factors is fairly constant through time, adding up to a little less than 40%.

For the pure factor models, figure 10.3 shows that the two information criteria IC_1 and IC_2 select a fairly modest number of common factors which varies between one and three.

Figures 10.4 and 10.5 show monthly forecasts for the inflation rate and unemployment rate series. We use the sample 1948:01–1969:12 for initial parameter estimation and the period 1970:01–2010:12 to evaluate the forecasts out-of-sample.

We show results for pure factor models including either models that include one or four factors, a VAR, a dynamic factor model, and two Ridge regressions with small ($\lambda_1 = 300$) and large ($\lambda_2 = 5,000$) penalty terms, respectively. For each variable, the single factor forecast is generally quite smooth, particularly when compared against the forecast with multiple factors. The VAR and dynamic factor model (DFM) forecasts are nearly identical, suggesting that once autoregressive terms are included, the factor terms are relatively less important. Among the Ridge forecasts, the effect of applying a heavy penalty term is to substantially smooth the forecasts.

Table 10.1 reports the forecasting performance of factor models selected by IC_1 or IC_2 in addition to principal components models with one or four factors, Ridge regressions, a VAR(1), a VAR with lag length selected by the AIC, dynamic factor models, and random walk and prevailing mean benchmarks.

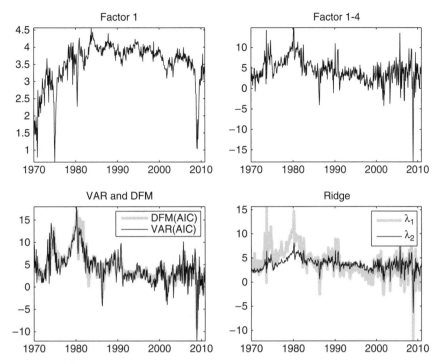

Figure 10.4: Recursive forecasts of the inflation rate using different combinations of the factors (top), a VAR and a factor-augmented VAR, and Ridge regression (bottom).

For the inflation rate series, the best models are the univariate autoregressive models closely followed by the VAR and DFM specifications, all of which beat the random walk benchmark. The pure factor models do comparatively worse with RMSE values above those of the best models, although the model that includes four factors still beats the random walk benchmark. This highlights the importance of including autoregressive terms for many macroeconomic variables. The performance of the Ridge regressions depends on the value of the penalty or shrinkage factor with weak amounts of shrinkage working best for this series. For stock returns, the Ridge regression with the largest amount of shrinkage is the only method that performs better than the benchmark prevailing mean method, although a number of approaches register RMSE performance similar to this benchmark. For stock returns, the most parsimonious models generate the most accurate forecasts, consistent with earlier findings for this variable.

The best unemployment rate forecasts come from the dynamic factor models, followed closely by the AR and VAR forecasts. Pure factor-based forecasts perform poorly again as they fail to pick up the very high persistence in this series. A similar conclusion holds for the T-bill rate, for which the AR, VAR, and dynamic factor models perform best, while the pure factor and Ridge models produce poor out-of-sample forecasts.

Table 10.2 reports Diebold–Mariano test statistics comparing the mean squared error performance of the forecasts in the previous table against a benchmark model. For persistent variables such as the inflation rate, unemployment, and the T-bill rate, the random walk model is a reasonable benchmark. Conversely, for

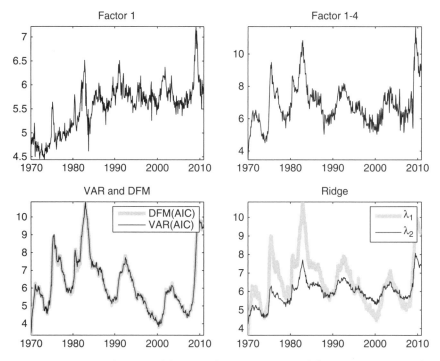

Figure 10.5: Recursive forecasts of the unemployment rate using different combinations of the factors (top), a VAR, a dynamic factor model, and Ridge regression (bottom).

TABLE 10.1:

Out-of-sample root mean squared forecast error performance for different models used to predict the monthly inflation rate, stock returns, unemployment rate, and the short interest rate. AR refers to univariate autoregressive models with lag length selected by the AIC or BIC, Ridge refers to Ridge regression, PC refers to principal components methods with the number of factors selected by the information criteria of Bai and Ng (2002) (IC_1 and IC_2), one principal component (PC_1), four principal components (PC_{1-4}), vector autoregressions (VAR(AIC) and VAR(1)), and two dynamic factor models (DFM(AIC), DFM(1)).

Method	Inflation	Stock	Unemployment	Interest rate
Random walk	3.4581	6.2488	0.1835	0.5001
Prevailing mean	4.2462	4.5388	1.8031	3.4816
AR(AIC)	3.0279	4.5720	0.1744	0.4978
AR(BIC)	3.1065	4.5390	0.1727	0.4901
Ridge, λ_1	3.1069	4.5917	0.4721	2.1419
Ridge, λ_2	3.5641	4.5269	1.1647	3.0255
PC (IC_1)	4.3079	4.5380	1.4095	3.5074
PC (IC_2)	4.2546	4.5406	1.3675	3.4308
PC_1	4.2062	4.5393	1.6985	3.4707
PC_{1-4}	3.3065	4.5592	0.9504	2.9615
VAR(AIC)	3.1260	4.6694	0.1769	0.4869
VAR(1)	3.0743	4.5742	0.1856	0.5061
DFM(AIC)	3.2278	4.7372	0.1626	0.4763
DFM(1)	3.1252	4.6033	0.1575	0.4845

TABLE 10.2:
Diebold–Mariano test statistics for quarterly out-of-sample mean squared error performance measured relative to the random walk benchmark for the inflation, unemployment, and interest rate series and relative to the prevailing mean benchmark for stock returns.

Method	Inflation	Stock	Unemployment	Interest rate
Random walk	0.0000	−7.0860	0.0000	0.0000
Prevailing mean	−2.6991	0.0000	−7.8383	−7.5985
AR(AIC)	2.4778	−1.0894	1.9847	0.0793
AR(BIC)	2.1590	−1.6005	2.3919	0.4114
Ridge, $k = 300$	3.5015	−0.7848	−10.4994	−8.1223
Ridge, $k = 5,000$	−0.5370	0.7163	−9.2411	−8.1120
PC (IC$_1$)	−3.1299	0.0347	−9.6665	−7.8576
PC (IC$_2$)	−2.8699	−0.0922	−8.3682	−7.4224
PC$_1$	−2.6468	−0.0322	−8.3236	−7.5509
PC$_{1-4}$	1.5718	−0.6082	−11.0552	−9.1946
VAR(AIC)	2.0430	−2.0898	0.9606	0.5711
VAR(1)	2.6658	−0.8326	−1.0256	−1.4500
DFM(AIC)	1.8846	−2.9401	2.5033	1.0641
DFM(1)	3.1808	−1.4957	3.3383	2.0652

stock returns that are not serially correlated, a better benchmark is the prevailing mean. Once again, for the stock return series there is no evidence that any of the forecasting methods is capable of beating the prevailing mean forecast's mean squared error performance. In contrast, the dynamic factor models in particular generate substantially more accurate point forecasts than the random walk forecasts for the inflation, unemployment, and interest rate series. For the inflation and unemployment rate series there is also evidence that the univariate AR models beat the benchmark random walk.

These results indicate that, for the data considered here, once autoregressive terms have been included in the forecasting model, there is little evidence that adding factors improves on the accuracy of the forecasts.

10.6 FORECASTING WITH PANEL DATA

Although our analysis has thus far focused on time-series forecasting, nothing prevents the forecasting methods from being used in a different context such as cross sections or panel data. The key point is that the predictor variables are predetermined either in the time dimension or in a cross-sectional sense. For example, we could build a forecasting model on a large cross-section of credit-card holders using data on household characteristics, past payment records, etc. Here the implicit time dimension is that we know whether a payment in the data subsequently turned out fraudulent.

In a predictive context, panel regressions may take the form

$$y_{it+1} = c + X'_{it}\delta + u_{it+1}, \quad i = 1, \ldots, N, \quad t = 1, \ldots, T, \tag{10.28}$$

where i refers to individual units such as households, stocks, etc., while t refers to the time dimension. Stacking the data into an $(NT \times 1)$ vector

$y = (y_{11}, \ldots, y_{1T}, y_{21}, \ldots, y_{2T}, \ldots, y_{N1}, \ldots, y_{NT})'$, and letting $Z = (\iota_{NT} \ X)$, $\beta' = (c', \delta')$, with X being an $(NT \times K)$ matrix of the data, (10.28) can be written more compactly as

$$y = Z\beta + u,$$

where u is an $(NT \times 1)$ vector stacked in the same way as y. For the random effects model $u_{it} = \omega_i + v_{it}$, where $\omega_i \sim \text{iid}(0, \sigma_\omega^2)$, $v_{it} \sim \text{iid}(0, \sigma_v^2)$, $i = 1, \ldots, N$, with ω_i and v_{it} being mutually independent across i and t, as well as independent of X_{it}.[6] The vector of error terms can then be written as

$$u = (I_N \otimes \iota_T)\omega + v,$$

where $\omega = (\omega_1, \ldots, \omega_N)$ and $v = (v_{11}, \ldots, v_{1T}, v_{21}, \ldots, v_{2T}, \ldots, v_{N1}, \ldots, v_{NT})'$. Moreover, the variance–covariance matrix for u simplifies to

$$\Sigma = E(uu') = \sigma_\omega^2 (I_N \otimes (\iota_T \iota_T')) + \sigma_v^2 (I_N \otimes I_T).$$

Assuming a known covariance matrix Σ, the best linear unbiased estimator of β is obtained by generalized least squares, $\hat{\beta}_{\text{GLS}} = (Z'\Sigma^{-1}Z)^{-1}Z'\Sigma^{-1}y$; see Baltagi (2013). Moreover, as shown by Goldberger (1962), the best linear unbiased predictor of y_{iT+1} is

$$f_{iT+1} = Z_{it}'\hat{\beta}_{\text{GLS}} + \gamma_i'\Sigma^{-1}\hat{u}_{\text{GLS}}, \qquad (10.29)$$

where $\hat{u}_{\text{GLS}} = y - Z\hat{\beta}_{\text{GLS}}$, and $\gamma_i = E[u_{iT+1}u]$ captures any ability of the current vector of errors to predict future shocks to the ith variable in period $T + 1$. For the random effects model, $u_{iT+1} = \omega_i + v_{iT+1}$, and so $\gamma_i = \sigma_\omega^2(l_i \otimes \iota_T)$, where l_i is an $(N \times 1)$ vector of 0s, except for a 1 in the ith place. See Baltagi (2013) for further details and discussion.

Two issues arise with the approach to forecasting in (10.29). First, this approach assumes that Ω is known, an assumption that is very unlikely to hold, and so introduces estimation errors when implemented in practice. Second, the forecast is best among unbiased estimators but, as we have seen throughout the book, there is often no reason to require forecasts to be unbiased. Even under MSE loss, bias can usually be traded off against forecast error variance in a way that reduces the expected loss.

Work by Baillie and Baltagi (1999) suggest that despite these deficiencies, what they label a "full-fledged GLS predictor" of $y_{i,T+1}$ that uses plug-in maximum likelihood estimates in place of unknown parameters, produces better forecasting performance compared with OLS or fixed effect predictors that ignore the random error structure in the data. The performance of the GLS estimator is particularly strong in the presence of large contributions from the random error, i.e., when $\sigma_\omega^2/(\sigma_\omega^2 + \sigma_v^2)$ is high.

---

[6] Baltagi and Li (1992) extend this case to allow for first-order serial correlation in v_{it} so that $v_{it} = \rho v_{i,t-1} + \varepsilon_{it}$.

10.7 CONCLUSION

Many methods have been developed for reducing the dimension of a set of conditioning predictor variables deemed too large to be subject to a comprehensive model search or even viable for parameter estimation. First and foremost among these are factor approaches which use a much smaller set of common factors, extracted from a large-dimensional list of variables, to predict the outcome variable of interest. Additional variables can be added to such factors, including own lags, which has given rise to factor-augmented vector autoregressions. Such models allow the simultaneous inclusion of ARMA terms and common factors and so can be used to combine the strength of two very different types of models.

In practice, forecasters are confronted with the decision whether to adopt model selection (regularization) methods that attempt to identify a small set of variables included in the preferred model, while the remaining variables get dropped, or, instead, to first aggregate the information in a large set of potential predictor variables in the form of common factors and then use these in the prediction model. Factor-augmented models represent a middle way in that they facilitate the inclusion of a few key predictors along with aggregate information extracted in some factors.

Which method works best will surely depend on the underlying data-generating process and how this relates to the variables in the forecaster's information set. If the predicted variable is driven by a small number of variables contained in the forecaster's information set, then regularization methods are likely to perform better than factor methods provided that these variables can be identified. This conclusion could be hampered, of course, if the predictors are strongly correlated, but in this case, the specific identity of the selected variables may not matter too much to the predictive accuracy since the predictor variables are close substitutes. Conversely, if the predicted variable depends on common factors, as opposed to individual predictors, then the true coefficients of relatively many predictors will be nonzero, and methods based on identifying a scarce set of predictors will not work well. For example, in the case with a large set of predictor variables, many of which are strongly correlated, factor methods that dilute the "noise" in the individual predictors can be expected to perform better than methods that attempt to identify a small set of individual predictors.

11

<><><><><><><><><><><><><><><><><><><><><><><><><><><><><><><><><><><><><><><><><><><>

Nonparametric Forecasting Methods

The methods examined in the preceding chapters have all been either fully parametric—in which case the forecasting model is specified up to a finite-dimensional vector of unknown parameters, β—or close to fully parametric, involving a search over a fixed set of parametric models (as in chapter 6). In chapter 4 we noted the possibility that any given parametric forecasting model $f(z, \beta)$ might not include the true model. Indeed, to know the true model one must know all or a substantial part of the joint density of Z—a requirement that typically does not hold in practical forecasting situations.

The loss function for a given problem at hand indicates which features of the joint distribution of Z we are interested in. For MSE loss, this is the conditional mean of Y given Z. For lin-lin loss, it is a conditional quantile. This chapter examines methods that have been used to approximate such objects nonparametrically or semi-non-parametrically with minimal information on the underlying model. These methods use the data to estimate the forecasting model in a way that can approximate as many of the potentially true models as possible. There are still restrictions on the set of functions that can be handled, but nonparametric approaches aim to find methods that work for a wide class of functions. By widening the set of models that can be estimated, there is a greater chance that the estimated forecasting model is close to the optimal model. Naturally there is a price to pay for the wider search adopted by nonparametric forecasting models. First, a practical consideration is the dimension of the variables available for constructing forecasts. Since many methods become difficult to implement with a large set of predictors, they are primarily used when the list of predictors is relatively short. Related to this, the wider search over functional forms means that there is much greater risk of overfitting the models in-sample, and hence of constructing models that deliver poor forecasting performance when used in practice.

For any nonparametric method there is a very large set of variations and modifications to the benchmark methods. It is not possible to examine all of these here, so instead we present the simplest forms of the methods supplemented with discussions of their advantages and disadvantages. We focus on three approaches. The first approach, used less commonly in forecasting situations, is kernel estimation. Kernel estimation can be employed in two ways. First, we can estimate the conditional density of Y given Z, then use this density to construct the forecast, just as is done in estimation of density forecasts. Alternatively, we can use kernel methods to directly estimate the feature of the conditional distribution we are interested in, e.g., the conditional mean. The second approach, sieve estimation, is far more commonly used in forecasting studies. Sieve estimators include neural nets as well as other regression methods that use basis functions for approximation. A third approach is to use methods developed in the statistical (machine) learning literature such as boosted regression trees. These can accommodate forecasts even in the presence of large-dimensional predictors.

Nonparametric approaches to forecasting require large data samples and so can be expected to yield better results for such situations. Electricity demand and electricity prices is one such area where a large number of published papers use nonparametric forecasting methods. Electricity loads predicted by temperature variations exhibit a clear nonlinearity as loads are expected to be high for both very cold and very hot weather.[1] Because of the strong nonlinearity in this relationship, nonparametric procedures provide better forecasts than linear models which are not considered reasonable. However, there appears to be little empirical evidence to suggest that one approach is dominant. There is less evidence of nonlinearity in electricity price forecasting. Despite a very large number of applications of various nonparametric procedures there is not much evidence to suggest that one nonparametric approach dominates other approaches or even improves upon linear models; see Aggarwal, Saini, and Kumar (2009) for a review.

Section 11.1 reviews kernel models and section 11.2 goes over the estimation of sieve models. Boosted regression trees are covered in section 11.3, while section 11.4 concludes.

11.1 KERNEL ESTIMATION OF FORECASTING MODELS

Local linear regression methods can be used to produce forecasts under MSE loss. These methods are essentially weighted least squares estimators that assign large weights to previous data for which the predictor variables are "close" to the values observed at the point where the current forecast is made. Conversely, less weight gets assigned to observations with very different values for the predictor variables. The idea is that if the true model really is nonlinear, then observations that are not close to the current predictor variables are less useful in estimating the conditional mean at the current levels of the predictor variables. Let z_t be the predictors for y_{t+1}, excluding a constant. We can directly estimate the conditional mean, and hence produce a forecast at time T, from

$$f_{T+1|T}(z_T) = \frac{\sum_{t=1}^{T-1} y_{t+1} K(z_t - z_T)}{\sum_{t=1}^{T-1} K(z_t - z_T)}, \tag{11.1}$$

where $K(z_t - z_T)$ is a multivariate kernel. For example, the Gaussian kernel sets

$$K(z_t - z_T) = |B|^{-1/2} \exp\{-0.5(z_t - z_T)' B^{-1}(z_t - z_T)\}, \tag{11.2}$$

where B is a bandwidth matrix chosen by the forecaster. In practice, often a product kernel is chosen, for which we have $K(z) = K_1(z_1) \times \cdots \times K_k(z_k)$, where $K_i(\cdot)$ is a

---

[1] Engle et al. (1986) use a variation of cubic splines to model this type of data.

univariate Gaussian kernel. Choosing B to be diagonal in (11.2) results in a product kernel with $K_i(\cdot)$ being the univariate Gaussian kernel.

The method can be extended to locally weighted linear regression to obtain estimates of $\beta = (\beta_0', \beta_1')$ by solving

$$(\hat{\beta}_0, \hat{\beta}_1) = \arg\min_{\beta_0, \beta_1} \sum_{t=0}^{T-1} \left(y_{t+1} - \beta_0 - \beta_1'(z_t - z_T)\right)^2 K(z_t - z_T), \qquad (11.3)$$

so that the forecast at time T is the estimated value $\hat{\beta}_0$. This follows because $(z_t - z_T) = 0$ at z_T. For calculation purposes let $y = (y_1, \ldots, y_T)'$, $\tilde{z} = ([1 \ (z_0 - z_T)], [1 \ (z_1 - z_T)], \ldots, [1 \ (z_{T-1} - z_T)])$ and let K be a diagonal matrix whose (i, i) element is $K(z_i - z_T)$. Then the estimator for the locally weighted regression coefficients is $\hat{\beta} = (\tilde{z}'K\tilde{z})^{-1}\tilde{z}'Ky$ and the forecast is the first element of $\hat{\beta}$, i.e., $\hat{\beta}_0$.[2]

Kernel regression methods were first proposed by Nadaraya (1965) and Watson (1964). Stone (1977) introduced local linear regression. Pagan and Ullah (1999) provide an excellent introduction and overview. The methods are appropriate under a wide range of assumptions on the data, allowing for heterogeneity and dependence in the data. See Hansen (2008b) for a general treatment.

For local linear regression methods to work well, we clearly require that there is a reasonable amount of data with predictors near the values we wish to condition on, i.e., close to z_T. As always with kernel-based methods, both the kernel and bandwidth must be chosen. For both the conditional mean estimator (11.1) and the local linear regression estimator (11.3), a larger bandwidth choice means averaging over more data and hence getting closer to either the unconditional mean for (11.1) or the OLS regression estimator for (11.3). Smaller bandwidths average over data with predictor variables very close to z_T, the current predictor variables. A trade-off therefore arises between a larger bias when averaging over more of the data (if the model is truly nonlinear) versus a larger variance when averaging over less of the data. The optimal bandwidth lies somewhere in the middle, depending on what is optimized. Minimizing MSE results in an optimal bandwidth that is proportional to $T^{1/5}$; see Pagan and Ullah (1999) for a discussion. A natural approach in the context of forecasting is to choose the bandwidth to minimize pseudo out-of-sample MSE, typically calculated using some proportion of the latter sample observations. This method is the forecast equivalent of cross validation, although its properties have not, as far as we know, been systematically evaluated.[3]

11.2 ESTIMATION OF SIEVE MODELS

Sieve estimation, due to Grenander (1981), seeks to approximate an unknown function by combinations of functions of the data. Applied to nonparametric

---

[2] Diebold and Nason (1990) examine nearest neighbor forecasts for exchange rates. Their method is a variation of locally weighted linear regression. They present some evidence that this approach can produce gains in forecasting performance over a random walk model. Satchell and Timmermann (1995) find similar evidence using a nearest neighbor algorithm.

[3] Chapter 16 discusses various designs of out-of-sample MSE estimators.

forecasting, the idea is to construct a forecasting model of the form

$$f(z_T) = \beta_0' z_T + \sum_{j=1}^{J_T} \beta_j g(z_T, \gamma_j), \qquad (11.4)$$

where J_T is the number of scalar nonlinear terms, each denoted $g(z_T, \gamma_j)$, and β_j are weights on those terms. Variations in choice of the g functions capture different approaches to the nonlinear approximation. Note that we could set $\beta_0 = 0$, although often it is better in practice to let this coefficient be estimated. The inclusion of a linear lead term $\beta_0' z_T$ reflects that linear models often perform well empirically and many of the choices for the g functions do not approximate linear models well unless J_T is very large. The image of a sieve is useful here—think of a larger number of terms as a more finely meshed sieve; the number of functions the sieve will "catch" is larger for large values of J_T because it is able to better approximate a wider set of possible functions. A sieve with fewer terms will catch fewer functional forms.

Once the functions in (11.4) are determined, estimation involves solving an extremum problem based on the loss function. Specifically, the free parameters $\{\beta_0, \beta_j, \gamma_j\}$, and perhaps the fineness of the mesh, J_T, are chosen by minimizing the average sample loss,

$$\bar{L}_T = (T-1)^{-1} \sum_{t=0}^{T-1} L(f(z_t), y_{t+1}). \qquad (11.5)$$

Most often the loss criterion is MSE, and so sieve estimators will approximate the conditional mean of y_{t+h} given z_t. Nonlinear regression can be used in this case to construct estimates of the forecasting model.

Theoretical results suggest that for the right choice of g functions, $E[(f^*(z_t) - f(z_t))^2]$ can become arbitrarily small as J_T gets large for any member of a given set of families of models. This suggests that as $J_T \to \infty$, the forecasting model becomes a better and better approximation to any model in some set of nonlinear models, $\mathcal{M}$. This feature of being a good approximator for a very large set of models is often used to justify the use of nonparametric methods. However, any empirical application must use a finite number of terms in the approximation, thus introducing both approximation and estimation errors.[4]

The number of terms in (11.4), J_T, is subscripted by the sample size, T, because the approximating properties are established asymptotically by letting the number of terms increase with the sample size. From a practical perspective, J_T needs to be small relative to the sample size to ensure that estimation of the parameters (β_j, γ_j) is not so imprecise that it overwhelms any gains from obtaining a better approximation to the optimal forecast model. If J_T is chosen to be too small, the model can be a poor approximation to the true conditional mean even when the model has attractive properties for larger values of J_T.

---

[4] Choices between different g functions rest on the properties of the unknown forecasting model itself. The notion that the sieve can capture all possible functions is really that it can capture all functions within a particular class of functions.

Complications might arise when estimating γ_j which, depending on the selected functional forms, can enter the specification nonlinearly and hence requires using search methods. Notice that for a given value of γ_j, the model is linear in β_j and hence these parameters can be estimated by OLS or by any of the shrinkage methods examined in chapter 6.

Sieve methods, of which there are many, differ in their specification of the functional form for g. These functions have the property that as J_T gets large the models are dense in some set $\mathcal{M}$. Not all choices of functions have useful properties in this regard. The desire for good approximating properties leads directly to the use of basis functions as specifications for g. Basis functions can be mutually orthogonal or correlated. We next provide a partial list of functions that can be employed.

11.2.1 Polynomials

When the form of the forecasting model, g, is unknown, a seemingly reasonable approach is to take a Taylor-series approximation to the function. For a univariate predictor, z_t, this suggests using the forecasting model,

$$y_{t+1} = \sum_{i=0}^{m} \beta_i z_t^i + u_{t+1}. \tag{11.6}$$

Although this estimator can have useful approximation properties— particularly if the true function is very smooth—in most cases it is really a local approximation. When the parameters β_i are estimated over a range of data, the estimated weights are not the local parameters at any particular point but instead an average of them. In practice, the method can therefore prove to be a poor predictor. To remedy that the parameter estimates are a data-weighted average obtained over many points, estimation can focus on a single point by extending the local linear regression in (11.3) to include polynomial terms. This approach is the most common form of application in empirical work.

11.2.2 Splines

Splines provide a method for effectively partitioning the space $\{y, z\}$ so that different models are estimated on separate partitions in such a way that the models remain continuous over the full range of z. For example, consider a forecasting regression that allows the model to be one linear regression for $z < z^*$ and another for $z > z^*$, such that the curves meet at z^*. In practice, often a cubic spline is used so that the model is a polynomial in z up to z^3. The partition points are known as knots.

Consider the problem of predicting y_{t+h} with a univariate predictor, z_t. The simplest cubic spline would involve estimating the model,

$$y_{t+1} = \beta_0 + \beta_1 z_t + \beta_2 z_t^2 + \beta_3 z_t^3 + \sum_{i=1}^{m} \beta_{3+i}(z_t - c_i)^3 \mathbb{1}(z_t \geq c_i) + u_{t+1}, \tag{11.7}$$

where the m knots are values of c_i, $i = 1, \ldots, m$ in the support of the predictor variable. Application of the cubic spline method requires choosing the location of the knots, and hence selecting m. A standard approach is to simply choose them as evenly spaced percentiles of z with m dependent on the sample size; larger values for

m result in a less smooth model and also require a greater number of parameters to be estimated. A common choice for a sample size of 100 is to use knots at the 20th, 40th, 60th, and 80th percentiles. Given such knots, estimation of (11.7) can proceed simply by OLS.

Two issues are often considered in spline regression of simple forms such as (11.7). First, near the boundaries of the support for the observed predictors, the fitted model can give very erratic results since the data are not influential in fitting the curve near these points. Hence, the cubic terms can result in large slopes at these points. To overcome this, a standard procedure is to place knots at the ends of the support and use linear functions for the partition between these and the closest knots. It is not clear that this is so helpful since it involves generating forecasts for situations that have hardly ever been previously observed. In such situations a forecaster probably does not want to rely on extrapolating from a model whose main property is that it is picking up nonlinearities and using them to extrapolate over unobserved data.

The second issue that arises is that if the coefficients $\beta_4, \ldots, \beta_{3+m}$ in (11.7) are vastly different from each other, then the fitted model can vary quite a bit. To counter this, differences in the parameter estimates can be penalized, e.g., by minimizing a weighted sum of squared errors and the penalty term. Penalties usually are of the form $\lambda \int [\tilde{g}(x)]^2 dx$, where $\tilde{g}$ is the derivative or second derivative of the estimated function. For example, the second derivative of the cubic spline in (11.7) is $2\beta_2 + 6\beta_3 z + 6 \sum_{i=1}^{m} \beta_{3+i}(z - c_i)\mathbb{1}(z \geq c_i)$. Integrating the square of this over z_t from the lower to the upper points of the support of the data results in a penalty $\lambda \beta' D \beta$. The estimation problem now is in the form of a generalized Ridge regression which has a simple closed-form solution (see chapter 6).

A final difficulty in using spline models is that the model gets very complicated as the dimension of z increases. Even with only two predictors, we could include not only polynomials in both predictors but also their cross products. This also complicates the choice of the knot positions since we now need to partition a larger space. One approach is to partition along each of the z-variables independent of the other predictors; however this introduces a large number of terms and hence more β coefficients to estimate.

11.2.3 Artificial Neural Networks

Artificial neural network (ANN) models are the most frequently used sieve method in economic forecasting. The term ANN refers not to a single choice for g but to a class of models. Their common thread is that the g functions are chosen such that their output is confined to the range $[0, 1]$.

The most common ANN method is to use what is known as a feedforward ANN with a single hidden layer. The notion of hidden layers refers to the possibility that rather than letting g directly be a function of z_t, we can let it be a function of another sigmoid $k(\cdot)$ which in turn is itself a function of z_t, so $g(z_t) = g(k(z_t))$. The feedforward property is that the output prediction does not feed back into g.

It is common to let the g functions be logistic, i.e., for $z_t = \gamma_{0j} + \sum_{i=1}^{k} \gamma_{ij} z_{it}$,

$$g(z_t, \gamma_j) = \frac{1}{1 + \exp\{-z_t\}}. \tag{11.8}$$

Different sigmoid functions than (11.8) can be used, for example, the Gaussian sigmoid sets,

$$g(z_t, \gamma_j) = (2\pi)^{-1/2} \int_{-\infty}^{z_t} \exp(-w^2/2) dw.$$

The on/off (Heaviside function) switch sets

$$g(z_t, \gamma_j) = \mathbb{1}(z_t > 0).$$

Nonsigmoid functions can also be employed. For example the Ridgelet ANN typically sets $g(z_t, \gamma_j) = \tilde{g}(\tilde{z}_t)$, where $\tilde{g}(\tilde{z}_t)$ is a so-called Ridge function and $\tilde{z}_t = \gamma_{j+1}^{-1} z_t$ where γ_{j+1} is the standard deviation of z_t and so is a scaled version of z_t. One example is to set $g(\tilde{z}_t)$ equal to the $(k-1)$th derivative of a smooth density function such as the normal distribution, so $g(\tilde{z}_t) = (d^{k-1}/d\tilde{u}^{k-1})e^{-\tilde{z}_t^2/2}$. See Chen, Racine, and Swanson (2001) for properties and an application to inflation forecasting.

The popularity of ANN models derives in large part from their very general approximating properties. Hornik, Stinchcombe, and White (1989) show that even with one hidden layer and an arbitrary choice of g, with enough terms included, ANN models are able to approximate any Borel-measurable function with very good accuracy. Hence, these models have global approximation properties unlike, for example, Taylor expansions that approximate functions at a single point. As forecasting models we might therefore expect ANN models to work well when we do not know the shape of the nonlinear function at all points in the data.

The ability of ANN models to approximate unknown nonlinear functions was established for a wide variety of choices for the functional form g, so this result gives no indications on how to choose these functions. Similarly, the choice between single and multiple layer models is not well guided by theory. Again it is reasonable to add a linear model in addition to the terms that pick up any nonlinear components (Kuan and White, 1994). Not surprisingly, an extraordinarily large set of variations on these methods are used in practice, with little theory to guide any choice between them. White (1996) discusses choices related to expected smoothness of the underlying function.

Applications of ANN models require specifying the values of the β and γ_j coefficients in (11.4). For given values of γ_j, the regression becomes linear and hence OLS could be applied. The difficulty lies in estimation of the parameters inside the g functions. This clearly complicates estimation, especially when large numbers of terms are included.

We also need to select J_T when applying the ANN models. Given values for γ_j (however estimated) the model is a linear regression and the techniques for model selection in chapter 6 apply. Information criteria and cross-validation methods can therefore be used.

Finally, a note on terminology. It should be clear from the above discussion that, approximation results not withstanding, ANN models are simply a family of nonlinear regression models that relate the predicted variable, y_{t+1}, to available data, z_t. However, many papers adopt different jargon. The g functions are known as squashing functions since they keep to the range $[0, 1]$ regardless of the support of the data. Estimation is known as learning. Once parameterized, the functions themselves are often referred to as nodes.

11.2.3.1 White's QuickNet

White (2006) suggests a convenient QuickNet algorithm that provides an easy and convenient way to estimate ANN models. The algorithm was proposed by White (2006) as a way to deal with nonlinearities in ANNs which can greatly complicate estimation of these models. Rather than estimating the values of γ_j the approach simply draws these coefficients randomly from a reasonable distribution, thereby limiting the estimation part of the problem to running linear regressions.

The algorithm makes use of the leave-one-out cross-validation MSE, CVMSE(q), defined as[5]

$$\text{CVMSE}(q) = \frac{1}{T-1} \sum_{t=1}^{T-1} \hat{\varepsilon}^2_{qt+1(-t-1)}, \tag{11.9}$$

where

$$\hat{\varepsilon}_{qt+1(-t-1)} = y_{t+1} - \hat{\beta}'_{0q(-t-1)} z_t - \sum_{j=1}^{q} g(\hat{\gamma}'_j z_t) \hat{\beta}_{qj(-t-1)}, \tag{11.10}$$

and the estimates $\hat{\beta}_{0q(-t-1)}$ and $\hat{\beta}_{qj(-t-1)}$ are fitted to the data that omit observation $t+1$. Here q refers to the number of nonlinear terms and $\hat{\beta}'_{0q}, \hat{\gamma}'_j, \hat{\beta}_{qj}$ are parameter estimates defined below. More general cross-validation techniques, including methods that leave out blocks of the data, could also be considered; see White (2006). As described by White (2006), the algorithm involves the following steps, none of which involves any nonlinear optimization.

1. Compute initial OLS estimates $\hat{\beta}_{00}$ by regressing y_{t+1} on an intercept and z_t. Also compute regression residuals, $\hat{\varepsilon}_{0t+1} = y_{t+1} - \hat{\beta}'_{00} z_t$ and the cross-validation MSE value, CVMSE(0), defined in (11.9) under the assumption that $\hat{\gamma}_j = 0$, for $j = 1, \ldots, q$. This defines the linear benchmark. Set $q = 1$.
2. Randomly generate m sets of coefficients, $\gamma_j = \{\gamma_{0j}, \gamma_{1j}\}_{j=1}^m$. For each γ_j, regress the residuals from iteration $q - 1$, $\hat{\varepsilon}_{q-1,t+1}$, on a constant and $g(\gamma'_j z_t)$. Pick $\hat{\gamma}_q$ as that value of γ_j, $j = 1, \ldots, m$, that maximizes the R^2 of this OLS regression.
3. Compute OLS regression coefficients, $\hat{\beta}_{0q}, \hat{\beta}_q = (\hat{\beta}_{q1}, \ldots, \hat{\beta}_{qq})'$, and residuals,

$$\hat{\varepsilon}_{qt+1} = y_{t+1} - \hat{\beta}'_{0q} z_t - \sum_{j=1}^{q} g(\hat{\gamma}'_j z_t) \hat{\beta}_{qj},$$

by regressing y_{t+1} on z_t and $g(\hat{\gamma}'_j z_t)$, $j = 1, \ldots, q$. Also compute the CVMSE(q). Increase q to $q + 1$, or stop in the case $q > \bar{q}$. Otherwise, go back to step 2.

---

[5] This is a special case of the more general cross-validation methods considered by White (2006).

4. Choose $\hat{q}$ by cross validation, i.e., by finding the value of q that minimizes

$$q = \arg\min_{q \in [1,...,\bar{q}]} \text{CVMSE}(q).$$

Using this value, $\hat{q}$, let $\hat{\theta}_{\hat{q}} = (\hat{\beta}'_{0\hat{q}}, \hat{\beta}'_{\hat{q}}, \hat{\gamma}'_1, \ldots, \hat{\gamma}'_{\hat{q}})'$.

White suggests that a nonlinear optimization step can be added after the fourth step. He also provides specific advice on how to avoid multicollinearity in the regressions by properly scaling the distribution from which the random coefficients γ_j are drawn in step 2. Specifically, to avoid multicollinearity between the terms in $g(\gamma_0 + \gamma'_1 z_t)$, in the univariate case, γ_1 should be selected to be of the same order of magnitude as the standard deviation of the data, $\text{sd}(z_t)$, or possibly larger, while γ_0 should be of roughly the same order of magnitude as $\text{sd}(\gamma_1 z_t)$. White notes that using $m = 500$ or $m = 1000$ values to estimate γ in step 2 tends to work well.

Racine (2001) finds that neural networks do not improve on linear forecasts of monthly stock returns by means of a variety of macroeconomic and financial predictor variables. When used to guide the positions of an investment rule that switches in and out of stocks and T-bills depending on the sign of the predicted excess return on stocks over T-bills, Racine finds that recursive neural net forecasts result in lower wealth and higher risks than forecasts from a linear model.

11.2.4 Projection Pursuit Regression

When the dimension of the predictor variables becomes moderately large, the set of approximating models also can become very large. This is a problem known as the curse of dimensionality. Choosing between models in this situation becomes problematic, as does implementation of many of the procedures. Projection pursuit regression, introduced by Friedman and Stuetzle (1981), is a simplified approach that aims to capture the gains from allowing for the estimation of a flexible function without encountering the problems that arise from the curse of dimensionality. The approximation they consider takes the form

$$y_{t+1} = \beta_0 + \sum_{i=1}^{m} g_i(\beta'_i z_t) + u_{t+1}, \tag{11.11}$$

where g_i is a nonlinear function of the linear index, $\beta'_i z_t$, with different values of the "weights" β_i for each term. Typically the predicted variable $\{y_{t+1}\}$ is first demeaned, giving an estimate for β_0. An iterative approach is used to building the model, starting with one term and adding terms until the gain from additional terms becomes smaller than a user-defined threshold for the minimum required improvement in the in-sample MSE.

To construct the first term, an initial guess at β_1 is made and $w_t = \beta'_1 z_t$ is constructed using this guess. Next, a nonparametric model is fitted to explain $(y_{t+1} - \hat{\beta}_0)$ by w_t. Given this model, β_1 is estimated by minimizing the sum of squared residuals $\sum_{t=1}^{T-1} (y_{t+1} - \hat{\beta}_0 - \hat{g}_1(\beta'_1 z_t))^2$. The procedure is then repeated to obtain the second term replacing $y_{t+1} - \hat{\beta}_0$ with $y_{t+1} - \hat{\beta}_0 - \hat{g}_1(\hat{\beta}'_1 z_t)$. Computational gains arise because the nonparametric procedure is a function only of a univariate series regardless of the dimension of z_t. As with most of these ad hoc procedures, a wide range of variations exist and the actual nonparametric methods used to construct estimates of $\hat{g}$ vary from application to application.

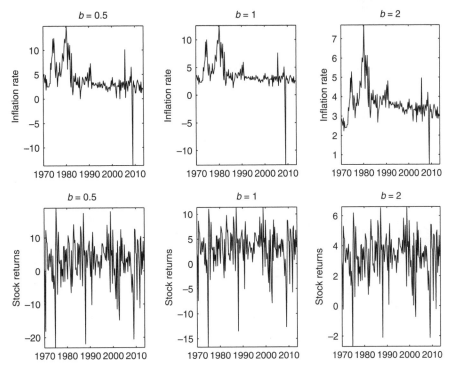

Figure 11.1: Kernel forecasts of inflation (top) and stock returns (bottom) for three different choices of bandwidth.

11.2.5 Empirical Illustration

As an illustration of the nonparametric approaches, we consider forecasting the quarterly CPI inflation rate and value-weighted returns on the US stock market using their respective lagged values. We choose these series because they have very different dynamic properties, with inflation having a highly persistent mean, while stock returns have little or no autocorrelation.

Figure 11.1 shows forecasts of inflation and stock returns using kernel bandwidths of $b = 0.5\hat{\sigma}$, $b = \hat{\sigma}$, and $b = 2\hat{\sigma}$, where $\hat{\sigma}$ is the estimated standard deviation of the underlying variable. The inflation forecasts are considerably more volatile, the narrower the bandwidth, and the more "local" the weighting under this approach. For $b = 0.5\hat{\sigma}$, the inflation rate forecasts are quite extreme as they are based on a narrow local average. In contrast, for $b = 2\hat{\sigma}$ the range of forecasts falls in a narrower band from 0 to 8% per annum. The sensitivity of the range of predicted value to the choice of bandwidth is equally large for the stock return series for which the volatility of the kernel forecasts is far higher for the smallest bandwidth compared to the largest bandwidth as can be noticed from the difference in scales in the three panels.

Figure 11.2 shows sequences of forecasts generated by artificial neural network models where we use an initial period 1947–1969 to estimate the first set of parameters before recursively expanding the estimation window and generating forecasts out-of-sample over the period 1970–2013. The number of terms in the neural network is selected either by the AIC or by the BIC. The two sets of inflation forecasts are quite similar with a time-series correlation of 0.94.

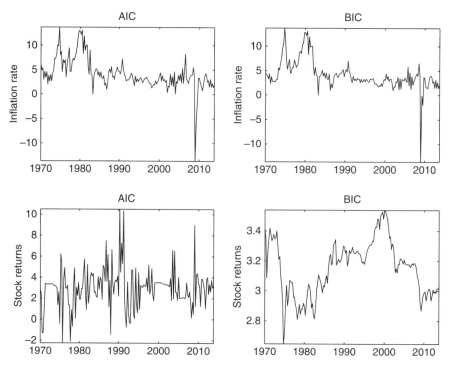

Figure 11.2: Artificial neural network forecasts of inflation and stock returns with network terms selected by the AIC or BIC criteria.

Figure 11.3 shows the number of terms selected by the ANN using either the AIC or the BIC. For the inflation series, the neural network selected by the AIC includes up to 12 terms (the maximum), although it frequently includes far fewer terms. The number of terms selected also tends to vary quite a bit through time. The BIC selects far fewer terms, typically three or four terms. For stock returns, the BIC includes no lags while the AIC typically includes one or two lags.

The top panel in figure 11.4 shows recursively generated inflation rate forecasts from a cubic spline with nodes at the 20th, 40th, 60th, and 80th percentiles. The cubic spline inflation forecasts generate an unexpected negative forecast around 1980 and an extremely large negative value around -0.25 in 2008. Cubic spline forecasts of stock returns, shown in the bottom panel in figure 11.4 also record extreme forecasts, namely a large negative value below -40% in 1970 and a very large positive value above 60% in 1975.

Sensible forecasters would arguably have been skeptical about using such forecasts and might have resorted instead to using a historical average (stock returns) or the previous value (inflation) in place of the extreme forecast. This is akin to using what is sometimes called the "insanity filter" and is a strategy that can be adopted in real time—the forecaster overrules a model-generated forecast if it is too implausible.[6]

Table 11.1 reports the root mean squared error performance of a range of nonparametric forecasts along with those of a random walk and prevailing mean

---

[6] An alternative way to constrain the forecast is by imposing exogenous information as proposed by González, Hubrich, and Teräsvirta (2011).

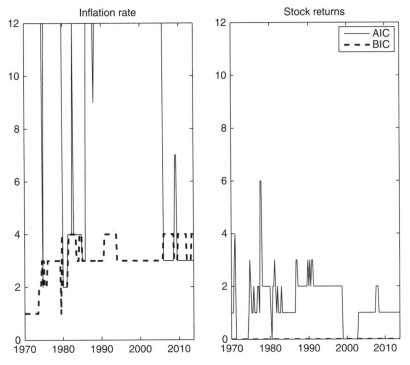

Figure 11.3: Number of terms in the artificial neural network selected by the AIC or BIC models fitted to the inflation rate or stock return forecasts.

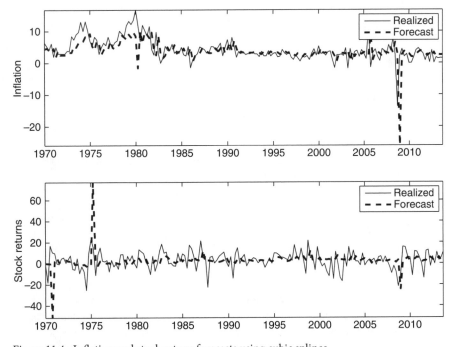

Figure 11.4: Inflation and stock return forecasts using cubic splines.

TABLE 11.1:

Root mean squared error performance for two benchmarks (random walk and prevailing mean) and a range of nonparametric models: artificial neural networks (ANN) with terms selected by the AIC or BIC information criteria, kernel forecasts with three different bandwidths, and cubic spline forecasts using four nodes and truncation of the most extreme forecast (marked Spline**).

Method	Inflation	Stock
Random walk	3.1646	11.4595
Prevailing mean	3.6395	8.4834
ANN(AIC)	3.0572	8.7907
ANN(BIC)	2.9281	8.4878
Kernel $b = 0.5\sigma$	3.0167	10.5425
Kernel $b = \sigma$	3.0052	9.2402
Kernel $b = 2\sigma$	3.2141	8.5243
Spline	3.6831	10.6889
Spline**	3.0944	8.4862

model. For the inflation rate, the best forecasts are generated by the ANN with terms recursively selected by the BIC. The kernel approaches perform relatively well, although they get worse for the largest value of the bandwidth. The cubic spline results are extremely poor if the outlier forecast is relied on but are otherwise quite good, illustrating the importance of filtering extreme forecasts from such approaches.

For stock returns, the best forecasts are generated by the prevailing mean, closely followed by forecasts from the ANN with terms selected by the BIC and the cubic spline forecasts that truncate extreme values. Turning to the kernel forecasts, the narrower the bandwidth, the worse the forecast, i.e., the nearest neighbors contain very little information on stock returns.

11.3 BOOSTED REGRESSION TREES

Regression trees provide a simple way to map a $(K \times 1)$ vector of predictors $z_t = (z_{t1}, z_{t2}, \ldots, z_{tK})'$ to some univariate outcome, y_{t+1}. We provide here a brief description of such methods following Hastie, Tibshirani, and Friedman (2009) and Rossi and Timmermann (2015).

Each regression tree splits the sample space defined by the predictors into "flat spots," so that the predicted value is modeled as a constant, c_j, within each state, S_j. If the sample is split into J separate subregions or states, $S_1, S_2, \ldots, S_J$, the fitted value from a regression tree, $g(z, \theta_J)$, with J terminal nodes and parameters, $\theta_J = \{S_j, c_j\}_{j=1}^{J}$, takes the form

$$g(z, \theta_J) = \sum_{j=1}^{J} c_j \mathbb{1}(z \in S_j), \qquad (11.12)$$

where $\mathbb{1}(z \in S_j)$ is an indicator variable that equals 1 if $z \in S_j$ and is 0 otherwise. Implementation of (11.12) requires deciding on which predictor variables to use to split the sample space and which split points to use. For example, if $J = 2$, a forecast may be based on a split of the predictors according to whether a particular variable takes a high or a low value.

Given a set of split points, $S_1, \ldots, S_J$, the constant term, c_j, is easily estimated. Under MSE loss, the estimated constant, $\widehat{c}_j$, is simply the sample average of y_{t+1} in state S_j:

$$\widehat{c}_j = \frac{1}{\sum_{t=1}^{T-1} \mathbb{1}(z_t \in S_j)} \sum_{t=1}^{T-1} y_{t+1} \mathbb{1}(z_t \in S_j). \tag{11.13}$$

Split points are more difficult to determine, particularly if the list of predictors, $z_{kt}, k = 1, \ldots, K$, is large. Often a sequential algorithm is used to split the sample space. For a given starting model, predictor, z_k, and split point s, the algorithm would construct half-planes,

$$S_1(k, s) = \{z | z_k \leq s\} \quad \text{and} \quad S_2(k, s) = \{z | z_k > s\},$$

so as to minimize the sum of squared residuals:

$$\min_{k,s} \left[\min_{c_1} \sum_{z_t \in S_1(k,s)} (y_{t+1} - c_1)^2 + \min_{c_2} \sum_{z_t \in S_2(k,s)} (y_{t+1} - c_2)^2 \right]. \tag{11.14}$$

Given choices of k and s the fitted values, $\hat{c}_1$ and $\hat{c}_2$, are then

$$\widehat{c}_1 = \frac{1}{\sum_{t=1}^{T-1} \mathbb{1}(z_t \in S_1(k, s))} \sum_{t=1}^{T-1} y_{t+1} \mathbb{1}(z_t \in S_1(k, s)),$$

$$\widehat{c}_2 = \frac{1}{\sum_{t=0}^{T-1} \mathbb{1}(z_t \in S_2(k, s))} \sum_{t=1}^{T-1} y_{t+1} \mathbb{1}(z_t \in S_2(k, s)). \tag{11.15}$$

The best pairing of splitting variables and split points (k, s) used in the first iteration can be determined by searching through each of the predictors, $k = 1, \ldots, K$. Given the best partition from the first step, the data can next be partitioned into two additional states and the splitting process is repeated for each of the subsequent partitions. Predictor variables that are never used to split the sample space do not influence the forecast so the choice of splitting variable is similar to variable selection. This process is known as boosting.

Boosted regression trees are very flexible and can capture local features of the data that linear models may overlook. Boosting methods can be used to identify which of a large number of possible variables help to improve forecasting performance. They build on the idea that combining a series of simple prediction models can lead to more accurate forecasts than those available from any individual model.

A boosted regression tree is simply the sum of individual regression trees:

$$f_B(z) = \sum_{b=1}^{B} g_b(z; \theta_{J,b}), \tag{11.16}$$

where $g_b(z; \theta_{J,b})$ is a regression tree of the form (11.12) used in the bth boosting iteration and B is the number of boosting iterations. Given the previous model, $f_{B-1}(z)$, the subsequent boosting iteration searches for parameters $\theta_{J,B} = \{S_{j,B}, c_{j,B}\}_{j=1}^{J}$ for the next tree to solve a problem of the form

$$\hat{\theta}_{J,B} = \arg\min_{\theta_{J,B}} \sum_{t=1}^{T-1} \left[y_{t+1} - (f_{B-1}(z_t) + g_B(z_t; \theta_{J,B})) \right]^2. \tag{11.17}$$

For a given set of state definitions ("splits"), $S_{j,B}$, $j = 1, \ldots, J$, the optimal constants, $c_{j,B}$, in each state are derived iteratively by solving the problem

$$\hat{c}_{j,B} = \arg\min_{c_{j,B}} \sum_{z_t \in S_{j,B}} \left[e_{t+1,B-1} - c_{j,B} \right]^2, \tag{11.18}$$

where $e_{t+1,B-1} = y_{t+1} - f_{B-1}(z_t)$ is the forecast error remaining after $B-1$ boosting iterations. The solution to this problem is the regression tree that most reduces the average of the squared residuals $\sum_{t=0}^{T-1} e_{t+1,B-1}^2$ and $\hat{c}_{j,B}$ is the mean of the residuals in the jth state.

Boosting algorithms iteratively reweight data used in the initial fit by adding new trees in a way that increases the weight on observations modeled poorly by the existing collection of trees. However, since the approach is sequential and successive splits are performed on fewer and fewer observations, this increases the risk of fitting idiosyncratic data patterns. Furthermore, there is no guarantee that the sequential splitting algorithm leads to the globally optimal solution.[7]

Shrinkage in this context means that each iteration of the model moves only a small fraction of the optimal step of the learning algorithm

$$f_B(z_t) = f_{B-1}(z_t) + \delta \sum_{j=1}^{J} c_{j,B} \mathbb{1}(z_t \in S_{j,B}), \tag{11.19}$$

where δ is a small number such as $\delta = 0.001$. Subsampling means that each tree is fitted on a randomly drawn subset of the training data. Fitting the tree only on a subset of the data reduces the risk of overfitting or getting stuck in a local optimum. Finally, by minimizing mean absolute errors, $T^{-1} \sum_{t=0}^{T-1} |y_{t+1} - f(z_t)|$, the algorithm fits the conditional median of y_{t+1} rather than the conditional mean used under MSE loss. The latter is often found to place too much weight on outliers in the data.

Forecasts from the boosted regression trees are simple to generate. The boosted regression tree is first estimated using data from $t = 1, \ldots, T$. Then a forecast of y_{T+1} is based on the model estimates and the value of the predictor variable at time T, z_T.

Rossi and Timmermann (2015) use boosted regression trees to predict time variations in the US equity premium. They find strong evidence that linear prediction models are misspecified, whereas boosted regression trees manage to pick up nonlinearities. Out-of-sample evidence suggests that the boosted regression trees yield better out-of-sample forecasts of both stock returns and stock market volatility

---

[7] Friedman (2001, 2002) propose a stochastic gradient approach that can be used to estimate such models. To avoid overfitting, a number of insights from the statistical learning literature can be adopted, including shrinkage, subsampling, and minimization of absolute forecast errors as opposed to squared forecast errors.

than a range of benchmark models. Bai and Ng (2009) is another application of this method to diffusion indexes and macro data.

11.4 CONCLUSION

Sieve methods such as artificial neural networks have powerful approximating capabilities and are able to approximate a very wide set of nonlinear models. This property relies on including an infinite number of terms. However, it is worth realizing that any estimated sieve model is itself an approximation to this infinite-order approximation. Finite sample applications approximate the infinite series with a finite series and must rely on estimated parameters that are then subject to estimation error. As a result, there is a real risk that sampling error overwhelms any gains from being able to approximate the underlying model in a more flexible manner. Model selection methods can be used to decrease the effects of overparameterization, but the actual usefulness of nonparametric forecasting methods over other less flexible methods needs to be evaluated rather than taken for granted.

The main difficulty with nonparametric methods is the so-called curse of dimensionality. Even with a single predictor, these methods are not particularly parsimonious, and with multiple predictors a very large number of parameters may have to be estimated (in the series-type approaches) or be influenced by sparse data (in the kernel approaches). Methods such as projection pursuit regression attempt to avoid this problem, but there is limited experience with their performance in forecasting.

Another issue is that it can be difficult to interpret the results from nonparametric estimation. This need not be an issue to the extent that the methods are regarded as an automatic forecasting device. However, if interpretability of the model's estimated relations is important, nonparametric methods are not as straightforward to use as parametric methods. In part, such issues can be addressed by using graphs to illustrate how input variables map into predictions, although this involves more effort than simply looking at estimates of individual regression coefficients.

12

⨯⨯

Binary Forecasts

Many economic applications involve data with a restricted support. Examples include a consumer's decision to buy an automobile chosen from a small set of possibilities or the Fed's decision to change the Federal funds rate in multiples of 25 basis points. When the outcome variable has restricted support, this needs to be taken into account in constructing as well as evaluating a forecasting model. It also has implications for the choice of loss function. For illustration, consider the binary prediction problem in which the observed outcome, Y, takes one of two values. For example, we might forecast whether there is a recession, whether an asset price rises, whether a company or a household goes bankrupt, or whether a student is admitted to a college. In each of these cases a particular outcome either happens or does not happen. Clearly the forecast cannot sensibly take any value on the real number line for these cases.

As for all forecasting problems, we can consider either density forecasts or point forecasts of the outcome. In the binary model the density of Y given z is fully described by the conditional mean, so the literature on binary forecasts has focused on density forecasts.[1] Moreover, in contrast with the majority of forecasting problems, the conditional mean is not (except in trivial cases) a possible outcome for binary variables and hence does not provide a point forecast for Y. Standard methods for obtaining the conditional mean therefore result in a density forecast rather than a point forecast. This unusual dichotomy extends to forecast evaluation; most methods for forecast evaluation of binary variables amount to density rather than point forecast evaluation.

Interesting issues arise for point forecasting of binary outcomes. First, there is a direct relationship between the density forecast and the point forecast. Since both the outcome variable and forecast can take only two possible values, the loss function is extremely simple and so it is much easier to match the loss function with the losses that could be incurred. For scoring rules—loss functions for distributional forecasting—direct relationships between utility functions and proper scoring rules have been developed. For point forecasting, the simplicity of the loss function gives rise to a fixed class of reasonable loss functions. Although the loss function is simple, it is not completely well behaved because it depends on the sign function, which

---

[1] This holds because the mean also defines the entire distribution for a Bernoulli random variable.

is discontinuous. This makes estimation somewhat more challenging and has led to shortcuts in estimation which in many cases could result in poor forecasting models.

Much of the early work on binary predictions comes from weather forecasting and it is useful to bridge different areas of the forecasting literature by including a note on differences in nomenclature. In the weather forecasting literature the unconditional distribution of Y is called a climatological forecast and is often used as a baseline; a point forecast is referred to as a deterministic forecast, while a distributional forecast is called a probabilistic forecast.

Chapter 12 proceeds as follows. Section 12.1 covers point and probability forecasts in the case with binary outcomes, while section 12.2 discusses density forecasting for binary variables. The estimation and construction of point forecasts for binary outcome variables is further discussed in section 12.3 which also covers an empirical application. Section 12.4 presents an empirical application and section 12.5 concludes.

12.1 POINT AND DENSITY FORECASTS FOR BINARY OUTCOMES

We first introduce some notation needed in the analysis. Let $Y = 1$ if some event occurs, while $Y = 0$ if the event does not occur, and let the random variable $p(Z)$ denote the probability that $Y = 1$ given Z. The choice of how we map the two outcomes to specific numbers is arbitrary, some methods in the literature use the normalization that the outcome equals -1 when the event does not occur. To cover this case we also define $\tilde{Y} = 2Y - 1$ which transforms the outcome space to $\{-1, 1\}$. The literature on binary forecasting uses both of these codings; either leads to the same results, although some of the expressions change. We focus on Y, but also provide some results for $\tilde{Y}$ to map back to the original papers.

Typically the conditional mean $E[Y|Z = z]$ provides a point forecast for the outcomes of Y whereas $P[Y|Z = z]$ gives the density forecast. For binary outcomes, however, this is not the case. Since Y takes one of only two values, then $E[Y|Z = z] = P[Y|Z = z]$ and so estimating one is the same as estimating the other. Point forecasts on the other hand should have the same support as the outcome, so point forecasts for forecasting Y should be either 0 or 1. This will never be the conditional mean for the Bernoulli distribution except in trivial cases where all outcomes are identical or the outcome is known with certainty, i.e., we have $E[Y|Z = z] = P[Y = 1|Z = z]$, and hence $0 < E[Y = 1|Z = z] = P[Y = 1|Z = z] < 1$, excluding trivial cases.

A density forecast along with a utility function can be used to generate a point forecast, so the standard relation between these two objects holds despite the different relations they individually bear with the conditional expectation. As usual, we are interested in predicting the outcome with a forecast function $f(Z)$. The utility function of the decision maker, $U(f, Y, Z)$, depends on the action, f; the outcome, Y; and potentially all or some subset of the covariates, Z. If the forecast and outcome are both binary, utility can take only four possible values $U_{f,y}$ for any z:

$$U(f, y, z) = \begin{cases} u_{1,1}(z) & \text{if } f = 1 \text{ and } y = 1, \\ u_{1,0}(z) & \text{if } f = 1 \text{ and } y = 0, \\ u_{0,1}(z) & \text{if } f = 0 \text{ and } y = 1, \\ u_{0,0}(z) & \text{if } f = 0 \text{ and } y = 0. \end{cases} \tag{12.1}$$

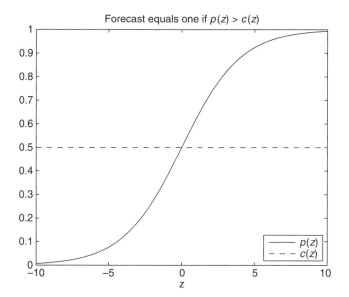

Figure 12.1: Probability forecast versus cutoff.

Sensible loss functions satisfy that $u_{1,1}(z) > u_{0,1}(z)$ and $u_{0,0}(z) > u_{1,0}(z)$ for all z so that a correct forecast is always superior to an incorrect one. The utility from correctly predicting a negative outcome need not be equal to the utility from correctly predicting a positive outcome, so we could have $u_{1,1}(z) \neq u_{0,0}(z)$. For example, if the predicted outcome is whether a stock price goes up ($y = 1$) or down ($y = 0$), we would have $u_{1,1}(z) < u_{0,0}(z)$ if being correct when the market falls is better than being correct when it rises. This simply says that avoiding losses is better for investors than making gains and might reflect a concave utility function.

Recalling from chapter 3 that risk can be defined as the negative of expected utility, $R(\theta, f, Z) = E[-U(f(Z), Y, Z)]$, a simple result lets us characterize the optimal density forecast with binary outcomes. Conditioning on Z, the risk is minimized by setting $f(Z) = 1$, i.e., forecasting a positive outcome, when

$$p(Z) > c(Z) \equiv \frac{u_{0,0}(Z) - u_{1,0}(Z)}{u_{1,1}(Z) - u_{0,1}(Z) + u_{0,0}(Z) - u_{1,0}(Z)}. \tag{12.2}$$

We refer to $c(Z)$ as the cutoff point at which the forecast switches between its two possible outcomes. When the probability that $Y = 1$ is greater than some cutoff, $c(Z)$, determined by the utility function, the optimal forecast is $f(Z) = 1$.

A common choice of cutoff is $c(Z) = 0.5$. This choice is illustrated in figure 12.1, which shows for a univariate Z the situation where $p(Z)$ is monotonically increasing in Z with $c(Z) = 0.5$. The model forecasts an outcome of $y = 1$ for $p(z) > c(z)$. This choice is optimal when $u_{0,0}(Z) - u_{1,0}(Z) = u_{1,1}(Z) - u_{0,1}(Z)$, i.e., when the relative utilities from a correct forecast versus an incorrect one are equal[2] regardless of the

---

[2] This calculation has appeared many times, at least when the utility function does not depend on Z; see Schervish (1989), Boyes, Hoffman, and Low (1989), Granger and Pesaran (2000), and Pesaran and Skouras (2002). The extension to dependence on Z is in Elliott and Lieli (2013).

direction of Y. Choices of cutoff other than 0.5 are relevant in situations where these marginal gains differ. For example, if the gain for $y = 1$ is bigger than that for $y = 0$, we could set the cutoff below 0.5 so as to "overweight" the more valuable forecasts, $f = 1$.

When the utility function does not depend on Z, $c(Z) = c$, and the utility-maximization problem can be reduced through a variety of renormalizations. Without loss of generality, we can subtract $u_{1,1}$ from the utility for $y = 1$, so that the utility equals 0 for a correct positive forecast, while for a false negative it is equal to $\tilde{u}_{0,1} = u_{0,1} - u_{1,1} < 0$. Similarly, for $y = 0$ we can subtract $u_{0,0}$ from utility, thereby setting the utility for a correct negative forecast to 0 and $\tilde{u}_{1,0} = u_{1,0} - u_{0,0} < 0$ for a false positive. This change leaves the numerator and denominator of c in (12.2) unchanged and allows us to write

$$c \equiv \frac{\tilde{u}_{1,0}}{\tilde{u}_{0,1} + \tilde{u}_{1,0}}.$$

In this case we can use that utility has no natural units to normalize $\tilde{u}_{1,0} + \tilde{u}_{0,1} = -1$. This leaves us with $c = -\tilde{u}_{1,0}$, $\tilde{u}_{0,1} = -(1 - c)$, and the simplified representation[3]

$$U(f, y, c) = \begin{cases} 0 & \text{if } f = 1 \text{ and } y = 1, \\ -c & \text{if } f = 1 \text{ and } y = 0, \\ -(1 - c) & \text{if } f = 0 \text{ and } y = 1, \\ 0 & \text{if } f = 0 \text{ and } y = 0, \end{cases} \qquad (12.3)$$

where $c > 0$ and the utility function is expressed directly as a function of the cutoff value, c.

If we construct distributional forecasts of the outcome $p(Z)$, we must employ a utility function on the probability for both estimation and forecast evaluation purposes. One probability forecast $p(Z)$ is better than another if it results in a higher utility for all possible cutoffs, c, i.e., $p(Z)$ is the dominant rule regardless of the utility function. If $p(Z)$ were known, this would be the dominant rule. More likely, however, $p(Z)$ has to be estimated and the model is misspecified and so $p(Z)$ is not equal to the true conditional probability. In this situation, some models could be best for certain regions of c, while other models could be best for other regions of c.

The scoring rule used for estimating a loss function, if proper, can be related directly to a weighting function over the possible cutoffs, c, which range from 0 to 1. Proper scoring rules take the form

$$L(p, y) = y f_1(p) + (1 - y) f_2(p), \qquad (12.4)$$

where $\partial f_1(p)/\partial p > 0$ for $p \in (0, 1)$ and

$$\frac{\partial f_2(p)}{\partial p} = -\frac{\partial f_1(p)}{\partial p} \left(\frac{p}{1 - p} \right).$$

---

[3] This normalization does not generally work for utilities that depend on z because it imposes a restriction on such utilities.

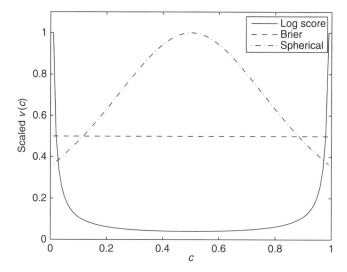

Figure 12.2: Weights for different scoring rules.

This relation was first shown in Shuford Jr, Albert, and Massengill (1966) and restated in Schervish (1989, Theorem 4.1). Schervish (1989) further showed that strictly proper scoring rules can be written as

$$U(y, p) = \begin{cases} -\int_p^1 (1 - c) v(c) dc & \text{for } y = 1, \\ -\int_0^p c v(c) dc & \text{for } y = 0, \end{cases} \tag{12.5}$$

where $v(c) > 0$ for $c \in (0, 1)$. This equation interprets proper scoring rules as weighted averages of utility functions. Different choices of $v(c)$ yield different weighting functions. For example, setting $v(c) = [c(1 - c)]^{-1}$ results in the log score function— better known as the maximum likelihood objective function given a model for the conditional probability—whereas $v(c) = 1$ yields the quadratic score. Notice the very different weights on these two scoring rules. The log score puts very high weights on individuals whose loss functions yield cutoffs close to 0 or 1 relative to those with loss functions that result in cutoffs near 0.5. The quadratic or Brier score (Brier, 1950) weighs all individuals evenly, while the spherical score weighs cutoffs close to 0.5 more heavily than cutoffs near the tail. The weights for the log score, Brier, and spherical scoring rules are shown in figure 12.2.[4]

The relationship between the weights $v(c)$ and the scoring rule can be shown to be

$$v(c) = \frac{\partial f_1(c)}{\partial c} \left(\frac{1}{1 - c} \right). \tag{12.6}$$

These results hold for the conventional scoring rules applied to binary problems such as the log score, Brier score, and spherical score, all of which weigh utility functions symmetrically around $p = 0.5$. Moreover, the results can be employed to construct a variety of proper scoring rules that need not treat costs symmetrically.

---

[4] See Toda (1963) for a definition of the spherical scoring rule.

12.2 DENSITY FORECASTS FOR BINARY OUTCOMES

As noted in the previous section, the distribution of a binary outcome is described entirely by its mean, so density estimation and estimation of the mean amount to the same estimation problem. Hence, the most common form of forecast reported for 0–1 outcomes is an estimate of the conditional probability that $Y = 1$, i.e., $p(z) = E[Y|Z = z]$.

Forecasters with MSE loss could also be interested in reporting the conditional probability that $Y = 1$ constructed by choosing $f(Z)$ as

$$p^*(Z) = \arg \min_{p(Z)} E[(Y - p(Z))^2|Z],$$

whose solution is the conditional mean, $p^*(Z) = E[Y|Z]$. This is simply a special case of the result in chapter 3 pertaining to the Bernoulli distribution. For the 0–1 case, the density forecast and the conditional mean forecast are identical.[5]

12.2.1 Parametric Density Forecasting Models

Parametric models of the conditional mean of Y are popular since they can be constructed to ensure that the probability lies in the 0–1 interval provided that they are nonlinear functions of the data. The most popular methods are the probit and logit models. Linear models truncated to fall between 0 and 1 can also be employed.

Estimation of the parameters of a model for the conditional distribution requires some form of loss function. Typically we choose a strictly proper scoring rule as reviewed in chapter 2. Recall that scoring rules take the form $S(y, p)$, where $E[S(y, p)]$ is finite and p is maximized when it is set equal to the true conditional probability that generates y. The sample analog is

$$Q_T(\beta) = \sum_{t=0}^{T-1} S(p(z_t, \beta), y_{t+1}). \tag{12.7}$$

Sample estimates of the parameters, $\hat{\beta}$, are then given by

$$\hat{\beta}_T = \arg \max_{\beta \in B} \sum_{t=0}^{T-1} S(p(z_t, \beta), y_{t+1}). \tag{12.8}$$

Logit and probit models are typically estimated by maximum likelihood (log scoring rule) methods using an index model. Given a parametric function $p(z_t'\beta)$ for the probability that $Y = 1$ and a one-step-ahead forecasting model, this approach chooses β to maximize

$$Q_T(\beta) = \frac{1}{T} \sum_{t=0}^{T-1} (y_{t+1} \ln p(z_t'\beta) + (1 - y_{t+1}) \ln(1 - p(z_t'\beta))). \tag{12.9}$$

---

[5] Lahiri, Peng, and Zhao (2013) give an overview of the issues discussed in this (and the next) section.

The probit specification for the linear index model sets

$$p(z_t'\beta) = \Phi(z_t'\beta), \tag{12.10}$$

where $\Phi(\cdot)$ is the c.d.f. of a normal distribution; the logit model sets

$$p(z_t'\beta) = \frac{\exp(z_t'\beta)}{1 + \exp(z_t'\beta)}. \tag{12.11}$$

Choices between these specifications are usually motivated by some background model $y_{t+1}^* = z_t'\beta + \varepsilon_{t+1}$, where y_{t+1}^* is unobserved, while the indicator $y_{t+1} = \mathbb{1}(y_{t+1}^* > 0)$ is observed. The probit or logit model (or other specifications) then follow from distributional assumptions on ε_{t+1}; see Maddala (1986) for an overview.

Under assumptions on the data-generating process, general properties can be established for estimates of the conditional probability (12.7) using different models and scoring rules. If the data are strictly stationary and sufficiently well behaved, $\hat\beta \to \beta^* = \arg\max_{\beta \in B} E[S(y_{t+1}, p(z_t, \beta))]$. Such results rely on different proofs of laws of large numbers, an example of which is given in Elliott, Ghanem, and Krüger (2014). If the data are covariance stationary rather than strictly stationary, it is still possible that the estimator converges to the value that minimizes average expected loss, $\hat\beta \to \beta^* = \arg\max_{\beta \in B} \sum_{t=0}^{T-1} E[S(y_{t+1}, p(z_t, \beta))]$. Use of a strictly proper scoring rule is necessary to ensure identification. de Jong and Woutersen (2011) present consistency results for the probit model with lagged values for y (which are binary) added.

For all strictly proper scoring rules, $p(z_t, \beta^*)$ is the true conditional probability provided that the model is correctly specified. Regardless of the scoring rule, it follows that the forecasts should be similar in sufficiently large samples. This gives little reason to choose between scoring rules as long as they are strictly proper. However, the log scoring rule yields an efficient estimate for β since it is the maximum likelihood objective and so would be the preferred scoring rule in finite samples.

Correct specification of the conditional probability is a strong assumption and is difficult to defend unless there is good economic theory guiding the choice of the model. If the model is not correctly specified, β^* depends on the chosen scoring rule. Section 12.1 examined how scoring rules are derived from weighting different utility functions. As the weighted average utility functions change, so do the approximate models that maximize them. Hence, the choice of scoring rule depends on which of these weighting schemes over utility functions is most relevant to the problem at hand.[6]

Multistep forecasts of binary variables engender the same choice between using either a direct or an iterated method for constructing forecasts as discussed in chapter 7. The direct approach uses the likelihood

$$Q_T(\beta) = \frac{1}{T-h} \sum_{t=0}^{T-h} (y_{t+h} \ln p(z_t'\beta) + (1 - y_{t+h}) \ln(1 - p(z_t'\beta))), \tag{12.12}$$

---

[6] Trade-offs between situations with correctly specified and misspecified models have been analyzed in Elliott and Lieli (2013) who show that there can be large differences between the methods when the forecasting model used to construct the conditional distribution of the outcome variable is not correctly specified.

and hence computation of forecasts is straightforward. Iterated forecasts require taking expectations over multiple paths of $y_{t+1}, \ldots, y_{t+h}$. Kauppi and Saikkonen (2008) note that because of the binary nature of y such calculations are simpler than in the general case and provide (model-specific) formulas for constructing iterated forecasts. As noted in chapter 9, it is more likely that the direct method yields better forecasts when the model is misspecified.

When parametric specifications such as the probit or logit are employed to model the conditional probability, maximum likelihood (log scoring) is typically chosen as the objective function. Examples include Estrella and Mishkin (1998) and Wright (2006) who use probit models to forecast recessions with various financial variables.

12.2.2 Bayesian Approaches

Given a conditional likelihood $p_Y(y_{t+1}|z_t, \beta)$ and a set of priors on the parameters, Bayesian methods can be used to construct posterior distributions for β and hence construct a predictive distribution $p_Y(y_{t+1}|z_t)$. A uniform prior on β results in the MLE as the posterior mean; for a normal prior the posterior mode is used as an asymptotic approximation to the mean of β. Following Albert and Chib (1993), a more typical approach is to use Gibbs sampling to directly estimate a distribution for some latent variable y_{t+1}^* underlying the observed outcome y_{t+1}. Using a normal prior for β and replacing the unknown y_{t+1}^* with draws from the sampler, we can characterize properties of the posterior density such as its mode in ways similar to those for the normal linear regression model discussed in chapter 5. Expressions for the posterior mean of β would replace the unknown outcomes with such draws. Geweke and Whiteman (2006) give a brief discussion of this point.

A number of papers on event forecasting have adopted Bayesian methods. Chauvet and Potter (2005) use Bayesian methods to predict recessions conditional on information from the term structure of interest rates. Let $y_t = \{0, 1\}$ be an indicator variable that tracks recessions ($y_t = 1$) and expansions ($y_t = 0$), while y_t^* is the underlying, latent state of the economy. We then have

$$
\begin{aligned}
y_t &= 0 \quad \text{if } y_t^* < 0, \\
y_t &= 1 \quad \text{if } y_t^* \geq 0.
\end{aligned}
\tag{12.13}
$$

In turn, y_t^* follows the process

$$
y_{t+1}^* = \beta_0 + \beta_1 S_t + \varepsilon_{t+1}, \quad \varepsilon_{t+1} \sim \mathrm{N}(0, \sigma_\varepsilon^2),
\tag{12.14}
$$

where S_t is a variable such as the spread between 10-year and 3-month Treasury rates.

It follows from (12.13) and (12.14) that the probability that the economy is in a recession next period is $\Pr(y_{t+1}^* \geq 0|S_t, \beta) = \Phi(\beta_0 + \beta_1 S_t)$, where Φ is the standard Gaussian cumulative distribution function.

Chauvet and Potter also entertain a dynamic probit specification that changes (12.13) to

$$
y_{t+1}^* = \beta_0 + \beta_1 S_t + \beta_2 y_t^* + \varepsilon_{t+1},
\tag{12.15}
$$

for $|\beta_2| < 1$. Chauvet and Potter (2005) use the Gibbs sampler to evaluate the likelihood function and estimate the parameters of this model. An empirical analysis of the 2001 US recession suggests that information in the yield curve helped to predict an economic slowdown and that probit models that do not account for persistence in different phases of the business cycle succeeded in predicting the recession with a high probability.

Dueker (2005) proposes an approach to generating dynamic forecasts of qualitative variables embedded in a VAR, labeled Qual VAR. The approach is based on a dynamic probit specification that includes lagged values of the dependent variable. Let y^* be some continuous latent variable that determines the sign of the binary dependent variable, $y \in \{0, 1\}$, and assume that y_t^* is generated by a dynamic probit model very similar to that in (12.13),

$$y_{t+1}^* = \rho y_t^* + \beta' z_t + \varepsilon_{t+1}, \quad \varepsilon_t \sim N(0, 1), \tag{12.16}$$

where z_{t-1} is a set of predictors. Dueker (2005) embeds this specification within a Qual VAR for $Y_t = (X_t'\, y_t^*)'$:

$$\sum_{i=0}^{p} A_i Y_{t-i} = \mu + \varepsilon_t, \quad \varepsilon_t \sim N(0, \Sigma).$$

Dueker uses MCMC estimation to draw sequences of values for $A = (A_1, \ldots, A_p)$, Σ, and y^*, using the following blocks:

$$p(A^{i+1} | \{y_t^{*(i)}\}_{i=1}^T, \{z_t\}_{t=1}^T, \Sigma^{(i)}) \sim \text{Normal},$$

$$p(\Sigma^{(i+1)} | \{y_t^{*(i)}\}_{i=1}^T, \{z_t\}_{t=1}^T, A^{(i+1)}) \sim \text{Inverted Wishart}, \tag{12.17}$$

$$p(y_t^{*(i+1)} | \{y_j^{*(i+1)}\}_{j<t}, \{y_k^{*(i)}\}_{k>t}, \{z_t\}_{t=1}^T, A^{(i+1)}, \Sigma^{(i+1)}) \sim \text{Truncated Normal}.$$

In an empirical exercise to forecast US recessions where y is the NBER's binary recession indicator, Dueker finds that a Qual VAR model did well in predicting the 2001 US recession out-of-sample. One advantage of this approach is that it generates recession probabilities not only for the next period but for multiple periods ahead in time.

12.2.3 Nonparametric Approaches

Nonparametric approaches for estimating distributional forecasts of binary variables parallel those discussed in chapter 11 adapted to the binary forecasting problem, the key difference being that the probability forecasts must be constrained to lie on the unit interval.

For example, the local linear or local polynomial regressions from chapter 11 could be applied after truncating forecasts outside the unit interval to equal 0 or 1. As an alternative, Gozalo and Linton (2000) suggest replacing the local linear polynomial with the probit or logit objective function. Their approach retains the property of the logit and probit models that it falls between 0 and 1, but allows the model to vary with the predictors. Estimation of the model parameters involves computing

$$\hat{\beta} = \arg\min_{\beta} \sum_{t=0}^{T-1} \left(y_{t+1} - \phi(\beta'(z_t - z_T)) \right)^2 K(z_t - z_T), \qquad (12.18)$$

where ϕ is a function restricted to the 0–1 interval. The forecasting model depends on z_T which, as discussed in chapter 11, may be useful especially when the true functional form is unknown.

12.3 CONSTRUCTING POINT FORECASTS FOR BINARY OUTCOMES

Estimation problems involving point forecasts generally require that the forecasts have the same support as the outcome. For the binary variable $\tilde{Y}$, this suggests forecasts $f(Z)$ that predict either -1 or 1, while for Y the two values are $\{0, 1\}$. This makes it very simple to set up the forecasting problem. The loss function need cover only four possible situations—two where the forecast is correct and two where it is false. This, as we saw in section 12.1, permits a general setting in which the universe of loss functions can easily be characterized. Only loss functions of this form have the properties discussed in chapter 2. For example MSE and MAE loss are applicable when $u_{1,1}(z) = u_{0,0}(z) = 0$ and $u_{1,0}(z) = u_{0,1}(z) > 0$.

Utility functions with binary outcomes complicate estimation because they are discontinuous in the forecast. The forecasting problem reduces to finding a function that tells us for which values of Z we have $p(Z) > c(Z)$. This again brings out the direct relation between density forecasting and point forecasting, since an estimate of $p(Z)$ is a density forecast. This relationship motivates the most common approach which we next describe.

12.3.1 Forecasts via $\hat{p}(Z)$

Estimation of the density forecast $p(Z)$ along with the form of equation (12.2) suggest that a forecast of $Y = 1$ can be constructed by choosing a forecasting model through the indicator variable

$$f(z) = \mathbb{1}\left(\hat{p}(z) > c(z) \right). \qquad (12.19)$$

This is an indirect approach since $\hat{p}(z)$ is estimated based on loss functions such as MSE or log score and not on the loss function in (12.1). Hence, there is no guarantee that the estimated coefficients are chosen optimally.

There are numerous examples of this approach in the literature. Dimitras, Zanakis, and Zopounidis (1996) survey business failure prediction models and find that 17 of 66 of the studies surveyed employed this method. Boyes, Hoffman, and Low (1989) use logit models to predict credit default, while Leung, Daouk, and Chen (2000) use both probit and logit models to predict the direction of the stock market. Martin (1977) and Ohlson (1980) use this approach to predict corporate bankruptcies. The choice of a cutoff probability, above which we assign a forecast of 1, tends to be arbitrary in these studies. Leung, Daouk, and Chen (2000) and Qi and Yang (2003) both choose 0.5 as their cutoff, while Boyes, Hoffman, and Low (1989) suggest a loss-based cutoff.

12.3.2 Discriminant Analysis

Discriminant analysis methods are popular in statistics and applied fields other than economics, and date back to work by Fisher (1936).[7] These methods split the joint distributions of the covariates Z into two different groups, one for $Y = 1$, the other for $Y \neq 1$, and arise from considering a hypothesis test between these two populations of covariates. Modeling the population joint densities parametrically, we can compute the likelihood that any subsequent observed set of covariates are generated from the density associated with the $Y = 1$ group or the other group. A likelihood ratio test between the two groups yields the forecasting rule that $Y = 1$ if the likelihood evaluated for this group at $Z = z$ exceeds that of the other group. If Z is joint normally distributed with common covariance matrices across groups, the prediction rule is linear in the observed z-variables and hence leads to decisions based on linear "scores" that are linked one-to-one with decisions based on the underlying likelihoods. Rather than weighting both likelihoods evenly, one can be weighted higher than the other to yield a procedure that alters the balance between false positive and false negative predictions. The loss function can be brought to bear on the decision through such weights.[8]

Discriminant analysis is often criticized because of its parametric assumptions of joint normality of the covariates. However, this really amounts to the same thing as choosing a parametric model for the conditional probability as becomes clear through the relationship with the logit model. Amemiya (1985, section 9.2.8) shows that under normality of Z conditional on Y, discriminant analysis is equivalent to using a logit model that includes the Z covariates linearly as well as quadratically. Under the assumption that the variance–covariance matrices are identical across groups, the quadratic terms drop out. When the group variances are identical, there is a one-to-one (population) relation between the logit specification based on a linear index and the discriminant analysis method. Dimitras, Zanakis, and Zopounidis (1996) note the similarity of predictions using these two methods, where differences arise due to differences in estimation methods for the unknown parameter weights.

12.3.3 Maximum Utility Estimation

Maximum utility estimation makes use of the M-estimator to minimize risk. Using homogeneity of the risk function, minimizing risk amounts to choosing a function, $g \in G$,

$$\max_{g \in G} E_{\tilde{Y}, Z}\big\{b(Z)[\tilde{Y} + 1 - 2c(Z)]\,\text{sign}[g(Z)]\big\}, \tag{12.20}$$

where G is the set of measurable functions from $\mathbb{R}^k$ to $\mathbb{R}$, $b(z) = u_{1,1}(z) - u_{0,1}(z) + u_{0,0}(z) - u_{1,0}(z)$, and $\text{sign}(a) = 1$ for $a > 0$, $\text{sign}(a) = -1$ for $a \leq 0$. Having chosen the best function $g(Z)$ in G, forecasts are constructed as $\text{sign}(g(Z))$. In practice, we choose a set of parameterized functional forms for $g(Z)$, $g(Z, \beta)$, and maximize over β.

---

[7] For general reviews of the methods, see Amemiya (1985) or Maddala (1986).

[8] It may seem odd that the focus of these methods is on the distribution of the covariates rather than on the conditional distribution of the outcome variable, but the methods are best understood as getting to this conditional distribution via the complete joint distribution of Y and Z.

The sample analog of the objective function in (12.20) is

$$Q_T(\beta) \equiv \frac{1}{T} \sum_{t=0}^{T-1} b(z_t)[\tilde{y}_{t+1} + 1 - 2c(z_t)] \, \text{sign}[g(z_t, \beta)]. \qquad (12.21)$$

This method was suggested by Manski (1975, 1985) and Manski and Thompson (1989) for the case where $c(z) = 0.5$, $b(z)$ is constant, and $g(z, \beta) = g(z'\beta)$. Under these conditions the estimator that maximizes (12.21) is the maximum score estimator. Elliott and Lieli (2013) extend this analysis to the general case.

Estimation of β in (12.21) depends on the utility function since different values of $b(z_t)$ and $c(z_t)$ affect the estimates of the parameters, β. This means that the value of each match varies as a function of the utility function through the weights $b(z_t)[\tilde{y}_{t+1} + 1 - 2c(z_t)]$. The elements $b(z_t)$ and $c(z_t)$ play different roles in the estimation: $c(z_t)$ determines the relative values of true positives versus true negatives, while $b(z_t)$ reweights the objective function, assigning relatively higher weights to those values of z_t for which correct prediction yields the largest benefits.

Regardless of the specification of $g(Z, \beta)$, the presence of the sign function in (12.21) makes the objective function nondifferentiable at points where the sign changes. This complicates both estimation and inference. For example, gradient methods will not be useful for estimation. Elliott and Lieli (2013) suggest simulated annealing methods for the general case; see also Corana et al. (1987) and Goffe, Ferrier, and Rogers (1994).

Primitive conditions that ensure convergence of $Q_T(\beta)$ to $E[b(z_t)[\tilde{y}_{t+1} + 1 - 2c(z_t)] \, \text{sign}[g(z_t, \beta)]]$ are given in Elliott and Lieli (2013). The assumptions that guarantee consistency of the estimator are slightly more restrictive than those usually entertained, e.g., strict stationarity and ergodicity of $\{\tilde{Y}_t, Z_t\}$.

12.3.4 Comparing Estimation Methods

Provided that the forecasting model is correctly specified, estimation without use of the loss function yields consistent parameter estimates with efficiency properties that are likely to be difficult to improve upon in practice.[9] Correct specification here means not just including the correct predictors but also having the correct functional form for the conditional probability of $Y = 1$. Conversely, when the model is not correctly specified, use of the loss function will generally improve on the forecasting performance.

In the context of binary forecasts, there can often be large gains from using the correct loss function given the practice of employing the arbitrarily chosen MSE loss function for parameter estimation. Unlike the linear regression case, using MSE loss never generates maximum likelihood or pseudo maximum likelihood results. So, unless squared error loss really reflects the forecast user's preferences, use of the correct loss function for estimation will likely yield improvements to the results.

These issues can be given a visual interpretation for the binary case. Returning to figure 12.1, we do not need very precise estimates of $p(z)$ everywhere to generate point forecasts, except at the point at which this function cuts $c(z)$, which equals 0.5 for all values of z in the figure. Outside this region, all we require is that $p(z) - c(z)$

---

[9] See the broader discussion of this issue in chapter 4.

has the correct sign—not that it is particularly close to its true value. Maximum likelihood estimation attempts to fit $p(z)$ as closely as possible given the flexibility of the model over all values of z, not just for z near the cutoff. Similar issues arise when squared loss is employed for estimation. Only use of the loss function in the estimation will focus the attention of the estimators on the cutoff.

Elliott and Lieli (2013) explore these issues analytically and through Monte Carlo analysis. In situations with misspecified models, they show that differences between loss-based and non-loss-based estimators can be quite large even when the misspecification is small enough to be difficult to detect with conventional tests. Loss-based and non-loss-based estimation methods have also been contrasted using actual data; Leung, Daouk, and Chen (2000) consider stock market returns, Srinivasan and Kim (1987) consider credit extension, and Lieli and Springborn (2013) study management of invasive plants.

12.4 EMPIRICAL APPLICATION: FORECASTING THE DIRECTION OF THE STOCK MARKET

We apply the maximum utility approach to out-of-sample forecasts of quarterly forecasts of the sign of quarterly excess stock returns, defining the indicator function as $y_{t+1} = \mathbb{1}(z_{t+1} > 0)$, where z_{t+1} is the quarterly value-weighted US stock return in excess of the three-month T-bill rate. The data are the same as those used earlier in the book. As before the out-of-sample period is 1970–2013 and forecasts are generated recursively using an expanding estimation window and a constant and the lagged T-bill rate as predictors.

The top left window in figure 12.3 shows the time series of the indicator variable we are interested in predicting. There are many shifts in this indicator variable during 1970–2013. The remaining windows in the figure show predicted values based on marginal utility estimation with cutoffs of $c = 0.1$, $c = 0.25$, and $c = 0.5$. As expected, when the cutoff is set as low as 0.1, corresponding to a low hurdle rate for predicting positive excess stock returns, there are far fewer predictions of negative returns. The incidence of negative predicted values rises steadily as the value of c is raised and the hurdle for predicting positive excess returns goes up.

Table 12.1 shows the accuracy for three maximum utility (MU) estimators with cutoff values $c = 0.1, 0.25$, and 0.5 along with results for a logit model. The proportion of positive returns whose signs are correctly predicted is 55% for the MU estimator with $c = 0.5$ and 50% for the logit model. This percentage increases to 58% as c is lowered and the MU method predicts more positive outcomes. The opposite pattern is seen for the accuracy of the predicted negative outcomes, underscoring how one cannot simultaneously increase the accuracy of the positive and negative return outcomes by changing the threshold, c. The total accuracy is very similar across the different methods. Looking at the values of the PT-statistic of sign predictability proposed by Pesaran and Timmermann (1992), which asymptotically follows a normal distribution under the null, we see that the null of no ability to predict the direction of quarterly excess stock returns is rejected at the 5% level for the MU estimator that uses the middle hurdle rate ($c = 0.25$) and also by the logit model.

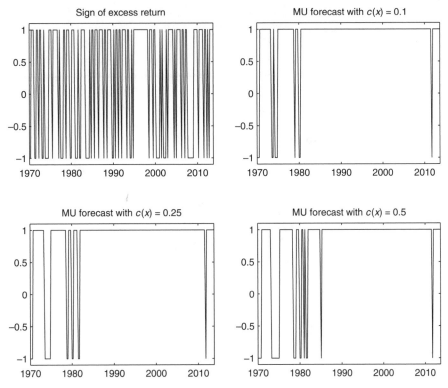

Figure 12.3: Indicator function and predicted values under maximum utility (MU) approach with different hurdle rates.

TABLE 12.1:
Out-of-sample forecast performance of different estimation methods applied to quarterly US stock returns.

Method	Accuracy $y = 1$	Accuracy $y = -1$	Total accuracy	PT	p-val
MU estimation $c(x) = 0.1$	58.5227	3.4091	61.9318	0.8844	0.1882
MU estimation $c(x) = 0.25$	57.9545	5.6818	63.6364	1.8596	0.0315
MU estimation $c(x) = 0.5$	55.1136	7.3864	62.5000	1.5533	0.0602
Logit	50.5682	11.9318	62.5000	1.9859	0.0235

12.5 CONCLUSION

Forecasting a binary outcome is interesting in its own right because the highly restrictive space of outcomes allows interesting simplifications of the loss functions.

Because the conditional mean is the probability of a particular outcome, and because in binary situations the probability of one outcome completely defines the distribution of the outcomes, estimating the conditional mean is equivalent to predictive density estimation. This contrasts with the usual case where the focus is on point forecasts which leads to estimating the conditional mean under MSE loss.

Under binary loss, the conditional mean estimate is a probability whereas outcomes are (typically) 0 or 1 and so the conditional mean is not a point forecast.

Loss functions relevant to the binary forecasting problem are very simple because there are only four outcomes, two of which are correct forecasts, two of which are not. Often, writing down a loss function therefore becomes a question of how to trade off between two possible mistakes. The simplicity of the loss function means that transforming a distributional (or conditional mean) forecast to a point forecast simplifies to whether the probability of an outcome is above a cutoff that is determined solely from the loss function.

Because of the simplicity of the loss function, it is possible to construct a one-to-one relationship between averages over loss functions for point forecasts and loss functions for distributional forecasts. This tight relationship allows a deep understanding of how scoring rules (loss functions for distributional forecasts) operate.

13

Volatility and Density Forecasting

The preceding chapters mostly focused on methods for generating point forecasts. Point forecasts were motivated as solutions to a problem of the form

$$\min_{f(z)} \int L(f(z), y) p_Y(y|z) dy, \tag{13.1}$$

and hence depend on both the loss function $L(f(z), y)$ and the density of the outcome conditional on available data, $p_Y(y|z)$. Point forecasts are a feature of the predictive density, $p_Y(y|z)$, and in some situations this kind of summary statistic is sufficient, most notably under squared error loss where only a location measure is required for the forecast.

This chapter presents the object of the forecasting exercise as that of providing a density forecast rather than a point forecast. A number of reasons have been suggested in the literature for why a forecaster might provide a predictive density, $p_Y(y|z)$, rather than a point forecast. The primary reason is that the forecasts will be employed by a variety of users with different loss functions. Point forecasts obtained as the solution to (13.1) are loss function specific and so providing a point forecast or even a few summary features of the predictive density is insufficient for many of the prospective uses of the forecast.

Second, just as with point estimates, point forecasts convey no sense of the precision of the forecast. Consider an inflation forecast reported to a policy maker. If current inflation is running at 3% per annum and the predicted inflation rate is 4%, then the policy maker may be tempted to raise interest rates to keep inflation in check. However, if the density of the forecast is such that outcomes anywhere between 2% and 6% are likely, then the information in the point forecast is quite imprecise and the policy maker may be less likely to undertake decisive action. Policy makers' inherent need for full distribution forecasts is recognized by the former Chair of the Federal Reserve, Alan Greenspan (2004): "A central bank needs to consider not only the most likely future path for the economy, but also the distribution of possible outcomes about that path."

Similarly, a portfolio manager whose point forecast of stock returns over some holding period is 5% will want to know the degree of uncertainty surrounding both this forecast and possible future outcomes. The former will depend on the estimation error of the forecast model and it matters greatly whether the standard error of the mean forecast is 2% or 10%—in the latter case, estimation uncertainty essentially swamps the "signal" in the point forecast. This matters, particularly to risk-averse investors. Risk-averse investors' portfolio selections will generally be more cautious if uncertainty about the future is perceived to be high, since this will increase the risk of suffering large losses.

A third reason for being interested in density forecasts arises when we are interested in multistep forecasting with nonlinear models. As explained in chapter 8, the full density matters whenever we iterate on a nonlinear prediction model since the nonlinear effects typically depend not just on the conditional mean, but also on where in the set of possible outcomes future values occur.

Density forecasts—forecasts of the likelihood of different outcomes—provide information on the uncertainty surrounding a forecast and hence can be used to address these issues. Alternatively, we could provide a summary measure of the spread of the distribution rather than the entire distribution. This leads to interval forecasts which are more informative than point forecasts but, except for special cases such as the Gaussian or other parsimoniously parameterized distributions, not as informative as density forecasts. Interval forecasts, like confidence intervals, give an idea of the uncertainty surrounding the outcome without requiring the complete information embedded in the density forecast.

The basic density forecasting problem involves a single outcome variable, y_{t+1}, and conditioning variables, z_t. A density forecast characterizes the conditional distribution of y_{t+1}, given Z_t:

$$p_Y(y_{t+1}|Z_t) = P(y_{t+1}|Z_t). \tag{13.2}$$

As written here, the conditional distribution or predictive density makes use of all relevant variables in the information set. In practice, a subset of conditioning variables is generally used. In the simplest case where only autoregressive dynamics is considered, this would comprise the past history of the variable itself.

A very popular approach to constructing density forecasts is to first model any conditional dynamics in the mean and volatility of the series and then apply flexible parametric or nonparametric methods to model the "normalized" residual, i.e., the demeaned series scaled by the conditional volatility. This conditional location–scale approach has given rise to a large family of volatility models which have proved successful in financial forecasting in particular, but also in recent macroeconomic forecasting studies.

This chapter considers some of the most popular families of volatility models and density specifications that have been used in academic studies and discusses how they can be used to construct density forecasts. We concentrate on parametric modeling of both the volatility and density, but also discuss alternatives involving semiparametric and nonparametric methods and their usage in constructing forecasts. We first cover a range of parametric volatility models in common use. As is typical of the arguments for and against parametric versus nonparametric estimates, the trade-off in density estimation is between obtaining better estimates for the parametric method when the parametric form is close to the true but unknown density versus the flexibility (and lower risk of misspecification) of the nonparametric methods.

Section 13.1 discusses the role of the loss function in constructing density forecasts. Section 13.2 goes over a range of parametric models for volatility forecasting. Section 13.3 provides a brief introduction to forecasting methods based on realized variance measures. Parametric, semiparametric, and nonparametric estimation of density models is covered in section 13.4. Section 13.5 turns to methods for generating interval and quantile forecasts. Multivariate density models are discussed in section 13.6, and copula models are covered in section 13.7. Section 13.8 concludes the chapter.

13.1 ROLE OF THE LOSS FUNCTION

The conditional density in (13.2) is a population object and is constructed without reference to the loss function. It would seem that provision of a predictive density is superior to reporting a point forecast since it both (a) can be combined with a loss function to produce any point forecast; and (b) is independent of the loss function. In classical estimation of the predictive density, neither of these points really holds up in practice. First, given the predictive density it is possible to generate point forecasts. Unless the predictive distribution is parametric, however, there are practical issues with the presentation and communication of predictive densities to facilitate such calculations. Moreover, in the classical setting the estimated predictive distributions depend on the loss function. All parameters of the predictive density need to be estimated and these estimates require some loss function, so loss functions are thrown back into the mix. The catch here is that the loss functions that are often employed in density estimation do not line up with those employed for point forecasting which can lead to inferior point forecasts.

Even when decisions are ultimately based on a point forecast, the conditional density is still worth reporting if the forecast user's loss function is unknown. Alternatively, the forecast may be intended for multiple users whose losses are known and could differ across end users. In these situations, the provision of the conditional density forecast can be viewed as the step before the loss function necessarily gets involved. Such a two-step procedure has obvious limitations, however. For example, the variables in the information set that are relevant could be different for different loss functions.

Example 13.1.1 (Optimal forecasts with dynamics in first and second moments under different loss functions). *Suppose the density forecast is fully characterized by the conditional mean and volatility given current information, denoted by $\mu_{t+1|t}$ and $\sigma_{t+1|t}$, so that*

$$y_{t+1} = \mu_{t+1|t} + \sigma_{t+1|t}\eta_{t+1}, \quad \eta_{t+1} \sim (0, 1).$$

Under MSE loss, the optimal forecast would be the conditional mean

$$f_{t+1|t} = \mu_{t+1|t}.$$

In contrast, under an asymmetric lin-lin loss function of the type

$$L(e_{t+1}) = (1 - \alpha)|e_{t+1}|\mathbb{1}(e_{t+1} > 0) + \alpha|e_{t+1}|\mathbb{1}(e_{t+1} \leq 0), \quad 0 < \alpha < 1,$$

the optimal forecast takes the form

$$f_{t+1|t} = \mu_{t+1|t} + \sigma_{t+1|t} P_\eta^{-1}\left(\frac{1-\alpha}{\alpha}\right),$$

where P_η^{-1} is the quantile function of the innovation, η. The forecast under lin-lin loss generally differs from $\mu_{t+1|t}$, assuming that $\alpha \neq 0.5$, even when ϵ has a symmetric distribution. Hence a forecaster with squared error loss will only be interested in information that helps predict the conditional mean, whereas a forecaster with asymmetric lin-lin loss will want to make use of information on variables that help forecast the conditional volatility, $\sigma_{t+1|t}$.

Moreover, conditional distributions are difficult to estimate well, and so point forecasts based on estimates of the conditional density may be highly suboptimal from an estimation perspective. It is also unclear what constitutes a "good" density forecast when we abstract from loss functions. Any estimate of the conditional density will have errors, and errors that are innocuous for some applications may be very important in other applications. Even if the conditional density avoids reference to the loss function, it is hard to imagine that optimal estimation of the density will be independent of the loss function. The loss function (or decision problem) will generally be central to the metric used to evaluate the estimator of the density.

From the perspective of generating point forecasts for a user with squared error loss, seemingly not much is lost by ignoring heteroskedasticity in the residuals. This is not quite true, however, since more efficient estimates of the parameters of the conditional mean can be obtained by accounting for time-varying heteroskedasticity. Moreover, in cases where forecasts require iterating multiple steps ahead on a model that involves nonlinear dynamics in the conditional mean, heteroskedasticity will directly affect the point forecast; see the discussion in chapter 8. In this chapter we mostly ignore such issues.

13.2 VOLATILITY MODELS

Often density modeling is separated into two steps: first construct a model for the conditional mean and conditional volatility. Then, in a second step, model the density of the residuals obtained after subtracting the conditional mean (or predicted value) and dividing by the conditional volatility. Different approaches for modeling the conditional mean have been described in chapters 6–11. This section describes a variety of approaches to modeling volatility dynamics, before approaches to modeling the density of the normalized residuals are covered in subsequent sections.[1]

13.2.1 Location–Scale Models of Density Forecasts

The most popular approach for generating density forecasts assumes that the predicted variable is generated by a conditional location–scale process of the form

---

[1] For a survey of density forecasting, see Tay, Wallis et al. (2000).

seen in Example 13.1.1

$$y_{t+1} = \mu_{t+1|t} + \sigma_{t+1|t}\eta_{t+1}, \quad \eta_{t+1} \sim (0, 1), \tag{13.3}$$

where $E[\eta_{t+1}|Z_t] = 0$ and $E[\eta_{t+1}^2|Z_t] = 1$. Hence $\mu_{t+1|t}$ is the conditional mean of y_{t+1} given conditioning information, Z_t, while $\sigma_{t+1|t}$ is the conditional standard deviation or volatility of y_{t+1}, again given Z_t. Both the conditional mean and volatility can be time varying and will depend on a finite-dimensional vector of parameters, θ, which we suppress in the notation here. The distribution function of η, P_η, is usually assumed to be constant (time invariant), although the approach can easily be extended to allow for time-varying conditional skew, kurtosis, or tail risks.

Assuming that $\eta_{t+1}|Z_t$ has a time-invariant distribution function, P_η, we can derive the conditional distribution function for y_{t+1} given Z_t as follows:

$$P(y_{t+1} \leq y|Z_t) = P\left(\frac{y_{t+1} - \mu_{t+h|t}}{\sigma_{t+1|t}} \leq \frac{y - \mu_{t+1|t}}{\sigma_{t+1|t}}\right)$$

$$\equiv P_\eta\left(\frac{y - \mu_{t+1|t}}{\sigma_{t+1|t}}\right).$$

This can readily be computed if a parametric model for P_η is available. For example, if the density of η is a standard normal, we have for $\eta_{t+1} = (y_{t+1} - \mu_{t+1|t})/\sigma_{t+1|t}$,

$$P_\eta(\eta_{t+1}) = (\sqrt{2\pi})^{-1} \int_{-\infty}^{\eta_{t+1}} \exp(-0.5x^2)dx.$$

Semiparametric methods, on the other hand, do not make distributional assumptions about η, instead assuming that this can be approximated by the empirical distribution function of $\hat{\eta}_{t+1|t} = (y_{t+1} - \hat{\mu}_{t+1|t})/\hat{\sigma}_{t+1|t}$.

Construction of an estimate for the conditional mean $\mu_{t+1|t}$ is standard and has already been covered. What is new in (13.3) is the presence of a time-varying conditional volatility, $\sigma_{t+1|t}$. The parameters of the volatility process are often estimated using maximum likelihood or QMLE methods.

Example 13.2.1 (Estimation of parameters of location–scale model). *Suppose the mean and variance functions and the density of the standardized innovations, η_{t+1}, are specified up to a finite-dimensional vector of unknown coefficients, θ, and consider a volatility model whose normalized innovations η_{t+1} are assumed to be independent N(0, 1). For a sample of T observations $\{y_1, \ldots, y_T\}$, the log-likelihood function is*

$$\mathrm{LL}(\theta|y_1, y_2, \ldots, y_T) = -\frac{1}{2}\sum_{t=1}^{T-1}\left(\ln(2\pi\sigma_{t+1|t}^2) + \frac{(y_{t+1} - \mu_{t+1|t}(\theta))^2}{\sigma_{t+1|t}^2(\theta)}\right). \tag{13.4}$$

This gives rise to a set of nonlinear first-order conditions. Maximization of the log-likelihood function therefore requires using numerical methods. Notice that even if one is only interested in estimating the parameters of the conditional mean, OLS methods are not efficient in the presence of volatility dynamics.

In the following we describe some simple and popular models for dynamics in the conditional volatility. With these in place, we then consider ways to generate distribution forecasts using various density forecasting models for the "normalized innovation," η_{t+1}.

13.2.2 GARCH Models

A large class of models for volatility forecasting make use of some variant of the autoregressive conditional heteroskedasticity (ARCH) model introduced by Engle (1982). Consistent with (13.3), suppose that the volatility of shocks to the predicted variable is time varying and takes the form

$$\varepsilon_{t+1} = \sigma_{t+1|t}\eta_{t+1}, \quad \eta_{t+1} \sim \text{ind } N(0, 1). \tag{13.5}$$

Here $\sigma_{t+1|t}$ is the conditional variance of ε_{t+1} given information at time t, Z_t. The ARCH(q) model proposed by Engle (1982) takes the form

$$\sigma_{t+1|t}^2 = \omega + \alpha_1\varepsilon_t^2 + \alpha_2\varepsilon_{t-1}^2 + \cdots + \alpha_q\varepsilon_{t-q+1}^2, \quad \omega > 0, \alpha_1, \ldots, \alpha_q \geq 0. \tag{13.6}$$

Since the α_j-values are positive, a large shock, ε_t^2, will induce higher future values of the conditional variances, $\sigma_{t+1|t}^2, \ldots, \sigma_{t+q|t}^2$. ARCH models can therefore capture clustering in the volatility of forecast errors: large squared errors tend to be followed by large squared errors and small errors tend to be followed by small errors. The sign of future errors is not predictable, however, as the model does not specify whether positive or negative shocks are more likely to occur.

The ARCH(q) model may require a large number of lag coefficients, α_i, to fit series with highly persistent volatility. A more parsimonious model that can capture persistent volatility dynamics is the Generalized ARCH or GARCH specification introduced by Bollerslev (1986). The GARCH(p, q) model with p autoregressive lags of the conditional variance and q lags of squared innovations takes the form

$$\sigma_{t+1|t}^2 = \omega + \sum_{i=1}^{p} \beta_i\sigma_{t+1-i|t-i}^2 + \sum_{i=1}^{q} \alpha_i\varepsilon_{t+1-i}^2. \tag{13.7}$$

In empirical work, by far the most popular specification is the GARCH(1,1) model:

$$\sigma_{t+1|t}^2 = \omega + \beta_1\sigma_{t|t-1}^2 + \alpha_1\varepsilon_t^2 \tag{13.8}$$

$$= \omega + (\alpha_1 + \beta_1)\sigma_{t|t-1}^2 + \alpha_1\sigma_{t|t-1}^2(\eta_t^2 - 1).$$

The term in the final bracket has zero mean since $E[\eta_t^2] = 1$. It follows from (13.8) that $\alpha_1 + \beta_1$ is a measure of the persistence of the conditional variance process, while α_1 is a measure of the "news" impact of shocks, i.e., the effect of current (normalized) shocks on the forecast of next period's conditional variance.

Many studies have examined the empirical performance of the GARCH(1,1) model and found it difficult to outperform. Hansen and Lunde (2005) compare 330 ARCH-type specifications, including very sophisticated volatility models. They find no significant evidence that any of these models outperforms the GARCH(1,1) model for daily exchange rate predictions. Conversely, for predictions of daily returns on IBM, models that account for leverage effects (discussed below) are found to be better than the GARCH(1,1) model. Given the prominence of this class of models, we next cover details of how such models can be used to generate density forecasts.

Note that recursive backward substitution in the first line in (13.8) allows us to express the conditional variance forecast as a sum of lagged squared innovations:

$$\sigma^2_{t+1|t} = \frac{\omega}{1-\beta_1} + \alpha_1 \sum_{i=0}^{\infty} \beta_1^i \varepsilon^2_{t-i}.$$

Hence the GARCH(1,1) model implies an ARCH model of infinite order with a particular decay structure in the coefficients on past squared innovations. This is very similar to the geometric decay seen for the AR(1) model analyzed in chapter 7.

As long as $\alpha_1 + \beta_1 < 1$, it is clear from the last line in (13.8) that the volatility process converges. Taking unconditional expectations on both sides, the steady state—or unconditional—variance (if it exists) must satisfy

$$E[\sigma^2_{t+1|t}] = \omega + (\alpha_1 + \beta_1)E[\sigma^2_{t|t-1}].$$

Thus, assuming that the process is covariance stationary, $E[\sigma^2_{t+1|t}] = E[\sigma^2_{t|t-1}] \equiv \sigma^2$, and so

$$E[\sigma^2_{t+1|t}] = \frac{\omega}{1-\alpha_1-\beta_1} = \sigma^2,$$

which is the unconditional variance. Using this, we can rewrite (13.8) as

$$\sigma^2_{t+1|t} = \sigma^2 + (\alpha_1+\beta_1)(\sigma^2_{t|t-1} - \sigma^2) + \alpha_1 \sigma^2_{t|t-1}(\eta^2_t - 1). \tag{13.9}$$

This allows us to write the future one-step-ahead conditional variance as follows (for $h \geq 1$):

$$\sigma^2_{t+h|t+h-1} = \sigma^2 + (\alpha_1+\beta_1)^h(\sigma^2_{t|t-1} - \sigma^2)$$

$$+ \alpha_1 \sum_{j=1}^{h} (\alpha_1+\beta_1)^{j-1} \sigma^2_{t+h-j|t+h-j-1}(\eta^2_{t+h-j} - 1). \tag{13.10}$$

Taking expectations conditional on period-t information, the expected one-period variance h-periods ahead, $\sigma^2_{t+h|t}$, is

$$\sigma^2_{t+h|t} = E_t[\sigma^2_{t+h|t+h-1}] = \sigma^2 + (\alpha_1+\beta_1)^{h-1}(\sigma^2_{t+1|t} - \sigma^2). \tag{13.11}$$

Hence, if the one-step-ahead conditional variance forecast exceeds the average variance forecast, σ^2, the multi-step-ahead variance forecasts will exceed the average forecast by an amount that is declining in the forecast horizon. This mean-reverting tendency is of course a defining property of stationary processes and so the importance of the assumption that $\alpha_1 + \beta_1 < 1$ becomes clear from (13.11).

Equation (13.11) gives the expected value of the future conditional variance given current information. The conditional density of the future variance is more complicated to characterize. Moving one step ahead and ignoring that the parameters are unknown, conditional on period-t information the only unknown variable in the last line in (13.9) is η^2_{t+1} and so next period's one-step-ahead conditional variance forecast follows a chi-squared distribution with one degree of freedom:

$$\sigma^2_{t+2|t+1} = \sigma^2 + (\alpha_1 + \beta_1)\left(\sigma^2_{t+1|t} - \sigma^2\right) + \alpha_1 \sigma^2_{t+1|t}(\eta^2_{t+1} - 1).$$

Moving one period further ahead to $\sigma^2_{t+3|t+2}$, from (13.10) we have

$$
\begin{aligned}
\sigma^2_{t+3|t+2} = {} & \sigma^2 + (\alpha_1 + \beta_1)\left\{(\sigma^2 + \alpha_1 + \beta_1)(\sigma^2_{t+1|t} - \sigma^2) + \alpha_1 \sigma^2_{t+1|t}(\eta^2_{t+1} - 1)\right\} \\
& + \alpha_1\left\{\sigma^2 + (\alpha_1 + \beta_1)(\sigma^2_{t+1|t} - \sigma^2) + \alpha_1 \sigma^2_{t+1|t}(\eta^2_{t+1} - 1)\right\}(\eta^2_{t+2} - 1).
\end{aligned}
\tag{13.12}
$$

Notice the presence of cross-product terms such as $\eta^2_{t+1}\eta^2_{t+2}$ involving future shocks that are unknown at time t. Such terms mean that the conditional multiperiod variance is no longer distributed as a chi-squared variable. In fact, the GARCH process can be viewed as a mixture of normals with time-varying weights. This leads to a distribution that can be considerably more fat tailed than the normal distribution. For example, as shown by Bollerslev (1986), the coefficient of excess kurtosis for the GARCH(1,1) process, measured relative to the Gaussian distribution, is[2]

$$\frac{E\left[\varepsilon^4_t\right]}{E\left[\varepsilon^2_t\right]} - 3 = \frac{6\alpha^2_1}{(1 - \beta^2_1 - 2\alpha_1\beta_1 - 3\alpha^2_1)}.$$

This expression is always positive and so shows that even a GARCH process with a conditionally Gaussian one-step-ahead forecast can generate fat tails for multiperiod or unconditional forecasts.

Example 13.2.2 (Estimation of GARCH parameters based on a loss function). *Skouras (2007) proposes to fit the parameters of a GARCH(1,1) model so as to minimize the expected loss of the forecast as used in an investor's portfolio decision. The investor can invest in a risky asset paying a random excess return y_{t+1} over the risk-free rate, r_f. The investor has initial wealth $W_0 = 0$ with wealth evolving according to the equation $W_{t+1} = 1 + r_f + w_t y_{t+1}$. Following Skouras (2007), consider the GARCH(1,1) model for the return on the risky asset, y_{t+1}:*

$$y_{t+1} = \mu_{t+1|t} + \sigma_{t+1|t}\varepsilon_{t+1}, \quad \varepsilon_{t+1} \sim (0, 1),$$

$$\mu_{t+1|t} = b_0 + b_1 y_t,$$

$$\sigma^2_{t+1|t} = \omega_0 + \alpha_1 \varepsilon^2_t + \beta_1 \sigma^2_{t|t-1}.$$

Suppose this approach is used by an investor with constant absolute risk aversion (CARA) utility

$$u(W_{t+1}) = -\exp(-A W_{t+1}),$$

where A is the investor's coefficient of absolute risk aversion. As pointed out by Skouras, under these assumptions, the investor's Bayes' rule (optimal holding of the risky asset)

---

[2] Bollerslev (1986, Theorem 1) shows that a necessary condition for the fourth moment to exist is that $1 - \beta^2_1 - 2\alpha_1\beta_1 - 3\alpha^2_1 > 0$.

takes the form

$$\frac{1}{A} \frac{\left(b_0 + b_1 y_t\right) y_{t+1}}{\omega_0 + \alpha_1 \varepsilon_t^2 + \beta_1 \sigma_{t|t-1}^2},$$

where $\theta' = (b_0, b_1, \omega_0, \alpha_1, \beta_1)'$ are the unknown parameters. If the investor estimates the parameters that minimize the sample average loss, we get what Skouras calls the maximum utility estimator,

$$\hat{\theta}^*(Z_T) = \arg\min_{\theta \in \Theta} \frac{1}{T} \sum_{t=1}^{T-1} L(f(z_t, y_{t+1}, \theta)).$$

For the GARCH(1,1) model this estimator takes the form

$$\hat{\theta}^*(z_T) = \arg\max_{\theta \in \Theta} \frac{1}{T-1} \sum_{t=1}^{T-1} -\exp\left(\frac{-(b_0 + b_1 y_t) y_{t+1}}{\omega_0 + \alpha_1 \varepsilon_t^2 + \beta_1 \sigma_{t|t-1}^2}\right)$$

$$= \arg\max_{\theta \in \Theta} \frac{1}{T-1} \sum_{t=1}^{T-1} -\exp\left(\frac{-(b_0 + b_1 y_t) y_{t+1}}{\omega_0 \sum_{j=0}^{t-1} \beta_1^j + \beta_1 \sigma_{1|0}^2 + \alpha_1 \sum_{j=0}^{t-1} \beta_1^j (y_{t-j} - b_0 - b_1 y_{t-j-1})^2}\right).$$

One issue with this estimator is that it identifies only the ratio of the conditional mean to the conditional variance. In empirical results based on a GARCH(1, 1) model, Skouras finds that the volatility dynamics implied by the empirical maximum utility estimates tend to be less persistent than their QMLE counterparts. When used in an out-of-sample investment rule, the maximum utility estimates often lead to higher average utility than under the QMLE approach, although this does not hold during the last 10 years of the sample analyzed by Skouras.

13.2.3 Refinements to GARCH Models

Numerous refinements to (13.7) that account for asymmetric effects of positive and negative volatility shocks have been proposed in the literature. For example, the threshold GARCH model allows negative and positive shocks to have different impact on future volatility:

$$\sigma_{t+1|t}^2 = \omega + \alpha_1 \varepsilon_t^2 + \lambda \varepsilon_t^2 \mathbb{1}(\varepsilon_t < 0) + \beta_1 \sigma_{t|t-1}^2, \tag{13.13}$$

where $\mathbb{1}(\cdot)$ is an indicator function that equals 1 if the condition in the bracket holds, and otherwise is 0. Here the additional news effect of negative shocks on the conditional variance is λ. In empirical work it is frequently found that λ is positive, as negative shocks affect the conditional volatility more strongly than positive shocks. This is sometimes labeled the leverage effect.[3] Forecasting volatility with (13.13) requires

---

[3] This term comes from the analysis of stock price volatility: negative shocks reduce equity values and increase the leverage of a stock as measured by its debt-to-equity ratio, thereby making the firm's equity (which is a residual claim on the firm's underlying assets) more risky.

predicting the probability of positive versus negative shocks whenever these affect future volatility differently. Under the assumption that negative and positive shocks are equally likely, i.e., $\Pr(\eta_t < 0) = \Pr(\varepsilon_t < 0) = 0.5$, it follows from (13.13) that

$$\sigma^2_{t+1|t} = \omega + (\alpha_1 + 0.5\lambda)\varepsilon^2_t + \lambda\varepsilon^2_t[\mathbb{1}(\varepsilon_t < 0) - 0.5] + \beta_1\sigma^2_{t|t-1} \qquad (13.14)$$

$$= \sigma^2 + (\alpha_1 + 0.5\lambda + \beta_1)\left[\sigma^2_{t|t-1} - \sigma^2\right]$$

$$+ (\alpha_1 + 0.5\lambda)\sigma^2_{t|t-1}[\eta^2_t - 1] + \lambda\varepsilon^2_t[\mathbb{1}(\varepsilon_t < 0) - 0.5],$$

where now $\sigma^2 = \omega(1 - \alpha_1 - 0.5\lambda - \beta_1)^{-1}$. Using that $E_t[\eta^2_{t+i} - 1] = 0$ and $E_t[\mathbb{1}(\varepsilon_{t+i} < 0) - 0.5] = 0$ for $i \geq 1$, we get the h-step-ahead forecast of the one-period conditional variance as (see Andersen et al., 2006)

$$\sigma^2_{t+h|t} = \sigma^2 + (\alpha_1 + 0.5\lambda + \beta_1)^{h-1}\left(\sigma^2_{t+1|t} - \sigma^2\right). \qquad (13.15)$$

Compared with the earlier formula for multistep forecasts from the GARCH(1,1) model (13.11), multistep forecasts from the threshold GARCH model in (13.15) are anchored on a different mean value and also can have different persistence, i.e., $\alpha_1 + 0.5\lambda + \beta_1$ versus $\alpha_1 + \beta_1$, although it should be noted that the estimates of α_1 and β_1 in the two models are likely to be different due to the inclusion of the asymmetry term.

Since the conditional variance cannot be negative, models for the conditional variance must impose nonnegativity of the variance. This is usually not a concern in practice for specifications such as the GARCH(1,1) model since volatility is often highly persistent and ω, α_1, and β_1 are all clearly positive. Another concern may be that the conditional variance is close to following an integrated process with $\alpha_1 + \beta_1$ close to 1.

One way to deal with the nonnegativity constraint on the conditional variance is to instead model the logarithm of volatility which is not subject to such concerns. This gives rise to the EGARCH model of Nelson (1991):

$$\log(\sigma^2_{t+1|t}) = \omega + \alpha_1(|\eta_t| - E[|\eta_t|]) + \beta_1 \log(\sigma^2_{t|t-1}) + \lambda\eta_t. \qquad (13.16)$$

Again this model allows for asymmetric news effects of positive and negative shocks: positive shocks ($\eta_t > 0$) impact the log conditional variance by $\lambda + \alpha_1$, while the effect of negative shocks is $\lambda - \alpha_1$.

An important advantage of the EGARCH specification is that there is no need to impose constraints on the parameters to ensure that the conditional volatility remains nonnegative. Conversely, a disadvantage of (13.16) is that while it easily delivers conditional forecasts of the h-step log-variance, $\log(\sigma^2_{t+h|t})$, typically the object of interest is not to predict the logarithm of the variance, but rather the variance itself, $\sigma^2_{t+h|t}$. There are no analytical expressions for $\sigma^2_{t+h|t}$ under the EGARCH model. Instead Monte Carlo simulation of the sequence of one-step density forecasts can be used to generate multistep volatility forecasts. This requires using numerical methods and so is a bit more involved.[4]

---

[4] Another flexible class of volatility models makes use of the semiparametric spline approach of Engle and Gonzalez-Rivera (1991). An excellent coverage of these and other models can be found in Andersen et al. (2006).

GARCH-type models can easily be generalized to allow for predictability from other state variables, z_t, or to let the volatility forecast affect the forecast of the conditional mean. For example, Glosten et al. (1993) consider an EGARCH-type model for the trade-off between risk and returns on stocks:

$$y_{t+1} = \mu_0 + \mu_1 \sigma_{t+1|t} + \varepsilon_{t+1}, \quad \varepsilon_{t+1} \sim N(0, \sigma^2_{t+1|t}),$$

$$\log(\sigma^2_{t+1|t}) = \omega_0 + \beta_1 \log(\sigma^2_{t|t-1}) + \delta_1 \left| \frac{\varepsilon_t}{\sigma_{t|t-1}} \right| + \delta_2 \frac{\varepsilon_t}{\sigma_{t|t-1}} + \delta_3 z_t. \quad (13.17)$$

In this model the log conditional variance, $\sigma^2_{t+1|t}$, depends on the state variable, z_t, the lagged conditional variance, $\sigma^2_{t|t-1}$, as well as current innovations, ε_t, whose effect may depend on whether the shocks are positive or negative. Moreover, the conditional mean is affected by the conditional volatility forecast—a phenomenon often labeled the ARCH-in-mean effect. This is consistent with the notion that investors expect higher returns, the higher the predicted volatility.

A property of the volatility models described so far is that the effect on future average volatility of a shock decays very fast, i.e., at an exponential rate as can be seen from formulas such as (13.11) and (13.15). Empirical studies of absolute or squared security returns sometimes find that their autocorrelations decay at a slower hyperbolic rate rather than at an exponential rate, suggesting that there is long memory in the volatility process.[5] To capture this, Baillie, Bollerslev, and Mikkelsen (1996) propose a so-called fractionally integrated, FIGARCH(1,d,1) process for the conditional variance:

$$\sigma^2_{t+1|t} = \omega + \beta_1 \sigma^2_{t|t-1} + [(1 - \beta_1 L - (1 - \alpha_1 L - \beta_1 L))(1 - L)^d] \varepsilon^2_t.$$

Slow decay in autocorrelations of the variance occurs if $0 < d < 1$. These authors also show that variance forecasts can be generated recursively using a chain rule of the form

$$\sigma^2_{t+h|t+h-1} = \frac{\omega}{1 - \beta_1} + \lambda(L) \sigma^2_{t+h-1|t+h-2}, \quad h > 0,$$

where the coefficients of the polynomial $\lambda(L) = 1 - (1 - \beta_1 L)^{-1}(1 - \alpha_1 L - \beta_1 L)(1 - L)^d$ are generated recursively:[6]

$$\lambda_1 = \alpha_1 + d,$$

$$\lambda_j = \beta_1 \lambda_{j-1} + [(j - 1 - d)j^{-1} - (\alpha_1 + \beta_1)]\delta_{j-1}, \quad j \geq 2,$$

$$\delta_j = \delta_{j-1}(j - 1 - d)j^{-1}.$$

For many GARCH models the multistep predictive density is not obtainable in closed form. In such cases, numerical methods can be used to generate multistep volatility forecasts. As explained by Andersen et al. (2006), such forecasts can be computed by using the convolution of the one-step conditional distributions which

---

[5] See Ding, Granger, and Engle (1993) and Andersen and Bollerslev (1997).
[6] See Andersen et al. (2006) for further discussion and details.

TABLE 13.1:
Parameter estimates for GARCH(1,1) and GJR(1,1) models fitted to daily stock returns on the S&P500 index.

Parameter	GARCH(1,1)	se	GJR(1,1)	se
GARCH	0.8769	0.0064	0.8920	0.0058
ARCH	0.1102	0.0055	0.0277	0.0070
Leverage	−	−	0.1607	0.0098

are typically fully specified by the GARCH models:

$$p_Y(y_{t+h}|Z_t) = \int \int \cdots \int p_Y(y_{t+h}|z_{t+h-1}) p_Y(y_{t+h-1}|z_{t+h-2}) \cdots p_Y(y_{t+1}|Z_t)$$
$$\times \, dy_{t+h-1} \ldots dy_{t+1}.$$

The procedure is to draw normalized residuals, $\eta_{t+1}^b, \ldots, \eta_{t+h}^b$, and then recursively generate values of the conditional volatility, $\sigma_{t+h+1|t+h}^b$, using the preferred GARCH model, g:

$$y_{t+j+1}^b = \mu + \sigma_{t+j+1|t+j}^b \eta_{t+j+1}^b,$$

$$\sigma_{t+j+1|t+j}^b = g\left(\left\{ \sigma_{t+i|t+i-1}^b, \eta_{t+i}^b \right\}_{i=1}^j ; \theta \right).$$

This generates a simple Monte Carlo estimate of the predictive density $p_Y(y_{t+h}|Z_t)$. For example, an estimate of the h-step-ahead conditional variance given current information, $\sigma_{t+h+1|t}^2$, can be obtained by iterating on the above equations and averaging across Monte Carlo simulations,

$$\hat{\sigma}_{t+h+1|t}^2 = \frac{1}{B} \sum_{b=1}^{B} \left(\sigma_{t+h+1|t}^b \right)^2, \quad b = 1, \ldots, B.$$

In the simplest case, η_{t+i}^b is drawn from a normal distribution. However, since the innovations need not be Gaussian, another possibility is to use estimated, standardized residuals, $\hat{\eta}_t = (y_t - \hat{\mu}_{t|t-1})/\hat{\sigma}_{t|t-1}$ to construct the c.d.f. for the residuals, $\hat{P}_\eta$, and then draw with replacement from this distribution. This can help capture features of the normalized residuals such as skews and fat tails.

Empirical estimates for GARCH models applied to many security returns suggest a high degree of persistence in the conditional variance. As an example, we estimated GARCH(1,1) and GJR models (described in equations (13.8) and (13.17)) for daily stock returns on the S&P500 index over the period 1990:01:01–2015:03:31. The resulting parameter estimates are reported in table 13.1. The volatility process is highly persistent, with GARCH(1,1) estimates of $\hat{\alpha}_1 = 0.110$, $\hat{\beta}_1 = 0.877$, so their sum (0.987) is close to unity. Figure 13.1 shows a plot of the associated (in-sample) conditional one-step-ahead volatility forecasts. Periods of low volatility around 2005 and, later, after 2012, are interspersed with periods of extremely high volatility such as during the fall of 2008. The GARCH(1,1) and GJR(1,1) estimates share common trends and are broadly similar.

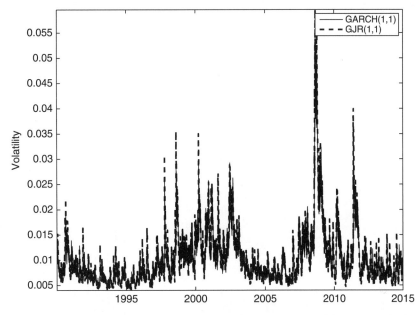

Figure 13.1: One-step-ahead conditional volatility forecasts generated by GARCH(1,1) and GJR models fitted to daily stock market returns.

Figure 13.2 plots the conditional volatility estimates implied by the GARCH(1,1) and GJR models during a few months in 2014. Focusing on this shorter sample allows us to better highlight the differences between the volatility estimates implied by these two models. Differences are largest following days with large negative shocks to returns because these have a larger effect on the GJR volatility forecast than on the forecast implied by the GARCH(1,1) model.

13.2.4 Stochastic Volatility Models

Stochastic volatility models assume that time-varying volatility is driven not only by shocks to the mean of the modeled process but by an additional source of randomness. In place of (13.5), a stochastic volatility model could take the form

$$\varepsilon_{t+1} = u_{t+1}\sqrt{V_{t+1}}, \tag{13.18}$$

$$\log(V_{t+1}) = \alpha + \beta \log(V_t) + \xi_{t+1}, \tag{13.19}$$

where V_{t+1} is the volatility, the logarithm of which follows an AR(1) process, and

$$u_{t+1} \sim \mathrm{N}(0, \sigma_u^2), \quad \xi_{t+1} \sim \mathrm{N}(0, \sigma_\xi^2), \quad \mathrm{Cov}(u_{t+1}, \xi_{t+1}) = 0.$$

Since these models involve an unobserved Markov process (V_{t+1}), Monte Carlo Markov chain algorithms are typically used to estimate the parameters (σ_u^2, σ_ξ^2) and generate future draws $\varepsilon_{t+1}, \ldots, \varepsilon_{t+h}$ as may be required; see Kim, Shephard, and Chib (1998). These models go back to Taylor (1982). For an early survey, see Ghysels, Harvey, and Renault (1995).

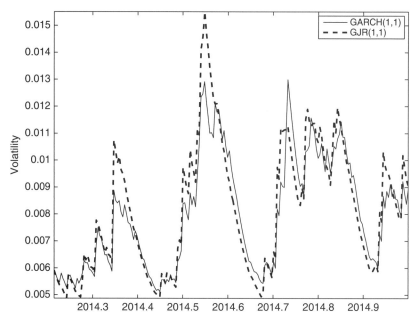

Figure 13.2: One-step-ahead conditional volatility forecasts generated by GARCH(1,1) and GJR models fitted to daily stock market returns.

13.3 FORECASTS USING REALIZED VOLATILITY MEASURES

Alternative ways exist for measuring variance based on data collected at a higher frequency than the observation period.[7] Such measures can be motivated from an underlying continuous time representation such as a generalized Wiener process with instantaneous drift μ_t and volatility σ_t:

$$dy_t = \mu_t dt + \sigma_t dW_t, \tag{13.20}$$

where dW_t is the increment to a standard Wiener process. For example, if $y_t = \log(P_t)$ and P_t is the price of a financial asset, dy_t becomes the continuously compounded rate of return on the asset. Suppose that μ_t and σ_t are both independent of W_t and

$$y_t | \bar{\mu}_t, \mathrm{IV}_t \sim \mathrm{N}(\bar{\mu}_t, \mathrm{IV}_t), \tag{13.21}$$

where $\bar{\mu}_t = \int_{t-1}^{t} \mu_s ds$, and $\mathrm{IV}_t = \int_{t-1}^{t} \sigma_s^2 ds$ measures the integrated variance which can be viewed as the true value of the variance over the interval $[t-1, t]$; see, e.g., Barndorff-Nielsen and Shephard (2002). The integrated variance is unobserved, but an estimate of it can be obtained by sampling y_t at increasingly small intervals defined on a grid $t - 1 < \tau_0 < \tau_1 < \cdots < \tau_N = t$, whose longest interval goes to 0, i.e., $\max_{1 \le j \le N} |\tau_j - \tau_{j-1}| \to 0$ as the number of grid points, N, increases: $N \to \infty$.

---

[7] See Hansen and Lunde (2011) for a review of the literature.

Quadratic variation is defined as

$$QV_t = p \lim_{N \to \infty} \sum_{j=1}^{N} (y_{\tau_j} - y_{\tau_{j-1}})^2. \tag{13.22}$$

This is not a feasible object to measure since we never observe the limit as the number of sampling points goes to infinity, i.e., $N \to \infty$. The equivalent measure for a finite number of intervals, N_t, is called the realized variance and is defined as the sum of squared intra-period changes:

$$RV_t = \sum_{j=1}^{N_t} (y_{\tau_j} - y_{\tau_{j-1}})^2. \tag{13.23}$$

Authors such as Barndorff-Nielsen (2002) have shown that RV_t is a consistent estimate of QV_t for semimartingales, a broad family of processes that includes Brownian motion and Poisson processes. In turn, QV_t equals IV_t for processes with time-varying volatility such as (13.20). See Hansen and Lunde (2011) for further discussion.

Recent empirical work uses RV estimates to predict future volatility of asset returns. Practical issues have to be addressed before computing RV, however. In principle the extent to which RV proxies for QV (and thus IV) can be expected to improve as N_t gets larger and data gets sampled at a higher frequency. However, in practice there are limits to how frequently data should be sampled. Consider the case of stock returns. At very high frequencies, market microstructure effects introduce noise into the estimator (13.23), so sampling stock prices more often is not guaranteed to improve the ability of RV to approximate QV. Rather, benefits from more frequent sampling should be traded off against increasingly large market microstructure effects and the optimal sampling frequency will depend on the trading volume of the underlying asset and a variety of market microstructure factors.[8] In some applications, asset returns are sampled at five-minute intervals and used to obtain an estimate of the daily realized variance, so N_t is a little under 100 observations on a typical trading day. At the monthly frequency it is common to use daily squared returns to obtain an estimate of the monthly realized variance, in which case N_t averages 22 observations.

The top window in figure 13.3 provides a plot of daily realized volatilities (the square root of realized variances) on the S&P500 index constructed using five-minute sampling (obtained from the Oxford-Man institute). There is clear evidence of volatility clustering and outliers such as during the fall of 2008. The bottom window of figure 13.3 shows the predicted volatility from an autoregressive model fitted to the realized volatility series. While these forecasts do not pick up the outliers in the realized series, they are broadly consistent with the movements in the realized series and identify a high level of persistence in this series.

Viewing RV_t as an observed, albeit noisy, estimate of the variance, σ_t^2, we can go ahead and use many standard forecasting tools to predict future volatility, σ_{t+1}^2. Typically, RV is found to be highly persistent at daily and longer horizons with

---

[8] See Andersen et al. (2003) for a discussion of how to model and forecast realized volatility series.

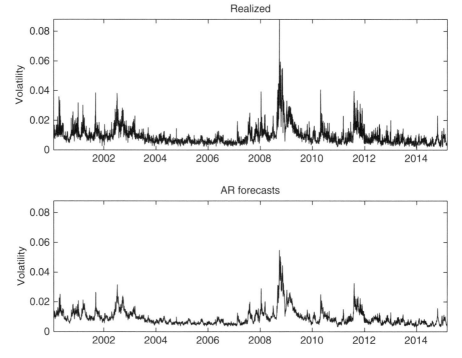

Figure 13.3: Realized volatility versus predicted values from an autoregressive model with lag
length selected by the AIC.

autocorrelations that decay only slowly. To capture this property, one option is to
model log RV$_t$ as a long-memory process using autoregressive fractionally integrated
moving average (ARFIMA) models of the form

$$\phi(L)(1 - L)^d \left(\frac{1}{2} \log(\text{RV}_t) - \mu \right) = \eta_t, \quad d \in [0, 1],$$

where η_t is white noise. If $d = 0$, this amounts to a simple AR model for $\log(\text{RV}_t)$
with the largest eigenvalue likely to be quite large due to the persistence in the realized
variance.

One approach to deal with measurement errors in the volatility measure is to
consider the joint dynamics in alternative volatility estimates. Engle and Gallo (2006)
develop a multiplicative error forecasting model based on the joint dynamics in daily
absolute returns, the daily high–low range and the daily realized volatility.

Another possibility is to add RV terms to GARCH models. For example, the
GARCH(1,1) model could be extended to

$$\sigma_{t+1|t}^2 = \omega + \alpha_1 \varepsilon_t^2 + \beta_1 \sigma_{t|t-1}^2 + \gamma \, \text{RV}_t \,. \tag{13.24}$$

As pointed out by Hansen and Lunde (2011), this can be attractive because the
filtration underlying the GARCH estimates is usually based on past returns sampled
at a relatively low frequency, whereas the filtration underlying RV$_t$ can be quite
different and is based on sampling at a different (higher) frequency.

13.4 APPROACHES TO DENSITY FORECASTING

Fully parametric approaches to density estimation assume that the conditional density $p_Y(y|z, \theta)$ is known apart from a finite-dimensional vector of parameters, θ. Classical approaches use the data, z, to obtain parameter estimates, $\hat{\theta}(z)$, and estimate the predictive density, $p_Y(y|z, \hat{\theta}(z))$, conditional on these plug-in estimates.

To estimate θ, we require some form of loss function on the estimates: something is maximized or minimized to obtain the estimates, $\hat{\theta}(z)$. The most popular loss function relating how "close" a candidate density, $p(y|z, \theta)$, is to the true density, $p_0(y|z, \theta^0)$, is the Kullback–Leibler (KL) distance. The KL distance between the true distribution, p_0, and the parametric distribution, p, is

$$\mathrm{KL}(p_0, p) = E_{p_0}\left[\ln\left(\frac{p_0}{p}\right)\right] = E_{p_0}[\ln(p_0(y|z, \theta^0))] - E_{p_0}[\ln(p(y|z, \theta))]. \quad (13.25)$$

Since the first term in (13.25) does not depend on θ, minimizing the KL distance over θ is the same as maximizing $E_{p_0}[\ln(p(y|z, \theta))]$, the expected log of the likelihood, over θ. This is known as the expected log score.[9] Hence, using the MLE or quasi-maximum likelihood estimation (QMLE), $\hat{\theta}_{\mathrm{MLE}}(z)$, as a plug-in estimator to construct the estimated predictive density is the same as minimizing the KL distance between the densities.[10] MLE and QMLE methods are well known and well understood which helps explain the popularity of this approach.

For outcomes that are continuously distributed, a wide range of models could be employed. An obvious first approach is to assume normality; for example $p(y|z, \theta)$ could be a conditional normal model with mean $\beta'z$ and variance σ^2, and so maximum likelihood methods would give the usual OLS plug-in estimator, $p(y|z) \sim N(\hat{\beta}'_{\mathrm{MLE}}z, \hat{\sigma}^2_{\mathrm{MLE}})$. For many problems this distribution is considered too restrictive, so many other distributions have been considered. We next cover some of the most popular of these parametric models.

In situations where the density of η_{t+1} is unknown, we can use quasi-maximum likelihood estimation to obtain the parameters of the density model. This works by first estimating the parameters of the conditional mean and conditional variance equations, assuming a normal density. Provided that the conditional mean and variance equations are correctly specified, this will yield consistent estimates even if the density for η is misspecified. Density forecasts can then be generated based on the standardized residuals, $\hat{\eta}_{t+1} = (y_{t+1} - \mu_{t+1|t}(\hat{\theta}))/\sigma_{t+1|t}(\hat{\theta})$. For example, a bootstrap can be used to draw from the empirical distribution function.

Given a set of estimates $\{\hat{\mu}_{t+1|t}, \hat{\sigma}_{t+1|t}\}_{t=0}^{T-1}$, we can construct standardized residuals,

$$\hat{\eta}_{t+1} = \frac{y_{t+1} - \hat{\mu}_{t+1|t}}{\hat{\sigma}_{t+1|t}}, \quad (13.26)$$

and use these to estimate the distribution of η_{t+1}.

[9] This should not be confused with the score of the log-likelihood function, i.e., the first derivative of the log-likelihood with respect to the parameter vector.

[10] If the distribution is known, maximum likelihood estimation can be used. If the distribution is unknown, we can employ the normal distribution to construct the density and use QMLE methods.

The simplest approach is to use the standardized residuals $\{\hat{\eta}_{t+1}\}$, $t = 0, \ldots,$ $T - 1$ as raw data to estimate a parametric density, p_η. In fact, since the standardized residuals are constructed to have zero mean and unit variance, if we assume a normal distribution for η, p_η would be fully known without requiring data on the residuals. More commonly, a less restrictive density could be chosen—for example the t-distribution with an estimated number of degrees of freedom.

Alternatively, any nonparametric approach to density estimation can be used on the raw data $\{\hat{\eta}_{t+1}\}$, $t = 0, \ldots, T - 1$, to obtain an estimate for $\hat{p}_\eta$. A typical approach is to use a kernel estimator for the density. Estimates for the density p_η at η would then be given by

$$\hat{p}_\eta(\eta) = \frac{1}{Tb} \sum_{t=0}^{T-1} K \left(\frac{\hat{\eta}_{t+1} - \eta}{b} \right), \tag{13.27}$$

for some bandwidth b and kernel $K(\cdot)$. A standard choice of kernel is either the Gaussian kernel $K(x) = (2\pi)^{-1} \exp(-0.5x^2)$ or the Epanechnikov kernel $K(x) = 0.75(1 - x)\mathbb{1}(|x| < 1)$, where $\mathbb{1}(a) = 1$ if a is true and is 0 otherwise. For either choice—or any choice in which the kernel integrates to 1—the mean of the estimated density equals the mean of $\{\hat{\eta}_{t+1}\}$, $t = 0, \ldots, T - 1$. The choice of kernel is generally not considered too important for the properties of the density estimate. The choice of the bandwidth parameter b is considered more critical. Larger values for b cause the estimate, $\hat{p}_\eta(\eta)$, to put larger weights on values of $\hat{\eta}_{t+1}$ further away from η and hence provide a smoother distribution. This, however, comes at the cost of adding a bias to the estimate. Optimal choices of bandwidth trade off these effects. A standard choice of the bandwidth for the Gaussian kernel is $1.06\hat{\sigma}_\eta T^{1/5}$, where $\hat{\sigma}_\eta$ is the standard deviation of $\{\hat{\eta}_{t+h}\}_{t=0}^{T-1}$, which should be 1 given the centering and standardization in (13.26). It should be recalled, however, that such choices are "optimal" not in regards to obtaining the best density forecast, but in terms of some criterion defined over the density of $\hat{\eta}_{t+1}$ itself. This is only one component of the density forecast, so it would not be surprising to find that optimal choices of the bandwidth from the kernel literature do not result in better density forecasts on some relevant criterion for the density forecast. A thorough exposition of density estimation is available in Pagan and Ullah (1999, chapter 2).

13.4.1 Parametric Density Models

We next cover some popular parametric density models that have found widespread use particularly in finance applications, including the student-t, two-piece normal, and mixtures of normals.

13.4.1.1 Non-Gaussian Density Models

Even after accounting for volatility dynamics, the standardized residuals, $\eta_{t+1|t}$, are often found not to be normally distributed. To account for this, a variety of alternative parametric density models have been proposed. These typically seek to capture "stylized features" of the forecast errors such as skew or fat tails by means of flexible yet parsimonious densities that depend on only a few judiciously chosen parameters. We briefly describe some of the parametric methods that have been found to be useful in generating forecasts of economic and financial time series.

Hansen (1994) proposed the skewed-t distribution with zero mean and unit variance which takes the form

$$
p(\eta_{t+1}|\gamma, \lambda) =
\begin{cases}
bc \left(1 + \frac{1}{\gamma-2} \left(\frac{b\eta_{t+1}+a}{1-\lambda}\right)^2\right)^{-(\gamma+1)/2} , & \eta_{t+1} < -a/b, \\
bc \left(1 + \frac{1}{\gamma-2} \left(\frac{b\eta_{t+1}+a}{1+\lambda}\right)^2\right)^{-(\gamma+1)/2} , & \eta_{t+1} \geq -a/b.
\end{cases}
\tag{13.28}
$$

The skewness (λ) and kurtosis (γ) parameters are subject to the restrictions $2 < \gamma < \infty$, $-1 < \lambda < 1$, while the scalar constants a, b, c are functions of λ and γ:

$$
a = 4\lambda c \left(\frac{\gamma-2}{\gamma-1}\right),
$$

$$
b^2 = 1 + 3\lambda^2 - a^2,
$$

$$
c = \frac{\Gamma((\gamma+1)/2)}{\sqrt{\pi(\gamma-2)}\Gamma(\gamma/2)}.
$$

Here Γ is the gamma function. The parameters in (13.28) can be generalized to depend on lagged innovations, e.g., $\lambda(\varepsilon_{t-1})$, $\gamma(\varepsilon_{t-1})$, which would produce an autoregressive conditional density model.

The two-piece normal distribution assumes that the predicted variable has a density function

$$
p_Y(y_{t+1}|Z_t) =
\begin{cases}
\dfrac{\exp(-(y_{t+1} - \mu_{t+1|t})^2/2\sigma_1^2)}{\sqrt{2\pi}(\sigma_1 + \sigma_2)/2} & \text{for } y_{t+1} \leq \mu_{t+1|t}, \\
\dfrac{\exp(-(y_{t+1} - \mu_{t+1|t})^2/2\sigma_2^2)}{\sqrt{2\pi}(\sigma_1 + \sigma_2)/2} & \text{for } y_{t+1} > \mu_{t+1|t}.
\end{cases}
\tag{13.29}
$$

The mean and variance of this distribution is

$$
E_t[y_{t+1}] = \mu_{t+1|t} + \sqrt{\frac{2}{\pi}}(\sigma_2 - \sigma_1),
\tag{13.30}
$$

$$
\text{Var}_t(y_{t+1}) = \left(1 - \frac{2}{\pi}\right)(\sigma_2 - \sigma_1)^2 + \sigma_1\sigma_2.
\tag{13.31}
$$

If $\sigma_2 > \sigma_1$, the distribution is positively skewed and large positive values become more likely than large negative values. The distribution has fat tails provided that $\sigma_1 \neq \sigma_2$. Only one extra parameter is introduced relative to the standard normal distribution whose critical values can still be used subject to a scaling factor. This approach has been used by the Bank of England to generate the so-called fan charts which communicate the degree of uncertainty surrounding the Bank's macroeconomic forecasts.[11]

For this family of distributions the so-called balance of risk, i.e., the probability of experiencing an outcome below the mean, is given by $\Pr(y_{t+1} \leq \mu_{t+1|t}) = \sigma_1/(\sigma_1 + \sigma_2)$. This equals 0.5 for $\sigma_1 = \sigma_2$, but grows bigger if the volatility of outcomes below the mean is higher than that of outcomes above the mean.

---

[11] See Wallis (2003) for an analysis of the Bank of England's fan charts.

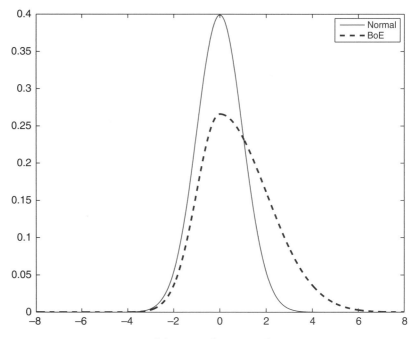

Figure 13.4: Two-piece exponential density with $\mu = 0$ and $\sigma_1 = 2, \sigma_2 = 1$.

As an illustration of this model, figure 13.4 compares the two-piece exponential density with $\mu = 0$ and $\sigma_1 = 2, \sigma_2 = 1$ to a standard normal distribution. The two densities are very different with the two-piece density displaying a notably slower decay for negative values and a faster decay for positive values relative to the symmetric normal distribution. This type of two-piece density can thus be used to capture a pronounced left skew in the distribution.

13.4.1.2 Mixtures of Normals

Mixtures of normals assume that y_{t+1} is a mixture of Gaussian components:

$$y_{t+1} = \mu_{s_{t+1}} + \sigma_{s_{t+1}} \eta_{t+1}, \quad \eta_{t+1} \sim \text{ind} \, N(0, 1), \tag{13.32}$$

where $\mu_{s_{t+1}}$ is the mean conditional on being in state s_{t+1} while $\sigma_{s_{t+1}}$ is the volatility in state s_{t+1}. The state variable, S_{t+1}, takes a finite number of values, $S_{t+1} \in \{1, \ldots, K\}$ and is typically assumed to be generated by a first-order homogeneous Markov chain:[12]

$$\Pr(s_{t+1} = i | s_t = j) = p_{ij}. \tag{13.33}$$

Note the crucial distinction between a weighted sum of normally distributed variables, which will be normally distributed, and a mixture of normal distributions. Mixtures of Gaussian distributions are not Gaussian. Instead, they resemble compound lotteries: first nature draws a state s_{t+1}, then it draws an outcome from the resulting state distribution. Only one of the states occurs at each point in time, but it

---

[12] For further discussion, see chapter 8.

TABLE 13.2:
Estimates of two-state Markov switching fitted to daily US stock market returns (1990–2015).

Parameter	Coefficient	Standard errors
σ_1	0.0047	0.0002
σ_2	0.0318	0.0016
μ_1	0.0777	0.0112
μ_2	−0.0773	0.0416
P_{11}	0.9877	0.0796
P_{22}	0.9709	0.0826

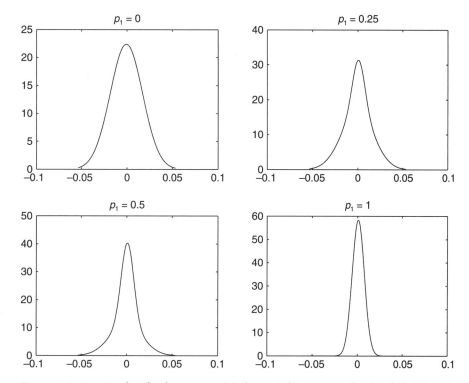

Figure 13.5: Density plots for the two-state Markov switching process fitted to daily US stock market returns, using four different probability weights for the two states.

is not known ahead of time which one will occur. This property can be used to create a flexible set of density forecasts.

We next estimate a two-state Markov switching model on daily US stock returns over the period 1990–2010, i.e., the same data used to generate the volatility plot in figure 13.1. The parameter estimates for this model are shown in table 13.2; the estimates indicate that state two is a low-mean, high-volatility regime, while state one is a high-mean, low-volatility state. As revealed by the state transition probabilities, both states are highly persistent although the high-mean, low-volatility state is notably more persistent ($\hat{p}_{11} = 0.988$) than the low-mean, high-volatility state ($\hat{p}_{22} = 0.971$).

Figure 13.5 shows the density implied by this model for four different values of the probability of state one, namely $p_1 = \{0, 0.25, 0.5, 1\}$. When $p_1 = 0$ or $p_1 = 1$,

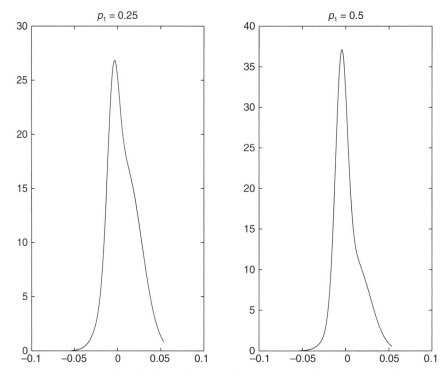

Figure 13.6: Density plots for the Markov switching process with $\mu_1 = -0.5\%$ and $\mu_2 = 1\%$ and volatility parameters as in figure 13.5.

the densities are Gaussian and differ only because the standard deviation is much higher in state two than in state one. However, when $p_1 = 0.25$ or $p_1 = 0.5$, there is clear evidence of kurtosis, with a more peaked distribution and a slower tail decay than under the normal distribution.

To further highlight this point, figure 13.6 plots two mixture distributions for $p_1 = 0.25$ and $p_1 = 0.5$, using the same volatility parameters as in the previous plot, but setting $\mu_1 = -0.5\%$ and $\mu_2 = 1\%$. Using these more extreme differences in mean parameters, we clearly see how the two-state mixture distribution is right skewed.

In fact, the density of a mixture is a weighted average of the individual densities, with weights that represent the probability of being in the respective states conditional on current information:

$$p_Y(y_{t+1}|Z_t) = \sum_{j=1}^{K} p_Y(y_{t+1}|s_{t+1} = j, Z_t) P(s_{t+1} = j|Z_t). \qquad (13.34)$$

Given the state transition probabilities in (13.33) the conditional state probabilities can be derived from the total probability theorem:

$$\Pr(s_{t+1} = j|Z_t) = \sum_{j=1}^{K} p_{ij} P(s_t = i|Z_t). \qquad (13.35)$$

Moments of mixture distributions are easily derived. For example, the centered unconditional moments of the Markov switching process (13.32)–(13.33) are given by

$$E\left[(y_{t+1} - \mu)^n\right] = \sum_{i=1}^{K} \pi_i \sum_{j=0}^{n} {}_nC_j \, \sigma_i^j \, E[\eta_t^j](\mu_i - \mu)^{n-j}, \tag{13.36}$$

where ${}_nC_j = n!/((n-j)! \, j!)$ and π_i is the steady-state probability of being in state i; see Timmermann (2000).

Suppose $k = 2$ so that there are two states and assume that the innovations, η, are normally distributed. Then the steady state probabilities are given by

$$\pi_1 = \frac{1 - p_{22}}{2 - p_{11} - p_{22}}, \quad \pi_2 = \frac{1 - p_{11}}{2 - p_{11} - p_{22}}. \tag{13.37}$$

The unconditional mean and variance of y take the forms

$$\mu = \pi_1 \mu_1 + \pi_2 \mu_2,$$

$$\sigma^2 = \pi_1 \sigma_1^2 + (1 - \pi_1)\sigma_2^2 + (1 - \pi_1)\pi_1(\mu_2 - \mu_1)^2.$$

This is not simply a weighted average of σ_1^2 and σ_2^2 and also depends on the difference in means $(\mu_1 - \mu_2)^2$.

Similarly, the centered skew is given by

$$\text{skew} = E\left[(y - \mu)^3\right]$$

$$= \pi_1(1 - \pi_1)(\mu_1 - \mu_2)\left\{3(\sigma_1^2 - \sigma_2^2) + (1 - 2\pi_1)(\mu_2 - \mu_1^2)^2\right\}.$$

For this to be nonzero requires that $\mu_1 \neq \mu_2$.

Conditional moments can be derived by using conditional state probabilities $p_{1t+1|t}$, such as those in (13.35), instead of the steady-state probabilities, π_i. As an illustration of this, figure 13.7 uses the smoothed-state probabilities to plot the time series of the conditional one-step-ahead volatility for daily US stock market returns. Given the relatively modest difference in the mean return estimates in table 13.2, the volatility estimates are close to $\sigma_{t+1|t} = [(1 - p_{1t+1|t})\sigma_2^2 + p_{1t+1|t}\sigma_1^2]^{1/2}$ and so effectively are bounded by σ_1 and σ_2. The step-like behavior of the plot reflects shifts in the smoothed-state probabilities—i.e., most of the time the underlying state is quite precisely estimated.

13.4.2 Nonparametric and Semiparametric Density Estimation

Conditional distributions can be estimated fully nonparametrically by kernel density methods. From Bayes' rule, the conditional distribution of y given z is

$$p(y|z) = \frac{p(y, z)}{p(z)}. \tag{13.38}$$

The standard approach to estimating conditional densities is thus to combine two density estimates—one for $p(y, z)$ and one for $p(z)$. For a random $(k \times 1)$ vector Z

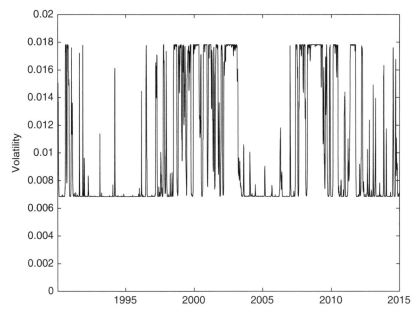

Figure 13.7: Time-series plots of one-step-ahead conditional volatility estimates for daily US stock market returns implied by a two-state Markov switching model.

and observations $\{z_t\}$, $t = 1, \ldots, T$, the joint density at any point, z, can be estimated from a weighted average around that point:

$$\hat{p}_Z(z) = \frac{1}{Tb^k} \sum_{t=1}^{T} K\left(\frac{z_t - z}{b}\right), \tag{13.39}$$

where the multivariate kernel K is nonnegative, integrates to 1, and often is assumed to be symmetric. To allow for different bandwidths, a product kernel might be used:

$$\hat{p}_Z(z) = \frac{1}{Tb_1 b_2 \cdots b_k} \sum_{t=1}^{T} K\left(\frac{z_{1t} - z_1}{b_1}\right) K\left(\frac{z_{2t} - z_2}{b_2}\right) \times \cdots \times K\left(\frac{z_{kt} - z_k}{b_k}\right).$$

$$\tag{13.40}$$

When the scales of the different variables in Z are different, it can be useful to choose individual bandwidths. The product kernel in (13.40) also ensures internal consistency in the use of kernels for the conditioning variables since the same kernels appear in the numerator and denominator of the approximation to (13.38).

Some methods mix purely parametric and purely nonparametric approaches. Gallant and Nychka (1987) proposed what they call a semi-non-parametric (SNP) approach to constructing conditional densities. The motivation for their method is broader than constructing forecast densities—it is a general approach to robust maximum likelihood estimation—but is a useful procedure for this problem as well. The idea is to construct a model for the mean and variance, just as in section 13.2, and then apply a series approximation to the density of the standardized data. Note that the mean, variance, and distribution are estimated simultaneously in a single maximum likelihood setting.

The SNP method approximates the density p_Y by means of a series approach. Gallant and Nychka (1987) consider many types of series, but we restrict the exposition here to the most popular version which uses Hermite polynomials. The density can then be written as

$$p_{\eta_{t+1}}^{\text{SNP}} = \frac{c^{-1}}{\sigma_{t+1|t}} \left(\sum_{i=0}^{m} \omega_i \eta_{t+1}^i \right)^2 \phi(\eta_{t+1}), \tag{13.41}$$

where ϕ is the standard normal distribution and $\eta_{t+h} = \sigma_{t+1|t}^{-1}(y_{t+1} - \mu_{t+1|t})$. For example, if we approximate the mean by βz_t, and assume a constant variance, σ^2, we get $\eta_{t+1} = \sigma^{-1}(y_{t+1} - \beta' z_t)$. The normalizing constant $c = \int \left(\sum_{i=0}^{m} \omega_i \eta_{t+1}^i \right)^2 \phi(\eta_{t+1}) d\eta_{t+h}$ ensures that $\int p_{\eta_{t+1}}^{\text{SNP}} d\eta_{t+1} = 1$. Using squared values of the weights on the standard normal terms $\phi(\eta_{t+1})$ ensures that the density is nonnegative everywhere. Parameter estimation for this type of model involves a constrained maximum likelihood problem,

$$(\hat{\beta}, \hat{\sigma}^2, \hat{\omega}_1, \ldots, \hat{\omega}_m) = \arg\max T^{-1} \sum_{t=0}^{T-1} \log \left[\frac{c^{-1}}{\hat{\sigma}} \left(\sum_{i=0}^{m} \omega_i \eta_{t+1}^i \right)^2 \phi(\eta_{t+h}) \right]. \tag{13.42}$$

As stated in (13.42), the weights ω_i are identifiable only up to a scalar and so it is standard to use the normalization $\omega_0 = 1$. If we set $m = 0$, it is clear that the method nests standard quasi-maximum likelihood estimation. Also note that c is a function of the weights. For example, if $m = 1$, we have

$$c = \int \left(\sum_{i=0}^{m} \omega_i \eta^i \right)^2 \phi(\eta) d\eta$$

$$= \int (1 + \omega_1 \eta)^2 \phi(\eta) d\eta$$

$$= \int (1 + \omega_1^2 \eta^2 + 2\omega_1 \eta) \phi(\eta) d\eta$$

$$= (1 + \omega_1^2).$$

The remaining problem is to select the order of the polynomial, m. Standard model selection procedures such as AIC or BIC can be employed. Coppejans and Gallant (2002) also suggest a cross-validation method.

Figure 13.8 plots SNP densities fitted to daily US stock market returns on the S&P500 index over the period 1990–2015. The model allows for GARCH dynamics in the conditional volatility and assumes a constant mean. We show results for $m = 1, 5, 10$ for a day with high volatility (left panels) and a day with low volatility (right panels). The densities for $m = 5, 10$ are notably flatter than the Gaussian density ($m = 0$) which is superimposed on the graphs.

Extensions of the SNP method allow the weights ω_i to depend on a set of conditioning variables; see Gallant and Tauchen (1989) for an exposition and application. As stated above, all of the variation in y due to the conditioning z-variables arises from centering on the conditional mean. However, extensions also

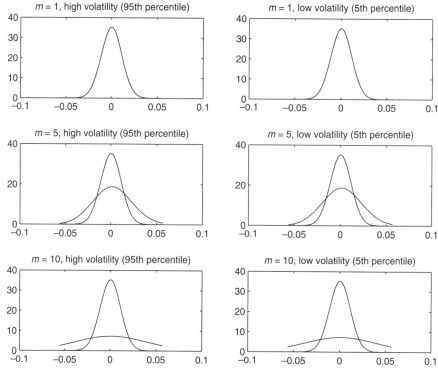

Figure 13.8: Semi-non-parametric (SNP) density plots for $m = 1, 5, 10$ at high and low volatility levels.

allow the variance as well as the density of the centered and standardized outcome to depend on conditioning information.

The SNP approach has been used in a number of empirical applications. Using models for expected stock returns and conditional volatility, Harrison and Zhang (1999) use the SNP approach to model the risk-return trade-off on stocks at long horizons, while Gallant, Rossi, and Tauchen (1992) use the approach to model the relation between stock price movements and trading volume.

13.4.3 How to Report Density Forecasts

A problem that frequently arises in density forecasting is how to report the predictive density. Point estimation typically requires reporting only a single number, for example the predicted number of jobs created next month may be 100,000, and is a number easily communicated to the user of the forecast. Density forecasting, in contrast, requires the entire distribution of the forecast to be communicated. If the density forecast is parametric, the functional form of the density along with the estimated parameters can be reported. For less parametric or Bayesian approaches, this becomes more difficult.

Often only partial information is transmitted at the end of the forecasting process. For example, the Bank of England's fan charts report selected percentiles. Alternatively, a graph of the prediction distribution could be presented. A difficulty with these methods is that they cannot be directly used by any forecaster without a loss function to generate their optimal forecast. If we take seriously the motivation of density forecasting—that it allows us to evaluate the expected loss (13.1) for a broad array of loss functions—then the full density must be communicated to the user. For methods that result in a simulated set of pairs $\{y_i|z, p_{yi}(y|z)\}$ for a range of y-values, one approach is to provide d such pairs to the decision maker. These can be used to approximate (13.1) by the sum

$$d^{-1} \sum_{i=1}^{d} L(f, y_i) p_{yi}(y_i|z),$$

which in turn can be minimized to find the optimal forecast, f, given L. The difficulties with this approach are twofold. First, we need a large number of pairs d in order to obtain a satisfactory approximation to the expected loss. This means choosing a large value for d and so requires a computational approach, e.g., making draws available electronically. When y is multivariate, this becomes more of an issue. Second, the pairs $\{y_i|z, p_{yi}(y|z)\}$, $i = 1, \ldots, d$ must be computed for all useful sets of z, on which they are conditioned. For an agency that provides density estimates in real time this is not too difficult since the relevant z will be known.

13.5 INTERVAL AND QUANTILE FORECASTS

Interval forecasts fall somewhere between density forecasts and point forecasts. They typically provide information about the most likely outcome as well as the degree of uncertainty surrounding a forecast as measured by the center and width of the interval forecast, respectively, assuming a symmetric distribution.

Example 13.5.1 (Conditional interval forecasts for Gaussian variable). *For conditional location–scale models, $y_{t+1} = \mu_{t+1|t} + \sigma_{t+1|t}\eta_{t+1}$, $\eta_{t+1} \sim P_\eta(0, 1)$ a typical interval forecast is that the outcome y_{t+1} falls in the interval $[p^l_{t+1|t}(\alpha), p^u_{t+1|t}(\alpha)]$ for some probability $1 - \alpha$, $\alpha \in (0, 1/2)$, where*

$$p^l_{t+1|t} = \mu_{t+1|t} + \sigma_{t+1|t} P_\eta^{-1}(\alpha/2),$$

$$p^u_{t+1|t} = \mu_{t+1|t} + \sigma_{t+1|t} P_\eta^{-1}(1 - \alpha/2). \tag{13.43}$$

If P_η is Gaussian and $\alpha = 0.05$, this simplifies to

$$p^l_{t+1|t} = \mu_{t+1|t} - 1.96\sigma_{t+1|t},$$

$$p^u_{t+1|t} = \mu_{t+1|t} + 1.96\sigma_{t+1|t}.$$

Example 13.5.2 (Interval forecasts using a two-piece normal distribution). *If the density follows the two-piece normal distribution in (13.29) with mean $\mu_{t+1|t}$ and variances below and above the mean of σ_1^2, σ_2^2, respectively, the α quantiles q_α are*

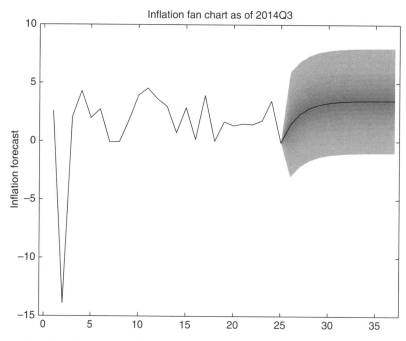

Figure 13.9: Fan charts generated by the two-piece exponential density, showing the predicted median and the 75% and 90% ranges for the predictive density.

given by

$$
q_\alpha = \begin{cases} \mu_{t+1|t} + \sigma_1 \Phi^{-1}\left(\dfrac{\alpha}{C\sqrt{2\pi}\sigma_1}\right) & \text{for } \alpha \le \dfrac{\sigma_1}{\sigma_1+\sigma_2}, \\[3ex] \mu_{t+1|t} + \sigma_2 \Phi^{-1}\left(\dfrac{\alpha + C\sqrt{2\pi}\sigma_2 - 1}{C\sqrt{2\pi}\sigma_2}\right) & \text{for } \alpha > \dfrac{\sigma_1}{\sigma_1+\sigma_2}, \end{cases}
$$

where $C = \sqrt{2/\pi}(\sigma_1 + \sigma_2)^{-1}$; see Banerjee and Das (2011).

Figure 13.9 plots a fan chart for quarterly inflation as of 2014Q3, using a two-piece exponential distribution fitted to quarterly inflation data. The solid line tracks the actual inflation rate during the six years leading up to 2014Q3 (observation 24) and tracks the point forecast for the subsequent three years (12 quarters). The different shades indicate 5% probability ranges for future inflation. While the point forecast for inflation is quite smooth, it is surrounded by considerable uncertainty, particularly at horizons greater than one year.

To construct interval forecasts for location–scale models, three estimates are required, namely an estimate of the conditional mean, $\mu_{t+1|t}$, an estimate of the conditional volatility, $\sigma_{t+1|t}$, and an estimate of the distribution function of the normalized innovation, P_η, so that $P_\eta^{-1}(\alpha/2)$ and $P_\eta^{-1}(1-\alpha/2)$ can be evaluated. Here P_η^{-1} is the quantile function. Hansen (2006) discusses ways to allow for parameter estimation uncertainty in the construction of interval forecasts.

Many parametric density forecast models lead to quantile forecasts that are simple to derive. For example, conditional location–scale models with Gaussian innovations imply quantiles of the form

$$q_\alpha(y_{t+1}|z_t) = \mu_{t+1|t} + \sigma_{t+1|t} P_N^{-1}(\alpha), \quad \alpha \in (0, 1), \tag{13.44}$$

where P_N is the standard normal distribution function and P_N^{-1} is the associated quantile function.

An alternative to this procedure is to separately model individual quantiles. This approach has gained interest particularly in value at risk (VaR) calculations in finance. Under the recommendations of the Basel committee, VaR estimates should be reported by banks as part of their risk management practices. VaR estimates are essentially left-tail quantile forecasts and so require banks to have ways to predict the quantiles for their asset values.

Predictability in individual quantiles can be captured in different ways by modeling $q_\alpha(y_{t+1}|Z_t)$, the conditional quantile for y_{t+1} given current information, Z_t. Since the full conditional distribution function does not need to be specified, such regressions are semiparametric. Typically the conditional quantile $q_\alpha(y_{t+1}|Z_t, \beta)$ is specified up to some unknown finite-dimensional parameter vector, β. Given an estimate, $\hat{\beta}$, quantile forecasts can be computed as $q_\alpha(y_{t+1}|Z_t, \hat{\beta})$. For example, a linear quantile model would take the form

$$q_\alpha(y_{t+1}|Z_t, \beta) = \beta_{0\alpha} + \beta_{1\alpha} z_t. \tag{13.45}$$

Since the slope coefficient ($\beta_{1\alpha}$) can differ across quantiles, this model is quite flexible and nests existing models from the literature, including the benchmark model $\beta_{1\alpha} = 0$ that assumes a constant distribution.

Generalizations of the quantile model that admit autoregressive dynamics have been proposed by Engle and Manganelli (2004). The so-called CAViaR models include last period's conditional quantile and the absolute value of last period's realization, $|y_t|$, as predictor variables. For example, the symmetric absolute value and asymmetric slope models of Engle and Manganelli take the form

$$q_\alpha(y_{t+1}|Z_t) = \beta_{0\alpha} + \beta_{1\alpha} q_\alpha(y_t|Z_{t-1}) + \beta_{2\alpha}|y_t|, \tag{13.46}$$

$$q_\alpha(y_{t+1}|Z_t) = \beta_{0\alpha} + \beta_{1\alpha} q_\alpha(y_t|Z_{t-1}) + \beta_{2\alpha} \max(0, y_t) + \beta_{3\alpha} \min(0, y_t),$$

where $q_\alpha(y_t|z_{t-1})$ is the lagged α-quantile. If $\beta_{1\alpha} > 0$, this specification is consistent with persistence in the α-quantile for the predicted variable. Notice that it is important to let the coefficients depend on α. For example, the tail dynamics observed in many financial time series tend to be highly persistent and can be captured by letting α be close to either 0 (left tail) or 1 (right tail). Conversely, for such series it is often found that there is little persistence in the conditional distribution of the center of the distribution as captured by the median ($\alpha = 0.5$).

13.5.1 Estimation

Following Koenker and Bassett (1978), the parameters of quantile models can be estimated by replacing the conventional quadratic loss function underlying most empirical work on predictability with the so-called "tick" loss function,

$$L_\alpha(e_{t+1}(\beta)) = (\alpha - \mathbb{1}(e_{t+1}(\beta) < 0))e_{t+1}(\beta), \tag{13.47}$$

where $e_{t+1}(\beta) = y_{t+1} - q_\alpha(y_{t+1}|Z_t, \beta)$ is the forecast error and $\mathbb{1}(\cdot)$ is the indicator function. Under this objective function, the optimal forecast is the conditional quantile. To see this, note that the first-order condition associated with minimizing the expected value of (13.47) with respect to the forecast, $q_\alpha(y_{t+1}|Z_t, \beta)$, is the α-quantile of the return distribution,

$$q_\alpha(y_{t+1}|Z_t, \beta) = P_{t+1|t}^{-1}(\alpha), \tag{13.48}$$

where $P_{t+1|t}$ is the conditional distribution function for e_{t+1}. In fact, for the forecast to be represented by the conditional α-quantile of y, it is necessary for the forecaster's loss to take the slightly more general form,

$$L(f, y) = [\alpha - \mathbb{1}(G(y) \le G(f))]\,(G(y) - G(f)),$$

where G is a strictly increasing function; see the discussion in Komunjer (2013). Under the loss function in (13.47), estimates can be obtained by solving a linear programming problem.

Conversely, specifications such as (13.46) are highly nonlinear functions in the parameters, θ, and so do not lend themselves to be solved by means of linear programming methods. Instead Markov chain Monte Carlo or minimax methods can be used; see Komunjer (2013) for further discussion.

Empirical evidence on the performance of various procedures for constructing quantile forecasts is provided in a number of studies. Kuester, Mittnik, and Paolella (2006) consider returns on the NASDAQ composite index over a 30-year period. They find that GARCH specifications generally underestimate the likelihood of extreme returns, particularly if the innovations are assumed to be Gaussian. Assuming instead that the innovations follow a skewed-t distribution leads to somewhat better results. Bao, Lee, and Saltoglu (2006) report shortcomings for CaViaR models fitted to five Asian stock markets during the Asian crisis in 1997–1998, although the models perform substantially better prior to the crisis.

13.6 MULTIVARIATE VOLATILITY MODELS

So far we have focused on univariate density forecasting problems. However, some applications require predicting joint distributions of two or more variables. For example, investors may be interested in pricing options with multiple underlying assets or computing Value at Risk at the portfolio level for many risky assets. In such situations, the outcome will depend on the degree of dependency across multiple underlying variables. This section discusses different ways to model multivariate volatility, while the next section covers copula modeling.

First, consider extending the conditional location–scale models to the multivariate case by modeling the conditional mean and volatility of an $(n \times 1)$ vector of variables y_{t+1}:

$$y_{t+1} = \mu_{t+1|t}(\theta) + H_{t+1|t}^{1/2}(\theta)\eta_{t+1}, \quad \eta_{t+1} \sim (0, I_n),$$

where θ is a vector of underlying parameters. Here $H_{t+1|t}^{1/2}$ is an $(n \times n)$ positive-semidefinite matrix with the property that $\text{var}(y_{t+1}|Z_t) = H_{t+1|t} = H_{t+1|t}^{1/2}(H_{t+1|t}^{1/2})'$, where $H_{t+1|t}^{1/2}$ can be obtained from the Cholesky decomposition of $H_{t+1|t}$. The question is how to best model $H_{t+1|t}$ in the multivariate case where $n > 1$. Bauwens, Laurent, and Rombouts (2006) review the large literature on this issue and we shall simply highlight a few key models from their review.

The so-called BEKK(1,1,1) specification takes the form

$$H_{t+1|t} = C'C + A'\varepsilon_t\varepsilon_t'A + G'H_{t|t-1}G, \qquad (13.49)$$

where C, A, G are $(n \times n)$ matrices and C is upper triangular and $\varepsilon_t = H_{t|t-1}^{1/2}(\theta)\eta_t$. This specification has $n(5n + 1)/2$ parameters and can readily be generalized to allow for additional lags of ε_t and $H_{t|t-1}$.

A parsimonious model can be obtained by assuming a factor structure in the conditional variance. For example, Lin (1992) studies a K-factor GARCH model of the form

$$H_{t+1|t} = C'C + \sum_{k=1}^{K} \lambda_k\lambda_k'(\alpha_k^2\omega_k'\varepsilon_t\varepsilon_t'\omega_k + \beta_k^2\omega_k'H_{t|t-1}\omega_k), \qquad (13.50)$$

where $\omega_k'\iota = 1$ serves as an identification restriction. Provided that $C'C$ is positive definite, $H_{t|t-1}$ will be of full rank. This specification has $n(n + 5)/2$ parameters.

Not only the variance parameters, but also the correlation parameters may vary over time. Early work such as Bollerslev (1990) assumed constant pairwise correlations and time-varying volatilities:

$$H_{t+1|t} = D_{t+1|t}RD_{t+1|t}, \qquad (13.51)$$

$$D_{t+1|t} = \text{diag}(h_{11t+1|t}^{1/2}, \ldots, h_{nnt+1|t}^{1/2}).$$

Here $h_{iit+1|t}$ can be obtained from a univariate GARCH model and the elements of the correlation matrix R are $R_{ij} = \rho_{ij}$ with $\rho_{ii} = 1$, so that the (i, j) element of $H_{t+1|t}$ takes the form $\rho_{ij}\sqrt{h_{iit+1|t}h_{jjt+1|t}}$. In this model the conditional correlation is constant, but the conditional covariance will vary over time because of time-varying variances.

Recent work has focused on modeling time-varying correlations. For example, the multivariate dynamic conditional correlation GARCH model proposed by Engle and Sheppard (2001) and Engle (2002) takes the form $y_{t+1} \sim N(0, H_{t+1|t})$,

$$H_{t+1|t} \equiv D_{t+1|t}R_{t+1|t}D_{t+1|t}, \qquad (13.52)$$

where $D_{t+1|t}$ is an $(n \times n)$ diagonal matrix of time-varying standard deviations with ith diagonal element $\sqrt{h_{iit+1|t}}$, and $R_{t+1|t}$ is now a time-varying correlation matrix.

The diagonal elements of $D_{t+1|t}$ are assumed to be generated by univariate GARCH processes:

$$h_{iit+1|t} = \omega_i + \sum_{j=1}^{q_i} \alpha_{ij}\varepsilon_{it+1-j}^2 + \sum_{p=1}^{p_i} \beta_{ip}h_{iit+1-p|t-p}, \qquad (13.53)$$

whereas the dynamics in the correlations take the form

$$Q_{t+1|t} = \left(1 - \sum_{j=1}^{J} \alpha_j - \sum_{k=1}^{K} \beta_k\right)\bar{Q} + \sum_{j=1}^{J} \alpha_j \varepsilon_{t+1-j}\varepsilon'_{t+1-j} + \sum_{k=1}^{K} \beta_k Q_{t+1-k|t-k},$$

(13.54)

$$R_{t+1|t} = (Q^*_{t+1|t})^{-1} Q_{t+1|t} (Q^*_{t+1|t})^{-1}.$$

Here $\bar{Q}$ is the unconditional covariance of the standardized residuals, the α_j terms measure the news impact of previous shocks, and the β_k terms capture persistence in the correlations. Finally, $Q^*_{t+1|t}$ is a diagonal matrix of the form

$$Q^*_{t+1|t} = \begin{pmatrix} \sqrt{q_{11t+1|t}} & 0 & 0 & \cdots & 0 \\ 0 & \sqrt{q_{22t+1|t}} & 0 & \cdots & 0 \\ \vdots & \vdots & \ddots & & \vdots \\ 0 & 0 & 0 & \cdots & \sqrt{q_{nnt+1|t}} \end{pmatrix},$$

(13.55)

so that the individual elements of the dynamic conditional correlation matrix $R_{t+1|t}$ can be written as $\rho_{ijt+1|t} = q_{ijt+1|t}/\sqrt{q_{iit+1|t}q_{jjt+1|t}}$.

Estimation of these models proceeds by maximum likelihood methods. For example, the log-likelihood function of the dynamic conditional correlation model is

$$LL = -\frac{1}{2}\sum_{t=1}^{T}(n\log(2\pi) + \log(|H_{t|t-1}|) + y'_t H_{t|t-1}^{-1} y_t)$$

$$= -\frac{1}{2}\sum_{t=1}^{T}(n\log(2\pi) + 2\log(|D_{t|t-1}|) + \log(|R_{t|t-1}|) + \varepsilon'_t R_{t|t-1}^{-1}\varepsilon_t),$$

(13.56)

where $\varepsilon_t \sim N(0, R_{t|t-1})$ is the standardized residual. Engle and Sheppard advocate using two-stage QMLE estimation. In a first stage, univariate GARCH models are estimated for each residual series and the estimates are used to normalize the residuals by their standard deviation. In the second stage, the normalized residuals are used to estimate dynamic correlations.

A related literature has also considered multivariate quantile models. For example, White Jr, Kim, and Manganelli (2008) use a multiquantile CAViaR specification to study conditional skewness dynamics in daily stock returns, while Cappiello et al. (2014) use time-varying conditional quantiles to study comovements in returns on Latin American equity markets.

13.7 COPULAS

Copulas provide an alternative representation to multivariate distribution functions or densities in a way that may be helpful in generating forecasts. Consider the case where $y_{t+1} = (y_{1t+1}, \ldots, y_{nt+1})$ has a multivariate distribution function P.

By Sklar's theorem (Sklar, 1959), we can decompose P into its individual univariate marginal distributions, $P_1(y_{1t+1}), \ldots, P_n(y_{nt+1})$, and an n-dimensional copula, C, capturing the joint distribution of the marginal distributions, $P(y_{t+1}) = C(P_1(y_{1t+1}), \ldots, P_n(y_{nt+1}))$. While P and C both have n-dimensional inputs, the key distinction is that the arguments in the copula function have uniform marginals. Each of the $P_i(y_i)$ functions are probability integral transforms (see chapter 18) and so will have uniform marginals.

The copula is simply a multivariate cumulative density function with uniform $(0,1)$ marginals. Intuitively, it contains all the dependence information that is not captured in the marginal distributions of the individual variables. An advantage of copulas is that they are invariant under increasing and continuous transformations of the marginals. Hence if $(y_{1t+1}, \ldots, y_{nt+1})'$ has copula C and $G_1, \ldots, G_n$ are increasing continuous functions, $(G_1(y_{1t+1}), \ldots, G_n(y_{nt+1}))'$ also has copula C; see Embrechts, McNeil, and Straumann (2002).

Multivariate ARCH models such as (13.52) capture dependencies across variables through their correlations. This suffices in the context of elliptical distributions which include the Gaussian family. Outside such restrictive families of densities, correlation will not, however, suffice to capture dependencies across variables. In particular, whereas independence of two random variables implies that they are uncorrelated (zero linear correlation), zero correlation does not in general imply independence. For example, if $y \sim N(0, 1)$, y and y^2 are uncorrelated but clearly not independent of each other.

Most relevant for forecasting situations with conditional dynamics in the distribution of the variables is the copula representation conditional on a set of variables Z_t. Assume that $y_{t+1}|Z_t \sim P_{t+1|t}(y_{t+1})$ with marginal distributions $P_{it+1|t}(y_{it+1})$. Then the conditional copula representation takes the form (see Patton, 2006)

$$P_{t+1|t}(y_{t+1}) = C_{t+1|t}(P_{1t+1|t}(y_{1t+1}), \ldots, P_{nt+1|t}(y_{nt+1})). \qquad (13.57)$$

From a forecasting perspective, there are potential benefits admitted from the decomposition in (13.57) of the joint distribution into the marginal distributions and the copula. For example, the marginal distributions may be fairly easy to estimate using the large literature on estimation of univariate distributions. A two-stage estimation approach could first estimate the marginal distributions and then use $u_{it+1|t} = P_{it+1|t}(y_{it+1})$ as input into the conditional copula model. One option here is to estimate the marginal distributions nonparametrically and fit a parametric model to the copula. This approach is appealing given that the marginal distributions are univariate and hence more easily modeled using nonparametric methods than the n-dimensional copula function. The copula approach can also be applied to multivariate density modeling. Multiplying the univariate conditional density estimates, $p_{it+1|t}(y_{it+1})$, by the copula estimates yields the multivariate joint conditional density, $p_{t+1|t}(y_{t+1})$,

$$p_{t+1|t}(y_{t+1}) = c_{t+1|t}(u_{1t+1}, \ldots, u_{n_t+1}) \times p_{1t+1|t}(y_{1t+1}) \times \cdots \times p_{nt+1|t}(y_{nt+1}).$$

$$(13.58)$$

Decompositions such as these may be helpful particularly in cases where the focus is on modeling dependencies for high-dimensional vectors of variables, i.e., when n is very large.

Another advantage from the copula representation in (13.57) is that it affords great flexibility in pairing well-known marginal distributions (e.g., a conditional Gaussian and a skewed-t distribution for two asset returns) with an altogether different copula such as the Gumbel or logistic copula which takes the form

$$C^{\text{Gu}}(u_{1t+1}, \ldots, u_{nt+1}|\beta)$$

$$= \exp\left[-\left\{(-\log(u_{1t+1}))^{1/\beta} + \cdots + (-\log(u_{nt+1}))^{1/\beta}\right\}^{\beta}\right],$$

where $0 < \beta \leq 1$.

Patton (2013) reviews empirical applications of copula models. Most studies of copulas have been to financial data with numerous applications in areas such as risk management, pricing of derivatives, and portfolio selection. The jury is still out on whether, in practice, advantages such as those listed above translate into better multivariate forecasts being produced by copula models than if the forecasts were based on conventional multivariate distributions. Of course, given the one-to-one correspondence between the copula and multivariate distribution function representations, ultimately which approach is most useful may be a question of convenience, i.e., which approach lends itself best to estimation and implementation. For example, the bivariate Gaussian copula takes the form

$$C_\rho(y_1, y_2) = \int_{-\infty}^{\Phi^{-1}(y_1)} \int_{-\infty}^{\Phi^{-1}(y_2)} \frac{1}{2\pi(1-\rho^2)^{1/2}} \exp\left(\frac{-(s^2 - 2\rho st + t^2)}{2(1-\rho^2)}\right) ds\, dt,$$

$$(13.59)$$

and so depends on only a single correlation parameter, ρ. Here Φ is the univariate c.d.f. of a standard Gaussian random variable. If the marginal distributions are also Gaussian, there is no obvious advantage from using the copula representation in (13.59) rather than the bivariate normal distribution function.

13.8 CONCLUSION

A stylized feature of many economic and financial time series is the presence of persistent volatility dynamics. Beginning with the ARCH model of Engle (1982), a large set of methods have been developed to incorporate such dynamics in density forecasts. Techniques have been developed to account for volatility persistence even for multivariate models of large dimension. As always, there is a bias–variance trade-off when deciding whether to use flexible and less biased semi- and nonparametric techniques for estimating density forecasting models versus using parametric models which may reduce the effect of estimation errors on the density forecast but lead to biased forecasts. And, once again, the trade-off involved in the choice between different estimators will ultimately depend on the forecaster's loss function.

Density forecasting has gained increased prominence in many areas of economic forecasting. It is now common for large institutions such as the Bank of England and the IMF to go beyond reporting simple point forecasts to also including indications of the uncertainty surrounding such forecasts. This requires a model for the full distribution of possible future outcomes. Density forecasting is also used in risk management and investment decisions as a way to track likely portfolio losses and determine optimal portfolio allocation given trade-offs between risk and returns.

Given the wide application of volatility and density forecasting in economics and finance, it is worth emphasizing that this is an area where tremendous progress has been made over the last couple of decades. We now possess sophisticated methods that allow us to generate predictive distributions for a wide variety of variables. How to assess the accuracy of such density forecasts is the topic of chapter 18.

14

◇◇

Forecast Combinations

The idea of combining multiple forecasts of the same outcome is intuitively appealing. Individual models are likely to be misspecified and it can often be difficult to identify a single best or "dominant" forecasting model. With two available forecasts, f_1 and f_2, it is thus quite likely that the combined forecast $f^c(f_1, f_2)$ generates a lower expected loss than the individual forecasts:

$$E\left[L(f_i, y)\right] > \min_{f^c(\cdot)} E\left[L(f^c(f_1, f_2), y)\right], \tag{14.1}$$

for $i = 1, 2$. The notation $f^c(f_1, f_2)$ is shorthand for $f^c(f_1(z), f_2(z))$ and f^c refers to the mapping from the two individual forecasts, f_1 and f_2, to the combined forecast. Forecast combination is essentially a model selection and parameter estimation problem that arises as a special case of the issues discussed in previous chapters—albeit a case in which special constraints on the estimation problem play an important role.

Why combine forecasts in the first place? Perhaps one of the oldest understandings in statistics is that when faced with multiple measurements of the same outcome, averaging is a better approach than choosing a single estimate. Empirically, many models or forecasts are often found to have similar predictive accuracy. Taking averages or weighted averages of such forecasts is likely to improve predictive accuracy. If a single model does not separate itself from a larger set of models by producing clearly superior forecasting performance, it makes sense to expect individual models to contribute information over and above what other models offer.

Situations where forecasts are combined can be divided into two cases—those where the data underlying the forecasts are not observed and those for which such data are observed. When the underlying data are not observed, the forecaster can simply treat the observed forecasts as data in the hopes of finding a combination that improves the forecast. This is the traditional view of forecast combination and arises, for example, when forecasts come from surveys. Typically the forecaster will not have access to the underlying information sets used by survey respondents and so the only feasible strategy is to treat the individual forecasts like any other conditioning information and estimate the best possible mapping from the individual forecasts (possibly augmented with other information) to the outcome.[1]

When the data underlying the model forecasts are observed, "model combination" is a more accurate description of the statistical problem. This case typically arises when the researcher constructs forecasts from different models, as in the study by Stock and Watson (1999). It may seem unreasonable to combine forecasts rather than simply gather the information used to construct those forecasts and use standard model procedures to directly map the underlying data to the forecasts. Using a middle step of first constructing forecasts does limit the flexibility of the final forecasting model and hence could increase the risk that the combined forecast does not optimally use all available information. However, model combination might still be attractive. For example, it may not be possible or even reasonable to construct the underlying data. This situation is well summarized by Diebold and Pauly (1990): "While pooling of forecasts is suboptimal relative to pooling of information sets, it must be recognized that in many forecasting situations, particularly in real time, pooling of information sets is either impossible or prohibitively costly."

Moreover, since estimation error plays a role in the final risk of any given forecasting method, model combination yields a different risk function which, through its more parsimonious use of the data, could be attractive to the forecaster. In this sense the combined forecast can be viewed simply as a different estimator of the final model, with a different—and perhaps better—risk for some parts of the parameter space. All estimation methods available when the underlying data are observed can be used in model combination. Researchers can therefore also utilize the underlying data in estimating model combination weights or as part of an extended regression model.

Forecast combination is closely related to the notion of forecast encompassing examined in chapter 17. In the context of equation (14.1), forecast f_1 encompasses forecast f_2 if the minimization results in no role being played by f_2 in the optimal combination; in this case (14.1) holds as an equality rather than as an inequality for $i = 1$. Tests for encompassing can be seen as tests for exclusion of a forecast from a forecast combination, or equivalently testing that there are no gains from taking a weighted average of the forecasts.

Conversely, if a decision is made to combine forecasts, what should be combined? Most obviously, if the information sets underlying the individual forecasts are unobserved, a generalized or "nesting" model cannot be constructed and so it is particularly likely that individual forecasts contribute distinct information. Combinations of forecasts based on different approaches—e.g., linear versus nonlinear forecasts—make it more likely that the combined forecast will be robust to changes in the data-generating process. A third possibility is to combine survey forecasts with forecasts from econometric models. Being based on subjective judgment, survey forecasts may better incorporate true forward-looking information, while formal econometric models have the advantage that they efficiently incorporate historical information.

---

[1] The issue of forecast combination also arises in the context of constructing an aggregate forecast from its individual components as discussed by Hubrich (2005). Hendry and Hubrich (2011) evaluate the effect of adding up forecasts of disaggregate variables to obtain an aggregate forecast versus using disaggregate information to directly forecast the aggregate variable. In the context of forecasting euro-area inflation and real activity, Marcellino, Stock, and Watson (2003) find that summing forecasts from country-specific models delivers more accurate forecasts than those based on euro-area aggregate forecasts.

The outline of the chapter is as follows. Section 14.1 considers the theory on optimal forecast combination. Section 14.2 introduces a variety of estimation schemes that have been proposed in the forecast combination literature. This section also examines the "forecast combination puzzle," i.e., the frequent empirical finding under MSE loss that averaging the forecasts is difficult to improve on. Section 14.4 examines classical model combination methods, section 14.5 examines classical density combination methods, while section 14.6 examines Bayesian model averaging which can provide both density and point forecasts. Section 14.7 provides an empirical example. Section 14.8 concludes.[2]

14.1 OPTIMAL FORECAST COMBINATIONS: THEORY

Results on optimal combinations of forecasts are similar to those discussed in chapter 3 for the construction of an optimal forecast, the key distinction being that the conditioning information is usually restricted to a set of forecasts of the outcome, so $z = \{f_1, \ldots, f_m\}$ if we have m forecasts to combine. The optimal forecast combination, f^{c*}, is a function of the forecasts that solves

$$\min_{f^c} E\left[L(f^c(f_1, f_2, \ldots, f_m), y)\right]. \tag{14.2}$$

Importantly, optimality of the combined forecast as defined in (14.2) is conditional on observing the forecasts, $\{f_1, f_2, \ldots, f_m\}$ rather than the underlying information sets that were used to construct the forecasts. When $f(\cdot)$ is a linear index, the combination is linear with weights $\omega_1, \ldots, \omega_m$. More generally, we can consider any function of the individual forecasts, although this is not often done in practice.

Additional restrictions are often placed on the search for combination schemes. A typical assumption is that the forecasts are unbiased, which reduces the space of linear combination models by constraining the weights to sum to 1. Moreover, because the underlying "data" are forecasts, they can be expected to obtain nonnegative weights that sum to unity, i.e., $0 \leq \omega_i \leq 1$, for $i = 1, \ldots, m$. Such considerations can be used to reduce the relevant parameter space for the combination weights in ways that rule out a variety of methods and may offer a more attractive risk function.

In general there is no need to constrain the information set to include only the set of observed forecasts $\{f_1, \ldots, f_m\}$. This vector could be augmented to include other observed variables, x, to extend (14.2) as follows:

$$\min_{f^c} E\left[L(f^c(f_1, f_2, \ldots, f_m, x), y)\right]. \tag{14.3}$$

Treating the forecasts as data makes forecast combination equivalent to the forecast problem described throughout this book.

Similar to the results in chapter 4, one should realize that the solution is only "optimal" in the sense that (14.2) or (14.3) is minimized. However, when the function needs to be estimated on data, we must also consider the effect of estimation error. Methods based on optimal combinations with suboptimal estimation techniques need not return the best possible forecast combination or have any optimality

---

[2] Reviews of the extensive literature on forecast combination are provided by Clemen (1989) and Timmermann (2006).

properties. Different estimators yield different risk functions that depend on the underlying data-generating process and typically no single optimal method will have a risk function that uniformly dominates all other methods across all possible parameter values. Instead, different families of forecasting methods typically have different risk properties in different parts of the parameter space. This will be borne out in the next section in which we discuss estimation methods for constructing the forecast combinations.

14.1.1 Optimal Combinations under MSE Loss

The majority of results in the forecast combination literature assume MSE loss. To establish intuition for the gains from forecast combination under MSE loss, consider two individual forecasts, f_1, f_2, with associated forecast errors $e_1 = y - f_1$, $e_2 = y - f_2$. Assuming that both forecasts are unbiased, we have $E[e_i] = 0$. Denote the variances of the forecast errors by σ_i^2, $i = 1, 2$ and their covariance by σ_{12}.

Since the individual forecasts are unbiased, the combined forecasts will also be unbiased if the combination weights add up to 1. Consider, therefore, a combination of the two forecasts that uses weights $(\omega, 1 - \omega)$:

$$f^c = \omega f_1 + (1 - \omega) f_2. \tag{14.4}$$

The associated forecast error is a weighted average of the individual forecast errors:

$$e(\omega) = y - \omega f_1 - (1 - \omega) f_2 = \omega e_1 + (1 - \omega) e_2. \tag{14.5}$$

Using that $E[e(\omega)] = 0$, the MSE loss becomes

$$\text{MSE}(e(\omega)) = \omega^2 \sigma_1^2 + (1 - \omega)^2 \sigma_2^2 + 2\omega(1 - \omega)\sigma_{12}. \tag{14.6}$$

The MSE loss in (14.6) is thus a weighted average of the elements of the variance–covariance matrix. Solving for the optimal combination weights, we have

$$\omega^* = \frac{\sigma_2^2 - \sigma_{12}}{\sigma_1^2 + \sigma_2^2 - 2\sigma_{12}}. \tag{14.7}$$

It follows from (14.7) that if the forecast errors have equal variance, $\sigma_1^2 = \sigma_2^2$, so neither forecast dominates the other, it is optimal to assign equal weights to the forecasts, regardless of their correlation.

Intuitively, greater weight is generally assigned to the more precise model, i.e., the one with the smallest σ_i^2. If the forecasts errors are weakly correlated ($\sigma_{12} \approx 0$), the best combination uses a weighted average that weights the individual forecasts in proportion with the inverse of their MSE values:

$$\omega^* \approx \frac{\sigma_2^2}{\sigma_1^2 + \sigma_2^2} = \frac{\sigma_1^{-2}}{\sigma_1^{-2} + \sigma_2^{-2}}. $$

Note that the combination weight can be negative in (14.7) if $\sigma_{12} > \sigma_1^2$ or $\sigma_{12} > \sigma_2^2$. Indeed, if forecasts are strongly correlated and variances are sufficiently different, neither weight will fall between 0 and 1, e.g., $\omega^* > 1$, $1 - \omega^* < 0$. A negative weight on a forecast does not mean that it has no value to the forecaster. It means that the forecast can be used to offset the prediction errors of other models.

Next, consider the optimal forecast combination weights for the more general case with m forecasts. Suppose the joint distribution for the vector of forecast errors $e = \iota_m y - f$ (where ι_m is an $(m \times 1)$ vector of 1s) has zero mean (unbiased forecasts) and variance covariance $\Sigma_e = E[ee']$. Minimizing the MSE subject to the weights adding up to 1 amounts to solving

$$\omega^* = \arg\min_{\omega} \left\{ \omega' \Sigma_e \omega \right\}, \quad \text{subject to} \quad \omega' \iota_m = 1. \tag{14.8}$$

The resulting optimal combination weights are given by

$$\omega^* = (\iota_m' \Sigma_e^{-1} \iota_m)^{-1} \Sigma_e^{-1} \iota_m; \tag{14.9}$$

see Bates and Granger (1969). The associated expected loss is $\omega^{*'} \Sigma_e \omega^* = (\iota_m' \Sigma_e^{-1} \iota_m)^{-1}$. Elliott and Timmermann (2005) show that the optimality of these weights holds for much broader classes of loss functions, including asymmetric loss, provided that the errors are drawn from elliptically symmetric distributions.

Equal weights play a special role in the forecast combination literature. Equation (14.9) allows us to analyze when such weights are optimal in population. One interesting case arises when the individual forecast errors have identical variance, σ^2, and identical pairwise correlations, ρ. Then

$$\Sigma_e^{-1} \iota_m = \frac{\iota_m}{\sigma^2(1 + (m-1)\rho)},$$

$$(\iota_m' \Sigma_e^{-1} \iota_m)^{-1} = \frac{\sigma^2(1 + (m-1)\rho)}{m},$$

and so equal weights are optimal:

$$\omega^* = \frac{1}{m} \iota_m.$$

Such a situation could hold to a close approximation when all forecasting models are based on similar data and hence produce forecasts with roughly the same accuracy. More generally, the optimal combination weights are equivalent to simple averaging over the forecasts when the unit vector lies in the eigenspace of Σ_e. To see this, note that when $\Sigma_e \iota_m = \lambda \iota_m$ for scalar λ, then $\Sigma_e^{-1} \iota_m = \lambda^{-1} \iota_m$, and

$$\omega^* = (\iota_m' \Sigma_e^{-1} \iota_m)^{-1} \Sigma_e^{-1} \iota_m$$

$$= (\lambda^{-1} \iota_m' \iota_m)^{-1} \lambda^{-1} \iota_m$$

$$= m^{-1} \iota_m.$$

That the unit vector lies in the eigenspace of Σ_e is both a sufficient and a necessary condition for equal weights to be optimal. To see this, note that for the optimal weights ω^* to be an eigenvector, we require that $\Sigma_e \omega^* = \lambda \omega^*$ for a scalar λ. However, $\Sigma_e \omega^* = (\iota_m' \Sigma_e^{-1} \iota_m)^{-1} \Sigma_e \Sigma_e^{-1} \iota_m = (\iota_m' \Sigma_e^{-1} \iota_m)^{-1} \iota_m$ and $\lambda \omega^* = \lambda (\iota_m' \Sigma_e^{-1} \iota_m)^{-1} \Sigma_e^{-1} \iota_m$. Equating and dividing both sides by $\lambda (\iota_m' \Sigma_e^{-1} \iota_m)^{-1}$, we have $\lambda^{-1} \iota_m = \Sigma_e^{-1} \iota_m$, so for

ω^* to be an eigenvector, ι_m must be an eigenvector. In the case with identical forecast error variances and identical pairwise correlations, the unit vector clearly lies in the eigenspace of Σ_e because the sums of the rows of Σ_e are identical across each row. The space of variance covariances for which equal weighting is optimal is, however, much wider than this special case. Variances and covariances need not be the same for each row of Σ_e; it is required only that the sums across rows must be equal.

14.1.2 Optimal Combinations under Linex Loss

In the same way that the shape of the loss function matters for the optimal forecast, it also matters to the forecast combination problem. Consider the case with Linex loss:

$$L(e) = \exp(ae) - ae - 1, \tag{14.10}$$

where a controls aversion against large positive ($a > 0$) or large negative ($a < 0$) forecast errors. Assume that the vector of forecast errors $e = y\iota_m - f$ is Gaussian with zero mean and covariance matrix Σ_e so that the forecasts are unbiased. Consider the linear forecast combination scheme

$$f^c = \omega_0 + \omega' f, \quad \text{subject to} \quad \omega' \iota_m = 1.$$

As we shall see, ω_0 can be used to capture an optimal bias. Using that the error from the combination $e^c = y - f^c = y - \omega' f - \omega_0 = \omega' e - \omega_0$, the expected loss becomes

$$E[L(e^c(\omega_0, \omega))] = \exp\left(-a\omega_0 + \frac{a^2}{2}\omega'\Sigma_e\omega\right) + a\omega_0 - 1. \tag{14.11}$$

Taking the derivative with respect to ω_0 and setting this to 0, we have

$$\omega_0^* = \frac{a}{2}\omega'\Sigma_e\omega.$$

In turn, inserting this into the expected loss in (14.11), we see that the weights, ω, should be chosen to minimize $\omega'\Sigma_e\omega$, subject to $\omega'\iota_m = 1$. This is identical to the earlier constrained optimization problem under MSE loss in (14.8) and so the combination weights are given by (14.9). Although the optimal combination weights, ω^*, are unchanged from the case with MSE loss, the intercept ω_0^* accounts for the shape of the loss function and is the only term that depends on the Linex asymmetry parameter, a. The optimal combination has a bias, $a(\iota_m'\Sigma_e^{-1}\iota_m)^{-1}/2$, that reflects the dispersion of the combined forecast error evaluated at the optimal combination weights.

In general, the combination weights need not be identical under MSE and asymmetric loss. For example, when the distribution of forecast errors is a mixture of two Gaussian distributions, the optimal combination is a solution to $m + 1$ nonlinear equations in ω_0 and ω. This setup with a mixture of distributions can be used to capture a situation where one particular forecast is correlated with the outcome only during times when other forecasts break down and so creates a role for this particular forecast as a hedge against model breakdown. See Timmermann (2006) for further discussion of this point.

14.2 ESTIMATION OF FORECAST COMBINATION WEIGHTS

The optimal forecast combination methods described in section 14.1 refer to the population models for the forecast combinations. In practice, the combination weights need to be estimated using past data, just as we do for regular forecasting problems. All the estimation issues treated earlier in the book are therefore directly relevant to the combination problem.

Once we use estimated parameters, solutions to problems such as (14.8) no longer have any optimality properties in a "risk" sense. For any forecast combination problem, there is typically no single optimal forecast method with estimated parameters. Risk functions for different estimation methods will typically depend on the data-generating process in such a way that we prefer one method for some processes and different methods for other data-generating processes.

Treating the forecasts as data means that all issues related to how we estimate forecasting models from data apply and are relevant. Many approaches can therefore be used to estimate the combination weights such as M-estimation or method of moment approaches using the first-order conditions for minimization of loss, plug-in methods based on least squares parameter estimates, or shrinkage methods. Many of the results in the literature on forecast combination simply apply standard estimation methods to the forecast combination problem.

The "data" used in forecast combination are not the outcome of a random draw but can, rather, be regarded as unbiased, if not necessarily precise, forecasts of the outcome. This suggests imposing special restrictions on the combination schemes. Specifically, under MSE loss, linear combination schemes might restrict the combination weights to sum to 1 and be nonnegative, so that $\omega_i \in [0, 1]$. Simple combination schemes such as equal weighting satisfy these constraints and do not require estimation of any parameters. Equal weighting can thus be viewed as a reasonable prior when no data have been observed and plays a similar role to putting zero weights on data in forecasting models.

14.2.1 Estimation of Forecast Combination Weights under MSE Loss

Many different ways exist for estimating the combination weights under MSE loss. The existence of such an extensive list of methods boils down to a number of previously discussed issues in constructing forecasts, namely, the role of estimation error, the lack of a single optimal estimation scheme, along with the empirical observation that simple methods are difficult to beat in practice.

A common baseline is to use a simple equal-weighted average of the forecasts:

$$f^{\text{ew}} = \frac{1}{m} \sum_{i=1}^{m} f_i. \tag{14.12}$$

An advantage of this approach is that it generates no estimation error since the combination weights are imposed rather than estimated. This has obvious intuitive appeal given the restrictions usually imposed on the combination weights. The method also has appeal if, when constructing forecast combinations over time, the panel of forecasts being combined changes dimension or if only a very short time series of the forecasts is available. Concerns about outlier forecasts can be addressed by using the median forecast or the trimmed mean—assuming that m is sufficiently large—instead of the mean.

The trimmed mean works as follows. Suppose the forecasts have been ranked from smallest to largest $f_1, \ldots, f_m$. Trimming a proportion ρ of the smallest and largest forecasts, the trimmed mean is computed as

$$f^{\text{trim}} = \frac{1}{\lfloor m(1 - 2\rho)\rfloor} \sum_{j=\lfloor \rho m\rfloor + 1}^{\lfloor m(1-\rho)\rfloor} f_j, \tag{14.13}$$

where $\lfloor . \rfloor$ rounds to the nearest (smaller) integer.

A natural alternative to these simple robust estimation methods is to use sample estimates for the population-optimal weights in (14.9). Bates and Granger (1969) suggest simply replacing the unknown variances and covariance in the formula for the optimal weights (14.9) with the equivalent sample estimates. More generally, for an $(m \times 1)$ vector of forecasts, the estimated variance–covariance matrix could be used in the formula for the combination weights (14.9). This plug-in solution turns out to be numerically identical to the restricted least squares estimator of the weights from a regression of the outcome on the forecasts and no intercept subject to the restriction that the coefficients sum to 1 ($\hat{\omega}'_{\text{ols}} \iota_m = 1$):

$$f^c = \hat{\omega}'_{\text{ols}} f = (\iota' \hat{\Sigma}_e^{-1} \iota)^{-1} \iota' \hat{\Sigma}_e^{-1} f, \tag{14.14}$$

where f is the vector of forecasts and $\hat{\Sigma}_{\varepsilon}$ is the usual sample estimator of the covariance matrix, $E[ee']$, e.g., $T^{-1} \sum_{t=0}^{T-1} e_{t+1} e'_{t+1}$.

To see the equivalence between the Bates and Granger approach and restricted least squares, consider the linear regression of the outcome on the forecasts:

$$y = f'\omega + \varepsilon. \tag{14.15}$$

Rearranging, we have

$$y = (f - y\iota'_m + y\iota'_m)\omega + \varepsilon$$
$$= -e\omega + y\iota'_m\omega + \varepsilon,$$
$$\text{so} \quad (1 - \omega'\iota_m)y = -e\omega + \varepsilon,$$

where e is the vector of forecast errors. Under the restriction that $\omega'\iota_m = 1$, it follows that $\varepsilon = e\omega$. Minimizing the sum of squared residuals subject to the restriction that the weights sum to 1 is therefore the same as minimizing $\omega'e'e\omega$, and thus gives the same result as Bates and Granger (1969); see Granger and Ramanathan (1984).[3] If there is suspicion that the individual forecasts are biased, a constant can be included in the regression.

Variants of least squares combination weights, much like variants of linear forecasting models with general data, revolve around attempts to reduce risk over some parts of the space of models, where the risk arises from the estimation error

---

[3] Sometimes it is incorrectly asserted that because estimates of the combination weights use an estimate of the $(m \times m)$-dimensional variance–covariance matrix, they are strongly affected by estimation error. However, the numerical equivalence with restricted OLS shows that actually only $m - 1$ estimates of the weights are involved in the estimation.

involved in constructing the weights. One possibility is to use Bayesian or empirical Bayes methods to estimate the combination weights. Clemen and Winkler (1999) propose one such approach that relies on the use of an inverse Wishart distribution on Σ_e.

Different assumptions on priors and model parameters yield different estimators. Diebold and Pauly (1990) suggest both Bayesian and empirical Bayes shrinkage-type methods. Using the results in chapter 5, it follows that for a Gaussian model and Gaussian priors the Bayesian estimator yields forecast combination weights formed as a weighted average of the prior, ω_p, and the least squares estimates, $\hat{\omega}_{\text{ols}}$. As noted above, the natural uninformative prior is to assign equal weights to the forecasts, so suppose that the prior weights on the m forecasts are $\omega_p = \iota_m/m$. Under the g-prior of Zellner (1986b) discussed in chapter 5, where g is a scalar prior that controls the degree of shrinkage with large values of g implying high precision and strong shrinkage towards the prior mean of ι_m/m, the posterior mean of the combination weights becomes

$$\hat{\omega} = m^{-1}\iota_m + \frac{1}{1+g}\left(\hat{\omega}_{\text{ols}} - m^{-1}\iota_m\right), \qquad (14.16)$$

where $\hat{\omega}_{\text{ols}}$ is the OLS estimate of ω in (14.14). More generally, assuming normal priors on ω, $N(\omega_p, \tau^2(Z_f'Z_f)^{-1})$, where Z_f is the $(T \times m)$ matrix of regressors in (14.14), Diebold and Pauly (1990) use empirical Bayes combination weights given by

$$\hat{\omega} = \omega_p + \frac{\hat{\tau}^2}{\hat{\sigma}^2 + \hat{\tau}^2}\left(\hat{\omega}_{\text{ols}} - \omega_p\right), \qquad (14.17)$$

where

$$\hat{\sigma}^2 = (y - Z_f\hat{\omega}_{\text{ols}})'(y - Z_f\hat{\omega}_{\text{ols}})/T,$$

$$\hat{\tau}^2 = (\hat{\omega}_{\text{ols}} - \omega_p)'(\hat{\omega}_{\text{ols}} - \omega_p)/\operatorname{tr}(Z_f'Z_f)^{-1} - \hat{\sigma}^2,$$

where $\hat{\sigma}^2$ is an estimator of the variance of the residuals in the regression model, σ^2. Equation (14.17) is similar to a shrinkage-type estimator for the combination weights.

Between data-free schemes such as equal weighting and methods attempting to approximate the optimal combination weights are methods that utilize data in the forecast combination scheme without attempting to asymptotically obtain the optimal combination weights. The simplest example is the trimmed mean in (14.13) which discards some fraction of the largest and smallest forecasts before taking the mean of the remaining forecasts.

Another frequently used approach simply ignores correlations across forecast errors and uses weights that are proportional to the inverse of the individual models' MSE values, MSE_i:

$$\omega_i = \frac{\text{MSE}_i^{-1}}{\sum_{i=1}^m \text{MSE}_i^{-1}}. \qquad (14.18)$$

A variant of this method is considered by Aiolfi and Timmermann (2006) who propose a robust weighting scheme that lets the combination weights be inversely proportional to the forecast models' rank, Rank_i:

$$\omega_i = \frac{\text{Rank}_i^{-1}}{\sum_{i=1}^{m} \text{Rank}_i^{-1}}. \tag{14.19}$$

Here the model with the lowest MSE value gets a rank of 1, the model with the second lowest MSE performance gets a rank of 2, and so forth. This combination scheme again ignores correlations across forecast errors.

Aiolfi and Timmermann (2006) also consider a factor-based clustering approach. If the outcome variable has a factor structure and the individual forecasts can be clustered according to which factors they track, in some cases little is lost by pooling forecasts within clusters. Their approach is to identify a small set of clusters, form equal-weighted forecasts within each cluster, and then apply least squares combination methods such as (14.14) to these pooled forecasts.

14.2.2 Estimation Methods for Time-Varying Combination Weights

If the joint distribution of the outcome and the forecasts varies through time, it seems attractive to let the combination weights change over time so that they can adapt to such changes. Bates and Granger (1969) propose several adaptive estimation schemes. One approach is to use a rolling window estimate of the models' forecasting performance over the most recent v observations:

$$\hat{\omega}_{it} = \frac{\left(\sum_{\tau=t-v+1}^{t} e_{i\tau}^2\right)^{-1}}{\sum_{j=1}^{m} \left(\sum_{\tau=t-v+1}^{t} e_{j\tau}^2\right)^{-1}}, \tag{14.20}$$

where $e_{i\tau}$ is the ith model's forecast error at time τ. Equation (14.20) is of course just a local estimate of the weights in (14.18). Using a short value for v means putting more weight on the models' recent track record. To account for the shorter data available for estimation, (14.20) simplifies the estimation problem by ignoring correlations between forecast errors.

Alternatively, correlations in forecast errors can be accounted for by using the following rolling window estimation scheme based on (14.9):

$$\hat{\omega}_t = \hat{\Sigma}_{et}^{-1} \iota_m / (\iota_m' \hat{\Sigma}_{et}^{-1} \iota_m),$$

$$\hat{\Sigma}_{et}[i, j] = v^{-1} \sum_{\tau=t-v+1}^{t} e_{i\tau} e_{j\tau}'. \tag{14.21}$$

A third adaptive updating scheme uses a smoothing parameter $\lambda \in (0; 1)$ to discount older forecasting performance:

$$\hat{\omega}_{it} = \lambda \hat{\omega}_{it-1} + (1 - \lambda) \frac{\left(\sum_{\tau=t-v+1}^{t} e_{i,\tau}^2\right)^{-1}}{\sum_{j=1}^{m} \left(\sum_{\tau=t-v+1}^{t} e_{j,\tau}^2\right)^{-1}}. \tag{14.22}$$

The closer to unity is λ, the smoother the combination weights will be.

Yang (2004) proposes an algorithm that aims to identify the best forecasts by minimizing a weighted MSE measure. Assuming equal priors, normal errors, and recursively updated error variance estimates $\hat{\sigma}_{it}^2$ (e.g., $\hat{\sigma}_{it}^2 = \sum_{\tau=1}^{t-1} e_{i\tau}^2/(t-1)$), the weights of the aggregated forecast through exponential reweighting (AFTER) algorithm are

$$\omega_{it} = \frac{\omega_{i1} \left(\prod_{\tau=1}^{t-1} \hat{\sigma}_{i\tau}^{-1} \right) \exp \left(-\frac{1}{2} \sum_{\tau=1}^{t-1} e_{i\tau}^2/\hat{\sigma}_{i\tau}^2 \right)}{\sum_{j=1}^{m} \left(\omega_{j1} \prod_{\tau=1}^{t-1} \hat{\sigma}_{j\tau}^{-1} \exp \left(-\frac{1}{2} \sum_{\tau=1}^{t-1} e_{j\tau}^2/\hat{\sigma}_{j\tau}^2 \right) \right)}, \tag{14.23}$$

where $i = 1, \ldots, m$ and $\tau \geq 1$. Note that this scheme weights the forecast errors relative to the estimated variance $\hat{\sigma}_{it}^2$ with weights that grow larger, the smaller the value of $\hat{\sigma}_{it}^2$. This also means that forecast errors that are large relative to the expected variance $\hat{\sigma}_{it}^2$ can lead to substantial declines in the weights. In an empirical study of the Survey of Professional Forecasters, Lahiri, Peng, and Zhao (2013) find that this method adjusts weights on individual survey participants' forecasts more aggressively following unexpectedly large squared forecast errors compared with least squares methods such as (14.14).[4]

Forecast combinations can work well empirically because they provide insurance against model instability or the types of extraneous structural breaks considered by Hendry and Clements (2004). Empirically, Elliott and Timmermann (2005) allow for regime switching in combinations of forecasts from surveys and time-series models and find strong evidence that the relative performance of the underlying forecasts changes over time.[5] Aiolfi and Favero (2005) study differences in forecasts of stock returns across multiple models and relate them to model uncertainty.

Further illuminating this point, the performance of combined forecasts tends to be more stable than that of individual forecasts used in the empirical combination study of Stock and Watson (2004). Interestingly, combination methods that attempt to explicitly model time variation in the combination weights often fail to perform well, suggesting that regime switching or model "breakdown" can be difficult to predict or even track through time.

14.2.3 Forecast Combination Puzzle

Empirical studies often find that simple equal-weighted forecast combinations perform well compared with more sophisticated combination schemes that rely on estimated combination weights. This finding is known as the forecast combination puzzle. To quote Smith and Wallis (2009), "Why is it that, in comparisons of combinations of point forecasts based on mean-squared forecast errors..., a simple average with equal weights, often outperforms more complicated weighting schemes." Since the optimal combination scheme of Bates and Granger (1969) amounts to restricted least squares under MSE loss, it is indeed puzzling that such a venerated method tends to provide combination weights that are inferior to simply averaging the forecasts.

---

[4] Guidolin and Timmermann (2009) propose to use Markov switching methods to model dynamics in combination weights applied to different forecasts.

[5] Ang, Bekaert, and Wei (2007) find that survey forecasts contain valuable information for forecasting inflation.

Although the least squares combination weights of Bates and Granger (1969) are optimal in population, estimation errors from constructing the weights from data mean that the optimal loss is not achieved in finite samples. Consider combinations of unbiased forecasts under MSE loss. The population loss from optimal combination weights can be expected to be smaller than the loss from using equal weights, i.e., $(\iota_m' \Sigma_e^{-1} \iota_m)^{-1} < m^{-2}(\iota' \Sigma_e \iota)$. However, it is not necessarily the case that $(\iota_m' \hat{\Sigma}_e \iota_m)^{-1} < m^{-2}(\iota' \Sigma_e \iota)$. Errors introduced by estimation of the combination weights could overwhelm any gains from setting the weights to their optimal values rather than using equal weights. Explanations of the forecast combination puzzle based on estimation error must therefore show that (a) estimation error is large and/or (b) the gains from setting the combination weights to their optimal values are small relative to using equal weights.

Consider showing that estimation error is large. In sufficiently large samples OLS estimation error should be of the order $(m - 1)/T$. Unless equal weights are close to being optimal, estimation error is unlikely to be the full story, however, at least when m/T is small. In many situations, m/T will be quite small, although in cases with survey data, m can be large relative to T and so estimation error could be important.

Of course if the optimal population weights are sufficiently close to equal weights, estimation error could still dominate the small gains from using estimated optimal weights; see Smith and Wallis (2009) for some Monte Carlo evidence.

In practice we might expect that poor forecasts get weeded out and so the forecasts included in most combinations have similar forecast error variances, leading to a nearly constant diagonal of Σ_e. In this situation, large differences across correlations would be required to cause deviations from equal weights. Typically the greatest gains from forecast combination arise when correlations are negative since forecasts can then be combined in a way that offsets individual errors. However, a large and unpredictable component of the outcome that is outside and therefore common across all the forecasts, pushes correlations towards positive numbers. Small differences between forecast error variances and positive correlations limit the possibility of large gains from using optimal combination weights rather than equal weights.

Explanations that aim to solve the forecast combination puzzle by means of large estimation errors instead require model misspecification or more complicated data-generating processes than is assumed when estimating the combination weights. One type of model misspecification occurs when the data-generating process changes over time in a way that affects the optimal weights. In this situation, full-sample estimates of the optimal weights will be biased with a bias that grows larger, the bigger and more recent the change in the data-generating process. For example, consider a process for which the constant term shifts discretely to a higher value at one point in the sample. If we use data from before the parameter shift to construct the forecast, the estimated parameters will be a weighted average of the current parameters and the parameters prior to the shift. Equal-weighted forecasts require no estimation and so the shift has no effect on the simple averaged forecast; see Hendry and Clements (2004) for Monte Carlo evidence on the importance of this effect.

14.2.4 Application to Survey Forecasts

We next illustrate some of the most popular combination methods in an empirical application that uses the type of survey data that are commonly used in forecasting.

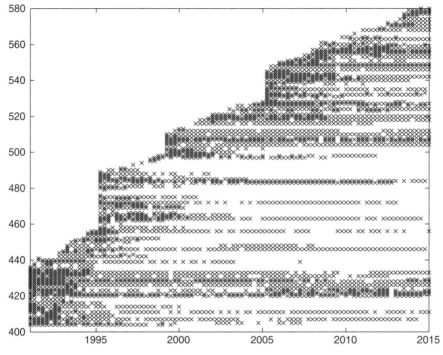

Figure 14.1: Reporting of GDP growth forecasts by participants with IDs above 400 in the Survey of Professional Forecasters. An "x" indicates that the survey participant reported a forecast for the following quarter, while an empty space indicates that the participant failed to report a prediction.

Primary sources of economic surveys used in macroeconomic forecasting include the Survey of Professional Forecasters and the Livingston Survey, both of which are maintained by the Federal Reserve Bank of Philadelphia, Blue Chip forecasts, Confederation of British Industry, Consensus Economics, and the University of Michigan survey of US consumers. In finance there is also the IBES data which survey analysts' earnings forecasts, along with the Gallup investor survey, the Duke survey of CFOs, and the American Association of Individual Investors survey.

Surveys typically take the form of panels of relatively large numbers of participants' forecasts. Importantly, the panels are unbalanced due to the frequent entry, exit, and reentry of individual participants.

As an empirical illustration, we consider one-quarter-ahead forecasts of the unemployment rate and growth in real GDP as reported by the Survey of Professional Forecasters. Forecasters includes commercial banks, individual experts, and professional forecasting firms and each forecaster is assigned a unique code that does not change over time. However, survey participants may exit and reenter the survey over time, and so forecast combination methods such as OLS estimation of the weights are not ideally suited for this type of unbalanced panel data.

Figure 14.1 illustrates how a subset of the individual forecasters (with IDs above 400) enter and exit the survey between 1991 and 2012. The majority of survey participants report real GDP growth forecasts for only relatively short periods of time, and even the forecasters with the longest track record experience some gaps in

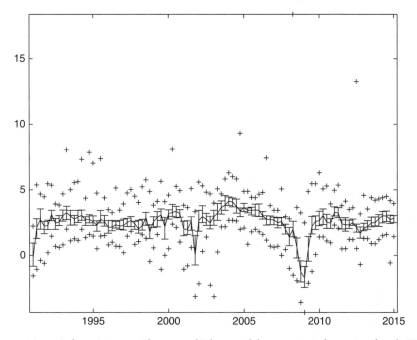

Figure 14.2: Median, interquartile range, highest and lowest point forecasts of real GDP growth from the Survey of Professional Forecasters. The middle of the box indicates the median forecast, outer bounds of the box show interquartile ranges, while the top and bottom "+" indicate the highest and lowest forecasts in a given quarter.

their reporting. The vertical trenches show when new groups of survey participants are added. Clearly the survey data constitute a highly unbalanced panel of forecasts.[6]

A purely statistical combination approach may miss out on any attrition bias that arises if forecasters exiting the survey—who do not subsequently reenter—exit because of poor forecasting performance. This behavior would resemble that observed among mutual funds which are more likely to close down if they have underperformed. If such attrition biases exist, forecast combinations might benefit from simply ignoring missing forecasts, unless they are randomly scattered in time.[7]

Figure 14.2 shows the median, interquartile range, and highest and lowest point forecasts for real GDP growth over the period 1991Q2:2012Q4. There are considerable differences between the most pessimistic and optimistic forecasts in the sample. While movements in the median forecast are much smoother than those of the individual forecasts, there are some notable declines around 2002 and again in 2008 and 2009, coinciding with the recessions during those periods. These are also the main periods where the forecasts of GDP growth turned negative.

Figure 14.3 shows the identity of the best forecaster of the real GDP growth rate using MSE values estimated over the most recent 5-year (top) and 10-year

[6] One way to deal with missing observations in this context is to assume a common factor structure and use an EM algorithm to fill out the missing forecasts. This is easily accomplished and could perform well since there is likely to be a strong commonality between individual survey participants' forecasts.

[7] In an empirical analysis of this issue, Capistrán and Timmermann (2009) find no evidence of attrition biases in the Survey of Professional Forecasters, however.

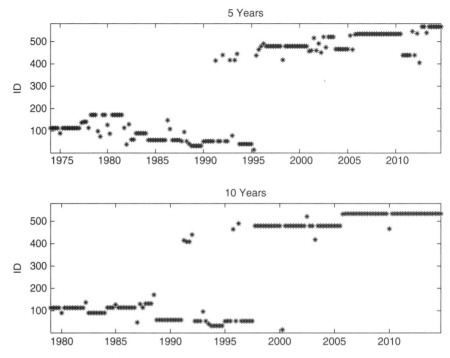

Figure 14.3: Identity of the participant in the Survey of Professional Forecasters with the best track record for GDP growth rate forecasts (measured by mean squared forecast error) over the previous 5 years (top) or the previous 10 years (bottom).

(bottom) periods. A short evaluation window has the advantage that it can quickly identify skilled forecasters as well as quickly eliminate forecasters starting to produce poor forecasts. Conversely, the longer 10-year window can be used to obtain a more precise estimate of the individual forecasters' average performance. In both cases there are periods with some forecasters dominating for a number of years, independently of whether a 5-year or a 10-year window is used. Note that some of this persistence in ranking is induced by the use of a rolling estimation window which is likely to lead to some persistence even in situations without persistence in skills.

Figure 14.4 provides the same plot of the previous best forecast for the unemployment rate data. Again there is evidence that the identity of the best forecaster is persistent, but also that it shifts over time. Note that the shift from low IDs to higher IDs is related to sample attrition—survey participants with the lowest IDs drop out of the sample during the 1990s, whereas participants with the highest IDs are present only during the later parts of the sample after the sample gets replenished. However, even within the two blocks of participants there is a fair amount of turnover despite the fact that the rolling windows induce a certain amount of persistence in the rankings.

Figures 14.5 and 14.6 plot forecasts from the previous best forecaster, the equal-weighted average computed across all survey participants that generate a forecast at a given point in time, and the inverse MSE-weighted average (14.18) for the unemployment rate (figure 14.5) and real GDP growth (figure 14.6). The inverse MSE weights and previous best forecaster variable use a 5-year rolling window.

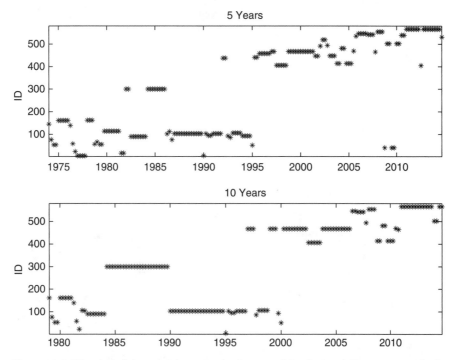

Figure 14.4: Identity of the participant in the Survey of Professional Forecasters with the best track record for unemployment rate forecasts (measured by mean squared forecast error) over the previous 5 years (top) or the previous 10 years (bottom).

For the unemployment series the long-run movements in the forecasts are very similar. This is to be expected given the highly persistent nature of this variable which means that a forecast based mainly on the current unemployment rate will capture most of the variation in this variable.

Conversely, we see bigger and quite pronounced differences in real GDP growth forecasts across the three approaches, suggesting that the choice of combination method is more important for this less persistent variable. Combining forecasts in proportion with the inverse of their MSE values leads to the most volatile forecasts for this variable.

14.3 RISK FOR FORECAST COMBINATIONS

The majority of the combination methods suggested in the literature are to some extent ad hoc. A choice between forecast combination schemes, as with forecast methods in general, is really a choice of risk functions over data-generating processes deemed likely to be relevant for the particular problem at hand.

As in the analysis of the model selection methods in chapter 6, we can examine the risk for the different forecast combination procedures through Monte Carlo simulation. One problem that immediately presents itself is that most combination problems involve a large set of parameters, and the risk could depend on these parameters in a complicated fashion. Rather than attempt to be comprehensive, we employ a simple Monte Carlo design that is representative of the situations faced in

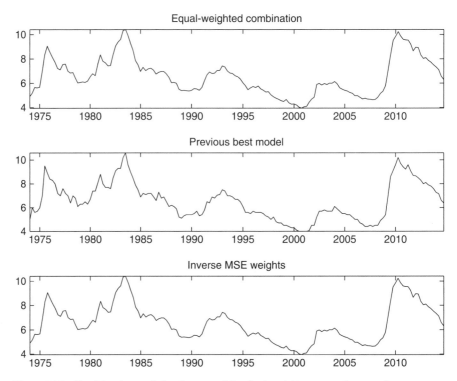

Figure 14.5: Combinations of the Survey of Professional Forecasters' unemployment rate forecasts using the equal-weighted average (top), the previous best forecaster (middle), and inverse MSE weights (bottom). Ranking and estimation is based on a 5-year rolling window.

practice and, more importantly, brings out some of the main practical issues. These are, first, that the Bates and Granger (1969) optimal forecast combination requires estimates of the m-dimensional combination weights and this added estimation error affects risk; second, equal-weighted forecast combinations often perform very well; and, third, no single combination method uniformly dominates for the same reasons as we discuss in chapter 6. In each Monte Carlo simulation there are 100 observations and for each model we report the average over 100,000 simulations.

The design of the Monte Carlo is as follows. We assume that the forecast errors follow a normal distribution $e_{t+1|t} \sim N(0, \Sigma_\alpha)$, where the variance–covariance matrix is such that each forecast has a variance of 1 and all forecasts are correlated with a correlation of 0.5 when $\alpha = 0$. Equal weights are optimal in the baseline case with when $\alpha = 0$. As α changes, the Bates–Granger optimal weights begin to spread out. The variance of the orthogonal and normally distributed residuals is chosen to be 1, which yields an R^2 for the regression of y_{t+1} on the forecasts (without the restriction that the coefficients sum to 1) of about 40%; this value rises slightly with α.

Results from these simulations are shown in figure 14.7. The first column of panels shows results for $m = 3$ forecasts while the second column assumes $m = 10$ forecasts are being combined. The first row of the figure presents MSE values computed relative to the infeasible optimal MSE value which uses the population optimal

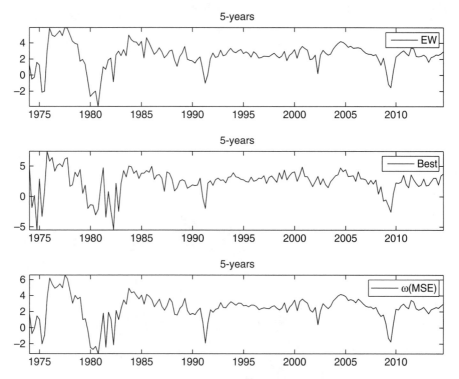

Figure 14.6: Combinations of the Survey of Professional Forecasters' GDP growth rate forecasts using the equal-weighted average (top), the previous best forecaster (middle), and inverse MSE weights (bottom). Ranking and estimation is based on a 5-year rolling window.

weights. The second row plots the combination weights. The bottom row of panels shows the power of a test for equal weights (solid line) and the R^2 for the regression (dashed line).

The first row of graphs in figure 14.7 shows the mean squared error risk relative to the risk that would obtain with the infeasible optimal weights. For example, a value of 1.02 means a 2% higher risk than this benchmark. We examine four combination methods, namely, (a) optimal weights estimated by restricted least squares, as in equation (14.14); (b) equal weights, as in equation (14.12); (c) shrinking the estimate in (a) towards the estimate in (b) as in equation (14.16) with $g = 0.5$; and (d) weighting each estimator by the inverse of the estimated variance of the forecast error, adjusted so that the weights sum to 1, as in equation (14.18). As expected from the properties of least squares estimates, the risk for the restricted least squares combination method in (a) is flat across model designs; for $m = 3$ the risk of this method is 1.02, while for $m = 10$ the risk is 1.1.[8] The risk for the combinations that use equal weights is also as expected. When the true weights are equal to each other ($\alpha = 0$), this scheme obtains the optimal weights without estimation error. However, as the optimal weights become more disperse, the risk of the

[8] In each case we expect that the risk is equal to $1 + (m - 1)/100$, where we subtract 1 because of the restriction on the weights. The difference is due to Monte Carlo error.

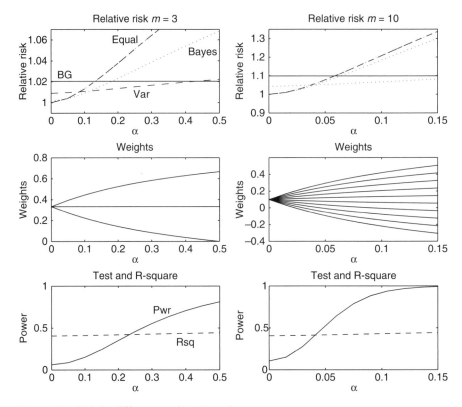

Figure 14.7: Risk for different combination schemes.

equal-weighted combination method increases due to the bias component of the MSE. Arguments that relate the better empirical performance of equal weights to the avoidance of estimation error rely on the weights being close enough to equal so that the bias component does not outweigh gains from reducing the variance component arising from not having to estimate the weights with data.

The panels in the second row in figure 14.7 show how the Bates–Granger optimal weights begin to spread out as we vary α along the horizontal axis.

As α rises the magnitude of a Wald test for equal weights increases to the point where the restriction would typically be rejected. This is illustrated in the third row of figure 14.7. It is noticeable that tests for equal weights need to reject with quite high power before the equal-weighted combination starts to produce higher risk than the combination schemes that rely on estimated weights. For $m = 10$ the weights must be far enough apart that the power of the test for equal weights is about 60%. For this case the optimal weights are quite disperse at this point. Shrinking the estimated weights towards the equal weights (combination scheme (c) in our simulations) has the expected effect, with risk typically falling between the risk of the two underlying methods that this shrinkage scheme is based on. However, the shrinkage combination method does not uniformly dominate either estimating the weights or imposing equal weights. Finally, ignoring correlations and using only the variances of the forecast errors (combination scheme (d)) does not result in a particularly attractive risk profile in these simulations.

When interpreting these results one should bear in mind that Monte Carlo studies reveal the risk at a few selected points in the parameter space, but often give a very incomplete picture of the trade-offs involved in choosing different combination schemes. Nevertheless, we think it is safe to conclude from these simulations that no combination method universally results in the lowest risk. Moreover, which method performs best will depend on the true data-generating process which of course is unknown. Hybrid methods that try to choose between using either estimated weights or equal weights do not uniformly dominate the underlying methods that they are based on.

14.4 MODEL COMBINATION

When the data underlying the individual forecasts are observed, we might consider constructing forecasts from many different models and averaging over the resulting forecasts. With the exception of the first step of constructing the individual forecasts, this setup is identical to the forecast combination problem discussed so far. Indeed, if we ignore how the forecasts were constructed, all the methods discussed in section 14.1 are available for combination of models. However, in model combination it is explicitly understood that the models depend on similar data and that such data are available for constructing the model weights. Treating the individual forecasts as if they are fixed therefore does not make sense when considering their sampling properties. Moreover, ignoring information about how the model forecasts were constructed might underutilize the available data. Model combination seeks to address this issue.

For linear combinations the model average forecast is

$$f^c = \sum_{i=1}^{m} \omega_i f_i,$$

where the individual forecasts f_i depend on some underlying data, z_t. We typically assume that the weights sum to 1 and often restrict them to be nonnegative.

One approach to constructing model averages uses weights that depend on the AIC. Hjort and Claeskens (2003) show that the resulting weights can be approximated by

$$\omega_i \approx \frac{\exp(-0.5\,\mathrm{AIC}_i)}{\sum_{i=1}^{m} \exp(-0.5\,\mathrm{AIC}_i)}, \tag{14.24}$$

so that models with the smallest value of AIC, and thus the best fit relative to the penalty factor, are assigned the greatest weight in the combination. This method does not require that the models in the combination are linear regressions; see chapter 6 on the generality of the AIC criterion. Basing the weights on the AIC means that the underlying data matter both through the fit of the forecasting models and through differences in the penalty applied to forecasting models of different dimensions. Other information criteria such as the BIC can also be used as we discuss below.

Hansen (2007, 2008a) suggest combining linear regression models with weights constructed to minimize the Mallows C_p criterion. His setup considers m covariates that have a natural ordering from 1 to m.[9] We can then construct sets of covariates z_i that contain all of the z-variables from 1 to $i \leq m$, so z_i is $i \times 1$. This method requires a nested setup for the models and ignores the possibility that variables 1 and 3 are included but variable 2 is not. Moreover, the method is not invariant to the ordering of the variables. Different orderings, even when based on the same method, might lead to different results.

The approach works as follows. For each model, project y onto z_i, yielding forecast errors e_i. Placing these forecast errors in a $(T \times m)$ matrix, e, the weights are selected as

$$\hat{\omega}_H = \arg\min_{\omega} \omega' e' e \omega + 2\hat{\sigma}^2 k' \omega,$$

$$\text{subject to} \quad \omega' \iota_m = 1, \quad \omega_i \geq 0 \text{ for } i = 1, \ldots, m.$$

Here ω are the weights, $\hat{\sigma}^2$ is an estimate of the variance of the residual for the true model—in Hansen (2007) this is a model with an infinite number of regressors—and k is an $(m \times 1)$ vector with elements k_i equal to the number of regressors in the ith regression. In practice, Hansen suggests estimating $\hat{\sigma}^2$ from a model that uses all m regressors. The objective function used is similar to that of Bates and Granger (1969) evaluated at the estimated variance–covariance matrix, with the addition of a term that penalizes the models differently for having different sizes through the vector k. The method is developed for outcomes and regressors that are i.i.d., but the method can be employed more generally although without the properties established in Hansen (2007).

14.4.1 Complete Subset Regressions

Elliott, Gargano, and Timmermann (2013) propose an estimation method that uses equal-weighted combinations of forecasts based on all possible models restricted to include a fixed (given) number of regressors, $k \leq K$. The approach, which they name complete subset regressions, first regresses the outcome, y_t, on a given subset of the regressors, then averages the results across all k-dimensional subsets of the regressors.

Assuming K regressors in the full model and k regressors chosen for each of the subset models, there will be $n_{k,K} = K!/(k!(K-k)!)$ subset regressions to average over. For example, the univariate case, $k = 1$, yields $n_{1,K} = K$ regressions, each of which includes a single variable.[10] All elements of $\hat{\beta}_i$ are 0 except for the least squares estimate of y on x_i in the ith row. The equal-weighted combination of forecasts from the individual univariate regression models becomes

$$f^c = \frac{1}{K} \sum_{i=1}^{K} x_i' \hat{\beta}_i. \tag{14.25}$$

Subset regression coefficients can be computed as averages over least squares estimates of the subset regressions. When the covariates are correlated, the individual regressions will be affected by omitted variable bias, but Elliott, Gargano, and

---

[9] This situation could occur if the models are successive lengths of an autoregression or from a series expansion.

[10] This approach is applied by Rapach, Strauss, and Zhou (2010) to forecast stock returns.

Timmermann (2013) show that the subset regression estimators are themselves approximately a weighted average of the full regression OLS estimator, $\hat{\beta}_{\text{ols}}$. Assume that K is fixed and let S_i be a $(K \times K)$ matrix with 0s everywhere except for 1s in the diagonal cells corresponding to included variables, so that if the (j, j) element of S_i is 1, the jth regressor is included, while if this element is 0, the jth regressor is excluded.

Provided that as the sample size gets large, $\hat{\beta}_{\text{ols}} \to^p \beta_0$ for some β_0 and $T^{-1}X'X \to^p \Sigma_X$, the estimator for the complete subset regression, $\hat{\beta}_{k,K}$, can be written as

$$\hat{\beta}_{k,K} = \Lambda_{k,K} \hat{\beta}_{\text{ols}} + o_p(1), \tag{14.26}$$

where

$$\Lambda_{k,K} \equiv \frac{1}{n_{k,K}} \sum_{i=1}^{n_{k,K}} \left(S_i' \Sigma_X S_i \right)^- \left(S_i' \Sigma_X \right).$$

In the special case where the covariates are orthonormal and $\hat{\beta}_{k,K} = \lambda_{k,K} \hat{\beta}_{\text{ols}}$ with $\lambda_{k,K} = 1 - (n_{k,K-1}/n_{k,K})$ being a scalar, subset regression reduces to Ridge regression.

The amount of shrinkage implied by $\lambda_{k,K}$ depends on both k and K and the smaller is k relative to K, the greater the amount of shrinkage. This result relates shrinkage provided by model averaging to shrinkage on the individual coefficients whereas a typical Bayesian approach would separate the two. In general $\Lambda_{k,K}$ reduces to the Ridge estimator, either approximately or exactly, only if the regressors are uncorrelated. If this does not hold, subset regression coefficients cannot be interpreted as the outcome of simple regressor-by-regressor shrinkage of the OLS estimates, and instead depend on the full covariance matrix of all regressors.

Figure 14.8 illustrates the complete subset regression approach for our earlier application to US stock returns. We use a list of 11 possible predictor variables, so $K = 11$ in this application. Along the horizontal axis we plot k, the number of included predictors which varies from $k = 0$ (the prevailing mean) to $k = 11$ (kitchen sink model). The root mean squared error is plotted on the vertical axis. For each value of k, the column of circles shows the RMSE values of all models with exactly k predictors, whereas the solid triangle shows the average RMSE value computed across these models. For example, there are 11 different RMSE values for $k = 1$ and for $k = 10$, and 55 different RMSE values for $k = 2$ and for $k = 9$. The range of values is larger in the middle, reflecting in part the bigger set of models being compared for these middle values of k. Note, however, that the average RMSE performance for a given value of k is trending upwards as k grows larger. This reflects the increased importance of estimation error for larger sets of regressors.

The curved line underneath the circles gives the RMSE value for the complete subset regressions corresponding to a given value of k. Notably, this line is lower than the lowest RMSE value of any individual model with the same number of regressors. The minimum value of the complete subset regression line is reached for $k = 2$. At this point (as well as for $k = 1$ or $k = 3$), the RMSE of the complete subset regression forecast is lower than that of the prevailing mean. It is also lower than the RMSE associated with the equal-weighted average forecast computed across all models, which tends to put too much weight on models with large numbers of regressors and poor forecasting performance.

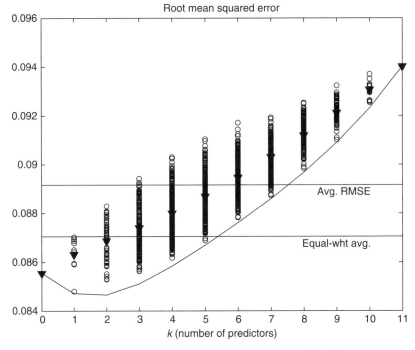

Figure 14.8: Complete subset regression combination forecasts of stock returns using 11 predictors.

In settings with large-dimensional sets of predictors with weak power, Elliott, Gargano, and Timmermann (2015) show analytically that the complete subset regression approach achieves variance reduction and find empirically in applications to US unemployment, GDP growth, and inflation (as well as in Monte Carlo simulations) that the approach establishes a more favorable bias–variance trade-off than univariate models or dynamic factor models.

14.4.2 Empirical Illustration

To illustrate the various model combination approaches, we study monthly growth in the industrial production index, $\Delta \log(IP_t)$. We consider three univariate and one multivariate approach to forecasting this variable, namely (AR) models (described in chapter 7); artificial neural net (ANN) models (chapter 11); and smooth threshold autoregressive (STAR) models (chapter 8), all with lag length selected by the AIC—and multivariate dynamic factor models (chapter 10). We first consider which of these models gets selected based on past MSE performance. This will of course vary with the length of the evaluation window, so we consider both 5- and 10-year windows. Our estimation sample runs from 1948:01 to 1969:12, which leaves the period 1970:01–2010:12 for out-of-sample forecast evaluation.

Figure 14.9 presents the results. If one model were dominant, we would expect it to get selected in most periods, barring random variation. This is not what we find. In fact, the dynamic factor model seems to dominate in the earliest part of the sample, followed by a period where the AR model performs best under the 5-year evaluation window method, while the STAR model is best under the 10-year evaluation window.

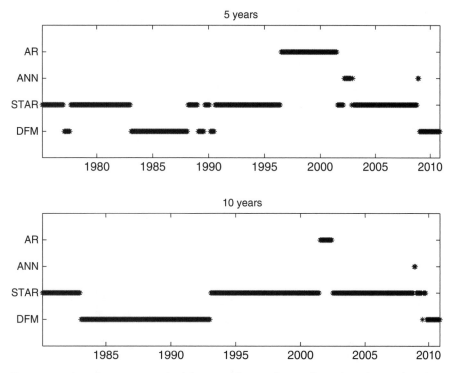

Figure 14.9: Best forecasting method for monthly growth in industrial production based on the root mean squared forecast error calculated over a rolling 5-year window (top) or a rolling 10-year window (bottom) for autoregressive (AR), artificial neural net (ANN), smooth threshold autoregression (STAR), and dynamic factor (DFM) models.

Figure 14.10 shows how the OLS estimates of the combination weights on STAR and DFM forecasts evolve over time. The weights show considerable variation over time, with the weight on the STAR forecasts being particularly volatile, and differ sharply from the value of 0.25 implied by equal weighting across the four forecasting methods.

How sensitive are the forecasts to using different weighting schemes? To address this issue, figure 14.11 plots time series of forecasts from combinations that use equal weights (top), OLS weights (second), inverse MSE weights (third), and the previous best model (bottom). The forecasts are quite similar but also show notable differences with the OLS weights leading to the greatest range of forecast variation. The similarities in performance across different combination schemes indicate that there are not great gains to be had by using the more complicated combination schemes such as OLS weighting or inverse MSE weighting compared with simply using equal weights.

Table 14.1 reports out-of-sample forecasting performance for the various forecast combination schemes in addition to the previous best model and the performance of the individual models. The left column reports RMSE values, while the right column shows values for the Diebold–Mariano test statistic, computed relative to the equal-weighted combination forecast which is thus the benchmark. Positive values

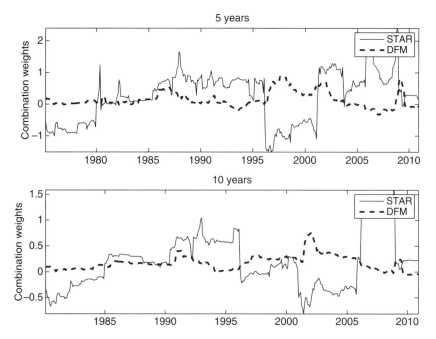

Figure 14.10: Estimated forecast combination weights on autoregressive (AR), artificial neural net (ANN), smooth threshold autoregression (STAR), and dynamic factor (DFM) models using rolling 5-year (top) and rolling 10-year (bottom) estimation windows applied to monthly growth in industrial production.

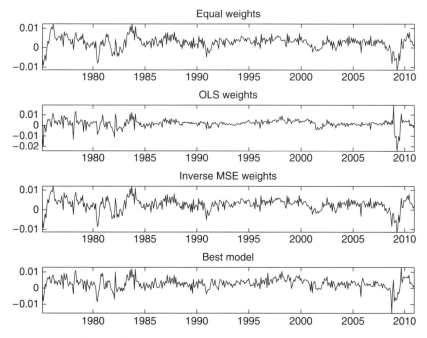

Figure 14.11: Combined forecasts using equal weights (EW), recursively estimated least squares weights (OLS), inverse MSE weights (MSE), and the previous best forecast method applied to the monthly growth in industrial production.

TABLE 14.1:
Root mean squared errors for out-of-sample forecasts of the monthly growth in industrial production based on rolling 10-year estimation windows. The top panel shows results for different combination methods, while the bottom panel shows results for the individual forecasting models with lag length selected by the AIC.

Method	RMSE	DM stats
EW	0.6685	0.0000
Previous best	0.7113	−1.4885
Inverse MSE	0.6672	0.3949
OLS	0.6933	−1.4792
AR	0.6720	−0.3420
ANN	0.6761	−0.5845
STAR	0.6972	−1.5199
DFM	0.8315	−3.4361

are indicative that a method generates more accurate forecasts than this benchmark, while negative values suggest the opposite. The results confirm the impression from figure 14.11. Indeed, the equal-weighted combination produces the second lowest RMSE value after the inverse MSE weighting and the two approaches differ only by a small margin.

Selecting the single model with the previous best forecast performance appears to be a bad forecasting strategy. It is also of interest to compare the combination approach to the performance of the individual models. From the bottom part of table 14.1 it is clear that the best combination strategy always performs better than the best individual model. This is again an argument for combining models, rather than attempting to select a single best model.

14.4.3 Risk of Model Combinations

We use the BIC to compare the choice between using a single model versus a combination of models. Specifically, we compare the outcomes when the BIC is used to select a single model against the result when the BIC is used to compute model combination weights, described below in (14.35). Consider the experiment in chapter 6, in which the data-generating process has eight uncorrelated regressors, three of which have coefficients that are local to 0—with parameter values shown on the x-axis in figure 14.12. The remaining five coefficients are 0. Risk functions under MSE loss are reported for four methods: (i) the correctly specified regression with coefficients estimated by OLS—this is the lower flat line; (ii) an approach that includes all eight variables in an OLS regression—the higher flat line; (iii) the forecast model selected by the BIC with parameters estimated by OLS—the humped line; (iv) the combination of all possible models using BIC weights and OLS estimation—the quadratic-looking line.

The shapes of the risk functions are as expected. Selection by BIC does well when all coefficients are 0, and also when the coefficients are large enough that the BIC reliably picks the correct model. Between these cases, the risk of the BIC approach is quite high, however, as discussed in chapter 6. The shape of the risk function is also as expected for the BIC-weighted combination. When all of the coefficients are 0, this

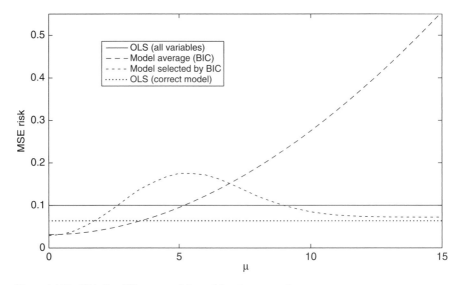

Figure 14.12: Risk for different model combination strategies.

approach puts large weights on the smaller models. As the coefficients become larger, the combination approach continues to place substantial weight on models that are not good predictors, and so the risk becomes large. The results show that the model selection and model combination methods differ both when the coefficients are near 0 and when they are further away from 0. Averaging effectively removes the hump from the risk function caused by the selection of a single model, but at the expense of doing poorly when the true model begins to reveal itself.

14.5 DENSITY COMBINATION

So far we have examined the combination of point forecasts generated by different models or forecasters. When individual forecasts are provided as densities rather than single points, we can also consider providing a combined—or pooled—density. Linear combinations of point forecasts take the form

$$f^c = \sum_{i=1}^{m} \omega_i f_i.$$

Similarly, linear combinations of density forecasts take the form

$$p^c(y) = \sum_{i=1}^{m} \omega_i p_i(y), \qquad (14.27)$$

where $p_i(y)$ are the individual density forecasts for an outcome y, and ω_i are the combination weights. To ensure that the combined density is itself a valid density, we require that it be nonnegative over the entire support of y and that it integrates to 1. We achieve this by restricting the weights to sum to 1, $\sum_{i=1}^{m} \omega_i = 1$, and by imposing that the weights are nonnegative, so $0 \leq \omega_i \leq 1$ for all i. The combined density is thus a mixture of the individual densities. Authors such as Wallis (2005) consider equal weighting, so $\omega_i = 1/m$. In the statistical literature (14.27) is known as a linear prediction pool or linear opinion pool.[11]

The key difference between point forecasting and density forecasting is that whereas in point forecasting the outcome is observed, in density forecasting the density of the outcome is not observed—only a single draw from this outcome is observed. It is from this difference that most of the different approaches to density forecast combination arise.

The problem of combining distributions has been a topic in the statistics literature for some time. In the prequential approach of Dawid (1984), the provision of a predictive distribution for variables rather than parameter estimation is the goal of statistical inference. This approach has been highly influential and led to the development of many of the results in this chapter.

Denote the mean of $p_i(y)$ by μ_i and its variance by σ_i^2. It follows from simple calculation in (14.27) that $p^c(y)$ has mean $\mu_c = \sum_{i=1}^{m} \omega_i \mu_i$ and variance $\sum_{i=1}^{m} \omega_i \left(\sigma_i^2 + (\mu_c - \mu_i)^2 \right)$. From this it can be seen that the combined density is centered between the individual densities. If the means of the individual distributions are disparate, the spread of the combined density will be wide, potentially even wider than that of any of the individual densities. This width represents the lack of information in the individual densities in pinpointing the best location of the actual density. If the means are all similar, the spread of the combined density will be somewhere in the middle of the spreads of the individual densities.

Clemen and Winkler (1999) discuss properties of linear aggregation methods. Linear aggregates of the form in (14.27) have the property of unanimity, which is that if all densities used in the combination give the same weight to an outcome, then so does the combined density.

We can also consider nonlinear density combinations, where $p^c(y) = H(p_1(y), p_2(y), \ldots, p_m(y))$. There are strong restrictions on the form that $H(\cdot)$ can take since we require $p^c(y)$ to be a valid density that is everywhere nonnegative and integrates to 1. A popular approach is the log combination method which sets

$$p^c(y) = \left(\int \prod_{i=1}^{m} p_i(y)^{\omega_i} d\mu \right)^{-1} \prod_{i=1}^{m} p_i(y)^{\omega_i}, \qquad (14.28)$$

where μ is the underlying counting measure. This is guaranteed to keep the density nonnegative and ensures that it integrates to 1. See Genest and Zidek (1986) for further discussion of this approach.

Many of the issues that arise in the combination of point forecasts are also important to the combination of density forecasts. First, the individual density forecasts might be the only statistics observed. Alternatively, we might actually observe the models and data used to generate the density forecasts, in which case density model combination would be the more appropriate term. The majority of combination methods rely on some form of loss function over the densities. This again brings up the question of whether the underlying data should be used rather than the forecast densities constructed from different models. Ideally, the loss function should play some role in the construction of the density combinations.

---

[11] In the context of combination of subjective probability distributions, the term opinion pool is usually attributed to Stone (1961).

14.5.1 Classical Approach to Density Combination

One approach combines densities by means of some loss function. Unlike in the point forecasting problem, we do not directly observe the outcome density—we observe only a draw from this—and so cannot directly choose the weights to minimize the loss between this object and the combined density. One way around this is to use a loss function that does not require knowing the density for the outcome variable; this leads directly to Kullback–Leibler loss.

The Kullback–Leibler (KL) loss for a linear combination of densities $\sum_{i=1}^{m} \omega_i p_i(y)$ relative to some unknown true density $p(y)$ is given by

$$
\begin{aligned}
\mathrm{KL} &= \int p(y) \ln \left(\frac{p(y)}{\sum_{i=1}^{m} \omega_i p_i(y)} \right) dy \\
&= \int p(y) \ln (p(y)) \, dy - \int p(y) \ln \left(\sum_{i=1}^{m} \omega_i p_i(y) \right) dy \\
&= C - E \ln \left(\sum_{i=1}^{m} \omega_i p_i(y) \right),
\end{aligned}
$$

where C is constant across all choices of the weights, ω_i. Hence, minimizing the KL distance is the same as maximizing the log score in expectation.

The use of the log score to evaluate the density combination is one of the more popular approaches in the literature. Geweke and Amisano (2011) use this approach to combine GARCH, hierarchical Markov normal mixture, and stochastic volatility models for predicting the density of daily stock returns. See also Hall and Mitchell (2007).

Under the log score criterion, estimation of the combination weights becomes equivalent to maximizing the log-likelihood. Given a sequence of observed outcomes for y, $\{y_t\}_{t=1}^{T}$, the sample analog is to maximize

$$
\hat{\omega}_T = \arg \max_{\omega_T} (T-1)^{-1} \sum_{t=1}^{T-1} \ln \left(\omega_{iT} \, p_{it+1|t}(y_{t+1}) \right),
$$

$$
\text{subject to} \quad \omega_{iT} \geq 0, \ \sum_{i=1}^{m} \omega_{iT} = 1, \ \text{for all } i.
$$

Estimation of these weights can be undertaken using a constrained optimization program that treats $p_{it}(y)$—the density evaluated at the outcome—as the data. In the case with $m = 2$, they note that if one model nests another and the smaller model is correctly specified, in the limit the two densities will be identical. Thus, in the limit the second-order condition is 0 for all sets of weights. In practice this might not be a problem since in this case the two densities are the same and so any weighting will provide the same results for the combined density.

The log score (or KL distance) is not the only candidate scoring rule that could be employed. Any proper scoring rule can be employed. Other scoring rules that have been suggested in the literature include quadratic scoring (QS) and the continuous ranked probability score (CRPS). See Gneiting and Raftery (2007) for further discussion.

14.6 BAYESIAN MODEL AVERAGING

Bayesian model averaging (BMA) typically examines combinations of the form

$$p^c(y) = \sum_{i=1}^{m} \omega_i \, p(y|M_i), \qquad (14.29)$$

where the BMA weights ω_i are posteriors for the individual models, M_i. The combined forecast is a weighted average of the individual models' forecasts with weights proportional to the posterior for the models. BMA is, as the name suggests, a model averaging procedure rather than a predictive density combination procedure per se. This means that it assumes the availability of both the data underlying the construction of each of the densities, $p_i = p(y|M_i)$, along with knowledge of how the data are employed to obtain a predictive density. BMA methods also apply more generally than indicated here—rather than y being the object of interest as it is in this book, we might instead be interested in a parameter which would then replace y in the derivations below. More broadly, the primary motivation for BMA is as a way of dealing with model uncertainty. Of course, this also explains its interest to forecasters.

Denote the m models by $M_1, \ldots, M_m$. Let $p(M_i)$ be the prior probability that model i is the true model, while Z is the data. Then the posterior probability for model i can be written

$$p(M_i|Z) = \frac{p(Z|M_i)p(M_i)}{\sum_{j=1}^{m} p(Z|M_j)p(M_j)}. \qquad (14.30)$$

The combined model average is then

$$p^c(y) = \sum_{i=1}^{m} p(y|M_i)p(M_i|Z). \qquad (14.31)$$

The marginal likelihood of model i in (14.30) is given by

$$P(Z|M_i) = \int P(Z|\theta_i, M_i)P(\theta_i|M_i)d\theta_i, \qquad (14.32)$$

where $p(\theta_i|M_i)$ is the prior density of model i's parameters, and $p(Z|\theta_i, M)$ is the likelihood of the data given the parameters and model i.

The difficulty in constructing BMA estimates lies in the complexity of obtaining the objects required to construct the weighted average given above; see Hoeting et al. (1999) for a detailed discussion. Initially a list of models, $M_1, \ldots, M_m$, considered in the combination must be constructed. After choosing the set of candidate models, three issues must be confronted in implementing BMA methods. First, computation of $p(M_i|Z)$ in (14.30) requires computation of $p(Z|M_i)$ in (14.32). Although this is a typical Bayesian estimation problem with plenty of algorithms available for different models, it is time consuming and must be undertaken separately for each model. Second, if m is large, repeated computation of these objects becomes difficult or infeasible unless there are closed-form solutions for the marginal likelihood. Finally, researchers must provide prior probabilities for all of the models, $p(M_1), \ldots, p(M_m)$ and (assuming the models are known) priors for the model parameters, $P(\theta_1|M_1), \ldots, P(\theta_m|M_m)$. For large values of m such choices are not obvious when many of the models are related to other models.

For linear regression models with normal priors, closed-form solutions are available to solve (14.32). Applying BMA methods to such forecasting models is therefore straightforward. This explains the popularity of the approach. For example, consider the set of forecasting models

$$y = X_i'\beta_i + W\gamma + u_i, \tag{14.33}$$

where the regressors in W are always included, X_i represents k_i additional regressors included in model i, constructed to be orthogonal to W by using the residuals from a regression of the individual X-variables on W. Assuming that the predictors are strictly exogenous, with $u_i \sim N(0, \sigma_i^2)$ and placing an uninformative prior on (γ, σ^2) and a Zellner (1986b) g-prior on β_i, the posterior for $y_1, \ldots, y_t$ given (X, W) has a closed-form solution—in the above notation this is $p(Z|M_i)$ for each model M_i. Following Magnus, Powell, and Prüfer (2010), apart from assigning equal prior probabilities to each model, the resulting weights are given by[12]

$$p(M_i|Z) = \frac{\left(\frac{1}{1+g_i}\right)^{k_i/2} \left(\frac{1}{1+g_i} \mathrm{SSR}_{-i}^R + \frac{g_i}{1+g_i} \mathrm{SSR}_i^U\right)^{-d/2}}{\sum_{i=1}^m \left(\frac{1}{1+g_i}\right)^{k_i/2} \left(\frac{1}{1+g_i} \mathrm{SSR}_{-i}^R + \frac{g_i}{1+g_i} \mathrm{SSR}_i^U\right)^{-d/2}}, \tag{14.34}$$

where, for each model M_i, SSR_i^U is the sum of squared residuals from regression (14.33) and SSR_{-i}^R is the sum of squared residuals from the same regression that omits the X_i-variables, and d is the number of degrees of freedom from the regression omitting the X_i-variables. To implement (14.34), we need to specify a value for g_i. Fernandez, Ley, and Steel (2001) and Magnus, Powell, and Prüfer (2010) suggest setting $g_i = \max(T, k_i^2)^{-1}$.

Raftery, Madigan, and Hoeting (1997) suggest a different set of priors that do not result in such closed-form solutions and instead provide an MC^3 algorithm to estimate the BMA weights. Koop and Potter (2007) consider a set of priors, which differ from the g-prior approach by using an informative prior for the variance. They also use principal components methods to first orthogonalize the X_i-variables since orthogonal components are required in their algorithm.

In cases where the models' marginal likelihoods in (14.32) are difficult to compute, one can use a simple approximation. Recall from chapter 6 that the Bayesian Information Criterion (BIC) is given by

$$\mathrm{BIC}_i = -2\,\mathrm{LL}_i / T + k_i \ln(T)/T,$$

where LL_i is the log-likelihood of model M_i, k_i is the number of parameters estimated for this model, and T is the sample size. The BIC provides an asymptotic approximation to the marginal likelihood, $\ln(P(Z|M_i)) \approx \mathrm{BIC}_i$. Hence, the BMA

---

[12] Note that Magnus, Powell, and Prüfer (2010) define g_i in the g-prior to be the inverse of how we have defined it elsewhere in this book, so their g_i is our $1/g_i$.

weights can be approximated by

$$\omega_i = P(M_i|Z) \approx \frac{\exp(-0.5 \, \mathrm{BIC}_i)}{\sum_{i=1}^{m} \exp(-0.5 \, \mathrm{BIC}_i)}. \tag{14.35}$$

One approach to lessening the computational workload, especially if m is large, is to consider only a subset of the models in the model averaging. If this approach is taken, a procedure for choosing which models to include and which models to ignore must be adopted. One method is to remove models from consideration if they appear not to be very good. Raftery, Madigan, and Hoeting (1997) suggest removing models for which $p(M_i|Z)$ is much smaller than the posterior probability of the best model. For example, a large model with a relatively low posterior probability would be excluded from the set of models under consideration. The final model average is not a weighted sum over all m original models, but over only a subset of them. An alternative method for including a subset of models is to use a simulation approach to approximating the average in (14.31). This approach uses Monte Carlo methods that require only a subset of the models to actually be evaluated.

Finally, consider how the prior probabilities are set. Any information that can guide this choice should of course be used, but often there are no particular reasons to ex ante prefer some models over others.[13] The linear regression model requires setting priors over the slope parameters. Since these parameters appear in many of the submodels, internal consistency requires the same coefficients to have the same priors across different models. Typically a conjugate prior is chosen. For the normal regression model it is common to assume that $p(\beta|\sigma^2) \sim N(\beta_0, \Omega)$ on the full set of parameters; for each model the prior is then a subset of these parameters. For example, the Zellner g-prior satisfies this internal consistency constraint.

Turning to the model priors, an obvious approach is to set the priors $p(M_i)$ equal to $1/m$, giving each model the same weight. A drawback of this is that many of the models under consideration might be very closely related, and hence as a group end up having a much higher weight than other different and potentially useful models that are not part of a similar cluster. This suggests paying close attention to the design of the list of models $M_1, \ldots, M_m$ considered in the combination, although we are not aware of papers that directly address this important issue.

14.7 EMPIRICAL EVIDENCE

Stock and Watson (1999) provide an extensive empirical comparison of the performance of a range of forecast methods, including linear and nonlinear ones, along with simple equal-weighted combined forecasts and combinations weighted by the inverse MSE values. The equal-weighted average of forecasts across all methods is found to produce the most attractive forecasts at 6- and 12-month horizons.

In their influential study of predictability of a large set of macroeconomic and financial variables, Stock and Watson (1999) conclude that "pooled forecasts were found to outperform the forecasts from any single method.... The pooling procedures that place weight on all forecasting methods (whether equal weighting, inverse

---

[13] Models deemed obviously inferior might not even make the list of models under consideration.

MSE weighting, or median) proved most reliable, while those that emphasized the recently best performing methods...proved least reliable."

Similarly, using a seven-country data set to forecast output growth, Stock and Watson (2004) find that combination forecasts perform better than individual autoregressive forecasts. Marcellino (2004) studies forecast pooling methods across a very large set of European macroeconomic series. He finds that pooled forecasts are often beaten by forecasts generated by nonlinear models although the combined forecasts perform well for a number of variables such as industrial production growth, inflation, and unemployment.

Related findings have been reported not just for model combination, but also for combinations of survey forecasts. For example, Genre et al. (2013) consider a range of combination schemes for the ECB Survey of Professional Forecasters and find little evidence that the simple equal-weighted average of survey forecasts is bettered by combinations using principal components, trimmed means, past-performance-based weighting, least squares estimates of the combination weights, or Bayesian shrinkage weights.

Bayesian model averaging has been used by Wright (2009) to forecast US inflation. Wright considers linear models that include the lagged inflation rate in addition to one predictor variable. Across 107 possible macroeconomic predictor variables Wright finds that BMA forecasts are more accurate than forecasts from equal-weighted combinations at longer horizons between one and two years, whereas they yield virtually identical results at shorter horizons of one through three quarters.

BMA methods have also been used to predict exchange rates (Wright, 2008) and stock returns by means of large sets of prediction models; see, e.g., Avramov (2002), Cremers (2002), and Elliott, Gargano, and Timmermann (2013). These studies typically combine all possible forecast models generated from K possible predictor variables, yielding 2^K possible specifications.

14.7.1 Application to Stock Returns

To illustrate the BMA approach, we consider quarterly stock market returns with $K = 11$ potential predictor variables and $2^{11} = 2048$ different models. We use the setup suggested by Ley and Steel (2009). Let $\mathbb{1}(i)$ be an indicator variable that takes a value of 1 if the predictor is included in the regression and 0 otherwise. Let π be the probability that a variable gets included so the prior probability of the jth model is $P(M_j) = \pi^{k_j}(1 - \pi)^{11-k_j}$, where k_j is the number of predictors in model j. A prior for π is obtained indirectly through a prior on the model size, $k = \sum_{i=1}^{K} \mathbb{1}(i)$. Here π is assumed to be random and drawn from a beta distribution with shape parameters $s_1 = 1$ and s_2. Ley and Steel (2009) show that under this specification, k will follow a binomial beta distribution. A prior on s_2 can be obtained indirectly by solving the equation for the expected model size, k, through $s_2 = (1 - \pi)/\pi$.

The marginal and predictive likelihoods have closed-form expressions only when using conjugate priors. We follow Fernandez, Ley, and Steel (2001), and adopt a combination of a "noninformative" improper prior on the common intercept and scale and a g-prior (Zellner, 1986b) on the regression coefficients. Under this specification, y given z and M_j follows a t-distribution. In the empirical exercise we set k equal to 1, 6, and 10 and, following Elliott, Gargano, and Timmermann (2013), set $g = 1$.

TABLE 14.2:
Inclusion of different predictors of quarterly US stock market returns weighted by the posterior model probabilities. The top 3 rows and first 11 columns show weighted inclusion frequencies for the individual predictors, using three different priors on the expected number of predictors in the forecasting model, $k = 1, 6, 10$. The last row and last column show the root mean squared forecast error for the individual prediction models (last row) and the Bayesian model averaging approach (last column).

Prior k	dp	dy	ep	bm	ntis	tbl	ltr	tms	dfy	infl	ik	RMSE
1	0.2156	0.2561	0.1584	0.1184	0.1301	0.2380	0.1191	0.1642	0.1390	0.1647	0.2156	8.5429
6	0.5912	0.5436	0.6066	0.5380	0.6352	0.6775	0.5184	0.5317	0.6156	0.5579	0.5025	8.6164
10	0.9098	0.8853	0.9240	0.9042	0.9307	0.9376	0.8896	0.8909	0.9247	0.8991	0.8815	8.7183
RMSE	8.5938	8.5949	8.6420	8.6866	8.6502	8.6943	8.6328	8.7025	8.6781	8.5922	8.4799	–

TABLE 14.3:
Indicators for inclusion of predictor variables in the highest posterior model for quarterly US stock market returns: 1 indicates variable inclusion, while 0 indicates variable exclusion. The last column shows the posterior probability for the most likely model.

Prior k	dp	dy	ep	bm	ntis	tbl	ltr	tms	dfy	infl	ik	Prob.
1	0.0000	0.0000	0.0000	0.0000	0.0000	0.0000	0.0000	0.0000	0.0000	0.0000	0.0000	0.1519
10	1.0000	1.0000	1.0000	1.0000	1.0000	1.0000	1.0000	1.0000	1.0000	1.0000	1.0000	0.2736

Table 14.2 shows the posterior probabilities for inclusion of individual variables cumulated across individual prediction models. For the first prior ($k = 1$) the biggest weights are assigned to the dividend yield (dy), the dividend–price ratio (dp), the T-bill rate (tbl), and the investment-capital ratio (ik), each of which gets a weight above 20%. Considerably less weight gets allocated to variables such as the book-to-market ratio (bm), long term returns (ltr), and the default yield (dfy). As the prior on k increases, more predictors are included so that for $k = 10$, all predictors are included close to 80% of the time.

Table 14.2 also shows the RMSE associated with the individual predictor variables (last row) along with the RMSE values for the three BMA forecasts (last column). The BMA approach based on the tightest prior, $k = 1$, performs better than all of the individual predictor models, except for the model that uses the investment-capital ratio as a predictor. However, the BMA approach with priors of $k = 6$ or $k = 10$ performs worse than many of the univariate prediction models as it gets affected more strongly by parameter estimation error. Effectively, how tightly k is set regulates the degree of shrinkage towards the prevailing mean model which tends to work well in this application.

To see how sensitive the forecasts are to the choice of the prior, k, figure 14.13 plots the recursively generated forecasts of stock returns for $k = 1, 6, 10$. The forecasts are clearly more stable, the smaller the value of k, and thus the fewer time-varying predictors are included in the model.

Finally, to get a sense of which model is most likely, for $k = 1$ and $k = 10$ table 14.3 shows the variables included in the model that, at the end of the sample, has the highest posterior probability. For example, for a prior of $k = 1$, the prevailing mean model that includes no time-varying predictors has a posterior probability of 15%, while for a prior of $k = 10$, a model that includes all variables gets a weight of 27%.

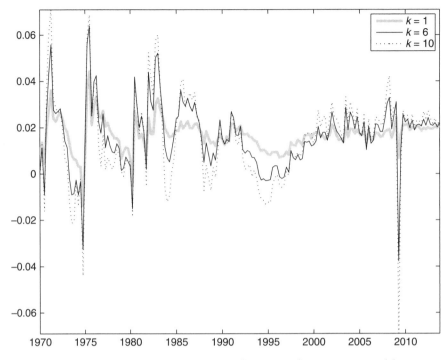

Figure 14.13: Forecasts of quarterly US stock market returns from Bayesian model averaging under different priors on the expected number of predictors included, $k = 1, 6, 10$.

14.8 CONCLUSION

Forecast combination has been widely found to be a reliable, and often simple, way to improve on the predictive accuracy of individual models. Moreover, simple combination methods such as equal weighting often perform well and can be difficult to beat in situations where combination weights are difficult to estimate with more precision or the precision of the underlying forecasts is broadly similar. This situation is often encountered with survey data for which individual forecasters' track records can be short and forecasts tend to cluster around similar points.

Model combination can be used in situations where the forecaster has more information about the underlying models used to generate the forecasts and so is not constrained to treat the observed forecasts simply as any other data, but can evaluate the likelihood of each model. Bayesian model averaging techniques have shown promise in many empirical applications as have predictive pooling methods for generating density forecasts.

Because forecasts from individual models are likely to be generated by misspecified models, it is unlikely that any particular model will dominate all other models across time and different economic states. This helps explain why, empirically, model and forecast combinations have been found to be a reliable device for generating "pooled" forecasts that are often more robust than the individual forecasts entering into the combination.

III
Forecast Evaluation
◇◇◇◇◇◇◇◇◇◇◇◇◇◇◇◇◇◇◇◇◇◇◇◇◇◇◇◇◇◇◇◇

◇◇◇

Desirable Properties of Forecasts

What constitutes a "good" forecast? When considering a sequence of forecasts, $f_{t+1|t}$, $t = 1, \ldots, T$, this question is related to how "close" the forecasts are to the outcome, y_{t+h}. If we have more than a single sequence of forecasts we can ask whether one sequence provides the best forecasts in the sense that it is, on average, closer to the outcomes that were subsequently observed. Quantifying what we mean by "closeness" requires a metric that trades off different forecasting mistakes. Empirical work often relies on somewhat arbitrary statistical measures although, as we emphasize throughout this book, it is preferable to use an economically motivated loss function to measure the distance between the forecast and outcome. In examining distributional forecasts one still requires some metric for closeness; the loss function provides a useful foundation although more arbitrary statistical measures such as the Kullback–Leibler distance are also popular. A related question that has occupied the literature is whether the forecasts are obviously deficient in the sense that they are systematically biased on average or in certain states of the world. Before admonishing a forecast because it is biased, recall, though, that even good forecasts may be biased—for example if they trade off bias against a reduction in the estimation error or due to asymmetries in the loss function.

We break these questions up over the following chapters according to the assumed loss function, the types of data available (including restrictions assumed on the data-generating process), and the questions being asked. A key issue is which testable implications follow from different assumptions on the loss function. We examine this in the present chapter. In situations where we observe additional data that were available to the forecaster, we can examine whether a particular sequence of forecasts efficiently exploited all information embedded in such data. Chapter 16 examines the case where a single sequence of forecasts is available for forecast evaluation and considers the estimation of expected loss.

When we observe more than a single set of forecasts or forecasting models, additional questions arise. We may be interested in examining whether one sequence of forecasts is better than others. Alternatively, even if one forecasting model is found to be better than individual alternatives, combining its forecasts with other forecasts might lead to improvements. Chapter 17 examines the evaluation and comparison of more than a single sequence of forecasts.

For forecast distributions, the issue of how close the forecasts are to the outcome becomes a question of how close the forecast distribution is to the conditional distribution of the outcomes. We examine this in chapter 18. Binary forecasting problems give rise to many interesting special case results. For the binary prediction problem, chapter 12 showed that forecasts of the probability of an outcome are distribution forecasts and so these are also considered in chapter 18.

There are many reasons why we need to evaluate forecasts. First, forecast evaluations can be valuable in their own right. Many statistical agencies provide forecasts as part of their mission, and it is important to examine whether such forecasts are any good. For example, an understanding of whether data are employed optimally to generate forecasts has implications for economic models of how decision makers behave.

A second reason for evaluating forecasts is that we are usually interested in examining whether we can improve the forecasts. Rejections of the rationality tests in this chapter provide some indication of how the forecasts can be improved and hence of how better forecasts can be constructed. In this sense forecast evaluation is simply part of the forecast estimation process. Similarly, if a comparison of multiple forecasts suggests that one set of forecasts contains information not available from another set of forecasts, this suggests either choosing the former or combining the information in the two sets so as to generate a better forecast.

Section 15.1 considers a variety of informal methods for examining forecasts, while section 15.2 presents loss decomposition methods which serve the same purpose. Section 15.3 describes testable efficiency properties that forecasts should have under known loss, while section 15.4 covers efficiency properties under unknown loss. By forecast efficiency we refer to population-optimal properties of the forecasts, ignoring the effect of estimation errors on the forecast. Sections 15.5 and 15.6 cover efficiency properties when the outcome is unobserved as well as the interpretation of efficiency tests. Section 15.7 concludes.

15.1 INFORMAL EVALUATION METHODS

There is a long tradition in economics for inspecting a model's forecasting performance as a way of evaluating its usefulness and fit. Informal graphical methods were considered by Theil (1961), while more formal inspections of forecast errors were proposed by Mincer and Zarnowitz (1969), Fair and Shiller (1989, 1990), and Meese and Rogoff (1983). Wilson (1934) is an early example of forecast evaluation. See Stekler (1991) for a broad discussion of macroeconomic forecast evaluation techniques.

Informal methods for forecast evaluation often provide a good precursor to more formal methods and can be helpful in providing pointers to ways in which a forecast may fail. The main approaches to informally examine the "goodness of fit" of a sequence of forecasts are graphical methods and decompositions of forecast errors. We first describe these before turning to more formal evaluation methods in subsequent sections.

15.1.1 Scatterplots and Time-Series Graphs

The most common graphical approach to examining closeness of forecasts and outcomes is a time-series graph which plots a sequence of forecasts and outcomes $\{f_{t+h|t}, y_{t+h}\}$, $t = 1, \ldots, T - h$ against the date where the forecast was made, t, or

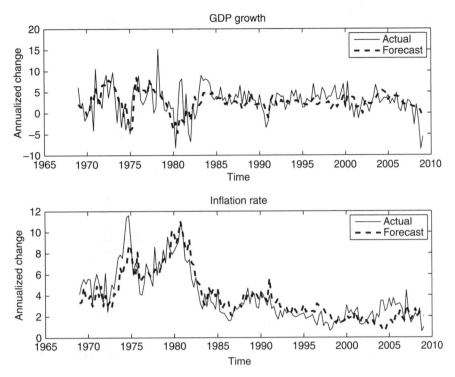

Figure 15.1: Time-series plots of actual values versus the Federal Reserve's Greenbook predictions of next quarter's GDP growth and inflation rate.

the date where the outcome was observed, $t + h$, where $h > 0$ is the (integer-valued) forecast horizon. Vertical differences between the two lines represent the forecast errors. Points in the sample where such differences are consistently of the same sign and/or unusually large indicate periods when the forecasts perform poorly and can be indicative of possible forecast breakdown. These graphs can, however, give a false sense of the performance of the forecast. When the predicted variable is highly persistent, simple autoregressive models will typically generate forecasts that appear to closely track the outcome, even though such forecasts might be relatively poor. For example, consider forecasts of stock prices which to a close approximation follow a random walk, so today's forecast of tomorrow's stock price is simply today's stock price. This is not a particularly informative forecast—in fact, it carries no information about the direction of the future change in the stock price. A time-series plot of forecasts against actual values could disguise this because it can be difficult to read the typical size of the forecast error off these graphs. For less persistent variables, time-series plots can help identify obvious lead-lag relations between forecasts and outcomes.

As an illustration of these time-series graphs, consider how the Federal Reserve's so-called Greenbook forecasts relate to subsequent outcomes. The Greenbook forecasts are part of the Federal Reserve's policy-making process and only get released after five years. Figure 15.1 plots the time series of one-quarter-ahead ($h = 1$) Greenbook forecasts of GDP growth and inflation against the actual values of these variables. Forecasts are smoother than outcomes, as one would expect if the forecasts reflect the conditional expectation of the outcome, but broadly track the level of both GDP growth and inflation.

Theil (1961) suggests several alternative graphical approaches to analyzing forecasts and their closeness to the outcome based on scatterplots of the sequence $\{f_{t+h|t}, y_{t+h}\}, t = 1, \ldots, T - h$. First consider a scatterplot of the forecast against the outcome. The 45° line represents the case where $f_{t+h|t} = y_{t+h}$, so deviations from the 45° line measure the size of the forecast error. With the forecast on the x-axis, the vertical distance of any point from the 45° line is the forecast error and so points above (below) this line indicate that the forecast underestimated (overestimated) the outcome. This scatterplot is useful for understanding the magnitude of the forecast errors, since the scale of the y-axis is measured in the same units as the outcome. It is also easy to glean the variation in forecast errors (deviations from the 45° line) relative to variation in outcomes (variation along the y-axis). Cases where the outcome is difficult to predict and the forecast does not change much will show great variation in the direction of the y-axis and little variation along the x-axis. Cases where the forecast varies much more than the outcome give rise to the opposite situation with large variation in the direction of the x-axis and less variation along the y-axis. For example, nonlinear forecasting models sometimes generate extreme forecasts and these will show up as outliers along the x-axis. A third use of this type of scatterplot is that it can uncover new information about the direction of systematic over- or underpredictions. For example, a tendency to overpredict when the outcome is large will be seen as points in the top right corner of the scatterplot that lie systematically above the 45° degree line. Finally, the outcome–forecast scatterplot gives an impression of the dispersion of the forecasts and whether this depends on the outcome variable or forecast. This can again be used to indicate ranges of the outcome variable for which forecasts are good versus ranges where they are poor.

Returning to the Federal Reserve's Greenbook forecasts, figure 15.2 provides a scatterplot of the GDP growth and inflation forecasts against the outcomes. Although forecast errors at times are very large, there is clearly a strongly positive relation between the predicted and actual values of GDP growth. The relation between forecasts and outcomes is a bit more tenuous for the inflation series.

An alternative to the scatterplot of forecasts, $f_{t+h|t}$, against outcomes, y_{t+h}, is to construct a scatterplot of the predicted change, $f_{t+h|t} - y_t$, against the actual change, $y_{t+h} - y_t$. In this graph, the 45° line still represents perfect forecasts, while the four quadrants now give an indication of directional accuracy. Points in the upper right quadrant (ordered around the f-, y-axes) show when the outcome is correctly predicted to increase. Similarly, points in the lower left quadrant show when the outcome is correctly predicted to decrease. The remaining quadrants show cases when the predicted direction is incorrect. Hence this graph decomposes forecast errors into groups based on directional accuracy.

As an illustration, figure 15.3 plots the actual versus predicted direction for the one-quarter-ahead Greenbook data, i.e., $y_{t+1} - y_t$ plotted against $f_{t+1|t} - y_t$. A positive relation here indicates that the Federal Reserve has the ability to predict whether GDP growth or the inflation rate is rising or falling. Again, a strong positive relationship emerges for the GDP series. While the correlation is also positive for the inflation rate series, the relation is clearly weaker.

Other plots can be based on forecast errors, $y_{t+h} - f_{t+h|t}$. For many loss functions, a simple transformation of the forecast error should be unpredictable. For example, under squared error loss, the forecast error should have a zero mean and be serially

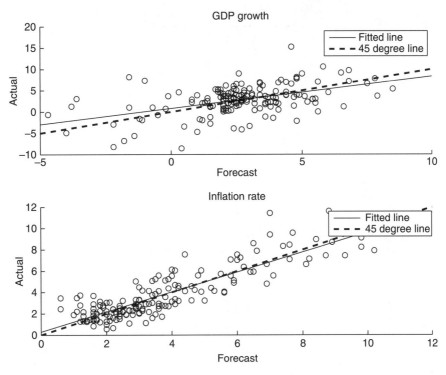

Figure 15.2: Scatterplots of actual values versus the Federal Reserve's Greenbook forecasts of next quarter's GDP growth and inflation rate.

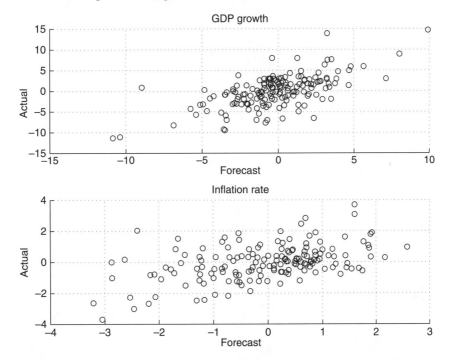

Figure 15.3: Scatterplots of changes in actual values versus the Federal Reserve's Greenbook forecasts of changes in next quarter's GDP growth and inflation rate.

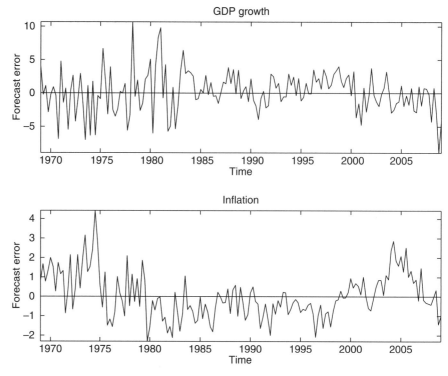

Figure 15.4: Time-series plots of one-quarter-ahead forecast errors (actual value minus the Federal Reserve's Greenbook forecast) for GDP growth and the inflation rate.

uncorrelated. This means that the time series of one-step-ahead forecast errors should not display periods with persistent negative or positive values. We illustrate this property for the Greenbook forecasts of GDP growth and the inflation rate in figure 15.4. While there is no obvious evidence of persistence in the forecast errors for GDP growth, the forecast errors appear to be serially correlated for the inflation series.

A density plot of the forecast error distribution can also be used to uncover evidence of bias, particularly if the distribution is not centered close to 0. As an illustration, figure 15.5 shows kernel smoothed plots of the densities for GDP growth and inflation rate forecast errors. While the density of the inflation rate forecast errors peaks at a negative value, the distribution is clearly right-skewed.

15.2 LOSS DECOMPOSITION METHODS

Methods for decomposing the loss are popular in the applied forecasting literature, particularly under squared error loss. Theil (1961) suggested the following decomposition:

$$E[y - f]^2 = E[(y - Ey) - (f - Ef) + (Ey - Ef)]^2$$

$$= E[y - Ey]^2 + E[f - E(f)]^2 + (Ey - Ef)^2$$

$$- 2E[(y - Ey)(f - Ef)]$$

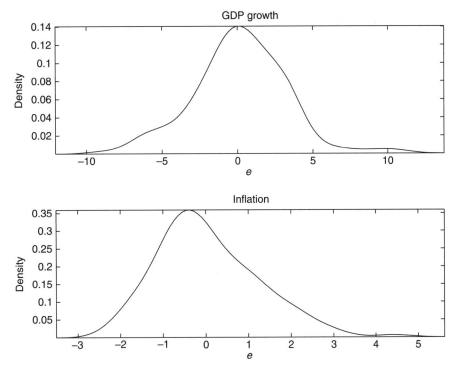

Figure 15.5: Density plots for the one-quarter-ahead forecast errors from the Federal Reserve's Greenbook forecasts of GDP growth and the inflation rate.

$$= (Ey - Ef)^2 + \left(\sqrt{E[y - Ey]^2} - \sqrt{E[f - E(f)]^2} \right)^2$$

$$+ 2\sqrt{E[y - Ey]^2}\sqrt{E[f - E(f)]^2}(1 - \rho)$$

$$= (Ey - Ef)^2 + (\sigma_y - \sigma_f)^2 + 2\sigma_y\sigma_f(1 - \rho), \tag{15.1}$$

where $\rho = \sigma_{yf}/(\sigma_f\sigma_y)$ is the correlation between y and f.[1] The sample analog to this expression is

$$\frac{1}{T-h}\sum_{t=1}^{T-h}(y_{t+h} - f_{t+h|t})^2 = \frac{1}{T-h}\sum_{t=1}^{T-h}((y_{t+h} - \bar{y}) - (f_{t+h|t} - \bar{f}) + (\bar{y} - \bar{f}))^2$$

$$= \hat{\sigma}_y^2 + \hat{\sigma}_f^2 + (\bar{y} - \bar{f})^2 - 2\hat{\sigma}_{yf}$$

$$= (\bar{y} - \bar{f})^2 + (\hat{\sigma}_y - \hat{\sigma}_f)^2 + 2(\hat{\sigma}_y\hat{\sigma}_f - \hat{\sigma}_{yf})$$

$$= (\bar{y} - \bar{f})^2 + (\hat{\sigma}_y - \hat{\sigma}_f)^2 + 2\hat{\sigma}_y\hat{\sigma}_f(1 - \hat{\rho}). \tag{15.2}$$

---

[1] Two cross products disappear in the second line since the expectation of deviations from the mean is 0.

Here $\bar{y} = (T-h)^{-1}\sum_{t=1}^{T-h} y_{t+h}$ and $\bar{f} = (T-h)^{-1}\sum_{t=1}^{T-h} f_{t+h|t}$ are sample means and $\hat{\rho} = \hat{\sigma}_{yf}/(\hat{\sigma}_y\hat{\sigma}_f)$, where $\hat{\sigma}_y$, $\hat{\sigma}_f$, $\hat{\sigma}_{yf}$ are sample estimates of σ_y, σ_f, and $\text{Cov}(y, f)$, respectively.

The first term in (15.2) measures the difference in the means of the forecast and outcome and so captures whether the average forecast is close to the average outcome. This term is 0 when the average outcome and forecast lie on the 45° line in the scatterplot of forecasts versus outcomes. A large value of this term indicates that average forecasts are off center, or biased. For forecasts constructed using lagged values of the outcome, this term is unlikely to be large.

The second term in (15.2) measures differences between the standard deviations of f and y and captures whether the variation in the forecasts is similar to that of the outcomes. For hard-to-predict variables such as stock returns, this term tends to be very large since the fluctuation in the outcome is an order of magnitude greater than that of the forecasts. Conversely, if forecasts are generated by a random walk model that sets $f_{t+h|t} = y_t$, this term will be close to 0 since the forecast and outcome display the same amount of variability.

The last term in (15.2) depends on the correlation between the forecast and the outcome and is smaller, the larger their correlation. This term will be large for hard-to-predict variables, although the scaling by $\hat{\sigma}_f$ may reduce this term.

An alternative approach, more commonly seen in binary prediction for which it was originally developed, decomposes mean squared errors into calibration and resolution terms:

$$E[y-f]^2 = E[(y-E[y]) - (f-E[y|f]) - (E[y|f]-E[y])]^2$$

$$= E[(y-E[y])^2] + E[(f-E[y|f])^2] + E\left[(E[y|f]-E[y])^2\right]$$

$$- 2E[(y-E[y])(E[y|f]-E[y])] + 2E[(f-E[y|f])(E[y|f]-y)]$$

$$- 2E[(y-E[y])(f-E[y|f])]$$

$$= E\left[(y-E[y])^2\right] + E\left[(f-E[y|f])^2\right] - E\left[(E[y|f]-E[y])^2\right].$$

$$(15.3)$$

Here unconditional expectations are taken over both y and f. The first term in this decomposition is the unconditional variance of the outcome variable. This does not depend on the forecast and so can be taken as given for the remainder of the analysis. Calibration is defined as $E[y-f|f]$. For any forecast, f, this measures the difference between the expected value of the outcome given the forecast and the forecast itself. Hence, the second term in (15.3) equals the average squared calibration error, where the average is taken over f. A well-calibrated model has a calibration measure of 0 for all f.

The last term in (15.3) is known as the resolution term and enters with a minus sign. Resolution measures the squared average (computed over all forecasts) of the difference between the average outcome conditional on the forecast and the unconditional average outcome. This term will be small, indicating poor resolution, if, conditional on the forecast, the average value of the outcome is equal to the unconditional average value of the outcome for a wide range of forecasts. In such cases, the forecast is not picking up much variation in the outcome variable apart from its mean. Conversely, high resolution is achieved when the forecast picks up a lot of the variation in the outcome variable and $E[y|f] - E[y]$ tends to be large.

Estimation of the terms in the decomposition in (15.3) requires estimates of the distribution of the outcome variable conditional on the forecast. A common approach is to discretize the forecast to enable such calculations. Galbraith and van Norden (2011) propose to use nonparametric methods for the case with continuous forecasts.

The decomposition can be modified for data that appear nonstationary or show trending behavior by setting $(T - h)^{-1} \sum_{t=1}^{T-h} (y_{t+h} - f_t)^2 = (T - h)^{-1} \sum_{t=1}^{T-h} ([y_{t+h} - y_t] - [f_t - y_t])^2$. The interpretation of the various components in the decompositions now applies to the actual and predicted change. This ensures that the variance and covariance terms can be estimated consistently when samples become large and is similar to first-differencing data to induce stationarity for variables with a unit root.

An important limitation of these decompositions is that there are no objective measures for how large or small the terms should be for any particular forecasting problem. Moreover, the terms are typically correlated so that one model's improvement in a specific term may result in a deterioration in the other terms. In this case, a reasonable forecast improvement would require that the improvement in one of the terms more than offsets any reductions in performance in the other terms.

15.3 EFFICIENCY PROPERTIES WITH KNOWN LOSS

To more rigorously discuss and conduct tests on the relationship between actual and predicted values, it is necessary to establish a benchmark for what constitutes an optimal or "good" forecast. As emphasized throughout the book, this issue is best addressed with reference to the forecaster's loss function and information set. We begin by discussing the properties that an optimal forecast should have for general loss functions and then address more specialized cases such as quadratic or homogenous loss.

The idea of rational or optimal forecasts originates from the rational expectations literature starting with Muth (1961) which was subsequently brought to the analysis of forecasts by Mincer and Zarnowitz (1969) and followed by papers such as Nordhaus (1987) and Batchelor and Dua (1991). The original notion was that a rational agent constructs forecasts of the outcome variable given knowledge of the true data-generating process (DGP) for the outcome—including the model and its parameters—using all currently available information. Rationality means optimal use of all information available to the forecaster in constructing the forecast, so "rational," "efficient," and "optimal" forecasts are synonymous in this setting. Forecasts are deemed rational if, given a loss function and a particular set of data, they fully capture all available information in the sense that these data cannot be used to construct a better forecast. Various flavors of rationality have been proposed, such as weak versus strong rationality, unbiasedness of forecasts and orthogonality of the forecast error to all available information. The resulting tests imply similar constructs from the perspective of the optimality property and amount to testing the first-order condition that the forecast cannot be improved upon using ex ante available information.

In the spirit of the rational expectations literature, the early literature assumed that efficient forecasts were based on knowledge of the true data-generating process, including the true parameter values. More recent work has relaxed this assumption to allow for parameter estimation errors. In the presence of uncertainty about the true data-generating process, the notion of efficient forecasts is that they are not obviously misspecified and thus dominated by other forecasting methods.

By definition, an efficient forecast has the property that no other forecast or combination of the forecast and the available data in the forecasters information set, Z_t, can be used to generate a smaller expected loss so that, consistent with (3.3),

$$f^*_{t+h|t} = \arg\min_{f(z_t)} E\left[L(f(z_t), y_{t+h})|Z_t\right]. \tag{15.4}$$

Equivalently, efficiency holds if f^* is sufficient for the best forecast given the information available in the extended set of data $z_t \in Z_t$, i.e., for any $\tilde{f}_{t+h|t} = f(z_t)$,

$$E\left[L(f^*_{t+h|t}(z_t), y_{t+h})|Z_t\right] \leq E\left[L(\tilde{f}_{t+h|t}(z_t), y_{t+h})|Z_t\right]. \tag{15.5}$$

If additional information in Z_t can be used to provide a better forecast than f^*, then the forecast is deemed not to be optimal in the sense that it fails to effectively utilize all data in Z_t. The definition is explicitly conditional on the information set considered, Z_t, and so any test of efficiency is conducted conditional on a particular information set. Finding that a prediction could be improved by adding information not available when the original forecast was computed does not prove that the original (smaller) information set was inefficiently utilized. It may of course help improve the original forecast if this information subsequently becomes available.

The composition of the information set lies behind the commonly used terminology of "weak" versus "strong" forecast efficiency. Tests of weak-form forecast efficiency refer to an information set that includes only past forecasts and past outcomes (and hence past forecast errors), i.e., $Z_t = \{y_{t-i}, f_{t+h-i|t-i}, e_{t-i|t-h-i}\}$, $i = 0, 1, \ldots, t$. Strong-form efficiency refers to extensions of the information set to include other variables, often all variables that were publicly available at the time the forecast was made.[2]

Rationality is also defined in the context of a given loss function: a forecast that is efficient under one loss function, L_1, need not be efficient under another loss function, $L_2 \neq L_1$. For example, one loss function may require predicting only the mean, while another loss function may require forecasts of both the mean and the variance. Forecast models that use a correct specification of the mean but not for the variance would then be efficient for the first loss function, but not for the second. In situations where the loss function underlying the forecast is unknown, evidence that a given forecast is inefficient with respect to one loss function, while it seems efficient with regard to another loss function might help establish the shape of the loss function that the forecaster implicitly used, at least under the null of forecast rationality.

Assuming that the loss function is once differentiable with regard to the forecast, the first-order condition for an optimal forecast becomes

$$E[L'(f_{t+h|t}(z_t), y_{t+h})|Z_t] = 0, \tag{15.6}$$

---

[2] Notice the similarity to the concepts of weak- and strong-form market efficiency used in finance. See Timmermann (2008) for a discussion of market efficiency in the context of forecasting.

where $L'(f_{t+h|t}(z_t), y_{t+h})$ is the derivative of the loss function with respect to the forecast, evaluated at the optimum forecast, $f^*_{t+h|t}$, i.e.,

$$L'_{t+h|t}(\cdot) \equiv \left. \frac{\partial L\left(f_{t+h|t}, y_{t+h}\right)}{\partial f_{t+h|t}} \right|_{f^*_{t+h|t}}. \tag{15.7}$$

The first-order condition in (15.6) forms the basis for many forecast rationality tests. Granger (1999) refers to the derivative in (15.7) as the generalized forecast error. Under a broad set of conditions that allow interchange between the expectation and differentiation operators, an implication of (15.6) is that the generalized forecast error is a martingale difference sequence and so has zero conditional mean with respect to all elements in the forecaster's information set. These conditions do not require that L is everywhere differentiable with respect to the forecast, nor is a unique optimum assumed.

The conditional moment condition (15.6) is written with respect to the information set Z_t and so does not lend itself directly to testing. If Z_t is generated by the variables z_t, then the conditional moment condition in (15.6) can be converted into an unconditional moment condition of the form

$$E[L'(f_{t+h|t}, y_{t+h})g(z_t)] = 0, \tag{15.8}$$

for all possible functions $g(z_t)$.[3] We use the notation $v_t = g(z_t)$ for a given choice of such functions and refer to these as "test functions" following White (2000). Different choices of test functions, v_t, change the direction of the power of tests of the moment conditions in (15.8). A specific test function, v_t, yields power in the direction of correlation between the derivative of the loss function and v_t but has zero power in directions that are orthogonal to v_t.

The most common way to implement a test of the orthogonality condition in (15.8) is to consider a regression,

$$L'(f_{t+h|t}(z_t), y_{t+h}) = \beta'v_t + u_{t+h}, \tag{15.9}$$

and testing $H_0 : \beta = 0$ versus $H_1 : \beta \neq 0$.

For MSE loss $L'(f_{t+h|t}(z_t), y_{t+h})$ is just the difference between the outcome and the forecast, i.e., the forecast error $e_{t+h|t}$. The main challenge in conducting inference lies in understanding the sampling distribution for $\hat{\beta}$ from such a regression. For example, inference generally depends on how the forecasts are generated. We discuss these issues below.

The implication that can be derived from rejections of rationality is that there is information in v_t that could potentially be used to improve the forecast. Including v_t in the information set for constructing the forecast and recomputing the optimal forecast could result in a forecast that has lower expected risk and could also result

---

[3] Conventional forecast efficiency tests are conducted in-sample and are typically undertaken to examine third-party forecasts. It makes less sense to examine in-sample efficiency of forecasts constructed from one's own model; if the forecast is chosen to minimize expected loss for a given loss function and information set, then examining whether this holds is really part of the estimation stage and not part of the forecast evaluation.

in a revised forecast for which $L'(f_{t+h|t}(z_t), y_{t+h})$ is orthogonal to v_t and hence is deemed rational.

While forecast efficiency tests are contingent upon the available information, they also critically depend on the assumed loss function. In the special case of MSE loss, the first-order condition in (15.6) does not involve any unknown parameters. However, for most other loss functions, additional parameters are involved. Even if these parameters are known, the first-order condition in (15.6) will typically depend on additional parameters capturing the shape of the loss function and so does not only involve the forecast error. Conversely, if the parameters of the loss function are unknown and have to be estimated, efficiency tests generalize to whether any parameters exist within a particular family of loss functions for which the forecast can be rationalized. Estimating these additional parameters then becomes part of the rationality test. Yet a third case arises if the shape of the loss function is unknown, or at least not known up to a few shape parameters. While the unrestricted case is untreatable, rationality tests are possible if restrictions can be imposed on the loss function and/or on the underlying data-generating process. We next discuss a variety of such cases.

15.3.1 Efficiency Properties under Squared Error Loss

Concrete and well-known results are available under squared error or MSE loss. Specifically, when the loss function is quadratic in the forecast error, $L(f, Y) = L(e) = e^2$, the first-order condition for an optimal forecast in (15.6) greatly simplifies:

$$\frac{\partial E[(y_{t+h} - f_{t+h|t})^2|Z_t]}{\partial f_{t+h|t}} = -2E[e_{t+h|t}|Z_t] = 0, \tag{15.10}$$

or, equivalently,

$$E[e_{t+h|t}v_t] = 0 \tag{15.11}$$

for any $v_t = g(z_t)$, where g is an arbitrary measurable function of z_t.

Several testable implications follow from this result. These are just different manifestations of the same first-order condition (15.10). Specifically, the following properties hold:[4]

1. Forecasts are unbiased, i.e., the forecast error $e_{t+h|t}$ has zero mean, both conditionally and unconditionally:

$$E[e_{t+h|t}] = E[e_{t+h|t}|Z_t] = 0. \tag{15.12}$$

2. The h-period forecast errors $(e_{t+h|t})$ are uncorrelated with information available at the time the forecast was computed (Z_t). In particular, the h-period forecast error is at most serially correlated of order $h - 1$:

$$\text{Cov}(e_{t+h|t}, e_{t-j|t-h-j}) = 0 \quad \text{for all } j \geq 0. \tag{15.13}$$

Hence, $e_{t+h|t}$ follows an MA($h - 1$) process. In the special case with a single-period horizon, $h = 1$, forecast errors, $e_{t+1|t}$, are serially uncorrelated:

$$E[e_{t+1|t}e_{t|t-1}] = 0.$$

---

[4] See Diebold and Lopez (1996) and Patton and Timmermann (2007a) for further discussion.

3. The variance of the forecast error ($e_{t+h|t}$) is a nondecreasing function of the forecast horizon, h:

$$\text{Var}(e_{t+h|t}) \geq \text{Var}(e_{t+h|t+1}) \quad \text{for all } h \geq 1. \tag{15.14}$$

It is instructive to illustrate these results using simple time-series representations as we do in the next examples.

Example 15.3.1 (Efficiency properties for a covariance stationary process). *Suppose that Y is a covariance stationary process and, without loss of generality, assume it has zero unconditional mean. The Wold representation theorem then establishes that Y can be represented as a linear combination of serially uncorrelated white noise terms (see chapter 7):*

$$Y_t = \sum_{i=0}^{\infty} \theta_i \varepsilon_{t-i}, \tag{15.15}$$

where, from chapter 7, $\varepsilon_t = Y_t - \text{Proj}(Y_t | y_{t-1}, y_{t-2}, \ldots)$ is the serially uncorrelated projection error[5] at time t.

Assuming that $Z_t = \{\varepsilon_t, \varepsilon_{t-1}, \ldots\}$ and the moving average parameters $\{\theta_0, \theta_1, \ldots\}$ are known, the h-period forecast becomes

$$f_{t+h|t} = \sum_{i=0}^{\infty} \theta_{h+i} \varepsilon_{t-i}. \tag{15.16}$$

This is an optimal forecast provided that ε_t is Gaussian or can be viewed as an optimal linear forecast given past values of the process $\{y_{t-1}, y_{t-2}, \ldots\}$. The associated forecast error is

$$e_{t+h|t} = y_{t+h} - f_{t+h|t} = \sum_{i=0}^{h-1} \theta_i \varepsilon_{t+h-i}. \tag{15.17}$$

Using that ε_t is serially uncorrelated mean-zero white noise, it follows that

$$E[e_{t+h|t}] = 0,$$

$$\text{Var}(e_{t+h|t}) = \sigma^2 \sum_{i=0}^{h-1} \theta_i^2, \tag{15.18}$$

$$\text{Cov}(e_{t+h|t}, e_{t+h-j|t-j}) = \begin{cases} \sigma^2 \sum_{i=j}^{h-1} \theta_i \theta_{i-j} & \text{for } 0 < j < h, \\ 0 & \text{for } j \geq h. \end{cases}$$

Our second example helps clarify the properties established in the first example.

---

[5] Although white noise is serially uncorrelated, this does not mean that its distribution is unpredictable. For example, it could have persistent second moments, e.g., $E[\varepsilon_t^2 | \varepsilon_{t-1}^2] = \theta \varepsilon_{t-1}^2$.

Example 15.3.2 (Efficiency properties for AR(1) process). *Consider the stationary first-order autoregressive process,*

$$y_t = \phi y_{t-1} + \varepsilon_t, \quad \varepsilon_t \sim ind\ N(0, \sigma^2), \quad |\phi| < 1, \tag{15.19}$$

where the information set is $Z_t = (y_t, y_{t-1}, \ldots)$, so that

$$y_{t+h} = \phi^h y_t + \sum_{i=1}^{h} \phi^{h-i} \varepsilon_{t+i}. \tag{15.20}$$

Using that $E[\varepsilon_{t+i}|Z_t] = 0$ for all $i \geq 1$, it follows from (15.20) that

$$f_{t+h|t} = \phi^h y_t,$$

$$e_{t+h|t} = \sum_{i=1}^{h} \phi^{h-i} \varepsilon_{t+i}.$$

It is easily seen that

$$E[e_{t+h}|Z_t] \equiv E[e_{t+h|t}] = E\left[\sum_{i=1}^{h} \phi^{h-i} \varepsilon_{t+i}\right] = 0.$$

Moreover, $\mathrm{Cov}(e_{t+1|t}, e_{t|t-1}) = 0$, while for $h > j \geq 1$,

$$\mathrm{Cov}(e_{t+h|t}, e_{t+h-j|t-j}) = \frac{\sigma^2 \phi^j (1 - \phi^{2(h-j)})}{1 - \phi^2},$$

which is increasing in h and shows that forecast errors will be serially correlated at horizons longer than one period. Finally, note from (15.20) that

$$\mathrm{Var}(e_{t+h|t}) = \frac{\sigma^2 (1 - \phi^{2h})}{1 - \phi^2},$$

which is a nondecreasing function of h, verifying the third property that the variance of the forecast error increases weakly in the forecast horizon.

The first two optimality properties, (15.12) and (15.13), are commonly tested by regressing forecast errors on elements in the forecaster's information set, $v_t = g(z_t)$:

$$e_{t+h|t} = \beta' v_t + u_{t+h}. \tag{15.21}$$

Tests of the null of forecast efficiency are of the form

$$H_0 : \beta = 0,$$

$$\text{versus} \quad H_1 : \beta \neq 0.$$

Tests for unbiasedness and orthogonality simply correspond to different choices for the test function, v_t. Tests for unconditional unbiasedness set v_t equal to a constant:

$$e_{t+h|t} = \beta_0 + u_{t+h}. \tag{15.22}$$

In a scatterplot of the forecasts against the outcome variable, this represents the case where the point described by the average of the forecast and outcome lies on the $45°$ line (see figure 15.2). A rejection of $\beta_0 = 0$ suggests that the forecast is a biased estimator of the outcome and thus explains why this procedure is called an unbiasedness test. Unbiasedness is also commonly viewed as a joint test of $\beta_0 = 0$, $\beta_1 = 1$ in the Mincer–Zarnowitz regression (Mincer and Zarnowitz, 1969) that adds the forecast, $f_{t+h|t}$, to both sides of (15.22),

$$y_{t+h} = \beta_0 + \beta_1 f_{t+h|t} + u_{t+h}, \tag{15.23}$$

and thus corresponds to setting $v_t = (1, f_{t+h|t})$ in (15.21).

As an empirical illustration, returning to the Greenbook forecasts, we use the Mincer–Zarnowitz test to check whether the forecasts are unbiased, adopting an F-test to test that $\beta_0 = 0$, $\beta_1 = 1$. The null of unbiased forecasts is strongly rejected for the GDP forecasts, but not for the inflation rate. From the individual t-tests applied separately to β_0 and β_1, it is clear that the intercept is nonnegative for the GDP series. As an alternative test, we check whether the forecast errors are serially uncorrelated. With autocorrelations around 0.5, we can strongly reject the null for both series, suggesting that the forecasts could be improved.

Extending the test function v_t in (15.21) to contain other information allows us to test whether the forecast errors are orthogonal to such information. For example, setting $v_t = (e_{t|t-h}, e_{t-1|t-h-1}, \ldots)$, gives a test for weak forecast rationality and so examines whether there is serial correlation in forecast errors over and above what would be expected due to any data overlaps resulting from the use of horizons exceeding a single period. As shown in (15.18), even optimal multistep forecasts may be serially correlated due to overlaps in forecast errors. Irrespective of this, the general rule is that rationality tests should use information dated at the point where the forecast was generated. Doing so always results in a valid specification of the rationality test.

Suppose the null of forecast rationality is rejected. This indicates that the forecaster failed to use all information in the test efficiently which implies that the forecast can be improved. This is perhaps most easily seen in the case of MSE loss and the regression,

$$y_{t+h} = \alpha + \beta f_{t+h|t} + \lambda v_t + \varepsilon_{t+h}. \tag{15.24}$$

Suppose we reject the null that $\alpha = 0$, $\beta = 1$, $\lambda = 0$, so the forecast is biased. A biased-adjusted forecast can then be computed as

$$\hat{f}^{\text{adj}}_{t+h|t} = \hat{\alpha} + \hat{\beta} \hat{f}_{t+h|t} + \hat{\lambda} v_t, \tag{15.25}$$

where "hats" indicate least squares estimates. The benefit of this approach is that it is a simple strategy for producing potentially improved forecasts. The disadvantage is that it is a mechanical adjustment that provides no explanation for the biases in the original model and does not attempt to produce a better forecasting model. Moreover, due to estimation error in $\hat{\alpha}, \hat{\beta}, \hat{\lambda}$, there is no guarantee that in practice this procedure will yield a more attractive risk function than the original (biased) forecast.

It is less common to test the third property, (15.14), that the variance of the forecast error should be weakly increasing in the forecast horizon, in part because such a test requires that forecasts are available at different horizons. This type of data is most common for economic surveys. For such situations, Patton and Timmermann (2012) propose a procedure that exploits the full information in the term structure of mean squared forecast errors, i.e., the full set of MSE values recorded for different horizons. Suppose MSE values corresponding to a set of forecast horizons of increasing length, $h = h_1, h_2, \ldots, h_H$ are available and denote the corresponding MSE population values by $\mu^e = \left[\mu_1^e, \ldots, \mu_H^e\right]'$, where $\mu_j^e \equiv E[e_{t+h_j|t}^2]$. Defining the associated MSE differentials as $\Delta_j^e \equiv \mu_j - \mu_{j-1} = E[e_{t+h_j|t}^2] - E[e_{t+h_{j-1}|t}^2]$, it follows from (15.14) that the expected value of the squared forecast errors under squared error loss is weakly increasing in the forecast horizon:

$$\Delta_j^e \geq 0 \quad \text{for } j = 2, \ldots, H. \tag{15.26}$$

This weak monotonicity property can be tested through the null hypothesis:

$$H_0 : \Delta^e \geq 0 \quad \text{versus } H_1 : \Delta^e \ngeq 0, \tag{15.27}$$

where the $((H-1) \times 1)$ vector of MSE differentials is given by $\Delta^e \equiv \left[\Delta_2^e, \ldots, \Delta_H^e\right]'$. The test uses the sample analogs to the unknown MSE differentials, $\hat{\Delta}_j^e = \hat{\mu}_j - \hat{\mu}_{j-1}$ for $\hat{\mu}_j \equiv (1/T) \sum_{t=1}^{T} e_{t+h_j|t}^2$. Standard critical values are not available for the test. However, results by Wolak (1987) show that these can be obtained under the null as a weighted sum of chi-squared variables, $\sum_{i=0}^{H-1} \omega(H-1, i)\chi^2(i)$, where $\omega(H-1, i)$ are the weights and $\chi^2(i)$ is a chi-squared variable with i degrees of freedom. The weights correspond to the probability that the vector $Z \sim N(0, \Sigma)$ has i positive elements, where Σ is the long-run covariance matrix of the estimated parameter vector, $\hat{\Delta}^e$. This can be computed either via simulation or in closed form; see Patton and Timmermann (2012) for details. Alternatively, the bootstrap methods of White (2000) or Hansen (2005) can be adopted; such methods can be useful particularly when the number of forecast horizons is large.

Figure 15.6 provides an empirical illustration of the bound applied to quarterly forecasts of the unemployment rate and real GDP growth obtained from the Survey of Professional Forecasters. We use the mean forecasts over the sample 1968Q4 to 2009Q4. As can be readily seen, the mean squared errors are monotonically increasing in the forecast horizon for the unemployment rate forecasts, though not, at the longest four-quarter horizon, for the GDP growth.[6]

---

[6] See also Joutz and Stekler (2000) for an empirical analysis of the predictions of the Federal Reserve under MSE loss.

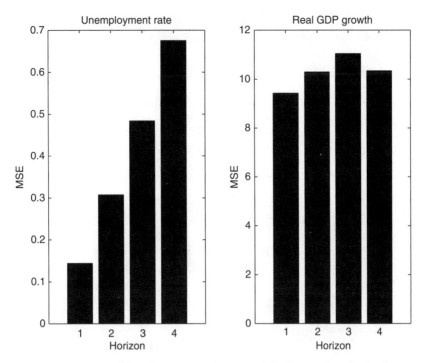

Figure 15.6: Mean squared forecast error as a function of the forecast horizon for the Survey of Professional Forecasters' mean forecasts.

Bounds such as (15.26) hold when the forecasting model is evaluated at the population values of the parameters. In the presence of parameter estimation error, the monotonicity properties could break down as shown by Hoque, Magnus, and Pesaran (1988) and Magnus and Pesaran (1989). A term structure of MSE values that is not weakly increasing therefore need not be indicative of inefficient forecasts and could be caused by estimation errors. In the reply to the discussion of their paper, Patton and Timmermann (2012) conduct Monte Carlo simulations for an AR(1) model and find that for estimation sample sizes of 100 or more all of the monotonicity and bounds results in Patton and Timmermann (2012) hold in the presence of parameter estimation error. They find that estimation error can overturn the bounds only in very small sample sizes such as 25 observations. In fact, tests based on inequality restrictions appear to be less sensitive to parameter estimation error than orthogonality tests based on equality restrictions.

15.3.2 Optimality Tests with Known Loss Shape, but Unknown Parameters

All of the results in section 15.3.1 rely on MSE loss which justified our use of the forecast error e in place of $L'(f, y)$. If the loss function were not in the MSE family, then orthogonality between the forecast error e_{t+h} and the test instruments v_t need not imply that the forecasts are efficient. Conversely, a rejection of orthogonality between e_{t+h} and v_t does not imply that the forecasts are inefficient if the loss function lies outside the MSE family.

In practice, the forecaster's loss function is often unknown. Such a situation arises when we evaluate forecasts that are constructed by third parties that have built their forecasts for their own (unknown) purposes. While the loss function may not be known, it is possible that it could be well approximated by a family of loss functions that are known apart from a few shape parameters. Alternatively, the loss function may be entirely unknown. We cover the first case here and subsequently turn to the second case.

When the forecaster's loss function is known up to a finite number of parameters, rationality tests that account for the unknown parameters can be used. For example, consider optimality tests in the context of the two-parameter loss function proposed by Elliott, Komunjer, and Timmermann (2005) and described in detail in chapter 2:

$$L(e_{t+1|t}, p, \alpha) \equiv [\alpha + (1 - 2\alpha)\mathbb{1}(e_{t+1|t} < 0)]|e_{t+1|t}|^p, \tag{15.28}$$

where p is a positive integer, while $\alpha \in (0, 1)$. Elliott, Komunjer, and Timmermann (2005) consider the case where $p = 1$ or $p = 2$. In their setting, rationality can only be tested jointly with an estimate of α and so their analysis addresses whether there exists an α for which forecast rationality is not rejected.

To obtain an estimate of α given a set of d instruments, v_t, a linear instrumental variable estimator can be used for the unknown loss parameter, $\hat{\alpha}_T$:

$$\hat{\alpha}_T \equiv \frac{\left[\frac{1}{T-1}\sum_{t=1}^{T-1} v_t |e_{t+1|t}|^{p-1}\right]' \hat{S}^{-1} \left[\frac{1}{T-1}\sum_{t=1}^{T-1} v_t \mathbb{1}(e_{t+1|t} < 0)|e_{t+1|t}|^{p-1}\right]}{\left[\frac{1}{T-1}\sum_{t=1}^{T-1} v_t |e_{t+1|t}|^{p-1}\right]' \hat{S}^{-1} \left[\frac{1}{T}\sum_{t=1}^{T} v_t |e_{t+1|t}|^{p-1}\right]}, \tag{15.29}$$

where $\hat{S}$ is a consistent estimate of the positive-definite weight matrix, $S = E[v_t v_t'(\mathbb{1}(e_{t+1|t} < 0) - \alpha)^2 |e_{t+1|t}|^{2p-2}]$, and the forecasts[7] run from $t = 1$ to $t = T$. Elliott, Komunjer, and Timmermann (2005) establish conditions under which, for a given value of $p = 1, 2$, a joint test of forecast rationality and the flexible loss function in (15.28) can be conducted based on the test statistic

$$J = \frac{1}{T-1} \left[\left(\sum_{t=1}^{T-1} v_t[\mathbb{1}(e_{t+1|t} < 0) - \hat{\alpha}_T]|e_{t+1|t}|^{p-1}\right)' \hat{S}^{-1} \right.$$

$$\left. \times \left(\sum_{t=1}^{T-1} v_t[\mathbb{1}(e_{t+1|t} < 0) - \hat{\alpha}_T]|e_{t+1|t}|^{p-1}\right)\right] \sim \chi_{d-1}^2. \tag{15.30}$$

The test requires that the number of instruments, $d > 1$ (the test is a test for overidentification), and assumes that the forecasts are constructed using a recursive estimation scheme. As with the earlier rationality tests, the test has power only for directions implied by the instruments chosen for the test.

Tests based on an assumption of MSE loss arise as a special case when $p = 2$ and $\alpha = 0.5$ in (15.28). The difference is that if indeed $\alpha = 0.5$, tests based on MSE loss impose this restriction, whereas the test in (15.30) uses a consistent estimate of α which is treated as unknown and hence has lower power than a test that imposes $\alpha = 0.5$. On the flip side, if $\alpha \neq 0.5$ then conventional tests based on MSE loss will asymptotically wrongly reject the null of forecast rationality with probability 1.

---

[7] Notice that when v_t is a constant and $p = 1$, this expression computes the proportion of negative forecast errors, which yields a very simple estimator for α.

In contrast, the test in (15.30) is consistent and avoids this problem, controlling for size if the forecaster's loss function reflects a different value of the true α. Asymptotically there is no loss from relaxing the assumption that $\alpha = 0.5$, but there is clearly a gain in terms of directing power in the desired direction.

When we apply the approach of Elliott, Komunjer, and Timmermann (2005) to a sample of current-quarter GDP growth forecasts from the Survey of Professional Forecasters, using a constant and the lagged forecast error as instruments, the estimated value for α is 0.35 with an associated J-test statistic from (15.30) of 0.25 which is statistically insignificant. A test of the overidentifying restriction that $\alpha = 0.5$ yields a statistic of 8.93 which means that the null of rational forecasts and quadratic error loss is strongly rejected. For current-quarter inflation forecasts the estimated value of α is 0.55 and the associated tests are 12.3 and 13.2, which in both cases reject the null of forecast rationality irrespective of whether α is constrained to equal 0.5. This illustrates how different shapes of the loss function can lead to different inference on whether the forecasts were rational or not.

The test in (15.30) has been applied to a number of forecasting problems, including applications to energy forecasts (Auffhammer, 2007), economic growth (Elliott, Komunjer, and Timmermann, 2008), and EU commission forecasts (Christodoulakis and Mamatzakis, 2009).

15.4 OPTIMALITY TESTS UNDER UNKNOWN LOSS

If the shape of the forecaster's loss function is not specified up to a few unknown parameters, it can be very difficult to conduct tests of forecast optimality. One strategy is to impose restrictions on the loss function and/or on the underlying DGP and develop testable implications subject to such restrictions.

Patton and Timmermann (2007b) characterize the optimal forecast when both the loss function and the underlying data-generating process can be restricted in this manner. They show that if predictability is constrained to the mean of the outcome, then the optimal forecast takes a very simple form for loss functions that depend only on the forecast error.

Specifically, suppose the loss function depends only on the forecast error,

$$L(f, y) = L(e), \tag{15.31}$$

while the data-generating process has dynamics only in the conditional mean,

$$Y_{t+h} = \mu_{t+h|t} + \sigma_{\varepsilon,h}\varepsilon_{t+h}, \quad \varepsilon_{t+h}|Z_t \sim p_{\varepsilon,h}(0, 1), \tag{15.32}$$

where $p_{\varepsilon,h}(0, 1)$ is the density of ε_{t+h} which has mean 0 and variance 1. This density may depend on h, but does not depend on Z_t. Patton and Timmermann (2007b) show that, under (15.31) and (15.32),

1. the optimal forecast takes the form

$$f_{t+h|t} = \mu_{t+h|t} + \alpha_h,$$

where the constant α_h depends only on the density $p_{\varepsilon,h}$ and the loss function;

2. forecast errors associated with the optimal forecasts, $e_{t+h|t}$, are independent of all $z_t \in Z_t$; in particular, $\text{Cov}(e_{t+h|t}, e_{t+h-j|t-j}) = 0$ for all $j \geq h$ and any $h > 0$;

3. the variance of the forecast error associated with the optimal forecast, $V(e_{t+h|t})$, is nondecreasing in the forecast horizon, h.

The first result has also been shown by Granger (1969b) and Christoffersen and Diebold (1997), while the result that the optimal bias is time invariant follows by noting that the forecast error associated with the optimal forecast takes the form

$$e_{t+h|t} = y_{t+h} - f_{t+h|t} = \sigma_{\varepsilon,h}\varepsilon_{t+h} - \alpha_h,$$

where α_h is a constant and so is independent of all $z_t \in Z_t$. This property can be tested through the constraint $\beta_h = 0$ in regressions such as

$$e_{t+h|t} = \alpha_h + \beta_h' v_t + u_{t+h}, \tag{15.33}$$

where $v_t = g(z_t)$. The regression in (15.33) generalizes the conventional efficiency regression in (15.21) to allow for a nonzero constant. A less formal test could be based on a plot of the forecast against the realized value. The best fitting line should be parallel with the $45°$ line, although it need not fall on top of it since the optimal bias could be nonzero.

The three properties in (1)–(3) make the strong assumption of no predictive dynamics in second- or higher-order moments of the DGP. This assumption is too strict for many macroeconomic and financial time series which display time-varying heteroskedasticity. On the other hand, the result only imposes weak assumptions on the loss function. If more structure can be imposed on the loss function, the assumptions on the DGP can be relaxed. Patton and Timmermann (2007b) provide forecast optimality results for a more general class of DGPs with time-varying mean and variance.

Specifically, suppose the loss function is homogeneous in the forecast error,

$$L(ae) = g(a)L(e), \tag{15.34}$$

while the DGP can have conditional mean and variance dynamics,

$$y_{t+h} = \mu_{t+h|t} + \sigma_{t+h|t}\varepsilon_{t+h}, \quad \varepsilon_{t+h}|Z_t \sim p_{\varepsilon,h}(0, 1), \tag{15.35}$$

where the density $p_{\varepsilon,h}(0, 1)$ has zero mean and unit variance and can depend on h, but not on elements in Z_t. Then the optimal forecast takes the following form:

$$f_{t+h|t} = \mu_{t+h|t} + \sigma_{t+h|t} \cdot \gamma_h,$$

where the constant γ_h depends only on the density $p_{\varepsilon,h}$ and the loss function. This result relies heavily on homogeneity of the loss function, (15.34), combined with the conditional scale-location properties of the underlying DGP in (15.35).

Let the standardized forecast error associated with the optimal forecast be given by $\tilde{e}_{t+h|t} = e_{t+h|t}/\sigma_{t+h|t}$. Then $\tilde{e}_{t+h|t}$ is independent of any element $z_t \in Z_t$. In particular, $\text{Cov}(\tilde{e}_{t+h|t}^r, \tilde{e}_{t+h-j|t-j}^s) = 0$ for all $j \geq h$, any $h > 0$, and all r, s for which the covariance exists.

This result follows from noting that $\tilde{e}_{t+h|t} = \varepsilon_{t+h} - \gamma_h$, where γ_h is a constant for fixed h and, by assumption, ε_{t+h} is independent of all elements in Z_t and has unit variance. Data-generating processes covered by this result include ARCH models like those proposed by Engle (1982).

Even if the assumptions underlying these results are valid, it follows that the forecast error will generally not be unbiased, serially uncorrelated, or homoskedastic. However, the forecast error scaled by the conditional standard deviation, $\tilde{e}_{t+h|t}$, is independent of any $z_t \in Z_t$ and so this scaled forecast error, $\tilde{e}_{t+h|t}$, will be serially uncorrelated and homoskedastic. Complicating matters, tests based on $\tilde{e}_{t+h|t}$ require that an estimate of $\sigma_{t+h|t}$ is available. For many types of financial data, the conditional variance can be estimated from time series on the outcome variable using GARCH-type models, nonparametric methods, or a realized volatility estimator; see chapter 13.

For situations where a reliable estimate of $\sigma_{t+h|t}$ is difficult to construct, Patton and Timmermann (2007b) show that under the same conditions leading to the previous results, the optimal forecast can be expressed as a conditional quantile of the outcome variable. Specifically, while the optimal forecast depends on both the forecast horizon and on the shape of the loss function, it is constant over time. Let $P_{t+h|t}$ be the conditional distribution function for y_{t+h} given Z_t and suppose that either (i) the loss function depends only on the forecast error $L(e)$ as in (15.31), while the DGP has dynamics only in the conditional mean as in (15.32); or (ii) the loss function is homogeneous in the forecast error as in (15.34), while the DGP can have conditional mean and variance dynamics as in (15.35). Then the optimal forecast, $f_{t+h|t}^*$, has the property that, for all t,

$$P_{t+h|t}\left(f_{t+h|t}^*\right) = q_h^*, \tag{15.36}$$

where $q_h^* \in (0, 1)$ depends only on the density $p_{\varepsilon,h}$ and the loss function. If $P_{t+h|t}$ is continuous and strictly increasing, then we can alternatively express this as

$$f_{t+h|t}^* = P_{t+h|t}^{-1}\left(q_h^*\right). \tag{15.37}$$

To facilitate tests of this property, define the indicator variable $\mathbb{1}(y_{t+h} \leq f_{t+h|t})$ which equals 1 if the forecast is greater than or equal to the outcome, and 0 otherwise. It follows that, for an optimal forecast, $\mathbb{1}(y_{t+h} \leq f_{t+h|t})$ is independent of all $z_t \in Z_t$ and $\mathbb{1}(y_{t+h} \leq f_{t+h|t})$ is a martingale difference sequence with respect to all information in Z_t.

Even though q_h^* is typically unknown, it is easy to construct a test based on this result by projecting the indicator function $\mathbb{1}(y_{t+h} \leq f_{t+h|t}^*)$ on elements $v_t = g(z_t) \in Z_t$, and an intercept and test that $\beta_h = 0$ in the regression

$$\mathbb{1}(y_{t+h} \leq f_{t+h|t}^*) = \alpha_h + \beta_h' v_t + u_{t+h}. \tag{15.38}$$

The likelihood ratio test of independence proposed by Christoffersen (1998) could also be employed to test for serial dependence in the indicator variable $\mathbb{1}(y_{t+h} \leq f_{t+h|t}^*)$. This test does not require knowledge of the unknown conditional distribution, $P_{t+h|t}$, nor does it require that the conditional mean or variance of Y is known.

15.5 OPTIMALITY TESTS THAT DO NOT RELY ON MEASURING THE OUTCOME

Conventional forecast efficiency tests based on forecast errors such as (15.22) require that we observe the realizations of the outcome variable so we can compute $e = y - f$. Such data may not always be available. For example, many macroeconomic variables are subject to data revisions and so first release, second release, or the latest data vintage could be used to measure the outcome. This raises some fundamental questions related to whether forecasters are trying to predict the first data release or some underlying "true" variable that may never be known with certainty.

These issues can be ignored when evaluating forecasts under MSE loss provide that multiple forecasts of the same "event," Y_t, produced at different points in time, are available. As shown by Nordhaus (1987), the forecast revision should itself be unpredictable and follow a martingale process. To see this under MSE loss, note that the rational forecast satisfies $f_{t+h|t} = E[Y_{t+h}|Z_t]$ and $f_{t+h|t+1} = E[Y_{t+h}|Z_{t+1}]$. By the law of iterated expectations, $E[f_{t+h|t+1}|Z_t] = E[E[Y_{t+h}|Z_{t+1}]|Z_t] = E[Y_{t+h}|Z_t] = f_{t+h|t}$. Hence the optimal forecast of a fixed event Y_{t+h} is itself predicted not to change over time:

$$E[f_{t+h|t+1} - f_{t+h|t}|Z_t] \equiv E[\Delta f_{t+h}|Z_t] = 0. \tag{15.39}$$

Stated differently, the best current forecast of next period's prediction is the current forecast. If we expect next period's forecast to change from the current value in a manner that is predictable, this information should lead us to revise the current forecast which therefore could not have been rational in the first instance.

The martingale difference condition in (15.39) can be tested by means of a simple regression that does not involve the outcome:

$$\Delta f_{t+h|t+1} = \alpha_h + \delta_h v_t + u_{t+h}, \tag{15.40}$$

where $\Delta f_{t+h|t+1} = f_{t+h|t+1} - f_{t+h|t}$, $v_t = g(z_t) \in Z_t$ and, under the null of forecast rationality, $\alpha = \delta = 0$.

Patton and Timmermann (2012) suggest an alternative regression test of this property which replaces the actual outcome with the short-run forecast in the Mincer–Zarnowitz regression:

$$f_{t|t-h_S} = \alpha + \beta f_{t|t-h_L} + \varepsilon_t, \tag{15.41}$$

where $h_S < h_L$ and $\alpha = 0, \beta = 1$ under the null of forecast rationality. If there are more than two forecast horizons, this regression will take the form of a stacked set of regressions or, alternatively, previous forecasts or forecast revisions can all be included on the right-hand side of equation (15.41).

15.6 INTERPRETING EFFICIENCY TESTS

Care needs to be exercised when interpreting the outcome of forecast efficiency tests. Suppose we fail to reject the null hypothesis of forecast efficiency. Because any efficiency test is conditional on a particular choice of information set, it is possible that the information set simply was too limited and that a well-chosen augmentation of the information set could overturn the result. In other words, even if we fail to reject $H_0 : \beta_{1h} = 0$ in the regression

$$e_{t+h|t} = \beta_{1h}v_{1t} + u_{1t+h}, \tag{15.42}$$

it is possible that we would reject the null hypothesis $H_0 : \beta_{1h} = \beta_{2h} = 0$ in the regression

$$e_{t+h|t} = \beta_{1h}v_{1t} + \beta_{2h}v_{2t} + u_{2t+h}, \tag{15.43}$$

where $v_{1t}, v_{2t} \in Z_t$. This simple point, that tests of forecast efficiency are contingent upon the specified information set, raises several issues. First, in the common situation where we do not observe the specific information available to the forecaster at the time when the forecast was generated, it can be very difficult to conduct a strong-form test of efficiency, i.e., a test of whether forecasters efficiently exploited *all* information at their disposal.

Conversely, conducting the efficiency test based on data that actually were not available to the forecaster in real time could lead us to wrongly reject that forecasts were efficient. This issue arises in forecast rationality tests with macroeconomic data which are often based on revised data as opposed to the original vintage data. If forecast errors and data on realized values were not in the forecaster's information set, then an apparent rejection of forecast rationality is of course meaningless. At a minimum, current and past values of the forecasts are known to the forecaster which suggests using this variable, or possibly the change in the forecast, $f_{t+h|t} - f_{t+h-1|t-1}$, as a predictor.

Weak power of the forecast rationality test is a second important issue. Macroeconomic data are typically recorded at monthly or quarterly frequency which limits us to small sample sizes and reduces the power of efficiency tests. This small sample concern is particularly strong in survey data such as the Survey of Professional Forecasters or Blue Chip forecasts where the forecast record of individual forecasters typically is very short and often not contiguous.

Short sample sizes and lack of power is also a concern with pseudo out-of-sample forecast experiments. These experiments typically split the full data sample into estimation and evaluation samples so that only a portion of the full data is held back for the actual forecast evaluation test. Ideally, the estimation sample is large enough to obtain precise estimates, while the evaluation sample is sufficiently large to obtain high power for the test. However, macroeconomic and many finance applications clearly impose severe limits on the available data. Another issue is the fact that macroeconomic data get revised and so an evaluation that uses data that were unavailable to the forecaster in "real time" can lead to wrong conclusions. Clark and McCracken (2009) address the importance of this issue both theoretically and for an empirical application involving inflation forecasts.

A related issue arises when the outcome distribution perceived by the forecaster differs from the empirical distribution observed in a particular evaluation sample, as in the case of the famous "peso" problem. Suppose that a currency forecaster puts a nonzero weight on the possibility that there will be a catastrophic event such as a substantial devaluation of the Mexican peso against the US dollar, perhaps due to an economic meltdown leading to a run on the currency. Forecasts that account for this possibility will lead to peso predictions that are on average lower than if this possibility was ignored. This makes rational forecasts appear biased if the meltdown does not occur in a given evaluation sample. The bias arises because the evaluation sample is not sufficiently representative in the sense that it does not contain a currency crash as stipulated by the forecaster. In this sense the peso problem is a small sample problem in which the evaluation sample differs significantly from the population distribution. If a very long sample was available with sufficiently many crash events to match the forecaster's prediction, the bias would vanish.

We might also be limited by not trusting data or forecasts too far in the past to have been generated by the same process as current values. The forecast methods used by survey participants or institutions can undergo change, leading to a failure to statistically reject the null of forecast rationality, even though the forecasts are poor from an economic perspective. Conversely, if rejections based on full-sample information reflect the forecaster's learning process, it is not clear that the forecaster used historically available information inefficiently.

A final issue in interpretation of forecast rationality tests is that any test of rationality is a joint test of rationality and the assumed loss function. As in the case with the forecaster's information set, the forecaster's loss function is typically unknown. This can lead to wrong rejections or failures to reject the null of forecast rationality. An immediate implication of a rejection of forecast rationality is that the forecaster did not optimally use all information and that a better forecast could have been produced. Suppose that the loss function that was actually used by the forecaster differs from that assumed by the evaluator. If the forecaster has asymmetric loss so the cost of over- and underpredictions are not the same, it would typically have been rational to generate biased forecasts; see section 15.2. Forecast efficiency tests based on MSE loss would reject the null of forecast rationality due to such bias and so lead to the wrong conclusion. We illustrate this point in the following example.

Example 15.6.1 (MSE evaluation of asymmetric quadratic loss). *Suppose a forecaster has the following asymmetric quadratic loss function:*

$$L(e_{t+1|t}) \equiv [\alpha + (1 - 2\alpha)\mathbb{1}(e_{t+1|t} < 0)]e^2_{t+1|t}.$$

This gives rise to the following first-order condition:

$$E[v_t (\alpha - \mathbb{1}(e_{t+1|t} < 0)) |e_{t+1|t}|] = 0. \tag{15.44}$$

The generalized forecast error in (15.7) now takes the form

$$
\begin{aligned}
2\left((\alpha - \mathbb{1}(e_{t+1} < 0)) |e_{t+1|t}|\right) &= 2\left(\alpha|e_{t+1|t}| - \mathbb{1}(e_{t+1|t} < 0)|e_{t+1|t}|\right) \\
&= 2\alpha|e_{t+1|t}| - \left(|e_{t+1|t}| - e_{t+1|t}\right) \\
&= (2\alpha - 1)|e_{t+1|t}| + e_{t+1|t}.
\end{aligned}
$$

Hence the first-order condition in (15.44) can be rewritten as

$$E[v_t ((2\alpha - 1)|e_{t+1|t}| + e_{t+1|t})] = 0,$$

which is the first-order condition from the regression

$$e_{t+1|t} + (2\alpha - 1)|e_{t+1|t}| = v_t \delta + u_{t+1}.$$

Efficiency tests based on MSE loss simply use the forecast error in the regression $e_{t+1|t} = v_t \delta + \tilde{u}_{t+1}$. They therefore omit the regressor $(1 - 2\alpha)|e_{t+1|t}|$ and induce an omitted variable bias in the estimate of δ. The omitted variable is nonzero except when loss is quadratic ($\alpha = 0.5$) and hence will cause the constant term (if v_t includes an intercept) to be nonzero, inducing a bias. The omitted variable could also be correlated with other terms in v_t and in a large enough sample the null of rationality will be rejected due to the use of an incorrect loss function.

Should we conclude from these considerations that forecast rationality is essentially empirically untestable due to the twin problems arising from joint hypothesis tests (the forecaster's loss function and information set are unknown) and weak power due to short samples or model instability? While these issues clearly complicate forecast rationality tests, this is taking the critique too far. For example, flexible loss functions of the type in (15.28) can be used to capture most interesting deviations from quadratic error loss, at least in so far as error-based loss is concerned. Issues related to unobservable or nonstationary data can in part be dealt with by basing the forecast rationality test on observables such as forecast revisions; see (15.40).

While we here consider tests of forecast rationality given the loss function and show how to extend the tests to allow for flexibility in the loss function, an alternative question might be to consider whether we can recover the forecaster's loss function, assuming that rationality holds. In the context of a parametric set of loss functions, this is what Elliott, Komunjer, and Timmermann (2005) allows. More generally, we might be interested in finding out whether it is possible to recover the forecaster's loss function without constraining this to be parameterized up to a finite set of unknown parameters. This question is addressed in Lieli and Stinchcombe (2013) who provide conditions under which identification of the loss function is possible.

15.7 CONCLUSION

Forecast evaluation is an important part of constructing, monitoring, and improving individual forecasting models. In-sample methods for forecast evaluation are similar to diagnostic testing in econometric analysis and include assessing whether forecast errors are serially correlated (or, more generally, predictable), in which case a better model could be constructed. Out-of-sample methods simulate models' "real-time" performance, using only part of the sample to generate a sequence of forecasts so as to reduce the possible effect of data-mining on the forecasting performance.

Forecast evaluation methods should reflect the forecaster's loss function. In fact, given a sequence of observed forecasts, it is sometimes possible to reverse engineer the forecaster's unknown loss function and to conduct tests of forecast rationality under much weaker assumptions than knowledge of the forecaster's specific loss function. In the case with mean squared error (quadratic) loss, a large literature has suggested tests for forecast optimality based on unbiasedness and lack of serial correlation in forecast errors. More broadly, assumptions about the underlying data generating process and the forecaster's loss function can also be traded off so as to establish testable implications of forecast rationality.

16

✦✦✦✦✦✦✦✦✦✦✦✦✦✦✦✦✦✦✦✦✦✦✦✦✦✦✦✦✦✦✦✦✦✦✦

Evaluation of Individual Forecasts

Measurement of predictive accuracy is closely related to forecast evaluation. Both absolute and relative measures of forecasting performance can be considered. Absolute performance measures are concerned with the accuracy of an individual forecast relative to the outcome, using either an economic (loss-based) or a statistical metric. Relative performance measures compare the performance of one or several forecasts against some benchmark. The present chapter is concerned with individual models' absolute forecasting performance, while the next chapter deals with comparisons of predictive accuracy across multiple forecasts.

Forecast evaluation amounts to understanding whether the loss from a given forecast is "small enough." Both formal and informal methods can be employed. Informal methods such as the graphical approach of Theil (1961) described in chapter 15 yield "big picture" answers to this question and can help point to directions in which a set of forecasts is clearly deficient. For example, a plot of the realized value against the predicted value could reveal a systematic tendency for over- or underprediction.

More formal methods that use the data to estimate average loss can also be examined. Examination of such averages has a long history, but only in the last few years have researchers begun to place standard errors on loss estimates in a way that facilitates rigorous inference about predictability. A key complication is that the distribution of the test statistic for these sample averages may depend on how the forecasts were constructed, specifically which estimation method the forecasts were based on. This has led to the recognition that not only the forecasting model, but also the forecasting method matters. For example, whether an expanding or a fixed estimation window was used to generate the forecast can affect the subsequent inference concerning predictive accuracy.

Formal evaluation of an individual forecast is concerned with testing whether the forecast is optimal with respect to some loss function and a specific information set. If forecast optimality is rejected, the implication is that the forecast can be improved upon. Forecast optimality tests have a long history reflected in a vast literature with its own nomenclature. As with the calculation of standard errors on average loss, construction of such tests requires understanding the method (and information set) used to generate forecasts and forecast errors. Often this is ignored in practice, and for many interesting situations the precise method for constructing the tests is unknown. One exception is the use of so-called pseudo out-of-sample forecasting methods which simulate the process by which forecasts could have been generated in "real time." By construction, this setup assumes that the methods used for model estimation and forecast construction are known to the evaluator.

Sampling properties of forecast evaluation statistics, such as the consistency and standard error, may well depend not only on the model but also on how the parameters were estimated and what data were used to construct the forecast. This is important because there are several different methods for constructing forecasts. A natural approach is to simulate the real-time forecasting problem by using only historically available data to construct forecasts. This backtesting approach contrasts with an approach of using the full data sample for estimation and forecast evaluation purposes.

The outline of the chapter is as follows. Section 16.1 reviews some issues that arise in analyzing the sampling distribution of average losses. Section 16.2 turns to different schemes for simulating out-of-sample forecasts, while section 16.3 pursues more formal methods for evaluating the magnitude of average loss from a sequence of forecasts and conducting inference on out-of-sample loss. These methods reflect both the properties of the data-generating process and the method used to construct the forecasts, where the latter explicitly accounts for the fact that the forecasts are themselves generated from some forecasting model and so parameter uncertainty must be taken into account. Section 16.4 discusses asymptotics for out-of-sample forecast rationality tests with generated forecasts. Section 16.5 covers evaluation of aggregate and disaggregate forecasts and Section 16.6 concludes.

16.1 THE SAMPLING DISTRIBUTION OF AVERAGE LOSSES

Good forecasting models produce "small" expected losses, while bad models produce "large" expected losses, where "small" and "large" loss are naturally defined with respect to the loss that would be incurred using an optimal forecast.[1] To evaluate a forecasting model, we therefore need to estimate its expected loss. The measure used for this purpose is the sample average loss. This, however, is a random variable that will fluctuate across different samples. Small average losses in a given sample could just be due to luck or could, alternatively, reflect the performance of a genuinely good model. To distinguish between these alternatives, we need to know more about the sampling distribution of average losses.

Risk was defined as

$$R(\theta, f) = E_{Y,Z}[L(f(Z), Y)], \tag{16.1}$$

in the notation of chapter 3. Clearly it is useful to understand the risk associated with the forecast at the time this is computed. While risk is unobserved, we can construct an estimate of it through the average loss from a sequence of forecasts and outcomes

---

[1] This definition accounts for the fact that some variables are easier to predict than others. A perfect forecast of an i.i.d. variable could have a "large" loss, though not compared to the optimal forecast. Conversely, a suboptimal forecast of a highly persistent variable may generate a "small" loss, even though its performance is much worse than that of the optimal forecast.

$\{f_{t+h|t}, y_{t+h}\}$, $t = 1, \ldots, T - h$, as

$$\hat{R}(f) = (T - h)^{-1} \sum_{t=1}^{T-h} L(f(z_t, \hat{\beta}_t), y_{t+h}). \tag{16.2}$$

Typical examples of the types of expected losses that are estimated empirically include the mean squared error (MSE) or root mean squared error (RMSE), which preserves the unit of the outcome variable, or mean absolute error (MAE). Such measures are sample averages based on forecast errors, $e_{t+h|t} = y_{t+h} - f_{t+h|t}$, measured over a sample, $t = 1, \ldots, T - h$:

$$\text{MSE} = (T - h)^{-1} \sum_{t=1}^{T-h} e_{t+h|t}^2,$$

$$\text{RMSE} = \left((T - h)^{-1} \sum_{t=1}^{T-h} e_{t+h|t}^2 \right)^{1/2},$$

$$\text{MAE} = (T - h)^{-1} \sum_{t=1}^{T-h} |e_{t+h|t}|. \tag{16.3}$$

Other loss functions have similar sample analogs.

In addition to average losses, other measures are sometimes reported even though they do not pertain to any particular loss function. Sometimes the forecast error is scaled by the outcome variable which gives rise to the percentage error $\text{pe}_{t+h|t} = e_{t+h|t}/y_{t+h}$, and the associated root mean squared percentage error (RMSPE),

$$\text{RMSPE} = \left((T - h)^{-1} \sum_{t=1}^{T-h} \text{pe}_{t+h|t}^2 \right)^{1/2}. \tag{16.4}$$

Unless based on the forecaster's loss function, these measures can be viewed more as informal summary statistics that can be useful for giving some sense of the degree of predictability of the outcome variable and the magnitude of forecast errors in the same sense as the standard error from a regression model. Great care must be exercised, however, in interpreting and basing statistical inference on such sample averages.

16.1.1 In-Sample Forecast Evaluation

In-sample, or full-sample, forecasts use the entire data from $t = 1, \ldots, T - h$ to estimate model parameters, $\hat{\beta}_T$, and evaluate forecasts constructed off such estimates:

$$f_{t+h|T} = \hat{f}(z_t, \hat{\beta}_T). \tag{16.5}$$

Because data at time $T > t$ were not available in real time to construct the forecast at time t, $\hat{f}(z_t, \hat{\beta}_t)$, such forecasts could not have been constructed in real time and thus are infeasible. Nevertheless, by making use of the full data set, these forecasts make efficient use of all data that is available at time T and eliminate the variation in the sequence of forecasts arising from revisions to model parameters. Hence, these forecasts represent the best forecasts available to a forecaster with access to the full information set, which we denote by Z_T.

Chapter 6 showed that in-sample evaluation of forecasting models—the practice of using the same sample for model estimation and forecast evaluation—results in a bias towards overparameterized models. By virtue of the properties of minimization, the in-sample estimate, $\hat{\beta}_T$, minimizes the sample estimate of the average loss, i.e.,

$$\hat{R}(f) = (T-h)^{-1} \sum_{t=1}^{T-h} L(f(z_t, \hat{\beta}_T), y_{t+h}) \leq (T-h)^{-1} \sum_{t=1}^{T-h} L(f(z_t, \beta), y_{t+h}),$$

$$(16.6)$$

for any $\hat{\beta}_T$, including the limiting value β^*. It follows that in-sample evaluation measures typically underestimate the unconditional expected loss.

In many situations $\hat{R}(f)$ provides a consistent estimate of the unconditional expected loss, as the effect of parameter estimation error through the variance term disappears asymptotically. Indeed, as discussed in chapter 4, estimation error disappearing asymptotically is precisely what justifies estimation of the parameters of the forecasting model by minimizing the forecast loss. If the in-sample average loss failed to be consistent for the unconditional loss, this would suggest using a different estimator.

The general problem with in-sample forecast evaluation methods is that they underestimate the true unconditional expected loss and hence yield an inaccurate picture of the likely future loss that a given forecasting model produces. This has led most researchers to consider out-of-sample forecasting methods for evaluating the expected loss, which we next turn to.

16.2 SIMULATING OUT-OF-SAMPLE FORECASTS

Assuming that the forecasts, $f_{t+h|t}$, are based on model estimates, $\hat{f}(x_t, \hat{\beta}_t)$, statistics that are a function of the forecasts will have sampling properties that depend on the estimation scheme used to generate such forecasts. The key observation is that the estimated parameters of the forecasting model, $\hat{\beta}_t$, typically get updated as time passes since they are based on information in the data set available for making the forecast. Time variation in $\hat{\beta}_t$ introduces a new source of variation in the forecast. Moreover, recursive updating of the parameters of the forecasting model induces a correlation between shocks to the outcome variable, y_{t+h}, and future parameter estimates, $\hat{\beta}_{t+h}$, $\hat{\beta}_{t+h+1}$, etc. These effects extend the problem from one of simply evaluating a sample mean to one that depends in a more complicated way on the data.

Two possible scenarios arise. First, sampling errors in the parameters of the forecasting model may be asymptotically irrelevant. In this case inference can be based on average loss assuming that the forecast errors come from the true model. Second, how the forecast was constructed may matter asymptotically, in which case estimation of the parameters of the forecasting model provides a second source of randomness in the average loss. For the second scenario, several different methods for how the parameters of the forecasting model are estimated have been studied. Each method varies in the sampling distribution of the loss $L(\hat{f}(x_t, \hat{\beta}_t), y_{t+h})$ due to differences in how the estimates $\hat{\beta}_t$ are arrived at. Often such differences are either not asymptotically negligible or, even when they are, still have different second-order asymptotic effects.

To account for the criticism that in-sample forecasts are not feasible in real-time, out-of-sample (OoS) forecasts impose the constraint that the parameter estimates of the forecasting model use only information available at the time the forecast was computed, which we denote time t. Hence, only information included in Z_t can be used to estimate the forecasting model at time t and generate forecasts $f_{t+h|t}$. Advancing one period to time $t+1$, only information included in Z_{t+1} can be used to generate forecasts $f_{t+h+1|t+1}$, and so forth. The same argument holds for choice of forecasting model, i.e., only information known at time t can be used to select a model for generating a forecast $f_{t+h|t}$. Only at the very end of the sample, at time T, is the full sample available for selecting and estimating the parameters of the forecasting model.

The many variants of OoS forecast estimation methods differ in how they account for possible model instability by discounting past data more or less strongly. Differences between the various weighting methods can be illustrated in the context of the linear regression model with a one-period forecast horizon ($h = 1$),

$$y_{t+1} = \beta' x_t + \varepsilon_{t+1},$$

which leads to one-step forecasts of the form $\hat{f}_{t+1|t} = \hat{\beta}'_t x_t$, where

$$\hat{\beta}_t = \left(\sum_{s=1}^{t} \omega(s, t) x_{s-1} x'_{s-1} \right)^{-1} \left(\sum_{s=1}^{t} \omega(s, t) x_{s-1} y_s \right). \tag{16.7}$$

Different methods are defined by different weight functions $\omega(s, t)$ which determine the importance of recent versus older data. We next describe the most common weighting schemes.

16.2.1 Expanding Estimation Window

Expanding or recursive estimation windows put equal weight on all observations from the beginning of the sample to the point of the forecast, $s = 1, \ldots, t$, to estimate the parameters of the forecasting model. The following period, the same information plus the extra observation, $z_{t+1} = z_t \cup \{y_{t+1}, x_{t+1}\}$, is used to update the model parameters and generate a new forecast. For this case the weights in equation (16.7) take the form

$$\omega(s, t) = \begin{cases} 1, & 1 \le s \le t, \\ 0 & \text{otherwise.} \end{cases} \tag{16.8}$$

For linear regressions the recursive coefficient estimates simplify to

$$\hat{\beta}_t = \left(\sum_{s=1}^{t} x_{s-1} x'_{s-1} \right)^{-1} \left(\sum_{s=1}^{t} x_{s-1} y_s \right). \tag{16.9}$$

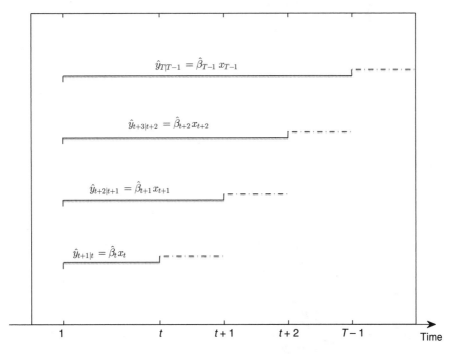

Figure 16.1: Estimation sample under an expanding estimation window.

As time progresses, the estimation sample grows larger, $Z_t \subseteq Z_{t+1}$ and so the expanding window approach mimics what many forecasters are likely to do in practice. Figure 16.1 illustrates this case.

In a stationary world where the parameters of the DGP do not change, the expanding window approach makes efficient use of the data and leads to consistent parameter estimates. Conversely, in a nonstationary world in which the parameters of the model are subject to change, the approach leads to biased forecasts. However, the approach can still be difficult to improve upon due to its use of all available data which reduces the effect of estimation error on the forecasts. In empirical applications, producing relatively small parameter estimation errors often dominates the effect of reducing the (squared) bias, unless the change in the model parameters is very large. See Pesaran and Timmermann (2007) for an analysis of this issue.

16.2.2 Rolling Estimation Window

A rolling estimation window refers to the practice of using an equal-weighted window of the most recent $\bar{\omega}$ observations to estimate the parameters of the forecasting model. For example, to generate a forecast of y_{t+1} at time $t > \bar{\omega}$, data (y_s, x_{s-1}), $s = t - \bar{\omega} + 1, \ldots, t$ is used for parameter estimation. As time progresses and new observations become available, older observations get dropped so that the size of the sample used for parameter estimation remains constant at $\bar{\omega}$. Hence, at time $t + 1$, the observation at time $t - \bar{\omega} + 1$ is dropped, while the new data point at time $t + 1$ is added, so the updated data set $\{y_s, x_{s-1}\}$, $s = t - \bar{\omega} + 2, \ldots, t + 1$ is used to generate a forecast of y_{t+2}. The rolling window weights in (16.7) are rectangular

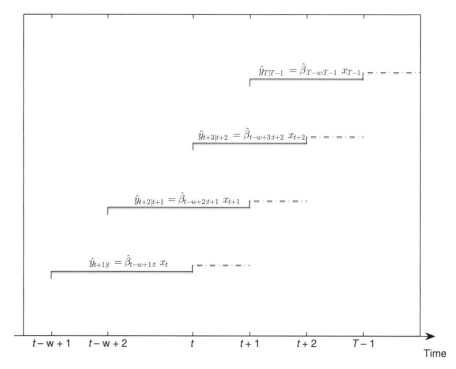

Figure 16.2: Estimation sample under a rolling estimation window.

and take the form

$$\omega(s, t) = \begin{cases} 1, & t - \bar{\omega} + 1 \leq s \leq t, \\ 0 & \text{otherwise.} \end{cases} \tag{16.10}$$

For a linear regression model this yields coefficient estimates,

$$\hat{\beta}_t = \left(\sum_{s=t-\bar{\omega}+1}^{t} x_{s-1} x'_{s-1} \right)^{-1} \left(\sum_{s=t-\bar{\omega}+1}^{t} x_{s-1} y_s \right).$$

Figure 16.2 illustrates this case.

The rolling window estimation method requires choosing a single parameter, namely the length of the estimation window, $\bar{\omega}$. This is commonly set to some fixed number, e.g., 5, 10, or 20 years of observations in the case of monthly or quarterly data. Alternatively, one could use cross-validation methods to optimize over the value of $\bar{\omega}$, but this is rarely done.

The rolling window method is typically used when forecasters are not convinced that the underlying DGP is stationary and so do not want to "contaminate" the model forecasts too much by basing them on old and potentially irrelevant data. The practice of dropping past data comes, however, at the cost of using parameter estimates that fluctuate more than under the expanding window scheme and so typically parameter estimation error is a greater concern for the rolling window method. Moreover, it is not possible to write down a general DGP under which it is optimal to use rolling window estimation, which complicates decisions on when and whether to use this approach versus other approaches designed to handle nonstationarities.

16.2.3 Fixed-Proportion Estimation Window

Rather than using a fixed-length window to estimate the parameters of the forecasting model, a fixed proportion of the data can be used. For example, the most recent 50% of the data could be used for parameter estimation. This has the advantage that the number of observations used for parameter estimation increases as the sample grows, thus dampening the effect of parameter estimation error. The data weights for this case take the form

$$\omega(s, t) = \begin{cases} 1, & (1 - \lambda)t + 1 \leq s \leq t, \\ 0 & \text{otherwise}. \end{cases} \tag{16.11}$$

Like the rolling (fixed) window method, this method relies on only one parameter, namely the value of λ, the proportion of the data sample used for estimation. This method is less widespread in applied work than the rolling window method, but is sometimes used in analytical work to characterize the sampling distribution of various test statistics.

16.2.4 Fixed Estimation Window

The fixed window estimation method includes only the first $\bar{\omega}$ observations to once and for all estimate the parameters of the forecasting model used to generate all subsequent forecasts. Newer data that could be used to reestimate the parameters of the forecasting model are ignored and instead the same parameters are used indefinitely. The fixed window weights can be written as

$$\omega(s, t) = \begin{cases} 1, & 1 \leq s \leq \bar{\omega}_0, \\ 0 & \text{otherwise}. \end{cases} \tag{16.12}$$

For linear regression models, the fixed window regression coefficients take the form

$$\hat{\beta}_t = \left(\sum_{s=1}^{\bar{\omega}_0} x_{s-1} x'_{s-1} \right)^{-1} \left(\sum_{s=1}^{\bar{\omega}_0} x_{s-1} y_s \right).$$

This method is typically employed when the costs of estimation are very high and reestimating the model with new data is prohibitively expensive or impractical in real time.[2] Figure 16.3 illustrates this case.

16.2.5 Exponentially Declining Weights

In the presence of model instability, it is common to discount past observations using weights that get smaller, the older the data. A simple scheme for doing this is to use

---

[2] Anecdotal evidence suggests a variation of this method that is used in practice. Forecast errors are monitored at each point in time and the parameters of the forecasting model are reestimated only when the errors get too large over a period of time, indicating evidence of model breakdown; see, e.g., Pesaran and Timmermann (2000).

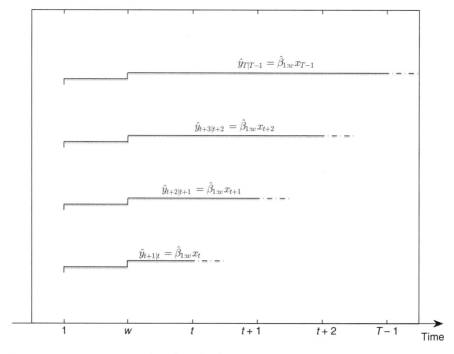

Figure 16.3: Estimation sample under a fixed estimation window.

exponentially declining weights of the following form:

$$\omega(s, t) = \begin{cases} \lambda^{t-s}, & 1 \leq s \leq t, \\ 0 & \text{otherwise,} \end{cases} \tag{16.13}$$

where $0 < \lambda < 1$. Notice that the most recent observation gets a weight of $\lambda^0 = 1$, the previous data point gets a weight of λ, two-period-old data are weighted by λ^2, and so forth.

This method is sometimes referred to as discounted least squares as the discount factor, λ, puts less weight on past observations.

16.3 CONDUCTING INFERENCE ON THE OUT-OF-SAMPLE AVERAGE LOSS

The simulated (or "pseudo") out-of-sample (OoS) approach described in the previous section seeks to mimic the real-time updating scheme underlying most forecasts. The basic idea is to split the data into an initial estimation sample (the in-sample period) and a subsequent evaluation sample (the out-of-sample period). Forecasts are based on parameter estimates that use data only up to the date when the forecast is computed. As the sample expands, the model parameters get updated, resulting in a sequence of forecasts. Comparing realized values to these forecasts, we can compute the average loss.

West (1996) provides the main set of results that establishes conditions under which the estimated loss is both consistent and asymptotically normal under expanding (recursive), rolling, and fixed estimation windows. The assumptions involve conventional restrictions on the data-generating process, but impose further limitations on the form of the forecasting model. The analysis assumes that the initial sample for estimating $\hat{\beta}_t$ has T_R observations, and that this allows the construction of $T_P = T - T_R - h$ out-of-sample forecast errors, where h is the forecast horizon.[3] If the full sample is used for parameter estimation, each forecast is computed using $\hat{\beta}_T$.

Let $l_{t+h|t}(\beta) = L(f(z_t, \beta), y_{t+h})$ be a vector of losses whose individual elements are denoted $l_{t+h|t,i}(\beta)$. The observed losses depend on the parameter estimates, $\hat{\beta}_t$, and are denoted $l_{t+h|t}(\hat{\beta}_t)$. The analysis requires that there exists a pseudo-true vector, β^*, for the model used to generate the forecasts; β^* is the limiting value of $\hat{\beta}_t$ as the sample size gets very large. Define $l_{t+h|t}(\beta^*)$ as the loss function evaluated at this pseudo-true value, while $F = E\left[\partial l_{t+h|t}(\beta)/\partial\beta\right]$ is the derivative evaluated at β^*. Also, let η_{t+h} be the orthogonality conditions used to estimate the model parameters so that $\eta_{t+h}(\beta^*)$ is a zero-mean process. The following assumptions summarize the technical conditions needed for West's result (West, 1996, Theorem 4.1).

1. The function $l_{t+h|t}(\beta)$ is twice differentiable in a neighborhood around β^*.
2. The estimate $\hat{\beta}_t$ can be written as a moment-type estimator of full rank. Specifically, $\hat{\beta}_t - \beta^* = B(t)H(t)$, where $B(t)$ is $k \times q$, $H(t)$ is $q \times 1$ with $B(t) \to^{as} B$, for B of rank k; $H(t) = (t-h)^{-1}\sum_{s=1}^{t-h}\eta_{s+h}(\beta^*)$; and $E[\eta_s(\beta^*)] = 0$.
3. The second derivative, $|\partial^2 l_{t+h|t}(\beta)/\partial\beta\,\partial\beta'|$, is bounded.
4. The derivative, $\partial l_{t+h|t}(\beta)/\partial\beta$, when evaluated at the pseudo-true value β^*, satisfies certain mixing, moment, and stationarity conditions. Moreover, letting $\Gamma(j) = E[(l_{t+h|t}(\beta^*) - E[l_{t+h|t}(\beta^*)])(l_{t-j+h|t-j}(\beta^*)' - E[l_{t-j+h|t-j}(\beta^*)'])]$ and $S_y(0) = \sum_{j=-\infty}^{\infty}\Gamma(j)$, $S_y(0)$ is assumed to be positive definite.
5. We have $T_R, T_P \to \infty$ and $T_P/T_R \to \pi$. Define $\Pi = 1 - \ln(1+\pi)/\pi$ if $0 < \pi < \infty$ and $\Pi = 0$ if $\pi = 0$ and $\Pi = 1$ if $\pi = \infty$.

Under assumptions (1)–(5), West (1996) establishes that

$$T_P^{-1/2}\left(\sum_{t=T_R}^{T-h} l_{t+h|t}(\hat{\beta}_t) - E[l_{t+h}(\beta^*)]\right) \to^d N(0, \Omega),$$

where, in general,

$$\Omega = S_y(0) + \Pi(FBS'_{yh}(0) + S_{yh}(0)B'F') + 2\Pi F V_\beta F', \qquad (16.14)$$

and $S_{yh}(0) = \sum_{j=-\infty}^{\infty} E[\eta_t\eta'_{t-j}]$, and V_β is the limiting variance–covariance matrix of the estimators, i.e., asymptotically $T^{1/2}(\hat{\beta} - \beta) \to^d N(0, V_\beta)$. If either $\pi = 0$ or $F = 0$, then $\Omega = S_y(0)$.

The result establishes that asymptotically, we can conduct inference about forecast accuracy using standard normal distributions provided that the correct (asymptotically valid) estimate of Ω is used. From (16.14), Ω consists of three components: $S_y(0)$ is the long-run variance of the loss under known model parameters, the third term reflects how parameter estimation affects the variance of the loss, while the second

---

[3] For simplicity we do not use an h subscript on T_P.

term reflects the covariance between the first and third terms. Since the second and third terms reflect estimation error, they will depend on the underlying estimation scheme—fixed, rolling, or expanding—via Π.

To understand the result, it is useful to go through the heuristics of the proof. The proof works by expanding the average OoS loss around the pseudo-true parameter value, β^*, at each data point. Assumption (1) in West's theorem allows a mean value theorem expansion around β^* so that, for some intermediate value, $\tilde{\beta}$,

$$l_{t+h|t}(\hat{\beta}_t) = l_{t+h|t}(\beta^*) + \left.\frac{\partial l_{t+h|t}(\beta)}{\partial \beta}\right|_{\beta^*}' (\hat{\beta}_t - \beta^*)$$

$$+ \frac{1}{2}(\hat{\beta}_t - \beta^*)'\left(\left.\frac{\partial^2 l_{t+h|t}(\beta)}{\partial \beta\, \partial \beta'}\right|_{\tilde{\beta}}\right)(\hat{\beta}_t - \beta^*). \qquad (16.15)$$

The first term in (16.15) is the contribution to the average loss evaluated at the pseudo-true value, i.e., the average loss when the parameters are known. Under West's conditions, this converges to its expected value and contributes the term $S_y(0)$ to the covariance matrix. This is similar to the usual covariance for the mean of a stationary series. The second term in (16.15) involves the term $(\hat{\beta}_t - \beta^*)$ and need not be identically equal to 0 since parameter estimates are periodically updated.[4] In some cases this term is not only nonzero but does not vanish asymptotically when scaled by $T^{1/2}$, resulting in the additional term in the variance in (16.14). The third term in (16.15) involves a quadratic in $(\hat{\beta}_t - \beta^*)$ and also does not disappear asymptotically.

In cases where the second and third terms in Ω equal 0, estimation error does not contribute to the variance of the average out-of-sample loss and so the result captures only first-order effects, while ignoring terms of order T^{-1} such as parameter estimation error. In such cases, in-sample and out-of-sample average loss have identical means and approximately identical variances, which makes it difficult to determine what is a better way to evaluate predictive performance in general.

One case of particular interest arises when the same loss function (e.g., squared error loss) is used for parameter estimation as well as forecast evaluation. In this case the extra terms in West's variance drop out and so the expression simplifies a great deal.

When West's theorem applies, $\hat{R}(f) \to^P E[L_{t+h}]$, and so the result establishes that the estimated average loss is a consistent estimator for the actual average loss.

West's result deals with inference about the expected loss evaluated at the population value of the model parameters, β^*, i.e., $E[L_{t+h|t}(\beta^*)]$. Complications arise because the inference cannot be based on the unobserved population value of the parameters but instead is based on finite sample information for which parameter estimation error can play an important role.

West's result does not cover inference about the finite-sample predictive ability of a model which is related to the model's expected loss evaluated at the current parameter values, $E[L_{t+h|t}(\hat{\beta}_t)]$. This case is considered by Giacomini and White (2006).

West (1996, table 2) presents Monte Carlo results for a dynamic bivariate model with exogenous regressors. For his design $\Omega \neq S_c(0)$, and so the variance–covariance

---

[4] Hence, this term is not the first-order condition used for estimation, although in the in-sample case it would be 0.

matrix should account for parameter estimation error in the construction of the forecasts. Across a range of cases West shows that without this correction, the size of the test can be far greater than its nominal size, e.g., with rejection rates of 20–50% instead of 5%. With the correction for estimation error, size is well controlled unless the number of observations in the initial regression model is small. Specifically, the test is undersized if T_p is small and oversized if T_p is relatively large.

16.3.1 West's Result under Squared Error Loss

Conditions (1)–(5) in West's theorem may appear somewhat abstract and hard to verify. To make the result more accessible, we next discuss West's theorem for the common case with squared error loss and univariate forecasts based on a linear regression model, $y_{t+1} = \beta' x_t + \varepsilon_{t+1}$, whose parameters are estimated by recursive OLS. Assumption (1) in West's theorem involves both the loss function and the method for constructing the forecast. Under squared error loss, and assuming $h = 1$,

$$l_{t+1|t}(\beta) = (y_{t+1} - \beta' x_t)^2,$$

and so

$$\frac{\partial l_{t+1|t}(\beta)}{\partial \beta} = -2(y_{t+1} - \beta' x_t)x_t,$$

$$\frac{\partial^2 l_{t+1|t}(\beta)}{\partial \beta \, \partial \beta'} = 2x_t x_t',$$

showing that the loss is twice differentiable.

Turning to the second assumption in West's theorem, the parameter estimate, $\hat{\beta}_t$, obtained under an expanding window takes the form

$$\hat{\beta}_t - \beta^* = \left((t-1)^{-1} \sum_{s=1}^{t-1} x_s x_s' \right)^{-1} \left((t-1)^{-1} \sum_{s=1}^{t-1} x_s (y_{s+1} - \beta^{*\prime} x_s) \right).$$

This case is covered by assumption (2) with $B(t) = ((t-1)^{-1} \sum_{s=1}^{t-1} x_s x_s')^{-1}$; $B(t)$ is the inverse of the variance–covariance matrix of x_t and so has limit B under relatively mild conditions on x_t. This leaves the definition of $\eta_{s+1} = \eta_{s+1}(\beta^*)$ to be $\eta_{s+1} = x_s(y_{s+1} - \beta^{*\prime} x_s)$, where the dependence on β^* is explicit. We define β^* as the linear projection of y_{s+1} on x_s, so $E[\eta(\beta^*)] = 0$ by construction. If the regressors were nonstationary, $B(t)$ would not converge to B and so this case is ruled out by assumption (2).

Assumption (3) in West's theorem is a smoothness condition. In the example here, the second derivative does not depend on the parameters and so this assumption follows directly given assumptions on the regressors. Assumption (4) places limited dependence and moment restrictions on the regressors and forecast errors, which again follows under weak assumptions on the DGPs. For example, in the very common case where $\{x_t, \varepsilon_t\}$ are covariance stationary, these conditions will hold and the theorem applies.

West's theorem shows that in the special case where $\Omega = S_y(0)$, the covariance matrix of the sample mean can be approximated by the usual spectral density estimate, ignoring sampling variation when we construct the estimates. One such special case arises when the training (estimation) sample used to construct the forecasts (T_R) overwhelms the out-of-sample period (T_P) so $\pi = 0$. Intuitively it makes sense that parameter estimation error is not relevant in this situation.

A second special case is less obvious. Under squared error loss, the forecasts are generated so that the prediction error is uncorrelated with the predictors and so

$$
F = E\left[\left.\frac{\partial l_{t+1|t,1}(\beta)}{\partial \beta}\right|_{\beta*}\right] = -2E\,(y_{t+1} - \beta^{*\prime}x_t)x_t' = 0,
$$

and so the usual asymptotic results apply. This combination of mean squared error loss and forecasts based on a linear regression model is very popular in applied work. For this pairing it is straightforward to compute standard errors for the expected loss, even though this is uncommon to do in practice. One only need treat the time series of squared error losses as raw data, compute the mean and spectral density at zero frequency in the usual way (e.g., by applying the methods of Newey and West (1987) or Andrews (1991)), and report the associated standard error.

In other cases, sampling error in the parameter estimates must be taken into account. Indeed, when the second and third terms in (16.15) are nonzero, the usual variance estimator is not consistent as it omits the extra two terms in the result. For such cases, West (1996) suggests estimators for the additional terms.

We next present a simple example that illustrates the individual terms in West's theorem.

Example 16.3.1 (Forecasting a univariate i.i.d. variable by its mean under squared error loss). *Let* $y_t \sim ind\ N(\mu, \sigma^2)$ *and suppose the one-step-ahead forecast model is based on the sample mean,*

$$
y_{t+1} = \mu + \varepsilon_{t+1},
$$

with $\hat{\mu}_t = t^{-1}\sum_{\tau=1}^{t} y_\tau$. *Under squared error loss,* $L(\mu) = E[L\,(f(z_t, \beta^*), y_{t+1})] = E[(y_{t+1} - \mu)^2] = \sigma^2$. *The model is correctly specified in this case and so* $\beta^* = \mu$. *Under squared error loss the mean value expansion is exact. Using that*

$$
\frac{\partial l_{t+1|t}(\beta)}{\partial \beta} = \frac{\partial(y_{t+1} - \mu)^2}{\partial \mu} = -2(y_{t+1} - \mu),
$$

$$
\frac{\partial^2 l_{t+1|t}(\beta)}{\partial \beta\,\partial \beta'} = 2,
$$

the three terms in (16.15) are therefore given by

$$
(y_{t+1} - \hat{\mu}_t)^2 = ([y_{t+1} - \mu] - [\hat{\mu}_t - \mu])^2
$$
$$
= (y_{t+1} - \mu)^2 - 2(y_{t+1} - \mu)(\hat{\mu}_t - \mu) + (\hat{\mu}_t - \mu)^2.
$$

Averaging over the T_P out-of-sample observations, we get

$$T_P^{-1} \sum_{i=1}^{T_P} (y_{T_R+i} - \hat{\mu}_{T_R+i-1})^2 = T_P^{-1} \sum_{i=1}^{T_P} (y_{T_R+i} - \mu)^2$$

$$-2T_P^{-1} \sum_{i=1}^{T_P} (y_{T_R+i} - \mu)(\hat{\mu}_{T_R+i-1} - \mu)$$

$$+T_P^{-1} \sum_{i=1}^{T_P} (\hat{\mu}_{T_R+i-1} - \mu)^2. \tag{16.16}$$

The first of these terms is the average loss with no uncertainty about μ. Contributions from parameter uncertainty come from the remaining terms and will disappear asymptotically.

West's result excludes some interesting cases where the assumptions of the theorem fail to hold. One such situation arises when a vector of forecasts is considered, one forecasting model nests other models, and $\pi \neq 0$. Suppose the training sample used for parameter estimation is large so the asymptotic approximation sets the coefficients in the model used to generate the forecasts ($\hat{\beta}_t$) at their pseudo-true values, β^*. For nested models where the small model is the true one, these parameter values are the same and hence the two sets of forecasts are identical and the covariance matrix will be singular. This is ruled out by assumption (4) in West's theorem since $S_y(0)$ is assumed to be nonsingular. This situation is not relevant when evaluating a single forecast, but becomes important in the comparison of multiple forecasts described in the next chapter.

For some cases the loss function is not twice differentiable. Examples of loss functions that do not satisfy this property are the MAE, lin-lin, and asymmetric quadratic loss functions, that are not differentiable at a single point. To some extent this requirement reflects the proof in West (1996) which assumes a twice continuously differentiable loss function in order to apply a second-order mean value theorem. Indeed, other methods of proof are available. McCracken (2000) relaxes the differentiability condition with a smoothness condition that requires the expected loss (or difference in losses) to be continuously differentiable around the probability limits of the parameter estimates, while maintaining other conditions similar to those in West (1996).[5] Other loss functions, such as the binary forecasting loss function (see chapter 2) and profit functions that rely on discrete actions cannot be handled in this way, and require a separate approach to establishing the consistency of expected loss, its rate of convergence, and also conditions under which expected loss is asymptotically normal.

16.4 OUT-OF-SAMPLE ASYMPTOTICS FOR RATIONALITY TESTS

West and McCracken (1998) develop asymptotic results that facilitate inference on regressions of the form

$$e_{t+h|t}(\hat{\beta}_t) = \gamma v_t(\hat{\beta}_t) + u_{t+h}, \tag{16.17}$$

---

[5] It is not completely clear for which loss functions this result holds since the method uses the high-level assumption that the limiting covariance matrix Ω is positive definite instead of establishing this as a result of primitive conditions on the functions of the losses examined.

where both the right- and left-hand-side variables can depend on the sequence of parameter estimates from a forecasting model, $\hat{\beta}_t$. Examples of such regressions include many of the bias and orthogonality regressions discussed in chapter 15. For example, $e_{t+h|t}(\hat{\beta}_t)$ could be the first derivative of the loss function evaluated each period, where the forecasts depend on estimated parameters, $\hat{\beta}_t$. In such a regression $v_t(\hat{\beta}_t)$ could be the lagged forecast errors (such as in a weak exogeneity test) which would also depend on the estimated model parameters. The setup in (16.17) is general and allows either the right- or left-hand-side variable to be independent of $\hat{\beta}_t$. For in-sample regressions where the parameters, $\hat{\beta}_t$, are estimated once over the entire sample we know that standard methods apply when v_t is independent of β. In such cases corrections must typically be made for the standard errors when the regressor, $v_t(\beta)$, is a function of estimated parameters; this is known as the generated regressor problem; see Pagan (1984).

West and McCracken (1998) extend the standard results to the forecasting problem by explicitly considering how the forecasts were generated and how this could impact inference on $\hat{\gamma}$ from the regression (16.17). We will use the notation $e_{t+h|t}$ for the dependent variable since in most applications the dependent variable is the forecast error. However, the definition of $e_{t+h|t}$ can be extended to include other functions of the forecast errors. West and McCracken (1998, Theorem 4.1) gives results for the case with general regression functions and multistep forecasts. We list the essential assumptions of this result below.

1. The variables $e_{t+h|t}(\beta)$ and $v_t(\beta)$ are measurable and twice differentiable in a neighborhood around β^*. Moreover, $E[e_{t+h|t}(\beta^*)v_t(\beta^*)] = 0$; $E[e_{t+h|t}(\beta^*)\partial e_{t+h|t}(\beta^*)/\partial\beta^*] = 0$; $E[e_{t+h|t}(\beta^*)\partial v_t(\beta^*)/\partial\beta^*] = 0$; and $E[v_t(\beta)v_t(\beta)']$ has full rank k.
2. The estimate $\hat{\beta}_t$ takes the form of a moment-type estimator of full rank: $\hat{\beta}_t - \beta^* = B(t)G(t)$, where $B(t)$ is $k \times q$, $G(t)$ is $q \times 1$ with $B(t) \to^{as} B$, B of rank k; under recursive estimation $G(t) = t^{-1}\sum g_s(\beta^*)$ with $E[g_s(\beta^*)] = 0$.
3. The second derivative $\left|\partial^2 e_{t+h|t}(\beta)/\partial\beta\,\partial\beta'\right|$ is bounded.
4. The quantity $w_t = ((\partial e_{t+h|t}(\beta)/\partial\beta)', \text{vec}(\partial v_t(\beta)/\partial\beta)', e_{t+h|t}(\beta)', v_t(\beta)', g_t')'$ satisfies certain moment, mixing, and stationarity conditions. Moreover, $S_c(0) = \sum_{j=-\infty}^{\infty}\Gamma(j)$ is positive definite, where $\Gamma(j) = E[c_{t+h|t}(\beta^*)c_{t-j+h|t-j}(\beta^*)']$ and $c_{t+h|t}(\beta) = e_{t+h|t}(\beta)v_t(\beta)$.
5. We have $T_P, T_R \to \infty$ and $T_P/T_R \to \pi$, where (a) $0 \le \pi \le \infty$ under an expanding estimation window; (b) $0 \le \pi < \infty$ for rolling and fixed windows.

Under these assumptions, West and McCracken show that

$$T^{1/2}\hat{\gamma} \to^d N(0, V), \tag{16.18}$$

where

$$V = E[X_t X_t']\Omega E[X_t X_t'],$$

$$\Omega = S_c(0) + \lambda_{cg}(FBS_{cg}'(0) + S_{cg}(0)B'F') + \lambda_{gg}FV_\beta F'. \tag{16.19}$$

This result is quite general, which explains the cumbersome notation. The theorem uses the notation

$$F = E \, \partial c_{t+h|t}(\beta)/\partial \beta,$$

$$\Gamma_{cg}(j) = E \left[c_{t+h|t}(\beta^*) g'_{t-j} \right],$$

and so

$$S_{cg}(0) = \sum_{j=-\infty}^{\infty} \Gamma_{cg}(j), \qquad \Gamma_{gg}(j) = E \left[g_t g'_{t-j} \right],$$

$$S_{gg}(0) = \sum_{j=-\infty}^{\infty} \Gamma_{gg}(j), \qquad V_\beta = B S_{gg}(0) B'.$$

The definition of $\left(\lambda_{cg}, \lambda_{gg} \right)$ depends on the method used for constructing the forecasts:

Estimation window	λ_{cg}	λ_{gg}	
Expanding window	$1 - \ln(1+\pi)/\pi$	$2 \left(1 - \ln(1+\pi)/\pi \right)$	
Rolling window ($\pi \leq 1$)	$\pi/2$	$\pi - \pi^2/3$	(16.20)
Fixed window	0	π	

Inference on regressions of the form (16.17) commonly assumes that the coefficient estimates $\hat{\gamma}$ are asymptotically normal and use robust standard error methods to construct hypothesis tests. This is a valid approach provided that $\Omega = S_y(0)$—a situation that only applies to special cases. More generally, the variance–covariance matrix must be corrected according to (16.19).

The leading case where one can proceed with the usual standard errors is when the forecasts are generated from the recursive estimation scheme and the residuals of orthogonality regressions such as (16.17) are conditionally homoskedastic. Assuming an expanding estimation window, it can be established that $S_c(0) = -FBS'_{cg}(0) = -S_{cg}(0)B'F' = FV_\gamma F'$, and the second and third terms of (16.19) sum to 0 since $\lambda_{cg} = \lambda_{gg}/2$. For the rolling window estimation scheme, these terms sum to $-\pi^2/3$ and so the variance–covariance matrix is $(1 - \pi^2/3)S_c(0)$. For this case, conventional tests based on $S_c(0)$ will use too large a variance–covariance matrix and hence will be undersized. The reverse happens for a fixed window for this model, resulting in oversized tests. It is also true for all models that if $\pi = T_P/T_R = 0$, so that asymptotically the proportion of the sample used for forecast evaluation (T_P) is overwhelmed by the sample used to construct the initial model estimates (T_R), conventional methods for inference apply since the effect of estimation error vanishes.

As for the results in West (1996), upon which these results build, there is a large number of assumptions that limit the applicability of the results in (16.18) and (16.19). The relevant functions of the parameters of the forecast model must be twice differentiable at β. This rules out some loss functions although for orthogonality regressions under MSE loss, the left-hand side of (16.17) becomes the forecast error which is linear in the forecast and hence this condition restricts only the form of the forecasting model itself. The second assumption is the same as in West (1996) and restricts attention to forecasting models of the least squares type (including GMM) but rules out many shrinkage estimators as well as Bayesian, semiparametric, and nonparametric estimators. The third and fourth assumptions require moment and dependence conditions on the data which rule out many nonstationarities in the data.

Assumption (1) requires that the population value for γ is 0 which explains the lack of centering of $\hat{\gamma}$ in the theorem. This means that the result is constructed under only the null hypothesis that $\gamma = 0$ and that the instruments v_t are not useful in predicting $e_{t+h|t}$. This is the standard form of the null hypothesis in orthogonality tests. Results are not available under the alternative hypothesis.

Very few results are available for more complicated loss functions and alternative forecasting techniques. A common approach is to simply ignore variation due to how the forecast is constructed. However, the theoretical results above show that this is not necessarily an appropriate course of action. Nonetheless, the results in West and McCracken (1998)) allow us to construct confidence intervals for commonly used out-of-sample estimates of average loss.

16.5 EVALUATION OF AGGREGATE VERSUS DISAGGREGATE FORECASTS

In many situations a multitude of forecasts emerges from individual forecasting models or from a survey. Forecasters then face the choice of either basing their models and inference on the individual forecasts or using some aggregate consensus measure of the forecasts. Often the only reason for restricting the analysis to the aggregate forecasts is that individual forecasts are unavailable since some agencies report only cross-sectional averages of forecasts.

To analyze this situation, suppose that data are available on individual forecasts, denoted $f_{i,t+h|t}$, for $i = 1, \ldots, m$. Individual forecast errors are denoted by $e_{i,t+h|t}$ and these are typically different across forecasters. Individual forecasts can be jointly examined in a panel regression model for $e_{it+h|t} = y_{it+h|t} - f_{it+h|t}$:

$$e_{it+h|t} = z'_{it}\beta_i + u_{it+h}, \tag{16.21}$$

where $i = 1, \ldots, m$ and $t = 1, \ldots, T - h$. As a starting point, suppose the coefficients are different for each forecaster. Rationality tests under squared error loss involve the null hypothesis $H_0 : \beta_i = 0$, for $i = 1, \ldots, m$. A multitude of alternative hypotheses can be tested, reflecting various departures from rationality. For example, a subset of the forecasters might depart from rationality, in which case the alternative hypothesis is that $H_1 : \beta_i \neq 0$, $i \in I$, where I is the subset of irrational forecasters. If all forecasters differ from rationality in the same way, we have $\beta_i = \beta \neq 0$. Alternatively, we can consider testing rationality separately for each individual forecaster by studying the β_i coefficients. Further, we can split tests of biasedness and orthogonality by running a fixed effects regression, where the fixed effects are individual effects.

The regression in (16.21) gives rise to a seemingly unrelated regression (SUR) problem because the error terms, u_{it+h}, are likely to be correlated due to the fact that y_{t+h} is identical across individuals which induces cross-sectional dependence among the u_{it+h} terms. The individual regressions can be stacked to form a system,

$$
e_{t+h|t} = \begin{pmatrix} e_{1t+h|t} \\ e_{2t+h|t} \\ \vdots \\ e_{mt+h|t} \end{pmatrix} = \begin{pmatrix} z_{1t} & 0 & \cdots & 0 \\ 0 & z_{2t} & 0 & 0 \\ \vdots & 0 & \ddots & \vdots \\ 0 & \cdots & 0 & z_{mt} \end{pmatrix} \begin{pmatrix} \beta_1 \\ \beta_2 \\ \vdots \\ \beta_m \end{pmatrix} + \begin{pmatrix} u_{1t+h} \\ u_{2t+h} \\ \vdots \\ u_{mt+h} \end{pmatrix}
$$

$$
= Z_t \beta + u_{t+h}, \tag{16.22}
$$

where $u_{t+h} = [u_{1t+h}, \ldots, u_{mt+h}]'$. Under the assumption of no serial correlation in the forecast errors beyond that accounted for in z_{it}, the SUR estimator for β is $\hat{\beta}_{\text{SUR}} = \left(\sum_t Z_t \Omega_c Z_t' \right)^{-1} \left(\sum_t Z_t \Omega_c e_{t+h} \right)$, where $\Omega_c = E[u_{t+h} u_{t+h}']$. In practice, Ω_c can be estimated directly as the covariance matrix of the regression residuals, initially setting the variance to the identity matrix.[6] Some authors have proposed more elaborate schemes based on assumptions on the form of the covariance matrix. For example, the regression residuals might have a common component due to variations in $e_{t+h|t}$ that arise from variations in the common component, y_{t+h}. This suggests modeling the residuals as $u_{it+h} = c_{t+h} + v_{it+h}$ and hence $E[u_{it+h} u_{jt+h}] = E[c_{t+h}^2] + E[v_{it+h} v_{jt+h}]$. The second term can be set to 0 for $i \neq j$ and σ_i^2 for $i = j$ for each $i = 1, \ldots, m$, so Ω_c takes the form

$$
\Omega_c = \sigma_c^2 \iota \iota' + \begin{pmatrix} \sigma_1^2 & 0 & \cdots & 0 \\ 0 & \sigma_2^2 & 0 & 0 \\ \vdots & 0 & \ddots & \vdots \\ 0 & \cdots & 0 & \sigma_m^2 \end{pmatrix}, \tag{16.23}
$$

where ι is an $(m \times 1)$ vector of 1s. Estimation of this matrix can proceed by first obtaining the OLS residuals from each individual regression and then estimating the restricted parameters in (16.23) from the OLS residuals.

This analysis can be extended in yet another direction by stacking forecast errors from different horizons for each individual and each time period. This extension is examined in Davies and Lahiri (1995). Further assumptions can be made on the structure of the variance–covariance matrix and exploited to obtain better estimates.

In many cases, data on individual forecasts are not reported, and sample averages $\bar{f}_t = m^{-1} \sum_{i=1}^m f_{it}$ are the only data available for forecast evaluation. Averaging cross-sectionally in (16.21), we obtain

$$
\bar{e}_{t+h|t} = \frac{1}{m} \sum_{i=1}^m e_{it+h|t} = \frac{1}{m} \sum_{i=1}^m z_{it}' \beta_i + \frac{1}{m} \sum_{i=1}^m u_{it+h}
$$

$$
= \frac{1}{m} \sum_{i=1}^m z_{it}' \beta_i + \bar{u}_{t+h}. \tag{16.24}
$$

If there is heterogeneity across the β_i coefficients, the weighted estimate in (16.24) will differ from the regression on the averaged data,

$$
\bar{e}_{t+h|t} = \left(\frac{1}{m} \sum_{i=1}^m z_{it}' \right) \beta + \bar{u}_{t+h}. \tag{16.25}
$$

---

[6] This is the same as estimating each regression individually by OLS and using the OLS residuals to estimate Ω_c.

Under the null of forecast rationality ($\beta_1 = \cdots = \beta_m = 0$) this does not cause any problem. However, unless all the deviations from rationality are in the same direction, it is unlikely that results from regressions (16.24) and (16.25) would be identical.

Interpreting results established for the average, as with the individual results, takes care. First, a failure to reject the null of forecast rationality clearly does not imply that each of the individual forecasts are rational. The averaged regression parameters in (16.24) and (16.25) will be consistent for a weighted average of the individual parameters, and hence this weighted average could be 0 even when its components are not. Researchers understand this and consider the average forecast to be an estimate of the consensus forecast and hence the test is really that the consensus forecast is rational, overcoming this issue.

One can also compare the aggregate and individual results. Rejecting the hypothesized forecast rationality for individual forecasts but not for the aggregate forecast might indicate a lack of power in the aggregated data, or simply suggest that the average coefficient is small even though individual coefficients can stray away from 0. Rejecting for the average forecast but not for individual forecasts could also be due to differences in the power of the tests. If there is a large amount of individual heterogeneity in the forecasts, so each of the u_{it} terms vary a great deal, the power of the individual tests could be low. However, this variation could average out, so the power could be greater for tests based on the average data.

16.6 CONCLUSION

It is common to evaluate sequences of forecasts generated either from survey data or from econometric models. Such evaluations differ from conventional specification analysis in econometrics in that they are typically conducted on out-of-sample forecasts. Out-of-sample forecasts restrict the information set—including the data used to estimate model parameters on—to the data available at the point in time where the forecasts are generated. As new data arrives, typically the parameters get reestimated using the most recent data. This out-of-sample approach is meant to simulate the forecasts generated by a forecaster in "real time" and to avoid look-ahead biases in so far as possible.

In situations where learning effects are important because the parameters of the forecasting model are updated recursively through time and the estimation window is not very large, care needs to be exercised when conducting inference about rationality for the underlying forecasting model. Results by West (1996) and West and McCracken (1998) address these issues, although they also impose tight restrictions on the types of models used to generate the forecasts.

17

Evaluation and Comparison of Multiple Forecasts

In many situations two or more competing forecasts of the same outcome are available and we are interested in comparing the forecasts. We could be interested in asking whether one forecast is better than the other forecast or whether they result in similar losses. If more than two forecasts are available, we can ask whether one particular forecast dominates all other forecasts.

In fact, we often have an embarrassment of riches when it comes to forecasts of the same outcome. Many of the forecast methods discussed in the previous chapters can be used to construct different forecasts of the same outcome even with the same data. Using different data sets further enriches the set of forecasts available for predicting an outcome. For example, ARIMA models or naive "no change" models are routinely used to generate baseline forecasts against which more sophisticated forecast methods can be compared.

Consider the case with m competing forecasts, each of which gives rise to a risk function which we can stack in an $(m \times 1)$ vector,

$$R(\theta, f) = E_{Y,Z} \left[L(f(Z), Y) \right]. \tag{17.1}$$

A common approach to choosing between forecasts is to select the method with the smallest expected loss. Other criteria could also be examined, such as stochastic dominance of one forecast over another. These questions can be examined using a sample analog of the risk, previously defined by

$$\hat{R}(f) = (T - h)^{-1} \sum_{t=1}^{T-h} L(f(z_t, \hat{\beta}_t), y_{t+h}). \tag{17.2}$$

Since we have a vector of forecasts, this is now an $(m \times 1)$ vector of estimated risks and $\hat{R}(f)$ is a vector of the same dimension as the vector of forecasts, f.

Suppose we are comparing the performance of two or multiple forecasting methods and are interested in finding out whether one of the methods performed better than the other over some sample period. Provided that certain stationarity conditions hold for the sequence of loss differentials, we can use results in Diebold and Mariano (1995) which develop simple regression-based tests of equal predictive accuracy based on the mean difference in sample average losses.

In contrast, suppose we are interested in using the sequence of forecasts generated by two or multiple forecasting models to answer which model provides a better fit to the data. This requires taking into account that the forecasts $f(z_t, \hat{\beta}_t)$ in (17.2) are constructed from estimates, and hence estimation error in the construction of the forecasts may contribute to the sampling distribution of the average risk estimates. This is of course parallel to the case with a single forecast. When out-of-sample methods are used to generate the forecasts, the results of West (1996) and West and McCracken (1998) can then be applied since they were derived for vectors of losses. However, it is possible that two or more forecasts become asymptotically equivalent, resulting in a variance–covariance matrix of the limiting risks that is not of full rank. This happens if two or more models nest the true model. In this case the two models' parameters converge to the same point and hence their forecasts become asymptotically equivalent. A second case arises with two linear forecasting models where the first model is the best predictor and the second model contains the same predictors plus additional variables that are irrelevant. The coefficient estimates on these irrelevant variables will, asymptotically, converge to 0, making the two models identical. West (1996) and West and McCracken (1998) rule out such possibilities and their results cannot be employed in this situation. Alternative approximations to the test statistics are instead required.

Comparisons of the predictive accuracy of two forecasting methods can lead to three outcomes. First, one forecast method may completely dominate the other method, in which case we would choose the dominant method. The notion that one method dominates another is typically labeled "encompassing." Hoel (1947) seems to have first considered this problem and Chong and Hendry (1986) made significant advances to understanding encompassing tests. Second, one forecast may be best, but does not contain all useful (forecast-relevant) information available from the second forecast. In this case, we may not wish to discard the second forecast. Third, it is possible that the two forecast methods achieve the same expected loss, in which case we would be indifferent between the two methods and might want to use a combined forecast, as discussed in chapter 14.

This chapter first examines methods for comparing two forecasts, for which there are many results available in the literature. The two basic questions asked in such comparisons are, first, does one forecast dominate—or encompass, in the forecasting terminology—the other forecast? Second, are the losses generated by the two sequences of forecasts the same on average? These questions are covered in section 17.1 (forecast encompassing tests) and section 17.2 (tests of equivalent loss using the Diebold–Mariano test), respectively. Section 17.3 introduces an approach to comparing forecast methods suggested by Giacomini and White (2006) while section 17.4 discusses comparisons of forecasting performance with nested models. Section 17.5 extends the analysis to comparisons involving multiple forecasting models. Section 17.6 discusses ways to address data mining when multiple forecasting models are being compared, while section 17.7 covers recent stepwise methods for identifying superior forecasting models. Choice of sample split in out-of-sample forecast evaluation experiments is discussed in section 17.8, while section 17.9 links forecast evaluation issues to questions from forecast combination and model selection and section 17.10 compares in-sample to out-of-sample methods.[1] Section 17.11 concludes.

---

[1] Clark and McCracken (2013) provide an excellent survey of the extensive literature on many of the topics covered in this chapter.

Throughout the chapter we will mostly assume a single-period forecast horizon and so set $h = 1$. For direct forecasting models the horizon makes little difference to most results and this assumption helps us keep notation simple.

17.1 FORECAST ENCOMPASSING TESTS

The general idea of encompassing relates to the notion that one model not only fully explains what another model can explain but provides additional explanation of some phenomenon.[2] In a predictive context, the idea of forecast encompassing is similar to the notion of orthogonality in the efficiency regressions discussed in chapter 15, the only difference being that the additional information now consists of forecasts or forecast errors from other forecast methods. If an additional forecast contains information relevant for predicting the outcome and not already contained in the original forecast, then such a forecast will enter the orthogonality regression with a nonzero weight. In this situation, the original forecast did not include all relevant information. Conversely, if orthogonality holds, then the original forecast is said to "encompass" the other forecast since it incorporates all relevant information that the other forecast embodies.

With two competing forecasts, the condition that $f_{1t+1|t}$ encompasses $f_{2t+1|t}$ can, under general loss, be stated as

$$E\left[L(f_{1t+1|t}, y_{t+1})\right] \leq \min_{g(\cdot)} E\left[L(g(f_{1t+1|t}, f_{2t+1|t}), y_{t+1})\right]. \qquad (17.3)$$

If (17.3) holds, then the first forecast is "sufficient" given the pair of forecasts $(f_{1t+1|t}, f_{2t+1|t})$ in the sense that there is no information in the second forecast that is useful once we have access to the first forecast.

Note that forecast encompassing depends on the loss function, L. Hence, we might well find that forecast $f_{1t+1|t}$ encompasses $f_{2t+1|t}$ for some loss function, L_1, but not for another loss function $L_2 \neq L_1$.

Chong and Hendry (1986) consider forecast encompassing under MSE loss. For this case (17.3) reduces to

$$E\left[(y_{t+1|t} - f_{1t+1|t})^2\right] = \min_{g(\cdot)} E\left[(y_{t+1|t} - g(f_{1t+1|t}, f_{2t+1|t}))^2\right]. \qquad (17.4)$$

Under the null of forecast encompassing, it follows that the expected loss from the forecast that is encompassed exceeds the expected loss associated with the forecast that encompasses it. This means that if $f_{1t+1|t}$ encompasses $f_{2t+1|t}$, then the MSE from $f_{1t+1|t}$ is less than that for $f_{2t+1|t}$. If the MSE for $f_{2t+1|t}$ were less than that for $f_{1t+1|t}$, clearly $E(y_{t+1} - f_{1t+1|t})^2 > E(y_{t+1} - f_{2t+1|t})^2 \geq \min_{g(\cdot)} E(y_{t+1} - g(f_{1t+1|t}, f_{2t+1|t}))^2$ and so $f_{1t+1|t}$ could not encompass $f_{2t+1|t}$. Under the alternative, both forecasts are useful and hence it would be better to combine the forecasts rather than use a single forecast.

17.1.1 Encompassing Tests under MSE Loss

A simple linear regression of the outcome on the two forecasts can be used to test forecast encompassing under MSE loss:

$$y_{t+1} = \beta_1 f_{1t+1|t} + \beta_2 f_{2t+1|t} + \varepsilon_{1t+1}. \qquad (17.5)$$

---

[2] See Mizon and Richard (1986) for the extension of this idea to hypothesis testing.

The first forecast encompasses the second provided that $\beta_1 = 1$ and $\beta_2 = 0$. This regression test in levels of the variables provides a useful link to forecast combinations.[3] Forecast encompassing occurs when one forecast gets a weight of 1 and the other forecast gets a weight of 0. This could arise, for example, if one forecast was just a noisy proxy (where the noise is independent of the forecast and outcome) of the other forecast. In this situation it is optimal to rely on only a single forecast. For all other situations, it is potentially better to combine the two forecasts.

Chong and Hendry (1986) suggest imposing $\beta_1 = 1$ in (17.5) and testing $\beta_2 = 0$ after subtracting $f_{1t+1|t}$ from both sides,

$$y_{t+1} - f_{1t+1|t} = e_{1t+1t} = \beta_2 f_{2t+1|t} + \varepsilon_{2t+1|t}. \tag{17.6}$$

A more common forecast encompassing test is to run the regression

$$e_{1t+1|t} = \beta(e_{1t+1|t} - e_{2t+1|t}) + \varepsilon_{3t+1|t}. \tag{17.7}$$

The null hypothesis is $H_0 : \beta = 0$ versus the alternative $H_1 : \beta > 0$. The levels specifications in (17.5) and (17.7) are identical under the restriction that $\beta_1 + \beta_2 = 1$ (which includes the null hypothesis of $\beta_1 = 1$ and $\beta_2 = 0$), but will otherwise differ.

Harvey, Leybourne, and Newbold (1998) propose the out-of-sample test statistic

$$T_P^{1/2} \frac{\bar{c}}{S^{1/2}}, \tag{17.8}$$

where S is a consistent estimator of the long-run variance of $c_{t+1} = \hat{e}_{1t+1}(\hat{e}_{1t+1} - \hat{e}_{2t+1})$ and $\bar{c} = T_P^{-1} \sum_{t=T_R}^{T-1} \left(\hat{e}_{1t+1} - \hat{e}_{2t+1} \right) \hat{e}_{1t+1}$. As in the previous chapter we assume that the sample T has been split into an estimation sample of length T_R and an evaluation sample $T_P = T - T_R$. We retain hats on the errors to indicate that they are based on estimated forecasts. For one-step-ahead forecasts with serially uncorrelated and homoskedastic errors ($h = 1$), this becomes what Clark and McCracken (2001) refer to as the ENC-T test:

$$\begin{aligned} \text{ENC-T} &= \frac{(T_p - 1)^{1/2}\bar{c}}{\left(T_p^{-1} \sum_{t=T_R}^{T-1} \left(c_{t+1}^2 - \bar{c} \right)^2 \right)^{1/2}} \\ &= \frac{(T_p - 1)^{1/2} T_p^{-1} \sum_{t=T_R}^{T-1} \left(\hat{e}_{1t+1}^2 - \hat{e}_{1t+1}\hat{e}_{2t+1} \right)}{\left(T_p^{-1} \sum_{t=T_R}^{T-1} \left(\hat{e}_{1t+1}^2 - \hat{e}_{1t+1}\hat{e}_{2t+1} \right)^2 - \bar{c}^2 \right)^{1/2}}, \end{aligned} \tag{17.9}$$

where the denominator is the usual variance estimator for $\bar{c}$. This is a regression of c_{t+1} on a constant, scaled by $(T_p - 1)^{1/2}$. Notice that c_{t+1} is the element being summed in the numerator of the regression coefficient from (17.7) and so ENC-T tests the restriction that $\beta = 0$ in that regression.

---

[3] The levels specification in (17.5) is not popular due to issues related to spurious regressions which are more likely to arise for strongly persistent variables.

An alternative, regression-based test, labeled the ENC-REG test, takes the form

$$\text{ENC-REG} = \frac{(T_p - 1)^{1/2} T_p^{-1} \sum_{t=T_R}^{T-1} \left(\hat{e}_{1t+1}^2 - \hat{e}_{1t+1} \hat{e}_{2t+1} \right)}{\left(T_p^{-1} \sum_{t=T_R}^{T-1} \left(\hat{e}_{1t+1} - \hat{e}_{2t+1} \right)^2 \left(T_p^{-1} \sum_{t=T_R}^{T-1} \hat{e}_{1t+1}^2 \right) - \bar{c}^2 \right)^{1/2}}. \quad (17.10)$$

Clark and McCracken (2001) suggest a different test when forecasts are based on estimates that arise from nested models:

$$\text{ENC-NEW} = \frac{T_p \bar{c}}{\left(T_p^{-1} \sum_{t=T_R}^{T-1} \hat{e}_{2t+1}^2 \right)}. \quad (17.11)$$

Apart from scaling by T_p rather than $T_p - 1$, the difference is that the usual variance estimator is removed from the denominator of the t-statistic and replaced with the MSE of the encompassed (under the null) forecast. Clark and McCracken suggest that this test will have better properties than the t-test when the parameters of the models generating the forecasts are estimated and the models are nested.

These tests assume that the encompassing forecasts are unbiased. The tests can be modified if this assumption does not hold. For tests based on the regressions (17.5), (17.6), and (17.7), a constant can be added to the regression. For the statistic in (17.8) an adjustment needs to be made to the forecast error $\hat{e}_{1t+1}$, so that it has a mean of 0 (see Marcellino, 2000).

When deriving limit distributions for these test statistics, care needs to be taken with the standard errors since the statistics are functions of objects (data) that were themselves constructed from previously estimated forecasting models.[4] Such estimation errors need not disappear asymptotically, depending on how the forecasts were constructed. We might therefore have to adjust the standard errors or, alternatively, use different distributional approximations for nested forecasting models.

These concerns matter if we are interested in drawing conclusions, from sample statistics on models' relative forecasting performance, about which model best fits the data. However, if we are interested in testing which forecasting method performed best over a particular sample period, estimation error only matters indirectly in so far as it affects the sampling distribution of the models' relative losses. As we shall see below, this is the perspective taken by Diebold and Mariano (1995) and Giacomini and White (2006).

Many empirical applications assume that the forecasts are "given," or taken as primitives, and so regard parameter estimation error as a fundamental feature of the forecast. For example, Chong and Hendry (1986) reference the potential need to adjust for estimated forecasts, but do not account for estimation errors in the forecasts in their analysis. The main application they have in mind is examining forecasts from large complicated models, for which no results are available for accounting for estimation error. Where results are available (e.g., West (2001) for nonnested tests), this approximation is still reasonable if the size of the sample on which the model is estimated is large relative to the evaluation sample, a result that

---

[4] Hoel (1947) recognized this problem and conditioned on the data used to construct the forecasts to avoid the effect of sampling error on the distributions of his statistics.

arises because the estimation error becomes negligible in large estimation samples. Harvey, Leybourne, and Newbold (1998) assume that the forecasts are constructed without estimation error, which yields asymptotically normal results with the usual variance–covariance matrix. They suggest using a student-t distribution to construct critical values as is common for nonnormal forecasts and small sample sizes.[5] Size distortions caused by using the asymptotic approximation can be quite substantial in such cases.

When models are not nested, the results of West and McCracken (1998) may apply to the regression tests in (17.5), (17.6), and (17.7) for recursively constructed forecasts that use rolling regressions or a fixed estimation window. Forecast models must satisfy the requirements of West (1996, Theorem 4.1) discussed in chapter 16, as must the underlying data. In addition, the models that generate the two forecasts must not be nested, nor both nest the true model. Under such conditions the results of West and McCracken apply directly to the statistic in (17.8) which, apart from the asymptotically irrelevant correction to the scaling by the sample size, yields a robust t-test on the coefficient from regressing c_{t+1} on a constant. West (2001) applies these results to this test, showing that when the forecasts are constructed recursively, a correction to the denominator is typically required to achieve the correct size asymptotically.

Under the conditions of West and McCracken (1998), consider forecasts constructed from nonnested regression models,

$$y_{t+1} = \beta_1 x_{1t} + e_{1t+1},$$

$$y_{t+1} = \beta_2 x_{2t} + e_{2t+1},$$

so the forecasts are $\hat{\beta}_i x_{it}$ for $i = 1, 2$ and the parameters are estimated using either a fixed, rolling or recursively expanding window with the evaluation sample starting at observation $T_R + 1$, so T_R observations are available for the initial estimates and T_P observations are available for evaluation.

The results of West and McCracken (1998) applied to the problem in West (2001) show that

$$\sqrt{T_P}(\bar{c} - E(c_{t+1})) \rightarrow^d N(0, S + \pi D V_\beta D'),$$

where $D = [E(e_{1t+1}x_{2t}), E(e_{2t+1}x_{1t})]$, e_{it+1} is the forecast error from the ith model, $\pi = T_P/T_R$, and V_β is the variance–covariance matrix of $(\hat{\beta}_1, \hat{\beta}_2)'$. This can be made operational by estimating D from the sample analogs $\hat{D} = [T_p^{-1} \sum \hat{e}_{2t+1}x_{1t}, T_p^{-1} \sum \hat{e}_{1t+1}x_{2t}]$, where the sums are over the evaluation sample; V_β can be estimated in the usual way considering the two univariate forecasting models as a system.

If the evaluation sample is small relative to the estimation sample (say 10% or less) and the forecasts are generated recursively, size distortions are typically not large. However, when this ratio gets closer to 0.5, the effect of estimation error on the size of the test is not negligible.

Monte Carlo simulations in Clark and McCracken (2001, 2005a) and Clark and West (2007) suggest that the tests generally have the right size with reasonable

---

[5] Their suggestion is not based on theoretical considerations but serves the role of increasing the critical values.

power when the forecast horizon covers only a single period ($h = 1$). Conversely, the tests are often oversized for multiperiod forecasts ($h > 1$). For this case, simulations reported by the same studies have found that bootstrap methods such as the fixed-regressor bootstrap seem to work quite well.

When we construct the competing forecasts from nested linear regressions and account for the sampling error that arises from estimating the parameters of the underlying regressions used to construct the forecasts, distributions are no longer asymptotically normal. Clark and McCracken (2001) provide asymptotic distribution theory and tables of critical values for the ENC-T, ENC-REG, and ENC-NEW tests when the parameters of the underlying forecasting models are updated using the recursive scheme throughout the evaluation sample.

17.2 TESTS OF EQUIVALENT EXPECTED LOSS: THE DIEBOLD–MARIANO TEST

Rather than focusing on the null that one of the forecasts dominates the other, an alternative is to examine whether the forecasts perform equally well, i.e., test whether the losses are equivalent across the two methods. Such tests for equivalent loss can be quite useful. For example, we might not bother to use a new and complicated forecast method if it only attains the same expected loss as a simpler, existing method. This section covers tests that assume estimation errors arising from the sampling scheme used to generate the forecasts can largely be ignored. The next section explicitly focuses on tests that account for such effects.

17.2.1 Tests of Loss Equivalence under MSE Loss

Using ideas in Morgan (1939), Granger and Newbold (1973) suggest an approach that is based on correlations of variables constructed from the forecast errors. Consider two forecast errors $e_{t+h} = (e_{1t+h}, e_{2t+h})$, with zero mean (so they are unbiased) and a variance–covariance matrix whose elements are labeled σ_{ij}. Regardless of the correlation between the two forecast errors, we have

$$E\left[(e_{1t+1} + e_{2t+1})(e_{1t+1} - e_{2t+1})\right] = \sigma_{11}^2 - \sigma_{22}^2, \tag{17.12}$$

i.e., the correlation between these two constructed variables is equal to the difference between the variances. Under MSE loss, this is also the difference between the two loss functions. Thus a test based on the correlation between the sum of the forecast errors and the difference between them amounts to a test of the null hypothesis $H_0 : \sigma_{11}^2 = \sigma_{22}^2$ versus $H_1 : \sigma_{11}^2 \neq \sigma_{22}^2$, i.e., that the expected losses are identical versus one model producing lower losses than the other.[6] Alternatively, a simple regression can be used to test this hypothesis:

$$e_{1t+1} + e_{2t+1} = \beta(e_{1t+1} - e_{2t+1}) + \varepsilon_{t+1}. \tag{17.13}$$

This regression has no constant since the forecast errors are assumed to have zero mean. The t-statistic for the slope coefficient can be used to test that β equals 0 and

---

[6] If the forecast errors follow a bivariate normal distribution, then the uniformly most powerful test of this hypothesis exists; see Lehmann and Romano (2006).

this will follow an approximate normal distribution under the null. As pointed out by Harvey, Leybourne, and Newbold (1998), unless the regressor and regressand are independent (e.g., the forecasts are bivariate normal), then robust standard errors such as those in White (1982) need to be used since the variances of the residuals and the regressor are related. Since the forecasts are often generated from estimated models, the issues in West (1996) also arise here.

17.2.2 The Diebold–Mariano Test

The approach of Diebold and Mariano (1995) explicitly takes into account the underlying loss function as well as sampling variation in the average losses. Suppose that two forecasts are available so we have two sets of losses, $L(f_{1t+1|t}, y_{t+1})$ and $L(f_{2t+1|t}, y_{t+1})$. Consider the difference between the two losses:

$$d_{t+1} = L(f_{2t+1|t}, y_{t+1}) - L(f_{1t+1|t}, y_{t+1}).$$

Samples of time-series observations on the two losses and the associated loss differential, d_{t+1}, form the basis of a test. Specifically, we can test the null hypothesis,

$$H_0 : E[d_{t+1}] \equiv \mu_d = 0, \tag{17.14}$$

against either a one-sided alternative—if we want to see whether a particular method is better than the other—or against a two-sided alternative if we want to see whether the performances are different on average.

Diebold (2015) discuss conditions under which a set of simple tests of equal predictive performance can be conducted. The key assumptions are that, for all t,

$$E[d_{t+1}] = \mu_d, \tag{17.15}$$

$$\text{Cov}(d_t, d_{t-j}) = \gamma(j), \tag{17.16}$$

$$0 < \text{var}(d_t) = \sigma^2 < \infty. \tag{17.17}$$

Under these assumptions, a variety of methods are available to conduct the hypothesis test. The most obvious idea is to use a t-statistic which requires an estimate of the variance of the individual losses for scaling purposes. When the suitably scaled vector of out-of-sample losses $\hat{R}(f)$ defined in (17.2) satisfies a central limit theorem, $(T_p)^{1/2} \hat{R}(f) \to^d N(\mu, \Omega)$, then

$$\bar{d} \sim N(\mu_2 - \mu_1, \Omega_{22} + \Omega_{11} - 2\Omega_{12}), \tag{17.18}$$

where $\mu = (\mu_1, \mu_2)'$ and the covariance matrix Ω is partitioned after the first row and first column. Diebold and Mariano (1995) suggest estimating the scale nuisance parameter directly from the sequence of data $\{d_{t+1}\}$, using the method of Newey and West (1987), although they note that any consistent estimator of the long-run variance would be applicable. For h-step-ahead forecasts with overlapping data, an MA($h-1$) structure is induced in d_{t+h} if the underlying forecasts are rational so a window of at least $h-1$ observations should be used to construct the standard errors in (17.18).

Diebold and Mariano (1995) take forecasts as primitives. This means that models whose forecasts are strongly affected by parameter estimation error tend to be deemed inferior relative to models that are less strongly affected by estimation error, even if the latter model could provide the best fit to the data in large samples. Thus, we cannot conclude from the outcome of the Diebold–Mariano test which model is "best"—we can only make statements about which method generates the best forecast in a particular sample. Diebold and Mariano (1995) use the usual variance estimator as a consistent estimator for the scale of the difference, $\bar{d}$, in (17.18).

When are the assumptions in (17.15)–(17.17) likely to hold? Suppose the parameters of a small and a large forecasting model have been estimated using a very short initial sample (e.g., 20 observations) and we are interested in studying the subsequent sequence of forecasts generated by the two models. In this situation, the initial forecasts from the large model are likely to be particularly strongly affected by estimation error. This effect will be reduced as the length of the estimation sample size increases, provided an expanding estimation window is used. In this situation, the sequence of loss differentials will not be stationary and (17.15)–(17.17) is unlikely to provide a good characterization of the behavior of the loss differentials. Specifically, the variance of the differential loss will decline over time, violating the second assumption in (17.17).

In other, less extreme, situations where either the initial estimation window is large or remains fixed so that the distribution of the sequence of loss differentials does not change over time (a case covered by Giacomini and White (2006) as we shall see below), assumption (17.17) is far more likely to be a good approximation to the data. Comparison of the accuracy of survey forecasts is another example in which the DM test can be useful. The methods that account for estimation error in the evaluation of forecast performance require that forecasts were generated according to a tight set of conditions that can be very hard to verify for such data.

If the focus is on finding out which method provides the best fit to the data and forecast errors are constructed using estimated model parameters, standard errors may have to be adjusted as suggested by West (1996) or West and McCracken (1998). In some cases one can use the corrected version of Ω from West (1996), replacing the usual estimator of Ω with that suggested in West (1996). Once again, nested models cannot be compared; if the models are nested, Ω will not be of full rank, and the long-run variance of d_{t+1} converges to 0. The results of West and McCracken (1998) would be relevant for the Morgan–Granger–Newbold regression test, while those of West (1996) are appropriate for the Diebold–Mariano test.

Harvey, Leybourne, and Newbold (1997) modify the Diebold and Mariano t-test in two ways; first, by altering the divisor on the variance term and, second, by suggesting that the t-distribution with $T_P - 1$ degrees of freedom should be used to construct the critical values. The modification follows from noting that the Diebold–Mariano test does not use degrees-of-freedom-adjusted variances. The suggestion to use the t-distribution is not based on theoretical concerns but serves to increase the critical values for tests that appear oversized in Monte Carlo experiments. For a general h-period forecast horizon, their modified t-statistic, labeled t_{HLN}, is

$$t_{\mathrm{HLN}} = \left(1 + T_P^{-1}(1 - 2h) + T_P^{-2}h(h-1)\right)^{1/2} t_{\mathrm{DM}}, \qquad (17.19)$$

where t_{DM} is the original Diebold–Mariano t-statistic. Notice that the correction adds second- and third-order terms which will have little effect except in very small sample sizes or for long horizons. As $(1 - 2h) < 0$ for all h, the first-order effect is to reduce the size of the test statistic.[7]

Monte Carlo evidence in Harvey, Leybourne, and Newbold (1998) shows that their corrections have the desired directional effect on size—the corrections reduce the rejection rate under the null hypothesis by both increasing the critical value and decreasing the value of the test statistic. Size is not controlled for all values of h and all sample sizes, but the distortions are smaller than for the uncorrected t-statistic.

Most of the simulation evidence has been conducted under MSE loss, so d_{t+h} is the difference between two squared terms. Squared errors tend to be quite skewed since they are bounded below at 0, and hence it is unsurprising that small sample tests based on the asymptotic normal distribution are oversized. This effect is exacerbated when the underlying forecast errors are fat tailed. Diebold and Mariano (1995) present simulation evidence that illustrates these effects when the forecast errors are drawn from stable distributions so the Monte Carlo design does not allow estimation error in the construction of the forecasts. Busetti and Marcucci (2013) conduct a Monte Carlo study of the size and power properties of a variety of tests for equal predictive accuracy under squared error loss for nested regression models. They find that the ranking of different tests is quite robust across settings with misspecified models and across different forecast horizons. They also find that highly persistent regressors give rise to a loss in power but do not affect the size of the test.

17.3 COMPARING FORECASTING METHODS: THE GIACOMINI–WHITE APPROACH

Giacomini and White (2006) propose a fundamentally different but highly relevant approach to testing between alternative forecasts. They do not rely on asymptotic results that replace parameter estimates by their probability limits—an approach that basically tests which model is better in population. Instead Giacomini and White (2006) retain the effect that estimation errors have on the forecasts and ask whether two forecasting methods produce the same quality of forecasts (according to the chosen loss function) or if instead one method is better. Their test takes as given an observed sequence of forecasts from the two methods that are being compared and assumes that the parameters of the models are estimated using a rolling window of fixed length. This preserves estimation errors and can be viewed as a sequence of observations on the methods' performance. Tests for equal expected loss as well as tests of orthogonality of forecast errors with respect to all information available when the forecasts were produced can then be performed. The distribution of such tests is approximated under the assumption that the observed sequence of forecasts gets large.

More formally, consider two models that at time t are used to generate one-step-ahead forecasts $f_{1t+1|t}$ and $f_{2t+1|t}$ using a fixed window of ω observations. Each forecast $f_{it+1|t}$ is a function of the data $(z_t, z_{t-1}, \ldots, z_{t-\omega+1})$ and parameter estimates $\hat{\beta}_{1t}, \hat{\beta}_{2t}$ and is denoted by $f_{it+1|t}(\hat{\beta}_{it})$, $i = 1, 2$ for short. From these forecasts we can construct losses $L(f_{it+1}(\hat{\beta}_{it}), y_{t+1})$ for $t = T_R, \ldots, T - 1$. These can be used

---

[7] In addition to this test, Harvey, Leybourne, and Newbold (1998) suggest tests based on the median difference instead of the mean difference in losses, and also consider signed rank tests of the difference.

to compare the models' finite sample predictive accuracy evaluated at the current parameters, $\hat{\beta}_{1t}$, $\hat{\beta}_{2t}$, through the following null:

$$H_0 : E\left[L(f_{1t+1|t}(\hat{\beta}_{1t}), y_{t+1}) - L(f_{2t+1|t}(\hat{\beta}_{2t}), y_{t+1})\right] = 0. \qquad (17.20)$$

It is useful to contrast the null hypothesis in (17.20) with the null of equal predictive accuracy at the population parameters, β_1^*, β_2^*, in the analysis of West (1996) and many subsequent papers:

$$H_0 : E\left[L(f_{1t+1|t}(\beta_1^*), y_{t+1}) - L(f_{2t+1|t}(\beta_2^*), y_{t+1})\right] = 0. \qquad (17.21)$$

The null in (17.20) tested by Giacomini and White (2006) is fundamentally different from the null in (17.21). The key difference is that the effect of estimation error does not vanish in (17.20), which assumes a fixed estimation window, whereas it does so for (17.21) which evaluates the expected losses at the (probability) limits of the estimators, $\hat{\beta}$, as the estimation sample gets very large. For example, suppose that the finite-sample bias in the small model due to the omission of relevant predictor variables balances exactly against the reduced effect of estimation error, both measured relative to a larger, unrestricted model. Then, the null hypothesis tested by Giacomini and White should not be rejected. In contrast, the null tested by West should be rejected as the estimation sample expands and the effect of estimation error vanishes.

Conversely, when comparing nested models, (17.20) can set a higher standard relative to tests such as (17.21) since the large model is now required to outperform the small model by a margin big enough to make up for the greater effect that estimation error has on the large model's forecasting performance.

Giacomini and White (2006) establish that, under a finite estimation window,

$$T_P^{-1/2} \sum_{t=T_R}^{T-1} \left[\Delta L_{t+1}(\hat{\beta}_{1t}, \hat{\beta}_{2t}, y_{t+1}) - E[\Delta L]\right] \to^d N(0, \tilde{S}_y(0)),$$

where $\Delta L_{t+1}(\hat{\beta}_{1t}, \hat{\beta}_{2t}, y_{t+1}) = L(f_{1t+1|t}(\hat{\beta}_{1t}), y_{t+1}) - L(f_{2t+1|t}(\hat{\beta}_{2t}), y_{t+1})$ measures the differential loss, while the variance $\tilde{S}_y(0)$ is given by

$$\tilde{S}_y(0) = \lim_{T_P \to \infty} \text{Var}\left(T_P^{-1/2} \sum_{t=T_R}^{T-1} \left[L(f_{1t+1|t}(\hat{\beta}_{1t}), y_{t+1}) - L(f_{2t+1|t}(\hat{\beta}_{2t}), y_{t+1})\right.\right.$$
$$\left.\left. - E[\Delta L_{t+1}]\right]\right).$$

Note that this result is obtained in the limit for $T_P \to \infty$ but without the assumption that T_R expands asymptotically. Hence, Giacomini and White (2006) do not need to make assumptions such as positive-definiteness of Ω and so their approach allows for both nested and nonnested comparisons. Moreover, a much wider class of forecast methods that do not necessarily fit in the mold of the analysis of West (1996) can be considered, including Bayesian, nonlinear, and nonparametric models, as well as forecasts based on a variety of nonstandard estimators. In each case it is important that the effect of estimation error does not vanish so that $\tilde{S}_y(0)$ does not become degenerate.

17.3.1 Conditional Test of Forecasting Performance

Giacomini and White (2006) introduce conditional tests for predictive accuracy that are conditional on current information, Z_t. For these tests the null hypothesis in (17.20) is altered to

$$E\left[\Delta L_{t+1}(\hat{\beta}_{1t}, \hat{\beta}_{2t}, y_{t+1})|Z_t\right] = 0, \qquad (17.22)$$

where $Z_t = \{z_1, \ldots, z_t\}$ is the information set available at time t. For a single-period forecast horizon, $h = 1$, the null is that the loss difference is a martingale difference sequence with respect to Z_t. For longer horizons, the null implies that information available at time, t, is not correlated with the difference in the losses.

The hypothesis in (17.22) is interesting from an economic point of view since it allows us to test whether certain forecasting models are better in some economic states than others. For example, Henkel, Martin, and Nardari (2011) find that stock returns are predictable during economic recessions but not during expansions. This could be tested by letting the conditioning information include a recession indicator, $\mathbb{1}(\text{NBER}_t = 1)$, that equals 1 if the NBER views period t as a recession, and otherwise equals 0, although the NBER indicator is not available in real time.

To make the conditional null hypothesis in (17.22) operational, we need to choose a set of test functions, v_t, which are functions of data available at the time the forecast is made, i.e., functions of Z_t. Letting v_t be a ($q \times 1$) vector, we can test the moment restriction in (17.22) using a standard GMM quadratic form,

$$\text{GW}(T_P) = T_P \left(T_P^{-1} \sum_{t=T_R}^{T-1} v_t \Delta L_{t+1} \right)' W^{-1} \left(T_P^{-1} \sum_{t=T_R}^{T-1} v_t \Delta L_{t+1} \right), \qquad (17.23)$$

where W is the optimal weight matrix for the GMM problem and $\Delta L_{t+1} = L(f_{1t+1|t}(\hat{\beta}_{1t}), y_{t+1}) - L(f_{2t+1|t}(\hat{\beta}_{2t}), y_{t+1})$. Under relatively mild and standard conditions, Giacomini and White show that this statistic has a limiting χ_q^2 distribution under the null hypothesis.[8]

An interesting aspect of this test is that different choices for the window length in the rolling regressions, ω, change what is being tested. The reason is that if we change the window length, we also alter $\hat{\beta}_{1t}, \hat{\beta}_{2t}$ and thus the sequence of forecasts, $\{f_{1t+1|t}(\hat{\beta}_{1t}), f_{2t+1|t}(\hat{\beta}_{2t})\}$, and the null hypothesis. The upshot of this is that with the same models but different window lengths, forecasters might find that the tests yield different results. However, this property is part of the point of undertaking the test for the forecast method (which includes the choice of estimation window) rather than attempting to learn which forecasting model is best when evaluated at the limit of the parameter estimates.

A failure of finding that the test in (17.23) detects superior performance for a model whose parameters are estimated using a rolling window does not imply, of course, that the same model, with parameters estimated on an expanding window, would not have generated better forecasts. Using a rolling window estimator in such situations can worsen the performance of large models with a greater number of estimated parameters and so can impair the test's ability to identify these models

---

[8] For example, strict stationarity is not needed for this result.

as being superior relative to more parsimonious models with fewer estimated parameters, even if the large model is the best specification. For example, forecasts based on rolling window estimation with 10 years of observations might lead to rejections of the large model, while the large model could be preferred with a rolling estimation window of 20 years of observations.

17.4 COMPARING FORECASTING PERFORMANCE ACROSS NESTED MODELS

When comparing the finite-sample performance of two nested models, estimation error can cause the large model to produce less precise forecasts—generate higher MSE values—than the small model which requires estimation of fewer parameters. The test statistics proposed by McCracken (2000) take this into account. Specifically, the distribution of test statistics that account for estimation error shifts further to the left and in many cases takes on negative values, the greater the number of additional parameters that have to be estimated for the large model.

This property means that a possible outcome of the test of equal predictive accuracy could be to favor a large forecasting model even though this model generates less precise forecasts in a particular finite sample than a smaller model. The logic in such cases is that although the large model underperformed the small model in a finite sample, its performance was not as bad as one would have expected given the additional number of parameters that require estimation by the large model.

From the point of conducting inference about two models, this is a valid point. However, from the perspective of a forecaster who is deciding on which model to use, it seems risky to choose the large model in situations where it is underperforming the smaller model. This holds even if the sample evidence suggests that the larger model eventually will be preferred when enough data are available to estimate its additional parameters with greater precision.

Two approaches have been proposed to address these issues for nested models. One approach suggested by Clark and West (2007) recenters the test statistic in a way that explicitly adjusts the test for the greater effect of parameter estimation error on the large model. The second approach is to directly focus the test on finite-sample performance, as suggested by Giacomini and White (2006). We first explain how recursive parameter estimation induces standard evaluation test statistics to follow nonstandard distributions and next describe these approaches.

17.4.1 Complications Arising from Nested Models

West (1996) established that two nonnested models' relative predictive accuracy will asymptotically be normally distributed, albeit with standard errors that need to account for estimation error. When models are nested, this result, or the results of West and McCracken (1998), need no longer hold. Under the null that the additional predictors of the larger model have zero coefficients and so are irrelevant, the forecasts from the large and small model will be identical. In the limit as the effect of estimation error vanishes, the standard error of the difference between the two models' forecast performance will therefore be 0. Test statistics based on differential MSE performance will therefore have nonstandard limiting distributions.

To deal with such situations, Clark and McCracken (2001) consider the t-test for $\beta = 0$ in (17.7) along with the ENC-T and ENC-NEW statistics for testing whether one model encompasses another smaller model that it nests. The distributions of such tests are generally nonstandard and the limit distributions for the ENC-T and ENC-REG methods in (17.9) and (17.10) are asymptotically equivalent under the null. The nonstandard distributions depend on the difference in the number of parameters in the two forecasting models, the estimation method used to generate out-of-sample forecasts (i.e., static, rolling, or recursive windows), and the proportion of out-of-sample to in-sample observations, T_P / T_R. As this last ratio becomes small, the test statistic becomes more like a standard normal distribution. Clark and McCracken provide critical values constructed from Monte Carlo approximations to the null distribution for a number of cases.

To see how such nonstandard distributions arise, we follow the analysis in Hansen and Timmermann (2012) and consider a simple regression model with only a constant:

$$y_{t+1} = \beta + \varepsilon_{t+1}, \quad \varepsilon_{t+1} \sim (0, \sigma_\varepsilon^2). \tag{17.24}$$

Suppose that β is estimated recursively by least squares, so that $\hat{\beta}_t = t^{-1} \sum_{s=1}^{t} y_s$. Using this model, the one-step-ahead forecast of y_{t+1} given information at time t becomes the sample average, i.e., $\hat{f}_{t+1|t} = \hat{\beta}_t$. Following Hansen and Timmermann, we compare this forecast to a simple benchmark forecast $\hat{f}_{t+1|t}^b = 0$, which does not require any parameters to be estimated.

Once again, suppose that T_R observations are used for initial estimation, while the remainder of the sample, $T_P = T - T_R$, is used for forecast evaluation, and let $\lambda = T_R / T$ be the fraction of the sample used for initial estimation, while $1 - \lambda$ is used for out-of-sample evaluation.

We evaluate the forecasts through their out-of-sample MSE values measured relative to those of the benchmark forecasts:

$$D_T(\lambda) = \sum_{t=T_R}^{T-1} \left(y_{t+1} - \hat{f}_{t+1|t}^b \right)^2 - \left(y_{t+1} - \hat{f}_{t+1|t} \right)^2. \tag{17.25}$$

Using the form of the two forecast errors in (17.25), we have

$$D_T(\lambda) = \sum_{t=T_R}^{T-1} \left(y_{t+1} - \hat{f}_{t+1|t}^b \right)^2 - \left(y_{t+1} - \hat{f}_{t+1|t} \right)^2$$

$$= \sum_{t=T_R}^{T-1} (y_{t+1} - \beta + \beta)^2 - \left(y_{t+1} - \beta - (\hat{\beta}_t - \beta) \right)^2$$

$$= \sum_{t=T_R}^{T-1} (\varepsilon_{t+1} + \beta)^2 - \left(\varepsilon_{t+1} - \frac{1}{t-1} \sum_{s=1}^{t-1} \varepsilon_{s+1} \right)^2$$

$$= \sum_{t=T_R}^{T-1} \beta^2 + 2\beta\varepsilon_{t+1} - \left(\frac{1}{t-1} \sum_{s=1}^{t-1} \varepsilon_{s+1} \right)^2 + 2\left(\frac{1}{t-1} \sum_{s=1}^{t-1} \varepsilon_{s+1} \right)\varepsilon_{t+1}.$$

TABLE 17.1:
Simulated critical values for out-of-sample MSE test statistic for nested model comparison (large model has two extra regressors).

λ	0.909	0.833	0.625	0.500	0.417	0.357	0.333
π	0.1	0.2	0.6	1	1.4	1.8	2
$\alpha = 0.99$	2.168	2.830	3.851	4.146	4.225	4.214	4.191
$\alpha = 0.95$	1.198	1.515	1.880	1.870	1.766	1.633	1.563

Next, define the partial sum,

$$W_T(u) = \frac{1}{\sqrt{T}} \sum_{s=1}^{\lfloor uT \rfloor} \varepsilon_s, \qquad u \in [0, 1].$$

From Donsker's theorem, $W_T(u) \Rightarrow \sigma_\varepsilon B(u)$, where $B(u)$ is a standard Brownian motion. Hence, as shown by Hansen and Timmermann (2012),

$$\sum_{t=T_R}^{T-1} \left(\frac{1}{t-1} \sum_{s=1}^{t-1} \varepsilon_{s+1} \right)^2 = \frac{1}{T} \sum_{t=T_R}^{T-1} \left(\frac{T}{t-1} W_T\left(\frac{t-1}{T} \right) \right)^2 \tag{17.26}$$

$$\rightarrow^d \sigma_\varepsilon^2 \int_\lambda^1 u^{-2} B(u)^2 du;$$

$$\sum_{t=T_R}^{T-1} \left(\frac{1}{t-1} \sum_{s=1}^{t-1} \varepsilon_{s+1} \right) \varepsilon_{t+1} = \sum_{t=T_R+1}^{T} \frac{T}{t-1} W_T\left(\frac{t-1}{T} \right) \left[W_T\left(\frac{t}{T} \right) - W_T\left(\frac{t-1}{T} \right) \right]$$

$$\rightarrow^d \sigma_\varepsilon^2 \int_\lambda^1 u^{-1} B(u) dB(u). \tag{17.27}$$

Let $\hat{\sigma}_\varepsilon^2 = (1-\lambda)^{-1} T^{-1} \sum_{t=T_R}^{T-1} (y_{t+1} - \hat{f}_{t+1|t})^2$ be a consistent estimator of σ_ε^2. Under the null, $H_0 : \beta = 0$, it follows from (17.27) that

$$\frac{D_T(\lambda)}{\hat{\sigma}_\varepsilon^2} \rightarrow^d 2 \int_\lambda^1 u^{-1} B(u) dB(u) - \int_\lambda^1 u^{-2} B(u)^2 du, \tag{17.28}$$

where $B(u)$ is a standard Brownian motion. Hence the test statistic in (17.28) converges to an integral of Brownian motion and will not have a standard normal distribution. This happens because of the recursive updating in the parameter estimates and the fact that innovations to the dependent variable are correlated with future revisions to the parameter estimates.

   This simple derivation from Hansen and Timmermann (2012) is a special case of the general results in McCracken (2007). McCracken tabulates the critical values for cases with fixed, rolling, and expanding estimation windows and covers regressions with multivariate extensions to the baseline model. Using the earlier notation, let $\pi = T_P/T_R$, while $\lambda = T_R/(T_R + T_P)$. Table 17.1 shows a few select critical values for McCracken's OOS-F test, simulated using the methods of Hansen and Timmermann (2015), for the linear regression model with two additional variables in the large prediction model for 95 and 99% critical values.

Note, first, how sensitive the critical values are to the sample split parameter, λ, varying from around 2 to 4 at the 99% critical level as the sample split fraction decreases from around 0.90 to one-third. Second, and as a result, these critical values can be very different from conventional critical values used in hypothesis testing under the assumption that $\pi = 0$ so $\lambda = 1$. With two additional predictor variables in the large model, these critical values are 4.826 for $\alpha = 0.95$ and 7.910 for $\alpha = 0.99$; see McCracken (2007, table 4).

17.4.2 Recentered Test Statistic

Clark and West (2007) argue that encompassing tests should account for the covariance of $\hat{e}_{1t+1}$ and $(\hat{e}_{2t+1} - \hat{e}_{1t+1})$ in cases where the (large) model used to construct $f_{2t+1|t}$ nests the (smaller) model used to construct $f_{1t+1|t}$. They note that the difference in the squared forecast errors is

$$\hat{e}_{1t+1}^2 - \hat{e}_{2t+h}^2 = -2\hat{e}_{1t+1}(\hat{e}_{2t+h} - \hat{e}_{1t+1}) - (\hat{e}_{2t+1} - \hat{e}_{1t+1})^2. \tag{17.29}$$

The term entering the numerator for $\hat{\beta}$ in (17.7) is the first term in (17.29). When the restricted (small) model is true, we expect the variance of the forecasts generated by the large model to be bigger since this model needs to estimate a greater number of parameters. When the small model encompasses the large model, we expect the differences in average MSE values to be negative, so the left-hand side in (17.29) is expected to be negative on average even though both models are "true," one being more profligately parameterized. When the forecasts are equal on average (when weighted), the first term on the right-hand side of (17.29) is expected to be 0. The last term on the right-hand side in (17.29) is clearly positive on average. Clark and West (2007) argue that we should correct the difference in MSE values by the second term in (17.29) which accounts for the negative bias, suggesting a test of the sample average of $\hat{e}_{1t+1}^2 - \hat{e}_{2t+h}^2 + (\hat{e}_{2t+1} - \hat{e}_{1t+1})^2 = -2\hat{e}_{1t+1}(\hat{e}_{2t+1} - \hat{e}_{1t+1})$. This motivates a test of the covariance of $\hat{e}_{1t+h}$ and $(\hat{e}_{2t+1} - \hat{e}_{1t+1})$ to be 0 as a test of equal MSE in situations with nested forecasting models.

Clark and West (2007) propose the following adjusted MSE test statistic:

$$\text{MSE}^{\text{adj}} = T_P^{-1} \sum_{t=T_R}^{T-1} \hat{e}_{1t+1}^2 - \left[T_P^{-1} \sum_{t=T_R}^{T-1} \hat{e}_{2t+1}^2 - T_P^{-1} \sum_{t=T_R}^{T-1} (\hat{f}_{1t+1|t} - \hat{f}_{2t+1|t})^2 \right]$$

$$= -2T_P^{-1} \sum_{t=T_R}^{T-1} \hat{e}_{1t+1} \left(\hat{f}_{1t+1|t} - \hat{f}_{2t+1|t} \right)$$

$$= 2T_P^{-1} \sum_{t=T_R}^{T-1} \hat{e}_{1t+1} \left(\hat{e}_{1t+1|t} - \hat{e}_{2t+1|t} \right). \tag{17.30}$$

The term $T_P^{-1} \sum_{t=T_R}^{T-1} (\hat{f}_{1t+1|t} - \hat{f}_{2t+1|t})^2$ is a measure of the extent to which parameter estimation error affects the second (large) model more than the nested first (small) model. Since this term gets subtracted from the MSE performance of the second model, the adjusted MSE test will of course make the larger model look better than the conventional MSE test which does not include such an adjustment term.

Specifically, define

$$\tilde{d}_{t+1} = (y_{t+1} - \hat{f}_{1t+1|t})^2 - \left[(y_{t+1} - \hat{f}_{2t+1|t})^2 - (\hat{f}_{1t+1|t} - \hat{f}_{2t+1|t})^2 \right]. \qquad (17.31)$$

We can then run an OLS regression of the adjusted MSE difference, $\tilde{d}_{t+1}$, on a constant,

$$\tilde{d}_{t+1} = \mu + \varepsilon_{t+1}, \qquad (17.32)$$

and use a one-sided t-test for μ. Clark and West propose to compare this adjusted MSE test against standard normal critical values of the normal distribution, i.e., 1.282 for a test with a size of 10%, and 1.645 for a 5% test, although these result in a size slightly below the nominal size in sufficiently large samples.

The adjusted test statistic is closely related to the earlier tests for encompassing. In fact, the t-statistic for the adjusted test for equal predictive accuracy based on (17.31) and (17.32) is the same as the ENC-T statistic and Clark and West (2007) establish conditions under which the distribution of the ENC-T test is asymptotically normal.[9]

Again this test addresses whether one model is better than another model, when evaluated at the pseudo-true probability limits. By construction, the test favors the larger model over the smaller one, relative to the unadjusted MSE test. Even if it is concluded from the test that the larger model is best, it does not follow that, in any given finite sample, it is best to use this model to generate out-of-sample forecasts. This is because the adjustment term does not actually reduce the forecast errors of the larger model—it only serves the purpose of sharpening inference about the relative performance of the two models in an environment where parameter estimation error is not a factor.

17.4.3 Finite Sample Behavior of Tests

The results described thus far are asymptotic, but the size of the forecast evaluation tests in finite samples has been examined in various Monte Carlo experiments. For situations where the forecast errors are given, differences across various test statistics have been analyzed in Harvey, Leybourne, and Newbold (1998). These authors do not replicate the forecast method but instead draw forecast errors directly as coming from a joint t-distribution with few degrees of freedom. For small samples they find that size distortions in (17.7) can be severe, although distributions must be quite fat tailed for this to hold.

West (2001) generates data from the model $y_{t+1} = x_{1t} + e_{1t+1}$ and compares this model (with an estimated effect of x_{1t} on y_{t+1}) against a model that uses x_{2t} to predict y_{t+1} with x_{2t} independent of y_{t+1}. The variables $(e_{1t+1}, x_{1t}, x_{2t})$ are drawn from an independent normal distribution using a variance–covariance matrix with diagonal elements $(1, 1, 2)$. West examines the test statistic (17.8) as well as this same statistic with its standard error, S, replaced by the adjusted standard error indicated by the results of West and McCracken (1998). Standard errors change with the relative size of the evaluation sample to the estimation sample, T_P / T_R, and depend on the method

---

[9] Clark and West (2007) show that if the null model is a martingale difference and so does not require any parameters to be estimated, and the alternative model uses rolling window estimates to generate forecasts, the ENC-T test has an asymptotic standard normal distribution. In other cases, the test statistic will be approximately normal, provided that T_P / T_R is not too extreme.

used to construct the forecasts. For this model (17.8) is theoretically oversized since the estimation error in constructing the forecasts adds a nonnegative component to the standard error. This is borne out by Monte Carlo results. The size of the corrected test statistic is well controlled as long as the evaluation sample is not too small; it is undersized for large estimation samples and oversized for small estimation samples.

For nested models, Clark and McCracken (2001) examine data-generating processes where $\{y_t, x_t\}$ are generated by a VAR(1) or VAR(2) with independent (across time and variables) residuals. The forecasting models are an autoregression (of correct order) in y_t or the correctly specified VAR.[10] To examine the size of the test, the VAR is chosen such that lags of x_t have no predictive power. Using tests based on the regression (17.7), the ENC-T and ENC-NEW statistics with critical values constructed from their asymptotic results, Clark and McCracken find that the size of these tests is well controlled.

Clark and McCracken (2005a) propose a restricted VAR bootstrap to deal with cases where serial correlation and conditional heteroskedasticity in the forecast errors introduce nuisance parameters in the asymptotic distribution of the test statistic. The bootstrap uses a VAR specification for $\{y_t, x_t\}$ whose parameters are estimated using full-sample OLS on the restricted model. Resampled residuals from this model are used to recursively generate bootstrapped time series of $\{y_t, x_t\}$. In turn these bootstrapped series are used to estimate the restricted and unrestricted forecasting models and the process is repeated a large number of times to compute the full distribution of test statistics bootstrapped under the null of no predictive power for the variables included only in the large model. Tests based on the (relative) forecast performance of the restricted and unrestricted models in the actual data are then compared with the percentiles of this distribution to compute p-values.

The power of various forecast evaluation tests has also been examined in Monte Carlo experiments. For the nested case, Clark and McCracken (2001) use the Monte Carlo design above but allow lags of x_t to affect y_t. They find that the ENC-NEW test has higher power than the tests based on the regression (17.7) and the ENC-T statistics. They also show that a full sample Granger causality test has considerably more power than any of the out-of-sample tests. This is not surprising since we are examining tests statistics for which classical assumptions apply so full sample tests will generally have higher power.

Hansen and Timmermann (2015) establish analytical results for power in the case with two nested linear regression models whose parameters are recursively estimated. Their results show that, for a fixed length of the total sample size (T), the power of out-of-sample tests decreases in the size of the data sample used for initial parameter estimation and conversely increases, the more data are used for out-of-sample forecast evaluation.

These out-of-sample tests have been extensively used to compare forecasts of stock returns (Lettau and Ludvigson, 2001; Hansen, Lunde, and Nason, 2011) and inflation and exchange rates (Rossi, 2013b).

---

[10] Clark and McCracken (2001) also examine results with data-determined lag lengths, but these results are more difficult to interpret.

TABLE 17.2:
Root mean squared error performance of univariate prediction models for monthly stock returns along with tests of equal predictive accuracy measured against the prevailing mean benchmark, pm. For each regression, the identity of the predictor variable is listed in the left column. HLN uses the finite-sample correction to the DM test proposed by Harvey et al. (1998), DM is the Diebold–Mariano test for equal predictive accuracy, while GW is the Giacomini–White test of equal predictive accuracy. The latter test is based on models estimated using a rolling window with 20 years of data.

Predictor	RMSE roll	RMSE enl	HLN	p-val	DM	p-val	GW	p-val
dp	4.5191	4.4994	−0.4535	0.6504	−0.4539	0.6501	0.5128	0.4739
dy	4.5150	4.5088	−0.6478	0.5174	−0.6484	0.5170	0.2662	0.6059
ep	4.5544	4.5276	−0.9967	0.3194	−0.9976	0.3189	1.9519	0.1624
bm	4.5546	4.5676	−2.0238	0.0435	−2.0258	0.0433	4.5548	0.0328
ntis	4.5073	4.5176	−1.1467	0.2520	−1.1477	0.2516	0.0898	0.7644
svar	4.5842	4.5027	−1.0688	0.2856	−1.0698	0.2852	1.7795	0.1822
dfr	4.5429	4.4854	0.1240	0.9014	0.1241	0.9013	3.6078	0.0575
ltr	4.4902	4.4830	0.2280	0.8198	0.2282	0.8196	0.1039	0.7472
infl	4.5107	4.4792	0.8307	0.4065	0.8315	0.4061	0.0507	0.8219
tms	4.4953	4.4852	0.0961	0.9235	0.0962	0.9234	0.0184	0.8920
tbl	4.5131	4.4900	−0.0915	0.9271	−0.0916	0.9271	0.0943	0.7588

17.4.4 Empirical Application

Table 17.2 reports the RMSE values associated with a rolling estimation window along with p-values for encompassing, the Diebold–Mariano and Giacomini–White tests for 11 univariate prediction models fitted to stock returns. Each model includes the predictor listed in the rows in the table, while the benchmark prevailing mean only includes an intercept. For the DM tests the parameters are estimated using an expanding window, while for the Giacomini–White test we use a rolling window with 20 years of monthly observations (120 data points). The out-of-sample evaluation period is 1970–2013.

Many of the models generate RMSE values comparable to those of the benchmark prevailing mean model (whose RMSE value is 4.4871) with the models based on the default spread (dfr), long term return (ltr), inflation (infl), and the term spread (tms) performing slightly better. However, neither the Diebold–Mariano test, nor the HLN or Giacomini–White test reject the null of equal predictive accuracy for any of the predictor variables.

17.5 COMPARING MANY FORECASTS

In cases with more than two forecasts to compare, we need to examine a vector of forecasts. Some of the methods discussed above extend to the general case with m forecasts (e.g., encompassing) while others do not (e.g., the Granger–Newbold comparison). This section discusses the effect on the tests of having an arbitrary number of forecasts.

With two forecasts, it is natural to test a null of equal predictive accuracy. In contrast, in the presence of multiple alternative forecasts, it is natural to ask whether there exists *any* forecast that is superior to the benchmark. This results in a composite hypothesis which is generally more difficult to test than the simple pairwise test of equal predictive accuracy.

17.5.1 Forecast Encompassing

Under MSE loss, forecast encompassing generalizes readily to testing that the first forecast encompasses the remaining forecasts for a general $(m \times 1)$ vector of forecasts. The vector analogs to (17.5), (17.6), and (17.7) become

$$y_{t+1} = \beta_1 \hat{f}_{1t+1|t} + \beta_2' \hat{f}_{2t+1|t} + \varepsilon_{1t+1}, \tag{17.33}$$

$$y_{t+1} - \hat{f}_{1t+1|t} = \beta_2' \hat{f}_{2t+1|t} + \varepsilon_{2t+1}, \tag{17.34}$$

$$\hat{e}_{1t+1|t} = \beta'(\hat{e}_{1t+1|t} - \iota_{m-1}\hat{e}_{2t+1|t}) + \varepsilon_{3t+1}, \tag{17.35}$$

respectively, where $\hat{f}_{2t+1|t}$ and $\hat{e}_{2t+1|t}$ are $((m-1) \times 1)$ vectors of the forecasts and forecast errors, respectively, ι_{m-1} is an $((m-1) \times 1)$ vector of 1s and β or β_2 are $((m-1) \times 1)$ vectors of regression coefficients. The null hypotheses $H_0 : \beta = 0$ or $H_0 : \beta_2 = 0$ yield tests that the first forecast encompasses the remaining $m-1$ forecasts.

17.5.2 Testing for Superior Predictive Ability

White (2000) studies the case with a vector of forecast errors or, more generally, losses that relate to these errors. However, he examines a very different question, namely how confident we can be that the best forecast, among a set of competing forecasts, is genuinely better than a pre-specified benchmark, given that the best forecast is selected from a potentially large set of models. That the best model has been drawn from a potentially large pool can be very important when assessing its performance: in any given sample, a forecast model may produce a smaller average loss even though in expectation (i.e., across all samples we could have seen) the model would not have been so good. A search across multiple forecast models may result in the recovery of a genuinely good model, but it may also uncover a bad model that just happens to perform well in a given sample. More broadly, this is the issue of skill versus luck, i.e., of having a genuinely superior model versus having an inferior model that just happens to perform well in a given sample.

The Reality Check setup considered by White (2000) closely mimics how many economists go about model building. Many different specifications are typically examined on a given data set. The tests used in model comparisons often ignore the specification search that may have preceded the selection of the prediction models although such models could be survivors from previous tests.

White uses a recursive setup for construction of the forecasts and considers the joint distribution of the performance of the individual forecasting models. With m models, there are m sample estimates of the out-of-sample (average) losses. Let $d_{kt+1|t}(\hat{\beta}_t) = L(f_{0t+1|t}(\hat{\beta}_{0t}), y_{t+1}) - L(f_{kt+1|t}(\hat{\beta}_{kt}), y_{t+1})$ be the loss difference in period $t+1$ for the benchmark model (numbered as model 0) measured relative to model k, so that we obtain a zero value if the average loss of model k equals that of the benchmark. Negative values suggest higher loss of model k relative to the benchmark, while positive values indicate that model k beats the benchmark. Moreover, let $\bar{d}_k$ denote the sample average of $d_{kt+1|t}$ for $t = T_R, \ldots, T - 1$, and let $\bar{d} = (\bar{d}_1, \ldots, \bar{d}_m)'$ be an $(m \times 1)$ vector of sample averages computed over some (out-of-sample) evaluation period with T_p observations. Finally, let $\beta_k^* = plim(\hat{\beta}_{kT})$ be the pseudo-true value for β_k, given the estimation method. The null hypothesis tested by the Reality Check is that the benchmark model is not inferior to *any* of the m alternatives:

$$H_0 : \max_{k=1,\ldots,m} E[d_{kt+1|t}(\beta_k^*)] \leq 0, \tag{17.36}$$

whereas the alternative is that at least one model produces lower expected loss than the benchmark:

$$H_1 : \max_{k=1,\ldots,m} E[d_{kt+1|t}(\beta^*)] > 0. \tag{17.37}$$

If all models perform as well as the benchmark, the $\bar{d}$ vector has zero mean and so the maximum of the vector also has zero mean. By examining the maximum of the vector of losses, the hypothesis reflects the practice that researchers are likely to search for the best model among a large set of competing specifications. The alternative hypothesis is that the best model outperforms the benchmark model, i.e., that there exists a superior model.

Under the assumption that $T_p^{1/2}(\bar{d} - E(\bar{d}^*)) \Rightarrow N(0, \Omega)$ as $T_p \to \infty$, where $\Rightarrow$ denotes convergence in distribution and $d_{t+1}^* = L(f_{0t+1|t}(\beta_0^*), y_{t+1}) - L(f_{t+1|t}(\beta^*), y_{t+1})$ with $\beta^* = plim(\hat{\beta}_T)$ as $T \to \infty$, White (2000) establishes conditions under which

$$\max_{k=1,\ldots,m} T_p^{1/2}(\bar{d}_k - E[\bar{d}_k^*]) \Rightarrow \max_{k=1,\ldots,m} \{U_k\}, \tag{17.38}$$

where U is an $(m \times 1)$ vector whose components U_k are distributed as $N(0, \Omega)$. White's high-level assumption is similar to the assumptions in West (1996) and so rules out a number of interesting cases, including comparisons of nested models.[11]

Even if we can characterize the limiting distribution of the vector of sample averages, we cannot easily determine the distribution of the maximum of this vector due to the correlation between the models captured by the unknown covariance matrix Ω. From a testing perspective, Ω is a nuisance parameter that we do not care about other than in so far as it affects inference about the predictive performance. White (2000) addresses this problem by making the high level assumption that the vector of losses is asymptotically normal and by developing a bootstrap approach for drawing the maximum from the distribution in (17.38) and computing the p-value that the null is true.

To see how the bootstrap works, denote by $\bar{d}_k^b$ the average differential loss computed in the bth bootstrap, $b = 1, \ldots, B$ and consider the following statistics:

$$\bar{d}_{\max,m} = \max_{k=1,\ldots,m} \{T_p^{1/2}\bar{d}_k\}, \tag{17.39}$$

$$\bar{d}_{\max,m}^b = \max_{k=1,\ldots,m} \{T_p^{1/2}(\bar{d}_k^b - \bar{d}_k)\}, \quad b = 1, \ldots, B. \tag{17.40}$$

---

[11] As pointed out by Hansen (2005), this high-level assumption is not innocuous and rules out cases where the parameters of the alternative models are estimated recursively using an expanding window and the alternative models nest the benchmark model. This is the situation considered by Clark and McCracken (2001) in which the limiting distribution becomes a function of Brownian motions. See also Granziera, Hubrich, and Moon (2014) for an approach to comparing a small number of nested models.

We can then compare the best performance of any model from the actual data in (17.39) to the quantiles from the bootstrap in (17.40) to obtain White's bootstrap Reality Check p-value for the null hypothesis in (17.36). By considering the sampling distribution of the maximum value of the relative loss, computed across the m models, we account for the effect of data mining over models.

White suggests using the stationary bootstrap of Politis and Romano (1994) to construct bootstrap samples. The stationary bootstrap resamples blocks of random length from the original data, letting the block length be drawn from a geometric distribution whose mean block length is $1/q$. Large values of q are appropriate for data with little (time-series) dependence, while smaller values of q can appropriately be used for more strongly dependent data.

Draws from the stationary bootstrap proceed as follows. Define a set of the random time indexes τ_t, which are numbers between T_R and T. Each bootstrap, b, then generates a sample estimate $\bar{L}_k^b = \sum_{t=T_R}^T L(f_{k\tau_t-1}, y_{\tau_t})$, as follows.

1. Set $t = T_R + 1$. Draw $\tau_t = \tau_{T_R}$ at random, independently, and uniformly from $\{T_R + 1, \ldots, T\}$.
2. Increase t by 1. If $t > T$, stop. Otherwise, draw a standard uniform random variable, U, independently of all other random variables.

   a) If $U < q$, draw τ_t at random, independently, and uniformly, from $\{T_R + 1, \ldots, T\}$.
   b) If $U \geq q$, expand the block by setting $\tau_t = \tau_{t-1} + 1$; if $\tau_t > T$, reset $\tau_t = T_R + 1$.

3. Repeat step (2).

This bootstrap is simple to implement because it requires resampling only from the forecast errors (or, more broadly, losses), as opposed to resampling from the original data, $\{y_t, z_{t-1}\}$, reestimating forecasting models, and generating sequences of forecasts and forecast errors. Hence, no estimation is involved.

Hansen (2005) notes that the bootstrap procedure in White (2000) means that, in practice, the assumption under the null hypothesis is that $E[d_k(\beta^*)] = 0$. He shows that if the maximum of $E(\bar{d})$ is negative, then $T_p^{1/2} \max_{k=1,\ldots,m} \bar{d}_k \to^P -\infty$. Thus with probability 1 we get a degenerate distribution when the benchmark model is better than all other models. Hansen's superior predictive ability (SPA) test modifies the Reality Check by normalizing and recentering the test statistic. First, he proposes to use a studentized test statistic,

$$\text{SPA} = \max \left[\max_{k=1,\ldots,m} \frac{T_p^{1/2}\bar{d}_k}{\hat{s}_k}, 0 \right], \tag{17.41}$$

where $\hat{s}_k^2$ is a consistent estimator of $s_k^2 = \text{var}(T_p^{1/2}\bar{d}_k)$. Second, Hansen's SPA test bases the null distribution on

$$N_m(\hat{\mu}^c, \hat{\Omega}), \tag{17.42}$$

where $\hat{\mu}_k^c = \bar{d}_k \mathbb{1} \left(T_p^{1/2}\bar{d}_k/\hat{s}_k \leq -\sqrt{2\log\log(T_p)} \right),$

where $\mathbb{1}(\cdot)$ is an indicator function. By recentering the null distribution for poorly performing models, the distribution becomes sample dependent under the null. The test does not discard poor models (models for which the indicator function equals 1) but reduces their influence through the recentering, while maintaining the influence of the models for which $\hat{\mu}_k^c = 0$.

Hansen presents Monte Carlo simulations that illustrate potentially large power gains from applying these modifications to the Reality Check test statistic. How important these modifications are depends on the particular application at hand and the number of "poor" forecasting models under consideration. Even in the absence of obviously inferior models, it is generally a good idea for many financial and economic time series to use a studentized test as in (17.41).

17.6 ADDRESSING DATA MINING

White's Reality Check provides a way to address a question that arises when selecting which variables, z_t, to include in the orthogonality regression. The vast array of possible covariates along with the wide set of choices of models means that one can search over many possible specifications. Indeed, this is exactly how the literature has proceeded with different researchers using different forecasting models. Suppose that a researcher finds a superior model. How should we interpret this evidence if the model were preceded by numerous other specifications? One way is to consider the model as the (potentially) best model among a larger set of competing specifications and use White's Reality Check approach to correct for the effect of the search across multiple models. In other words, we would examine whether the best of the specifications really does outperform the baseline, taking into account the other models that were tried out. This is the approach taken by Sullivan, Timmermann, and White (2001) to study the performance of technical trading rules applied to daily stock returns.

An alternative to the White–Hansen approach is to use a Bonferroni bound. Let p_k be the p-value associated with the null that model k does not produce lower expected loss than the benchmark. For arbitrary correlations between the performance measures, $\bar{d}_1, \ldots, \bar{d}_m$, the Bonferroni bound implies that the p-value for the joint null that none of the m models is superior to the benchmark satisfies an upper bound,

$$p \leq \min(m \times \min(p_1, \ldots, p_m), 1). \tag{17.43}$$

Equivalently, the test rejects at the α% critical level if $\min(p_1, \ldots, p_m) < \alpha/m$. Note that the smallest of the p-values, which produces the strongest evidence against the null that no model beats the benchmark, gets multiplied by the number of models under consideration. The Bonferroni approach tends to be conservative and guards against "worst case" scenarios. For example, in the case of perfectly correlated forecasts, the p-values are identical and so the correct procedure is to reject if $p < \alpha$, rather than rejecting only for $p < \alpha/m$.

Both equations (17.42) and (17.43) illustrate that, from the perspective of being able to identify a truly superior model, it is not innocuous to search across a large set of prediction models, many of which have no hope of producing good results. Every time a new alternative model is considered, the yardstick for beating the benchmark

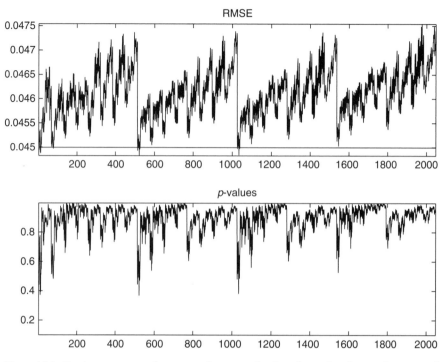

Figure 17.1: Root mean squared error performance (top) and p-value (bottom) measured against the prevailing mean benchmark and based on all possible combinations of 11 predictor variables. All forecasts are based on estimates using a rolling window with 20 years of monthly observations.

gets adjusted, thereby imposing a "tax" on mindless data mining efforts. Procedures that can direct the search for a forecasting model by using economic theory to identify either functional form or predictor variables, therefore have a better hope of being successful.

17.6.1 Empirical Application

To illustrate these ideas, we undertook an empirical application to monthly stock returns using the 11 predictor variables from the Welch and Goyal (2008) data set included in the earlier application. We consider all possible $2^{11} = 2048$ models. The out-of-sample period is 1970–2013 and estimates are updated using a rolling estimation window with 20 years of monthly observations. This ensures that nested models do not become an issue when applying White's Reality Check or Hansen's SPA test. We use the prevailing mean model of Welch and Goyal (2008) as our benchmark. This includes an intercept but no time-varying predictors.

The top panel in figure 17.1 plots the RMSE performance with the value for the benchmark prevailing mean model shown as a horizontal line. The patterns in the plots reflect the ordering of the models which is not random but has small models followed by larger models within different blocks comprising the different predictors. Very few models manage to produce a lower RMSE performance than the prevailing mean benchmark.

The bottom panel in figure 17.1 plots the p-values associated with the individual models. None of the models appear able to generate p-values close to the conventional 5% cutoff. Thus it is not surprising for this application that none of the models beat the prevailing mean benchmark after accounting for model search. In fact, when we use White's Reality Check, this yields a p-value of 1, confirming that the best forecasting model does not outperform the prevailing mean benchmark.

17.7 IDENTIFYING SUPERIOR MODELS

The approach taken by White (2000) and Hansen (2005) asks whether a superior model exists. By using the max-statistic, both White and Hansen identify models that are significantly better than the benchmark, i.e., models whose individual t-statistics exceed the appropriate critical value. Their approach does not go beyond this first step in an attempt to identify which particular model is better than the benchmark, nor does it address how many benchmark-beating models exist. This issue is addressed by Romano and Wolf (2005) who develop a stepwise approach that iterates on White's bootstrap in a way that controls the so-called familywise error rate, i.e., the event of wrongly identifying at least one forecasting model as superior, and can be used to identify additional significant alternatives by tightening the critical value in subsequent steps. Like White's approach, their method achieves power gains relative to the Bonferroni bound by accounting for correlation among the individual models' test statistics.

To see how the Basic StepM method of Romano and Wolf (2005) works, without loss of generality suppose that we have ordered the models from largest to smallest by their out-of-sample forecasting performance, $\bar{d}_1, \ldots, \bar{d}_m$. The first step in the procedure estimates the critical value, $c_{1\alpha}$, associated with the null hypothesis that not even the best model is superior using the one-step White bootstrap conducted at the $\alpha\%$ critical level. If this step does not result in a rejection of the null, there is no need to continue because none of the models beats the benchmark. Conversely, if the null is rejected, all models with performance $\bar{d}_j < c_{1\alpha}$ are removed.[12] Next, the previous step is repeated including only those models that remain in the candidate set to establish a new cutoff, $c_{2\alpha}$, for these models. The procedure continues until no additional models are removed. Romano and Wolf propose algorithms that asymptotically identify all models that are better than the benchmark, while removing inferior models and maintaining control over the familywise error rate.

Hansen, Lunde, and Nason (2011) avoid the need for having a random or fixed benchmark against which a multitude of models are compared. Their model confidence set identifies the subset of models that includes the best, but usually unknown, model with a certain level of confidence. The model confidence set is constructed given an equivalence test and an elimination rule. The equivalence test is a test for equal predictive performance of the models contained in some set of (superior) models. If the equivalence test rejects, the models in the maintained set are not equally good and the elimination rule identifies which of the models to eliminate.

---

[12] Recall that a small value of $\bar{d}_j$ suggests poor performance for model j relative to the benchmark.

Specifically, let $\mathcal{M}_0 = \{M_1, \ldots, M_m\}$ denote the initial set of models under consideration. Each model, i, generates a loss in period t of $L_{it+1|t}$, so the differential loss when comparing pairs of models i and j at time t is

$$d_{ij,t+1} = L_{it+1|t} - L_{jt+1|t}, \quad i, j \in \mathcal{M}_0. \tag{17.44}$$

Hansen, Lunde, and Nason (2011) propose a simple algorithm for constructing the model confidence set. The first step sets $\mathcal{M} = \mathcal{M}_0$, i.e., the full set of models under consideration. The next step uses the equivalence test to test $H_{0,\mathcal{M}} : E[d_{ij,t+1}] = 0$ for all $i, j \in \mathcal{M}$ at a critical level α. If $H_{0,\mathcal{M}}$ is accepted, the estimated model confidence set is $\hat{\mathcal{M}}^*_{1-\alpha} = \mathcal{M}$. If the null is rejected, the elimination rule is used to reject one model from $\mathcal{M}$ and the procedure is repeated on the reduced set of models. The procedure continues until the equivalence test does not reject and no further model needs to be eliminated.

This description still leaves the issue of which test to use to eliminate forecast models and construct the model confidence set. A natural approach is to consider the models' out-of-sample forecasting performance. To this end, Hansen, Lunde, and Nason (2011) define two relative sample loss measures, $\bar{d}_{ij} = T_P^{-1} \sum_{t=T_R}^{T-1} d_{ij,t+1}$, which captures the relative sample loss of models i and j, and $\bar{d}_{i\bullet} = m^{-1} \sum_{j \in \mathcal{M}} \bar{d}_{ij}$, which captures the relative sample loss of model i against the average loss across the m models in $\mathcal{M}$. Studentized test statistics can be used in the tests:

$$t_{ij} = \frac{\bar{d}_{ij}}{\sqrt{\widehat{\text{var}}(\bar{d}_{ij})}}, \quad i, j \in \mathcal{M}, \tag{17.45}$$

$$t_{i\bullet} = \frac{\bar{d}_{i\bullet}}{\sqrt{\widehat{\text{var}}(\bar{d}_{i\bullet})}},$$

where $\widehat{\text{var}}(\bar{d}_{ij})$ and $\widehat{\text{var}}(\bar{d}_{i\bullet})$ are sample estimates of the corresponding population objects. The first of the test statistics in (17.45) is similar to the t-test proposed by Diebold and Mariano (1995) for comparing the predictive accuracy of models i and j and testing the null that $E[\bar{d}_{ij}] = 0$. To convert the many t-tests in (17.45) into simpler objects that allow inspection of the null that all models have equivalent forecast performance, Hansen, Lunde, and Nason (2011) propose the following test statistics for $H_{0,\mathcal{M}}$:

$$T_{\max,\mathcal{M}} = \max_{i \in \mathcal{M}} \{t_{i\bullet}\},$$

$$T_{R,\mathcal{M}} = \max_{i,j \in \mathcal{M}} |t_{ij}|.$$

These test statistics have a nonstandard asymptotic distribution whose critical values can be bootstrapped along the lines described in White (2000) and Hansen (2005). The natural elimination rule associated with $T_{\max,\mathcal{M}}$, denoted $e_{\max,\mathcal{M}}$, is to set $e_{\max,\mathcal{M}} = \arg\max_{i \in \mathcal{M}} t_{i\bullet}$, so that in the case of rejection of $H_{0,\mathcal{M}}$, the model with the largest t-statistic against the average loss (and hence the worst performance) gets eliminated. For the $T_{R,\mathcal{M}}$ test statistic, Hansen, Lunde, and Nason (2011) propose the elimination rule $e_{R,\mathcal{M}} = \arg\max_{i \in \mathcal{M}} \sup t_{ij}$, thus eliminating the model whose performance looks worst relative to some other model.

17.8 CHOICE OF SAMPLE SPLIT

White's Reality Check bootstrap approach can be used to address the effect on inference of searching for a superior model across many different model specifications. Another dimension along which forecasters could have searched for superior performance is the sample split, i.e., the decision how to split a sample with $T = T_R + T_P$ observations into an initial estimation and model selection period that uses the first T_R observations, and a forecast evaluation period that uses the remaining T_p observations. Instead of studying the specific starting date for the forecast evaluation period, T_R, we can equivalently consider $\lambda = T_R / T \in (0, 1)$ which is the fraction of the sample used for initial estimation. To obtain well-behaved test statistics, it is common to assume that the choice of sample split λ is limited to an interval $\lambda \in [\underline{\lambda}, \bar{\lambda}]$, typically leaving out 10–15% of the sample on each side. This ensures sufficient data for initial model estimation and for subsequent forecast evaluation.

Hansen and Timmermann (2012) study the size of tests such as (17.28) when the p-value is chosen as the smallest value associated with all possible split points, i.e.,

$$p_{\min} = \min_{\lambda \in [\underline{\lambda}, \bar{\lambda}]} P_\lambda^{-1} \left(\frac{D_T(\lambda)}{\hat{\sigma}_\varepsilon^2} \right), \tag{17.46}$$

where $D_T(\lambda)$ is defined in (17.25), $\hat{\sigma}_\varepsilon^2$ is a consistent estimate of the variance of the forecast errors, P_λ^{-1} is the inverse of the c.d.f. of the test statistic $D_T(\lambda)/\hat{\sigma}_\varepsilon^2$. This is a quantile function and so gives the p-value of the test for a given value of λ. A single randomly selected p-value will follow a uniform distribution but this is no longer the case when we consider the *smallest* p-value selected from a potentially large number of test statistics. Overlaps in the estimation and evaluation windows used by the tests, $t = T_R, T_R + 1, \ldots, T$, introduce further complications since the individual p-values will be strongly correlated. Thus, if the reported p-value is the smallest value chosen from many possible sample splits, conventional inference will no longer be valid.

Hansen and Timmermann show that conventional tests of the predictive accuracy of nested models that account for nonstandard limiting distributions but ignore the effect of sample split mining can be greatly oversized. For example, with one additional predictor variable in the large model, a test with a nominal size of 5% can actually reject close to 15% of the time as a result of such sample split mining. Inflation in the size of the test grows even larger when the number of additional predictor variables in the large forecasting model is increased.

As a constructive way to account for the effect of sample split mining on inference, Hansen and Timmermann (2012) suggest an adjusted minimum p-value test corresponding to the statistic in (17.46). The test is based on the $p_{\min}$ statistic whose critical values can be derived using Monte Carlo simulations of the asymptotic distribution. Hansen and Timmermann compute adjusted p-values from the quantiles of the sorted distribution of $p_{\min}$-values simulated from a large number of sample paths.

For example, for a test with a critical level of 5% and one additional predictor variable, the $p_{\min}$-value adjusted for sample split mining in the interval $\lambda \in [0.1, 0.9]$ would have to fall below 1.3% for there to be significant evidence that the larger model dominates the small model. This result is intuitive: if only a single p-value had been inspected, there would be no distortion to inference, and we could simply use the critical values reported by McCracken (2007). On the other hand, if the reported p-value is pre-selected from a large set of candidate p-values, then we require stronger evidence—a larger test statistic and a smaller p-value—to be confident in the strength of the evidence.

A similar message comes out of Rossi and Inoue (2012) who consider test statistics computed either from averages or from the maximum of test statistics across different sample splits in a manner analogous to Hansen and Timmermann (2012). Rossi and Inoue also provide sample split mining-robust test statistics and show through Monte Carlo simulations that conventional tests that ignore such mining can lead to large size distortions.

17.9 RELATING THE METHODS

Differences between forecast encompassing tests and tests for equal predictive accuracy are perhaps best understood by considering the relation between these tests and forecast combination under MSE loss for a pair of forecasts. As we saw in chapter 14, if two forecasts have the same forecast error variance and we fail to reject the null of equal forecast accuracy, then it is optimal to use equal weights in a combined forecast, rather than use only one or the other forecast. In this case the combined forecast will reduce the forecast error variance, at least asymptotically. Conversely, forecast encompassing tests inspect whether it is optimal to assign a weight of 1 on one forecast and 0 on the other. These tests therefore examine very different hypotheses regarding the relative usefulness of the forecasts.

This reasoning does not extend to the situation with more than two forecasts in the comparison. With multiple forecasts, a combined forecast need not assign nonzero weights to all forecasts even if these have the same accuracy and it is possible for a forecast to produce the same forecast error variance as the remaining forecasts, yet still be encompassed by these forecasts.

Tests for forecast encompassing are equivalent to pre-testing a model. The forecast encompassing test addresses whether there is useful information in a forecast, just as pre-testing asks whether there is useful information in a candidate regressor. The general approach is to subsequently ignore models that are encompassed, just as regressors are ignored if they do not contribute enough to be marginally helpful in explaining the outcome.

Tests for equal predictive accuracy are more difficult to consider since neither a rejection nor a failure to reject imply a specific course of action. If the proposal is to replace one model with another, equal predictive accuracy might be regarded as a failure of the competing model to improve on the benchmark forecast. However, equal predictive accuracy does not mean that a new model is not useful, since it is possible that a combination of forecasts could lead to improvements. Moreover, even if we reject that the forecasts are equally good, it still may be that the forecasts can be usefully combined to provide a better forecast.

17.10 IN-SAMPLE VERSUS OUT-OF-SAMPLE FORECAST COMPARISON

When we are interested in evaluating the expected loss or some other statistic that involves data generated by any of the above estimation schemes, the sampling behavior of the resulting test statistics must account for which estimation scheme was used by the forecasting model. It is less clear whether the "pseudo" out-of-sample approach based on any of the recursive schemes is better than simply basing the forecast evaluation on models that are estimated on the full data sample.

It might seem natural to mimic the forecaster's problem when testing whether one model provides better forecasts than another model. However, a well-understood set of optimality results establishes that under quite general conditions, the optimal model comparison test should use the entire data set for model estimation. Typically the conditions required for this result are satisfied by the assumptions made to establish the sampling properties of out-of-sample test statistics. Hence, if the objective is to examine which forecasting model is better, the power of in-sample tests for the difference in the models' performance is higher than the power of out-of-sample tests. This point has been made in the forecasting context by Inoue and Kilian (2005) and, more recently, by Hansen and Timmermann (2015). Hansen and Timmermann (2015) demonstrate that commonly used out-of-sample test statistics for relative MSE performance are equivalent to the difference between two Wald statistics, one based on the full sample, the other based on only part of the sample. One implication of this is that out-of-sample forecast evaluation tests can imply a substantial loss of power compared to full-sample tests that do not split the sample in this manner.

When the forecast evaluation tests are used to choose between different methods for constructing a forecasting model, the problem becomes essentially a variation on model selection. As we saw in chapter 6, there is no optimal approach to model selection, so it is possible that different methods have different, possibly desirable, properties in different circumstances. However, this issue has not yet been examined in the literature.

Tests for equally precise forecasts may be better examined by means of full-sample regressions rather than using the pseudo out-of-sample experiments that underline many of the methods detailed above. The null and alternative models are presented in terms of model parameters with a large number of regularity conditions on the data and models which are often tested more powerfully using the full sample.

Why are out-of-sample tests then so popular in the forecasting literature? One reason is the (healthy) skepticism among economists when presented with a forecast model that provides a suspiciously impressive in-sample fit. As we saw in the previous chapter, in-sample results tend to exaggerate a model's likely future forecasting performance. This holds even if only a single forecast model is considered.

If, in fact, multiple models were considered and only the best model's performance gets presented, such data mining can greatly exaggerate that model's true expected forecasting performance. In some situations, out-of-sample forecasts can be used to address this data-mining concern. Specifically, if it can be certified that the forecaster did not in any way use the out-of-sample data to select and estimate a model, this evaluation sample is not contaminated and so can be used as a relatively "clean" sample on which to evaluate the model. There are, however, many ways in which the evaluation sample can get contaminated. For example, suppose we estimate a prediction model for US T-bill rates based on data up to 2000, but we include variables that we know (based on subsequent information) were correlated with monetary policy during the financial crisis of 2008–2009. This benefit of hindsight could in turn favor the selected model in a way that is unlikely to reflect its future predictive performance. Moreover, if a researcher splits the data into separate estimation and evaluation samples, but studies different models' performance over the evaluation sample, this would again mean that the best model's forecasting performance is no longer a single independent draw from a fresh data sample.

Such practice is a concern for any pseudo out-of-sample test and blurs the line between in-sample and out-of-sample forecast evaluation tests. However, it does not remove the practical point that the effect of data-mining can be far stronger for in-sample tests—since the model parameters are being tailored to the evaluation sample—than for out-of-sample tests.

A second reason for continuing with the out-of-sample approach is the belief that the conditions under which the in-sample tests are optimal are invalid. For example, the process generating the outcome might not be stationary and hence the correct forecasting model might not be constant over time. Examining the out-of-sample performance of the models might suggest a model that performs better more often than an in-sample test that—due to the failure of assumptions underlying the construction of the null distribution—might not control the test's size and hence performs poorly. While this argument has its merits, unfortunately the construction of null distributions for the out-of-sample tests also requires fairly strong assumptions and hence these tests could also fail to properly control size in such situations.

A third reason for using out-of-sample tests is that these allow us to address whether a forecasting model is practically useful even after accounting for recursive estimation error. Suppose the question is not whether the parameters of a large prediction model are different from 0 in the limit, but whether the associated forecasts are better than those generated by another, possibly nested, model. This is the question that is relevant in many forecasting situations and one that can be addressed using the out-of-sample forecast evaluation framework of Giacomini and White (2006).[13]

17.11 CONCLUSION

Forecasters often work with multiple competing models or observe multiple forecasts from survey data. In such a situation it is not only of interest to ask whether the individual forecasts are "optimal," using the methods from chapters 15 and 16, but also to ask whether there exists a single dominant forecasting model, or perhaps a set of models that are better than the other ones (as in the model confidence set).

The Diebold–Mariano test has become a convenient and popular tool for comparing the predictive accuracy across pairs of models. It is easy to implement and can be tailored to the underlying loss function (if known). Subsequent work by West (1996), Clark and McCracken (2001), and others quantify the effect of sampling error on the distribution of nonnested and nested model's relative forecasting performance in situations where nonstationarities induced by recursive updating in parameter estimates can be important.

---

[13] This is one of the reasons Ashley, Granger, and Schmalensee (1980) emphasize out-of-sample predictions as being more closely aligned with Granger causality tests.

When the performance of multiple models is being studied, an immediate concern is that the best model may appear to beat some benchmark simply by luck, or as a result of inspecting multiple models. In practice, the sampling distribution of the joint performance across multiple models is complex to characterize, but White (2000) and subsequent papers have constructed easily implemented bootstrap methods that handle the multiple hypothesis problem and so can be used to control for data mining. Stepwise methods can also be used to identify which models (if any) have superior performance compared to some benchmark or to identify a set of "best" models.

18

⌖⌖⌖

Evaluating Density Forecasts

Chapters 12 and 13 considered the situation where a predictive distribution, $p_Y(y|z)$, rather than a point forecast, was provided. This chapter examines how we can evaluate such predictive densities. For a single density forecast this means evaluating whether the density is correctly specified and leads to good forecasting performance. If there are multiple density forecasts, we may be interested in comparing them and perhaps selecting the best. Although the ideas of density forecast evaluation mirror those for point forecasts, the literature on density forecast evaluation is less well developed.

The primary difficulty that arises when evaluating density forecasts is that we never actually observe the density of an outcome; only a single draw from the distribution is observed. Further complicating matters, when we observe outcomes over a period of time the predictor variables change and so we obtain density forecasts $\hat{p}_{Yt}(y_{t+h}) = \hat{p}_Y(y_{t+h}|z_1, \ldots, z_t)$ and outcomes y_{t+h} conditional on different values of z_t.

One way to evaluate density forecasts is to explicitly rely on a loss function that maps the density forecast and outcome to a single number that can be the basis for an examination of average loss. Such loss functions are typically known as scoring rules, especially in the statistics literature, and were discussed in chapters 2 and 13. Loss functions should be chosen to address the particular forecaster's problem as different forecasters may use different loss functions. In practice, however, most studies rely on a small set of loss functions, the most popular being the log score, i.e., the average likelihood given certain distributional assumptions. Other methods that map the density forecast and outcome to a single number do not have an explicit loss function in mind but result in statistics that trade off different types of errors.

A second approach looks for desirable properties of the density forecast such as calibration or sharpness or matching the distribution function of the outcome. These features are often examined separately, with "good" density forecasts possessing as many desirable properties as possible.

Section 18.1 discusses density evaluation methods based on loss functions. Density forecasts are sometimes evaluated using features such as calibration, resolution, and sharpness. We cover this in section 18.2. Probability integral transform tests use information on the full density and are covered in section 18.3. Section 18.4 covers multicategory forecasts, while section 18.5 discusses how to evaluate interval forecasts, and section 18.6 concludes. Again, we focus on the case with a single-period forecast horizon, $h = 1$, to keep notation simple.

18.1 EVALUATION BASED ON LOSS FUNCTIONS

A direct approach to the evaluation of density forecasts would be to apply loss functions to a sequence of observed values of the difference between what actually occurs and the density forecasts. As we noted in the introduction to this chapter, what we observe is not a sequence of distributional outcomes but, rather, a single draw from that distribution. So the loss function applied to this setup needs to map single outcomes and density forecasts to the real line. One option is to transform the density forecast into a point forecast which can then be evaluated using standard procedures. Specifically, suppose we have in mind a particular loss function that allows us to map the density forecast into a point forecast. We can then, first, transform the density forecast to a point forecast and second, evaluate this point forecast with the same loss function. Alternatively, we could use a scoring rule which takes density forecasts as inputs.

For the first of these approaches, discussed more fully in section 18.1.1 below, it is important to note that the results will depend on the loss function outside the special (and unlikely) case that the density forecast is correctly specified. The comparison of misspecified density forecasts is discussed in Diebold, Gunther, and Tay (1998). The correctly specified density forecast is preferred over a misspecified density forecast by any loss function. In contrast, when the models generating the density forecasts are misspecified, the ranking of the associated forecasts may well differ across different loss functions—i.e., two forecasters with different loss functions will rationally disagree on their ranking of two sets of density forecasts. For example, consider the MSE and lin-lin loss functions. If one of the density forecasts is accurate for the conditional mean but not for the conditional variance, whereas the other is accurate for the conditional variance but is a little off-center, it could easily be that the MSE forecaster prefers the first density forecast whereas the lin-lin forecaster prefers the second.

Under the second approach, discussed in section 18.2 below, different scoring rules will prioritize accuracy at different points of the outcome distribution, and hence may differ in their ranking of misspecified density forecasts. For the binary forecasting problem there is a simple relation between loss functions applied to point forecasts and scoring rules. However, for more general problems there is not an obvious relationship between the two formulations (point forecasts evaluated using loss functions versus density forecasts evaluated using scoring rules). In practice, in situations where it is not straightforward to convert a density forecast into a point forecast, the scoring rule approach would seem appropriate.

18.1.1 Evaluation of Individual Density Forecasts

To empirically evaluate a density forecast, we require an observed sequence of outcomes and density forecasts $\{y_{t+1}, \hat{p}_{Yt}(y_{t+1})\}$, $t = 1, \ldots, T - 1$. One way to proceed would be to convert the density forecast into a point forecast and use the methods for point forecast evaluation covered in chapter 16. Using this approach, we would first generate the optimal point forecast, $f(\hat{p}_{Yt}(y_{t+1}))$, implied by the density forecast, $\hat{p}_Y(y_{t+1}|Z_t)$, and the loss function, $L(f(\hat{p}_{Yt}(y_{t+1})), y_{t+1})$. For example, under MSE loss, the point forecast $f(z_t)$ is simply the conditional mean of y_{t+1} computed using $\hat{p}_{Yt}(y_{t+1})$. The average loss associated with the density forecast then becomes

$$\bar{L}_T = (T-1)^{-1} \sum_{t=1}^{T-1} L(f(\hat{p}_{Yt}(y_{t+1})), y_{t+1}), \tag{18.1}$$

which is in the form of an average loss, as examined in chapter 16.

This simple approach to evaluating density forecasts might be appropriate for a number of reasons. First, as we saw in chapter 13, density forecasts can be justified on the grounds that there are multiple users with different loss functions. Any one of these users might examine the performance of a density forecast with reference to the specific loss function deemed appropriate for their problem. The relevant measure of forecast performance is the average loss calculated from each user's specific loss function. Second, even if a density forecast works well for some loss functions, it need not do so for all loss functions. For example, a density forecast that works well under MSE loss—meaning it is well centered—may be very poor for loss functions based on quantiles near the tails. This is just another way of saying that evaluation is specific to the loss function assumed in (18.1).

Understanding the sampling properties of (18.1) is difficult since the realized loss is a complicated function of the underlying density forecast and loss function. Moreover, the density forecasts typically depend on models whose estimates are recursively updated. The assumptions of West (1996) may not apply to situations with density forecasts, so actually assessing the correct sampling distribution and its dependence on the underlying estimates used to construct the density forecasts requires extensions of these methods, at least for situations where recursive updating in parameter estimates introduces nonstationarities. A typical approach is to ignore estimation error and simply evaluate the sampling error treating the observations on the realized loss, $L(f(z_t), y_{t+1})$, as data. However, this may understate the true sampling variability of the sample mean.[1]

Rather than converting the density forecast to a point forecast, an alternative is to use loss functions that are directly related to densities, such as the scoring rules discussed in chapter 2, sometimes known as skill scores. Scoring rules are functions that map the outcome y_{t+1} and the density forecast $\hat{p}_{Yt}(y_{t+1})$ to the real number line. If proper, they are maximized in expectation when the density forecast and the distribution of the outcome are the same.

For binary outcomes, distributional forecasts are equivalent to conditional mean forecasts. Since many loss functions for point forecast result in proper scoring rules, the two approaches are often equivalent. For example, under MSE loss the sample average loss associated with the distributional forecast of a binary variable is

$$Q_T^{MSE} = (T-1)^{-1} \sum_{t=1}^{T-1} (y_{t+1} - \hat{p}_{Yt}(y_{t+1}))^2. \tag{18.2}$$

This is often referred to as the Quadratic Probability Score (QPS) statistic or the Brier QPS after Brier (1950). As discussed in chapter 12, there is a direct link between

---

[1] If the density forecasts are generated from a rolling estimation window with fixed length, the methods of Giacomini and White (2006) along with assumptions on the dependence and moments of $L(f(z_t), y_{t+1})$, can be used to justify treating the observations on the realized loss as data.

scoring rules for the binary forecasting problem and the underlying loss functions for the point forecasts in which the scoring rule can be viewed as a weighted average taken over the loss of the underlying point forecasts.

For variables with continuous outcomes, there is no simple relationship between the scoring rule and the underlying loss function of the point forecasts. Thus, forecast evaluation usually rests on an arbitrarily chosen scoring rule. The most popular of these is the log scoring rule which leads to the sample average

$$Q_T^{LS} = (T-1)^{-1} \sum_{t=1}^{T-1} \log(\hat{p}_{Yt}(y_{t+1})), \tag{18.3}$$

where $\hat{p}_{Yt}(y_{t+1})$ is the conditional density forecast evaluated at the outcome y_{t+1}. For binary variables (18.3) becomes

$$Q_T^{LS} = (T-1)^{-1} \sum_{t=1}^{T-1} \left(y_{t+1} \log(\hat{p}_{Yt}(y_{t+1})) + (1 - y_{t+1}) \log(1 - \hat{p}_{Yt}(y_{t+1})) \right). \tag{18.4}$$

This is effectively the average likelihood. As with most scoring rules, we use the negative of the loss and so look for a large average likelihood or average log score. More generally, any scoring rule $S(y_{t+1}, \hat{p}_{Yt}(y_{t+1}))$ mapping $(y_{t+1}, \hat{p}_{Yt}(y_{t+1}))$ to a single number results in the average score

$$Q_T = (T-1)^{-1} \sum_{t=1}^{T-1} S(y_{t+1}, \hat{p}_{Yt}(y_{t+1})). \tag{18.5}$$

As with the average loss in (18.1), understanding the sampling properties of these objects is complicated by their dependence on estimated objects.

18.1.2 Comparing Density Forecasts

The method of Amisano and Giacomini (2007) compares two density forecasts, $\hat{p}_{Y1}(y|z)$ and $\hat{p}_{Y2}(y|z)$, using the log scoring rule. Using a setup similar to Giacomini and White (2006) for their distribution theory, Amisano and Giacomini (2007) assume that each successive forecast is based on a rolling window of observations which ensures that estimation error does not disappear asymptotically. Letting y_{t+1} be the outcome variable whose density is being predicted, Amisano and Giacomini (2007) base density evaluations on the studentized weighted average differences in log scores, i.e.,

$$t_{AG} = \hat{\sigma}_{T_P}^{-1} \sqrt{T_P} \sum_{t=T_R}^{T-1} w \left(\frac{y_{t+1} - \hat{\mu}_t}{\hat{\sigma}_t} \right) \left(\log \left[\hat{p}_{Y1t}(y_{t+1}) \right] - \log \left[\hat{p}_{Y2t}(y_{t+1}) \right] \right), \tag{18.6}$$

where $\log \left[\hat{p}_{Yit}(y_{t+1}) \right]$ is the log of the ith predictive distribution evaluated at the outcome y_{t+1}, $\hat{\mu}_t$ and $\hat{\sigma}_t$ are estimates of the mean and variance of y_{t+1}, respectively, based on the same rolling estimation window used to construct the forecasts, and $\hat{\sigma}_{T_P}^2$

is an estimate of the long-run variance of

$$
\left\{ w \left(\frac{y_{t+1} - \hat{\mu}_t}{\hat{\sigma}_t} \right) \left(\log \left[\hat{p}_{Y1t}(y_{t+1}) \right] - \log \left[\hat{p}_{Y2t}(y_{t+1}) \right] \right) \right\}
$$

for $t = T_R, \ldots, T - 1$. Using notation from chapters 16 and 17, $T_P = T - T_R$ is the length of the evaluation sample, and T_R is the start of the prediction sample.

Amisano and Giacomini (2007) suggest estimating $\hat{\sigma}^2_{T_P}$ using standard methods such as Newey and West (1987). Should it be desired, $w(\cdot)$ can be chosen to put more or less weight on different parts of the distribution. For example, a symmetric zero-mean density for $w(\cdot)$ would weight observations near the mean of y_{t+1} more heavily than the tails. This might be appropriate for a forecaster with MSE loss. The authors suggest a range of other weighting functions corresponding to alternative choices for where the focus of the test should be. Under fairly general assumptions they provide results showing that the limiting distribution for t_{AG} is standard normal and so can be compared to standard critical values.

Gneiting and Ranjan (2011) propose an adjustment to the approach of Amisano and Giacomini (2007) which is based on the sum of a different function of the data and density forecasts. Their approach towards weighting regions of the support of the density is guaranteed to be proper, i.e., it ranks the true predictive density highest, if this is included among the density models being compared. Once again, this leads to a test statistic that is asymptotically normally distributed.

Chapter 17 showed that pairwise comparisons of point forecasts have been extended to comparisons of multiple point forecasts. Similar extensions have been proposed for comparing the accuracy of multiple density forecasts. Employing the Reality Check of White (2000), Corradi and Swanson (2006a,b) propose ways to test whether the density forecast generated by one out of possibly many misspecified models is better in the sense that it more closely approximates the data than some benchmark model. Their approach considers parametric density models, $\hat{p}_{Yit}(y_{t+1}, \theta_i)$, $i = 1, \ldots, n$, whose parameters are updated recursively using, e.g., quasi-maximum likelihood estimators $\hat{\theta}_{it}$ that minimize $-\sum_{\tau=1}^{t-1} \ln p_{Yi\tau}(y_{\tau+1}, \theta_i)$. Each density model is associated with a conditional distribution, $\hat{F}_{Yit}(u, \theta_i) = \Pr(y_{t+1} \leq u | Z_t, \theta_i)$, where $F_{0t}(u, \theta_0)$ is the true conditional probability distribution. Corradi and Swanson propose to use squared errors to measure the distance between probability distributions and the data and assume that the first model is the benchmark we are interested in beating. Proceeding as in White (2000), they test the composite null that even the best among the alternative models, $k = 2, \ldots, m$, cannot generate distribution forecasts that are closer to the "true" distribution than the distribution forecasts implied by the benchmark model:

$$
\max_{k=2,\ldots,m} \int_U E \left[\left(\hat{F}_{1t}(u, \theta^*_1) - F_{0t}(u, \theta^*_0) \right)^2 - \left(\hat{F}_{kt}(u, \theta^*_k) - F_{0t}(u, \theta^*_0) \right)^2 \right] \varphi(u) du \leq 0,
$$

$$(18.7)$$

where θ^*_i is the probability limit of $\hat{\theta}_{it}$. The alternative is that this expression exceeds 0. Here $\varphi(u) \geq 0$ and $\int_U \varphi(u) du = 1$.

The test statistic in (18.7) tests whether the mean squared error between the cumulative distribution function values for the kth model measured relative to the

Table 18.1:
Diebold–Mariano test applied to GARCH(1,1), risk metrics, and rolling window forecasts of daily US stock market volatility.

Methods	t-stat	p-value (right tail)
Risk metrics ($\lambda = 0.94$) vs GARCH	-0.0870	0.5347
Risk metrics ($\lambda = 0.94$) vs AR	0.9668	0.1669
Rolling window (300 days) vs GARCH	0.9313	0.1759
Rolling window (300 days) vs AR	1.5919	0.0558
GARCH vs AR	1.7110	0.0437
Rolling window (300 days) vs risk metrics ($\lambda = 0.94$)	2.9121	0.0018

Note: The out-of-sample range is 2000–2010 using daily data.

true conditional distribution are smaller than that of the first (benchmark) model. Negative values indicate that none of the models perform better than the benchmark and so suggest that the benchmark model should be preferred. In practice, the true conditional distribution is of course unknown—otherwise we would not have a model selection problem in the first place—so Corradi and Swanson propose testing the null in (18.7) through the statistic

$$W_{T_P} = \max_{k=2,\dots,m} \frac{1}{\sqrt{T_P}} \int_U \sum_{t=T_R}^{T-1} \left[\left(\hat{F}_{1t}(u, \hat{\theta}_{1,t}) - \mathbb{1}(y_{t+1} \leq u) \right)^2 \right.$$

$$\left. - \left(\hat{F}_{kt}(u, \hat{\theta}_{k,t}) - \mathbb{1}(y_{t+1} \leq u) \right)^2 \right] \varphi(u)du, \quad (18.8)$$

where the indicator function $\mathbb{1}(\cdot)$ equals 1 if the condition inside the brackets is true, and 0 otherwise. Hence, the probability forecasts are directly compared to the rate at which outcomes of a certain magnitude occur in the evaluation sample. Corradi and Swanson (2006c) survey the theory and implementation of inference with this test statistic which, as in White (2000), is based on bootstrap methods.

18.1.3 Empirical Application to Volatility Forecasting

Applications of density forecasting in finance have often focused on volatility modeling. As discussed in chapter 2, Patton (2011) establishes that the MSE and QLIKE loss functions can be used to consistently rank volatility forecasts even when the outcome is measured with noise but can be proxied through the realized variance. Patton (2011) suggests using Diebold–Mariano tests applied to these loss functions.

Table 18.1 provides an illustration of this approach applied to daily stock market returns measured by the S&P500 index. As benchmark we use the risk metrics model which downweights past squared returns exponentially by a factor $\lambda = 0.94$ along with a 300-day rolling window volatility estimator. These forecasts are compared to a GARCH(1,1) and an AR model with lag length selected by AIC estimated on the realized variance series, using MSE loss. The initial estimation window uses 10 years of data from 2000 to the end of 2009, while the out-of-sample evaluation period runs from 2010 through 03/31/2015 and so covers more than five years. Forecast precision is measured using the realized variance as a proxy for the outcome. Positive values of the Diebold–Mariano test show that the squared errors of the model listed first are higher than those of the model listed last. The results show that the AR model performs best and in fact beats the GARCH and rolling window models with p-values close to 5%. Conversely, the rolling window method performs quite poorly in this application.

18.2 EVALUATING FEATURES OF DISTRIBUTIONAL FORECASTS

An alternative to examining the density forecast by means of some loss function is to review certain features of the density forecast. The idea is to check whether certain features of the distribution of the outcomes line up well with features implied by the distributional forecasts. This can be done either by directly relating the predicted and "actual" distributions and examining whether they are identical, or by considering certain features of the probability distribution.

Feature-based evaluation has been most fully developed for the case where Y is either 0 or 1 and so is a binary random variable with a probability forecast $\hat{p}_t = p(Y_{t+1} = 1 | z_1, \ldots, z_t)$. Murphy (1973) showed that the standard quadratic probability score, $E[(Y_{t+1} - \hat{p}_t)^2]$, can be decomposed as follows (see equation (15.3)):

$$E[(Y_{t+1} - \hat{p}_t)^2] = \mathrm{Var}(Y_{t+1}) + E[(\hat{p}_t - E[Y_{t+1}|\hat{p}_t])^2]$$
$$- E[E[Y_{t+1}|\hat{p}_t] - E[Y_{t+1}]]^2. \tag{18.9}$$

The first term in (18.9) is the unconditional variance of the outcome variable and so is independent of the forecast; the second term is the average squared calibration error; the last term is known as the resolution term and is the squared average difference between the conditional mean given the forecast and the unconditional mean. Calibration and resolution are examined below; the hope is that calibration is small (0) while resolution is large, leading to a smaller MSE.

To compute the decomposition in (18.9), for the case where p_i follows a discrete distribution we divide the line from 0 to 1 into m bins with centers p_i, $i = 1, \ldots, m$. Suppose again that we have T_P (out-of-sample) observations to evaluate forecasting performance and observe n_i observations in the ith bin so that $T_P = \sum_{i=1}^{m} n_i$. For each bin we predict $p_i n_i$ of the outcomes to be equal to 1. For each i, let the outcomes be y_{ij}, $j = 1, \ldots, n_i$, and let $\bar{y}_i = n_i^{-1} \sum_{j=1}^{n_i} y_{ij}$ be the associated sample mean of the outcomes. For the special case with $Y = 0, 1$, Murphy (1973) suggests the following decomposition:

$$T_P^{-1} \sum_{t=T_R}^{T-1} (y_{t+1} - p_t)^2 = T_P^{-1} \sum_{i=1}^{m} n_i(\bar{y}_i - p_i)^2 - T_P^{-1} \sum_{i=1}^{m} n_i(\bar{y}_i - \bar{y})^2 + \bar{y}(1 - \bar{y}).$$
$$\tag{18.10}$$

A good forecast, i.e., one with a small MSE, has calibration as close to 0 as possible and a resolution as high as possible. Calibration and resolution are correlated and it can be unclear how to adjust these measures to minimize the mean squared loss since any attempts to minimize the calibration term might also decrease the resolution.

To derive the decomposition in (18.10), note that

$$T_P^{-1} \sum_{t=T_R}^{T-1} (y_{t+1} - p_t(z_t))^2$$

$$= T_P^{-1} \sum_{i=1}^{m} \sum_{j=1}^{n_i} \left(p_i - y_{ij} \right)^2$$

$$= T_P^{-1} \sum_{i=1}^{m} \left(n_i p_i^2 + \sum_{j=1}^{n_i} y_{ij}^2 - 2p_i \sum_{j=1}^{n_i} y_{ij} \right)$$

$$= T_P^{-1} \sum_{i=1}^{m} \left(n_i p_i^2 + \sum_{j=1}^{n_i} y_{ij} - 2p_i \sum_{j=1}^{n_i} y_{ij} \right)$$

$$= T_P^{-1} \sum_{i=1}^{m} \left[n_i \left((p_i - \bar{y}_i)^2 - (\bar{y}_i^2 + \bar{y}_i) \right) \right]$$

$$= T_P^{-1} \sum_{i=1}^{m} \left[n_i (p_i - \bar{y}_i)^2 - n_i (\bar{y}_i^2 + \bar{y}_i) \right]$$

$$= T_P^{-1} \sum_{i=1}^{m} \left[n_i (p_i - \bar{y}_i)^2 - n_i (\bar{y}_i - \bar{y})^2 + n_i (\bar{y}^2 + \bar{y}_i - 2\bar{y}\bar{y}_i) \right]$$

$$= T_P^{-1} \sum_{i=1}^{m} n_i (p_i - \bar{y}_i)^2 - T^{-1} \sum_{i=1}^{m} n_i (\bar{y}_i - \bar{y})^2 + T^{-1} \sum_{i=1}^{m} n_i (\bar{y}^2 + \bar{y}_i - 2\bar{y}\bar{y}_i)$$

$$= T_P^{-1} \sum_{i=1}^{m} n_i (p_i - \bar{y}_i)^2 - T_P^{-1} \sum_{i=1}^{m} n_i (\bar{y}_i - \bar{y})^2 + \bar{y}(1 - \bar{y}).$$

Here we used that $T_P^{-1} \sum_{i=1}^{m} n_i \bar{y}_i = \bar{y}$. The first term is the calibration (ignoring the scaling by $p_i(1 - p_i)$), while the second term is the resolution.

Other decompositions of the Brier score exist (see, e.g., Sanders, 1963), one of which results in a property known as sharpness which refers to how concentrated the distributional forecast is. Sharpness is a feature of the forecasts themselves rather than how they relate to the outcomes. It is commonly evaluated based on a histogram of the probability forecasts on [0, 1]. A sharp forecast has a lot of probability mass near 1 or 0, the idea being that the forecast is giving decisive signals on which outcome will occur.

Extensions from the binary problem to general distributions have only recently been tackled. Our discussion reflects the small formal literature on such extensions and ignores some less used properties of density forecasts. We first cover calibration, then resolution, and finally sharpness.

18.2.1 Calibration

Calibration requires that if a density forecast assigns a certain probability to an event, then the event should occur with the stated probability over successive observations. This idea first arose in predictions of binary outcomes. Consider forecasting whether it will rain or shine, so a density forecast is just the probability that it will rain. If the weather forecaster predicts a 70% chance of rain, then over all the days for which this is the density forecast, we should see rain occurring 70% of the time. More generally, for a well-calibrated forecast, $E[Y|p(z)] = p(z)$.

This idea can be extended by transforming any event for the outcome to a binary variable. For any such event, A, if the associated density forecast $\int_A p_Y(y|z)(y)dy = p$, calibration requires that $P[y_{t+1} \in A]$ is indeed equal to p, conditional on the same information. For example, let A be the set of outcomes for which we predict an increase in the value of the outcome, $y_{t+1} > y_t$. Then, for all periods where the predicted probability that $y_{t+1} - y_t > 0$ is, say, $1/4$, we should see an increase in y exactly 25% of the time. For a well-calibrated forecast this should hold for all values of p and any event, A. Clearly, this only holds if the forecast distribution is precisely the distribution of the outcomes.

Example 18.2.1 (Comparing Gaussian density forecasts). *Following Gneiting and Raftery (2007), consider two possible density forecasts for y_{t+1}. The first is the true unconditional density, $p_{Y1t+1} \sim N(0, 2)$. The second is a correctly specified conditional density, $p_{Y2t+1|t} \sim N(\mu_t, 1)$, where the marginal distribution of μ_t is drawn from a standard Gaussian distribution, i.e., $\mu_t \sim N(0, 1)$. Let $A = \{y_{t+1} > 0\}$. Then p_{Y1t+1} implies a probability forecast $\int_A p_{Y1t+1}(y)dy = 0.5$ in every period. Correct calibration requires that $y_{t+1} > 0$ holds half the time on average. For the second model, $\int_A p_{Y2t+1}(y)dy = \Phi(\mu_t)$, which varies over time. Hence, calibration requires that $E[y_{t+1} > 0|\Phi(\mu_t) = p] = E[y_{t+1} > 0|\mu_t = \Phi^{-1}(p)] = p$ for all periods where $\Phi(\mu_t) = p$. This example has sufficient variation in μ_t so the condition can be checked for many different values of p.*

Most attempts to examine calibration lead to informal rather than formal hypothesis tests. An issue that arises is that $P\left[y_{t+1} \in A| \int_A p_{t+1}(y)dy = p\right]$ is a function of $p \in [0, 1]$ but often a given sample will have very few observations for any specific value of p. In the binary forecasting literature this has often been overcome by examining the property for a range of values for p to create a histogram as in the Murphy decomposition in (18.10). Using this approach, calibration can be measured as

$$\frac{1}{T} \sum_{i=1}^{m} n_i (\bar{y}_i - p_i)^2, \tag{18.11}$$

where a value of 0 means perfect calibration. Formal tests based on this statistic have a nonpivotal distribution. To get around this, Seillier-Moiseiwitsch and Dawid (1993) suggest the following standardized statistic:

$$\sum_{i=1}^{m} \frac{n_i (\bar{y}_i - p_i)^2}{p_i(1 - p_i)}. \tag{18.12}$$

Using a martingale difference sequence central limit theorem, these authors show that the statistic in (18.12) is approximately χ^2_m. Their result does not account for estimation error in the construction of the distributional forecast, however.

For forecasts converted into binary predictions, Galbraith and van Norden (2011) suggest using kernel methods. Standard kernel approaches to estimate the conditional mean are appropriate for this problem; see Pagan and Ullah (1999) for a review of the general problem. For general continuously distributed outcomes, y_{t+1}, a large number of choices exist for A. Calibration means that the result should hold for any such choice, although it is not feasible to try out every single choice for A.

Calibration suffers from the shortcoming that it ignores information in the conditioning variables. A forecast can be well calibrated even though the density forecast is not the best available one.

Example 18.2.2 (Comparing Gaussian density forecasts, continued). *For $A = \{y_{t+1} > 0\}$, the first density forecast, p_{Y1t+1}, is well calibrated since $P[y_{t+1} > 0] = 0.5$ which is the predicted probability each period. The second density forecast, p_{Y2t+1}, is also well calibrated. Whenever $\mu_t = \mu$, then $y_{t+1} \sim N(\mu, 1)$ and so $P[y_{t+1} > 0] = \Phi(\mu)$, resulting in a well-calibrated model.*

Calibration thus does not measure whether the density forecast is good in the sense that it assigns high probability to events that are likely to happen. Rather, it can be used to measure whether the density forecast makes systematic mistakes in some situations. For this reason, calibration is often termed "reliability"; a well-calibrated forecast is reliable in the sense that it avoids predicting events that do not happen, even if it can be a poor indicator of what will actually happen. In this sense calibration is really more a tool for specifying a good distribution rather than a way to persuade a user that the density forecast is optimal.

18.2.2 Resolution

Resolution asks the following question: Is the conditional distribution different from the unconditional distribution? We saw in the example that calibration is unable to distinguish between correct specification of a conditional density and correct specification of the unconditional density. Resolution attempts to resolve this issue. Resolution is usually examined through the difference in the conditional and unconditional means, $E[Y|\hat{p}] - E[Y]$, thus making it a function of the forecast, $\hat{p}$. Average resolution relies on taking the average of this squared difference over different values of $\hat{p}$. High resolution for a binary outcome requires that the density forecast can differentiate the chance that $Y = 1$ in different situations. Resolution equals 0 if the density forecast is equivalent to the unconditional distribution for the outcome.

Following the same path as for calibration, we can construct binary outcomes from any continuous distribution by focusing on some event, A. For any such event, A, we can then consider the difference between $P[y_{t+1} \in A| \int_A p_{t+1}(y)dy = p]$ and $P[y_{t+1} \in A]$.

Example 18.2.3 (Comparing Gaussian density forecasts, continued). *When $A = \{y_{t+1} > 0\}$, we know that for the second forecast, $\int_A p_{Y2t+1}(y)dy = \Phi(\mu_t)$. Unconditionally $P[y_{t+1} \in A] = 0.5$. The difference between the conditional and unconditional forecasts of A is then $\Phi(\mu_t) - 0.5$. Clearly the conditioning information (knowledge of μ_t) results in different forecasts, which is the idea behind resolution. This example also shows that squaring the difference makes sense since the difference can be both positive (if $\mu_t < 0$) and negative (if $\mu_t > 0$).*

Once again, "bins" or ranges of values for p can be used to test resolution. The use of bins allows for multiple observations for each comparison. Using the same definitions of terms as in (18.11), resolution with m bins is measured as

$$\frac{1}{T}\sum_{i=1}^{m} n_i(\bar{y}_i - \bar{p})^2,\tag{18.13}$$

where $\bar{p}$ is the (unconditional) sample average of the event that $y_{t+h} \in A$. As for calibration, nonparametric procedures can be used to estimate the resolution as a function of p.

18.2.3 Sharpness

Sharpness is a property of the distributional forecast and so does not depend on the outcome y_{t+1}. This property gets at whether the distributional forecasts discriminate relatively clearly between different outcomes. For binary outcomes, forecasts of $y_{t+1} = 1$ with a high probability such as 80% would be sharper than forecasts assigning a 55% chance to this event. When directed at continuously distributed outcomes, the forecasts are considered "sharp" if they assign zero probability to a large set of all possible outcomes, and a high probability to those outcomes predicted to happen. Another way to state this is that if, for any probability p, there exists an interval A on the support of y_{t+1}, where $\int_A p_{t+1}(y)dy = p$, then the length of the interval A is short.

Example 18.2.4 (Comparing Gaussian density forecasts, continued). *Let $p = 0.9$. For the first forecast, $\int_{A_1} p_{Y1t+1}(y)dy = 0.9$ for $A_1 = \{-2.33, 2.33\}$. For the second forecast, $\int_{A_2} p_{Y2t+1}(y)dy = 0.9$ for $A_{2t} = \{\mu_t - 1.645, \mu_t + 1.645\}$. Clearly the second forecast is sharper than the first.*

Since one can always present very sharp forecasts by assigning a probability of 1 to a single point, the sharpness property must be (and is in practice) used in concert with the other properties of a desirable forecast. Mitchell and Wallis (2011) raise other issues with the use of sharpness in practice.

18.2.4 Receiver Operator Characteristic (ROC) curve

The Receiver Operator Characteristic (ROC) curve provides a popular way to evaluate binary forecasts. The unusual name arises from the method's origination in the analysis of radio signals. The method has since become a common tool in medical diagnosis and weather forecasting. Consider a density forecast method that yields $p(z)$, and recall that for any cutoff, $c(z)$, the forecast is generated as $f(z) = \mathbb{1}\left(\hat{p}(z) > c(z)\right)$ as shown in chapter 12. For any density forecast $p(z)$ we can therefore compute the following table of outcomes.

	$Y = 1$	$Y = -1$
Forecast $f = 1$	TP	FP
Forecast $f = -1$	FN	TN

Here TP is the number of true positives, i.e., the number of forecasts of $Y = 1$ for which the method correctly predicts the outcome; TN is the number of true negatives, i.e., correct forecasts of $Y = -1$. FN and FP are the number of false negatives and false positives, respectively. Since the forecast depends on $c(z)$, numbers in this table are a function of $c(z)$.

Using this table we can construct estimates of different features of the forecasting method. First, consider the ratio of true positives to the actual number of times the outcome is indeed positive, TP/(TP+FN). This is known as the true positive rate (or sensitivity) and is a sample estimate of the population object $P[F = 1|Y = 1]$. We can also consider the false positive rate FP/(FP+TN) (often defined as 1 minus the sensitivity) which is a sample estimate of the population object $E[F = 1|Y = -1]$. Naturally, we would like the true positive rate to be 1 and the false positive rate to be 0. Without a perfect classifier or forecasting method, increasing the cutoff, $c(z)$, results in fewer positive forecasts and more negative forecasts. Suppose we set the cutoff $c(z) = 0$, so that all forecasts are equal to 1. Then both the true positive rate and the false positive rate are equal to 1, since FN=TN=0. At the other extreme, suppose we set $c(z) = 1$ so all forecasts are equal to -1. Then both the true positive rate and the false negative rate are 0, since TP=FP=0. Between these extreme choices for $c(z)$, there is a positive relation between these two measures: increasing $c(z)$ reduces the number of positive forecasts, reducing both the true positive and false positive rates. Tracing the curve that relates the two measures as a function of $c(z)$, where moves to the right decrease $c(z)$, produces the ROC curve. The closer this curve is to being a step function that immediately shifts to 1 as $c(z)$ moves away from 1, the better. A common measure reported for the ROC curve is the area underneath the curve.

As derived, the estimated ROC curve is a step function. However, both parametric and nonparametric methods have been considered in the statistical literature for generating smooth ROC curves and estimates of the area under the curve. Higher ROC curves are generally taken to be better estimators of the forecast distribution because they classify outcomes more correctly across different cutoffs, $c(z)$. The curves can be viewed as sequences of (correlated) averages over the data, and hence should be accompanied by standard errors. Further, since the forecasts are themselves a function of estimated parameters, estimation error should be taken into account. In practice, bootstrap methods are popular for inference.

Empirically, the ROC curve has been used by Jordà and Taylor (2012) to examine carry trades set up to exploit interest rate differentials between pairs of currencies.

18.3 TESTS BASED ON THE PROBABILITY INTEGRAL TRANSFORM

The probability integral transform[2] (PIT) of a continuous cumulative density function $P_Y(y_{t+1}|Z_t)$ evaluated at some outcome, y_{t+1}, is defined as $U = P_Y(y_{t+1}|z_1, \ldots, z_t)$. Given a density forecast $\hat{p}_{Yt}(y_{t+1})$ and an outcome y_{t+1}, we can compute u_{t+1} as the probability of observing a value less than or equal to y_{t+1}. If the density forecast comes from a parametric model, this number can be calculated directly. If the density estimate is provided as a set of simulated pairs $\{y_i|z, \hat{p}_{Yi}(y|z)\}$, $i = 1, \ldots, m$ for a range of y-values, as we discuss in chapter 13, the PIT value can

---

[2] The idea of using the probability integral transformation to test whether a sample of observations comes from a particular distribution goes back to at least Pearson (1938) and Rosenblatt (1952).

be estimated as

$$\hat{P}_{Yt}(Y < y_{t+1}) = m^{-1} \sum_{i=1}^{m} \hat{p}_{Yt}(y_i) \mathbb{1}(y_i \le y_{t+1}) dy_i, \qquad (18.14)$$

where dy_i is the difference in the values of y_i.

The PIT has the useful property that if Y is truly distributed as $P_Y(y|z)$, then U is uniformly distributed on $[0, 1]$. To see this, notice that $P[U \le u] = P[P_Y(Y) \le u] = P[Y \le P_Y^{-1}(u)] = P_Y[P_Y^{-1}(u)] = u$, and $P[U \le u]$ is the uniform density. Since $P_Y(y)$ has support on $[0,1]$, it follows that $U \sim \text{Uniform}[0, 1]$. The key assumption here is that the density used to compute the PIT is identical to that of the actual outcome.

Moreover, provided that the sequence of conditional densities is correctly specified each period, a sequence of PIT values, $\{\hat{u}_{t+1}\}, t = T_R, \dots, T - 1$, generated from a sample of density forecasts, $\hat{p}_{Yt}(y_{t+1})$, and outcomes, $\{y_{t+1}\}, t = T_R, \dots, T - 1$, will also be Uniform $[0, 1]$ and mutually independent: $\hat{u}_{t+1} \sim$ i.i.d. Uniform$[0, 1]$. For this to hold requires that the conditional density is correctly specified at each point in time; misspecified densities lead to violations of this property. For example, if the densities do not condition correctly on prior information, values of $\hat{u}_t$ can be serially correlated.

Example 18.3.1 (PIT score for GARCH(1, 1) process). *Suppose that the true density model is a GARCH(1, 1),*

$$y_{t+1} = \mu_{t+1|t} + \sigma_{t+1|t} \eta_{t+1}, \quad \eta_{t+1} \sim ind \, N(0, 1),$$

$$\sigma_t^2 = \omega + \alpha_1 \sigma_{t|t-1} \eta_t^2 + \beta_1 \sigma_{t-1}^2.$$

If a forecaster uses a homoskedastic density model of the form

$$y_{t+1} \sim N(\mu_{t+1|t}, \sigma^2),$$

then the PIT becomes

$$\Phi\left(\frac{\mu_{t+1|t} + \sigma_{t+1|t}\varepsilon_{t+1} - \mu_{t+1|t}}{\sigma}\right) = \Phi\left(\frac{\sigma_{t+1|t}}{\sigma}\eta_{t+1}\right) \ne \Phi(\varepsilon_{t+1}),$$

where Φ is the standard Gaussian c.d.f. Specifically, at times when σ_t is higher than σ, the average volatility, there is a higher than predicted chance of observing large forecast errors of either sign, and so this misspecification will show up in the form of higher probabilities of very large or very small PIT values at such times.

These results suggest a simple way of testing whether the density forecasts are correctly specified. Given a sequence of PIT values, $\{\hat{u}_{t+1}\}, t = T_R, \dots, T - 1$, we can examine whether they are drawn from a uniform distribution.

As an empirical illustration, we use our daily data on S&P500 stock returns and generate one-step-ahead out-of-sample density forecasts from a GARCH(1,1) model with standard normal innovations and computed PIT values. A plot of these values for the last year of the sample preceding 03/31/2015, along with their squares, are shown in figure 18.1. There is no noticeable pattern in these.

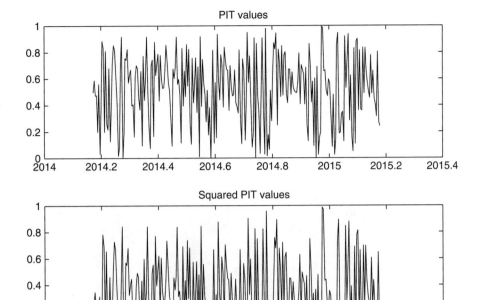

Figure 18.1: Time-series plot of probability integral transform (PIT) values in 2010 from a GARCH(1, 1) model fitted to daily US stock market returns. The top window plots the PIT values, while the bottom window shows the squared PIT values from one-step-ahead density forecasts.

Figure 18.2 shows a histogram of the PIT values[3] using 20 bins, each of which should cover 5%. There is a slight overrepresentation of values near 0.5, suggesting that the GARCH(1,1) model misses the many days with very small return outcomes. Conversely, the model seems to perform reasonably well in the tails of the return distribution, perhaps with a slight tendency to overestimate the probability of large positive outcomes. Of course, the histogram shown here does not reveal what happens in the extreme tails.

To more formally test the hypothesis of correct specification, we can use a Kolmogorov–Smirnov or Cramer–von Mises test. For the Kolmogorov–Smirnov (KS) test, we construct the cumulative density function for U as $\hat{P}_T(u) = T_P^{-1} \sum_{t=T_R}^{T-1} \mathbb{1}(\hat{u}_{t+1} < u)$ as a function of u. The cumulative density function of a uniform variable is simply u on $[0, 1]$, so the KS test for this problem is

$$KS = \sup_u \left| \hat{P}_T(u) - u \right|. \tag{18.15}$$

When the predictive distribution $p_{Yt}(y_{t+1})$ is known, the limit distribution for the KS test statistic in (18.15) is $\sup_{s \in [0,1]} |W(s) - s\,W(1)|$, where $W(s)$ is a standard

---

[3] Diebold, Gunther, and Tay (1998) suggest examining histograms of PIT values, which is a common approach in weather forecasting.

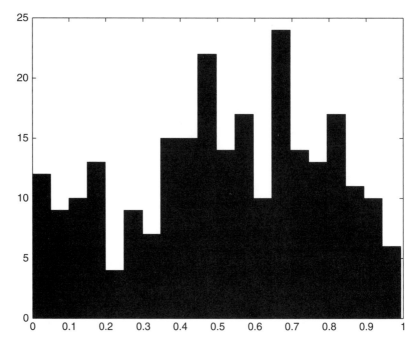

Figure 18.2: Histogram of one-step-ahead probability integral transform (PIT) values from a GARCH(1, 1) model with recursively estimated parameter values.

Brownian motion process. When parameters of the forecast distribution are estimated, the asymptotic distribution of the KS statistic must account for parameter estimation errors, leading to different critical values; see Durbin (1973). Bai (2003) shows that when the density estimate comes from a distribution known up to a finite set of parameters that must be estimated, the limiting distribution of the Kolmogorov test statistic depends on the true parameters and the true underlying distribution which are of course unknown. This makes it difficult to approximate percentiles of the limit distribution.[4] Bai's analysis is in-sample, whereas Corradi and Swanson (2006c) address the effect of parameter estimation error when such tests are applied to out-of-sample forecasts.

For the Cramer–von Mises test statistic we compute

$$\text{CvM} = \int_0^1 \left[\hat{P}_T(\hat{u}) - u \right]^2 du. \qquad (18.16)$$

The integral in (18.16) can be approximated numerically by using a fine mesh for $u \in [0, 1]$. Alternatively, given a sample of T_P density forecasts, the expression

$$\text{CvM} = \sum_{t=T_R}^{T-1} \left(\hat{p}_{Yt}(y_{t+1}) - \frac{t - 0.5}{T_P} \right)^2 + \frac{1}{12 T_P} \qquad (18.17)$$

---

[4] Bai proposes a nonparametric specification test for conditional distributions of dynamic models. Hong (2000) derives a generalized spectral test that can detect violations of independence in the form of serial dependence.

TABLE 18.2:
Tests of the i.i.d. and zero-mean property of standardized forecast errors from a GARCH(1,1) model with Gaussian shocks estimated on daily US stock market returns.

Equation, null hypothesis	μ	ρ	Test	p-value
$\tilde{u}_{t+1} = \mu + \epsilon_{t+1}, \mu = 0$	0.0350	–	1.3238	0.1858
$\tilde{u}_{t+1} = \mu + \rho * \tilde{u}_t^2 + \epsilon_{t+1}, \mu = \rho = 0$	0.0165	0.0210	1.6934	0.1934
$\tilde{u}_{t+1}^2 = \mu + \rho * \tilde{u}_t^2 + \epsilon_{t+1}, \rho = 0$	0.9494	−0.0252	−1.1104	0.2670

can be employed. The limit distribution for the CvM statistic is $\int_0^1 (W(s) - sW(1))^2 ds$, which is the integral of a Brownian bridge. The critical value for a test with a size of 5% is approximately 0.461, with larger values leading to rejections.

Berkowitz (2001) suggests transforming the PIT values through the inverse of the standard Gaussian c.d.f., Φ^{-1}. Defining

$$\tilde{u}_{t+1} = \Phi^{-1} \left(\int_{-\infty}^{y_{t+1}} \hat{p}_{Yt}(v) dv \right) = \Phi^{-1}(\hat{u}_{t+1}), \tag{18.18}$$

and noting that $\hat{u}_{t+1} \sim$ i.i.d. Uniform(0, 1), it follows that $\tilde{u}_{t+1} \sim$ ind N(0, 1). This suggests simple likelihood ratio tests for correct specification of the distribution forecast. For example, one can run a simple unconstrained regression of $\tilde{u}_t$ on a constant and its lagged value,

$$\tilde{u}_t = \mu + \rho \tilde{u}_{t-1} + \varepsilon_t, \quad \varepsilon_t \sim (0, \sigma^2), \tag{18.19}$$

and use conventional likelihood ratio tests to see whether the mean and variance of $\tilde{u}_t$ are 0 and 1, respectively:

$$LR_{0,1} = -2 \left(\ell(0, 1, \hat{\rho}) - \ell(\hat{\mu}, \hat{\sigma}, \hat{\rho}) \right) \sim \chi_2^2, \tag{18.20}$$

where $\ell(\mu, \sigma, \rho)$ denotes the likelihood function in (18.19); $\tilde{u}_t$ should also be independent of its lagged values which suggests using the test statistic

$$LR_{\rho} = -2 \left(\ell(0, 1, 0) - \ell(\hat{\mu}, \hat{\sigma}, \hat{\rho}) \right) \sim \chi_3^2. \tag{18.21}$$

Even if the density model passes these tests, it is possible that the distribution forecasts ignore time-varying volatility. This can be detected by considering persistence in the squared values of $\tilde{u}_t$:

$$\tilde{u}_t^2 = \sigma + \rho \tilde{u}_{t-1}^2 + v_t,$$

where, under the null of a correctly specified density, $\sigma^2 = 1$ and $\rho = 0$. These regression tests are convenient and easy to conduct, but do not, of course, change the size or power of the original tests for uniformity.

As an empirical illustration of these tests, table 18.2 applies simple regression tests to GARCH(1,1) forecasts of daily US stock returns. We use 2000–2009 as an initial estimation period and 2010–2015 as the forecast evaluation period and assume a constant daily mean return. Tests of zero mean and no serial correlation in $\tilde{u}_{t+1}$ are not rejected, nor does there appear to be evidence of serial dependence in the squared value $\tilde{u}^2_{t+1}$.[5]

Constructing a correctly specified density forecast may be too tall an order; after all, correctly specifying the conditional mean is a hard problem. We might therefore expect that tests based on the assumption of a correct density forecast would mostly reject. However, tests such as (18.15) and (18.16) are notorious for having low power unless the sample size is very large, so a failure to reject the null hypothesis may not be very informative. Another problem, detailed in examples by Hamill (2001) and Gneiting and Raftery (2007) is that it is entirely possible that forecast distributions that are not particularly informative about the outcome can look reasonable in tests based on the PIT. We illustrate this by returning to the example from Gneiting and Raftery (2007).

Example 18.3.2 (Comparing Gaussian density forecasts, continued). *Consider the two density forecasts from Example 18.2.1, $p_{Y1t+1} \sim N(0, 2)$ and $p_{Y2t+1t} \sim N(\mu_t, 1)$. Both the density forecasts p_{Y1t+1} and p_{Y2t+1t} yield probability integral transforms that are uniformly distributed, despite the second forecast clearly being a better one. Unconditionally, $y_{t+1} \sim N(0, 2)$, so the first density forecast, p_{Y1t+1}, is correctly specified and results in a uniform distribution for $u_{1t+1} = \int_{-\infty}^{y_{t+1}} p_{Y1t+1}(y)dy$. However, conditional on observing μ_t, $y_{t+1} \sim N(0, 1)$, so p_{Y2t+1t} is also correctly specified and $u_{2t+1} = \int_{-\infty}^{y_{t+1}} p_{Y2t+1t}(y|\mu_t)dy$ is also uniformly distributed.*

These examples show that methods based on the PIT may not be able to distinguish between density forecasts that are correctly specified, but use different conditioning variables. Passing the test of uniformity does not imply that conditioning information has been utilized well, or even at all. For this reason, Hamill (2001) regards the PIT uniformity property as a necessary but not sufficient condition for a good forecast density.

18.4 EVALUATION OF MULTICATEGORY FORECASTS

Pesaran and Timmermann (2009) consider a range of dependency tests for multicategory variables that directly apply to predictability tests for such variables. Suppose that the outcome variable falls in m_y categories, y_{it+1}, $i = 1, 2, \ldots, m_y$, while the forecast falls in m_f categories, $f_{jt+1|t}$, $j = 1, 2, \ldots, m_f$. For serially independent outcomes, a test of independence between y_{t+1} and $f_{t+1|t}$ can be based on the canonical correlation coefficients between y_{t+1} and $f_{t+1|t}$. For serially dependent outcomes, Pesaran and Timmermann (2009) show that a multicategory predictability test can be constructed using canonical correlations of suitably filtered versions of y_{t+1} and $f_{t+1|t}$ after accounting for the effect of lagged values of $(y'_{t+1}, f'_{t+1|t})'$. Specifically, they propose trace and maximum canonical correlation tests that use dynamically augmented reduced rank regression and are simple to compute. The tests hold under general conditions and require only that outcomes and forecasts are generated by ergodic, finite-order Markov processes.

---

[5] González-Rivera, Senyuz, and Yoldas (2011) propose to use autocontours for dynamic specification testing of densities of forecasting models. By jointly considering a battery of such tests, we may possibly get a better idea of which parts of a density model are misspecified.

To see how the test works, let $Y = (y_2, y_3, \ldots, y_T)'$ and $F = (f_{2|1}, f_{3|2}, \ldots, f_{T|T-1})'$ be $(T-1) \times (m_y - 1)$ and $((T-1) \times (m_f - 1))$ observation matrices tracking the qualitative indicators, respectively. Also, let $M_\iota = I_{T-1} - \iota_{T-1}(\iota'_{T-1}\iota_{T-1})^{-1}\iota'_{T-1}$, where ι_{T-1} is a $((T-1) \times 1)$ vector of 1s. Finally, define $S_{yf} = S'_{fy} = (T-1)^{-1}Y'M_\iota F$, $S_{yy} = (T-1)^{-1}Y'M_\iota Y$, $S_{ff} = (T-1)^{-1}F'M_\iota F$.

In the absence of serial dependencies in the outcome, a trace test of independence between the forecast and the outcome has an asymptotic χ^2 distribution, i.e.,

$$(T-1) \times \text{trace}(S_{yy}^{-1}S_{yf}S_{ff}^{-1}S_{fy}) \stackrel{a}{\sim} \chi^2_{(m_y-1)(m_f-1)}. \tag{18.22}$$

In the presence of serial dependencies, a test of predictability (i.e., independence between y_{t+1} and $f_{t+1|t}$) can be based on the maximum or the average of the canonical correlation coefficients of Y and F after filtering both variables for the effects of lagged values. For example, in the presence of first-order dependencies we first compute the eigenvalues of $S_w = S_{yy,w}^{-1}S_{yf,w}S_{ff,w}^{-1}S_{fy,w}$, where

$$S_{yy,w} = (T-1)^{-1}Y'M_w Y,$$

$$S_{ff,w} = (T-1)^{-1}F'M_w F,$$

$$S_{fy,w} = (T-1)^{-1}F'M_w Y,$$

$$M_w = I_{T-1} - W(W'W)^{-1}W',$$

with $W = (\iota, F_{-1}, Y_{-1})$; F_{-1} and Y_{-1} are $((T-1) \times (m_f - 1))$ and $((T-1) \times (m_y - 1))$ matrices containing the lagged values $f_{t|t-1}$ and y_t, respectively.

Pesaran and Timmermann show that the trace test based on S_w is equivalent to testing $\Pi = 0$ in the dynamically augmented reduced rank regression,

$$Y = F\Pi' + WB + U, \tag{18.23}$$

where U is a $((T-1) \times (m_y - 1))$ matrix of serially uncorrelated errors and W controls for the effects of lagged variables. Pesaran and Timmermann (2009, Theorem 1) show that, asymptotically as $T \to \infty$,

$$(T-1) \times \text{trace}(S_{yy,w}^{-1}S_{yf,w}S_{ff,w}^{-1}S_{fy,w}) \stackrel{a}{\sim} \chi^2_{(m_y-1)(m_f-1)}, \tag{18.24}$$

where S_{yy}, $S_{yf,w}$, and $S_{ff,w}$ are defined above.

This intuitive result shows that provided the trace test is conducted on the residuals from the dynamically augmented regressions so that any dynamics is filtered out, the standard results for the trace canonical correlation test in the static case, (18.22), go through.

In the special case with only two outcomes for the dependent variable, Pesaran and Timmermann (1992) derive a simple test statistic. For example, suppose we are interested in predicting the sign of y_{t+1} by means of the sign of a forecast $f_{t+1|t}$. Let P be the probability of a correctly predicted sign, while P_y and P_f are the probabilities of observing positive values of the outcome and forecast, respectively. Further, let

$$\hat{P} = (T-1)^{-1} \sum_{t=1}^{T-1} y_{t+1} f_{t+1|t} > 0,$$

$$\hat{P}_y = (T-1)^{-1} \sum_{t=1}^{T-1} y_{t+1} > 0,$$

$$\hat{P}_f = (T-1)^{-1} \sum_{t=1}^{T-1} f_{t+1|t} > 0$$

be the corresponding sample estimates of these probabilities. Under the null that the signs of the outcome and the forecast are independently distributed, $P = P_* \equiv P_f P_y + (1 - P_f)(1 - P_y)$. A test can therefore be based on the difference $(P - P^*)$. Pesaran and Timmermann (1992) show that, asymptotically as $T \to \infty$,

$$S_T = \frac{\hat{P} - \hat{P}_*}{\sqrt{\widehat{\mathrm{var}}(\hat{P}) - \widehat{\mathrm{var}}(\hat{P}_*)}} \overset{a}{\sim} N(0, 1),$$

where

$$\hat{P}_* = \hat{P}_y \hat{P}_f + (1 - \hat{P}_y)(1 - \hat{P}_f),$$

$$\widehat{\mathrm{var}}(\hat{P}) = (T-1)^{-1} \hat{P}_*(1 - \hat{P}_*),$$

$$\widehat{\mathrm{var}}(\hat{P}_*) = (T-1)^{-1}(2\hat{P}_y - 1)^2 \hat{P}_f(1 - \hat{P}_f) + (T-1)^{-1}(2\hat{P}_f - 1)^2 \hat{P}_y(1 - \hat{P}_y)$$
$$+ 4(T-1)^{-2} \hat{P}_y \hat{P}_f(1 - \hat{P}_y)(1 - \hat{P}_f).$$

This test is very simple to compute and has found use in studies of market timing of stock returns as well as in tests of whether survey participants can forecast if their firms' prices will go up or go down. The test does not account for serial dependence in the outcomes or forecasts, however.

18.5 EVALUATING INTERVAL FORECASTS

Interval forecasts take the form of a statement that the future outcome will fall in some interval $[p_{t+1|t}^l(\alpha), p_{t+1|t}^u(\alpha)]$ with probability α for $\alpha \in (0, 1)$. Construction of such forecasts is examined in section 13.5.

To evaluate interval forecasts, define the indicator variable $\mathbb{1}_{y_{t+1}} = \mathbb{1}(y_{t+1} \in [p_{t+1|t}^l(\alpha), p_{t+1|t}^u(\alpha)])$ which equals 1 if the outcome falls inside the forecast interval and 0 otherwise. A testable implication that could serve as a null hypothesis is that

$$E[\mathbb{1}_{y_{t+1}}] = \alpha. \tag{18.25}$$

For any given sample of outcomes and interval forecasts, this suggests testing correct unconditional coverage, $(T-1)^{-1} \sum_{t=1}^{T-1} \mathbb{1}_{y_{t+1}} = \alpha$. This leads to a test that the outcome falls in the interval with the stated probability, precisely the same idea as calibration but for a fixed probability. Since the test statistic is a simple sample mean, one can use a standard t-test, perhaps with robust standard errors. Again this property cannot form the basis for a comparison of forecasts based on different conditioning information. For example, a confidence interval based on the unconditional distribution of y_{t+1} should pass this test.

Christoffersen (1998) extends the idea from correct unconditional coverage to correct conditional coverage given a set of information. This leads to a null hypothesis $E[\mathbb{1}_{y_{t+1}}|Z_t] = \alpha$, for any z_t. Specifically, Christoffersen refers to the sequence of interval forecasts, $\{p_{t+1|t}^l(\alpha), p_{t+1|t}^u(\alpha)\}_{t=1}^{T-1}$, as being efficient with respect to the conditioning information, $Z_t = z_1, \ldots, z_t$, if

$$E[\mathbb{1}_{y_{t+1}}|Z_t] = \alpha. \tag{18.26}$$

The key requirement is that conditional efficiency requires (18.26) to hold for all t. This is a much stronger requirement than the property of correct unconditional coverage in (18.25). In fact, under the null of conditional efficiency (18.26), Christoffersen shows that a test of $E[\mathbb{1}_{y_{t+1}}|z_1, \ldots, z_t] = E[\mathbb{1}_{y_{t+1}}|\mathbb{1}_{y_t}, \mathbb{1}_{y_{t-1}}, \ldots, \mathbb{1}_{y_1}] = \alpha$ for all t, is equivalent to testing that the sequence $\{\mathbb{1}_{y_t}\}$ is identically and independently distributed Bernoulli with parameter α, $\{\mathbb{1}_{y_t}\} \sim$ i.i.d. Bern(α). This suggests a simple test. Under the null hypothesis, the likelihood for the indicators $(\mathbb{1}_{y_1}, \ldots, \mathbb{1}_{y_{T-1}})$ is

$$L(\alpha; \mathbb{1}_{y_1}, \ldots, \mathbb{1}_{y_{T-1}}) = (1 - \alpha)^{n_0} \alpha^{n_1},$$

where n_0 is the number of cases for which $\mathbb{1}_{y_t} = 0$, and $n_1 = T - n_0 - 1$. No parameters need to be estimated under the null. Under the alternative of first-order Markov dependence in the indicators, we can define n_{ij} as the number of observations where value i was followed by value j, $i, j \in \{0, 1\}$ and $\pi_{ij} = \Pr(\mathbb{1}_{y_t} = j|\mathbb{1}_{y_{t-1}} = i)$. Then the approximate likelihood function becomes

$$L(\pi_{00}, \pi_{11}; \mathbb{1}_{y_1}, \ldots, \mathbb{1}_{y_{T-1}}) = \pi_{00}^{n_{00}} (1 - \pi_{00})^{n_{01}} (1 - \pi_{11})^{n_{10}} \pi_{11}^{n_{11}}.$$

This likelihood requires estimating two parameters, π_{00} and π_{11}. A joint likelihood ratio test for correct coverage and independence is then (Christoffersen, 1998)

$$\text{LR} = -2\log\left[L(1 - \alpha, \alpha; \mathbb{1}_{y_1}, \ldots, \mathbb{1}_{y_{T-1}})/L(\pi_{00}, \pi_{11}; \mathbb{1}_{y_1}, \ldots, \mathbb{1}_{y_{T-1}})\right],$$

which asymptotically has a χ_2^2 distribution, provided that we ignore issues related to estimation error due to how the forecasts were generated.

The ideas of resolution and sharpness have also been applied to evaluate interval forecasts, at least informally. Sharpness means having short intervals. Resolution means that the length of the interval forecasts varies with conditioning information.

18.6 CONCLUSION

Approaches to evaluating distributional forecasts differ in whether they conduct direct comparisons guided by a loss function (often called accuracy) or whether they examine properties of the density forecast as it relates to outcomes. Evaluations based on loss functions allow us to compare pairs of distribution forecasts which is useful in situations where some benchmark model exists. The unconditional distribution of the outcome is an obvious benchmark and it corresponds to the no-change forecast often used in point forecasting. In other areas, the difference between a distribution forecast and the unconditional forecast (evaluated by means of some loss function) is known as "skill."

Rather than using loss functions directly to examine density forecasts, various characteristics of distributional forecasts are often examined. Calibration refers to the "reliability" of a forecast and measures whether forecasts of various probabilities result in outcomes occurring with the same frequencies. This measure ignores the spread in the forecast distribution and well-estimated unconditional distributions of the outcome will have this property. Resolution refers to how the forecast varies with conditioning information and is usually gauged relative to the unconditional distribution. Sharpness refers to how well the distributional forecast manages to rule out unexpected events. By themselves, none of these measures delivers a verdict on whether the distributional forecast is good. However, each property is worth examining at the model-building stage, as they can suggest regions where the distributional forecast might be lacking.

IV
Refinements and Extensions

19

Forecasting under Model Instability

Previous chapters considered the possibility that the forecasting model was mis-specified in the sense that it differed from the data-generating process. Assuming a sufficiently stationary environment, the estimated parameters of the misspecified model will converge to their pseudo-true values and the resulting estimates are often useful for forecasting.

This chapter examines the frequently encountered situation where the parameters of the forecasting model change over time in such a way that the full-sample estimates of the forecasting model provide a poor representation of the forecasting model at the end of the sample when the forecast is computed. Model parameters may evolve over time due to phenomena such as shifting market conditions, changing regulations, new technologies, or changes in government policies.

Empirical evidence strongly suggests that parameter instability plagues commonly used forecasting models. In a large-scale study of forecasting models fitted to a wide range of macroeconomic variables, Stock and Watson (1996) find evidence of parameter instability for the majority of the variables.[1] In a frequently cited study, McConnell and Perez-Quiros (2000) document a sharp drop in the volatility of output and various components of GDP around 1984. This phenomenon is known as the "Great Moderation" and is reflected in a wide variety of macroeconomic variables and surely affects volatility forecasts for such variables.

Model instability, when neglected, can show up in the form of a disparity between a forecasting model's in-sample and out-of-sample performance or even in differences in the model's out-of-sample forecasting performance in different subsamples. Stock and Watson (2003a) conclude, "Forecasts based on individual indicators are unstable. Finding an indicator that predicts well in one period is no guarantee that it will predict well in later periods. It appears that instability of predictive relations based on asset prices (like many other candidate leading indicators) is the norm." Ang and Bekaert (2007), Paye and Timmermann (2006), and Rapach and Wohar (2006) find evidence of instability for prediction models fitted to stock market returns.

This chapter focuses on forecasting models of the form $f(z, \beta_t)$, where β_t follows some exogenous process, i.e., parameter changes are nonrandom or follow

---

[1] For example, one set of results rejects the null of parameter stability at the 10% significance level for more than 55% of a set of 5700 bivariate models. Parameter instability seems to affect prices and inflation particularly strongly.

a random process that is independent of the observed data. This contrasts with "observation driven models" (Cox, 1981) which allow the parameters to depend on observable data. Assuming that the parameters change in a stable manner, such models sometimes give rise to nonlinear forecasting models with stable parameters. For such cases, the modeling issues that arise are similar to those examined in chapter 8 on forecasting with nonlinear models.

Three difficulties arise when constructing good forecasts in the presence of model instability. First, it is generally very difficult to determine the exact form of the parameter instability. Tests of the null of model stability have power against many potential types of parameter instability and so rejections of the null of stability tend to be uninformative about the nature of the instability. Second, as a result, the forecaster often does not have a good idea of how to model parameter instability. We examine different approaches to modeling parameter instability in the second section of this chapter.

Finally, when the forecasting model is unstable, future values of the parameters might change again over the forecast horizon. In this situation, forecasting procedures—and even methods for calculating the risk of a particular forecasting approach—require modeling both the probability and magnitude of future breaks. Models with rare changes to the parameters—e.g., a single break—have little or nothing to say about the chance of a future break. For such models it can be reasonable not to consider the chance of additional breaks over the forecast horizon, assuming that the horizon is sufficiently short. For models with multiple breaks, such an approach is far less reasonable.[2]

Section 19.1 provides a broad discussion of how breaks affect forecasting performance and section 19.2 follows up by pointing out some limitations to in-sample tests for model instability. Procedures for handling single and multiple breaks are covered in sections 19.3 and 19.4, respectively. Forecasting methods that posit a model for the process generating past and future breaks are discussed in section 19.5, while the opposite approach—ad hoc methods for dealing with breaks—are covered in section 19.6. Section 19.7 discusses model instability and forecast evaluation and section 19.8 concludes.

19.1 BREAKS AND FORECASTING PERFORMANCE

To see how forecasts get affected when parameters undergo change, let β_t be the regression parameters of the forecasting model where the "t" subscript indicates that the parameters now vary over time. Assuming that parameter changes are not random, we would prefer to construct forecasts using the parameters, β_T, at the point of the forecast (T) which is typically at the end of the historical sample. Instead, the estimator based on full-sample information, $\hat{\beta}_T$, will typically converge not to β_T but, rather, to the average value for the β_t-values over the estimation period $t = 1, \ldots, T$.

Example 19.1.1 (Linear regression model with a single break). *Consider the model*

$$y_{t+1} = \beta_t' x_t + \varepsilon_{t+1}, \quad t = 1, \ldots, T-1, \tag{19.1}$$

---

[2] One could also consider the converse situation with a stable model in the historical sample but the possibility of future breaks. Without a model for the breaking process and without evidence of previous breaks this seems an unlikely situation, however.

where ε_{t+1} are i.i.d. $(0, \sigma^2)$ and are independent of $\{x_t\}_{t=1}^{T}$. Suppose that $\beta_t = \beta + d \times \mathbb{1}(t \leq \tau)$ so the regression parameters change from $\beta + d$ before the break to β after time τ. To generate a forecast of y_{T+1} at time T we would prefer to use the model $\beta' x_T$. However, the conditional expectation of the full-sample least squares estimates, $\hat{\beta}_T$, obtained by regressing y_{t+1} on x_t for $t = 1, \ldots, T - 1$, conditional on $\{x_t\}_{t=1}^{T}$, is equal to

$$
E[\hat{\beta}_T] = E\left[\left(\sum_{t=1}^{T-1} x_t x_t'\right)^{-1}\left(\sum_{t=1}^{T-1} x_t y_{t+1}\right)\right]
$$

$$
= E\left[\left(\sum_{t=1}^{T-1} x_t x_t'\right)^{-1}\left(\sum_{t=1}^{T-1} x_t\left(x_t'\beta + x_t'd\mathbb{1}(t \leq \tau) + \varepsilon_{t+1}\right)\right)\right]
$$

$$
= \beta + \Sigma_{X,T-1}^{-1}\Sigma_{X,\tau}d, \tag{19.2}
$$

where $\Sigma_{X,t} = \sum_{s=1}^{t} x_s x_s'$. If $E[\Sigma_{X,t}] = t\Sigma_X$ for all t, then (19.2) reduces to $\beta + (\tau/(T-1))d$. In general, the parameters of the forecasting model will be biased by $\Sigma_{X,T-1}^{-1}\Sigma_{X,\tau}d$ and the bias gets larger the larger the break size, d, and the later in the sample the break occurred (τ).

Model instability can give rise to a sudden "breakdown" in forecasting performance because the parameters of the data-generating process may have shifted while the estimated parameters put a heavy weight on data occurring prior to such a change, generating biased forecasts. For most loss functions such biases will increase the loss; for example, the expected loss is increased by the squared bias under MSE loss.

Example 19.1.2 (Linear regression with a single break, continued). *Using the setup from Example 19.1.1, note that, conditional on $\{x_t\}_{t=1}^{T}$,*

$$
y_{T+1} - \hat{\beta}_T' x_T = \varepsilon_{T+1} - (\hat{\beta}_T - \beta)' x_T
$$

$$
= \varepsilon_{T+1} + x_T'\Sigma_{X,T-1}^{-1}\Sigma_{X,\tau}d + \left(\sum_{t=1}^{T-1} \varepsilon_{t+1}x_t'\right)\Sigma_{X,T-1}^{-1}x_T
$$

$$
\sim \left(x_T'\Sigma_{X,T}^{-1}\Sigma_{X,\tau}d, \sigma^2\left(1 + x_T'\Sigma_{X,T-1}x_T\right)\right).
$$

It follows from this that the MSE is given by

$$
E[y_{T+1} - \hat{\beta}_T' x_T]^2 = d'\Sigma_{X,\tau}\Sigma_{X,T}^{-1}x_T x_T'\Sigma_{X,T}^{-1}\Sigma_{X,\tau}d + \sigma^2\left(1 + x_T'\Sigma_{X,T-1}x_T\right). \tag{19.3}
$$

Assuming $E[\Sigma_{X,t}] = t\Sigma_X$ for all t and taking expectations over $\{x_t\}_{t=1}^{T}$, then (19.3) simplifies to $(\tau/(T-1))^2 d'\Sigma_X d + \sigma^2(1 + (k/T))$.

Another consequence of a single break in the parameters within the historical sample is that a forecasting model that uses a good predictor might end up generating poor forecasts because the parameter estimates are a hybrid of the pre- and post-break models or, more generally, an average of time-varying coefficients. This can lead to situations where valuable predictor variables appear to be uninformative to the forecast because the hybrid parameter estimate is close to 0. Rossi (2013a) gives a simple example similar to (19.1) in which $\beta = -d \frac{\tau}{T-1}$ so that the full-sample test that x_t Granger causes y_{t+h} yields an OLS estimate that converges to 0 even though $\beta \neq 0$ and the predictor is useful for forecasting at each point in the sample.[3] This is, of course, a very special case in which the effect of parameter instability exactly eradicates any full-sample evidence of predictability. Nevertheless, the point holds more broadly that predictability can be present locally in time in a way that conventional full-sample tests may not have power to detect. The converse is also possible: full-sample tests might indicate that certain predictors are useful even though, at the time of the forecast, β_T is close to 0. This situation would occur in our example if $\beta = 0$, but $d \neq 0$.

19.2 LIMITATIONS OF IN-SAMPLE TESTS FOR MODEL INSTABILITY

Once we allow the parameters of the model, β_t, to change over time, there are many different ways to specify the precise way in which the parameters evolve. Parameters might shift from $\beta + d$ to β just once at time $t = \tau$ as in Example 19.1.1 in which case the model for the parameters is $\beta_t = \beta + d\mathbb{1}(t \leq \tau)$. Or, there could be multiple discrete shifts in the parameters:

$$
\beta_t = \begin{cases}
\beta + d_1 & \text{for } t \leq \tau_1, \\
\beta + d_2 & \text{for } \tau_1 < t \leq \tau_2, \\
\vdots & \vdots \\
\beta + d_k & \text{for } \tau_{k-1} < t \leq \tau_k, \\
\beta & \text{for } \tau_k < t.
\end{cases}
\tag{19.4}
$$

Rather than deterministic shifts in the parameters, we might consider a sequence of random perturbations,

$$
\beta_t = \beta_{t-1} + \varepsilon_t,
\tag{19.5}
$$

also known as random walk breaks. If $\varepsilon_t = \eta_t \tilde{\varepsilon}_t$, where η_t is a Bernoulli random variable and $\tilde{\varepsilon}_t$ is drawn from a continuous distribution and is independent over time, the random walk breaks model is similar in form to the multiple discrete shifts model with an expected number of pT breaks in the sample, where p is the probability parameter of the Bernoulli distribution. Mean reversion in the parameters can be captured by a specification of the form

$$
\beta_t = \kappa(\bar{\beta} - \beta_{t-1}) + \varepsilon_t,
\tag{19.6}
$$

where $|\kappa| < 1'$ is the speed of mean reversion and $\bar{\beta}$ is the long-run mean for β. An alternative to these models is that the coefficients follow a Markov switching process, oscillating between a finite number of states:

$$
\beta_t = \beta_{s_t}, \quad s_t \in \{1, \dots, K\},
\tag{19.7}
$$

$$
\Pr(s_t = i | s_{t-1} = j) = p_{ij}.
$$

---

[3] The example in Rossi (2013a) considers a univariate setting where $\beta = -1$, $d = 2$, and $\rho = 1/2$, but the result holds more generally.

The existence of many different models for the break process, along with the lack of a uniformly most powerful test against any of these specific alternatives, has led to a large set of tests that attempt to distinguish the stable parameter model from models where the parameters break. For linear regression specifications with a single break, ad hoc tests based on least squares estimates of the break date have been employed (e.g., Andrews, 1993b), while families of optimal tests have been suggested by Andrews and Ploberger (1994).[4] Sequential methods for estimating the time of the break and testing for additional breaks in the remaining portions of the data have been suggested by Bai and Perron (1998) for a fixed number of breaks. For random walk breaks, Nyblom (1989) suggests a locally best test for more general sets of models and Elliott and Müller (2006) provide a point optimal test. Rossi (2005a) provides a test that is optimal with respect to a weighted average of power in a well-chosen direction.

For each of these break processes, tests for a fixed number of breaks have local power against models that converge to the stable no-break model at rate $T^{1/2}$. Assuming a single break, this means that $\delta = d \times \mathrm{se}(\beta)$, where $\mathrm{se}(\beta)$ is the standard deviation of the estimator for β in the stable model. If we consider a break in the mean and $\mathrm{Var}(\varepsilon_t) = \sigma^2$, this translates into a local break with magnitude $\delta = d\sigma T^{-1/2}$. For the random walk model the variance of ε_t declines to 0 under the local alternative so $T\Delta\beta_t$ has a stable variance.

Important practical lessons emerge from the theoretical literature on break point testing and associated Monte Carlo studies. First, the power curves for optimal tests and many ad hoc tests are quite similar. This explains the continued use in practice of ad hoc tests for the single break model. Second, tests designed for one type of break process typically have power against other break processes. For example, tests for a single break often still reject under the alternative of random walk breaks. Elliott and Müller (2006) show that this conclusion extends to power equivalence between optimal tests; tests that are optimal for any member of a wide class of break processes have the same power against other break processes within this wide class. Rejections of a test for a particular break process therefore do not imply that the break process tested for is "correct". Rather, it could be one of many processes. For sufficiently large values of either the break magnitude, d, or the variance of $T\Delta\beta_t$, break tests effectively have a power of 1 and so the presence of breaks of such magnitude is essentially known. For breaks of an order smaller than this, there is uncertainty over whether or not breaks really affected the parameters.

These features of break tests can be examined through Monte Carlo simulations. Figure 19.1 uses four Monte Carlo designs to examine the asymptotic power of tests for different types of breaks. In each case we consider breaks in the mean of an independent, normally distributed series. The upper left panel assumes that the break occurs at the center of the sample ($\tau = T/2$); the upper right panel assumes two breaks, one at the 40th percentile of the sample, the other at the 60th percentile of the sample. Here δ is the sum of the magnitude of the two breaks. The lower panels assume that $T\Delta\beta_t$ is a random walk. In the lower left panel there is a 10% probability of a shock to $T\Delta\beta_t$, while in the lower right panel a shock occurs every period. In both cases δ refers to the variance of the shocks normalized by the probability that the shock occurs.

---

[4] These are families of tests rather than a single optimal test because the notion of optimality depends on how the alternatives are weighted.

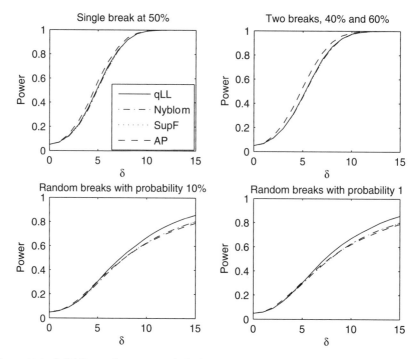

Figure 19.1: Solid line indicates qLL, dash-dot is Nyblom, dashes indicate the Andrews and Ploberger test, dots represent the SupF test power.

For each experiment figure 19.1 shows the asymptotic power for Andrews' SupF test and the Andrews–Ploberger (AP) test—both designed to detect a single break—along with the power for the qLL test of Elliott and Müller (2006) and the Nyblom test for random walk breaks. The points noted above emerge clearly from these plots. First, the power curves are indeed similar and all tests have power against different types of break processes. As a consequence, rejection of a test designed to detect one particular break sequence is not evidence that the break sequence is in fact of this type. Rejections of the tests are clearly not suggestive of any specific form of instability—only of instability of some form.

As noted above, estimation results might suggest that some regressors should not be included in a forecasting model because their full-sample estimates are near 0 even though the regressors contain information useful to forecasting at time T. For models with a single break, an alternative strategy is to test jointly that $\beta = \beta_0$ and $\delta = 0$. This tests jointly that the value of the parameter in the forecasting model equals 0 ($\beta_0 = 0$) and the absence of a break ($\delta = 0$). Hence, a test for whether x_t is useful in forecasting y_{t+h} in (19.1) that avoids failing to detect predictability due to an unknown break would involve testing both the parameter value ($\beta = 0$) and that there is no break ($\delta = 0$).

Instead of jointly testing for a break and lack of predictability after the break (as in Rossi's test if we set $\beta_0 = 0$), we could alternatively consider a hypothesis that tests the null of no predictability ($\beta = 0$) while controlling the test size regardless of the magnitude of δ. Elliott and Müller (2014) provide such a test when there is a break to a single element of β. The test controls size asymptotically regardless of the size of the break, including no breaks.

Giacomini and Rossi (2009) look at the related question of whether forecast models estimated over one particular period are useful for forecasting future outcomes. Their test compares the in-sample and out-of-sample forecasting performance and seeks to predict forecast breakdowns as a means to predicting future breaks.

19.3 MODELS WITH A SINGLE BREAK

For forecasting models with a single break to the parameters we can attempt to estimate the date and magnitude of the break. If the model truly has a single break, this approach has the potential—given a sufficiently accurate estimate of the break date—to provide a better forecasting model based on the post-break parameter values. Consider the linear regression

$$y_{t+1} = \begin{cases} (\beta + d)'x_t + \varepsilon_{t+1}, & t \leq \tau^0, \\ \beta'x_t + \varepsilon_{t+1}, & t > \tau^0, \end{cases} \quad t = 1, \ldots, T-1. \quad (19.8)$$

We could use the forecast $f_{T+1} = \hat{\beta}'x_T$, where $(\hat{\beta}, \hat{d})$ are estimated from a regression that replaces the single (unknown) break point in (19.8) with the estimated break point, $\hat{\tau}$. To estimate the break point, note that for an arbitrary break date, τ, the sum of squared residuals in (19.8) is

$$\text{SSR}(\tau) = \sum_{t=1}^{T-1} (y_t - \beta'x_{t-1} - d'x_{t-1}\mathbb{1}(t \leq \tau))^2. \quad (19.9)$$

For each value of τ we can obtain estimates of $(\hat{\beta}(\tau), \hat{d}(\tau))$ by minimizing $\text{SSR}(\tau)$ in (19.9). The least squares estimator for τ is then given by

$$\hat{\tau} = \arg\min_{\tau \in (\tau_{\min}, \tau_{\max})} \text{SSR}(\tau). \quad (19.10)$$

Note that we "trim" the data by searching only for breaks between lower and upper limits, $\tau_{\min}$ and $\tau_{\max}$. Some minimal amount of data is required, in part to make estimation feasible in both the pre- and post-break samples, and also for the asymptotic justifications to be reasonable. Typical choices for $\tau_{\min}$ and $\tau_{\max}$ exclude 10–15% of the sample at both ends.

In practice, estimates of the break date are often inaccurate. If the estimated break date exceeds the true value $\hat{\tau} > \tau^0$ the resulting parameter estimates are inefficient since we could have used more post-break observations to estimate the parameters. Conversely, if the estimated break date occurs prior to τ (i.e., $\hat{\tau} < \tau^0$) the estimates will use pre-break data and hence be biased towards $(\beta + d)$.

The location of the break date can be estimated by means of either least squares or maximum likelihood methods. Bai (1997) establishes conditions under which least squares estimates of the break proportion $T^{-1}\hat{\tau}$ are consistent for the true break proportion. This result does not imply that $\hat{\tau} \to^p \tau^0$, the true break date.[5]

---

[5] The linear regression model considered by Bai allows for lagged dependent variables among the regressors along with serially correlated errors.

Least squares methods are consistent for breaks that are an order of magnitude larger than those for which tests have local power, i.e., $\delta = T^{-1/2+r}\sigma d$ for $0 < r < 1/2$. Yao (1987) establishes results for correctly specified maximum likelihood estimates for independently distributed data.

Pesaran and Timmermann (2002) propose an alternative approach to estimating the break point. Rather than directly testing for a break, Pesaran and Timmermann address how much historical data to use, viewed from the perspective of the forecasting date, T, at the end of the sample. The idea is to perform a sequence of break tests and then limit the estimation sample to post-break data. Pesaran and Timmermann first reverse the ordering of the data and then employ a reverse-ordered CUSUM squared (ROC) break test. To see how this works, let $\tilde{Y}_t$ and $\tilde{X}_t$ denote the reverse-ordered data so that $\tilde{Y}_t = (y_t, y_{t-1}, \ldots, y_1)$ and $\tilde{X}_t = (x_t, x_{t-1}, \ldots, x_1)$. For linear forecasting models $y_{t+1} = \beta'x_t + \varepsilon_{t+1}$, the ROC method involves running a set of regressions using only post-break data $[\tau : T-1]$ for a sequence of break dates $\tau = \tau_{\min}, \tau_{\min} - 1, \ldots, 2, 1$, where $\tau = 1$ indicates using the full sample. Specifically, define $\tilde{Y}_{T,\tau} = (y_T, y_{T-1}, \ldots, y_\tau)'$ and $\tilde{X}_{T,\tau} = (x_T, x_{T-1}, \ldots, x_\tau)'$. Then the (backward) recursive least squares estimate of β is given by

$$\tilde{\beta}_\tau = (\tilde{X}'_{T,\tau}\tilde{X}_{T,\tau})^{-1}\tilde{X}'_{T,\tau}\tilde{Y}_{T,\tau}. \tag{19.11}$$

Pesaran and Timmermann suggest restricting the first break date, $\tau = \tau_{\min}$, to a certain multiple of the number of regressors to ensure that the parameter estimates associated with the shortest estimation window are not too imprecise.

Each of the regressions based on a given estimation window for the reverse-ordered data produces a standardized recursive residual,

$$\hat{v}_\tau = \frac{(y_\tau - \hat{\beta}_{\tau-1}x_{\tau-1})}{1 + x'_{\tau-1}\left(\tilde{X}'_{T,\tau-1}\tilde{X}_{T,\tau-1}\right)^{-1}x_{\tau-1}}. \tag{19.12}$$

Repeating this calculation for each τ results in a sequence $\{\hat{v}_\tau\}$, $\tau = \tau_{\min}$, $\tau_{\min}-1, \ldots, 1$. The associated sequence of reverse ordered CUSUM squared test statistics $\{\text{ROC}_{\tau,T}\}$ is

$$\text{ROC}_{\tau,T} = \frac{\sum_{j=\tau_{\min}}^{\tau} \hat{v}_j^2}{\sum_{j=\tau_{\min}}^{T} \hat{v}_j^2}. \tag{19.13}$$

Under fairly stringent assumptions—regressors fixed in repeated samples and i.i.d. normal errors—Brown, Durbin, and Evans (1975) provide critical values for this sequence. Values for $\text{ROC}_{\tau,T}$ outside the critical value bands indicate a break; Pesaran and Timmermann suggest using the first value of τ for which the test rejects the null of constant parameters as the beginning of the post-break sample. This sample can then be used to estimate the forecasting model. Note that this procedure does not yield a consistent estimate of the break date.

Instead of only including data after the estimated break date, $\hat{\tau}$, Pesaran and Timmermann (2007) note that the expected loss can sometimes be reduced by adding pre-break observations to the post-break observations used to estimate the parameters of the linear regression model. Adding such pre-break observations introduces a bias in the forecast but can also reduce the variance of the estimator. Provided that the magnitude of the break is small enough that the bias does not dominate and provided that the break occurs late enough in the sample that additional observations reduce the variance of the estimates by a large enough amount, the MSE of the forecast can be reduced by incorporating pre-break data points.

Pesaran and Timmermann (2007) characterize the size of the trade-offs analytically for a single break to the coefficient of a strictly exogenous regressor:

$$y_{t+1} = (\beta + d \times \mathbb{1}(t \le \tau^*)) x_t + \varepsilon_{t+1}, \tag{19.14}$$

$$\begin{pmatrix} \varepsilon_{t+1} \\ x_t \end{pmatrix} \sim \text{ind} \quad N \left[\begin{pmatrix} 0 \\ 0 \end{pmatrix}, \begin{pmatrix} \sigma^2 & 0 \\ 0 & \sigma_x^2 \end{pmatrix} \right].$$

Suppose that the starting point of the estimation window is τ, while τ^* is the time of the break. Assuming that τ^* is known, it will never be efficient to ignore post-break information and so $\tau \le \tau^* + 1$. Let $\omega_{\text{pre}} = \tau^* - \tau + 1$ and $\omega_{\text{post}} = T - \tau^*$ be the number of pre-break and post-break observations, respectively, so the total length of the estimation window equals $\omega = \omega_{\text{pre}} + \omega_{\text{post}} = T - \tau + 1$. Pesaran and Timmermann show that the unconditional MSE associated with an estimation window that starts at $\tau \le \tau^* + 1$ is given by

$$E[e_{T+1}^2(\tau)] = \sigma^2 + \sigma_x^2 d^2 \left(\frac{\omega_{\text{pre}}(\omega_{\text{pre}} + 2)}{\omega(\omega + 2)} \right) + \frac{\sigma^2}{\omega - 2}. \tag{19.15}$$

The second term in (19.15) captures bias from using pre-break information in the estimation. It is equal to 0 if $\omega_{\text{pre}} = 0$, and otherwise is positive and increasing in ω_{pre}. The third term represents estimation error and so is decreasing in the total length of the estimation window, ω. From this expression it follows that, in this simplest possible case, the optimal pre-break window that minimizes the MSE is longer the smaller the R^2 (lower σ_x^2/σ^2), the smaller the size of the break, d, and the shorter the post-break window, ω_{post}. This result is very intuitive: pre-break observations are more useful for estimation of the parameters of the forecasting model when the post-break parameters are imprecisely estimated (low R^2 and short post-break window, ω_{post}) and this gain in estimation precision is not overwhelmed by the bias effect (small d).

Pesaran and Timmermann (2007) also allow the variance of the residuals to break at the same point as the coefficients. This too impacts the usefulness of pre-break observations in minimizing the MSE. A larger post-break variance provides an additional incentive to include pre-break observations because of the greater estimation error in the post-break estimates.

To implement these ideas, Pesaran and Timmermann (2007) suggest the following stopping rule approach. First, estimate the time at which a break may have occurred, $\hat{\tau}$. If no break is detected, use all the data. If a break is found, proceed by estimating the MSE using only data after the break date, $\hat{\tau}, t = \hat{\tau} + 1, \ldots, T$. Next, compute the MSE by including an additional observation, i.e., by using sample observations from $\hat{\tau}$ to T. If the estimate suggests that this reduces the MSE, then continue by adding an additional data point ($\hat{\tau} - 1$) to the sample and again compute the MSE. This method is repeated until the data suggest that including additional pre-break data no longer reduces the MSE. Notice that this method produces an estimation window whose length is time varying: as the distance to the break gets larger, more (post-break) observations are used, while fewer observations are included closer to the estimated break date, $\hat{\tau}$.

Other methods can be used to select the estimation window when model instability is suspected. For example, if the last T_P observations are used for cross-validation purposes, one can choose the length of the rolling estimation window, ω, that minimizes the following pseudo out-of-sample criterion:

$$\text{MSE}(\omega, T_p, T) = T_P^{-1} \sum_{t=T-T_P}^{T-1} (y_{t+1} - x_t' \hat{\beta}_{t-\omega+1:t})^2, \tag{19.16}$$

where $\hat{\beta}_{t-\omega+1:t}$ is the OLS estimate of β that uses observations $[t - \omega + 1 : t]$. A limitation of this approach is that it requires a sufficiently long evaluation window, T_p, to yield precise MSE estimates. Oftentimes, this will be difficult to obtain, particularly if the time of the break point is close to the end of the sample. As a result, this cross-validation procedure may not yield precise estimates of the optimal estimation window.

A very different procedure that partially handles this issue is to use model averaging to deal with the underlying uncertainty surrounding the selection of the estimation window. Pesaran and Timmermann (2007) propose a simple procedure that combines forecasts associated with estimation windows $\omega \in [\omega_0, \omega_1]$:

$$\hat{y}_{T+1|T} = \frac{\sum_{\omega=\omega_0}^{\omega_1} (x_T' \hat{\beta}_{T-\omega+1:T}) \text{MSE}(\omega, T_p, T)^{-1}}{\sum_{\omega=\omega_0}^{\omega_1} \text{MSE}(\omega, T_p, T)^{-1}}. \tag{19.17}$$

As in chapter 14, the combination weights are proportional to the inverse of the MSE of the forecasts. If the break is very large, models that start the estimation sample after the break will receive greater weight than models that include pre-break data and thus get affected by a large (squared) bias term.

Procedures that base the forecasting model on an estimator for the break point might not work well if the breaks are small and the date of the break is imprecisely estimated. The results of Bai (1997) noted above show that breaks that are local in magnitude (i.e., of order $T^{-1/2}$) are not consistently estimated by least squares methods. To justify conditioning on the break estimates, breaks therefore need to be large enough that tests reject with probability 1. Elliott and Müller (2007) show that confidence intervals for the break date can be very wide for breaks small enough (local) that tests will detect them only some of the time. Of course, if the breaks are sufficiently small, ignoring them will not be too harmful to the forecast. For intermediate values of the break size, ignoring breaks will result in a larger MSE while estimating the break yields sufficiently imprecise values to also strongly impact the MSE of the forecast and so there are no dominant forecasting strategies for this case.

19.4 MODELS WITH MULTIPLE BREAKS

The single break model in (19.8) can be extended to a model that breaks at multiple points in time:

$$
y_{t+1} = \begin{cases}
(\beta + d_1)'x_t + \sigma_1\varepsilon_{t+1}, & t \le \tau_1, \\
\vdots & \vdots \\
(\beta + d_k)'x_t + \sigma_k\varepsilon_{t+1}, & \tau_{k-1} < t \le \tau_k, \\
\beta'x_t + \sigma\varepsilon_{t+1}, & t > \tau_k,
\end{cases}
\tag{19.18}
$$

where $\varepsilon_t \sim (0, 1)$ and $t = 1, \dots, T$. Assuming no breaks between periods T and $T + 1$, the ideal forecasting model under MSE loss for period $T + 1$ is $f_{T+1} = \beta'x_T$. As in the previous section, we do not know the timing of the breaks. Note that (19.18) allows the variance of the regression residuals to change discretely at the time of the breaks. We can also augment (19.18) to include variables (v_t) with constant coefficients; this is known as a partial break model:

$$
y_{t+1} = \begin{cases}
(\beta + d_1)'x_t + \lambda'v_t + \sigma_1\varepsilon_{t+1}, & t \le \tau_1, \\
\vdots & \vdots \\
(\beta + d_k)'x_t + \lambda'v_t + \sigma_k\varepsilon_{t+1}, & \tau_{k-1} < t \le \tau_k, \\
\beta'x_t + \lambda'v_t + \sigma\varepsilon_{t+1}, & t > \tau_k.
\end{cases}
$$

Bai and Perron (1998) provide a procedure for estimating multiple break dates $\{\tau_1, \dots, \tau_k\}$ in linear regressions when k, the number of breaks, is unknown and y is univariate.[6] For a given number of breaks, Bai and Perron's procedure chooses the break dates by minimizing the sum of squared residuals across potential break dates. This is a direct extension of the method discussed previously for the case with a single break. Their procedure estimates an entire set of break dates $\{\hat{\tau}_1, \dots, \hat{\tau}_k\}$. Given this set of break dates $\{\hat{\tau}_1, \dots, \hat{\tau}_k\}$, the parameters of (19.18) can be estimated by OLS and the sum of squared residuals can be computed:

$$
\text{SSR}(\tau_1, \dots, \tau_k) = \sum_{t=1}^{T-1} \sum_{j=1}^{k} \left(y_{t+1} - \beta_j'x_t - d_j'x_t \mathbb{1}(\tau_{j-1} \le t < \tau_j)\right)^2,
\tag{19.19}
$$

$$
\hat{\tau}_1, \dots, \hat{\tau}_k = \arg\min \text{SSR}(\tau_1, \dots, \tau_k),
$$

subject to the constraint that $\tau_1 < \tau_2 < \cdots < \tau_k$. As in the case with a single break, some trimming of the data is required—now not only at the endpoints but also to ensure a sufficient distance between the individual breaks to allow consistent estimation of the break parameters.

Under relatively standard assumptions on the predictors and the residuals, and assuming that the break points are asymptotically distinct and exist, Bai and Perron show that their method consistently estimates the true p break proportions,[7] i.e., they consistently estimate $T^{-1}\hat{\tau}_i$ for $i = 1, \dots, k$.

---

[6] Qu and Perron (2007) generalize the analysis to cover multivariate regression models with multiple breaks.

[7] This requires that the number of breaks is correctly specified and does not imply that the break date, $\hat{\tau}_k$, is consistently estimated.

To overcome the difficulty that the number of breaks is unknown, Bai and Perron suggest a sequential procedure that tests for k versus $k+1$ breaks until no further breaks are detected. With k breaks, there are $k+1$ periods for which the parameters are potentially stable. Each of these periods is then tested for a break using a largest F test (SupWald) statistic. Critical values for this test depend on the number of breaks under the null. For details on algorithms to undertake these methods, see Bai and Perron (2003).[8] The need to estimate the break date adds to the risk function of the OLS approach so this method again relies on having a good estimate of the final break date. This is most likely to be true in situations with large breaks that are easily identified in the data.

Noting that the last break of the sequence, τ_k, is most important when it comes to generating out-of-sample forecasts, the reverse CUSUM test discussed in section 19.3 could also be used. This method can also provide estimates of the remaining break dates, although these are of course not required.

19.5 FORECASTS THAT MODEL THE BREAK PROCESS

Suppose we suspect that there are breaks to the parameters, or, alternatively, that we have rejected the null of no breaks in a pre-test. We can then consider constructing models of the break process that would allow us to construct better forecasts than if we ignore model instability. One approach is to select and estimate a particular parametric specification for the break process with the hope that this provides a good approximation of the break process and improves forecasts. Different break processes give rise to different estimation methods. This section examines the properties of some popular break processes.

19.5.1 Markov Switching Models

The first-order Markov switching VAR, MSVAR for short, takes the form

$$y_{t+1} = \mu_{s_{t+1}} + A_{s_{t+1}} y_t + \varepsilon_{t+1}, \quad \varepsilon_{t+1} \sim \mathrm{N}(0, \Sigma_{s_{t+1}}). \tag{19.20}$$

Here s_{t+1} is a scalar state variable. Typically it is assumed that s_{t+1} moves around between one of K different values, $s_{t+1} \in \{1, 2, \ldots, K\}$, where $K \geq 2$ is a fixed number. Most empirical applications set $K = 2$. Transitions between states are often assumed to be governed by a homogenous first-order Markov process with state transitions $\Pr(s_{t+1} = i | s_t = j) = p_{ij}$. The key assumption here is that the same K states repeat so that we can learn something from previous visits to the current state and other states (such as their means, variances and transition probabilities). However, as shown in section 8.3, the optimal forecast is a complex nonlinear function of all the data even under MSE loss.

---

[8] Note the computational complexity of solving (19.19) for large values of k. With only a single break there are $T-1$ possible break points (ignoring endpoint restrictions). With two breaks, there are $(T-1)(T-2)$ possible break points and so the number of possible break points increases rapidly in k and T.

19.5.2 Change Point Models

The change point models considered by Chib (1998) provide an alternative to this class of models. Change point models allow the number of states to increase over time and so do not impose that the states are drawn repeatedly from the same fixed set of values, or that "history repeats." An example from this class of models is

$$y_{t+1} = \mu_i + \Sigma_i \varepsilon_{t+1}, \quad \tau_i \le t \le \tau_{i+1}, \tag{19.21}$$

for $i = 1, \ldots, K$ and assuming K states in the sample up to time T. Assuming that the probability of remaining within a particular state is constant, but possibly state-specific, the transitions for this class of models are

$$P = \begin{pmatrix} p_{11} & p_{12} & 0 & \cdots & & 0 \\ 0 & p_{22} & p_{23} & \cdots & & 0 \\ \vdots & \vdots & \vdots & \vdots & & \vdots \\ 0 & \cdots & 0 & p_{K-1,K-1} & p_{K-1,K} \\ 0 & 0 & \cdots & & 0 & 1 \end{pmatrix}. \tag{19.22}$$

Here $p_{i,i+1} = 1 - p_{ii}$ is the probability of exiting from state i to state $i + 1$. According to this model the state variable either remains in the current state or moves to a new one. Usually the model is estimated under the assumption of k regime shifts occurring during the historical sample $t = 1, \ldots, T$. However, the implication of nonrepeated states is that the number of unique states can be expected to grow as the sample size expands.

Because the process could shift from state K at time T to a new state $K + 1$ at time $T + 1$, forecasts generated by this model require us to make assumptions about the distribution from which future parameter values, μ_{k+1} and Σ_{k+1}, are drawn in case of a break. Moreover, if forecasting two or more periods ahead, one also needs assumptions about the distribution from which $p_{k+1,k+1}$ and future values are drawn. Pesaran, Pettenuzzo, and Timmermann (2006) propose ways to model both the magnitude of shifts in parameters and the duration of new regimes. Given the paucity of detectable break points for most economic variables, in practice this approach requires combining prior information with empirical evidence on the frequency and magnitude of breaks. Pesaran, Pettenuzzo, and Timmermann (2006) and Koop and Potter (2007) are examples of this latter approach.

Bauwens, Korobilis, and Koop (2011) find extensive evidence of structural breaks for the majority of series they investigate; more than three-quarters of their series display evidence of one or more breaks. They compare the performance of a range of approaches that formally model the instability process such as the Bayesian discrete break models of Pesaran, Pettenuzzo, and Timmermann (2006) and Koop and Potter (2007) versus ad hoc approaches based on rolling window methods. Empirically, no particular approach is found to be dominant across all variables, as the results depend on the particular variable being considered.

19.5.3 Time-Varying Parameter Models

The simple time-varying parameter (TVP) random walk model takes the form

$$y_t = x'_{t-1}\beta_t + \varepsilon_{yt}, \tag{19.23}$$

$$\beta_t = \beta_{t-1} + \varepsilon_{\beta t}.$$

This model is in state-space form with y_t being the observable process and β_t being the latent "state," so we can rewrite (19.23) using the notation from the Kalman filter appendix:

$$y_t = H_t \xi_t + w_t, \tag{19.24}$$

$$\xi_t = \xi_{t-1} + v_t. \tag{19.25}$$

Moreover $w_t \sim N(0, R_t)$, $v_t \sim N(0, Q_t)$. Assuming that y_t and $H_t = x'_{t-1}$ are observable while ξ_t is a latent variable, (19.24) is the observation equation and (19.25) is the state equation. The model can readily be estimated using Kalman filter methods.[9]

Several variations exist on how to estimate the TVP model and are routinely used to forecast vector-valued variables. As discussed in chapter 9, Sims (1993) proposed a Bayesian approach to computing forecasts. Assuming normally distributed innovations ε_{yt} and $\varepsilon_{\beta t}$ in (19.23), it is standard to use conjugate priors with a normal prior on the initial value for β_t and an inverse Wishart prior on the variance–covariance matrix. This yields a model that can easily be estimated by Gibbs sampling methods; see our discussion of this topic in section 9.3.4. A fuller (book-length) examination of the formulation and estimation of these models is given in West and Harrison (1998).

Let $Z_t = (y_t, y_{t-1}, \dots, x_t, x_{t-1}, \dots)$ be the data available at time t. First consider the simple case with known covariance matrix, and suppose a normal prior has been used to initialize the recursion, i.e., $\xi_0 \sim N(\xi_{0|0}, P_{0|0})$ in the notation from the Kalman filter appendix.[10] The posterior predictive distribution for y_{t+1} given Z_t is

$$p_Y(y_{t+1}|Z_t) \sim N(y_{t+1|t}, G_{t+1|t}),$$

where formulas for the arguments in the normal distribution are given in the Kalman filter appendix.

In the more realistic case with an unknown covariance matrix, we also require priors over the covariance parameters. Suppose that Q_t is time varying and consider the normalization $Q_t = R Q_t^*$, where R is an invertible matrix. Using the inverse Gamma priors

$$R|Z_0 \sim IG \left[\tfrac{1}{2}, \tfrac{1}{2} S_0 \right],$$

---

[9] Note that if the shocks are not normally distributed, then estimates can be considered pseudo MLE values.

[10] Recall that the subscript $t|s$ refers to the mean of the time-t random variable given information at time s.

where S_0 is some preliminary estimate such as the MLE based on past data, the posterior distribution for the outcome is

$$p_Y(y_{t+1}|Z_t) \sim T_{n_t}(y_{t+1|t}, G_{t+1|t}).$$

Here T_{n_t} is the multivariate t-distribution with n_t degrees of freedom, mode $y_{t+1|t}$, and scale matrix $G_{t+1|t}$.[11] We replace R in the above Kalman filter formulas by the MLE estimate of the covariance matrix, S_t. West and Harrison (1998) also consider multiperiod forecasts, although these rely on knowing H_{t+h-1} for the h-step-ahead forecast.[12]

A number of studies have applied these methods. Stock and Watson (1996) find that time-varying parameter models with a random walk component, as well as forecasting models based on a rolling estimation window, in many cases produce better out-of-sample forecasts than models with fixed parameters. Models that allow for unstable parameters also tend to reduce the risks of extremely poor forecasting performance such as when large parameter breaks are present. Average gains relative to a recursively estimated constant parameter model are generally very small, however.[13]

Stock and Watson (2007) propose an unobserved components (univariate) stochastic volatility model of the form in (19.24) where $H = 1$. Variances are assumed to follow stochastic volatility processes

$$\ln(R_t) = \ln(R_{t-1}) + \psi_{rt}, \qquad (19.26)$$

$$\ln(Q_t) = \ln(Q_{t-1}) + \psi_{qt},$$

and the volatility shocks are mutually uncorrelated as well as uncorrelated through time: $(\psi_{rt}, \psi_{qt})' \sim \text{ind} \, N(0, I)$. The forecast of $y_{t+h|t}$ is obtained as the filtered estimate of ξ_t. The model can be estimated using MCMC methods. This model generalizes the simple TVP random walk model with an intercept, which does not allow for stochastic volatility.

Engle and Smith (1999) propose a stopbreak model with stochastic permanent breaks:

$$y_{t+1} = \xi_{t+1} + w_{t+1},$$

$$\xi_{t+1} = \xi_t + q_t w_t,$$

where $q_t = q(w_t)$ and w_t follows a martingale process. This model differs from the standard setup since the shocks in both equations are the same although q_t determines the effect of a shock, w_t, on y_{t+1}. If $q_t = 1$, we obtain a simple version of the random walk model with perfectly correlated shocks, while if $q_t = 0$, the shock w_t has no permanent effect on the mean of y.

---

[11] Here $n_t = n_{t-1} + 1$, where n_0 is the number of degrees of freedom used to estimate S_0.

[12] To generalize to cases with multiperiod forecasts we need a forecasting equation for $X_t = H_t$ as well.

[13] Dangl and Halling (2012) use a Zellner g-prior on $\xi_{0|0}$ in a model used to forecast stock returns.

19.6 AD HOC METHODS FOR DEALING WITH BREAKS

Each of the methods discussed in the previous section matches the estimation scheme to the model assumed for the break process. If the forecaster strongly believes that a particular break process generated the data, it makes sense to choose an estimation strategy that matches this particular break process. However, as noted above, it is often difficult to determine the break process most likely to have generated the data. Tests for a single break and tests for random walk breaks are almost equally likely to reject regardless of the break process. Rejections of parameter stability tests are therefore not an indication of the specific break process that generated the data.

In situations where the form of the break process is unknown, instead we might use ad hoc methods that do not relate directly to the type of break process. This section describes a variety of such approaches.

19.6.1 Weighting Schemes That Downweight Past Observations

When β_t is time varying we generally try to approximate β_T in the forecast regression through some "average" value for the parameters. A simple scheme is to put greater weight on recent observations than on past observations. This can be accomplished by adding weights to the objective function, i.e., by choosing parameters that minimize the weighted loss,

$$\hat{\beta}_T = \arg\min_{\beta \in \mathcal{B}} (T-1)^{-1} \sum_{t=1}^{T-1} \omega_t L(f_{t+1|t}(\beta), y_{t+1}). \tag{19.27}$$

The forecast $f_{T+1|T}(\hat{\beta}_T)$ is then based on the estimates, $\hat{\beta}_T$. The conventional approach for the stationary case arises as a special case with $\omega_t = 1$ for all t. As described in section 16.2, older observations can be downweighted in different ways. A prominent example is rolling regressions that set $\omega_t = \mathbb{1}(T - \bar{\omega} \le t \le T - 1)$, i.e., use a rectangular window (equal weights) for the most recent $\bar{\omega}$ observations and 0 otherwise. As the sample expands, this approach includes one new observation and drops one old observation, thereby keeping the estimation window constant at $\bar{\omega}$. Another approach is to let the estimation window be a fixed proportion, ρ, of the sample size, i.e., $\omega_t = \mathbb{1}((1-\rho)T + 1 \le t \le T)$. Discounted least squares sets $\omega_{\tau T} = \lambda^{T-\tau}$ for $\lambda \in (0, 1]$ for the MSE loss function, although clearly the same idea extends readily to the construction of forecasting models in more general situations. Estimation under discounted least squares objectives is straightforward. For linear regression models and MSE loss, it amounts to weighted least squares.

Rolling regressions employ an intuitive trade-off. Shorter estimation windows are likely to reduce the bias in the estimates due to the use of stale data that comes from a different data-generating process than the one that generates the data at the time the forecast is computed. This bias reduction is achieved at the cost of a decreased precision in the parameter estimates as less data get used. The hope is that the bias reduction more than makes up for the increased parameter estimation error. Discounted least squares estimation makes a similar trade-off, although this method downweights nearby observations and puts some weight on even the oldest data points, potentially mitigating the effects on the variance of the parameter estimates.

19.6.2 Intercept Correction

Forecast models whose parameters are based on all observations in a historical sample typically provide biased forecasts in situations where the model parameters are time varying. Consider the forecasting model $f_{T+1|T}(\beta)$, where β is estimated over some sample $t = 1, \ldots, T-1$, resulting in the forecasting model $f_{T+1|T}(\hat{\beta}_T)$. If the parameters change over time, typically $E[y_{T+1} - f_{T+1|T}(z_T, \hat{\beta}_T)] \neq 0$. Intercept corrections attempt to estimate this bias. Provided that the parameters do not break by a large amount every period, an estimator of the bias is the forecast error in the previous period, $y_T - f_{T|T-1}(\hat{\beta}_{T-1})$. Hence, we can use the intercept corrected forecast $f_{T+1|T}^{IC}(\hat{\beta}) = f_{T+1|T}(\hat{\beta}_T) + [y_T - f_{T|T-1}(\hat{\beta}_{T-1})]$. The bias of the intercept corrected forecast is

$$E\left[y_{T+1} - f_{T+1|T}(\hat{\beta}_T) - (y_T - f_{T|T-1}(\hat{\beta}_{T-1}))\right] \tag{19.28}$$

$$= E\left[y_{T+1} - f_{T+1|T}(\hat{\beta}_T)\right] - E\left[(y_T - f_{T|T-1}(\hat{\beta}_{T-1}))\right].$$

If the two terms are roughly similar—the bias in the forecasts does not change quickly—the bias will be close to 0.

Example 19.6.1 (Linear regression with a single break, continued). *Consider the model in (19.1) with a single break $\beta_t = \beta + d\mathbb{1}(t \leq \tau)$. For this model the bias in the forecast is $E[y_{T+1} - \hat{\beta}_T x_T] = T^{-1}\tau d' E x_T$ and hence the bias of the intercept corrected forecast is $d' E[T^{-1}\tau x_T - (T-1)\tau x_{T-1}]$. Assuming that x_t is covariance stationary, this is $\tau d' E x_T T^{-1}(T-1)^{-1}$. This will be close to 0 for large values of T.*

The intercept correction approach has been popularized and analyzed by Clements and Hendry (1996, 1998). Analytical results in these papers do not consider the impact of estimation error. For local breaks, the size of the bias is of the same order as the estimation error, so an understanding of this approach needs to consider both effects jointly. In essence though, the intercept correction approach can indeed reduce or remove the bias from estimating a model subject to infrequent breaks. However, this bias reduction comes at the cost of an increase in the variance of the forecast. Hence, the value of this approach depends on the size of the bias to begin with, and the method will be most useful when this bias is relatively large so that the bias correction is large enough to offset the increased variance.

The last line in (19.28) shows that the effect of adding the intercept correction to the forecast is to roughly double the variance of the forecast error relative to the case with no correction. This happens because there are now two forecast errors (one at time $T+1$, another at time T) and the variance of this is the sum of the variances minus twice their covariance. Forecast errors are typically either uncorrelated (if we have a very good model) or weakly positively correlated due to omitted (persistent) terms.

Example 19.6.2 (Linear regression with a single break, continued). *Consider again the linear regression with a single local break to the parameters $\beta_t = \beta + d\mathbb{1}(t \leq \tau)$.*

After considerable calculation along the lines of Examples 19.1.1 and 19.1.2, we have

$$(y_{T+1} - \hat{\beta}_T x_T, \, y_T - \hat{\beta}_{T-1} x_{T-1})'$$

$$\sim \left[\begin{pmatrix} \Sigma_{X,T-1}^{-1} \Sigma_{X,\tau} d' x_T \\ \Sigma_{X,T-2}^{-1} \Sigma_{X,\tau} d' x_{T-1} \end{pmatrix}, \right.$$

$$\left. \sigma^2 \begin{pmatrix} 1 + x_T' \Sigma_{X,T-1} x_T & 0 \\ 0 & 1 + x_{T-1}' \Sigma_{X,T-2} x_{T-1} \end{pmatrix} \right],$$

and so

$$(1 \; -1) \begin{pmatrix} y_{T+1} - \hat{\beta}_T' x_T \\ y_T - \hat{\beta}_{T-1}' x_{T-1} \end{pmatrix}$$

$$\sim \left[(\Sigma_{X,T-1}^{-1} \Sigma_{X,\tau} d' x_T - \Sigma_{X,T-2}^{-1} \Sigma_{X,\tau} d' x_{T-1}), \right.$$

$$\left. \sigma^2 (2 + x_T' \Sigma_{X,T-1} x_T + x_{T-1}' \Sigma_{X,T-2} x_{T-1}) \right].$$

The MSE for the intercept corrections approach is

$$\text{MSE} = (\Sigma_{X,T-1}^{-1} \Sigma_{X,\tau} d' x_T - \Sigma_{X,T-2}^{-1} \Sigma_{X,\tau} d' x_{T-1})^2$$

$$+ \sigma^2 (2 + x_T' \Sigma_{X,T-1} x_T + x_{T-1}' \Sigma_{X,T-2} x_{T-1}).$$

Notice that we get the bias reduction, but at the cost of essentially doubling the variance component.

These theoretical results show that breaks need to be very large for the gains from the intercept correction method to outweigh the increased variance of the forecast error—a situation unlikely to occur in practice. Such results appear to be borne out in practice. Examining a large number of variables, Rossi (2013a) finds that intercept corrections almost never improve upon univariate autoregressive forecasts.

19.6.3 Forecast Combination and Model Instability

A number of authors, including Diebold and Pauly (1987), Min and Zellner (1993), Hendry and Clements (2004), and Aiolfi, Capistrán, and Timmermann (2011) suggest that parameter instability could be among the reasons that forecast combinations are found to perform well in empirical studies. As an illustration, Aiolfi, Capistrán, and Timmermann (2011) consider the simple mixture model with two Gaussian predictors:

$$y_{t+1} = (1 - s_{t+1}) x_{0t+1} + s_{t+1} x_{1t+1} + \varepsilon_{t+1},$$

$$f_{0t+1} = x_{0t+1},$$

$$f_{1t+1} = x_{1t+1}.$$

Suppose that $x_{it+1} \sim N(0, \sigma_i^2)$, $i = 0, 1$, $\varepsilon_{t+1} \sim N(0, \sigma_\varepsilon^2)$, $E[\varepsilon_{t+1} x_{it+1}] = 0$, and $E[x_{0t+1} x_{1t+1}] = 0$. Finally, let $s_t = 0$ with probability p, while $s_t = 1$ with probability $(1 - p)$. The best forecast in this model is determined by the outcome of the state variable, s_{t+1}. If $s_{t+1} = 0$, f_{0t+1} is best, while f_{1t+1} is best if $s_{t+1} = 1$. The possibility of switching between states captures the notion of instability in the underlying data-generating process. Aiolfi, Capistrán and Timmermann show that the population MSE of the equal-weighted forecast combination $(f_{0t+1} + f_{1t+1})/2$ is lower than the population MSFE of the best individual forecasting model, f_{0t+1} or f_{1t+1}, provided that

$$\frac{1}{3}\left(\frac{p}{1-p}\right)^2 < \frac{\sigma_1^2}{\sigma_0^2} < 3\left(\frac{p}{1-p}\right)^2. \tag{19.29}$$

These inequalities ensure that neither of the forecasts dominates the other forecast "too much in population," in which case it would clearly be optimal to simply use the dominant forecast and not combine. In the simple case where $\sigma_1^2 = \sigma_0^2$, the equal-weighted forecast combination is optimal as long as $(p/(1-p)) \in (\sqrt{1/3}, \sqrt{3})$, i.e., as long as neither of the states (forecasting models) occurs far more often than the other one. Note that the result in equation (19.29) ignores estimation error, another reason often used to explain the good performance of equal-weighted combinations.

In an empirical analysis Clark and McCracken (2010) combine forecasts of output, inflation, and short-term interest rates across VAR specifications that allow for model instability in different ways, including the use of recursive lag selection, rolling estimation windows, and intercept corrections. They find that simple equal-weighted averaging yields consistently good results. In contrast, least squares estimation of the combination weights tends to yield poor forecasting results. These findings are consistent with Rossi (2013a) who finds that equal-weighted forecast combinations produce relatively good out-of-sample forecasts.

19.7 MODEL INSTABILITY AND FORECAST EVALUATION

Clark and McCracken (2005b) consider how structural breaks affect encompassing tests as well as tests for equal predictive accuracy. Building on the insight that the predictive accuracy of a model with time-varying parameters depends on the timing of the break(s) relative to the point of the forecast, they find that out-of-sample tests can miss genuine predictability in the presence of breaks even in situations where in-sample tests would detect such predictability. This situation is particularly likely to occur if the parameters break towards 0 during the part of the sample that is used for out-of-sample forecast evaluation. Their analysis suggests that parameter instability may be one reason for the common finding that in-sample predictability fails to translate into out-of-sample predictability.

Rossi (2005a) provides optimal tests for the joint null of no predictability (Granger causality) and model stability. Rossi's tests address whether x_t has predictive power over y_{t+1} in linear regression models $y_{t+1} = \beta_t x_t + \varepsilon_{t+1}$ in which β_t might be time varying. One form of parameter instability that is particularly tractable is when β_t shifts from β to $\bar{\beta}$ at an unknown point in time. Rossi's exponential Wald test proceeds as follows. Let $\hat{\beta}_{1\tau}$ and $\hat{\beta}_{2\tau}$ be the OLS estimators before and after the break, posited to occur at time τ,

$$\hat{\beta}_{1\tau} = \left(\frac{1}{\tau}\sum_{t=1}^{\tau-1} x_{t-1}x'_{t-1}\right)^{-1}\left(\frac{1}{\tau}\sum_{t=1}^{\tau-1} x_{t-1}y_t\right),$$

$$\hat{\beta}_{2\tau} = \left(\frac{1}{T-\tau}\sum_{t=\tau}^{T-1} x_{t-1}x'_{t-1}\right)^{-1}\left(\frac{1}{T-\tau}\sum_{t=\tau}^{T-1} x_{t-1}y_t\right).$$

The test proposed by Rossi uses two components. One component, $\hat{\beta} = (\tau/T)\hat{\beta}_{1\tau} + (1-\tau/T)\hat{\beta}_{2\tau}$, is simply the full-sample estimate of β. Testing that this component is nonzero amounts to a test that β is constant, but nonzero. However, such a test is unable to detect variation in β that causes this parameter to be 0 on average, even in situations where β at times is significantly different from 0. The other component, $\hat{\beta}_{1\tau} - \hat{\beta}_{2\tau}$, can detect such variation. This component measures the difference between the parameters estimated on two different subsamples and thus can identify variation in β over time.

The exponential Wald test statistic proposed by Rossi (2005a) takes the form

$$\text{Exp-W}_T^* = \frac{1}{T}\sum_{\tau=0.15T}^{0.85T} \frac{\exp(\frac{1}{2})}{0.7}\left(\left(\hat{\beta}_{1\tau} - \hat{\beta}_{2\tau}\right)', \left(\frac{\tau}{T}\hat{\beta}_{1\tau} + \left(1-\frac{\tau}{T}\right)\hat{\beta}_{2\tau}\right)'\right)\hat{V}^{-1}$$

$$\times \left(\begin{array}{c} \hat{\beta}_{1\tau} - \hat{\beta}_{2\tau} \\ \frac{\tau}{T}\hat{\beta}_{1\tau} + \left(1-\frac{\tau}{T}\right)\hat{\beta}_{2\tau} \end{array}\right),$$

where

$$\hat{V} = \left(\begin{array}{cc} \frac{\tau}{T}S'_{xx}\hat{S}_1^{-1}S_{xx} & 0 \\ 0 & \frac{T-\tau}{T}S'_{xx}\hat{S}_2^{-1}S_{xx} \end{array}\right),$$

$$S_{xx} = \frac{1}{T}\sum_{t=1}^{T} x_{t-1}x'_{t-1},$$

$$\hat{S}_1 = \left(\frac{1}{\tau}\sum_{t=2}^{\tau} x_{t-1}\hat{\varepsilon}_t\hat{\varepsilon}_t x'_{t-1}\right) + \sum_{j=2}^{\tau-1}\left(1-\left|\frac{j}{\tau^{1/3}}\right|\right)\left(\frac{1}{\tau}\sum_{t=2}^{\tau} x_{t-1}\hat{\varepsilon}_t\hat{\varepsilon}_{t-j}x'_{t-j-1}\right),$$

$$\hat{S}_2 = \left(\frac{1}{T-\tau}\sum_{t=\tau+1}^{T-\tau} x_{t-1}\hat{\varepsilon}_t\hat{\varepsilon}_t x'_{t-1}\right)$$

$$+ \sum_{j=\tau+1}^{T-\tau}\left(1-\left|\frac{j}{(T-\tau)^{1/3}}\right|\right)\left(\frac{1}{T-\tau}\sum_{t=j+1}^{T-\tau} x_{t-1}\hat{\varepsilon}_t\hat{\varepsilon}_{t-j}x'_{t-j-1}\right),$$

and $\hat{\varepsilon}_t = y_t - x'_{t-1}\hat{\beta}$ are the regression residuals from the fitted model. In the absence of serial correlation in the data, only the first term in $\hat{S}_1$ and $\hat{S}_2$ matter.

Rossi (2005a, table B1) tabulates the critical values for the Exp-W$_T^*$ test under the joint null hypothesis that x_t does not Granger cause y_{t+1} and no time-variation in the parameters, i.e., $\beta_t = \beta = 0$.

Empirically, Rossi (2013a) finds that Granger causality tests that are robust to instabilities can detect stronger empirical evidence of predictability—including out-of-sample evidence—for many macroeconomic series.

Rossi (2013a) undertakes a large-scale comparison of forecasting procedures that account for model instability. Like Pesaran and Timmermann (2007), she finds that the choice of estimation window is very important for forecasting performance. Overall, the empirical evidence presented by Rossi suggests that a simple equal-weighted average tends to perform as well as or better than several more sophisticated approaches.

Giacomini and Rossi (2010) suggest fluctuation tests for examining the stability of forecasting models using their out-of-sample performance. The basic idea is that, following Giacomini and White (2006), we can consider the differences in the out-of-sample losses generated by two different forecasting methods as raw data that can be examined in a test. Using this approach, Giacomini and Rossi present a number of tests. For example, their fluctuation test is a sequence of rolling Diebold–Mariano tests for equal predictive accuracy. The DM test is constructed from a window of observations around each point in the sample and so will fluctuate as the window moves. If the fluctuations are too large relative to the critical values from an asymptotic distribution, this is considered evidence of instability in the relationship between the two forecasting methods.

Rossi and Sekhposyan (2013) extend the analysis of model instability for point forecasts to cover evaluation of distribution forecasts. Their tests, which include Kolmogorov–Smirnov and Cramer–von Mises tests such as those described in chapter 18, have power against misspecified density models even if the misspecification affects only part of the sample due to model instability. Rossi and Sekhposyan (2015) develop tests for forecast rationality that are robust to instabilities in the forecast errors. If forecasts are inefficient in only part of the sample, traditional rationality tests lack power. By basing their tests on rolling windows of the sample, Rossi and Sekhposyan (2015) can detect more local evidence of deviations from forecast rationality.

19.8 CONCLUSION

The processes generating most economic and financial time series are likely to be changing over time. This raises some important issues. First, can model instability explain some of the empirical findings reported throughout the forecasting literature such as the good empirical performance of forecast combinations and the tendency of forecasting performance to worsen out-of-sample? Given the pervasiveness of model instability found in empirical research, it is natural to suspect that such instability is a key source of model misspecification.

Second, should a forecaster try to detect and model such instabilities and exploit them to generate more accurate forecasts? A variety of approaches have been used here, ranging from fully parametric methods that model the process giving rise to the change in parameters over time to more ad hoc, adaptive methods. A key challenge when deciding which method to use is that tests for model instability usually are not very informative about the nature of any detected instability, i.e., whether it takes the form of frequent small breaks to the parameters or, alternatively, rare but large breaks to the parameters which may even alternate between a few discrete states.

Third, how do we come up with robust forecasting approaches whose performance is not critically linked to getting the break point model exactly right? Model combination (covered in chapter 14) offers one way to achieve this. While using a rolling estimation window or a discounted least squares estimator offer some degree of robustness by putting more weight on recent data than on older data, these approaches are often not optimal and can amplify the effect of estimation error on the forecast which can lead to worse forecasting performance (compared to methods based on an expanding estimation window) in situations where parameter uncertainty is important.

20

Trending Variables and Forecasting

Many of the results presented in previous chapters made the implicit assumption that the data display enough lack of persistence and lack of heterogeneity that standard laws of large numbers apply, so that sums of random variables suitably scaled (usually by the square root of the sample size) converge to normal distributions. Many variables of interest in forecasting—macro variables such as income or money growth, financial variables such as stock prices and trading volume, even weather variables such as temperature—appear to be sufficiently persistent that we may not be confident in such assumptions. We refer to such variables as trending variables, by which we mean that the unconditional mean or variance of the predicted variable diverges over time. For example, if y_t has a unit root, then its variance increases linearly in time. If y_t is dominated by a time trend, then it has a mean that diverges over time.

In many ways, this persistence issue has little or no effect on many of the questions discussed so far. For example, there are no real issues for loss functions or the choice of loss functions. Expected loss still exists under well-defined assumptions, so the results on loss functions in chapter 2 still apply. Similarly, many of the issues discussed in chapters 4 and 5 continue to apply. For example, uncertainty over parameters remains of the same order in the sample size. Some things do change, however. Many of the trade-offs appearing in the expression for risk will now be different from those discussed earlier, both in magnitude and in terms of the techniques required to understand them. Persistent dynamics in the predicted variable therefore has implications for model building, model selection and comparison, and evaluation of risk.

Suppose the nature of the trending behavior is precisely known—for example we may know that the trend is a deterministic function of time or that the variable has one root on the unit circle and all others well outside the unit circle. In these cases, the complications that arise in the presence of trending variables are relatively straightforward. For example, if there is a single unit root driving the variables, methods such as differencing or cointegration can be applied to model the variables. If there is a deterministic time trend, this can simply be added to the model.

Chapter 3 discussed plug-in estimators and estimators for the parameters of the forecasting model that minimize average loss. We established general conditions under which such estimators converge to the pseudo-true value that minimizes the expected risk. Estimation of the parameters of the forecasting model that minimize average loss require the data to be either strictly stationary (for the average loss with estimated parameters to converge to the expected loss at time T) or weakly stationary (for the average loss with estimated parameters to converge to an average of expected losses). Similarly general results are not available when the variables have unit roots or exhibit other forms of trending behavior; specific results hinge on the locations of the unit roots, the number of unit roots among the variables and also on whether the forecasting model is correctly specified in the sense of being "balanced," ensuring that the trend in the predicted variable is correctly captured by the forecasting model.

Provided that the forecasting model for y_{T+h} is linear and the loss function is quadratic, some general points apply. First, if the trending behavior is correctly specified by the forecasting model, estimation error is unconditionally of the same order as in the ergodic case, i.e., of order T^{-1}. This is true both in- and out-of-sample and holds despite the fact that coefficients in models with unit roots (or time trends) converge at a rate faster than $T^{1/2}$. Second, when the trend is correctly specified the precise magnitude of the order T^{-1} term differs from model to model. In the ergodic case this term is equal to the number of coefficients estimated; in the nonergodic case this term will depend on the precise form of the trend.

Section 20.1 discusses expected loss in the presence of trending variables. Section 20.2 focuses the problem on univariate forecasting models, while section 20.3 covers multivariate forecasting models. Section 20.4 covers the case with highly persistent predictor variables and section 20.5 discusses how forecast evaluation is affected by the presence of trending or persistent variables. Section 20.6 concludes.

20.1 EXPECTED LOSS WITH TRENDING VARIABLES

To illustrate the first point, consider the following example where an autoregressive model with a root near 1 is the true data-generating process and we use a least squares estimator to obtain the model parameters; this can be thought of as a plug-in estimator or as the estimator that minimizes the average in-sample loss.

Example 20.1.1 (MSE with near-unit root process). *Consider an AR(1) model* $y_{t+1} = \beta y_t + \varepsilon_{t+1}$, *where* $\varepsilon_{t+1} \sim (0, \sigma^2)$. *The mean squared error for a one-step-ahead forecast at time T is*

$$E[(y_{T+1} - \hat{\beta}_T y_T)^2] = E[(\varepsilon_{T+1} - (\hat{\beta}_T - \beta)y_T)^2]$$

$$= E[\varepsilon_{T+1}^2 + (\hat{\beta}_T - \beta)^2 y_T^2] + o_p(1). \tag{20.1}$$

An exact result for this expression is difficult to establish even for the Gaussian case. As $T \to \infty$, let $\beta = \beta_T = 1 - \gamma/T$, so we are considering triangular array asymptotics. For $\gamma = 0$ we have a unit root; for $\gamma > 0$ we have a root local to unity. Then $T(\hat{\beta} - \beta) \Rightarrow (\int W_\gamma(s)^2 ds)^{-1} \int W_\gamma(s) dW(s)$ and $T^{-1/2} y_T \Rightarrow \sigma W_\gamma(1)$, where $W(s)$ is a standard Brownian motion and $W_\gamma(s) = \int_0^s e^{-\gamma(s-r)} dW(r)$.[1] Hence, the term

---

[1] The appendix at the end of the book provides more details on Brownian motion processes. All integrals over Brownian motion objects are 0 to 1 unless otherwise indicated.

inside the expectation in (20.1) can be approximated by

$$\sigma^2 \left(1 + T^{-1} W_\gamma(1)^2 \left(\int W_\gamma(s)^2 ds\right)^{-2} \left(\int W_\gamma(s) dW(s)\right)^2\right).$$

Again the order of the estimation error is T^{-1}, although for a unit root or root local to unity the magnitude of the effect is different from the case with a single stationary regressor.

This example illustrates our main points. Despite both y_{t+1} and $z_t = y_t$ having either a unit root or a near unit root, the expected loss exists and can be approximated by limit results in sufficiently large samples. As in the ergodic case, the term that arises from estimation error is of order T^{-1}. This is true even though our estimator for the autoregressive root is converging at rate T rather than $T^{1/2}$. The rate in the expected loss calculation remains at T^{-1} because the value of the regressor z_T also diverges. The order T^{-1} term no longer equals k, the number of regressors, but is instead the expectation of a function of Brownian motions. This function depends on the value for γ, the local-to-unity parameter, and so depends on the model parameters.[2]

The next example shows a similar result for the case with a time trend rather than a unit root.

Example 20.1.2 (Forecasting model with a deterministic trend). *Consider the model $y_t = \beta_1 + \beta_2 t + u_t = \beta' x_t + u_t$, where $u_t \sim (0, \sigma^2)$, $\beta = (\beta_1, \beta_2)'$, and $x_t = (1, t)$. The OLS estimators for the regression coefficients are jointly normal with $\Upsilon_T(\hat\beta - \beta) \to^d N(0, \sigma^2 \Sigma)$, where $\Upsilon_T = \text{diag}(T^{1/2}, T^{3/2})$ and $\Sigma = p\lim(\Upsilon_T^{-1}[\sum_{t=1}^T x_t x_t']\Upsilon_T^{-1})^{-1}$ is a (2×2) matrix whose elements are 1 and 1/3 on the diagonal with 1/2 on the off-diagonal. Since $T^{-3/2}(\hat\beta_2 - \beta_2)$ is $O_p(1)$, $\hat\beta_2$ converges faster than $\hat\beta_1$ and we might expect that the effect of estimation error is of lower order for β_2 than for β_1. However, this is not true because the additional T in the convergence rate offsets the time trend regressor which is also of order T. Assuming mean squared error loss and ignoring higher-order terms, we have*

$$E[(y_{T+1} - x_t'\hat\beta)^2] = \sigma^2(1 + T^{-1} \iota'\Sigma\iota) = \sigma^2\left(1 + \frac{4}{T}\right).$$

Here the order of the effects of estimation error are the same for each coefficient. However, the overall effect of estimation error is bigger than in the stationary case with two regressors, by $2(T)^{-1}$.

In this example the term of order T^{-1} differs from the corresponding term in the ergodic case. In the trended case, the term depends on the particular type of trend (a linear time trend) but not on the parameters of the model. Again, the faster rate of convergence on the coefficient on the time trend does not translate into an estimation error of lower order.

---

[2] If we were to include a constant in the forecasting model, the Ornstein–Uhlenbeck processes $W_\gamma(s)$ would be replaced with their projections onto a constant.

A third point to note is that when the trending behavior is not correctly specified, this typically results in a mean squared error that grows as the sample size increases, rather than converging to some expected MSE for the problem.

Example 20.1.3 (MSE with misspecified trend). *Consider again the model $y_t = \beta_1 + \beta_2 t + u_t = \beta' x_t + u_t$, where $u_t \sim (0, \sigma^2)$, $\beta = (\beta_1, \beta_2)'$, and $x_t = (1, t)$. However, suppose we misspecify the trend by including only a constant in the forecasting model, i.e., our forecast is the sample average of y_t using all available data. In this case we use $\hat{\beta}_1 = T^{-1} \sum_{t=1}^{T} y_t$ to forecast y_{T+1} which yields an MSE,*

$$E[y_{T+1} - \hat{\beta}_1]^2 = \sigma^2 + E[\beta_1 + \beta_2(T+1) - \hat{\beta}_1]^2$$

$$= \sigma^2(1 + T^{-1}) + \beta_2^2 \left(T + 1 - T^{-1} \sum_{t=1}^{t} t \right)^2$$

$$= \sigma^2(1 + T^{-1}) + \beta_2^2 T^2/4 + o(1),$$

and so the MSE diverges as T gets large.

Similar results hold for situations where y_t has a unit root but the forecasting model regards y_t as having a time trend, or vice versa. They also extend to situations where y_t has a unit root but the model for y_t as a function of other trending variables does not adequately account for the trending behavior in y_t, e.g., if the model is not cointegrating. As for the case with a correctly specified trend, each case needs to be constructed individually and there are no general results. However, a unifying theme is that the MSE diverges when the trend is misspecified as the trend comes to dominate. In these cases, typically the parameters do not converge to pseudo-true values and a subset of the parameter estimates is not consistent for any fixed value as the sample size grows.

Under an unknown trend, a simple forecasting approach that is almost always feasible and often results in a nondivergent MSE (or any loss function for which expectations are finite) is to use y_T to predict y_{T+h}. This prediction is known as the random walk forecast since it is optimal for that model. In this case, even though the mean or variance of y_{T+h} is diverging in T, the forecast error, $y_{T+h} - y_T$, does not diverge, provided that the trending behavior is due to unit roots or time trends. For other types of trending behavior, e.g., near unit roots, the divergent behavior of $y_{T+h} - y_T$ is often much smaller and hence less of a problem.

20.2 UNIVARIATE FORECASTING MODELS

Define d_t to be deterministic if d_t is perfectly predictable into the future. For example, d_t can be a constant, a time trend, or a sine wave. When the trending behavior of a series is caused by deterministic terms, model estimation and many of the aspects of forecast evaluation follow the discussions in earlier chapters. Because d_t is perfectly predictable (if there are no nondeterministic terms), we can consider the forecasting model $y_t = f_t(z_t, \beta) + \varepsilon_t$ to estimate β under MSE loss. For any horizon, forecasts can be constructed from $\hat{f}_{t+h|t} = f_t(z_{t+h}, \hat{\beta})$ since z_{t+h} is known at time t. Hence, no issues arise in relation to whether direct or iterated forecasts should be used. Estimates for $\hat{\beta}$ are consistent and asymptotically normal if the model is sufficiently smooth, so model selection issues are similar to those covered in earlier chapters.

Consider the following linear model that may have a unit root:

$$y_t = \phi' d_t + u_t, \quad t = 1, \ldots, T, \tag{20.2}$$

$$(1 - \rho L)u_t = v_t, \quad t = 2, \ldots, T,$$

$$u_1 = \xi.$$

Here d_t consists of strictly exogenous deterministic terms and $\beta = (\phi', \rho)'$. We consider models with either a constant or a constant and a time trend, so $d_t = 1$ or $d_t = (1, t)'$ and so ϕ is either univariate or $\phi = (\phi_1, \phi_2)'$; ξ is the initial condition. We can allow additional serial correlation through $v_t = c(L)\varepsilon_t$, where ε_t is a zero-mean white noise term with variance σ_ε^2. The lag polynomial describing the dynamic behavior of y_t has been factored so that $\rho = 1 - \gamma/T$ corresponds to the largest root of the polynomial, and we assume that $c(L)$ is one summable, i.e., $\sum_{i=0}^{\infty} |c_i| i < \infty$. We could alternatively assume that v_t is globally covariance stationary and that $T^{-1/2} \sum_{t=1}^{T} v_t \to^d N(0, \omega^2)$, where ω^2 is the spectral density of v_t at frequency 0, divided by 2π. In either case, an autoregressive model for $y_t - \phi' d_t$ is regarded as an approximation to the stationary dynamics of the model.

When y_t is known to have a unit root, many results are equivalent to those obtained in previous chapters with a unit root imposed. Specifically, in this case the predicted variable can be differenced and modeling can proceed with the differenced data. If we use the iterated forecasting method of section 7.3, we can predict $\Delta y_{t+1}, \ldots, \Delta y_{t+h}$ and use the sum $y_t + \sum_{\tau=1}^{h} \Delta y_{t+\tau}$ as our forecast for the level of y_{t+h}. The direct forecasting method regresses $y_{t+h} - y_t$ on variables known at time t, which may include lags of the change in y_t, as well as other terms that are not trending apart from deterministic terms, to produce a forecast $f_h(z_t, \beta)$. The forecast of the level of y_{t+h} is then obtained as $f_{t+h|t} = y_t + f_h(z_t, \beta)$. Similar results apply under loss functions other than MSE.

If we are unsure whether y_t contains a unit root, issues related to estimation error similar to those discussed in earlier chapters arise. Magnitudes of estimation errors are different in this setting, however, because parameter estimates are no longer asymptotically normally distributed and typically depend on how close the root is to unity. Forecasters have the choice between (i) ignoring the possibility that $\rho \neq 1$ and so estimating the autoregression in differences; (ii) estimating ρ from an autoregression in levels; or (iii) combining the two approaches with a pre-test for a unit root. Comparison of the risk function in (i) and (ii) is straightforward—for ρ close enough to 1, a smaller risk is obtained by imposing a value of 1 rather than estimating the parameter. As ρ moves further away from 1, the error from imposing the incorrect value of the largest root will increase and becomes larger than the loss due to estimation of the parameter. As in the stationary case, the risk function that arises from imposing $\rho = 1$ when it is not true is unbounded as ρ diverges from 1, whereas the risk from estimating ρ is bounded for all values of ρ.

By recursive substitution, the model in (20.2) with $c(L) = 1$ yields

$$y_{T+h} - y_T = \varepsilon_{T+h} + \rho\varepsilon_{T+h-1} + \cdots + \rho^{h-1}\varepsilon_{T+1} + (\rho^h - 1)(y_T - \phi' d_T)$$

$$+ \phi'(d_{T+h} - d_T)$$

$$= \sum_{i=1}^{h} \rho^{h-i}\varepsilon_{T+i} + (\rho^h - 1)(y_T - \phi' d_T) + \phi'(d_{T+h} - d_T), \tag{20.3}$$

and so the h-step-ahead forecast (with known parameters is) $f_{T+h|T} = y_T + (\rho^h - 1)(y_T - \phi' d_T) + \phi'(d_{T+h} - d_T)$. We next compare each of the three strategies discussed above. If we impose a unit root on the model and $d_t = 1$, then the forecast becomes simply y_T. If there is also a time trend, then the forecast is $y_T + \hat{\phi}_2 h$, where $\hat{\phi}_2$ is an estimator of ϕ_2. Under the second strategy that estimates the parameters (ρ, ϕ), the forecasts are $y_T + (\hat{\rho}^h - 1)(y_T - \hat{\phi}' d_T) + \hat{\phi}'(d_{T+h} - d_T)$. Different estimators can be used for (ρ, ϕ) in this case. There is no obvious "optimal" estimator for the autoregressive parameters and many estimators have been suggested. Typically, however, either OLS or median unbiased estimators are employed.[3] In addition, least squares can be used to estimate ϕ, although Canjels and Watson (1997) and Ng and Vogelsang (2002) have also suggested GLS estimators. Alternatively, we can consider estimating (ρ, ϕ) directly by simply regressing y_t on (y_{t-1}, d_t). The final strategy that has been considered in the literature is a hybrid of the first two approaches, namely selecting the relevant forecast using estimation or imposing a unit root after a pre-test for a unit root.

To analyze the behavior of the forecast errors, we employ large sample approximations for which $\rho = 1 + \gamma/T$, although we suppress the dependence of ρ on T as is typical in this literature. For the initial condition let

$$\xi = \alpha \omega (2\gamma)^{-1/2} T^{1/2},$$

where $\omega^2 = c(1)^2 \sigma_\varepsilon^2$ so the initial condition is asymptotically of the same order as the stochastic part of the model when $\alpha \neq 0$. Setting $\alpha = 1$ corresponds to drawing the initial condition from its unconditional distribution when $\rho < 1$. Under these conditions we have

$$T^{-1/2}(u_{[Ts]}) \Rightarrow \omega M(s) = \begin{cases} \omega W(s) & \text{for } \gamma = 0, \\ \omega \alpha e^{-\gamma s}(2\gamma)^{-1/2} + \omega \int_0^s e^{-\gamma(s-\lambda)} dW(\lambda) & \text{for } \gamma \neq 0, \end{cases}$$
(20.4)

where $W(\cdot)$ is a standard univariate Brownian motion and (20.4) defines $M(s)$. See Elliott (2006) for further details.

20.2.1 Short-Horizon Forecasts

When the model parameters are known, the optimal forecast in (20.3) is

$$f_{T+h|T} = y_T + (\rho^h - 1)(y_T - \phi' d_T) + \phi'(d_{T+h} - d_T).$$

This results in an h-step-ahead forecast error of $\sum_{i=1}^h \rho^{h-i} \varepsilon_{T+i}$. The expected squared error loss is $\sigma_\varepsilon^2 (1 - \rho^{2h})/(1 - \rho^2)$ which, as T becomes large, converges to $h\sigma_\varepsilon^2$; this result holds exactly if $\gamma = 0$. Hence the unpredictable component of y contributes a term that grows linearly in the forecast horizon. Local misspecification of the model retains this term and further adds a term that disappears at rate T.

Imposing a unit root is a common practice among forecasters. Under the assumption that $\rho = 1$, the forecast becomes $f_{T+h|T} = y_T + \phi'(d_{T+h} - d_T)$. If $d_t = 1$,

---

[3] See Andrews (1993a), Andrews and Chen (1994), Roy and Fuller (2001), and Stock (1991).

the second term is 0. If the model also contains a time trend, then $\phi'(d_{T+h} - d_T) = \phi_2 h$ and the natural estimator for ϕ_2 is the mean of the change in y_t—this is the MLE under the misspecified model. We can study the costs and benefits of imposing a unit root by examining the asymptotic approximation to the forecast error $\sum_{i=1}^{h} \rho^{h-i} \varepsilon_{T+i} + (\rho^h - 1)(y_T - \phi' d_T)$ for models where ρ is local to 1. As just discussed, the first term is unpredictable and of higher order than the second component when ρ is local to unity. These components contribute to the MSE but decline to 0 at rate T. To see this, note that

$$T^{1/2}(\rho^h - 1)(y_T - \phi' d_T) \Rightarrow -h\gamma\sigma_\varepsilon M(1),$$

$$E\left[-h\gamma\sigma_\varepsilon M(1)\right]^2 = \sigma_\varepsilon^2 \left\{ \frac{h^2\gamma(\alpha^2 - 1)e^{-2\gamma}}{2} + \frac{h^2\gamma}{2} \right\}, \tag{20.5}$$

where $M(1)$ is defined in (20.4). This second-order term is a function of how close ρ is to 1 given the sample size (through γ), the forecast horizon h, as well as the extent of the deterministic terms and the assumption on the initial condition. As expected, this term increases in both γ (how far the root is from 1) and the forecast horizon— the effect of misspecification of the model compounds as h increases. In large enough samples the contribution of the initial condition is small and disappears quickly as γ moves away from 0 and so the second-order term is roughly equal to $\sigma_\varepsilon^2 h^2 \gamma / 2$. Equation (20.5) increases linearly in γ and quadratically in h, though note that the contribution of the unpredictable part of the forecast error increases linearly in h.

The expression in (20.5) can be used to understand the percentage increase in MSE from imposing $\rho = 1$. For reasonable values of γ, the percentage increase in the MSE due to imposing a unit root rather than using the true value of ρ is approximately equal to $h\gamma/(2T)$. When d_t includes a time trend there is an additional effect through the estimation of ϕ_2. Using the mean of $y_{t+h} - y_t$, the additional second-order term in the MSE can be approximated[4] by $\sigma_\varepsilon^2 h^2(\gamma + 2)/2$. This expression suggests that imposing the unit root on ρ and estimating the coefficient on the time trend through the mean of the change in y_t increases the MSE[5] by $h(\gamma + 2)/(2T)$. In either case, if the process is strongly mean reverting or the forecast horizon is long enough, imposing a unit root on the model will not yield good forecasts.

Rather than imposing a unit root, we could estimate the model parameters (ρ, ϕ). Expressions under least squares estimation and serial correlation are available for this case in Phillips (1998). Ng and Vogelsang (2002) examine one-step-ahead forecast errors analytically for various OLS and GLS approaches and show that the asymptotic approximations to the first-order term (the term caused by estimation error) differ across estimation methods. Their simulation results suggest that GLS approaches (particularly ones incorporating the initial observation) outperform OLS approaches.

The third approach is to employ a pre-test for $\rho = 1$, imposing the unit root when the pre-test fails to reject, otherwise estimating the model parameters. Diebold and

---

[4] Some additional terms that turn out to be very small are ignored here; see Elliott (2006) for the full expression.

[5] Sampson (1991) points out that model uncertainty causes the squared forecast error to grow at a rate h^2 when $\rho = 1$ and extends the analysis to include stationary dynamics.

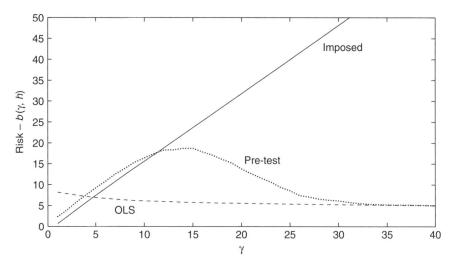

Figure 20.1: Short-horizon risk under three different approaches. The figure plots the risk
component b as a function of the local-to-unity parameter γ for three different approaches: (i) imposing a unit root (full line); (ii) estimating the model
parameters (dash-dotted line); (iii) pre-testing for a unit root (dotted line). The
figure assumes a short forecast horizon of $h = 3$ periods and includes a constant
deterministic term.

Kilian (2000) examine this approach in a Monte Carlo exercise and recommend pre-
testing for a unit root. As with all pre-test approaches (see chapter 6), the forecasting
model based on a pre-test can itself be considered as an estimator and we can examine
the resulting risk function. Elliott (2006) compares the risks for the three strategies
of imposing a unit root, estimating the model parameters, and pre-testing using the
Dickey and Fuller (1979) test for a unit root.

In each of these cases the risk for the AR(1) model is of the form $\sigma^2(1 +
T^{-1}b_i(\gamma, h))$, where $i \in \{$impose unit root, estimate parameters by OLS, hybrid
approach using a unit root pre-test$\}$. The accompanying figures report the size of
$b_i(\gamma, h)$ as a function of γ. The plots can be used to approximate the additional
percentage MSE loss after dividing by the sample size. Figure 20.1 shows results for
the model that only includes a constant, $d_t = 1$. The figure sets $h = 3$ and shows
results for various values of γ. Figure 20.2 repeats this exercise when $d_t = (1, t)$.
Some broad conclusions occur from these plots. First, imposing a unit root rather
than estimating it works only very close to the region where the assumption of a unit
root is true.[6] Compared to estimating the autoregressive model, imposing a unit root
is therefore likely to be a poor approach in practice. Second, as with all pre-testing
methods, the risk function associated with using a unit root pre-test is attractive when
the null of the pre-test is true or when the pre-test has power close to 1, i.e., for large
values for γ, but the pre-test does poorly in an intermediate range where the power
of the test is between the test size and 1. This is shown on the figures as a large hump
in the risk function for intermediate values for γ.

---

[6] Turner (2004) examines the cutoffs in γ for which estimating the model outperforms imposing a unit
root and finds that these are not particularly sensitive to the forecast horizon, h.

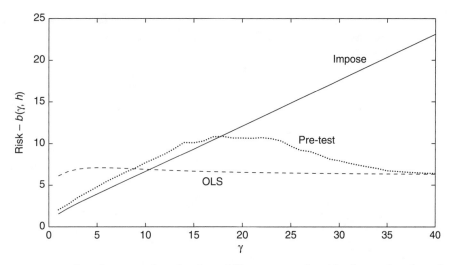

Figure 20.2: Short-horizon risk under three different approaches. The figure plots the risk component b as a function of the local-to-unity parameter γ for three different approaches: (i) imposing a unit root (full line); (ii) estimating the model parameters (dash-dotted line); (iii) pre-testing for a unit root (dotted line). The figure assumes a short forecast horizon of $h = 3$ periods and includes a constant and a trend as deterministic terms.

These calculations all assume a persistent autoregressive process with a root close to 1. Other models can generate persistence in the data in a way that mimics unit-root-type dynamics. For example, breaks in the parameters of the process can look like permanent shocks, which result in unit root or near unit root behavior (Perron, 1989). Breaks are examined in chapter 19. Long memory models also have similar properties.

20.2.2 Long-Horizon Forecasts

For stationary models with dynamic behavior that displays short memory, chapter 7 showed that the long-run forecast equals the unconditional mean of the variable. Thus, if we are interested in forecasting such variables far enough into the future, all we need to know about the variable is whether the dynamics have died out. For variables that are highly persistent, e.g., unit root processes, this conclusion is no longer true. For a model with a unit root, the long-run forecast is now the unconditional mean of the change in the variable plus the current observation and so the forecast depends on the present level of the data. For persistent variables, the model will have relevant information even at long horizons. As usual, we are most interested in forecasts conditional on the last observation.[7] Unfortunately, results are not available for the very persistent models analyzed here, so we restrict ourselves to follow the literature and examine unconditional MSE loss.

Suppose the model for the data is given by (20.2) so the recursion in (20.3) remains relevant. Forecasts are constructed in the same way as for the short-horizon case discussed above, but now for large values of h. For purposes of the asymptotic theory, we typically take h to be large relative to the sample size T, such that $h = [\lambda T]$,

---

[7] See Phillips (1987), which we discuss in section 7.3.2.

where λ is the ratio of the forecast horizon to the sample size. Since h now diverges as the sample size becomes large, so does the unpredictable component $\sum_{i=1}^{h} \rho^{h-i} \varepsilon_{T+i}$ in (20.3) and so the MSE diverges. However, rescaling the mean squared error by T results in a stable object that converges to a function of Brownian motions. The estimation error component in (20.3) also diverges at the same rate, so model estimation error is of the same order of magnitude as the unpredictable component, unlike in the short-horizon case. Analysis of the asymptotic properties of the MSE that use this approach to asymptotic theory, where ρ is local to unity and $h = [\lambda T]$, has been undertaken by Stock (1996) and Phillips (1998), using a more general setup than here, and in Kemp (1999) and Turner (2004). These studies are reviewed by Elliott (2006).

To establish some results, let $h = [T\lambda]$ but now assume that estimation uses the first $T - h = T_1$ observations[8] so we forecast y_T using observations $t = \{1, \ldots, T_1\}$. When the model is known, the forecast error scaled by $T^{-1/2}$ is

$$T^{-1/2} \sum_{i=1}^{h} \rho^{h-i} \varepsilon_{T_1+i} = T^{-1/2}(y_{T_1+[T\lambda]} - \rho^h y_{T_1})$$

$$= T^{-1/2}(y_T - \rho^h y_{T_1})$$

$$\Rightarrow \sigma_\varepsilon \{M(1) - e^{-\gamma\lambda} M(1 - \lambda)\}.$$

Hence, the long-horizon forecast diverges, as we might expect since h is diverging. The expectation of the square of this limit is $\sigma_\varepsilon^2 (1 - e^{-2\gamma\lambda})/(2\gamma)$ when $\rho < 1$ and is independent[9] of the initial condition, α. In the presence of a unit root, the mean of the squared forecast error divided by T equals $\lambda\sigma_\varepsilon^2$.

Suppose, alternatively, that we impose a unit root. When $d_t = 1$ this means that we use y_{T_1} to forecast y_T. The scaled forecast error is now

$$T^{-1/2}(y_T - y_{T_1}) \Rightarrow \sigma_\varepsilon \{M(1) - M(1 - \lambda)\}.$$

The expectation of this term is

$$\frac{1 - e^{-\gamma\lambda}}{\gamma} + \frac{(\alpha^2 - 1)e^{-2\gamma}(1 - e^{\gamma\lambda})^2}{2\gamma}. \tag{20.6}$$

The estimation error and the unpredictable component are now of the same order, unlike in the fixed horizon case. For $\rho < 1$, the expectation in (20.6) is greater than that for the known model. When $d_t = (1, t)$, the additional terms due to model misspecification error are

$$T^{-1/2}(y_T - y_{T_1} - \hat{\phi}_2 h) \Rightarrow \sigma_\varepsilon \left(M(1) - M(1 - \lambda) - \lambda(M(1 - \lambda) - M(0)) \right).$$

The mean of the square of this term is lengthy and not particularly informative.

---

[8] This setup differs from Stock (1996) and Elliott (2006) but only by relabeling the observations. The results are the same as if we forecast y_{T+h} using $t = \{1, \ldots, T\}$. The approach here provides two advantages. First, all Brownian motion results are on C[0,1], the set of continuous processes with outcomes falling between 0 and 1. Second, and as a result of this, we can more easily analyze out-of-sample forecasting results.

[9] This is because the model is correctly specified and the initial value appears in both the predicted outcome and the forecast itself.

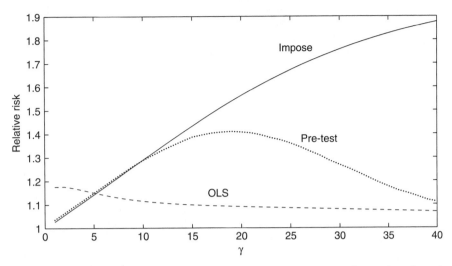

Figure 20.3: Long-horizon risk under three different approaches. The figure plots the risk component b as a function of the local-to-unity parameter γ for three different approaches: (i) imposing a unit root (full line); (ii) estimating the model parameters (dash-dotted line); (iii) pre-testing for a unit root (dotted line). The figure assumes a long forecast horizon of $\lambda = 0.1$, i.e., 10% of the full sample and includes a constant deterministic term.

Estimation of the model parameters results in the expressions becoming even more abstract, although they have been given in Stock (1996), Phillips (1998), and Turner (2004). Rather than state the results, we note that estimation error is again of the same order as the unpredictable component, similar to what we found when imposing the unit root. To visualize the results, we examine the trade-offs of the same methods examined for short horizons but now for much longer horizons up to $h = 40$ periods.

Figure 20.3 shows the risk for the three approaches—imposing a unit root, estimating the model parameters, or the hybrid approach based on a pre-test—measured relative to the infeasible risk under the known model. The first panel assumes $d_t = 1$, while the second is for $d_t = (1, t)'$. Each panel assumes $\lambda = 0.1$. The basic results are similar to the situation with a fixed horizon, namely that imposing a unit root works well if this is close to being the correct model. However, this approach quickly gets overwhelmed by simply estimating the parameters. Pre-testing does not really provide a useful way to combine the good properties of imposing the root when the root is close to 1 and estimating it when the root is far from 1, because the pre-test method (as seen in the stationary case) does not have the power to clearly distinguish between the two choices in the region where such a distinction becomes useful.

The main difference compared with the stationary case is that the cutoff point where imposing a unit root versus estimating it works equally well is now larger and occurs for values of γ further away from 1. The need to estimate the contribution of the trend component seems to further increase the cutoff value.

Because the distributions above depend on the unknown value of γ, it is difficult to construct confidence intervals for y_T given the data $\{y_1, \ldots, y_{T_1}\}$. When $\gamma = 0$ so there is an exact unit root,

$$T^{-1/2}(y_T - y_{T_1}) \Rightarrow \sigma_\varepsilon^2 \{W(1) - W(1 - \lambda)\} = \mathrm{N}(0, \lambda \sigma_\varepsilon^2).$$

In this case it makes sense to construct confidence intervals using $y_T \overset{a}{\sim} N(y_{T_1}, h\sigma_\varepsilon^2)$, so that a $(1-\alpha)\%$ confidence interval for y_T is $\{y_{T_1} \pm cv_\alpha \sqrt{h\sigma_\varepsilon^2}\}$, where cv_α is the $\alpha\%$ critical value. In the general case, however, the distribution of the forecast error obtained either by imposing a unit root or by estimating the root will depend on γ (and potentially α). There are no currently available methods to deal with this dependence.

20.3 MULTIVARIATE FORECASTING MODELS

When modeling a vector of persistent variables, a natural starting point is to use a vector autoregression, assuming MSE loss. We could simply allow the estimation method to determine the parameters, ignoring the possibility of unit roots. Such VARs in levels have a long history in forecasting; the original Litterman VAR used a prior that each of the variables followed an AR(1) process with unit roots (see section 9.3.2).

Recall that we can write the VAR in levels as $y_t = A(L)y_{t-1} + \varepsilon_t$. As for univariate models, the effect of estimation error on model risk differs from the stationary case but is of the same order and will thus disappear for short (fixed) horizons at rate T. To see this, note that the vector of one-step-ahead forecast errors is

$$y_{T+1} - f_{T+1|T} = \varepsilon_{T+1} + [A(L) - \hat{A}(L)]y_T. \qquad (20.7)$$

As in the univariate case, the term due to estimation error will disappear at rate $T^{1/2}$, and so the squared error term disappears at rate T.

When each of the n variables in y_t has a unit root, in the absence of cointegration between the variables we can simply impose the known unit roots on the system and estimate the VAR in differences. In this situation the results of chapter 9 are directly relevant. When the n variables are cointegrated and there are only $n - r$ unit roots $(n > r)$ in the model, the Granger representation theorem (Engle and Granger, 1987) shows that the correct specification is an error correction model (ECM). For this case, the VAR can be written as

$$\Delta y_t = \alpha\beta' y_{t-1} + \tilde{A}(L)\Delta y_{t-1} + \varepsilon_t, \qquad (20.8)$$

where $\beta' y_t$ are the r cointegrating vectors. These are linear combinations of y_t that have all roots outside the unit circle. Here α is an $(n \times r)$ vector of "impact" coefficients.

It is natural to ask how useful it is to impose the cointegrating restrictions for purposes of forecasting h steps ahead. This is similar to asking how different are forecasts using the VAR in levels (20.7) versus using the error correction model (20.8). A second question is how valuable the cointegrating vector is for forecasting h periods into the future, i.e., how different are forecasts using the VAR in differences—thus omitting information in the cointegrating vector—versus using the ECM. We address each question in turn.

The Granger representation theorem shows that r cointegrating relations between the n unit root variables imply $(n - r)^2$ restrictions on the parameters of the VAR in levels, including normalizing the cointegrating vector; these restrictions result in the error correction model. Hence, differences between forecasts based on the VAR and

ECM specification arise due to difference from imposing versus not imposing these restrictions. For the univariate model examined above, the analogy is the difference between imposing the unit root or estimating this parameter. In the univariate case we saw that such a constraint results in better forecasts when there is exactly a unit root, but can increase the expected loss when the restriction is false since any reduction in estimation error gets overwhelmed by additional biases. In the multivariate case considered here, a similar trade-off occurs. However, there are now a larger number of restrictions (allowing the gains to be bigger) and additional dimensions in which the restrictions might not hold exactly, making it more difficult to examine potential losses. Abadir, Hadri, and Tzavalis (1999) examine the impact of estimating the r^2 coefficients on estimation error and find that the effects can be large, essentially because the dimension of the restrictions is also large. They do not examine how forecasts are affected, however.

The second question relates to the value of using the information in the cointegrating vectors for forecasting versus simply ignoring cointegration but still imposing unit roots, i.e., compared to the misspecified model in differences. Using the misspecified model was (and to some extent remains) a standard approach to forecasting with persistent variables. This approach essentially asks whether omitting $\alpha\beta' y_{t-1}$ from the forecasting model (20.8) results in any loss. It would seem that if α is close to 0 and/or the cointegrating vector $\beta' y_{t-1}$ is not very persistent, omitting these variables is not going to have much effect. Conversely, if α is large and $\beta' y_{t-1}$ is very persistent, omitting the error correction term might have an effect on the forecast. This turns out to be true. To see this, consider the error correction model for a bivariate system with a single cointegrating relationship (i.e., $n = 2$, $r = 1$) and no additional dynamics (i.e., $\tilde{A}(L) = 0$). Through recursive substitution, we can write

$$y_{t+h} - y_t = \left(\frac{1 - \rho_c^h}{1 - \rho_c}\right) \alpha\beta' y_t + \sum_{i=1}^{h} (\alpha\beta' + I)^{h-i} \varepsilon_{t+i}, \tag{20.9}$$

where $\rho_c = 1 + \beta'\alpha$ is the autoregressive parameter for the AR(1) cointegrating vector $\beta' y_t$ and so measures the persistence in the cointegrating vector. This example helps clarify the earlier discussion. The bigger is α, the larger is the contribution of the cointegrating vector to the h-step-ahead forecast. Similarly, the bigger is ρ_c, the larger is the impact of the cointegrating vector on the forecast. This explains the seeming anomaly between results suggesting a small impact on the forecast from including the cointegrating vector versus results suggesting a larger impact. Engle and Yoo (1987) present Monte Carlo evidence which shows that the cointegrating term can be useful at moderate horizons—their choice for parameters has $\alpha = (-0.4, 0.1)$ and $\rho_c = 0.4$, so the cointegrating vector is moderately persistent. Christoffersen and Diebold (1998) set $\rho_c = 0$ so the cointegrating vector is not serially correlated in their simulations and so they obtain little value from including the cointegrating vector. Both Engle and Yoo (1987) and Christoffersen and Diebold (1998) make the point that as h gets large, the relative value of using the cointegrating vector decreases. This can easily be seen in the above model. Provided that $|\rho_c| < 1$, $\beta' y_t$ will be stationary with finite asymptotic variance and so the contribution of the error correction term has a bounded variance as h gets large. In contrast, the variance of the unpredictable component (the last term in (20.9)) is increasing in h and so the relative cost from ignoring the cointegrating vector goes to 0 as the forecast horizon increases.

The above analysis assumed that the cointegrating model is correctly specified. There are many ways in which a practitioner can misspecify the model. First, the persistence in the variables may not mean that they have exact unit roots. Second, we may not know the exact number of cointegrating relations in the model. As in the univariate case, one can still impose the misspecified model, or the forecaster could use pre-tests to attempt to estimate the most appropriate model. Such choices involve trade-offs in which imposing the restriction works well if it is close enough to being true. Pre-tests work well when either the null of the pre-test is correct or, alternatively, if the departure of the model from this null is large enough that the test has power close to 1; pre-tests perform poorly between these possibilities, however. Reinsel and Ahn (1992) provide a small Monte Carlo analysis with four variables and two cointegrating vectors. They find that underdifferencing (imposing too few cointegrating vectors) works well in the short run, while overdifferencing works well in the long run since the effect of the cointegrating vectors will to some extent have petered out. They also evaluate a pre-testing approach, although it is difficult to derive general conclusions from this. Lin and Tsay (1996) conduct a larger set of simulations, finding some gains from imposing cointegration constraints on the model; however they do not find any gains in an analysis of actual data.

20.3.1 Empirical Example

As an empirical illustration, we consider long-run forecasts of the quarterly inflation rate, i.e., the log-first difference in the CPI, the unemployment rate, and the interest rate. These time series are quite persistent as shown in previous chapters. We show results for forecast horizons $h = \{1, 2, 3, 4, 8, 12, 16, 20\}$ quarters and compare forecasts from a random walk, random walk with drift, an AR model with lag length selected by the AIC, and forecasts from AR(1) and AR(4) models. The out-of-sample results reported in table 20.1 are generated for the period 1970–2014 using an expanding estimation window.

First consider the inflation rate. Here the results show that the autoregressive models generally perform better than the random walk model for horizons of 1 through 3 quarters, but that the random walk model is better at the longest 20 quarter horizon. The random walk model with drift produces very poor forecasts, especially at long horizons. For the unemployment rate the AR(4) model dominates at all horizons and the random walk model produces RMSE values that are generally a bit higher than those from the AR models. Conversely, the random walk model produces the lowest RMSE values for the interest rate series at both short and long horizons.

In all cases the random walk with drift model performs very poorly because the series investigated here are not trending deterministically in any particular direction. Whether the simple random walk specification or the autoregressive specification is best varies, however, across variables and across sample periods. Which model produces the best forecasts will depend on the true, but unknown, degree of persistence of the underlying series; this is consistent with our theoretical results.

20.4 FORECASTING WITH PERSISTENT REGRESSORS

A common forecasting situation involves a regressor that displays persistence — the regressor is reverting to its mean only very slowly, if at all—but appears to

TABLE 20.1:
Root mean squared forecast errors (RMSE) for different forecasting models. The table reports RMSE values for the quarterly inflation, unemployment and interest rate series at different forecast horizons ranging from 1 through 20 quarters. The forecast evaluation period is 1970–2014; parameters are estimated using a recursively expanding estimation window for the models with unknown parameters.

Steps	RW	RW drift	AR(AIC)	AR(1)	AR(4)
Inflation rate					
1Q	4.144	4.513	3.316	3.626	3.432
2Q	4.560	5.776	3.488	3.803	3.477
3Q	4.196	6.760	3.543	3.752	3.467
4Q	3.653	7.912	3.735	3.825	3.487
8Q	4.277	14.532	4.243	4.239	4.034
12Q	4.229	21.210	4.361	4.384	4.286
16Q	4.370	27.952	4.365	4.401	4.346
20Q	4.118	34.777	4.188	4.221	4.180
Unemployment rate					
1Q	0.358	0.400	0.279	0.365	0.277
2Q	0.655	0.744	0.562	0.663	0.557
3Q	0.915	1.059	0.843	0.919	0.831
4Q	1.140	1.349	1.110	1.138	1.089
8Q	1.759	2.343	1.725	1.701	1.698
12Q	2.040	3.213	1.899	1.923	1.872
16Q	2.107	4.026	1.956	1.989	1.937
20Q	2.081	4.872	1.990	2.006	1.985
Interest rate					
1Q	1.164	1.207	1.398	1.201	1.269
2Q	1.516	1.652	1.680	1.564	1.649
3Q	1.632	1.926	1.762	1.643	1.766
4Q	1.975	2.403	2.204	1.982	2.108
8Q	2.876	3.988	3.082	2.809	3.083
12Q	3.351	5.302	3.662	3.381	3.731
16Q	3.506	6.442	4.122	3.632	4.145
20Q	3.403	7.521	4.457	3.898	4.565

have predictive power based on tests for the exclusion of that regressor in a linear regression. Examples include using the forward premium to predict changes in exchange rates (Bilson, 1981), short-run interest rates, consumption, and stock prices for forecasting changes in income (Chen, 1991; Hall, 1978), or the dividend–price ratio or earnings–price ratio for forecasting future stock returns (Stambaugh, 1999; Valkanov, 2003). In many cases, variation in the outcome variable captured by such predictor variables tends to be modest, although often economically interesting, as in the case of a small, but highly persistent risk premium on a financial asset.

To capture this setting, consider the model

$$y_t = \phi_y d_{yt} + \beta z_{t-1} + u_{yt}, \tag{20.10}$$

$$z_t = \phi_z d_{zt} + w_{zt},$$

$$(1 - \rho L) w_{zt} = u_{zt},$$

$$u_{z1} = \xi.$$

TABLE 20.2:
Size properties for one-sided test.

$\delta =$	-0.95	-0.75	-0.5
$\rho = 1$	0.416	0.289	0.180
$\rho = 0.9$	0.139	0.116	0.091
$\rho = 0.8$	0.105	0.092	0.079

Note: Size is 5% for a one-sided upper-tail test.

The regressor, z_t, follows the same process as y_t in (20.2). Assumptions on u_{zt} are the same as in the earlier section. Regressions such as (20.10) typically do not allow u_{yt} to be serially correlated. If u_{yt} were serially correlated, we would want to model this correlation to improve predictability. Moreover, in empirical applications there is usually little or no serial correlation to be found. The terms d_{zt} and d_{yt} are assumed to be deterministic, with $d_{zt} \subseteq d_{yt}$.

We further assume that the partial sums of the residuals $u_t = (u_{yt}, u_{zt})'$ converge to a bivariate Brownian motion process with variance–covariance matrix, Σ, given by[10]

$$\Sigma = \begin{pmatrix} \Sigma_{11} & \delta \Sigma_{11}^{1/2} \Sigma_{22}^{1/2} \\ \delta \Sigma_{11}^{1/2} \Sigma_{22}^{1/2} & \Sigma_{22} \end{pmatrix}; \tag{20.11}$$

δ is the correlation between u_{yt} and u_{zt}. This is also the long-run correlation between these shocks when u_{zt} is serially correlated but globally covariance stationary.

Monte Carlo simulation results have lead a number of authors to note that t-tests of the hypothesis $H_0 : \beta = 0$ versus $H_1 : \beta \neq 0$ are not well approximated by the standard normal distribution when ρ is close to 1 and δ is far from 0. For $\delta > 0$, the test underrejects in the upper tail and overrejects in the lower tail; the opposite holds for $\delta < 0$; see Mankiw and Shapiro (1986), Elliott and Stock (1994), and Stambaugh (1999). Table 20.2 shows upper-tail rejections for tests with a nominal 5% level for $T = 100$ and $\xi = 0$. The values for (δ, ρ) are selected to be relevant choices for forecasting changes in stock returns with the dividend–price ratio (Stambaugh, 1999).

Econometric analysis has explained such findings either as a small sample bias problem that disappears asymptotically or by modeling ρ as being local-to-unity and showing that there is always a region for ρ in which such tests will overreject, regardless of the sample size. Under both approaches, we have a SUR model for $\delta \neq 0$, and we can rotate u_t so $u_{yt} = \Sigma_{11}^{1/2}(\delta \Sigma_{22}^{-1/2} u_{zt} + (1 - \delta^2)^{1/2} u_{y.zt})$, where $u_{y.zt}$ is orthogonal to u_{zt}. If there are no deterministic terms in the model, this allows us to write the OLS estimate of β as

$$(\hat{\beta} - \beta) = \frac{\sum z_{t-1} u_{yt}}{\sum z_{t-1}^2} \tag{20.12}$$

$$= \Sigma_{11}^{1/2} \left(\delta \Sigma_{22}^{-1/2} (\hat{\rho} - \rho) + (1 - \delta^2)^{1/2} \frac{\sum z_{t-1} u_{y.zt}}{\sum z_{t-1}^2} \right),$$

---

[10] Σ is also the spectral density of $u_t = (u_{yt}, u_{zt})'$ scaled by 2π.

where $\hat{\rho}$ is the OLS estimate of ρ obtained from an AR(1) regression on z_t. The intuition behind the "small sample" approach becomes clear from (20.12). The second line has a sampling distribution centered on 0. The OLS coefficient is downward biased for $\rho > 0$, so if $\delta < 0$ then $\hat{\beta}$ will be upwards biased, as found in the simulations discussed above. The extent of the bias depends on the nature of the deterministic terms and is greater when constants are estimated in the regressions. Stambaugh (1999) presents analytical results for the size of the bias when $|\rho| < 1$. Amihud and Hurvich (2004) suggest a correction for the bias, and base tests on their corrected estimator. Each of these methods requires that $|\rho| < 1$. The problem with this approach is that for roots "close" to 1, the assumptions underlying the correction fail and the correction does not solve the overrejection problem and means that one needs to know whether ρ is close to 1. In general, if ρ is far enough away from 1, the original size distortion problem is small as is the correction. Hence, such methods seem applicable only for "moderate" values of ρ and it is difficult to tell the precise region where ρ is both close enough to 1 that we need to correct the statistic, yet far enough away from 1 that the correction solves the overrejection problem.

Asymptotic approaches allow for ρ smaller than 1 (but close to 1) as well as $\rho = 1$ uniformly. Following this approach and employing the expression (20.12), Elliott and Stock (1994) use the local-to-unity representation $\rho_T = 1 - \gamma / T$ to show that when $\beta = \beta_0$, t-statistics converge to the limiting distribution

$$t_{\beta=\beta_0} \Rightarrow \delta t^* + (1 - \delta^2)^{1/2} z^*, \tag{20.13}$$

where z^* is a standard (mixed) normal random variable that is independent of t^*, and t^* has a nonstandard distribution equivalent to the distribution of a t-test testing that z_t has a coefficient ρ_T when regressing z_t on z_{t-1} and lagged changes that correct for the serial correlation in u_{2t}. For $\rho = 1$, this is the well-known Dickey–Fuller distribution for a t-statistic in a unit root test. This nonstandard distribution is a function of γ, the local-to-unity parameter. Thus, when δ is small or 0, there is little size distortion in testing whether or not z_t is a good predictor of y_{t+1}; however, for values of δ further away from 0, we expect size distortions even asymptotically if ρ is sufficiently close to 1.

Understanding whether or not this problem arises empirically is relatively straightforward since the extent of the problem depends on the parameters (δ, ρ) and the sample size. We can estimate δ consistently from the data by using OLS on (20.10) and estimating the spectral density matrix using standard methods outlined in Newey and West (1987) or Andrews (1991). Estimates of the correlation from this estimated matrix are consistent, though biased towards 0. No consistent estimator is available for the local-to-unity parameter, γ. However, we can still understand empirically whether there is a problem because we can construct confidence intervals on ρ that are informative about which values of γ appear plausible. For any value of δ, size distortions in conventional t-tests are largest when ρ is near 1. For example, if $\delta = 0.5$, a nominal 10% equal-tailed test leads to lower-tail rejections of 11% and upper-tail rejections around 2%. When $\delta = 0.9$, the lower-tail rejections increase to 38% while the upper-tail rejections almost completely disappear—they are about one-tenth of 1%. As γ gets larger and ρ decreases, these size distortions disappear.

Different approaches have been suggested for constructing confidence intervals on β in (20.10). Cavanagh, Elliott, and Stock (1995) suggest a Bonferroni approach, using confidence intervals for ρ along with the distribution in (20.13) to provide intervals for β. Campbell and Yogo (2006) show gains over this method from a similar approach that is based on a rotated version of (20.10). Jansson and Moreira (2006) suggest a method that conditions on a sufficient statistic for ρ, which results in a test that maximizes power conditional on this statistic. Since this test is similar for all values of ρ, by construction it is unbiased.[11] However, this property comes at the cost of reduced power—Jansson and Moriera show that for many alternatives the Campbell and Yogo (2006) approach has better power. Elliott (2011) shows that additional stationary covariates that help explain the simultaneity leading to a nonzero δ can be used to mitigate or remove size distortions. Elliott, Müller, and Watson (2015) develop a method for constructing hypothesis tests on β that is optimal against a point in the alternative space and controls size for all values of δ. These latter two methods have the property that they do not necessarily require ρ to be near 1.

20.4.1 Empirical Application

The question of whether the dividend yield predicts stock returns has generated considerable interest in the finance literature. Intuitively, we would expect the dividend–price ratio to mean revert at least at longer horizons and so this variable could act as a measure of whether stocks are expensive (small dividend–price ratio) or cheap (large dividend–price ratio). Valkanov (2003) is one study that focuses on return predictability from the dividend–price ratio.

The return prediction model considered by Valkanov is a special case of (20.10):

$$y_{t+1} = \beta z_t + u_{1t+1},$$
$$z_{t+1} = \phi z_t + u_{2t+1}, \tag{20.14}$$

where $\phi = 1 - \gamma/T$ and γ is an unobserved nuisance parameter with $\gamma = 0$ in the unit root case, while $\gamma < 0$ for persistent regressors.

Define long-horizon variables $y_t^h = \sum_{i=0}^{h-1} y_{t+i}$, $z_t^h = \sum_{i=0}^{h-1} z_{t+i}$; Valkanov considers long-run regressions on either "short" predictors (z_t) or "long" predictors, z_t^h, which cumulate the predictor over the previous h periods:

$$y_{t+1}^h = \beta z_t + u_{1ht+1}, \tag{20.15}$$
$$y_{t+1}^h = \beta z_t^h + u_{2ht+1}. \tag{20.16}$$

Valkanov assumes that the overlap, h, is a constant fraction of the sample size, $h = \lfloor \lambda T \rfloor$, $\lambda \in (0, 1)$, and that the innovations u_t are martingale difference sequences.

Under these assumptions, Valkanov shows that the estimate $\hat{\beta}$ in regressions (20.15) of cumulated h-period returns on the single-period regressor, z_t, is not consistent and has a limiting distribution that depends on the unknown nuisance parameter, γ. Moreover, the t-statistic for β does not converge to a well-defined distribution; rather, it diverges at rate $T^{1/2}$. In practice, this means that longer horizons tend to produce higher t-statistics and that the R^2-value from the predictive regression (20.15) does not converge in probability under the null.

---

[11] Earlier tests are biased, i.e., there exist models with $\beta \neq 0$ which for some values of c have power less than size.

TABLE 20.3:

Test statistics for predictive regressions undertaken for monthly stock returns. The table reports the slope coefficient on the dividend yield (column 2) in a regression of monthly stock returns on an intercept and the dividend yield. Also reported is the t-statistic for the slope coefficient using Newey–West HAC standard errors (column 3) along with the t-statistic scaled by the square root of the sample size, T. The sample uses monthly data over the period 1926–2013.

Steps	$\hat{\beta}$	t-stat(NW)	$t/\sqrt{T}$
1M	0.0063	1.0730	0.0340
2M	0.0137	1.2625	0.0400
3M	0.0207	1.4366	0.0455
6M	0.0369	1.9525	0.0619
12M	0.0822	2.9893	0.0948
24M	0.1642	5.0512	0.1601
36M	0.2303	6.3122	0.2001
48M	0.2917	7.1642	0.2271
60M	0.3479	8.9445	0.2836

Conversely, the regression (20.16) that uses the long-run predictor z_t^h leads to a consistent estimator of β. Although the $t_{\hat{\beta}}$-statistic still does not converge to a well-defined distribution, the scaled statistic $t_{\hat{\beta}}/T^{1/2}$ converges weakly, so tests can be based on simulated critical values for this test statistic. In fact, under the alternative that $\beta \neq 0$, $\hat{\beta}$ is super-consistent and converges at rate T and the R^2 converges in probability to 1. These findings suggest that it is preferable to regress long-run variables (e.g., cumulative returns) on long-horizon predictors (cumulative dividend yields) to obtain consistent estimates of β.

As an illustration, we next consider results for an empirical application to monthly US stock returns. We use a linear model to predict stock returns by means of the dividend–price ratio at horizons $h = \{1, 2, 3, 6, 12, 24, 36, 48, 60\}$ months. Table 20.3 reports the test statistic recommended by Valkanov (2003) along with conventional t-statistics which, as we have seen, can be misleading. The highly persistent behavior for the dividend yield, together with the strongly negative correlation between innovations to stock returns and the dividend suggests that care should be exercised when interpreting the predictive regressions for this data. Indeed, although the conventional t-test appears to be highly significant at longer horizons, there is little evidence of predictability from the scaled t-test, $t_{\hat{\beta}}/\sqrt{T}$.

20.4.2 Results for Multivariate Long-Run Forecasts

A small literature has extended the univariate results to multivariate models. Stock (1996) and Phillips (1998) provide results for vector autoregressions which may or may not have unit roots—or roots close to unity—with cointegrated or near-cointegrated variables. The main result is that the forecasts and forecast errors have distributions that depend on the local-to-unity parameters, as they do in the univariate problem shown above. This makes it extremely difficult to construct uniformly consistent forecasts and confidence intervals that uniformly cover the outcome of the predicted variable. Rossi (2005b) employs results for the multivariate model to set up tests based on the difference between random walk and estimated models. This involves taking the unknown values for the local-to-unity parameters into account. Corradi, Swanson, and Olivetti (2001) study the Diebold–Mariano test in settings with cointegrated variables.

20.5 FORECAST EVALUATION

For univariate models the in-sample mean squared forecast error will converge to the variance of the unpredictable component for models that are correctly specified or close to being correctly specified (e.g., models that impose a unit root when ρ is local to unity). This is unsurprising and follows directly from the estimation error being of smaller order than variation due to the unpredictable error component.

Things get more complicated out-of-sample, although only a small body of research extends the out-of-sample results of chapters 16 and 17 to nonstationary models. We briefly discuss the main issues in a simple model to clarify the implications of using persistent data with a unit root or near unit root. A key issue with persistent data is that out-of-sample averages of squared errors typically no longer converge to the expected loss when forecasting a single outcome, so conventional estimates of performance are not necessarily indicative of the expected performance. At long horizons, sample averages of MSE values diverge as the sample size increases. These results have implications for commonly reported performance measures such as the MSE, ratios of MSE values, or R^2-values.

20.5.1 Out-of-Sample Evaluation for Univariate Models

To establish results for out-of-sample forecast evaluation, consider the simplest version of (20.2), where $d_t = 1$ and $c(L) = 1$ so the model is an AR(1) with a mean shift. We also set the initial condition to 0. The sample split point is $T_1 = [T \times r]$ so the first T_1 observations are used for the first estimation period and a recursively expanding estimation window is subsequently used up to $T + h$.

First, let h be fixed. This is a reasonable approach if we are approximating forecast horizons that are short relative to the sample size. As above,

$$y_{t+h} - y_t = (\rho^h - 1)(y_t - \phi) + \sum_{i=1}^{h} \rho^{h-i} \varepsilon_{t+i},$$

and so the infeasible forecast that uses the true values of ρ and ϕ produces an MSE of

$$\text{MSE}(\rho, \phi) = \frac{1}{T - T_1 - h} \sum_{t=T_1+1}^{T-h} \left(y_{t+h} - y_t - (\rho^h - 1)(y_t - \phi) \right)^2$$

$$= \frac{1}{T - T_1 - h} \sum_{t=T_1+1}^{T-h} u_{t+h}^2,$$

where $u_{t+h} = \sum_{i=1}^{h} \rho^{h-i} \varepsilon_{t+i}$. When u_{t+h} displays limited dependence, we expect that $\text{MSE}(\rho, \phi) \to^p E[u_{t+h}^2]$ under sufficient regularity conditions.

The MSE value associated with the random walk (rw) forecast that sets $f_{t+h|t} = y_t$ is

$$\text{MSE(rw)} = \frac{1}{T - T_1 - h} \sum_{t=T_1+1}^{T-h} (y_{t+h} - y_t)^2$$

$$= \frac{1}{T - T_1 - h} \sum_{t=T_1+1}^{T-h} \left(u_{t+h} + (\rho^h - 1)(y_t - \phi)\right)^2$$

$$= \frac{1}{T - T_1 - h} \sum_{t=T_1+1}^{T-h} \left(u_{t+h}^2 + T^{-1}\left[T(\rho^h - 1)(T^{-1/2}(y_t - \phi))\right]^2\right.$$

$$+ \left. 2T(\rho^h - 1)T^{-1}u_{t+h}(y_t - \phi)\right).$$

The second term disappears at rate T and the third term disappears even faster. Local misspecification of the model results in a term of order T^{-1} as in the regular case. Here this term has a random limit.

When ρ is estimated, the leading term remains the unpredictable component and again there will be a random term of order T^{-1} that enters the limit expression. The out-of-sample MSE now becomes

$$\text{MSE}(\hat{\rho}, \hat{\phi}) = \frac{1}{T - T_1 - h} \sum_{t=T_1+1}^{T-h} \left(y_{t+h} - (\hat{\rho}^h - 1)(y_t - \hat{\phi})\right)^2$$

$$= \frac{1}{T - T_1 - h} \sum_{t=T_1+1}^{T-h} \left(u_{t+h} + (\rho^h - 1)(y_t - \phi) - (\hat{\rho}^h - 1)(y_t - \hat{\phi})\right)^2$$

$$= \frac{1}{T - T_1 - h} \sum_{t=T_1+1}^{T-h} \left[u_{t+h} - T^{-1/2}\left[T(\hat{\rho}^h - \rho^h)T^{-1/2}(y_t - \phi)\right.\right.$$

$$\left.\left. - T(\hat{\rho}^h - 1)T^{-1/2}(\hat{\phi} - \phi)\right]\right]^2.$$

Again the leading term asymptotically will be the limit of the MSE for the known model. There is also a term disappearing at rate T which equals the limit of

$$\frac{1}{T - T_1 - h} \sum_{t=T_1+1}^{T-h} \left[T(\hat{\rho}^h - \rho^h)T^{-1/2}(y_t - \phi) - T(\hat{\rho}^h - 1)T^{-1/2}(\hat{\phi} - \phi)\right]^2.$$

The limit of this term will depend on γ; recall that $\rho = 1 - \gamma/T$. Analytic expressions that are functions of Brownian motions can be obtained but are sufficiently complicated to be of limited practical value.

Apart from the case with a known model, the limits of the $O_p(T)$ terms in the MSE expressions depend on r, the choice of the proportion for the sample split.

In this sense, the expected value of the first-order risk term from a single h-step-ahead forecast differs from the average of the out-of-sample h-step-ahead squared forecast errors. Average MSE values therefore may not be a good guide to estimating the true risk.

We can consider the same approaches when h is large relative to the sample size, so that $h = [T\lambda]$ grows at the same rate as the sample for the asymptotic results. Let the forecast error be $y_{t+h} - f_{t+h|t}$. Then the statistic of interest in the out-of-sample experiment is

$$\text{MSE} = \frac{1}{T - T_1 - h} \sum_{t=T_1+1}^{T-h} \left(y_{t+h} - f_{t+h|t}\right)^2.$$

To analyze this statistic and its large sample behavior, first assume that the model is known, so $y_{t+h} - f_{t+h|t} = y_{t+h} - \rho^h y_t$. Then we have, for known ρ,

$$T^{-1}\,\text{MSE}(\rho) = \frac{1}{T - T_1 - h} \frac{1}{T} \sum_{t=T_1+1}^{T-h} (y_{t+h} - \rho^h y_t)^2$$

$$= \frac{1}{1 - [Tr]/T - [T\lambda]/T} \frac{1}{T} \sum_{t=[Tr]+1}^{T-[T\lambda]} \left(T^{-1/2} y_{t+[T\lambda]} - \rho^h T^{-1/2} y_t\right)^2$$

$$\Rightarrow \frac{1}{1 - \lambda - r} \int_r^{1-\lambda} \left(M(s + \lambda) - e^{-\gamma\lambda} M(s)\right)^2 ds.$$

This is just the average of the limits of the unpredictable components. It depends on the split point (r), the forecast horizon (λ), as well as the degree of persistence, γ.

If instead we impose a unit root on the forecasting model and use $f_{t+h|t} = y_t$, we obtain

$$T^{-1}\overline{\text{MSE}}(\text{rw}) = \frac{1}{T - T_1 - h} \frac{1}{T} \sum_{t=T_1+1}^{T-h} (y_{t+h} - y_t)^2$$

$$= \frac{1}{1 - [Tr]/T - [T\lambda]/T} \frac{1}{T}$$

$$\times \sum_{t=[Tr]+1}^{T-[T\lambda]} \left(T^{-1/2} y_{t+[T\lambda]} - \rho^h T^{-1/2} y_t + (\rho^h - 1)M(s)\right)^2$$

$$\Rightarrow \frac{1}{1 - \lambda - r} \int_r^{1-\lambda} \left(M(s + \lambda) - e^{-\gamma\lambda} M(s)\right)^2 + (e^{-\gamma\lambda} - 1)^2 M(s)^2 ds$$

$$= \frac{1}{1 - \lambda - r} \int_r^{1-\lambda} \left(M(s + \lambda) - e^{-\gamma\lambda} M(s)\right)^2 ds$$

$$+ \frac{(e^{-\gamma\lambda} - 1)^2}{1 - \lambda - r} \int_r^{1-\lambda} M(s)^2 ds.$$

This depends on the same three parameters r, λ, and γ.

Again, we can compute the means of these limit expressions. These depend on r, the choice of sample split point, unless there is an exact unit root ($\gamma = 0$) in which case the mean is λ for all values of r. The means of these expressions are typically not the same as the means of the expressions for the same h-step-ahead forecast in a single outcome.

20.5.2 Cointegration between Forecasts and Outcomes

Under MSE loss we expect that the forecast errors $y_{t+h} - f_{t+h|t}$ are martingale difference sequences with respect to information observed at time t, i.e., $E[y_{t+h} - f_{t+h|t}|Z_t] = 0$. When y_t has a unit root, this implies that $f_{t+h|t}$ must also have a unit root and the series should be cointegrated with cointegrating vector $(1, -1)$. Some authors have used this implication to test for cointegration between outcomes and forecasts. Liu and Maddala (1992) and Aggarwal, Mohanty, and Song (1995) examine this in applications to exchange rates and macroeconomic data, respectively. Cheung and Chinn (1999) examine cointegration between macroeconomic outcomes and forecasts without imposing the cointegrating vector.

Such tests are unlikely to shed much light on whether the forecasts are efficient. For the forecasts and outcomes not to be cointegrated with the expected cointegration vector $(1, -1)$, the forecasts and outcomes would have to diverge over time. For nearly all forecasting problems we either observe y_t or a close proxy of it, so it is difficult to imagine that this could happen in practice. In this sense, the cointegration test does little to separate good from bad forecasts. For example, simply setting $f_{t+h|t} = y_t$ results in a forecast that satisfies the cointegrating restriction and the null of cointegration allows for a lot of serial correlation in the forecast errors, so the test would fail to reject for models that fail the orthogonality conditions described in chapter 16.

20.6 CONCLUSION

Forecasts based on estimated parameters of a model fitted to highly persistent data do not necessarily dominate forecasts of persistent data that impose a unit root. One reason is that the conventional autoregressive model fitted to persistent data is not necessarily the right model for departures from a unit root. Persistence could also be due to fractional integration, stochastic breaks, time-varying parameters, or some other form of model instability.

Considerations such as these have lead Stock and Watson (2003b, pages 466–467) to conclude, "The most reliable way to handle a trend in a series is to transform the series so that it does not have a trend.... Even though failure to reject the null hypothesis of a unit root does not mean the series has a unit root, it still can be reasonable to approximate the true autoregressive root as equaling one and therefore to use differences of the series rather than its levels."

21

◇◇

Forecasting Nonstandard Data

So far we have mostly concentrated on analyzing time-series forecasts where the outcome variable is real valued and follows a continuous distribution—the obvious exception being the binary case covered in chapter 12 which is sufficiently simple and tractable to warrant special treatment. There are other interesting cases of special interest. One example is count data for which the dependent variable is restricted to take on positive, integer values. This case requires its own class of prediction models and distributional assumptions—typically some variation on a Poisson or binomial model—and is covered in section 21.1. Another example is duration data which involves predicting the time before some event happens—e.g., the end of a recession or a change in the Federal funds rate. Here the outcome can follow a continuous distribution, but one that is restricted to only positive values. We cover such models in section 21.2.

Another complication arises due to data revisions. So far we have taken the information set Z_t used to generate forecasts as given and largely ignored complications arising from which pieces of information forecasters have access to and which pieces they do not observe. Section 21.3 considers practical issues related to the construction of forecasts with data that are in some ways irregular and thus require careful attention before being used by forecasters.

Data revisions is a key issue that has generated considerable interest among macro forecasters. Key variables such as GDP growth, industrial production, unemployment, and consumption expenditures are all subject to revisions. Data repositories are now being created for a number of variables to keep track of such revisions. Data revisions can affect forecasts through the conditioning information set, parameter estimation, and even model selection.

Economic data are published at different frequencies: GDP growth is published quarterly, industrial production is available on a monthly basis, payroll numbers are available weekly, while financial data such as stock prices and interest rates are available on a second-by-second basis. A set of recent papers have addressed how to construct forecasts with data observed on different dates and at different frequencies, e.g., at daily, weekly, monthly, or quarterly intervals. This gives rise to so-called mixed data sampling techniques as well as applications of the Kalman filter which can handle such issues. It also raises the issue of how we produce the best estimate—or summary measure—of the current state given the wealth of information observed at one point in time. This is an area commonly referred to as nowcasting and opens up the possibility of constructing a daily measure of the business cycle. We cover this topic in section 21.4. Section 21.5 concludes.

21.1 FORECASTING COUNT DATA

Often we are interested in forecasting outcomes for variables restricted to take on integer values. For example, y_t could have a support $\{0, 1, 2, \ldots, M\}$, where M could be infinite. In such situations it seems appropriate to take this support into account both for the elicitation of the loss function as well as in the construction of the forecasting model. It would seem as though nearly all forecasting problems fit this situation; for example, forecasting the number of jobs added to the economy fits this situation since the number of jobs is a natural number. This also holds when forecasting the level of GDP since this is often rounded to millions of dollars and in any case cannot be fractions of cents. However, for large values of M, the "count data" nature of the problem can appropriately be ignored because taking it into consideration considerably complicates the forecasting process with no hope of any gains to either predictive accuracy or our understanding of the problem. Hence, applications of count data really refer to situations where M is quite small, typically no more than 5 or 10. Examples include forecasting the size of a household, or the number of cars or computers owned by the household, or the number of individual stocks held by private investors.

There appears to be very little work done on understanding loss functions for count data problems. Nearly all point forecasting methods revolve around the provision of estimates of the conditional mean, implicitly assuming a squared error loss function.

21.1.1 Parametric Models for Count Data

Parametric approaches to modeling count data choose distributions for which the support includes only nonnegative integers. The parametric model of choice in this literature is the Poisson model. The Poisson(λ), $\lambda \geq 0$ model has support $y = \{0, 1, 2, \ldots\}$, so M is infinite and assigns probabilities $P[Y = y] = e^{-\lambda}\lambda^y/(y!)$. Both the mean and variance of the Poisson distribution equal λ and all moments exist for this distribution.

More generally, in a regression setting we could allow the Poisson parameter λ to be a function of conditioning variables, $\lambda = \lambda(z)$, once again imposing that $\lambda(z)$ is positive. The standard approach to modeling $\lambda(z)$ is to use the exponent of a linear index,

$$\lambda(z) = \exp\left(\beta'z\right). \tag{21.1}$$

Assuming that the parametric model is correctly specified, maximum likelihood procedures are available. Results are also available for other estimators. The literature on estimation of these models is specialized and lengthy; Cameron and Trivedi (1998) provide an excellent overview.

Models of the type in (21.1) can include lags of the counts y_t in z_t. In the Poisson model this would also make the variance of the outcome depend on lags of the counts. Alternatively, a wide set of dynamic models are aimed at generalizing autoregressive models. McKenzie (2003) provides a wide ranging review of such models.

A popular generalization of autoregressive specifications for use in modeling and forecasting count data is the integer autoregressive model of order p, denoted INAR(p), introduced by Al-Osh and Alzaid (1987). The most common version of this model takes the form

$$y_t = a_1 \circ y_{t-1} + a_2 \circ y_{t-2} + \cdots + a_p \circ y_{t-k} + \varepsilon_t, \tag{21.2}$$

where $a_i \circ y_{t-i} = \sum_{j=1}^{y_{t-i}} B_{j,i}$, where each of the $B_{j,i}$ terms are Bernoulli(a_i) 0–1 random variables with $0 < a_i < 1$. The motivation for this approach comes from $a_i \circ y_{t-i}$ always being integer valued—as opposed to, say, including a lagged dependent variable with a fixed coefficient. Typically, ε_t is drawn from a parametric distribution that is nonnegative and independent of $B_{j,i}$ and past values of y. This ensures that ε_t is independent of the lagged component of the model, which is integer valued, and so requires ε_t to also be integer valued. Again, the most common specification for ε_t is the Poisson(λ) distribution, although other distributions such as the binomial are also used. The distribution for ε_t is nonnegative and so has a nonzero mean, which explains the absence of a constant term in the model (21.2). Using that y_{t-i} and $B_{j,i}$ are independent, we have $E[a_i \circ y_{t-i}|y_{t-i}] = a_i y_{t-i}$. As $a_i < 1$, past values for the count have a damped effect on the current count.[1] For stationary models we require that $\sum_{i=1}^{p} a_i < 1$. Numerous variations on this model result in different properties; see McKenzie (2003).

Estimation of the INAR(1) model with T observations on y_t is relatively straightforward. Assuming ε_t to be Poisson(λ), the parameters (a, λ) can be estimated using either maximum likelihood or simply by OLS regression of y_t on a constant and y_{t-1} with $\hat{a}$ being the OLS coefficient on the lagged dependent variable, followed by setting $\hat{\lambda} = (T-1)^{-1}\sum_{t=2}^{T}(y_t - \hat{a}y_{t-1})$. Using these plug-in estimators, a prediction of the mean of y_{T+1} can be computed as $\hat{\alpha}y_T + \hat{\lambda}$, where the extra term arises through the mean of ε_T. Alternatively, since the model is fully parametric, we can construct the forecast distribution directly (Freeland and McCabe, 2004). This approach does not generally result in an integer-valued prediction, although the forecast can be rounded to the nearest integer value.

Using recursive substitution and taking expectations results in the h-step-ahead forecast,[2]

$$E[y_{t+h}|y_t] = a^h y_t + \frac{1-a^h}{1-a}\lambda, \tag{21.3}$$

where the first term is familiar from the AR(1) model and the second term arises due to the nonzero mean of ε_t.

---

[1] In the parlance of this literature, this is known as "thinning."

[2] To obtain these expressions note that $E[a \circ a \circ y_t|y_t] = E[a \circ \tilde{y}]$, where $\tilde{y} = \sum_{j=1}^{y_t} B_j$. Further, $E[a \circ \tilde{y}|y_t] = E\left[\sum_{i=1}^{\tilde{y}} \tilde{B}_i|y_t\right] = aE[\tilde{y}]$, where $\tilde{B}_i$ are independent Bernoulli(α) random variables since $\{\tilde{B}_i\}$ and $\{B_j\}$ are independent.

To construct the forecast distribution directly, consider the INAR(1) model with Poisson(λ) residuals:[3]

$$P\left(Y_{T+h} = y | y_T\right)$$

$$= \sum_{s=0}^{\min(y, y_T)} \binom{y_T}{s} a^{hs} (1 - a^h)^{y_T - s} \frac{1}{(y-s)!} \exp\left(-\lambda \frac{1 - a^h}{1 - a}\right) \left(\lambda \frac{1 - a^h}{1 - a}\right)^{y-s} \tag{21.4}$$

for each $y = 0, 1, 2, \ldots$. To derive this expression, note that there are a number of combinations of the autoregressive component and the residual that sum to y. For each of these combinations, the probability is simply the product of the binomial and Poisson terms that give rise to that sum. This follows from the independence of these terms. If the binomial part equals some value $\tilde{y} \le y$, then the Poisson part must be $(y - \tilde{y})$ for the total sum to be y. Plug-in estimates of $(\hat{a}, \hat{\lambda})$ can be used to generate an estimated h-step-ahead forecast distribution and, provided these parameters are consistently estimated, the probabilities constructed in this manner are also consistent. Bayesian prediction methods have also been developed for this class of models; see McCabe and Martin (2005).

Less parametric approaches have also been considered. McCabe, Martin, and Harris (2011) study the INAR(p) model (21.2) but leave the distribution of ε_t unrestricted apart from imposing that its support is the set of nonnegative integers. Instead they suggest a nonparametric MLE approach for estimating the distribution of the residuals; for details of this method, see section 2.3 of their paper.

21.2 FORECASTING DURATIONS

Interest in predicting the length of time it takes before some event unfolds arises in numerous situations. For example, we might be interested in predicting the length of an unemployment spell, the length of a bull market run for stock prices, or the time it takes before the Federal Reserve changes the Federal funds rate. This section studies the most common prediction models that have been used to model and predict duration data.

Specifically, let t_i denote an arrival time such as the time of execution of a financial transaction, the start of a recession, or the data for a change in the Federal Reserve's funds rate, while $y_i = t_i - t_{i-1}$ is the interval between two arrival times ("events"), the duration of which we are interested in modeling. Furthermore, following Engle and Russell (1998) let ψ_i be the conditional expectation of the ith duration given past durations,

$$\psi_i\left(y_{i-1}, \ldots, y_1; \theta\right) \equiv \psi_i = E\left[y_i | y_{i-1}, \ldots, y_1\right]. \tag{21.5}$$

---

[3] Estimation and the construction of forecast densities is more involved for the general INAR(p) model; see Bu and McCabe (2008).

Engle and Russell (1998) discuss various parameterizations of (21.5). For the case with a multiplicative error structure, they use the decomposition

$$y_i = \psi_i \varepsilon_i, \tag{21.6}$$

where $\varepsilon_i \sim$ i.i.d. has unit mean and density $p_\varepsilon(\phi)$ defined over a positive support since durations cannot be negative. Note that the duration, y_i, is modeled here as a latent variable (ψ_i) times a positive random variable (ε_i). The parameters θ and ϕ in (21.5) and (21.6) are assumed to be constant.

The autoregressive conditional duration (ACD) class of models specifies different densities $p_\varepsilon(\phi)$ in (21.6) and different functional forms for the expected duration in (21.5). The resulting duration models are very similar to the GARCH specifications considered in section 13.2. If the expected duration depends on only the most recent m durations (lags of y_i), we have

$$\psi_i = \omega + \sum_{j=1}^m \alpha_j y_{i-j}. \tag{21.7}$$

Engle and Russell (1998) also propose a dynamic ACD(m, q) specification without the limited memory feature of (21.7):

$$\psi_i = \omega + \sum_{j=1}^m \alpha_j y_{i-j} + \sum_{j=1}^q \beta_j \psi_{i-j}. \tag{21.8}$$

Under (21.8) and appropriate conditions ensuring stationarity, the unconditional expectation of the duration for this model becomes

$$E[y_i] = \frac{\omega}{1 - \sum_{j=1}^m \alpha_j - \sum_{j=1}^q \beta_j}.$$

As for GARCH models, (21.8) is similar to an ARMA(m, q) process for durations, and so we can use iterative methods such as the chain rule to form predictions of future durations.

One specification of particular interest is the ACD(1,1) model:

$$\psi_i = \omega + \alpha_1 y_{i-1} + \beta_1 \psi_{i-1}. \tag{21.9}$$

Assuming that $\alpha_1, \beta_1 \geq 0$ and $\omega > 0$, this model can capture excess dispersion in durations, consistent with much empirical evidence. Estimation of the parameters of the ACD model can be based on maximum likelihood methods provided that a distribution $p_\varepsilon(\phi)$—e.g., the exponential distribution—has been specified. Engle and Russell (1998) show empirically that ACD models can successfully be applied to model durations between transactions of IBM shares.

Bauwens et al. (2004) consider various extensions to these models. Within the context of the ACD(1,1) model (21.9) they consider densities P_ε such as the exponential, Weibull, and generalized gamma. The exponential distribution uses only a single parameter and yields a flat hazard function. The Weibull distribution nests the exponential distribution as a special case and implies a monotonic hazard function. The Weibull distribution $\varepsilon_i \sim W(\gamma, 1)$ has (noncentral) moments $E[\varepsilon_i^n] = \Gamma(1 + n/\gamma)$ and is easy to work with. The generalized gamma has two shape parameters and offers more flexibility.

Using any one of these densities, a parametric (conditional) density forecast of y can be computed as $p_\varepsilon(y_i \psi_i^{-1}) \psi_i^{-1}$.

Bauwens et al. (2004) discuss logarithmic ACD models of the form

$$\log(\psi_i) = \omega + \alpha_1 \log(y_{i-1}) + \beta_1 \log(\psi_{i-1}). \tag{21.10}$$

This specification has the advantage that it need not impose sign restrictions on the right-hand side; while durations must be nonnegative, log-durations need not satisfy this requirement. Given a density, p_ε, for the shocks ε_i in $y_i = \exp(\psi_i)\varepsilon_i$, density forecasts from log-ACD models can be generated from $p_\varepsilon(y_i(\exp(\psi_i))^{-1})(\exp(\psi_i))^{-1}$.

A third class of duration models that allows for a single dynamic stochastic factor has been proposed by Bauwens and Veredas (2004). The factor, $\tilde{\psi}_i$, is assumed to follow the process

$$\log(\tilde{\psi}_i) = \omega + \beta_1 \log(\tilde{\psi}_{i-1}) + u_i, \quad u_i \sim \text{ind } N(0, \sigma^2), \tag{21.11}$$

where, again, $y_i = \exp(\tilde{\psi}_i)\varepsilon_i$, and ε_i and u_i are mutually independent. This is labeled the stochastic conditional duration model. For example, Bauwens and Veredas show that the mean and variance of the durations implied by this model with a Weibull distribution, $\varepsilon_i \sim W(\gamma, 1)$, are

$$E[y_i] = \Gamma(1 + 1/\gamma) \exp\left(\frac{\omega}{1 - \beta_1} + \frac{\sigma^2}{2(1 - \beta_1^2)}\right),$$

$$\text{Var}(y_i) = E[y_i]^2 \left(\frac{\Gamma(1 + 2/\gamma)}{\Gamma(1 + 1/\gamma)^2} \exp\left(\frac{\sigma^2}{1 - \beta_1^2}\right) - 1\right).$$

These expressions can be used to assess the properties of the model and to generate forecasts of the mean and variance of the durations.

Bauwens et al. (2004) evaluate their duration forecasts using the probability integral transform described in chapter 18. Probability integral transform methods are well suited for the suite of models described above which are fully parametric and mostly available in closed form with the exception of the stochastic conditional duration model in (21.11), whose density forecasts have to be computed by simulation. As a benchmark a simple constant-parameter exponential distribution with i.i.d. increments (corresponding to a Poisson model) can be used, although more sophisticated dynamic benchmarks could be based on any one of the models described here.

21.3 REAL-TIME DATA

Real-time forecasting refers to the computation of forecasts by means of data restricted to be available at the point in time when the forecast is constructed. This may seem like an obvious requirement to impose and is automatically satisfied in the case of survey forecasts. Often, however, forecasts are constructed "after the fact," using simulated or pseudo out-of-sample methods—or backtests as they are called in finance—and it is for these exercises that the data availability restriction becomes relevant. Suppose, for example, that we find that we could have predicted some event, say the sharp decline in stock markets during the fall of 2008, by means of data that were not available at the time such as detailed information on banks' balance sheets or counterparty risk exposures, and the delinquency rates on mortgages. Clearly, we would not conclude from this finding that, historically, markets were not efficient. At most we could conclude that, had such data been available and used to construct a forecasting model, it might have helped investors and other decision makers predict the ensuing events.

Close attention therefore has to be paid to which data are available to forecasters in real time. Many types of macroeconomic data undergo substantial revisions. This leads to the concept of data vintages, i.e., snapshots of the data series available at a given point in time, v. For example, at the monthly frequency the 2012:12 data vintage might comprise all data available at the end of December 2012. This includes data on earlier observations known at that point in time. Data vintages can be represented as an expanding triangular shape, as shown in table 21.1. [4]

Data revisions come in different shapes. First, there are the regularly scheduled revisions for variables such as GDP. For example, in the US, an advance estimate of GDP in a given quarter is published by the Bureau of Economic Analysis near the end of the month following the end of the quarter. The following year, data from income tax records and economic census data allow this estimate to be updated to include more precise data. Second, benchmark revisions may reflect changes in how a variable is being measured. A prime example here is the change from measuring GDP using fixed weighting as opposed to chain weighting, which was introduced in 1996 for US GDP.

Let t be the date of the forecast and let z_{tv} refer to date-t observations from vintage v. Only the current data vintage—data available at time t—can be used to generate forecasts. Moreover, let β_{tv} be the parameter of the forecasting model associated with vintage v. Taking explicit account of data vintages, we can write the forecast for period $t+h$ given information at time t on the latest vintage v as

$$f_{t+h|tv} = f_v(z_{tv}, \beta_{tv}).$$

Here v refers to the vintage of data used for the model, z_{tv} is the data vintage available at time t, and β_{tv} are the parameters associated with this model.

As pointed out by Croushore (2006) and Stark and Croushore (2002), data revisions can affect the forecasting model, and the conditional forecast, $f_v(z_{tv}, \hat{\beta}_{tv})$, in three ways. First, data revisions directly affect the forecast through the conditioning information, z_{tv}. To illustrate this point, suppose we compare two forecasts from identical linear models, except that one forecast uses vintage v_1, while the other uses vintage v_2. Then the two forecasts would be $\hat{f}_{t+h|tv_1} = \hat{\beta}' z_{tv_1}$ and $\hat{f}_{t+h|tv_2} = \hat{\beta}' z_{tv_2}$, respectively. Second, the use of different data will almost certainly lead to different parameter estimates, $\hat{\beta}_{tv}$, i.e., $\hat{\beta}'_{v_1} \neq \hat{\beta}'_{v_2}$, and so $\hat{\beta}'_{v_1} z_{tv_1} \neq \hat{\beta}'_{v_2} z_{tv_2}$. Finally, the forecast model $f_v(\cdot)$ could itself change with the data vintage—a point that applies both to the choice of lag order for linear models and the inclusion of nonlinear terms for nonlinear models.

These considerations appear to matter empirically. In a study of predictability of

---

[4] In the US, the Federal Reserve Bank of Philadelphia keeps track of a real-time data set for macroeconomists; see Croushore and Stark (2001). Similar data sets have now been created for European

TABLE 21.1:
Data vintages for quarterly US real GNP.

DATE	ROUTPUT 12Q2	ROUTPUT 12Q3	ROUTPUT 12Q4	ROUTPUT 13Q1	ROUTPUT 13Q2	ROUTPUT 13Q3	ROUTPUT 13Q4	ROUTPUT 14Q1
2010:Q1	12937.7	12947.6	12947.6	12947.6	12947.6	14597.7	14597.7	14597.7
2010:Q2	13058.5	13019.6	13019.6	13019.6	13019.6	14738	14738	14738
2010:Q3	13139.6	13103.5	13103.5	13103.5	13103.5	14839.3	14839.3	14839.3
2010:Q4	13216.1	13181.2	13181.2	13181.2	13181.2	14942.4	14942.4	14942.4
2011:Q1	13227.9	13183.8	13183.8	13183.8	13183.8	14894	14894	14894
2011:Q2	13271.8	13264.7	13264.7	13264.7	13264.7	15011.3	15011.3	15011.3
2011:Q3	13331.6	13306.9	13306.9	13306.9	13306.9	15062.1	15062.1	15062.1
2011:Q4	13429	13441	13441	13441	13441	15242.1	15242.1	15242.1
2012:Q1	13502.4	13506.4	13506.4	13506.4	13506.4	15381.6	15381.6	15381.6
2012:Q2	−999	13558	13548.5	13548.5	13548.5	15427.7	15427.7	15427.7
2012:Q3	−999	−999	13616.2	13652.5	13652.5	15534	15534	15534
2012:Q4	−999	−999	−999	13647.6	13665.4	15539.6	15539.6	15539.6
2013:Q1	−999	−999	−999	−999	13750.1	15583.9	15583.9	15583.9
2013:Q2	−999	−999	−999	−999	−999	15648.7	15679.7	15679.7
2013:Q3	−999	−999	−999	−999	−999	−999	15790.1	15839.3
2013:Q4	−999	−999	−999	−999	−999	−999	−999	15965.6

money demand, Amato and Swanson (2001) find that the latest available data on the aggregate stock of money, as measured by M1 and M2, appear to predict output growth, while real-time measures of the money stock do not have such predictive power. This suggests that measures of growth in money should perhaps be omitted from real-time forecasting models. Swanson and White (1997) examine the effect of real-time data revisions on model selection.

Dependent on what is being modeled, data revisions can also lead to changes in the predicted variable. If the predicted variable is subject to revisions, what is considered the "actual" or outcome is no longer so clear-cut. Are forecasters trying to predict the first measurement of a variable because this is what will generate most publicity, or are they trying to predict some underlying, unobserved, "true" measure of the outcome which, over time, is measured with increasing precision? This important issue is often difficult to address.

Stark and Croushore (2002) consider using either the latest available data vintage, the most recent vintage prior to a benchmark revision, or the vintage obtained one year after the observation date. If information is improving over time, using the latest available vintage would seem to make most sense. In this case, data on older observation dates have had more time to "settle" and so could introduce heterogeneity in the quality of the data, with more recent data being subject to the greatest measurement errors. For GDP growth, Stark and Croushore (2002) find that forecasts are not notably improved if based on the latest available data. Conversely, for inflation forecasts, models based on the latest available data seem to lead to better forecasts than models based on the real-time data vintages.

21.4 IRREGULARLY OBSERVED AND UNOBSERVED DATA

Economic data are not always observed at equidistant points in time, and instead arrive at irregular times and may not even be observed on certain dates. Different methods have been developed to address this issue as we next describe.

21.4.1 Nowcasting

Nowcasting refers to "forecasting the present." Specifically, it is the attempt to extract information about the present state of some variable or system of variables and so is distinct from traditional forecasting; see Giannone, Reichlin, and Small (2008). Nowcasting makes sense only if the present state is unknown—otherwise nowcasting would trivially amount to checking the current value of the variable of interest. Hence, while at first nowcasting may seem like a strange concept, it is easily understood in the context of models with one or more unobserved state variables. Suppose there is a single state variable that summarizes the state of the economy, e.g., the daily point in the business cycle. Suppose, however, that this state variable is unobservable, yet related to variables that are observable. Extracting the best estimate of this "summary" state variable could well be of interest to the prediction of many other variables that depend on the current state of the economy.

There are two key reasons for approaching the nowcasting problem as a system of state variables. First, as we have seen in our discussion of real-time data, even

---

countries; see Giannone et al. (2012).

supposedly observed variables such as GDP are actually observed with measurement error. Second, because the economy is an interconnected system, information about underlying common factors can benefit from modeling the joint dynamics across multiple variables, many of which are affected by measurement error to varying degrees or simply not observed very frequently.

Many practical difficulties arise when constructing estimates of the current state of the economy or similar, unobserved, state variables at a relatively high frequency such as the daily horizon. Macroeconomic data such as GDP figures, monetary aggregates, consumption, unemployment figures, or housing starts, as well as financial data extracted from balance sheets and income statements, are published infrequently and sometimes at irregular intervals. Equivalently, the delay in the publication of macro variables differs across variables. Such nonsynchronous data releases give rise to what is often called "jagged edge" data (Banbura, Giannone, and Reichlin, 2011).

At any given point in time, a forecaster can use only such data as are available on that date and so needs to pay careful attention to which observables are in the information set. Let $Z_v = \{x_{i_{t_i}}, t_i = 1, \ldots, T_{iv}, i = 1, \ldots, n\}$ denote the information set containing the data available on day v, where T_{iv} is the date of the most recent release of variable i.

Suppose an $(n \times 1)$ vector of monthly data $x_t = (x_{1t}, x_{2t}, \ldots, x_{nt})'$ is available. Following Banbura, Giannone, and Reichlin (2011), assume that all variables have been transformed so that they are jointly stationary and lend themselves to a factor representation of the form

$$x_t = \mu + \Lambda F_t + \varepsilon_t. \tag{21.12}$$

As in chapter 10, F_t comprises r unobserved factors, Λ are factor loadings, and ε_t are idiosyncratic shocks. The factors have been demeaned, so $E[F_t] = 0$. We shall assume that the factors follow a first-order VAR process,

$$F_t = AF_{t-1} + u_t, \quad u_t \sim \text{ind } N(0, Q). \tag{21.13}$$

Finally, as in Banbura, Giannone, and Reichlin (2011), the idiosyncratic shocks in (21.12) are assumed to be driven by mutually uncorrelated AR(1) processes,

$$\varepsilon_t = \text{diag}(\alpha)\varepsilon_{t-1} + e_t, \quad e_t \sim \text{ind } N(0, \text{diag}(\sigma^2)), \tag{21.14}$$

so that $E[e_{it}e_{jt}] = 0$ for $i \neq j$. The terms $\text{diag}(\alpha)$ and $\text{diag}(\sigma^2)$ are both diagonal $(n \times n)$ matrices with values α_i and σ_i^2, respectively, in the (i, i) position on the main diagonals and 0s elsewhere.

The nowcasting approach can be illustrated by going from monthly to quarterly observations in a model for flow variables that are averaged across multiple periods. Denote monthly variables by a superscript M, Δy_t^M, and let $y_t = y_t^M - y_{t-1}^M$ be the monthly change—or growth rate if the variables are measured in logs. Suppose the monthly growth rates are unobserved but driven by the same factors as in (21.12). If the monthly data can be represented through a factor model with i.i.d. normal shocks, we have[5]

$$y_t^M = \mu^M + \Lambda^M F_t^M + \varepsilon_t^M,$$ (21.15)

$$\varepsilon_t^M = \alpha^M \varepsilon_{t-1}^M + u_t^M, \quad u_t^M \sim \text{ind } N(0, \sigma_M^2).$$

Suppose we are interested in modeling quarterly variables such as the GDP and denote such variables by a superscript Q, y_t^Q, so that $y_t^Q = (y_t^M + y_{t-1}^M + y_{t-2}^M)$. The quarter-on-quarter rate of change, $\Delta y_t^Q \equiv y_t^Q - y_{t-3}^Q$, can be approximated by Banbura, Giannone, and Reichlin (2011),

$$\Delta y_t^Q \approx y_t^M + 2y_{t-1}^M + 3y_{t-2}^M + 2y_{t-3}^M + y_{t-4}^M,$$ (21.16)

where t now increases in increments of 3, i.e., $t = 3, 6, 9, 12$. The term Δy_t is a weighted average of monthly growth rates. Notice how the weights peak in the middle and have a tent-shaped pattern. This is a typical pattern when we go from a higher frequency (monthly) to a lower frequency (quarterly) and sum across growth rates.

Defining $\bar{x}_t = (x_t', \Delta y_t^Q)'$, Banbura, Giannone, and Reichlin (2011) show that (21.12)–(21.16) can be written as a state-space model:

$$\bar{x}_t = \bar{\mu} + Z(\theta)\bar{\xi}_t,$$

$$\bar{\xi}_t = T(\theta)\bar{\xi}_{t-1} + \eta_t, \quad \eta_t \sim \text{ind } N(0, \Sigma_\eta(\theta)),$$

where the state vector $\bar{\xi}_t$ and the parameters θ are given by

$$\bar{\xi}_t = \left(F_t^M, F_{t-1}^M, F_{t-2}^M, F_{t-3}^M, F_{t-4}^M, \varepsilon_t', \varepsilon_t^M, \varepsilon_{t-1}^M, \varepsilon_{t-2}^M, \varepsilon_{t-3}^M, \varepsilon_{t-4}^M \right)',$$

$$\theta = \left\{ \mu, \mu^M, \Lambda, \Lambda^M, A, \text{diag}(\alpha), \alpha^M, \text{diag}(\sigma^2), \sigma_M^2 \right\}.$$

Note that four lags are needed due to the weights in (21.16). For the single-factor ($r = 1$) univariate case, the model gives rise to the following measurement equations:

$$\begin{pmatrix} x_t \\ \Delta y_t^Q \end{pmatrix} = \begin{pmatrix} \mu \\ 9\mu^M \end{pmatrix} + \begin{pmatrix} \Lambda & 0 & 0 & 0 & 0 & I_n & 0 & 0 & 0 & 0 & 0 \\ \Lambda^M & 2\Lambda^M & 3\Lambda^M & 2\Lambda^M & \Lambda^M & 0 & 1 & 2 & 3 & 2 & 1 \end{pmatrix} \begin{pmatrix} F_t^M \\ F_{t-1}^M \\ F_{t-2}^M \\ F_{t-3}^M \\ F_{t-4}^M \\ \varepsilon_t \\ \varepsilon_t^M \\ \varepsilon_{t-1}^M \\ \varepsilon_{t-2}^M \\ \varepsilon_{t-3}^M \\ \varepsilon_{t-4}^M \end{pmatrix}.$$

[5] Here we have simplified the model of Banbura, Giannone, and Reichlin (2011) by assuming first-order dynamics in the factors and i.i.d. shocks to y_t. Banbura et al. allow for higher-order factor dynamics and a moving average component in the innovations, ε_t^M.

Similarly, the state equations take the form

$$
\begin{pmatrix}
F_t^M \\
F_{t-1}^M \\
F_{t-2}^M \\
F_{t-3}^M \\
F_{t-4}^M \\
\varepsilon_t \\
\varepsilon_t^M \\
\varepsilon_{t-1}^M \\
\varepsilon_{t-2}^M \\
\varepsilon_{t-3}^M \\
\varepsilon_{t-4}^M
\end{pmatrix}
=
\begin{pmatrix}
A & 0 & 0 & 0 & 0 & 0 & 0 & 0 & 0 & 0 & 0 \\
I_r & 0 & 0 & 0 & 0 & 0 & 0 & 0 & 0 & 0 & 0 \\
0 & I_r & 0 & 0 & 0 & 0 & 0 & 0 & 0 & 0 & 0 \\
0 & 0 & I_r & 0 & 0 & 0 & 0 & 0 & 0 & 0 & 0 \\
0 & 0 & 0 & I_r & 0 & 0 & 0 & 0 & 0 & 0 & 0 \\
0 & 0 & 0 & 0 & 0 & \mathrm{diag}(\alpha) & 0 & 0 & 0 & 0 & 0 \\
0 & 0 & 0 & 0 & 0 & 0 & \alpha^M & 0 & 0 & 0 & 0 \\
0 & 0 & 0 & 0 & 0 & 0 & 1 & 0 & 0 & 0 & 0 \\
0 & 0 & 0 & 0 & 0 & 0 & 0 & 1 & 0 & 0 & 0 \\
0 & 0 & 0 & 0 & 0 & 0 & 0 & 0 & 1 & 0 & 0 \\
0 & 0 & 0 & 0 & 0 & 0 & 0 & 0 & 0 & 1 & 0
\end{pmatrix}
\begin{pmatrix}
F_{t-1}^M \\
F_{t-2}^M \\
F_{t-3}^M \\
F_{t-4}^M \\
F_{t-5}^M \\
\varepsilon_{t-1} \\
\varepsilon_{t-1}^M \\
\varepsilon_{t-2}^M \\
\varepsilon_{t-3}^M \\
\varepsilon_{t-4}^M \\
\varepsilon_{t-5}^M
\end{pmatrix}
+
\begin{pmatrix}
u_t \\
0 \\
0 \\
0 \\
0 \\
e_t \\
e_t^M \\
0 \\
0 \\
0 \\
0
\end{pmatrix}.
$$

Using these equations, the model can be estimated by means of a Kalman filter. In turn, the extracted states can be used to generate forecasts of monthly and quarterly growth rates. See Banbura, Giannone, and Reichlin (2011) for additional details and further discussion.

21.4.2 Mixed Data Sampling Methods

Can we improve on the forecasts of, say, monthly or quarterly variables, by utilizing data observed more often such as daily stock prices and interest rates? This is an important question since variables such as stock prices and interest rates are published on a daily basis, while payroll figures are published weekly, industrial production gets published monthly, and GDP figures are published quarterly and are subject to revisions. To make full use of all information, forecasters effectively have to use mixed frequency data. A string of papers summarized in Andreou, Ghysels, and Kourtellos (2011) have developed the so-called MIDAS—mixed data sampling—approach to estimation and forecasting that addresses this situation.[6]

Suppose we are interested in predicting a quarterly variable, Y_{t+1}^Q, using daily observations on a predictor, $X_{N_D-j,t}^D$, where N_D is the number of days in the quarter, $j = 0$ refers to the last day of quarter t, $X_{N_D,t}$, while $j = N_D - 1$ refers to the first day of quarter t, $X_{1,t}$. Note the double subscript X: the first subscript refers to days and counts backwards, while the second subscript refers to the quarter.

One option is to use only the average value of the daily variable,

$$
\bar{X}_t^Q = (X_{N_D,t}^D + X_{N_D-1,t}^D + \cdots + X_{1,t}^D)/N_D,
$$

as conditioning information in the prediction model. This measure puts the same weight on older and more recent daily observations and may not be the best approach because older information could be less relevant than more recent information.

To deal with this deficiency, another option would be to simply regress the quarterly outcome variable on all daily variables observed during the most recent and perhaps previous quarters, $\{X_{N_D,t}^D, \ldots, X_{1,t}^D, X_{N_D,t-1}^D, \ldots\}$. However, this introduces many new parameters and is likely to lead to large parameter estimation errors.

As an alternative solution to these two extremes, Ghysels, Sinko, and Valkanov (2007) propose to use data-driven weighting (or aggregation) schemes that in a

---

[6] See, for example, Ghysels, Santa-Clara, and Valkanov (2005) and Ghysels, Sinko, and Valkanov (2007).

parsimonious manner allow more weight to be placed on recent daily observations without discarding old data points by applying lag polynomials to high-frequency data. They consider an exponential Almon lag and a beta lag polynomial, both of which contain two unknown parameters (θ_1, θ_2).

The weight of the exponential Almon lag polynomial at lag j takes the form

$$w_j(\theta_1, \theta_2) = \frac{\exp(\theta_1 j + \theta_2 j^2)}{\sum_{j=1}^m \exp(\theta_1 j + \theta_2 j^2)}, \quad 1 \le j \le m, \tag{21.17}$$

where m is some truncation point. The weights of the beta lag are

$$w_j(\theta_1, \theta_2) = \frac{g(j; \theta_1, \theta_2)}{\sum_{j=1}^m g(j; \theta_1, \theta_2)}, \tag{21.18}$$

$$g(j; \theta_1, \theta_2) = j^{\theta_1 - 1}(1 - j)^{\theta_2 - 1} \frac{\Gamma(\theta_1 + \theta_2)}{\Gamma(\theta_1)\Gamma(\theta_2)},$$

$$\Gamma(\theta_1) = \int_0^\infty e^{-x} x^{\theta_1 - 1} dx.$$

Given a set of estimates of θ_1 and θ_2, the weights on the individual daily observations can be computed and the quarterly variable can be projected on the weighted average of the daily observations:

$$Y_{t+1}^Q = \mu + \beta \sum_{j=0}^{N_D - 1} w_j(\theta_1, \theta_2) X_{N_D - j, t}^D + u_{t+1}. \tag{21.19}$$

For simplicity we assumed here that only the daily data from the previous quarter are used in the forecast, but daily observations from prior periods can of course also be used with the weights (and the cutoff point, m) adjusted accordingly. For example, Ghysels, Santa-Clara, and Valkanov (2005) consider a cutoff of 250 data points.

The MIDAS approach is quite flexible and encompasses equal weights, for which (21.19) simplifies to

$$Y_{t+1}^Q = \mu + \beta \bar{X}_t^Q + u_{t+1}.$$

This case arises as a special case of the exponential Almon lag in (21.17) with $\theta_1 = \theta_2 = 0$.

It is clear from this description that once the parameters (θ_1, θ_2) have been determined, the prediction step in (21.19) is trivial and involves only linear projection, making the approach easy to use.

21.4.3 State-Space Approaches with Irregular Data

Kalman filter methods are ideally suited to handle irregularly observed data and have been used by Aruoba, Diebold, and Scotti (2009) to estimate a dynamic factor model that tracks the state of the economy at a higher frequency than that at which many variables are observed. Their approach allows for differences in observation frequencies of economic data as well as irregular patterns in the publication of observable data.

Suppose the scalar time-series process v captures the underlying state of the economy. Letting ξ_t measure the state of the economy on day t, this is assumed to follow an AR(p) process,

$$\xi_t = \sum_{i=1}^{p} \rho_i \xi_{t-i} + e_t, \quad e_t \sim \text{WN}(0, 1). \tag{21.20}$$

Here ξ_t is assumed to be unobserved and is treated as a latent variable. It is linked to a vector of observable variables, $y_t = (y_{1t}, \ldots, y_{nt})'$, each of which is a linear function of ξ_t, and a ($k \times 1$) vector of exogenous variables $w_t = (w_{1t}, \ldots, w_{kt})'$ through the equations

$$y_{it} = c_i + \beta_i \xi_t + \sum_{j=1}^{k} \delta_{ij} w_{jt} + \sum_{j=1}^{n_J} \gamma_{ij} y_{it-j \times D_{it}} + u_{it}. \tag{21.21}$$

Here D_{it} is the number of days per observation period for variable i at time t. For example, $D_{it} = 7$ for a variable measured weekly. The value of D_{it} will almost certainly vary across different variables and over time, but if we assume that $D_{it} = D_{jt} = D$, we can write (21.21) as a vector process for $y_t = (y_{1t}, \ldots, y_{nt})'$:

$$y_t = c + \beta \xi_t + \delta w_t + \sum_{j=1}^{n_J} \gamma_j y_{t-j \times D} + u_t, \tag{21.22}$$

where c, β, and u_t are ($n \times 1$) vectors, δ is ($n \times k$), and γ_j is ($n \times n$). This equation is the basis for the measurement equation of a state-space model comprising (21.20) and (21.22). Aruoba, Diebold, and Scotti (2009) provide details of how the Kalman filter and smoother can be used to extract estimates of the latent state.

Two complications arise when implementing the state-space model (21.20)–(21.22). First, suppose the model for y_{it} is tailored to the daily frequency. Many variables are not observed this often. To account for this, let $\tilde{y}_{it}$ denote the ith variable observed at the lower frequency. For stock variables $\tilde{y}_{it} = y_{it}$ if y_{it} is observed on day t; otherwise $\tilde{y}_{it} = \text{NA}$ ("not available" or missing). For flow variables, $\tilde{y}_{it} = \sum_{j=0}^{D_{it}-1} y_{it-j}$ if y_{it} is observed on day t, otherwise $\tilde{y}_{it} = \text{NA}$.

A second complication arises exactly because D_{it} will differ across variables measured at different frequencies and across time due to changes in the number of days per month or the effect of holidays. This leads to heteroskedasticity in the error terms in (21.21) and to time variation in some of the matrices of the model. Letting $z'_t = (w'_t \, y'_{t-1} \cdots y'_{t-JD})'$, while α_t captures the latent state variables, (21.20) and (21.22) lead to a state-space model of the form

$$y_t = \Psi_t \alpha_t + \Gamma_t z_t + u_t,$$

$$\alpha_{t+1} = J \alpha_t + R \eta_t,$$

for $t = 1, \ldots, T$, where $u_t \sim (0, H_t)$, and $\eta_t \sim (0, Q)$. Time variation in the matrices Ψ_t, Γ_t, and H_t reflects changes in the number of days across different months and quarters. If the model is tailored to daily data, y_t will mostly have missing observations since many variables are not observed this often. This means that the associated matrices of the state-space system (21.20)–(21.22) become sparse, a feature that can be exploited to simplify the estimation and updating equations.

Specifically, because most variables do not get observed on most days, the measurement equation on day t can be based on only the subset of those variables that are observed on this day, denoted $y_t^* = S_t y_t$, where the matrix S_t selects those elements of y_t that are observed on day t. Updates to the Kalman filter can then be based on a reduced subsystem for $y_t^* = S_t y_t$,

$$y_t^* = \Psi_t^* \alpha_t + \Gamma_t^* z_t + u_t^*, \quad u_t^* \sim N(0, H_t^*),$$

where $\Psi_t^* = S_t \Psi_t$, $\Gamma_t^* = S_t \Gamma_t$, $u_t^* = S_t u_t$, and $H_t^* = S_t H_t S_t'$. When the number of series being modeled, n, is large, this can considerable simplify updates to the model.

These methods have proved influential as the Federal Reserve Bank of Philadelphia publishes a daily time series summarizing the state of the US economy.

21.5 CONCLUSION

Recent improvements in computer power and access to large real-time data have translated into exciting developments allowing forecasters to produce daily estimates and forecasts of the state of the business cycle in a manner that would not have been feasible just a few years ago. These advances build on methods covered throughout this book such as dynamic factor models and Kalman filtering and only begin to scratch the surface of what are likely future usages of forecasting techniques in a wide area of applications.

Appendix

◇◇

This Appendix covers the Kalman filter along with some probability concepts that are used throughout the book.

A.1 KALMAN FILTER

The linear Kalman filter is essentially an algorithm for linear prediction. Introduced in 1960 by Kalman for engineering applications (Kalman, 1960), the method has found widespread use in many disciplines, including economics and finance. For models with normally distributed variables, the filter can be used to write down the likelihood function or, more generally, a pseudo likelihood. Many popular models can be rewritten in a form so that they fit in this framework. Our exposition draws on Hamilton (1994, chapter 13).

A.1.1 Basic Setting

The basic building block is what is called a model in state-space form. This assumes that the model can be written as a first-order vector autoregression in states, along with an equation relating the observed data (y) to the states (ξ). Recall from section 7.2.1 that the basic model comprises a state equation,

$$\xi_t = F\xi_{t-1} + v_t, \tag{A.1}$$

and a measurement equation,

$$y_t = H\xi_t + w_t, \tag{A.2}$$

where the error terms are both serially uncorrelated and mutually uncorrelated:

$$E\left[\begin{pmatrix} v_t \\ w_t \end{pmatrix}\begin{pmatrix} v_t' & w_t' \end{pmatrix}\right] = \begin{pmatrix} Q & 0 \\ 0 & R \end{pmatrix}. \tag{A.3}$$

Here y_t denotes observed values, while the states, ξ_t, can be either observed or unobserved. The basic setup can be generalized to let the parameters of the model F, H, Q, and R vary with time.

The state-space form is a flexible way to write many models. For example, the AR(1) model,

$$y_t = \rho y_{t-1} + \varepsilon_t, \tag{A.4}$$

can be written in state-space form as

$$\xi_t = \rho\xi_{t-1} + \varepsilon_t,$$

$$y_t = \xi_t,$$

with $F = \rho$, $H = 1$, $Q = \sigma_\varepsilon^2$, and $R = 0$. Similarly, the AR(2) model,

$$y_t = \rho_1 y_{t-1} + \rho_2 y_{t-2} + \varepsilon_t \qquad (A.5)$$

can be written in state-space form as

$$\begin{pmatrix} \xi_{1t} \\ \xi_{2t} \end{pmatrix} = \begin{pmatrix} \rho_1 & \rho_2 \\ 1 & 0 \end{pmatrix} \begin{pmatrix} \xi_{1t-1} \\ \xi_{2t-1} \end{pmatrix} + \begin{pmatrix} 1 \\ 0 \end{pmatrix} \varepsilon_t,$$

$$y_t = \xi_{1t},$$

with the obvious choice of parameters. This works out since $\xi_{2t} = \xi_{1t-1} = y_{t-1}$, so $\xi_{2t-1} = y_{t-2}$.

As a third example, the MA(1) model,

$$y_t = \varepsilon_t + \theta\varepsilon_{t-1}, \qquad (A.6)$$

can be written in state-space form

$$\begin{pmatrix} \xi_{1t} \\ \xi_{2t} \end{pmatrix} = \begin{pmatrix} 0 & 0 \\ 1 & 0 \end{pmatrix} \begin{pmatrix} \xi_{1t-1} \\ \xi_{2t-1} \end{pmatrix} + \begin{pmatrix} 1 \\ 0 \end{pmatrix} \varepsilon_t,$$

$$y_t = \begin{pmatrix} 1 & \theta \end{pmatrix} \begin{pmatrix} \xi_{1t} \\ \xi_{2t} \end{pmatrix}.$$

In this case the state (ε_t) is typically unobserved. Some models lend themselves to multiple forms of representations which, however, are identical up to a normalization.

As an example of a multivariate model, consider the VAR(2),

$$y_t = A_1 y_{t-1} + A_2 y_{t-2} + \varepsilon_t, \qquad (A.7)$$

where y_t and ε_t are $(n \times 1)$ vectors and A_i is an $(n \times n)$ matrix for $i = 1, 2$. Using the companion or state-space form, we can rewrite this as a first-order matrix autoregressive model:

$$\begin{pmatrix} \xi_{1t} \\ \xi_{2t} \end{pmatrix} = \begin{pmatrix} A_1 & A_2 \\ I_n & 0 \end{pmatrix} \begin{pmatrix} \xi_{1t-1} \\ \xi_{2t-1} \end{pmatrix} + \begin{pmatrix} I_n \\ 0 \end{pmatrix} \varepsilon_t,$$

$$y_t = \xi_{1t}.$$

As a final example, the unobserved components model,

$$\xi_t = \xi_{t-1} + v_t, \tag{A.8}$$

$$y_t = \xi_t + w_t,$$

is already in state-space form. In this example, the state is again unobserved.

Two reasons explain the popularity and usefulness of the Kalman filter. First, the state equation (A.1) is in AR(1) form which is easy to iterate forward. Specifically, the h-step-ahead forecast of the state is given by

$$E_t[\xi_{t+h}] = F^h \xi_t. \tag{A.9}$$

From a computational point of view, this greatly simplifies matters.

Second, updating the Kalman filter through newly arrived information is easy and relies on only the first two moments, essentially reducing to least squares (projection) methods. To establish the analogy, consider the bivariate normal distribution,

$$\begin{pmatrix} x_1 \\ x_2 \end{pmatrix} \sim N\left[\begin{pmatrix} \mu_1 \\ \mu_2 \end{pmatrix}, \begin{pmatrix} \Sigma_{11} & \Sigma_{12} \\ \Sigma_{21} & \Sigma_{22} \end{pmatrix} \right]. \tag{A.10}$$

Rotating the variables, we get the equivalent representation,

$$\begin{pmatrix} x_1 - \mu_1 \\ x_2 - \mu_2 \end{pmatrix} \sim N\left[\begin{pmatrix} 0 \\ \Sigma_{12}' \Sigma_{11}^{-1} (x_1 - \mu_1) \end{pmatrix}, \begin{pmatrix} \Sigma_{11} & 0 \\ 0 & \Sigma_{22} - \Sigma_{21} \Sigma_{11}^{-1} \Sigma_{21} \end{pmatrix} \right]. \tag{A.11}$$

Using this representation, it is easily seen that the optimal prediction for the second variable is

$$E[(x_2 - \mu_2)|x_1 - \mu_1] = \Sigma_{12}' \Sigma_{11}^{-1} (x_1 - \mu_1), \tag{A.12}$$

which is both the conditional mean and the formula for OLS regressions. Dropping the normality assumption, (A.12) becomes the optimal linear predictor.

A.2 KALMAN FILTER EQUATIONS

To establish the prediction and updating equations for the Kalman filter for some random variable, x, let $x_{t|t-1}$ denote the best prediction of x_t given $t-1$ information while $x_{t|t}$ is the best "prediction" (or nowcast) of x_t given time t information. Moreover, let the matrices P and G contain the MSE values associated with the forecasts of ξ_t and y_t, respectively, i.e., $P_{t|t-1} = E[(\xi_t - \xi_{t|t-1})(\xi_t - \xi_{t|t-1})']$ and $P_{t|t} = E[(\xi_t - \xi_{t|t})(\xi_t - \xi_{t|t})']$, while $G_{t|t-1} = E[(y_t - y_{t|t-1})(y_t - y_{t|t-1})']$.

Using the state (A.1), measurement (A.2), and error covariance (A.3) equations, we get the following set of prediction equations:

$$y_{t|t-1} = H\xi_{t|t-1}, \tag{A.13}$$

$$G_{t|t-1} = H P_{t|t-1} H' + R, \tag{A.14}$$

$$\xi_{t|t-1} = F\xi_{t-1|t-1}, \tag{A.15}$$

$$P_{t|t-1} = FP_{t-1|t-1}F' + Q. \tag{A.16}$$

Similarly, we have a pair of updating equations:

$$\xi_{t|t} = \xi_{t|t-1} + P_{t|t-1}H'G_{t|t-1}^{-1}(y_t - y_{t|t-1}), \tag{A.17}$$

$$P_{t|t} = P_{t|t-1} - P_{t|t-1}H'G_{t|t-1}^{-1}HP_{t|t-1}. \tag{A.18}$$

Recall that the states may be unobserved, so current-time predictions, $\xi_{t|t}$, make sense. On the other hand, there is no $y_{t|t}$ or $G_{t|t}$ since y_t is observed.

To see how the method works, start at $t = 0$. At this time we have not observed any data, so we must make our best guesses of $\xi_{1|0}$ and $P_{1|0}$ without data, which essentially means picking a pair of initial conditions. Using these along with the model parameters, the prediction equations (A.13) and (A.14) give us $y_{1|0}$ and $G_{1|0}$. Now all first period forecasts are in place.

At time $t = 1$ we observe y_1. The updating equations (A.17) and (A.18) provide us with $\xi_{1|1}$ and $P_{1|1}$. The prediction equations (A.13)–(A.16) then give us each of the forecasts for the second period.

At time $t = 2$ we observe y_2, and the cycle continues. The end result is a set of sequences of predictions of the states, $\{\xi_{t|t}\}$ and $\{\xi_{t|t-1}\}$.

A.2.1 Derivation of the Kalman Filter

Having described how the Kalman filter works, we briefly derive the prediction equations. Using (A.1) and (A.2), we have

$$\xi_{t|t-1} = E_{t-1}\xi_t = E_{t-1}[F\xi_{t-1} + v_t] = F\xi_{t-1|t-1},$$

$$y_{t|t-1} = E_{t-1}y_t = E_{t-1}[H\xi_t + w_t] = H\xi_{t-1|t-1},$$

which is (A.15) and (A.13), respectively. The MSE values follow from this. Notice that

$$\xi_t - \xi_{t|t-1} = F\xi_{t-1} + v_t - F\xi_{t-1|t-1}$$
$$= F(\xi_{t-1} - \xi_{t-1|t-1}) + v_t,$$

and so, using (A.3), we get (A.16):

$$P_{t|t-1} \equiv E[(\xi_t - \xi_{t|t-1})(\xi_t - \xi_{t|t-1})']$$
$$= FE[(\xi_{t-1} - \xi_{t-1|t-1})(\xi_{t-1} - \xi_{t-1|t-1})']F' + Q$$
$$= FP_{t-1|t-1}F' + Q,$$

where the covariance is 0 because v_t is white noise.

Turning to y_t,

$$
\begin{aligned}
G_{t|t-1} &\equiv E\left[(y_t - y_{t|t-1})(y_t - y_{t|t-1})'\right] \\
&= E\left[H(\xi_t - \xi_{t|t-1} + w_t)(\xi_t - \xi_{t|t-1} + w_t)'H'\right] \\
&= HP_{t|t-1}H' + R,
\end{aligned}
\tag{A.19}
$$

which yields (A.14).

For the updating equations, we need to work out the optimal way to update our forecast of the state given the observed y_t. The forecast errors for the state and the actual values are expected to be correlated, so

$$
\begin{pmatrix} y_t - y_{t|t-1} \\ \xi_t - \xi_{t|t-1} \end{pmatrix}
$$

has a nondiagonal variance–covariance matrix. This is where the linear projections matter. Once we know the variance–covariance matrix, we can use the observed forecast error in y_t to update ξ_t. The covariance is

$$
\begin{aligned}
E\left[(\xi_t - \xi_{t|t-1})(y_t - y_{t|t-1})'\right] &= E\left[(\xi_t - \xi_{t|t-1})(\xi_t - \xi_{t|t-1} + w_t)'H'\right] \\
&= E\left[(\xi_t - \xi_{t|t-1})(\xi_t - \xi_{t|t-1})'\right]H' \\
&= P_{t|t-1}H'.
\end{aligned}
$$

Hence, we have

$$
\begin{pmatrix} y_t - y_{t|t-1} \\ \xi_t - \xi_{t|t-1} \end{pmatrix} \sim \left[\begin{pmatrix} 0 \\ 0 \end{pmatrix}, \begin{pmatrix} G_{t|t-1} & HP_{t|t-1} \\ P_{t|t-1}H' & P_{t|t-1} \end{pmatrix} \right]
$$

and the linear predictor is

$$
\xi_t - \xi_{t|t-1} = P_{t|t-1}H'G_{t|t-1}^{-1}(y_t - y_{t|t-1}).
$$

This gives the updating equation for $\xi_{t|t}$ in (A.17).

By analogy with (A.11), the variance is[1]

$$
P_{t|t} = P_{t|t-1} - P_{t|t-1}H'G_{t|t-1}^{-1}HP_{t|t-1},
\tag{A.20}
$$

which is equation (A.18) and so completes the derivation of the prediction and updating equations.

To initialize the system, we need to choose a set of priors, i.e., starting values before we get to observe any data. We can choose from the unconditional distribution if the model is stationary. Provided that the roots of F fall outside the unit circle, this distribution is centered on 0 and hence we could just set $\xi_{1|0} = 0$ and use

$$
E[\xi_1\xi_1'] = FE[\xi_0\xi_0']F' + E[v_1v_1'],
$$

---

[1] This is the analog of $\mathrm{Var}(x_2|x_1) = \Sigma_{22} - \Sigma_{21}\Sigma_{11}^{-1}\Sigma_{12}$.

or, equivalently,

$$\Sigma_\xi = F\Sigma_\xi F' + Q,$$

so that

$$\mathrm{vec}(\Sigma_\xi) = [I_r - (F \otimes F')]^{-1}\,\mathrm{vec}(Q).$$

We could alternatively draw $\xi_{1|0}$ from a distribution with moments $(0, \Sigma_\xi)$. For nonstationary models the choice of initial values is not obvious. One approach is to leave the initial values as parameters to be estimated.

A.2.2 Examples

Any time we can write a model in state-space form, we are on our way to use the above methods. The only additional problems will be whether the model is identified and whether convergence can be achieved independent of the initialization.

A.2.2.1 *Constructing Coincident Indicators*

Common economic activity measures such as GDP are measured after the event, and so are really lagging indicators of the state of the economy. Stock and Watson (2002a) use the Kalman filter to construct an estimate of an unobserved component tracking the state of the economy, denoted C_t. Suppose we observe a set of macroeconomic variables, $Y_t = (Y_{1t}, \ldots, Y_{nt})'$ which have a common component, C_t, and idiosyncratic errors, χ_{it}, both of which follow AR(1) processes:

$$Y_{it} = \gamma_i C_t + \chi_{it},$$
$$C_t = \phi_c C_{t-1} + v_{ct},$$
$$\chi_{it} = \phi_i \chi_{it-1} + v_{it}.$$

Assuming that both C_t and χ_{it}, $i = 1, \ldots, n$ are unobserved, the state equation can be written

$$\xi_t = \begin{bmatrix} C_t \\ \chi_{1t} \\ \vdots \\ \chi_{nt} \end{bmatrix} = \begin{pmatrix} \phi_c & 0 & \cdots & 0 \\ 0 & \phi_1 & 0 & 0 \\ \vdots & 0 & \ddots & 0 \\ 0 & 0 & 0 & \phi_n \end{pmatrix} \xi_{t-1} + \begin{pmatrix} v_{ct} \\ v_{1t} \\ \vdots \\ v_{nt} \end{pmatrix},$$

while the measurement equation for the observed Y_t becomes

$$y_t = \begin{bmatrix} y_{1t} \\ y_{2t} \\ \vdots \\ y_{nt} \end{bmatrix} = \begin{pmatrix} \gamma_1 & 1 & 0 & 0 \\ \vdots & 0 & \ddots & 0 \\ \gamma_n & 0 & 0 & 1 \end{pmatrix} \xi_t.$$

A.2.2.2 Hodrick–Prescott Filter

The Hodrick–Prescott (HP) filter can be written in the form of a pair of equations,

$$\Delta^2 g_t = u_t, \tag{A.21}$$

$$y_t = g_t + w_t. \tag{A.22}$$

This is almost in state-space form, except that the unobserved state follows an AR(2) rather than an AR(1) process. This can be handled by writing the model in companion form as follows:

$$\begin{pmatrix} \xi_{1t} \\ \xi_{2t} \end{pmatrix} = \begin{pmatrix} 2 & -1 \\ 1 & 0 \end{pmatrix} \begin{pmatrix} \xi_{1t-1} \\ \xi_{2t-1} \end{pmatrix} + \begin{pmatrix} 1 \\ 0 \end{pmatrix} u_t,$$

and then notice that

$$\xi_{1t} = 2\xi_{1t-1} - 1\xi_{2t-1} + u_t$$
$$= 2\xi_{1t-1} - 1\xi_{1t-2} + u_t,$$

or, rearranging,

$$\Delta\xi_{1t} = \Delta\xi_{1t-1} + u_t,$$

so $g_t = \xi_{1t}$. The measurement equation takes the form

$$y_t = \begin{pmatrix} 1 & 0 \end{pmatrix} \xi_t + w_t,$$

which puts the HP filter in state-space form.

A.2.2.3 Missing Observations

One way to handle missing observations is to "fill out" the data using the Kalman filter to infer our best estimate of the missing data point. This can be done by treating the series that would have been observed as the state variable and relating this to the variables that are actually observed. The two must be identical for data that are observed but can otherwise differ. This means that the H matrix multiplying ξ_t in the measurement equation is not constant over time.

For example, consider a bivariate VAR(1) where some of the observations are missing for the first variable:

$$\begin{pmatrix} y_{1t} \\ y_{2t} \end{pmatrix} = \begin{pmatrix} a_{11} & a_{12} \\ a_{21} & a_{22} \end{pmatrix} \begin{pmatrix} y_{1t-1} \\ y_{2t-1} \end{pmatrix} + \begin{pmatrix} v_{1t} \\ v_{2t} \end{pmatrix}.$$

Written in state-space form, we have

$$\begin{pmatrix} \xi_{1t} \\ \xi_{2t} \end{pmatrix} = \begin{pmatrix} a_{11} & a_{12} \\ a_{21} & a_{22} \end{pmatrix} \begin{pmatrix} \xi_{1t-1} \\ \xi_{2t-1} \end{pmatrix} + \begin{pmatrix} v_{1t} \\ v_{2t} \end{pmatrix},$$

$$y_t = H_t \xi_t.$$

In periods where we observe the entire vector y_t, $H_t = I_2$. When we do not observe y_t, the measurement equation can be set to $y_{2t} = \xi_{2t}$, i.e., $y_{2t} = H_t \xi_t$, where $H_t = [0, 1]$. Both H_t and the dimension of the measurement equation change. This presents no problem for the Kalman filter, which adjusts accordingly.

When y_t is fully observed, $H_t = I$ (and $R = 0$), so the prediction equations are

$$y_{t|t-1} = \xi_{t|t-1},$$

$$G_{t|t-1} = P_{t|t-1},$$

while the updating equations become

$$\xi_{t|t} = \xi_{t|t-1} + P_{t|t-1} P_{t|t-1}^{-1}(y_t - y_{t|t-1})$$

$$= \xi_{t|t-1} + (y_t - \xi_{t|t-1})$$

$$= y_t.$$

Hence the interpolated value is the observed value. When y_{1t} is not observed, the updating equations provide an estimate of the missing observation.

A.2.3 Estimating Parameters

Many applications contain unknown parameters in the coefficient matrices F, H, Q, and R. These can be estimated using the Kalman filter which provides a convenient way to construct the likelihood or pseudo likelihood for the data.

Suppose that v_t and w_t are normally distributed. From equations (A.13) and (A.14) we then have that, given time $t - 1$ information,

$$y_{t|t-1} \sim N(H\xi_{t|t-1}, G_{t|t-1}),$$

which depends on the unknown parameter matrices F, H, Q, and R since

$$G_{t|t-1} = HP_{t|t-1}H' + R,$$

$$P_{t|t-1} = FP_{t-1|t-1}F' + Q.$$

Using the normality assumption, we can write down the likelihood for an observation, y_t, given the past elements:

$$f_{y_t}(y_t|y_{t-1}, \dots) = (2\pi)^{-n/2}|G_{t|t-1}|^{-1/2}$$

$$\times \exp\left\{-\frac{1}{2}(y_t - H'\xi_{t|t-1})'G_{t|t-1}^{-1}(y_t - H'\xi_{t|t-1})\right\}. \quad \text{(A.23)}$$

With an additional assumption on the distribution of the initial value, y_1, the likelihood for the observed data becomes

$$L = \log f_{y_1}(y_1) + \sum_{t=2}^{T} f_{y_t}(y_t|y_{t-1}, \dots). \quad \text{(A.24)}$$

This expression can be maximized to obtain estimates of the unknown parameter matrices. Of course, we need to make sure that the model is identified and also need to pay attention to the numerical method used to construct the maximum of (A.24). Complicated models may result in likelihood surfaces that are difficult to maximize over. Also, parameters such as the variances are bounded. One approach is to use regressions on the state-space model. Suppose we have "starting values" for $\{\xi_{t|t}\}$ and use seemingly unrelated regression on the model

$$\xi_t = F\xi_{t-1} + v_t,$$

$$y_t = H\xi_t + w_t,$$

resulting in estimates for F, Q, H, and R. These estimates are next used to generate new values for $\{\xi_{t|t}\}$. This is a special case of the EM algorithm (Dempster et al., 1977) and has been applied by authors such as Watson and Engle (1983).

A.2.4 Kalman Smoothing

So far we constructed estimates of the state variable $\xi_{t|t}$ using current and past data. In "real time," information dated at time t is of course the most up-to-date information available for computing estimates of period-t variables. In some situations, we might instead be interested in computing the best estimate of the unobserved state variable at time t given all past, current, and future data, $\xi_{t|T} : [\xi_{t|T} = E[\xi_t|y_1, \ldots, y_T], 0 \leq t \leq T]$.

The Kalman smoother accomplishes this using the recursive equations,

$$\xi_{t|T} = \xi_{t|t} + P_{t|t}F'P_{t+1|t}^{-1}(\xi_{t+1|T} - \xi_{t+1|t}), \tag{A.25}$$

$$P_{t|T} = P_{t|t} + P_{t|t}F'P_{t+1|t}^{-1}(P_{t+1|T} - P_{t+1|t})P_{t+1|t}^{-1}FP_{t|t}. \tag{A.26}$$

Constructing the sequences $\{\xi_{t|T}\}$ and $\{P_{t|T}\}$ is trivial and proceeds by backwards recursion, starting from the end ($t = T$). The last terms of the Kalman filter equations give the starting points for the Kalman smoother, $\xi_{T|T}$ and $P_{T|T}$. From these we can compute $\xi_{T-1|T}$ and $P_{T-1|T}$ using (A.25) and (A.26). Continuing in this fashion from the end to the start of the data, $t = T, T - 1, \ldots, 1$, gives the smoothed sequences.

The Kalman smoother equations can be derived in much the same way as the updating equations. Consider the objects $\xi_T - \xi_{T|T-1}$ and $\xi_{T-1} - \xi_{T-1|T-1}$. Given information in $y_1, \ldots, y_{T-1}$, the expectations of these are given by $E_{t-1}[(\xi_T - \xi_{T|T-1})(\xi_T - \xi_{T|T-1})'] = P_{T|T-1}$ and $E_{t-1}[(\xi_{T-1} - \xi_{T-1|T-1})(\xi_{T-1} - \xi_{T-1|T-1})'] = P_{T-1|T-1}$. Moreover, the expectation of the covariance is

$$E_{t-1}[(\xi_T - \xi_{T|T-1})(\xi_{T-1} - \xi_{T-1|T-1})']$$

$$= E_{t-1}[(F(\xi_{T-1} - \xi_{T-1|T-1}) + v_T)(\xi_{T-1} - \xi_{T-1|T-1})']$$

$$= FP_{T-1|T-1}.$$

The best linear projection of $\xi_{T-1|T} - \xi_{T-1|T-1}$ given $y_1, \ldots, y_{T-1}, \xi_T$ is

$$\xi_{T-1|T} - \xi_{T-1|T-1} = P_{T|T}F'P_{T|T-1}^{-1}(\xi_T - \xi_{T|T-1}). \tag{A.27}$$

Replacing the unobserved state, ξ_T, with our best linear projection $\xi_{T|T}$ given $y_1, \ldots, y_T$ results in (A.27). Similar arguments lead to the recursive equation for the MSE matrix. Such smoothed estimates therefore use all the information in the data up to time T. Notice a key difference: the Kalman filter is a one-sided, time-varying linear filter where the time variation arises through the updates to the variances. In contrast, the Kalman smoother is a two-sided time-varying filter.

A.3 ORDERS OF PROBABILITY

The orders of probability concept is a direct extension of the order of a nonrandom infinite sequence which we therefore use to motivate the former.

Definition. *For sequences* $\{x_n\}_{n=1}^{\infty}$ *and* $\{a_n\}_{n=1}^{\infty}$, *we say that* $x_n = o(a_n)$ *if* $\lim_{n\to\infty}(x_n/a_n) = 0$. *We say that* x_n *is* $O(a_n)$ *if there exists a constant* K *such that* $|x_n/a_n| < K$ *for all* n *that are sufficiently large.*

Examples

1. Since $\log(n)/n \to 0$ then $\log(n) = o(n)$.

2. For k fixed, $\binom{n}{k} = o(n^k)$. To see this, notice that

$$\binom{n}{k} n^{-k} = \frac{n(n-1)\cdots(n-k+1)(n-k)\cdots 1}{n^k k(k-1)\cdots 1(n-k)(n-k-1)\cdots 1}$$

$$= \frac{n(n-1)\cdots(n-k+1)}{n^k k(k-1)\cdots 1}$$

$$< \frac{n(n-1)\cdots(n-k+1)}{n^k}$$

$$\to 0.$$

We pronounce $o(a_n)$ as "little oh of order a_n" and $O(a_n)$ as "big oh of order a_n." The little oh terminology is shorthand for "disappears at this rate and any faster rate"; the big oh terminology means that for division by the specified rate the variable "hangs around," i.e., it does not get too large or too small.

Extensions to random sequences, x_n, follow naturally, although they give rise to a more complex idea of "convergence".

Definition. *For a random sequence* $\{X_n\}_{n=1}^{\infty}$ *and deterministic sequence* $\{a_n\}_{n=1}^{\infty}$, *we say that* $X_n = o_p(a_n)$ *if* $p\lim_{n\to\infty}(X_n/a_n) = 0$. *We say that* X_n *is* $O_p(a_n)$ *if there exists a constant* K *such that* $P(|x_n/a_n| < K) > 1 - \varepsilon$ *for all* $\varepsilon > 0$ *and all* n *sufficiently large.*

As an example, suppose $X_1, \ldots, X_n \sim$ ind N(0, 1), so $\bar{X} \sim N(0, n^{-1})$. Now $P[|\bar{X}| > \varepsilon] \to 0$ as $n \to \infty$ by Chebyshev, so $\bar{X}$ is $o_p(1)$. Further, consider $Z_n = n^{1/2}\bar{X}$. By the central limit theorem, $Z_n \to^d N(0, 1)$. Let $\mathcal{N}(t)$ be the c.d.f. of a standard normal variable so $P(n^{1/2}\bar{X}_n < K) \to \mathcal{N}(K)$. Choose K such that $P(|n^{1/2}\bar{X}_n| < K) \to \mathcal{N}(K) - \mathcal{N}(-K) > 1 - \varepsilon$, so $\bar{X}_n$ is $O_p(n^{-1/2})$.

We pronounce this convergence as "little oh p of order a_n." We typically use such convergence as shorthand, i.e., rather than expressing completely a term that disappears, we summarize it with a term that indicates the order at which it vanishes.

A.4 BROWNIAN MOTION AND FUNCTIONAL CENTRAL LIMIT THEORY

In chapters 17 and 20, we employ limit distributions of objects of interest that are expressed as functions of Brownian motions rather than through the usual asymptotic normal distribution. Here we give a short overview of the area, omitting technical details but providing pointers to the literature.

Just as sums (or averages) of suitably normalized random variables $\sum_{i=1}^{n} x_i$ are often well approximated in the limit by a normal distribution via the central limit theorem, suitably normalized partial sums $\sum_{i=1}^{[ns]} x_i$ (where $s \in (0, 1]$ and $[\cdot]$ takes the integer portion of its argument) are often well approximated by convergence to a Brownian motion using functional central limit theory (FCLT). In such cases, continuous functions of normalized sums will converge to that function of a normal random variable and—via the continuous mapping theorem—continuous functions of normalized partial sums converge to that function of a Brownian motion. The extension to the use of functional central limit theory allows a wider set of results to be established and is the natural tool for obtaining asymptotic distributional approximations in situations where partial sums arise.

Brownian motions are distributions for paths on $[0, 1]$ that satisfy some basic requirements. Consider $W(s)$ for $s \in [0, 1]$. If (a) $W(0) = 0$, (b) $W(b) - W(a) \sim N(0, b - a)$ for $b > a$ and (c) $W(c) - W(b)$ is independent of $W(b) - W(a)$ for $0 \leq a < b < c \leq 1$, then $W(s)$ is called a standard Brownian motion on $s \in [0, 1]$. Using (b) with $a = 0$, $b = 1$, this implies that $W(1) = N(0, 1)$, making standard Brownian motion an extension of the standard normal distribution.

Convergence of partial sums to Brownian motions via the FCLT can be written $n^{-1/2} \sum_{i=1}^{[ns]} x_i \Rightarrow W(s)$, where $\Rightarrow$ denotes weak convergence. Results require assumptions on the sequence $\{x_i\}_{i=1}^{n}$, and as with central limit distributions there exist a wide range of assumptions that result in convergence; a useful textbook reference is White (2001, chapter 7). A thorough examination is also provided in Davidson (1994).

The FCLT can be used to analyze the process $y_t = \rho y_{t-1} + u_t$, where $\rho = 1 - \gamma / T$. Let ω^2 equal the spectral density of u_t at frequency 0, which is nonnegative and assumed to be finite. If $\rho = 1$ ($\gamma = 0$) and $T^{-1/2} u_1 \to^p 0$, we have $T^{-1/2} \omega^{-1/2} y_t = T^{-1/2} \omega^{-1/2} \sum_{i=1}^{[Ts]} u_t \Rightarrow W(s)$ under suitable assumptions on the shocks u_t. If $\gamma > 0$, the FCLT can still be applied after some rearrangement and, under the same assumptions, $T^{-1/2} \omega^{-1/2} y_{[Ts]} \Rightarrow \int_0^s e^{-\gamma(s-r)} dW(r)$ via a continuous mapping theorem (Bobkoski, 1983; Phillips, 1987). This process is known as a standard Ornstein–Uhlenbeck process.

While some functions of standard Brownian motion have distributions that are normal, such as the endpoint in the previous paragraph, other cases such as the function $\int W(s)^2 ds$ are not normally distributed. In practice, many interesting functions map the Brownian motion to $\mathbb{R}$, and hence the resulting distribution can be characterized through its mean, variance, quantiles, and density even though it is typically not normal. Because the distributions are often not standard, well-known, and tabulated distributions, statistics that have these distributions as asymptotic limits require the provision of tables of critical values. See Tanaka (1996) for details on computing critical values.

Bibliography

Abadir, K. M., K. Hadri, and E. Tzavalis. 1999. The influence of VAR dimensions on estimator biases. *Econometrica* 67:163–81.

Abraham, B., and J. Ledolter. 1983. *Statistical methods for forecasting.* New York: Wiley & Sons.

Aggarwal, R., S. Mohanty, and F. Song. 1995. Are survey forecasts of macroeconomic variables rational? *Journal of Business* 68:99–119.

Aggarwal, S. K., L. M. Saini, and A. Kumar. 2009. Electricity price forecasting in deregulated markets: A review and evaluation. *International Journal of Electrical Power & Energy Systems* 31:13–22.

Aiolfi, M., C. Capistrán, and A. Timmermann. 2011. Forecast combinations. In M. P. Clements and D. F. Hendry (eds.), *Oxford Handbook of Economic Forecasting*, chap. 12, 355–88. Oxford University Press.

Aiolfi, M., and C. A. Favero. 2005. Model uncertainty, thick modelling and the predictability of stock returns. *Journal of Forecasting* 24:233–54.

Aiolfi, M., and A. Timmermann. 2006. Persistence in forecasting performance and conditional combination strategies. *Journal of Econometrics* 135:31–53.

Aït-Sahalia, Y., and M. W. Brandt. 2001. Variable selection for portfolio choice. *Journal of Finance* 56:1297–351.

Akaike, H. 1974. A new look at the statistical model identification. *IEEE Transactions on Automatic Control* 19:716–23.

Al-Osh, M., and A. A. Alzaid. 1987. First-order integer valued autoregressive (INAR(1)) process. *Journal of Time Series Analysis* 8:261–75.

Albert, J. H., and S. Chib. 1993. Bayesian analysis of binary and polychotomous response data. *Journal of the American Statistical Association* 88:669–79.

Amato, J. D., and N. R. Swanson. 2001. The real-time predictive content of money for output. *Journal of Monetary Economics* 48:3–24.

Amemiya, T. 1985. *Advanced econometrics.* Harvard University Press.

Amihud, Y., and C. M. Hurvich. 2004. Predictive regressions: A reduced-bias estimation method. *Journal of Financial and Quantitative Analysis* 39:813–41.

Amisano, G., and R. Giacomini. 2007. Comparing density forecasts via weighted likelihood ratio tests. *Journal of Business & Economic Statistics* 25:177–90.

Andersen, T. G., and T. Bollerslev. 1997. Heterogeneous information arrivals and return volatility dynamics: Uncovering the long-run in high frequency returns. *Journal of Finance* 52:975–1005.

Andersen, T. G., T. Bollerslev, P. F. Christoffersen, and F. X. Diebold. 2006. Volatility and Correlation Forecasting. In G. Elliott, C. Granger, and A. Timmermann (eds.), *Handbook of Economic Forecasting*, vol. 1, 777–878. Elsevier.

Andersen, T. G., T. Bollerslev, F. X. Diebold, and P. Labys. 2003. Modeling and forecasting realized volatility. *Econometrica* 71:579–625.

Andreou, E., E. Ghysels, and A. Kourtellos. 2011. Forecasting with mixed-frequency data. In M. Clements and D. Hendry (eds.), *Oxford Handbook of Economic Forecasting*, 225–45. Oxford University Press.

Andrews, D. W. 1991. Heteroskedasticity and autocorrelation consistent covariance matrix estimation. *Econometrica* 59:817–58.

——. 1993a. Exactly median-unbiased estimation of first order autoregressive/unit root models. *Econometrica* 61:139–165.

——. 1993b. Tests for parameter instability and structural change with unknown change point. *Econometrica* 71:821–56.

Andrews, D. W., and H.-Y. Chen. 1994. Approximately median-unbiased estimation of autoregressive models. *Journal of Business & Economic Statistics* 12:187–204.

Andrews, D. W., and W. Ploberger. 1994. Optimal tests when a nuisance parameter is present only under the alternative. *Econometrica* 62:1383–414.

Ang, A., and G. Bekaert. 2007. Stock return predictability: Is it there? *Review of Financial Studies* 20:651–707.

Ang, A., G. Bekaert, and M. Wei. 2007. Do macro variables, asset markets, or surveys forecast inflation better? *Journal of Monetary Economics* 54:1163–212.

——. 2008. The term structure of real rates and expected inflation. *Journal of Finance* 63:797–849.

Ang, A., and A. Timmermann. 2012. Regime Changes and Financial Markets. *Ann. Rev. Financ. Econ.* 4:313–337.

Artis, M., and M. Marcellino. 2001. Fiscal forecasting: The track record of the IMF, OECD and EC. *Econometrics Journal* 4:20–36.

Aruoba, S. B., F. X. Diebold, and C. Scotti. 2009. Real-Time Measurement of Business Conditions. *Journal of Business & Economic Statistics* 27:417–27.

Ashley, R., C. W. Granger, and R. Schmalensee. 1980. Advertising and aggregate consumption: An analysis of causality. *Econometrica* 48:1149–67.

Athanasopoulos, G., and F. Vahid. 2008. VARMA versus VAR for macroeconomic forecasting. *Journal of Business & Economic Statistics* 26:237–52.

Auffhammer, M. 2007. The rationality of EIA forecasts under symmetric and asymmetric loss. *Resource and Energy Economics* 29:102–21.

Avramov, D. 2002. Stock return predictability and model uncertainty. *Journal of Financial Economics* 64:423–58.

Bai, J. 1997. Estimation of a change point in multiple regression models. *Review of Economics and Statistics* 79:551–63.

——. 2003. Testing parametric conditional distributions of dynamic models. *Review of Economics and Statistics* 85:531–49.

Bai, J., and S. Ng. 2002. Determining the number of factors in approximate factor models. *Econometrica* 70:191–221.

——. 2006. Confidence intervals for diffusion index forecasts and inference for factor-augmented regressions. *Econometrica* 74:1133–50.

——. 2008. Forecasting economic time series using targeted predictors. *Journal of Econometrics* 146:304–17.

——. 2009. Boosting diffusion indices. *Journal of Applied Econometrics* 24:607–29.

Bai, J., and P. Perron. 1998. Estimating and testing linear models with multiple structural changes. *Econometrica* 66:47–78.

——. 2003. Computation and analysis of multiple structural change models. *Journal of Applied Econometrics* 18:1–22.

Baillie, R. T. 1979. Asymptotic prediction mean squared error for vector autoregressive models. *Biometrika* 66:675–8.

Baillie, R. T., and B. H. Baltagi. 1999. *Prediction from the regression model with one-way error components*, chap. 10, 255–67. Cambridge University Press.

Baillie, R. T., T. Bollerslev, and H. O. Mikkelsen. 1996. Fractionally integrated generalized autoregressive conditional heteroskedasticity. *Journal of Econometrics* 74:3–30.

Baltagi, B. H. 2013. Panel data forecasting. In G. Elliott and A. Timmermann (eds.), *Handbook of Economic Forecasting*, vol. 2, part B, 995–1024. Elsevier.

Baltagi, B. H., and Q. Li. 1992. Prediction in the one-way error component model with serial correlation. *Journal of Forecasting* 11:561–7.

Banbura, M., D. Giannone, and L. Reichlin. 2010. Large Bayesian vector auto regressions. *Journal of Applied Econometrics* 25:71–92.

——. 2011. Nowcasting. In M. P. Clements and D. F. Hendry (eds.), *Oxford Handbook of Economic Forecasting*, chap. 7, 193–224. Oxford University Press.

Banerjee, N., and A. Das. 2011. Fan Chart: Methodology and its application to inflation forecasting in India. working paper, Reserve Bank of India.

Bao, Y., T.-H. Lee, and B. Saltoglu. 2006. Evaluating predictive performance of value-at-risk models in emerging markets: A reality check. *Journal of Forecasting* 25:101–28.

Barberis, N. 2000. Investing for the long run when returns are predictable. *Journal of Finance* 55:225–64.

Barndorff-Nielsen, O. E. 2002. Econometric analysis of realized volatility and its use in estimating stochastic volatility models. *Journal of the Royal Statistical Society: Series B (Statistical Methodology)* 64:253–80.

Barndorff-Nielsen, O. E., and N. Shephard. 2002. Estimating quadratic variation using realized variance. *Journal of Applied Econometrics* 17:457–77.

Batchelor, R., and P. Dua. 1991. Blue Chip rationality tests. *Journal of Money, Credit and Banking* 23:692–705.

Bates, J. M., and C. W. Granger. 1969. The combination of forecasts. *OR* 20:451–68.

Bauer, M. D., G. D. Rudebusch, and J. C. Wu. 2012. Correcting estimation bias in dynamic term structure models. *Journal of Business & Economic Statistics* 30:454–67.

Bauwens, L., P. Giot, J. Grammig, and D. Veredas. 2004. A comparison of financial duration models via density forecasts. *International Journal of Forecasting* 20:589–609.

Bauwens, L., D. Korobilis, and G. Koop. 2011. A comparison of forecasting procedures for macroeconomic series: The contribution of structural break models. *CIRANO-Scientific Publications* No. 2011s-13.

Bauwens, L., S. Laurent, and J. V. Rombouts. 2006. Multivariate GARCH models: A survey. *Journal of Applied Econometrics* 21:79–109.

Bauwens, L., and D. Veredas. 2004. The stochastic conditional duration model: A latent variable model for the analysis of financial durations. *Journal of Econometrics* 119:381–412.

Belloni, A., and V. Chernozhukov. 2011. *High dimensional sparse econometric models: An introduction*. Springer.

Berkowitz, J. 2001. Testing density forecasts, with applications to risk management. *Journal of Business & Economic Statistics* 19:465–74.

Bernanke, B. S., J. Boivin, and P. Eliasz. 2005. Measuring the effects of monetary policy: A factor-augmented vector autoregressive (FAVAR) approach. *Quarterly Journal of Economics* 120:387–422.

Bhansali, R. J. 2002. Multi-step forecasting. *A Companion to Economic Forecasting* 206–21.

Bilson, J. F. 1981. The "Speculative efficiency" hypothesis. *Journal of Business* 435–51.

Bobkoski, M. 1983. *Hypothesis testing in nonstationary time series*. Ph.D. Thesis, Department of Statistics, University of Wisconsin. Unpublished.

Boivin, J., and M. Giannoni. 2006. DSGE models in a data-rich environment.working paper 12772, National Bureau of Economic Research.

Boivin, J., and S. Ng. 2005. Understanding and comparing factor-based forecasts. *International Journal of Central Banking* 1:117–51.

——. 2006. Are more data always better for factor analysis? *Journal of Econometrics* 132:169–94.

Bollerslev, T. 1986. Generalized autoregressive conditional heteroskedasticity. *Journal of Econometrics* 31:307–27.

——. 1990. Modelling the coherence in short-run nominal exchange rates: A multivariate generalized arch model. *Review of Economics and Statistics* 72:498–505.

Box, G. E., and G. M. Jenkins. 1970. *Time series analysis; Forecasting and control*. San Francisco: Holden-Day.

Boyes, W. J., D. L. Hoffman, and S. A. Low. 1989. An econometric analysis of the bank credit scoring problem. *Journal of Econometrics* 40:3–14.

Bregman, L. M. 1967. The relaxation method of finding the common point of convex sets and its application to the solution of problems in convex programming. *USSR Computational Mathematics and Mathematical Physics* 7:200–17.

Breiman, L. 1995. Better subset regression using the nonnegative garrote. *Technometrics* 37:373–84.

——. 1996. Bagging predictors. *Machine Learning* 24:123–40.

Breitung, J., and S. Eickmeier. 2006. Dynamic factor models. *Allgemeines Statistisches Archiv* 90:27–42.

Brier, G. W. 1950. Verification of forecasts expressed in terms of probability. *Monthly Weather Review* 78:1–3.

Brockwell, P. J., and R. A. Davis. 1996. *Introduction to time series and forecasting*. Springer.

Brown, B. W., and R. S. Mariano. 1989. Predictors in dynamic nonlinear models: Large-sample behavior. *Econometric Theory* 5:430–52.

Brown, R. 1962. *Smoothing, forecasting and prediction*. Prentice-Hall.

Brown, R. L., J. Durbin, and J. M. Evans. 1975. Techniques for testing the constancy of regression relationships over time. *Journal of the Royal Statistical Society. Series B (Methodological)* 149–92.

Brunnermeier, M. K., S. Nagel, and L. H. Pedersen. 2008. Carry trades and currency crashes. working paper 14473, National Bureau of Economic Research.

Bu, R., and B. McCabe. 2008. Model selection, estimation and forecasting in INAR(p) models: A likelihood-based Markov Chain approach. *International Journal of Forecasting* 24:151–62.

Bühlmann, P., and B. Yu. 2003. Boosting with the l_2 loss: Regression and classification. *Journal of the American Statistical Association* 98:324–39.

Burman, P., E. Chow, and D. Nolan. 1994. A cross-validatory method for dependent data. *Biometrika* 81:351–8.

Busetti, F., and J. Marcucci. 2013. Comparing forecast accuracy: A Monte Carlo investigation. *International Journal of Forecasting* 29:13–27.

Cameron, A. C., and P. Trivedi. 1998. *Regression analysis of count data*. Cambridge, UK and New York: Cambridge University Press.

Campbell, J. Y., and R. J. Shiller. 1988. The dividend-price ratio and expectations of future dividends and discount factors. *Review of Financial Studies* 1:195–228.

Campbell, J. Y., and S. B. Thompson. 2008. Predicting excess stock returns out of sample: Can anything beat the historical average? *Review of Financial Studies* 21:1509–31.

Campbell, J. Y., and M. Yogo. 2006. Efficient tests of stock return predictability. *Journal of Financial Economics* 81:27–60.

Campos, J., N. R. Ericsson, and D. F. Hendry. 2005. *General-to-specific modelling*, vol. 2. Edward Elgar.

Canjels, E., and M. W. Watson. 1997. Estimating deterministic trends in the presence of serially correlated errors. *Review of Economics and Statistics* 79:184–200.

Capistrán, C. 2008. Bias in Federal Reserve inflation forecasts: Is the Federal Reserve irrational or just cautious? *Journal of Monetary Economics* 55:1415–27.

Capistrán, C., and A. Timmermann. 2009. Forecast combination with entry and exit of experts. *Journal of Business & Economic Statistics* 27:428–40.

Cappiello, L., B. Gérard, A. Kadareja, and S. Manganelli. 2014. Measuring comovements by regression quantiles. *Journal of Financial Econometrics* 12:645–78.

Carriero, A., G. Kapetanios, and M. Marcellino. 2009. Forecasting exchange rates with a large Bayesian VAR. *International Journal of Forecasting* 25:400–17.

——. 2012. Forecasting government bond yields with large Bayesian vector autoregressions. *Journal of Banking & Finance* 36:2026–47.

Cavanagh, C. L., G. Elliott, and J. H. Stock. 1995. Inference in models with nearly integrated regressors. *Econometric Theory* 11:1131–47.

Chamberlain, G., and M. Rothschild. 1983. Arbitrage, factor structure, and mean-variance analysis on large asset markets. *Econometrica* 51:1281–304.

Chan, K.-S. 1993. Consistency and limiting distribution of the least squares estimator of a threshold autoregressive model. *Annals of Statistics* 21:520–33.

Chatfield, C. 1978. The Holt–Winters forecasting procedure. *Applied Statistics* 27:264–79.

Chauvet, M., and S. Potter. 2005. Forecasting recessions using the yield curve. *Journal of Forecasting* 24:77–103.

Chen, N.-f. 1991. Financial investment opportunities and the macroeconomy. *Journal of Finance* 46:529–54.

Chen, X. 2007. Large sample sieve estimation of semi-nonparametric models. In *Handbook of Econometrics*, vol. 6, 5549–632. Elsevier.

Chen, X., J. Racine, and N. R. Swanson. 2001. Semiparametric ARX neural-network models with an application to forecasting inflation. *IEEE Transactions on Neural Networks* 12:674–83.

Cheung, Y.-W., and M. D. Chinn. 1999. Are macroeconomic forecasts informative? Cointegration evidence from the ASA-NBER surveys. working paper, National Bureau of Economic Research.

Chib, S. 1998. Estimation and comparison of multiple change-point models. *Journal of Econometrics* 86:221–41.

Chong, Y. Y., and D. F. Hendry. 1986. Econometric evaluation of linear macro-economic models. *Review of Economic Studies* 53:671–90.

Christodoulakis, G. A., and E. C. Mamatzakis. 2009. Assessing the prudence of economic forecasts in the EU. *Journal of Applied Econometrics* 24:583–606.

Christoffersen, P. F. 1998. Evaluating interval forecasts. *International Economic Review* 39:841–62.

Christoffersen, P. F., and F. X. Diebold. 1997. Optimal prediction under asymmetric loss. *Econometric Theory* 13:808–17.

——. 1998. Cointegration and long-horizon forecasting. *Journal of Business & Economic Statistics* 16:450–6.

Clark, T., and M. McCracken. 2013. Advances in Forecast Evaluation. In G. Elliott and A. Timmermann (eds.), *Handbook of Economic Forecasting*, vol. 2, part B, 1107–1201. Elsevier.

Clark, T. E. 2011. Real-time density forecasts from Bayesian vector autoregressions with stochastic volatility. *Journal of Business & Economic Statistics* 29:327–41.

Clark, T. E., and M. W. McCracken. 2001. Tests of equal forecast accuracy and encompassing for nested models. *Journal of Econometrics* 105:85–110.

——. 2005a. Evaluating direct multistep forecasts. *Econometric Reviews* 24:369–404.

——. 2005b. The power of tests of predictive ability in the presence of structural breaks. *Journal of Econometrics* 124:1–31.

——. 2009. Tests of equal predictive ability with real-time data. *Journal of Business & Economic Statistics* 27:441–54.

——. 2010. Averaging forecasts from VARs with uncertain instabilities. *Journal of Applied Econometrics* 25:5–29.

Clark, T. E., and F. Ravazzolo. 2014. Macroeconomic forecasting performance under alternative specifications of time-varying volatility. *Journal of Applied Econometrics* 30:551–75.

Clark, T. E., and K. D. West. 2007. Approximately normal tests for equal predictive accuracy in nested models. *Journal of Econometrics* 138:291–311.

Clemen, R. T. 1989. Combining forecasts: A review and annotated bibliography. *International Journal of Forecasting* 5:559–83.

Clemen, R. T., and R. L. Winkler. 1999. Combining probability distributions from experts in risk analysis. *Risk Analysis* 19:187–203.

Clements, M. P., P. H. Franses, and N. R. Swanson. 2004. Forecasting economic and financial time-series with non-linear models. *International Journal of Forecasting* 20:169–83.

Clements, M. P., and D. F. Hendry. 1993. On the limitations of comparing mean square forecast errors. *Journal of Forecasting* 12:617–37.

——. 1996. Intercept corrections and structural change. *Journal of Applied Econometrics* 11:475–94.

——. 1998. Forecasting economic processes. *International Journal of Forecasting* 14:111–131.

Clements, M. P., and H.-M. Krolzig. 1998. A Comparison of the forecast performance of Markov-switching and threshold autoregressive models of US GNP. *Econometrics Journal* 1:47–75.

Cohen, M. A., T. H. Ho, Z. J. Ren, and C. Terwiesch. 2003. Measuring imputed cost in the semiconductor equipment supply chain. *Management Science* 49:1653–70.

Connor, G., and R. A. Korajczyk. 1986. Performance measurement with the arbitrage pricing theory: A new framework for analysis. *Journal of Financial Economics* 15:373–94.

Coppejans, M., and A. R. Gallant. 2002. Cross-validated SNP density estimates. *Journal of Econometrics* 110:27–65.

Corana, A., M. Marchesi, C. Martini, and S. Ridella. 1987. Minimizing multimodal functions of continuous variables with the "simulated annealing" algorithm. *ACM Transactions on Mathematical Software (TOMS)* 13:262–80.

Corradi, V., and N. R. Swanson. 2006a. Bootstrap conditional distribution tests in the presence of dynamic misspecification. *Journal of Econometrics* 133:779–806.

——. 2006b. Predictive density and conditional confidence interval accuracy tests. *Journal of Econometrics* 135:187–228.

——. 2006c. Predictive density evaluation. In G. Elliott, C. Granger, and A. Timmermann (eds.), *Handbook of Economic Forecasting*, vol. 1, 197–284. Elsevier.

Corradi, V., N. R. Swanson, and C. Olivetti. 2001. Predictive ability with cointegrated variables. *Journal of Econometrics* 104:315–58.

Cox, D. 1981. Statistical analysis of time series: Some recent developments. *Scandinavian Journal of Statistics* 8:93–115.

Cremers, K. M. 2002. Stock return predictability: A Bayesian model selection perspective. *Review of Financial Studies* 15:1223–49.

Croushore, D. 2006. Forecasting with real-time macroeconomic data. In G. Elliott, C. Granger, and A. Timmermann (eds.), *Handbook of Economic Forecasting*, vol. 1, 961–82. Elsevier.

Croushore, D., and T. Stark. 2001. A real-time data set for macroeconomists. *Journal of Econometrics* 105:111–30.

Dacco, R., and S. Satchell. 1999. Why do regime-switching models forecast so badly? *Journal of Forecasting* 18:1–16.

D'Agostino, A., and D. Giannone. 2006. *Comparing alternative predictors based on large-panel factor models.* ECB working paper.

Dangl, T., and M. Halling. 2012. Predictive regressions with time-varying coefficients. *Journal of Financial Economics* 106:157–81.

Davidson, J. 1994. *Stochastic limit yheory: An introduction for econometricians.* Oxford University Press.

Davies, A., and K. Lahiri. 1995. A new framework for analyzing survey forecasts using three-dimensional panel data. *Journal of Econometrics* 68:205–27.

Davies, R. B. 1977. Hypothesis testing when a nuisance parameter is present only under the alternative. *Biometrika* 64:247–54.

——. 1987. Hypothesis testing when a nuisance parameter is present only under the alternative. *Biometrika* 74:33–43.

Dawid, A. P. 1984. Present position and potential developments: Some personal views: Statistical theory: The prequential approach. *Journal of the Royal Statistical Society. Series A (General)* 278–92.

de Jong, R. M., and T. Woutersen. 2011. Dynamic time series binary choice. *Econometric Theory* 27:673–702.

De Mol, C., D. Giannone, and L. Reichlin. 2008. Forecasting using a large number of predictors: Is Bayesian shrinkage a valid alternative to principal components? *Journal of Econometrics* 146:318–28.

Del Negro, M., and F. Schorfheide. 2004. Priors from general equilibrium models for VARs. *International Economic Review* 45:643–73.

——. 2013. DSGE model-based forecasting. In G. Elliott and A. Timmermann (eds.), *Handbook of Economic Forecasting*, vol. 2, part A, 57–140. Elsevier.

Dempster, A. P., N. M. Laird, D. B. Rubin, et al. 1977. Maximum likelihood from incomplete data via the EM algorithm. *Journal of the Royal Statistical Society* 39:1–38.

Dickey, D. A., and W. A. Fuller. 1979. Distribution of the estimators for autoregressive time series with a unit root. *Journal of the American Statistical Association* 74:427–31.

Diebold, F. X. 2007. *Elements of forecasting*. 4th ed. Cengage Learning.

——. 2015. Comparing predictive accuracy, twenty years later: A personal perspective on the use and abuse of Diebold–Mariano tests. *Journal of Business and Economic Statistics* 33:1–8.

Diebold, F. X., T. A. Gunther, and A. S. Tay. 1998. Evaluating density forecasts with applications to financial risk management. *International Economic Review* 39:863–83.

Diebold, F. X., and L. Kilian. 2000. Unit-root tests are useful for selecting forecasting models. *Journal of Business & Economic Statistics* 18:265–73.

Diebold, F. X., J.-H. Lee, and G. C. Weinbach. 1994. Regime switching with time-varying transition probabilities. In *Business Cycles: Durations, Dynamics, and Forecasting*, 144–65. Princeton University Press.

Diebold, F. X., and J. A. Lopez. 1996. Forecast evaluation and combination. In G. Maddala and C. Rao (eds.), *Handbook of Statistics*. Amsterdam: North-Holland.

Diebold, F. X., and R. S. Mariano. 1995. Comparing predictive accuracy. *Journal of Business & Economic Statistics* 13:253–263.

Diebold, F. X., and J. A. Nason. 1990. Nonparametric exchange rate prediction? *Journal of International Economics* 28:315–32.

Diebold, F. X., and P. Pauly. 1987. Structural change and the combination of forecasts. *Journal of Forecasting* 6:21–40.

——. 1990. The use of prior information in forecast combination. *International Journal of Forecasting* 6:503–8.

Dimitras, A. I., S. H. Zanakis, and C. Zopounidis. 1996. A survey of business failures with an emphasis on prediction methods and industrial applications. *European Journal of Operational Research* 90:487–513.

Ding, Z., C. W. Granger, and R. F. Engle. 1993. A long memory property of stock market returns and a new model. *Journal of Empirical Finance* 1:83–106.

Doan, T., R. Litterman, and C. Sims. 1984. Forecasting and conditional projection using realistic prior distributions. *Econometric Reviews* 3:1–100.

Dobrev, D., and E. Schaumburg. 2013. Robust forecasting by regularization. working paper, Federal Reserve Board of Governors and Federal Reserve Bank of New York.

Dueker, M. 2005. Dynamic forecasts of qualitative variables: A Qual VAR model of US recessions. *Journal of Business & Economic Statistics* 23:96–104.

Dufour, J.-M. 1984. Unbiasedness of predictions from estimated autoregressions when the true order is unknown. *Econometrica* 52:209–15.

Durbin, J. 1973. Weak convergence of the sample distribution function when parameters are estimated. *Annals of Statistics* 1:279–90.

Durbin, J., and S. J. Koopman. 2012. *Time series analysis by state space methods.* No. 38 in Oxford Statistical Science Series. Oxford University Press.

Durland, J. M., and T. H. McCurdy. 1994. Duration-dependent transitions in a Markov model of US GNP growth. *Journal of Business & Economic Statistics* 12:279–88.

Edge, R. M., and R. S. Gürkaynak. 2010. How useful are estimated DSGE model forecasts for central bankers? *Brookings Papers on Economic Activity* CEPR Discussion Paper No. DP8158.

Ehrbeck, T., and R. Waldmann. 1996. Why are professional forecasters biased? Agency versus behavioral explanations. *Quarterly Journal of Economics* 111:21–40.

Elliott, G. 2006. Forecasting with trending data. In G. Elliott, C. Granger, and A. Timmermann (eds.), *Handbook of Economic Forecasting*, vol. 1, chap. 11, 555–604. Elsevier.

——. A control function approach for testing the usefulness of trending variables in forecast models and linear regression. *Journal of Econometrics* 164:79–91.

Elliott, G., A. Gargano, and A. Timmermann. 2013. Complete subset regressions. *Journal of Econometrics* 177:357–73.

——. 2015. Complete subset regressions with large-dimensional sets of predictors. *Journal of Economic Dynamics and Control* 54:86–110.

Elliott, G., D. Ghanem, and F. Krüger. 2014. Forecasting conditional probabilities of binary outcomes under misspecification. working paper, Department of Economics, UC San Diego.

Elliott, G., and T. Ito. 1999. Heterogeneous expectations and tests of efficiency in the yen/dollar forward exchange rate market. *Journal of Monetary Economics* 43:435–56.

Elliott, G., I. Komunjer, and A. Timmermann. 2005. Estimation and testing of forecast rationality under flexible loss. *Review of Economic Studies* 72:1107–25.

——. 2008. Biases in macroeconomic forecasts: Irrationality or asymmetric loss? *Journal of the European Economic Association* 6:122–57.

Elliott, G., and R. P. Lieli. 2013. Predicting binary outcomes. *Journal of Econometrics* 174:15–26.

Elliott, G., and U. K. Müller. 2006. Efficient tests for general persistent time variation in regression coefficients. *Review of Economic Studies* 73:907–40.

——. 2007. Confidence sets for the date of a single break in linear time series regressions. *Journal of Econometrics* 141:1196–218.

——. 2014. Pre and Post Break Parameter Inference. *Journal of Econometrics* 180:141–157.

Elliott, G., U. K. Müller, and M. W. Watson. 2015. Nearly optimal tests when a nuisance parameter is present under the null hypothesis. *Econometrica* 83:771–811.

Elliott, G., and J. H. Stock. 1994. Inference in time series regression when the order of integration of a regressor is unknown. *Econometric Theory* 10:672–700.

Elliott, G., and A. Timmermann. 2004. Optimal forecast combinations under general loss functions and forecast error distributions. *Journal of Econometrics* 122:47–79.

——. 2005. Optimal forecast combination under regime switching. *International Economic Review* 46:1081–102.

Embrechts, P., A. McNeil, and D. Straumann. 2002. *Correlation and dependence in risk management: properties and pitfalls*, 176–223. Cambridge: Cambridge University Press.

Engle, R. F. 1982. Autoregressive conditional heteroscedasticity with estimates of the variance of United Kingdom inflation. *Econometrica* 50:987–1007.

——. 2002. Dynamic conditional correlation: A simple class of multivariate generalized autoregressive conditional heteroskedasticity models. *Journal of Business & Economic Statistics* 20:339–50.

Engle, R. F., and G. M. Gallo. 2006. A multiple indicators model for volatility using intra-daily data. *Journal of Econometrics* 131:3–27.

Engle, R. F., and G. Gonzalez-Rivera. 1991. Semiparametric ARCH models. *Journal of Business & Economic Statistics* 9:345–59.

Engle, R. F., and C. W. Granger. 1987. Co-integration and error correction: Representation, estimation, and testing. *Econometrica* 5:251–76.

Engle, R. F., C. W. Granger, J. Rice, and A. Weiss. 1986. Semiparametric estimates of the relation between weather and electricity sales. *Journal of the American Statistical Association* 81:310–20.

Engle, R. F., and S. Manganelli. 2004. CAViaR: Conditional autoregressive value at risk by regression quantiles. *Journal of Business & Economic Statistics* 22:367–81.

Engle, R. F., and J. R. Russell. 1998. Autoregressive conditional duration: A new model for irregularly spaced transaction data. *Econometrica* 66:1127–62.

Engle, R. F., and K. Sheppard. 2001. Theoretical and empirical properties of dynamic conditional correlation multivariate GARCH. working papers 8554, National Bureau of Economic Research.

Engle, R. F., and A. D. Smith. 1999. Stochastic permanent breaks. *Review of Economics and Statistics* 81:553–74.

Engle, R. F., and M. Watson. 1981. A one-factor multivariate time series model of metropolitan wage rates. *Journal of the American Statistical Association* 76:774–81.

Engle, R. F., and B. S. Yoo. 1987. Forecasting and testing in co-integrated systems. *Journal of Econometrics* 35:143–59.

Estrella, A., and F. S. Mishkin. 1998. Predicting US recessions: Financial variables as leading indicators. *Review of Economics and Statistics* 80:45–61.

Fair, R. C., and R. J. Shiller. 1989. The informational context of ex ante forecasts. *Review of Economics and Statistics* 71:325–31.

——. 1990. Comparing information in forecasts from econometric models. *American Economic Review* 80:375–89.

Fan, J., M. Farmen, and I. Gijbels. 1998. Local maximum likelihood estimation and inference. *Journal of the Royal Statistical Society: Series B (Statistical Methodology)* 60:591–608.

Fan, J., and R. Li. 2001. Variable selection via nonconcave penalized likelihood and its oracle properties. *Journal of the American Statistical Association* 96:1348–60.

Fan, J., J. Lv, and L. Qi. 2011. Sparse high dimensional models in economics. *Annual Review of Economics* 3:291–317.

Fan, J., and Q. Yao. 2003. *Nonlinear time series*, vol. 2. Springer.

Ferguson, T. S. 1967. *Mathematical statistics: A decision theoretic approach*, vol. 7. New York: Academic Press.

Fernandez, C., E. Ley, and M. F. Steel. 2001. Benchmark priors for Bayesian model averaging. *Journal of Econometrics* 100:381–427.

Filardo, A. J. 1994. Business-cycle phases and their transitional dynamics. *Journal of Business & Economic Statistics* 12:299–308.

Fisher, R. A. 1936. The use of multiple measurements in taxonomic problems. *Annals of Eugenics* 7:179–88.

Forni, M., M. Hallin, M. Lippi, and L. Reichlin. 2000. The generalized dynamic-factor model: Identification and estimation. *Review of Economics and Statistics* 82:540–54.

Franses, P. H., and D. van Dijk. 2000. *Non-linear time series models in empirical finance*. Cambridge University Press.

Freeland, R. K., and B. P. McCabe. 2004. Forecasting discrete valued low count time series. *International Journal of Forecasting* 20:427–34.

Friedman, J. H. 2001. Greedy function approximation: A gradient boosting machine. *Annals of Statistics* 29:1189–232.

——. 2002. Stochastic gradient boosting. *Computational Statistics & Data Analysis* 38:367–78.

Friedman, J. H., and W. Stuetzle. 1981. Projection pursuit regression. *Journal of the American Statistical Association* 76:817–23.

Fuller, W. A., and D. P. Hasza. 1980. Predictors for the first-order autoregressive process. *Journal of Econometrics* 13:139–157.

Galbraith, J. W., and S. van Norden. 2011. Kernel-based calibration diagnostics for recession and inflation probability forecasts. *International Journal of Forecasting* 27:1041–57.

Gallant, A. R., and D. W. Nychka. 1987. Semi-nonparametric maximum likelihood estimation. *Econometrica* 55:363–90.

Gallant, A. R., P. E. Rossi, and G. Tauchen. 1992. Stock prices and volume. *Review of Financial Studies* 5:199–242.

Gallant, A. R., and G. Tauchen. 1989. Seminonparametric estimation of conditionally constrained heterogeneous processes: Asset pricing applications. *Econometrica* 57:1091–120.

Genest, C., and J. V. Zidek. 1986. Combining probability distributions: A critique and an annotated bibliography. *Statistical Science* 1:114–35.

Genre, V., G. Kenny, A. Meyler, and A. Timmermann. 2013. Combining expert forecasts: Can anything beat the simple average? *International Journal of Forecasting* 29:108–21.

George, E. I., D. Sun, and S. Ni. 2008. Bayesian stochastic search for VAR model restrictions. *Journal of Econometrics* 142:553–80.

Geweke, J. 1976. *The dynamic factor analysis of economic time series models.* University of Wisconsin.

——. 2005. *Contemporary Bayesian econometrics and statistics*, vol. 537. John Wiley & Sons.

Geweke, J., and G. Amisano. 2011. Optimal prediction pools. *Journal of Econometrics* 164:130–41.

Geweke, J., and C. Whiteman. 2006. Bayesian forecasting. In G. Elliott, C. Granger, and A. Timmermann (eds.), *Handbook of Economic Forecasting*, vol. 1, 3–80. Elsevier.

Ghent, A. C. 2009. Comparing DSGE-VAR forecasting models: How big are the differences? *Journal of Economic Dynamics and Control* 33:864–82.

Ghysels, E., A. Harvey, and E. Renault. 1995. *Stochastic volatility.* CIRANO.

Ghysels, E., D. R. Osborn, and P. M. Rodrigues. 2006. Forecasting seasonal time series. In G. Elliott, C. Granger, and A. Timmermann (eds.), *Handbook of Economic Forecasting*, vol. 1, 659–711. Elsevier.

Ghysels, E., P. Santa-Clara, and R. Valkanov. 2005. There is a risk-return trade-off after all. *Journal of Financial Economics* 76:509–48.

Ghysels, E., A. Sinko, and R. Valkanov. 2007. MIDAS regressions: Further results and new directions. *Econometric Reviews* 26:53–90.

Giacomini, R., and B. Rossi. 2009. Detecting and predicting forecast breakdowns. *Review of Economic Studies* 76:669–705.

——. 2010. Forecast comparisons in unstable environments. *Journal of Applied Econometrics* 25:595–620.

Giacomini, R., and H. White. 2006. Tests of conditional predictive ability. *Econometrica* 74:1545–78.

Giannone, D., J. Henry, M. Lalik, and M. Modugno. 2012. An area-wide real-time database for the euro area. *Review of Economics and Statistics* 94:1000–13.

Giannone, D., L. Reichlin, and L. Sala. 2005. Monetary policy in real time. In *NBER Macroeconomics Annual 2004*, vol. 19, 161–224. MIT Press.

Giannone, D., L. Reichlin, and D. Small. 2008. Nowcasting: The real-time informational content of macroeconomic data. *Journal of Monetary Economics* 55:665–76.

Girshick, M., and D. Blackwell. 1954. *Theory of games and statistical decisions.* McGraw Hill (1970).

Glosten, L. R., R. Jagannathan, and D. E. Runkle. 1993. On the relation between the expected value and the volatility of the nominal excess return on stocks. *Journal of Finance* 48:1779–801.

Gneiting, T., and A. E. Raftery. 2007. Strictly proper scoring rules, prediction, and estimation. *Journal of the American Statistical Association* 102:359–78.

Gneiting, T., and R. Ranjan. 2011. Comparing density forecasts using threshold- and quantile-weighted scoring rules. *Journal of Business & Economic Statistics* 29:411–422.

Goffe, W. L., G. D. Ferrier, and J. Rogers. 1994. Global optimization of statistical functions with simulated annealing. *Journal of Econometrics* 60:65–99.

Goldberger, A. S. 1962. Best linear unbiased prediction in the generalized linear regression model. *Journal of the American Statistical Association* 57:369–75.

González, A., K. Hubrich, and T. Teräsvirta. 2011. Forecasting inflation with gradual regime shifts and exogenous information. working papers, European Central Bank.

González-Rivera, G., Z. Senyuz, and E. Yoldas. 2011. Autocontours: Dynamic specification testing. *Journal of Business & Economic Statistics* 29:186–200.

Gozalo, P., and O. Linton. 2000. Local nonlinear least squares: Using parametric information in nonparametric regression. *Journal of Econometrics* 99:63–106.

Granger, C. W. J. 1969a. Investigating causal relations by econometric models and cross-spectral methods. *Econometrica* 37:424–438.

——. 1969b. Prediction with a generalized cost of error function. *Journal of the Operational Research Society* 20:199–207.

——. 1993. On the limitations of comparing mean square forecast errors: Comment. *Journal of Forecasting* 12:651–52.

——. 1999. Outline of forecast theory using generalized cost functions. *Spanish Economic Review* 1:161–73.

Granger, C. W. J., and A. P. Andersen. 1978. *An introduction to bilinear time series models.* Göttingen: Vandenhoeck und Ruprecht.

Granger, C. W. J., and M. J. Machina. 2006. Forecasting and decision theory. In G. Elliott, C. Granger, and A. Timmermann (eds.), *Handbook of Economic Forecasting*, vol. 1, 81–98. Elsevier.

Granger, C. W. J., and P. Newbold. 1973. Some comments on the evaluation of economic forecasts. *Applied Economics* 5:35–47.

——. 1986. *Forecasting economic time series.* Orlando: Academic Press.

Granger, C. W. J., and M. H. Pesaran. 2000. Economic and statistical measures of forecast accuracy. *Journal of Forecasting* 19:537–60.

Granger, C. W. J., and R. Ramanathan. 1984. Improved methods of combining forecasts. *Journal of Forecasting* 3:197–204.

Granziera, E., K. Hubrich, and H. R. Moon. 2014. A predictability test for a small number of nested models. *Journal of Econometrics* 182:174–85.

Gray, S. F. 1996. Modeling the conditional distribution of interest rates as a regime-switching process. *Journal of Financial Economics* 42:27–62.

Grenander, U. 1981. *Abstract inference.* Wiley, New York.

Guidolin, M., and A. Timmermann. 2006. An econometric model of nonlinear dynamics in the joint distribution of stock and bond returns. *Journal of Applied Econometrics* 21:1–22.

——. 2008. Size and value anomalies under regime shifts. *Journal of Financial Econometrics* 6:1–48.

——. 2009. Forecasts of US short-term interest rates: A flexible forecast combination approach. *Journal of Econometrics* 150:297–311.

Haldrup, N., and M. Ø. Nielsen. 2006. A regime switching long memory model for electricity prices. *Journal of Econometrics* 135:349–76.

Hall, R. 1978. Stochastic implications of the Life Cycle–Permanent Income hypothesis: Theory and evidence. *Journal of Political Economy* 86:971–87.

Hall, S. G., and J. Mitchell. 2007. Combining density forecasts. *International Journal of Forecasting* 23:1–13.

Hamill, T. M. 2001. Interpretation of rank histograms for verifying ensemble forecasts. *Monthly Weather Review* 129:550–60.

Hamilton, J. D. 1989. A new approach to the economic analysis of nonstationary time series and the business cycle. *Econometrica* 57:357–84.

——. 1994. *Time series analysis.* Princeton: Princeton University Press.

——. 1996. This is what happened to the oil price–macroeconomy relationship. *Journal of Monetary Economics* 38:215–20.

Hannan, E. J., and B. G. Quinn. 1979. The determination of the order of an autoregression. *Journal of the Royal Statistical Society. Series B (Methodological)* 41:190–95.

Hansen, B. E. 1994. Autoregressive conditional density estimation. *International Economic Review* 705–30.

——. 2006. Interval forecasts and parameter uncertainty. *Journal of Econometrics* 135:377–98.

——. 2007. Least squares model averaging. *Econometrica* 75:1175–89.

——. 2008a. Least-squares forecast averaging. *Journal of Econometrics* 146:342–50.

——. 2008b. Uniform convergence rates for kernel estimation with dependent data. *Econometric Theory* 24:726–48.

Hansen, P., and A. Lunde. 2011. Forecasting volatility using high frequency data. In M. P. Clements and D. F. Hendry (eds.), *Oxford Handbook of Economic Forecasting*, 525–56. Oxford University Press.

Hansen, P. R. 2005. A test for superior predictive ability. *Journal of Business & Economic Statistics* 23:365–80.

Hansen, P. R., and A. Lunde. 2005. A forecast comparison of volatility models: Does anything beat a GARCH(1,1)? *Journal of Applied Econometrics* 20:873–89.

——. 2006. Consistent ranking of volatility models. *Journal of Econometrics* 131:97–121.

Hansen, P. R., A. Lunde, and J. M. Nason. 2011. The model confidence set. *Econometrica* 79:453–97.

Hansen, P. R., and A. Timmermann. 2012. Choice of sample split in out-of-sample forecast evaluation. working paper ECO 2012/10, European University Institute.

——. 2015. Equivalence between out-of-sample forecast comparisons and Wald statistics. *Econometrica* 83 (6):2485–505.

Harrison, P., and H. H. Zhang. 1999. An investigation of the risk and return relation at long horizons. *Review of Economics and Statistics* 81:399–408.

Hartmann, P., K. Hubrich, M. Kremer, and R. J. Tetlow. 2014. Melting down: Systemic financial instability and the macroeconomy. Available at SSRN 2462567.

Harvey, D., S. Leybourne, and P. Newbold. 1997. Testing the equality of prediction mean squared errors. *International Journal of Forecasting* 13:281–91.

Harvey, D. S., S. J. Leybourne, and P. Newbold. 1998. Tests for forecast encompassing. *Journal of Business & Economic Statistics* 16:254–59.

Hastie, T., R. Tibshirani, and J. Friedman. 2009. *The elements of statistical learning.* 2nd ed. Springer.

Hendry, D. F. 1995. *Dynamic econometrics.* Oxford University Press.

Hendry, D. F., and M. P. Clements. 2004. Pooling of forecasts. *Econometrics Journal* 7:1–31.

Hendry, D. F., and K. Hubrich. 2011. Combining disaggregate forecasts or combining disaggregate information to forecast an aggregate. *Journal of Business & Economic Statistics* 29:216–27.

Henkel, S. J., J. S. Martin, and F. Nardari. 2011. Time-varying short-horizon predictability. *Journal of Financial Economics* 99:560–80.

Hjort, N. L., and G. Claeskens. 2003. Frequentist model average estimators. *Journal of the American Statistical Association* 98:879–99.

Hoel, P. G. 1947. On the choice of forecasting formulas. *Journal of the American Statistical Association* 42:605–11.

Hoeting, J. A., D. Madigan, A. E. Raftery, and C. T. Volinsky. 1999. Bayesian model averaging: A tutorial. *Statistical Science* 14:382–401.

Hong, H., and J. D. Kubik. 2003. Analyzing the analysts: Career concerns and biased earnings forecasts. *Journal of Finance* 58:313– 51.

Hong, Y. 2000. Generalized spectral tests for serial dependence. *Journal of the Royal Statistical Society: Series B (Statistical Methodology)* 62:557–74.

Hoover, K. D., and S. J. Perez. 1999. Data mining reconsidered: Encompassing and the general-to-specific approach to specification search. *Econometrics Journal* 2:167–91.

Hoque, A., J. R. Magnus, and B. Pesaran. 1988. The exact multi-period mean-square forecast error for the first-order autoregressive model. *Journal of Econometrics* 39:327–46.

Hornik, K., M. Stinchcombe, and H. White. 1989. Multilayer feedforward networks are universal approximators. *Neural Networks* 2:359–66.

Hubrich, K. 2005. Forecasting euro area inflation: Does aggregating forecasts by HICP component improve forecast accuracy? *International Journal of Forecasting* 21:119–36.

Hubrich, K., and R. J. Tetlow. 2015. Financial stress and economic dynamics: The transmission of crises. *Journal of Monetary Economics* 70:100–15.

Hylleberg, S. 1992. *Modelling seasonality*. Oxford University Press.

Hyndman, R., A. B. Koehler, J. K. Ord, and R. D. Snyder. 2008. *Forecasting with exponential smoothing: The state space approach*. Springer Science & Business Media.

Ingram, B. F., and C. H. Whiteman. 1994. Supplanting the "Minnesota" prior: forecasting macroeconomic time series using real business cycle model priors. *Journal of Monetary Economics* 34:497–510.

Inoue, A., and L. Kilian. 2005. In-sample or out-of-sample tests of predictability: Which one should we use? *Econometric Reviews* 23:371–402.

——. 2008. How useful is bagging in forecasting economic time series? A case study of US consumer price inflation. *Journal of the American Statistical Association* 103:511–22.

Jansson, M., and M. J. Moreira. 2006. Optimal inference in regression models with nearly integrated regressors. *Econometrica* 74:681–714.

Jordà, Ò., and A. M. Taylor. 2012. The carry trade and fundamentals: Nothing to fear but FEER itself. *Journal of International Economics* 88:74–90.

Joutz, F., and H. O. Stekler. 2000. An evaluation of the predictions of the Federal Reserve. *International Journal of Forecasting* 16:17–38.

Kadiyala, K. R., and S. Karlsson. 1997. Numerical methods for estimation and inference in Bayesian VAR-models. *Journal of Applied Econometrics* 12:99–132.

Kalman, R. E. 1960. A new approach to linear filtering and prediction problems. *Journal of Basic Engineering* 82:35–45.

Kandel, S., and R. F. Stambaugh. 1996. On the predictability of stock returns: An asset-allocation perspective. *Journal of Finance* 51:385–424.

Karlsson, S. 2013. Forecasting with Bayesian vector autoregression. In G. Elliott and A. Timmermann (eds.), *Handbook of Economic Forecasting*, vol. 2, part B, chap. 15, 791–897. Elsevier.

Kauppi, H., and P. Saikkonen. 2008. Predicting US recessions with dynamic binary response models. *Review of Economics and Statistics* 90:777–91.

Kemp, G. C. 1999. The behavior of forecast errors from a nearly integrated AR(1) model as both sample size and forecast horizon become large. *Econometric Theory* 15:238–56.

Kendall, M. G. 1954. Note on bias in the estimation of autocorrelation. *Biometrika* 41:403–04.

Kendall, M. G., and A. Stuart. 1961. *The advanced theory of statistics. Volumes II and III*. Hafner.

Kilian, L., and S. Manganelli. 2008. The central banker as a risk manager: Estimating the Federal Reserve's preferences under Greenspan. *Journal of Money, Credit and Banking* 40:1103–29.

Kilian, L., and M. P. Taylor. 2003. Why is it so difficult to beat the random walk forecast of exchange rates? *Journal of International Economics* 60:85–107.

Kim, C.-J., and C. R. Nelson. 1999. *State-space models with regime switching: Classical and Gibbs-sampling approaches with applications*. MIT Press.

Kim, S., N. Shephard, and S. Chib. 1998. Stochastic volatility: Likelihood inference and comparison with ARCH models. *Review of Economic Studies* 65:361–93.

Kinal, T., and J. Ratner. 1986. A VAR forecasting model of a regional economy: Its construction and comparative accuracy. *International Regional Science Review* 10:113–26.

Knight, K., and W. Fu. 2000. Asymptotics for Lasso-type estimators. *Annals of Statistics* 28:1356–78.

Koenker, R., and G. Bassett. 1978. Regression quantiles. *Econometrica* 46:33–50.

Komunjer, I. 2005. Quasi-maximum likelihood estimation for conditional quantiles. *Journal of Econometrics* 128:137–64.

———. 2013. Quantile Prediction. In G. Elliott and A. Timmermann (eds.), *Handbook of Economic Forecasting*, vol. 2, part B, chap. 17, 961–994. Elsevier.

Komunjer, I., and M. T. Owyang. 2012. Multivariate forecast evaluation and rationality testing. *Review of Economics and Statistics* 94:1066–80.

Koop, G. 2003. *Bayesian Econometrics*. New York: Wiley.

Koop, G., and D. Korobilis. 2010. *Bayesian multivariate time series methods for empirical macroeconomics*. Now Publishers.

Koop, G., and S. M. Potter. 2007. Estimation and forecasting in models with multiple breaks. *Review of Economic Studies* 74:763–89.

Koop, G. M. 2013. Forecasting with medium and large Bayesian VARs. *Journal of Applied Econometrics* 28:177–203.

Kuan, C.-M., and H. White. 1994. Artificial neural networks: An econometric perspective. *Econometric Reviews* 13:1–91.

Kuester, K., S. Mittnik, and M. S. Paolella. 2006. Value-at-risk prediction: A comparison of alternative strategies. *Journal of Financial Econometrics* 4:53–89.

Lahiri, K., H. Peng, and Y. Zhao. 2013. Machine learning and forecast combination in incomplete panels. Unpublished Discussion Paper.

Laster, D., P. Bennett, and I. S. Geoum. 1999. Rational bias in macroeconomic forecasts. *Quarterly Journal of Economics* 114:293–318.

Laurent, S., J. V. Rombouts, and F. Violante. 2013. On loss functions and ranking forecasting performances of multivariate volatility models. *Journal of Econometrics* 173:1–10.

Leeb, H., and B. M. Pötscher. 2005. Model selection and inference: Facts and fiction. *Econometric Theory* 21:21–59.

Lehmann, E. L., and J. P. Romano. 2006. *Testing statistical hypotheses*. Springer Science & Business Media.

Leitch, G., and J. E. Tanner. 1991. Economic forecast evaluation: Profits versus the conventional error measures. *American Economic Review* 81:580–90.

Leng, C., Y. Lin, and G. Wahba. 2006. A note on the Lasso and related procedures in model selection. *Statistica Sinica* 16:1273–84.

Lettau, M., and S. Ludvigson. 2001. Consumption, aggregate wealth, and expected stock returns. *Journal of Finance* 56:815–49.

Leung, M. T., H. Daouk, and A.-S. Chen. 2000. Forecasting stock indices: A comparison of classification and level estimation models. *International Journal of Forecasting* 16:173–90.

Ley, E., and M. F. Steel. 2009. On the effect of prior assumptions in Bayesian model averaging with applications to growth regression. *Journal of Applied Econometrics* 24:651–74.

Lieli, R. P., and M. Springborn. 2013. Closing the gap between risk estimation and decision making: Efficient management of trade-related invasive species risk. *Review of Economics and Statistics* 95:632–45.

Lieli, R. P., and M. B. Stinchcombe. 2013. On the recoverability of forecasters' preferences. *Econometric Theory* 29:517–44.

Lin, J.-L., and R. S. Tsay. 1996. Co-integration constraint and forecasting: An empirical examination. *Journal of Applied Econometrics* 11:519–38.

Lin, W.-L. 1992. Alternative estimators for factor GARCH models–A Monte Carlo comparison. *Journal of Applied Econometrics* 7:259–79.

Litterman, R. 1979. Techniques of forecasting using vector autoregressions. working paper, Federal Reserve Bank of Minneapolis.

Litterman, R. B. 1986. Forecasting with Bayesian vector autoregressions–Five years of experience. *Journal of Business & Economic Statistics* 4:25–38.

Liu, P. C., and G. S. Maddala. 1992. Rationality of survey data and tests for market efficiency in the foreign exchange markets. *Journal of International Money and Finance* 11:366–81.

Lütkepohl, H. 2006. Forecasting with VARMA models. In G. Elliott, C. Granger, and A. Timmermann (eds.), *Handbook of Economic Forecasting*, vol. 1, 287–325. Elsevier.

——. 2007. *New introduction to multiple time series analysis*. Springer.

Maddala, G. S. 1986. *Limited-dependent and qualitative variables in econometrics*. Cambridge University Press.

Maekawa, K. 1987. Finite sample properties of several predictors from an autoregressive model. *Econometric Theory* 3:359–70.

Magnus, J. R., and B. Pesaran. 1989. The exact multi-period mean-square forecast error for the first-order autoregressive model with an intercept. *Journal of Econometrics* 42:157–79.

Magnus, J. R., O. Powell, and P. Prüfer. 2010. A comparison of two model averaging techniques with an application to growth empirics. *Journal of Econometrics* 154:139–53.

Malinvaud, E. 1970. *Statistical methods of econometrics*. American Elsevier.

Mallows, C. L. 1973. Some comments on C_p. *Technometrics* 15:661–75.

Mankiw, N. G., and M. D. Shapiro. 1986. Do we reject too often?: Small sample properties of tests of rational expectations models. *Economics Letters* 20:139–45.

Manski, C. F. 1975. Maximum score estimation of the stochastic utility model of choice. *Journal of Econometrics* 3:205–28.

——. 1985. Semiparametric analysis of discrete response: Asymptotic properties of the maximum score estimator. *Journal of Econometrics* 27:313–33.

Manski, C. F., and T. S. Thompson. 1989. Estimation of best predictors of binary response. *Journal of Econometrics* 40:97–123.

Manso, G. 2013. Feedback effects of credit ratings. *Journal of Financial Economics* 109:535–48.

Marcellino, M. 2000. Forecast Bias and MSFE encompassing. *Oxford Bulletin of Economics and Statistics* 62:533–42.

——. 2004. Forecast pooling for European macroeconomic variables. *Oxford Bulletin of Economics and Statistics* 66:91–112.

Marcellino, M., J. H. Stock, and M. W. Watson. 2003. Macroeconomic forecasting in the euro area: Country specific versus area-wide information. *European Economic Review* 47:1–18.

——. 2006. A comparison of direct and iterated multistep AR methods for forecasting macroeconomic time series. *Journal of Econometrics* 135:499–526.

Marcucci, J. 2005. Forecasting stock market volatility with regime-switching GARCH models. *Studies in Nonlinear Dynamics & Econometrics* 9:1–55.

Marriott, F., and J. Pope. 1954. Bias in the estimation of autocorrelations. *Biometrika* 41:390–402.

Martin, D. 1977. Early warning of bank failure: A logit regression approach. *Journal of Banking & Finance* 1:249–76.

McCabe, B., and G. M. Martin. 2005. Bayesian predictions of low count time series. *International Journal of Forecasting* 21:315–30.

McCabe, B. P., G. M. Martin, and D. Harris. 2011. Efficient probabilistic forecasts for counts. *Journal of the Royal Statistical Society: Series B (Statistical Methodology)* 73:253–72.

McConnell, M. M., and G. Perez-Quiros. 2000. Output fluctuations in the United States: What has changed since the early 1980s? *American Economic Review* 90:1464–76.

McCracken, M. W. 2000. Robust out-of-sample inference. *Journal of Econometrics* 99:195–223.

——. 2007. Asymptotics for out of sample tests of Granger causality. *Journal of Econometrics* 140:719–752.

McKenzie, E. 2003. Discrete variate time series. In *Handbook of Statistics*, vol. 21, 573–606. Amsterdam: Elsevier Science.

Meese, R. A., and K. Rogoff. 1983. Empirical exchange rate models of the seventies: Do they fit out of sample? *Journal of International Economics* 14:3–24.

Min, C.-k., and A. Zellner. 1993. Bayesian and non-Bayesian methods for combining models and forecasts with applications to forecasting international growth rates. *Journal of Econometrics* 56:89–118.

Mincer, J. A., and V. Zarnowitz. 1969. The evaluation of economic forecasts. In *Economic Forecasts and Expectations: Analysis of Forecasting Behavior and Performance*, 1–46. NBER.

Mitchell, J., and K. F. Wallis. 2011. Evaluating density forecasts: Forecast combinations, model mixtures, calibration and sharpness. *Journal of Applied Econometrics* 26:1023–40.

Mizon, G. E., and J.-F. Richard. 1986. The encompassing principle and its application to testing non-nested hypotheses. *Econometrica* 54:657–78.

Morgan, W. 1939. A test for the significance of the difference between the two variances in a sample from a normal bivariate population. *Biometrika* 31:13–9.

Murphy, A. H. 1973. A new vector partition of the probability score. *Journal of Applied Meteorology* 12:595–600.

Muth, J. F. 1961. Rational expectations and the theory of price movements. *Econometrica* 29:315–35.

Nadaraya, E. 1965. On non-parametric estimates of density functions and regression curves. *Theory of Probability & its Applications* 10:186–90.

Nelson, D. B. 1991. Conditional heteroskedasticity in asset returns: A new approach. *Econometrica* 59:347–70.

Newey, W. K., and D. McFadden. 1994. Large sample estimation and hypothesis testing. In *Handbook of Econometrics*, vol. 4, 2111–2245. Elsevier.

Newey, W. K., and J. L. Powell. 1987. Asymmetric least squares estimation and testing. *Econometrica* 55:819–847.

Newey, W. K., and K. D. West. 1987. A simple, positive semi-definite, heteroskedasticity and autocorrelation-consistent covariance matrix. *Econometrica* 55 (3):703–8.

Ng, S. 2013. Variable selection in predictive regressions. In G. Elliott and A. Timmermann (eds.), *Handbook of Economic Forecasting*, vol. 2, part B, 752–89. Elsevier.

Ng, S., and T. J. Vogelsang. 2002. Forecasting autoregressive time series in the presence of deterministic components. *Econometrics Journal* 5:196–224.(ISSN 13684221)

Ni, S., and D. Sun. 2005. Bayesian estimates for vector autoregressive models. *Journal of Business & Economic Statistics* 23:105–17.

Nordhaus, W. D. 1987. Forecasting efficiency: Concepts and applications. *Review of Economics and Statistics* 69:667–74.

Nyblom, J. 1989. Testing for the constancy of parameters over time. *Journal of the American Statistical Association* 84:223–30.

Ohlson, J. A. 1980. Financial ratios and the probabilistic prediction of bankruptcy. *Journal of Accounting Research* 18:109–31.

Onatski, A. 2010. Determining the number of factors from empirical distribution of eigenvalues. *Review of Economics and Statistics* 92:1004–16.

Ottaviani, M., and P. N. Sørensen. 2006. The strategy of professional forecasting. *Journal of Financial Economics* 81:441–66.

Pagan, A. 1984. Econometric issues in the analysis of regressions with generated regressors. *International Economic Review* 25:221–47.

Pagan, A., and A. Ullah. 1999. *Nonparametric econometrics*. Cambridge University Press.

Patton, A. J. 2006. Modelling asymmetric exchange rate dependence. *International Economic Review* 47:527–56.

——. 2011. Volatility forecast comparison using imperfect volatility proxies. *Journal of Econometrics* 160:246–56.

——. 2013. Copula methods for forecasting multivariate time series. In G. Elliott and A. Timmermann (eds.), *Handbook of Economic Forecasting*, vol. 2, part B, chap. 16, 899–960. Elsevier.

——. 2015. Evaluating and comparing possibly misspecified forecasts.

Patton, A. J., and A. Timmermann. 2007a. Properties of optimal forecasts under asymmetric loss and nonlinearity. *Journal of Econometrics* 140:884–918.

——. 2007b. Testing forecast optimality under unknown loss. *Journal of the American Statistical Association* 102:1172–84.

——. 2012. Forecast rationality tests based on multi-horizon bounds. *Journal of Business & Economic Statistics* 30:1–40.

Paye, B. S., and A. Timmermann. 2006. Instability of return prediction models. *Journal of Empirical Finance* 13:274–315.

Pearson, E. 1938. The probability integral transformation for testing goodness of fit and combining independent tests of significance. *Biometrika* 30:134–148.

Perron, P. 1989. The great crash, the oil price shock, and the unit root hypothesis. *Econometrica* 57:1361–401.

Pesaran, M. H., D. Pettenuzzo, and A. Timmermann. 2006. Forecasting time series subject to multiple structural breaks. *Review of Economic Studies* 73:1057–84.

Pesaran, M. H., A. Pick, and A. Timmermann. 2011. Variable selection, estimation and inference for multi-period forecasting problems. *Journal of Econometrics* 164:173–87.

Pesaran, M. H., and S. M. Potter. 1997. A floor and ceiling model of US output. *Journal of Economic Dynamics and Control* 21:661–95.

Pesaran, M. H., and S. Skouras. 2002. *Decision-based methods for forecast evaluation*, 241–267. A Companion to Economic Forecasting. Oxford: Blackwell.

Pesaran, M. H., and A. Timmermann. 1992. A simple nonparametric test of predictive performance. *Journal of Business & Economic Statistics* 10:461–5.

——. 2000. A recursive modelling approach to predicting UK stock returns. *Economic Journal* 110:159–91.

——. 2002. Market timing and return prediction under model instability. *Journal of Empirical Finance* 9:495–510.

——. 2007. Selection of estimation window in the presence of breaks. *Journal of Econometrics* 137:134–61.

——. 2009. Testing dependence among serially correlated multicategory variables. *Journal of the American Statistical Association* 104:325–37.

Pettenuzzo, D., and A. Timmermann. 2011. Predictability of stock returns and asset allocation under structural breaks. *Journal of Econometrics* 164:60–78.

——. 2015. Forecasting macroeconomic variables under model instability. *Journal of Business and Economic Statistics*. Available at SSRN 2603879.

Phillips, P. C. 1979. The sampling distribution of forecasts from a first-order autoregression. *Journal of Econometrics* 9:241–61.

——. 1987. Towards a unified asymptotic theory for autoregression. *Biometrika* 74:535–47.

——. 1998. Impulse response and forecast error variance asymptotics in nonstationary VARs. *Journal of Econometrics* 83:21–56.

Politis, D. N., and J. P. Romano. 1994. The stationary bootstrap. *Journal of the American Statistical Association* 89:1303–13.

Politis, D. N., and H. White. 2004. Automatic block-length selection for the dependent bootstrap. *Econometric Reviews* 23:53–70.

Primiceri, G. E. 2005. Time varying structural vector autoregressions and monetary policy. *Review of Economic Studies* 72:821–52.

Qi, M., and S. Yang. 2003. Forecasting consumer credit card adoption: What can we learn about the utility function? *International Journal of Forecasting* 19:71–85.

Qu, Z., and P. Perron. 2007. Estimating and testing structural changes in multivariate regressions. *Econometrica* 75:459–502.

Quah, D., and T. J. Sargent. 1993. A dynamic index model for large cross sections. In *Business cycles, indicators and forecasting*, 285–310. University of Chicago Press.

Racine, J. 2000. Consistent cross-validatory model-selection for dependent data: hv-block cross-validation. *Journal of Econometrics* 99:39–61.

——. 2001. On the nonlinear predictability of stock returns using financial and economic variables. *Journal of Business & Economic Statistics* 19:380–2.

Raftery, A. E., D. Madigan, and J. A. Hoeting. 1997. Bayesian model averaging for linear regression models. *Journal of the American Statistical Association* 92:179–91.

Rapach, D. E., J. K. Strauss, and G. Zhou. 2010. Out-of-sample equity premium prediction: Combination forecasts and links to the real economy. *Review of Financial Studies* 23:821–62.

Rapach, D. E., and M. E. Wohar. 2006. Structural breaks and predictive regression models of aggregate US stock returns. *Journal of Financial Econometrics* 4:238–74.

Reinsel, G. C., and S. K. Ahn. 1992. Vector autoregressive models with unit roots and reduced rank structure: Estimation. likelihood ratio test, and forecasting. *Journal of Time Series Analysis* 13:353–75.

Robert, C. P. 2001. *The Bayesian choice: From decision-theoretic foundations to computational implementation.* Springer Texts in Statistics. New York: Springer.

Robertson, J. C., and E. W. Tallman. 2001. Improving federal-funds rate forecasts in VAR models used for policy analysis. *Journal of Business & Economic Statistics* 19:324–30.

Romano, J. P., and M. Wolf. 2005. Stepwise multiple testing as formalized data snooping. *Econometrica* 73:1237–82.

Rosenblatt, M. 1952. Remarks on a multivariate transformation. *Annals of Mathematical Statistics* 23:470–2.

Rossi, A. G., and A. Timmermann. 2015. Modeling Covariance Risk in Merton's ICAPM. *Review of Financial Studies* 28:1428–61.

Rossi, B. 2005a. Optimal tests for nested model selection with underlying parameter instability. *Econometric Theory* 21:962–90.

——. 2005b. Testing long-horizon predictive ability with high persistence, and the Meese–Rogoff puzzle. *International Economic Review* 61–92.

——. 2013a. Advances in forecasting under instability. In G. Elliott and A. Timmermann (eds.), *Handbook of Economic Forecasting*, vol. 2, part B, chap. 21, 1203–324. Elsevier.

Rossi, B. 2013b. Exchange rate predictability. *Journal of Economic Literature* 51:1063–119.

Rossi, B., and A. Inoue. 2012. Out-of-sample forecast tests robust to the choice of window size. *Journal of Business & Economic Statistics* 30:432–53.

Rossi, B., and T. Sekhposyan. 2013. Conditional predictive density evaluation in the presence of instabilities. *Journal of Econometrics* 177:199–212.

——. 2015. Forecast rationality tests in the presence of instabilities, with applications to Federal Reserve and survey forecasts. *Journal of Applied Econometrics.* doi:10.1002/jae.2440.

Roy, A., and W. A. Fuller. 2001. Estimation for autoregressive time series with a root near 1. *Journal of Business & Economic Statistics* 19:482–93.

Rudebusch, G. D. 1998. Do measures of monetary policy in a VAR make sense? *International Economic Review* 39:907–31.

Sampson, M. 1991. The effect of parameter uncertainty on forecast variances and confidence intervals for unit root and trend stationary time-series models. *Journal of Applied Econometrics* 6:67–76.

Sanders, F. 1963. On subjective probability forecasting. *Journal of Applied Meteorology* 2:191–201.

Sarantis, N. 1999. Modeling non-linearities in real effective exchange rates. *Journal of International Money and Finance* 18:27–45.

Sargent, T. J. 1987. *Macroeconomic theory*, vol. 2. New York: Academic Press.

——. 1989. Two models of measurements and the investment accelerator. *Journal of Political Economy* 97:251–87.

Sargent, T. J., and C. A. Sims. 1977. *Business cycle modeling without pretending to have too much a priori economic theory*, vol. 1 of *New Methods in Business Cycle Research*, 145–168. Minneapolis: Federal Reserve Bank of Minneapolis.

Satchell, S., and A. Timmermann. 1995. An assessment of the economic value of non-linear foreign exchange rate forecasts. *Journal of Forecasting* 14:477–97.

Scharfstein, D. S., and J. C. Stein. 1990. Herd behavior and investment. *American Economic Review* 80:465–79.

Schervish, M. J. 1989. A general method for comparing probability assessors. *Annals of Statistics* 17:1856–79.

Schorfheide, F. 2005. VAR forecasting under misspecification. *Journal of Econometrics* 128:99–136.

Schwarz, G. 1978. Estimating the dimension of a model. *Annals of Statistics* 6:461–4.

Seillier-Moiseiwitsch, F., and A. Dawid. 1993. On testing the validity of sequential probability forecasts. *Journal of the American Statistical Association* 88:355–9.

Shaman, P., and R. A. Stine. 1988. The bias of autoregressive coefficient estimators. *Journal of the American Statistical Association* 83:842–8.

Shao, J. 1993. Linear model selection by cross-validation. *Journal of the American Statistical Association* 88:486–94.

——. 1997. An asymptotic theory for linear model selection. *Statistica Sinica* 7:221–42.

Shibata, R. 1980. Asymptotically efficient selection of the order of the model for estimating parameters of a linear process. *Annals of Statistics* 8:147–64.

——. 1981. An optimal selection of regression variables. *Biometrika* 68:45–54.

Shuford Jr, E. H., A. Albert, and H. E. Massengill. 1966. Admissible probability measurement procedures. *Psychometrika* 31:125–45.

Sims, C. A. 1980. Macroeconomics and reality. *Econometrica* 48:1–48.

——. 1993. A nine-variable probabilistic macroeconomic forecasting model. In *Business Cycles, Indicators and Forecasting*, 179–212. University of Chicago Press.

Sims, C. A., and T. Zha. 2006. Were there regime switches in US monetary policy? *American Economic Review* 96:54–81.

Sklar, M. 1959. *Fonctions de répartition à n dimensions et leurs marges*. Université Paris 8.

Skouras, S. 2007. Decisionmetrics: A decision-based approach to econometric modelling. *Journal of Econometrics* 137:414–40.

Smets, F., and R. Wouters. 2003. An estimated dynamic stochastic general equilibrium model of the euro area. *Journal of the European Economic Association* 1:1123–75.

Smith, J., and K. F. Wallis. 2009. A simple explanation of the forecast combination puzzle. *Oxford Bulletin of Economics and Statistics* 71:331–55.

Srinivasan, V., and Y. H. Kim. 1987. Credit granting: A comparative analysis of classification procedures. *Journal of Finance* 42:665–81.

Stambaugh, R. F. 1999. Predictive regressions. *Journal of Financial Economics* 54:375–421.

Stark, T., and D. Croushore. 2002. Forecasting with a real-time data set for macroeconomists. *Journal of Macroeconomics* 24:507–31.

Stekler, H. O. 1991. Macroeconomic forecast evaluation techniques. *International Journal of Forecasting* 7:375–84.

Stock, J. H. 1991. Confidence intervals for the largest autoregressive root in US macroeconomic time series. *Journal of Monetary Economics* 28:435–59.

——. 1996. VAR, error correction and pretest forecasts at long horizons. *Oxford Bulletin of Economics and Statistics* 58:685–701.

Stock, J. H., and M. W. Watson. 1989. New indexes of coincident and leading economic indicators. In *NBER Macroeconomics Annual 1989, Volume 4*, –409. MIT Press.

——. 1991. A probability model of the coincident economic indicators. In G. Moore and K. Lahiri (eds.), *The Leading Economic Indicators: New Approaches and Forecasting Records*. Cambridge University Press.

——. 1996. Evidence on structural instability in macroeconomic time series relations. *Journal of Business & Economic Statistics* 14:11–30.

——. 1999. A comparison of linear and nonlinear univariate models for forecasting macroeconomic time series. In *Cointegration, Causality, and Forecasting. A Festschrift in Honour of Clive W.J. Granger*. Oxford University Press.

——. 2002a. Forecasting using principal components from a large number of predictors. *Journal of the American Statistical Association* 97:1167–79.

——. 2002b. Macroeconomic forecasting using diffusion indexes. *Journal of Business & Economic Statistics* 20:147–62.

——. 2003a. Forecasting output and inflation: The role of asset prices. *Journal of Economic Literature* 41:788–829.

——. 2003b. *Introduction to econometrics*, vol. 104. Boston: Addison Wesley.

——. 2004. Combination forecasts of output growth in a seven-country data set. *Journal of Forecasting* 23:405–30.

——. 2005. Implications of dynamic factor models for VAR analysis. working paper, National Bureau of Economic Research.

——. 2006. Forecasting with many predictors. In G. Elliott, C. Granger, and A. Timmermann (eds.), *Handbook of Economic Forecasting*, vol. 1, 515–54. Elsevier.

——. 2007. Why has US inflation become harder to forecast? *Journal of Money, Credit and Banking* 39:3–33.

——. 2009. Forecasting in dynamic factor models subject to structural instability. *Methodology and Practice of Econometrics. A Festschrift in Honour of David F. Hendry* 173–205.

——. 2011. Dynamic factor models. In M. P. Clements and D. F. Hendry (eds.), *Oxford Handbook of Economic Forecasting*, vol. 1, 35–59. Oxford University Press.

——. 2012. Generalized shrinkage methods for forecasting using many predictors. *Journal of Business & Economic Statistics* 30:481–93.

Stone, C. J. 1977. Consistent nonparametric regression. *Annals of Statistics* 5:595–620.

Stone, M. 1961. The linear opinion pool. *Annals of Mathematical Statistics* 32:1339–42.

Sullivan, R., A. Timmermann, and H. White. 2001. Dangers of data mining: The case of calendar effects in stock returns. *Journal of Econometrics* 105:249–86.

Svensson, L. E. 1997. Inflation forecast targeting: Implementing and monitoring inflation targets. *European Economic Review* 41:1111–46.

Swanson, N. R., and H. White. 1997. A model selection approach to real-time macroeconomic forecasting using linear models and artificial neural networks. *Review of Economics and Statistics* 79:540–50.

Tanaka, K. 1996. *Time series analysis: Nonstationary and noninvertible distribution theory*, vol. 309. University of Texas Press.

Tay, A. S., K. F. Wallis, et al. 2000. Density forecasting: a survey. *Journal of Forecasting* 19:235–54.

Taylor, S. J. 1982. Financial returns modelled by the product of two stochastic processes–a study of the daily sugar prices 1961–75. *Time Series Analysis: Theory and Practice* 1:203–26.

Teräsvirta, T. 2006. Forecasting economic variables with nonlinear models. In G. Elliott, C. Granger, and A. Timmermann (eds.), *Handbook of Economic Forecasting*, vol. 1, 413–457. Elsevier.

Teräsvirta, T., D. Tjøstheim, and C. W. J. Granger. 2010. *Modelling nonlinear economic time series*. Oxford University Press.

Theil, H. 1961. *Economic forecast and policy*. North Holland.

Tibshirani, R. 1996. Regression shrinkage and selection via the Lasso. *Journal of the Royal Statistical Society. Series B (Methodological)* 267–288.

Timmermann, A. 2000. Moments of Markov switching models. *Journal of Econometrics* 96:75–111.

——. 2006. Forecast combinations. In G. Elliott, C. Granger, and A. Timmermann (eds.), *Handbook of Economic Forecasting*, vol. 1, 135–196. Elsevier.

——. 2008. Elusive return predictability. *International Journal of Forecasting* 24:1–18.

Tipping, M. E., and C. M. Bishop. 1999. Probabilistic principal component analysis. *Journal of the Royal Statistical Society: Series B (Statistical Methodology)* 61:611–22.

Toda, M. 1963. Measurement of subjective probability distributions. working paper, DTIC Document.

Trueman, B. 1994. Analyst forecasts and herding behavior. *Review of Financial Studies* 7:97–124.

Turner, J. L. 2004. Local to unity, long-horizon forecasting thresholds for model selection in the AR(1). *Journal of Forecasting* 23:513–39.

Valkanov, R. 2003. Long-horizon regressions: Theoretical results and applications. *Journal of Financial Economics* 68:201–32.

van Dijk, D., T. Teräsvirta, and P. H. Franses. 2002. Smooth transition autoregressive models–A survey of recent developments. *Econometric Reviews* 21:1–47.

Varian, H. R. 1975. A Bayesian approach to real estate assessment. *Studies in Bayesian econometrics and statistics in honor of Leonard J. Savage* 195–208.

Villani, M. 2009. Steady-state priors for vector autoregressions. *Journal of Applied Econometrics* 24:630–50.

Waggoner, D. F., and T. Zha. 1999. Conditional forecasts in dynamic multivariate models. *Review of Economics and Statistics* 81:639–651.

Wallis, K. F. 2003. Chi-squared tests of interval and density forecasts, and the Bank of England's fan charts. *International Journal of Forecasting* 19:165–175.

——. 2005. Combining density and interval forecasts: A modest proposal. *Oxford Bulletin of Economics and Statistics* 67:983–94.

Watson, G. S. 1964. Smooth regression analysis. *Sankhyā: Indian Journal of Statistics, Series A* 26:359–72.

Watson, M. W., and R. F. Engle. 1983. Alternative algorithms for the estimation of dynamic factor, mimic and varying coefficient regression models. *Journal of Econometrics* 23:385–400.

Weiss, A. A. 1996. Estimating time series models using the relevant cost function. *Journal of Applied Econometrics* 11:539–60.

Welch, I., and A. Goyal. 2008. A comprehensive look at the empirical performance of equity premium prediction. *Review of Financial Studies* 21:1455–508.

West, K. D. 1996. Asymptotic inference about predictive ability. *Econometrica* 64:1067–84.

——. 2001. Tests for forecasts encompassing when forecasts depend on estimated regression parameters. *Journal of Business & Economic Statistics* 19:29–33.

West, K. D., H. J. Edison, and D. Cho. 1993. A utility-based comparison of some models of exchange rate volatility. *Journal of International Economics* 35:23–45.

West, K. D., and M. W. McCracken. 1998. Regression-based tests of predictive ability. *International Economic Review* 39:817–840. (ISSN 00206598)

West, M., and J. Harrison. 1998. Bayesian forecasting and dynamic models. *Journal of the Operational Research Society* 49:179–179.

White, H. 1982. Maximum likelihood estimation of misspecified models. *Econometrica* 50:1–25.

——. 1996. *Estimation, inference and specification analysis*. 22. Cambridge University Press.

——. 2000. A reality check for data snooping. *Econometrica* 68:1097–126.

——. 2001. *Asymptotic theory for econometricians*. New York: Academic Press.

——. 2006. Approximate nonlinear forecasting methods. In G. Elliott, C. Granger, and A. Timmermann (eds.), *Handbook of Economic Forecasting*, vol. 1, 459–512. Elsevier.

White Jr, H. L., T.-H. Kim, and S. Manganelli. 2008. Modeling autoregressive conditional skewness and kurtosis with multi-quantile CAViaR. working paper 957, European Central Bank.

Wilson, E. B. 1934. The periodogram of American business activity. *Quarterly Journal of Economics* 48:375–417.

Wolak, F. A. 1987. An exact test for multiple inequality and equality constraints in the linear regression model. *Journal of the American Statistical Association* 82:782–93.

Wooldridge, J. M. 1994. Estimation and inference for dependent processes. In *Handbook of Econometrics*, vol. 4, 2639–2738. Elsevier.

Wright, J. H. 2006. *The yield curve and predicting recessions*. Divisions of Research & Statistics and Monetary Affairs, Federal Reserve Board.

———. 2008. Bayesian model averaging and exchange rate forecasts. *Journal of Econometrics* 146:329–41.

———. 2009. Forecasting US inflation by Bayesian model averaging. *Journal of Forecasting* 28:131–44.

———. 2011. Term premia and inflation uncertainty: Empirical evidence from an international panel dataset. *American Economic Review* 101:1514–34.

———. 2013. Evaluating real-time VAR forecasts with an informative democratic prior. *Journal of Applied Econometrics* 28:762–76.

Yang, Y. 2004. Combining forecasting procedures: Some theoretical results. *Econometric Theory* 20:176–222.

———. 2005. Can the strengths of AIC and BIC be shared? A conflict between model indentification and regression estimation. *Biometrika* 92:937–50.

Yao, Y.-C. 1987. Approximating the distribution of the maximum likelihood estimate of the change-point in a sequence of independent random variables. *Annals of Statistics* 15:1321–8.

Zellner, A. 1962. An efficient method of estimating seemingly unrelated regressions and tests for aggregation bias. *Journal of the American Statistical Association* 57:348–68.

———. 1971. *Introduction to Bayesian inference in econometrics*. Wiley.

———. 1986a. Bayesian estimation and prediction using asymmetric loss functions. *Journal of the American Statistical Association* 81:446–51.

———. 1986b. On assessing prior distributions and Bayesian regression analysis with g-prior distributions. *Bayesian Inference and Decision Techniques: Essays in Honor of Bruno De Finetti* 6:233–43.

Zhao, P., and B. Yu. 2006. On model selection consistency of Lasso. *Journal of Machine Learning Research* 7:2541–63.

Zou, H., and T. Hastie. 2005. Regularization and variable selection via the elastic net. *Journal of the Royal Statistical Society: Series B (Statistical Methodology)* 67:301–20.

Index